SUSTAINABLE EVENT MANAGEMENT

A practical guide

Second edition

Meegan Jones

Routledge
Taylor & Francis Group

LONDON AND NEW YORK

earthscan

from Routledge

First edition published 2009

Second edition published 2014
by Routledge
2 Park Square, Milton Park, Abingdon, Oxon OX14 4RN

and by Routledge
711 Third Avenue, New York, NY 10017

Routledge is an imprint of the Taylor & Francis Group, an informa business

British Library Cataloguing in Publication Data
A catalogue record for this book is available from the British Library

Library of Congress Cataloging-in-Publication Data
Jones, Meegan.
Sustainable event management: a practical guide / Meegan Jones. — Second edition.
pages cm
Includes bibliographical references and index.
1. Special events—Management—Handbooks, manuals, etc.
2. Special events—Environmental aspects—Handbooks, manuals, etc. I. Title.
GT3405.J66 2014
394.2068—dc23   2013040607

ISBN13: 978-0-415-84019-4 (hbk)
ISBN13: 978-0-415-84020-0 (pbk)
ISBN13: 978-0-203-76872-3 (ebk)

Typeset in Adobe Garamond and Futura by
Keystroke, Station Road, Codsall, Wolverhampton

CONTENTS

ILLUSTRATIONS

FIGURES

TABLES

BOXES

ACKNOWLEDGEMENTS

I would like to thank all those who helped me produce this book, and who also put up with me while I produced this book. They include Jane, Pru and Cass at GreenShoot Pacific for not minding too much that I ignored them for a couple of months as the deadline for the book was looming. And to Helen and the team at Earthscan from Routledge for bearing with my fussy layout requirements for the book.

Tara, Caitlin, Dave, Courtney, Katie, Stephanie, Bianca, Ivan, Steve, Emiko and Greer: thanks for your research assistance and case study wrangling.

Special thanks to Chris Johnson of Shambala and Powerful Thinking – for your peer review and also the fantastic cover photo.

My thanks to all who contributed case studies and information for the book, and who shared their experiences and outcomes for you to read. A large amount of examples and case studies unfortunately didn't make it into the book due to the word count restriction, and so you can find mentions in the book and extended detail on the book's website.

And a great big thank you to all the photographers who captured wonderful images and allowed them to be used in the book. A special mention must go to Mik La Vage and Jakob Kalor for their fantastic images.

INTRODUCTION

Across the world each year events of every shape and size are held: community events, business functions, local sporting competitions and school fairs, through to the world's largest festivals, music concerts, conferences, expos and sporting events. These public parties use up resources, send out emissions, and generate mountain ranges of waste. They also cause a lot of smiles, community cohesion, celebration, give voice to issues, and everyone has a wonderful time. It may be said that the most 'environmentally friendly' event is no event at all, but that's no fun. Public parties always have and always will be a part of the human story.

Whether a meeting for 100 people in a hotel, a conference for 500, an exhibition for 10,000, a sporting match in an arena for 50,000, a street parade, a rock music festival, an arts festival, food fair, religious celebration or formal ball, every coming together of people for a purpose can be done with consideration for sustainability. If all event organisers placed the tenants of sustainability at the very core of their planning, recognising the contribution they can make to sustainable development, the cumulative positive outcomes of their efforts would be impressive.

Reducing the impacts of consumption is key. Be frugal, cut budgets, get creative. Use products, materials and supplies made from sustainable materials. Reuse. Repurpose. Salvage. Hire, don't buy. Reduce the amount of energy needed, conserve water, don't use toxic pollutants, reduce transportation needs, and use renewable energy. Buy organic, chemical-free, sustainably harvested and humanely produced catering supplies. Choose the 'green and fair' option.

Nurture the communities that host your events through giving back to them. Consult and communicate with the local community. Buy local. Be sensitive to noise, light, traffic congestion and other disruptions to local amenity. Involve local people, volunteers, contractors and businesses. Looking further afield, consider the conditions of workers who make the products, materials and supplies you use to create your event. Source fairly traded and fairly produced products.

Events have the power to show sustainability in action, and an attractive by-product of every sustainably produced event is the potential to inspire and motivate others to action. Lead by example. Demonstrate what's possible, and inspire attendees, contractors, suppliers, venues, talent and sponsors to take on sustainability solutions in their own homes, communities and workplaces.

There is an urgent need for the event industry to change our production and purchasing habits right now.

I hope this book inspires you to change the way you produce your events and to use your event to in turn inspire others.

ABOUT THIS BOOK

Sustainable Event Management: A practical guide offers discussion and thought-provoking insight into the areas of environmental and social responsibility in event management and production. It takes you and your event on a journey towards sustainably produced events with tips, production logistics, projects to undertake and practical solutions to common challenges.

You will benefit from first-hand experience of those who have put sustainable event management into action with real-life examples from event organisers who have tackled challenges and successfully reduced the impacts of their events.

To get where you need to go, questions need to be asked – of you, of suppliers, participants, venues and host destinations. Hopefully this book will shed light on areas previously left unconsidered and arm you if not with all the answers, at least with a lot of the questions.

When you break it right down, to successfully deliver your event sustainability goals, your tools are communications, management, and making the right choices. To achieve event sustainability success you don't need to be an expert in every aspect of the very broad and very deep subject that is 'sustainability'. Specialists exist to become part of your toolbox of solutions. Use them.

Scientists, environmental experts, activists and specialists in every field of sustainability, greening, environment, ecology, biodiversity and climate change have published volumes of books, papers, reports and documents on these subjects. There are thousands of websites, action groups, causes and campaigns online. This book doesn't attempt to re-create or duplicate this work or to teach environmental science. It is written assuming the reader has some understanding of the concepts of sustainable development and the pillars of sustainability (environmental, social, cultural and economic), or at least to have a passionate concern for and interest in finding out more.

WHO SHOULD READ THIS BOOK?

This book is aimed at individuals, committees and teams, agencies, PCOs, promoters, owners, contractors, suppliers and venue management. If you are involved in producing any type of event, of any scale of location, this book is for you.

If you are organising a gathering of people for a purpose and they need to be fed, watered, entertained, powered, moved and sanitised – this book will help you get it done sustainably.

Those who are studying event management, are on internships or in work experience and who plan to be change agents to move the event industry towards a sustainable future are prime candidates to read this book, as we want the new generation to enter the industry with a passion for sustainability and the knowledge to get it done.

Community, Cultural, Entertainment and Sports Events

Music festivals, film festivals, cultural festivals, multi-arts festivals, activist or cause-based festivals, music concerts, community fairs, open days, sports events, marathons, international matches, local leagues, scouting jamborees, large campouts, or even large gatherings of fire-fighters during bush fire season!

MICE (meetings, incentives, conventions, exhibitions)

Conventions, symposiums, summits, conferences, corporate hospitality, client functions, seminars, annual meetings, exhibitions, trade fairs.

Special Events and Brand Events

Launches, awards, celebrations, publicity events, sponsorship campaigns, promotional activities, brand activation, religious gatherings, ceremonies, graduations and balls.

Events such as Boom have a transforming potential in many ways. Firstly, the gathering of thousands of people in a specific place for a limited amount of time is an opportunity for reflection on the communitarian nature of our species: How do we live together? How do we relate? How do we occupy space? What do we leave behind? What is our ecological function in the web of life? How can we satisfy our survival needs in equilibrium with the needs of all other species? The answers to these questions become clearer when we can be away from the pressures of the consumer culture and surrounded by art, music and a culture of freedom of expression such as the Boom Festival.

Dr André Soares, EcoCentro IPEC, Boom Festival, Portugal

Figure 1.1 Welcome to Boom Festival.

Source: Jakob Kalor.

1

SUSTAINABILITY AND EVENTS

Events have the potential to be model examples of harmonious balance between human activity, resource use and environmental impact rather than hedonistic, resource gulping and garbage producing. There is a powerful opportunity, and an urgent imperative, for events to leave a lasting positive legacy, demonstrating a pathway to sustainable development and enabling and inspiring attendees, supply chain and host destinations to action.

Events are a gathering of people for a purpose. They are opportunities to celebrate and inspire. Their purpose can be to promote knowledge, to showcase excellence, to entertain, to compete, to inspire community pride, celebrate culture and enhance social cohesion.

But in the gathering of all those people for whatever purpose, resources are used, waste is created, people, environment and economies are affected. No matter the type of event – a conference, sports event, exhibition, or community celebration – or if held inside buildings, in closed off streets, central parks or sports stadiums – there is the opportunity for *every single event* to be a shining light of sustainability-in-action.

To look into the future and see one that is truly sustainable, our industry must play its part in responsible resource use, in protecting natural environments, and ensuring an equitable distribution of the earth's abundance for all.

The event industry can be a powerful catalyst in this story. With the sheer size of our industry globally, and the millions upon millions of people who attend events each year, the industry and all working within it have a responsibility to ensure that sustainability management is embedded in the event's planning and delivery.

If we ignore this urgent call of nature, we will surely play our part in the continual devastation of the natural environment and the diminishing of its resources, along with lopsided and far from fair distribution of resources, wealth and well-being among the humans and non-humans inhabiting the planet.

The chapters in this book will delve into the phases and facets of event planning and delivery, offer suggestions for ways to embrace all the pillars of sustainability, and for your event to play its part in supporting sustainable development.

We will also go into the detail of how to manage

specific sustainability issues to reduce the negative impacts and enhance positive outcomes and lasting legacies.

This book will arm you with the skills and knowledge you need to deliver a truly sustainable event. If you want to test your mettle, at the end of this chapter I have listed the competencies you should aim to achieve.

Moving beyond your actual event, as a result of your sustainability focus you can influence the ongoing behaviour and attitudes of your attendees, contractors, suppliers, and the event industry at large.

You have the power to effect change and leave participants with the inspiration to conduct business, and to live their lives more sustainably. This is your legacy, your contribution to our collective sustainable future.

Event Sustainability

Event sustainability practice has moved far beyond the early days of first a focus on recycling quickly followed by counting greenhouse gas emissions (GHGs). This was sustainability 1.0. If you have not yet progressed beyond this and plucking other low-hanging fruit, welcome to the new era of event sustainability practice. . . .

The industry now embraces the indicators of sustainability performance set down by the *Global Reporting Initiative's Event Organizers' Sector Supplement (GRI EOSS)*,[1] and has established its own framework for the systematic treatment of sustainability issues for events with the launch of the international standard *ISO 20121: Event Sustainability Management Systems*.[2]

This is underscored with the principles of sustainable development such as those prescribed in the *UN Global Compact*,[3] and embraces social responsibility and principles outlined in *ISO 26000 Social Responsibility*.[4]

We are talking the length and breadth of the sustainability spectrum; social, cultural, economic and environmental issues, along with taking on concepts such as ' governance, transparency and inclusivity. This ed up into a package offering 'soft' event knowledge transfer and societal cohesion legacies such as physical infrastructure. leading the charge and leveraging a their host cities. Hotels, stadia, n centres are leading the way in

the built environment. Local government has a role to play in supporting or incentivising local events to be operated sustainably, and the music industry, through outdoor festivals and events, is excelling in event sustainability practice.

There are still sectors of the industry or regions of the world that have not yet taken up the responsibility which events have towards society to be sustainably operated and to leave lasting positive legacies. And certainly there is a lot of difference in the level of success (or even uptake) of sustainability management from one hotel or venue to the next.

Most outdoor events in countries that have embraced sustainable development principles and have active sustainability in practice at a municipal level have started their sustainability journey. The only outdoor events that are at least not tackling simple and obvious things, such as recycling, are in those countries where there are other pressing issues at a societal and economic level and where concepts such as recycling have not yet become a priority for the community.

However, the event industry is an international one, and it is the responsibility of every event organiser who runs events across national borders to decide on their own minimum best practice and adhere to this no matter where the event is held. Issues management should be framed against both the local context and globally accepted responsible operating practice and norms of behaviour, and the values by which the organisation stands.

SUSTAINABILITY MANAGEMENT

'Sustainability management' represents the actions taken to address issues, impacts and opportunities needed to meet your social, cultural, environmental and economic performance outcomes. In other words it is balancing your event, venue or organisation's quadruple bottom-line performance.

By managing activities with consideration for its responsibility to society on an environmental, economic, cultural and social level, the organisation is set up to deliver a positive legacy – tangible and intangible benefits of the event's activities to society and the environment.

To do this, organisations must embrace ethical organisational governance.

Managing for sustainability requires an organisation to consider the sustainable development of the society within which it operates, as well as how its activities impact on sustainable development at a global level.

Issues, Impacts and Outcomes

When looking at sustainability management for an event we can break it down into **issues**, **impacts** and **outcomes**.

Issues are the specific actions that may need managing: for example, communication with local residents; recycling of cans; using energy-efficient equipment.

Impacts are the measureable outputs of those issues; negative if not managed and positive if managed well: for example,negative and disruptive public opinion; waste to be managed and increased waste to landfill; more GHGs produced than are necessary.

Outcomes are the final remains of the issues being managed and the impacts being reduced or enhanced: for example, the event enhances community cohesion; resources are conserved; climate change effects reduced.

The issues needed to be managed to control these impacts and to create positive outcomes or reduced negative outcomes are detailed in the next chapter, but here are a few examples of positive and negative impacts to whet your appetite:

- use of natural and renewable resources
- use of non-renewable resources
- use of synthetic resources
- emissions to air, land and water
- localised sound and light pollution
- localised congestion
- economic benefit to the local community and supply chain
- being complicit in human rights abuses through procurement choices
- being complicit in environmental pollution through procurement choices
- creation of social capital through event activities.

The following chapter provides guidance on how to evaluate and prioritise issues and impacts management.

You are not expected to deal with everything all at once. Continual improvement is a key principle of sustainability management and this premise includes a staged approach to managing impacts.

Disclosure is vital. Transparency is a key sustainable development principle and is an aspect of good governance. Even if you cannot manage all the issues and impacts immediately, communicating to those stakeholders who either may be affected or will have an opinion on your actions or the issues is key. Lay down what you have identified as sustainability issues and your plan of management, even if it is to say, "*this year we will be managing X for this reason, and next year we will introduce Y for this reason.*"

Management Pathway

Like any management or business plan, you will need to have a vision and a pathway to action. The following steps will help you to establish a framework to get you where you want to be:

At the top is envisioning where you want to get to. Ask yourself, "*Imagine if at the completion of the event . . .*" and fill in the blanks.

This is your **vision**. Your **mission** will describe how to get there, and your **values** will underscore your behaviour and actions. **Policies** help keep you on track. Your **goals** will set your key themes or aspects of concern for management, and **objectives** and **targets** will give you specific items to action. The **strategy** will outline how to set everything up to get where you need to be – the internal workings of your organisation and its interaction with stakeholders. The **framework** is your management system, including documentation and measurement systems. Read through the Management Pathway Steps in Box 1.1.

SUSTAINABILITY SELL-IN

Sustainability is an important aspect of event creation; however, the reality is that it must be balanced with delivering the event **on time** and **on budget**.

You may come up against those who don't want to change the way they do business. However, I encourage you to go forth and blaze trails. Offer opportunities to new and innovative suppliers and contractors who want to move with you into a sustainable future. Work with the old-school boys and coax them into the light.

If top management is not interested, no resources are being provided and no one else in the team is interested, you have an interesting challenge ahead. You may need to lead by example, forge ahead and show everyone what can be done, and work towards the 'contagious' approach. If you build it they will come. You will need to go on a deliberate behaviour and attitude change campaign within the organisation, before you can embed sustainability and have it working without you continually driving it.

If you find yourself organising an event for a client, a boss or company which is not really interested in sustainability, what do you do? How do you sell-in sustainability to get your new ideas off the table and into reality? Apart from the environmental benefits, the positives of producing an event sustainably may include the following:

- positioning and competitive advantage
- public relations opportunities
- financial savings.

Positioning and Competitive Advantage

You can appeal to the other green in your client or company: envy (the green monster). If financially motivated and in business for business's sake, top management are likely to have a keen competitive streak. This may lead to bouts of professional jealousy when a competitor stakes a claim before they do. Use the green monster to your advantage by demonstrating how your event and company becoming a sustainability leader is to its competitive advantage – you could otherwise end up being left behind by your competitors.

Reputational Benefits

As more people are becoming green at heart, they are voting with their wallets, supporting those companies which are doing the same. Event attendees are becoming more clued up about sustainability issues and expect events to toe the line. The government agencies regulating event licences are now placing environmental conditions on them. Your clients may demand that you produce their events sustainably.

If your event is not considering sustainability management, could this come back around and bite you? If asked by the media, attendees, clients or sponsors, are you able to report on what you are doing to reduce the impacts of the event and what that event is doing to contribute to sustainable development?

Financial Savings

The bottom line (as opposed to quadruple bottom line) may be a good place to start. Do your budgets and look for savings both on an immediate and long-term basis. Do cost comparisons in all the major areas such as energy, fuel supply, procurement, transport, hire costs, waste disposal etc. You may be surprised that the sustainable alternative can be cheaper than its conventional counterpart. Taken at its least complex:

* buy and use less stuff – reduce expenditure
* create less waste – save money on disposal
* use less power/fuel – reduce your energy bill

Where things may become a little more expensive is in procurement choices that are not yet as popular as they need to be to be price competitive with 'regular' products. But basic supply and demand may come into play here – the more of us who ask for organic, non-toxic, local, fairly produced and traded, and/or recyclable goods, the less 'premium' prices may be. The 'green' choice may not always be the most expensive. Don't assume that it is; go out and cost it.

Top Management Commitment

Top management can demonstrate commitment to sustainable development principles and implementing sustainability management at events through the following:

✓ Developing sustainability policies.
✓ Allocating enough time to research.
✓ Providing resources, including budget equipment or infrastructure.

✓ Developing the team's sustainability skills.
✓ Communicating with all stakeholders their commitment to sustainability and expectations for the stakeholder's involvement.
✓ Setting down a directive to commit to sustainable development principles and working with their team to devise strategies and plans.
✓ Placing sustainability objectives equal with financial and creative decisions, and creating a balance between these objectives to reach an improved triple-bottom-line performance.
✓ Designating a sustainability leader in all relevant teams.
✓ Encouraging suppliers to innovate sustainable solutions.
✓ Being prepared to invest a little more to be an innovator and sustainability leader, since cost benefits may follow.
✓ Aligning only with sponsors that have a demonstrated commitment to environmental protection and sustainable development principles.
✓ Requesting feedback, performance results and reports.
✓ Working with event management to define targets and priorities ensuring continued momentum towards meeting defined sustainability goals.

SUPPLIERS and CONTRACTORS

Clever suppliers and contractors are developing tailored products and services with event sustainability in mind. Conventional contractors and suppliers are well advised to look at what they offer events, to make sure that they keep up with the innovators entering the market.

Demand by events for sustainable solutions is pulling change up through the supply chain. To achieve good event sustainability outcomes, managers require suppliers and contractors to change their offerings. Rather than waiting for new sustainable products and service solutions to appear, demand them from your suppliers or create them yourself.

The soon-to-be-abundant availability of sustainable solutions for the event industry will cause competition among the suppliers as they look for outlets for their products and services. This will further increase the uptake of sustainability management in the event industry as more options that have been tested and proven will be on offer. Event organisers who may not have previously considered sustainability management of their events will find themselves with sustainable solutions without lifting a finger.

Help Grow the Market

By making the best purchasing and contracting decisions, your contribution to growing the demand for fledgling sustainable products and services for the event industry can help turn ideas into full-blown commercial success.

Certain pioneering suppliers have been offering perfect solutions for several years. They have been knocking on the same doors year in year out and it is only recently that they have been invited in. Recently 'tuned-in' event organisers may be shocked to hear that the solution they have just started to look for has been attempting to present to them for some time! Don't leave the innovators and sustainable designers out in the cold. Give a new contractor a go. This may shake up the old boys and get them thinking sustainably too.

Green-washing by those in it for a quick buck is something of which you need to be mindful. It may be obvious, but they will bombard you with technical details and confusing jargon. Keep yourself informed and conduct your own investigation if something seems confusing, or is an unjustified or outrageous claim.

By using your sustainable event know-how you will be empowered to keep the contractors honest, talk in realities and help keep the sector innovative and moving in the right direction.

Figure 1.2 In harmony with nature. Hortisculpture installation at Shambala Festival 2012 .
Copyright Shambala Festival 2012. Louise Roberts, Burst Photography.

SUSTAINABLE DEVELOPMENT

The terms 'Sustainability' and 'Sustainable Development' are understood by a wide and increasingly informed audience. Becoming buzzwords, along with terms and concepts like 'Climate Change' and 'Carbon Footprint', they are used as brands in media and marketing, and our event attendees are listening.

These concepts are working as 'green hooks' bringing the masses over to the green side. And that's a good thing. It gets event attendees thinking about sustainability issues and makes your job to tune in your event to sustainability a little easier through engaging an already warmed-up audience.

But while everyone 'knows' in essence what sustainability is, there is no formal agreement on a definition of 'sustainability' and its interplay with sustainable development. Some see sustainability as the journey taken to the final end point of 'sustainable development'. Others see a state of sustainability as the end goal and sustainable development as the means to get there.

'Sustainability', as a plain old word, means the *capacity to endure*. Sustainable development brings together a concern for the carrying capacity of our planet's natural systems to sustain life with humanity's progression to a more comfortable and thriving existence with equity, dignity, and happiness for all.

ISO 26000 explains it well: "*The objective of sustainable development is to achieve sustainability for society as a whole and the planet. It does not concern the sustainability or ongoing viability of any specific organization.*"

The term 'Sustainable Development' was first defined in 1987 through what is commonly known as the *Bruntland Report* or formally '*Our Common Future*'.[5] Its definition is as follows:

Sustainable development is development that meets the needs of the present without compromising the ability of future generations to meet their own needs. It contains within it two key concepts:

1   the concept of 'needs', in particular the essential needs of the world's poor, to which overriding priority should be given; and
2   the idea of limitations imposed by the state of technology and social organization on the environment's ability to meet present and future needs.

Sustainable development is global, cross-border and cross-generational equity and endurance. The report goes on to say:

A world in which poverty and inequity are endemic will always be prone to ecological and other crises. Sustainable development requires meeting the basic needs of all and extending to all the opportunity to satisfy their aspirations for a better life.

The sustainability pillars – environmental, social/cultural and economic – are inextricably linked, and in the overlapping sweet spots we are in a state that is at once *equitable*, *bearable* and *viable*.

Equitable in that all people have fair access to the earth's resources and a chance for economic prosperity. This must be **bearable** considering the earth's total resources and its regeneration ability. But the exploitation of the earth's resources need to be both economically and environmentally **viable** and ensure this exploitation does not come at an environmental cost.

Traditionally, sustainability had just three pillars: environmental, social and economic. In 2010 the fourth pillar, **culture**, was proposed, at the *World Summit of Local and Regional Leaders – 3rd World Congress* of *United Cities and Local Governments* (UCLG).[6] This fourth pillar celebrates the aspect of cultural diversity and the role of cultural policy in enhancing sustainable human development, and rightly so.

Since 2010 the inclusion of **culture** as a fourth pillar has proliferated. Culture is about creativity, heritage, knowledge and diversity – and including these aspects is vital to sustainable and thriving human development on our planet.

There is not one play-book for sustainable development – one size does not fit all. By including **culture** as a pillar you can start to build context, and obvious pathways towards sustainable human development will light up more brightly.

What better vehicle than events to celebrate cultural diversity, to help safeguard cultural heritage, to strengthen cultural and creative industries, and to promote cultural tourism? I would go so far as to say the inclusion of the fourth pillar of **culture** has been purpose-written for our industry.

Sustainable Development Principles

The first thing an event organisation should do is to establish a statement of purpose and values as these relate to the principles of sustainable development. These beliefs are the tenants that will govern or underscore the organisation's activities.

When setting your organisation's founding values and principles for supporting sustainable human development, you should look to the context in which you operate. You may wish to bring certain aspects to the fore depending on the geographic and cultural context in which the event or organisation exists.

If you are based in one specific geographic location, look at what that region has stated as its primary sustainable development values and what the sustainable development ambitions are for the region. You may then choose to either mirror those destination values, or if you believe some fundamental aspects are not being treated well or have been completely missed out, you may choose to highlight them as key features of your own organisation's values and principles when operating within the region.

For example, in a country that has a poor human rights reputation, you may decide, when operating within this country, to push that up to the top of the agenda and to do all that you can to ensure your activities don't contribute to human rights violations. This is an interesting situation if your organisation is headquartered in one country but operates in several other countries, each of which has different sustainable development issues and different localised prioritisation of issues.

When you break it down across many different protocols and guiding documents, the principles or values to enable sustainable human development include the following:

- inclusivity
- integrity
- environmental stewardship

- transparency
- equity
- human rights.

Different programmes dice it different ways, and use different words or themes, but if you address each of these values and interpret them for your own situation, you should be able to come up with a succinct and relevant set of values.

One of the outcomes of *Rio+20*, the *United Nations Conference on Sustainable Development*, was the report *Realizing the Future We Want for All*.[7] In it is laid out a vision based on three fundamental values: respect for **human rights**, **equality** and **sustainability**. It also brings in four core dimensions and a series of enablers to help us build a 'rights-based, equitable, secure and sustainable world for all people'. These are as follows:

- inclusive social development
- inclusive economic development
- environmental sustainability
- peace and security.

The *United Nations Global Compact* is a strategic policy initiative for businesses committed to aligning their operations and strategies with ten universally accepted principles in the areas of human rights, labour, environment and anti-corruption. The *UN Global Compact*'s ten principles cover human rights, labour, the environment and anti-corruption.

ISO 26000 Social Responsibility also offers great guidance on what could be included in an organisation's approach to ethical governance and its role as a responsible member of society. More details on the *UN Global Compact* and *ISO 26000* are given below.

A great example of setting down principles by which to stand is the *Burning Man* event. They are guided by *Ten Principles* meant to evoke the cultural ethos that has emerged from the event. Their principle for *Leaving No Trace* has respecting the environment at its core.

Let us now dive down into some of the sustainable development principles and establish some context on how they could apply within the event industry.

Integrity

Including integrity in sustainable development principles cuts to the core of ethical organisational governance. To ensure the highest level of integrity, events and their business dealings should be produced with professional conduct by all staff, with regard for the rule of law, and without bias.

Ethical conduct and operating with integrity will come down to three things: having policies in place, having a culture within the organisation that embraces ethical conduct, and having individuals working within the organisation and supply chain who personally embrace these ideals. Policies to assist could include the following:

- Anti-bribery and Corruption Policy
- Conflict of Interest Policy
- Standards of Conduct Policy
- Confidentiality Policy
- Anti-Money Laundering Policy
- Legal and Compliance Policy.

Ensuring fair labour and working conditions is also part of organisational governance with integrity. Examples within the event industry which speak to fair labour practices include the following:

- Not restricting or limiting the ability of staff, performers or supply chains to be involved in labour unions or collective bargaining groups.
- Playing your part in eliminating all forms of forced, compulsory or child labour through your procurement decisions.
- Ensuring discrimination is eliminated through your employment policy, that of subcontractors, and through your supply chain/procurement choices.

Inclusivity

Inclusivity means involving, informing or offering access to the event or event information by those who may be affected by your event activities, those who may have an opinion or form a view, and those who have a need or an expectation related to your activities.

These parties may include traditional landowners and first peoples, members of the local community, neighbouring businesses, government authorities and agencies, supply chain, venue, talent, staff, crew and attendees.

The first thing to do is to identify all potentially interested parties in the event activities through numerous routes. *ISO 20121* requests that you actually formally do this and to have a procedure written down to explain how these 'interested parties' are identified. See more in Chapter 11.

By addressing inclusion, you are addressing its counterpart: exclusion. By recognising inclusion as a founding sustainable development principle and enacting that within your organisation's activities, you are committing to not acting in any way that could exclude participation from your event by those who wish to. For example, you would enact the inclusivity principle through your tendering process to ensure that all who wish to do business with your organisation have transparent access routes.

If you are actually creating a ticketed event with limited numbers, and it is therefore exclusive by nature, this is where context comes into play. You must consider the outside looking in – and the context in which the event would be held. If it is socially acceptable to hold such an event and it would not impinge upon human rights or advance negatively any other aspects of sustainable development, then it's OK to hold your event!

You would embrace inclusivity through other aspects of your event such as the supply chain. If, on the other hand, it is a ticketed event where it is run for the whole of the community (e.g. a major sports event or a city-wide arts festival run by a community organisation or local municipality funded group) then it would be viewed as unacceptable for exclusion to occur because of either the price of the tickets or the routes through which tickets must be bought (e.g. credit card only or online only), and the fact that there are no low-price or open-access/free activities or event components.

The antidote to discrimination is inclusion. By embracing inclusivity into your organisation's values you are committing to anti-discrimination measures. This would be enacted through employment policies, programming policies and procurement policies.

Inclusivity brings in the cultural pillar for sustainability and, through celebrating culture and by embracing

Box 1.2

THE TEN PRINCIPLES – BURNING MAN

Radical Inclusion – Anyone may be a part of Burning Man. We welcome and respect the stranger. No prerequisites exist for participation in our community.

Gifting – Burning Man is devoted to acts of gift giving. The value of a gift is unconditional. Gifting does not contemplate a return or an exchange for something of equal value.

Decommodification – In order to preserve the spirit of gifting, our community seeks to create social environments that are unmediated by commercial sponsorships, transactions, or advertising. We stand ready to protect our culture from such exploitation. We resist the substitution of consumption for participatory experience.

Radical Self-reliance – Burning Man encourages the individual to discover, exercise and rely on his or her inner resources.

Radical Self-expression – Radical self-expression arises from the unique gifts of the individual. No one other than the individual or a collaborating group can determine its content. It is offered as a gift to others. In this spirit, the giver should respect the rights and liberties of the recipient.

Communal Effort – Our community values creative cooperation and collaboration. We strive to produce, promote and protect social networks, public spaces, works of art, and methods of communication that support such interaction.

Civic Responsibility – We value civil society. Community members who organise events should assume responsibility for public welfare and endeavour to communicate civic responsibilities to participants. They must also assume responsibility for conducting events in accordance with local, state and federal laws.

Leaving No Trace – Our community respects the environment. We are committed to leaving no physical trace of our activities wherever we gather. We clean up after ourselves and endeavour, whenever possible, to leave such places in a better state than when we found them.

Participation – Our community is committed to a radically participatory ethic. We believe that transformative change, whether in the individual or in society, can occur only through the medium of deeply personal participation. We achieve being through doing. Everyone is invited to work. Everyone is invited to play. We make the world real through actions that open the heart.

Immediacy – Immediate experience is, in many ways, the most important touchstone of value in our culture. We seek to overcome barriers that stand between us and a recognition of our inner selves, the reality of those around us, participation in society, and contact with a natural world exceeding human powers. No idea can substitute for this experience.

www.burningman.com

diversity, an organisation can achieve great rewards and advance sustainable development.

Inclusivity also embraces communication – ensuring that there are channels available for all interested parties to communicate with the event organiser over event-related activities. This would include communicating information about the event such as operating hours, traffic alterations, noise and lighting controls, protection of local biodiversity, waste management, security and safety.

Acknowledge traditional landowners and first peoples, and respect their rights, access and involvement. In some countries, in urban locations, this may mean an acknowledgement of traditional owners. In other regions it may include formally requesting permission to hold an event on land which by common law is owned by a private citizen but, by indigenous tradition, is under the custodianship of the indigenous people.

A great example of inclusion is bringing attendees into issues identification and solutions management. This is just what *Roskilde Festival* in Denmark has done in dealing with the ongoing and intense issues of campsite waste control at outdoor music festivals where the culture is to play hard and dirty! Read more on the book's website.

The annex to *ISO 20121* includes a table with questions to contemplate when addressing inclusivity for your event. Questions to ask are as follows:

- How to identify those who could affect or be affected by decisions and actions?
- How do interested parties contribute their views, and how do they do so on a continual basis?
- How to help interested parties understand the reasons for the organisation's decisions and the implications of its actions?
- How to ensure that no groups or individuals are disadvantaged or kept uninformed?
- Are there interests beyond the immediate interested parties that should be considered?
- How to take into account the interested parties' rights and interests?

Examples of actions taken to ensure inclusion within the context of event planning and delivery are as follows:

- Community stakeholder meetings to invite participation in the event and to share information about the event.
- Stakeholder involvement in identifying what the key sustainability issues may be for the event and their participation in establishing key sustainability performance indicators.
- Multiple routes for two-way communication with all stakeholder groups, tailored to suit each group.
- Having ticketing policies and procedures in place that do not discriminate access to the event, and as such having multiple ticketing options available to ensure accessibility by all.
- Ensuring access for attendees with mobility or sensory impairment.
- Including contractors, suppliers, staff and crew at various levels of event planning, and debriefing and providing the opportunity to express their opinions, give feedback, offer suggestions or to present grievances on decisions made by the organisation.

Transparency

Organisations are subject to greater scrutiny and being held to account for their actions than ever before. By having transparent processes, and transparency in performance outcomes, stakeholders can be confident that the organisation is acting ethically.

Transparency is also an essential aspect of ethical organisational governance and is a foundation of sustainability, as performance disclosure is key.

Transparency within the sporting sector of the event industry is also a major issue. Corruption can come in the form of match fixing or athlete doping. *Transparency International* work within the sports sector, particularly in major sporting events, on prevention and education in match fixing and good governance within sports bodies. In 2009 they published the paper *Corruption and Sport: Building Integrity and Preventing Abuses*.[8] They also have the *Integrity Pact* that may be used by events organisers.[9]

To achieve transparency, information about an event's operation should be available for interested parties as it applies to them, along with performance results.

- Potential attendees should be kept up to date with ticket release dates, event information, programming and other relevant information.
- Bidding and tendering processes should be transparent and not at risk of corruption.
- The supply chain should be informed of securing contracts in a timely fashion and with written confirmation.
- Staff and crew should have access to information about working hours and conditions, and be consulted and informed if any changes need to be made.
- Regulatory authorities should have access to relevant policies and plans at appropriate points throughout the event planning cycle.
- Local community should be kept informed of relevant information at key points during the event planning cycle.
- Performance outcomes should be disclosed.
- Assurance and scrutiny by external parties such as NGO observers and standards certifying bodies.
- Gifts and Invitations Policy.
- Whistleblower Protection Policy.
- Budget Transparency Policy.

Environmental Stewardship

At the heart of the concept of environmental stewardship is that we are temporary custodians of the land on which our activities take place, and that we are responsible for the resources consumed and waste streams created.

This can translate perfectly to the event industry. If our events occur in a natural setting it is our responsibility to ensure that no negative impacts occur from our event activities. We must be mindful that to produce our events we are using the earth's resources, and we must take a conservative and responsible approach to managing this consumption. We must also acknowledge that our event activities will create waste streams – liquid and solid waste and gaseous emissions.

To embrace environmental stewardship as a principle we must also ensure that our waste creation is minimised and that responsible management of those waste resources is undertaken.

Box 1.3

UN GLOBAL COMPACT

The *UN Global Compact* is a strategic policy initiative for businesses are committed to aligning their operations and strategies with ten universally accepted principles.

Human Rights

Principle 1: Businesses should support and respect the protection of internationally proclaimed human rights.

Principle 2: make sure that they are not complicit in human rights abuses.

Labour Standards

Principle 3: Businesses should uphold the freedom of association and the effective recognition of the right to collective bargaining.

Principle 4: the elimination of all forms of forced and compulsory labour.

Principle 5: the effective abolition of child labour.

Principle 6: the elimination of discrimination in respect of employment and occupation.

Environment

Principle 7: Businesses should support a precautionary approach to environmental challenges.

Principle 8: undertake initiatives to promote greater environmental responsibility.

Principle 9: encourage the development and diffusion of environmentally friendly technologies.

Anti-corruption

Principle 10: Businesses should work against corruption in all its forms, including extortion and bribery.

www.unglobalcompact.org

Actions to undertake to include environmental stewardship in your event planning and delivery are as include:

- undertaking an environmental impact assessment
- creating an environmental protection plan
- moderating consumption of natural resources
- having plans to ensure the reduction of solid, liquid and gaseous waste emissions
- encouraging the development and diffusion of sustainable technologies through supply chain management.

Give something back. *The Festival Wood* is a wild forest regeneration initiative from *A Greener Festival*. Rather than a carbon offset scheme, the project is an opportunity for the festival community to help protect, restore and nurture the great outdoors we so love to enjoy.

Trees for Life were selected to collaborate on the initiative due to their outstanding commitment to conserving and restoring the wild forests of the Scottish Highlands. *The Festival Woods* are beginning in Dundreggan on 10,000 acres of wild land near Loch Ness with a focus on native species grown from locally sourced seeds.

The vision is to see the *Festival Wood* become Festival Forest, a protected, flourishing forest rich with biodiversity. The whole Festival community, from festival-goers and artists to suppliers, are asked to donate a tree to enable this ongoing restoration (www.agreenerfestival.com).

SOCIAL RESPONSIBILITY

There is an increasing awareness by organisations and their stakeholders of the need for and benefits of socially responsible behaviour by organisations. This means that being responsible to society at an environmental, economic, cultural and sociopolitical level is in compliance with the rule of law, and is consistent with international norms of behaviour.

The very reason for considering social responsibility within an organisation is to contribute to sustainable development of the societal, economic, cultural and natural systems in which the organisation exists.

Social responsibility is the lens through which an organisation manages what has traditionally been called the 'triple bottom line', and now, with the inclusion of 'culture' as a pillar of sustainability, the 'quadruple bottom line'.

The concept of social responsibility has been around for as long as there have been people bringing personal morals, ethics and values into their businesses. The issues of concern within social responsibility, over history, have reflected the issues of the time or place.

The principles of sustainable development as they stand today are a sound basis for social responsibility. They reflect accepted international norms, and are continually reinforced and enhanced at each edition of international gatherings on sustainable development. Embedding these principles into the organisation's culture, policy, training and practice will set an organisation on an effective path.

In the business world in recent times, *Corporate Social Responsibility* (CSR) has been the name of the game. Things have progressed significantly during the past ten years or so, with CSR moving through many phases. CSR as we know it in the modern era started out as reactive or tokenistic before moving on to corporate philanthropy, which was closely tied to reputation management and public relations.

Now CSR means socially responsible management and quadruple bottom-line reporting and, at its ultimate, is transformative. *CSR International* takes you on this journey through its '*Ages and Stages of CSR*' (www.csrinternational.org).

In November 2010 the *International Standards Organization* released *ISO 26000 Social Responsibility*,[10] which provides guidelines on social responsibility for organisations. It defines social responsibility as follows:

> Responsibility of an organization for the impacts of its decisions and activities on society and the environment, through transparent and ethical behaviour that:
>
> - contributes to sustainable development, including health and the welfare of society;
> - takes into account the expectations of stakeholders;

Box 1.4

MEETINGS INDUSTRY CSR RESEARCH

CSR Research

Meetings Professionals International (MPI) conducted research into CSR in the meetings industry, in association with the *International Centre for Research in Events, Tourism and Hospitality at Leeds Metropolitan University.*

Their research included investigating the current status of the industry with regards to CSR policy and surveying industry professionals. Their survey received responses from 1100 meeting industry professionals and businesses, and 1500 from meetings delegates. The research has loads of great findings including that 80 per cent of industry professionals surveyed felt customer expectations for CSR would increase in the coming years. Also interesting was that more than 50 per cent of conference delegates would like CSR reports to be submitted, but only 25 per cent of organisers actually produced CSR reports.[11]

The approach the industry took to CSR, and its definition of CSR, was widely varied, with no one common definition or approach. There were two schools of thought that emerged; one being that formal structure could stifle innovation and excellence, with a prescriptive framework potentially leading to only minimum levels of compliance being met. The other school of thought was that without a frame of reference and an agreed approach the industry's effective treatment of CSR may falter.

www.mpiweb.org

- • is in compliance with applicable law and consistent with international norms of behaviour; and
- • is integrated throughout the organization and practised in its relationships.

Just as *ISO 26000* did, I too like to remove the word 'corporate' from CSR and just be left with SR – social responsibility. It is more than just companies or businesses that have a responsibility to society. It comes down to each and every one of us within an organisation, a community and a family to act with social responsibility. Individual social responsibility is where it's at.

Shangri-La Hotels and Spas demonstrate a well-integrated approach to CSR. *Shangri-La* run two divisions to their CSR activities – 'Embrace' which focuses on improving social disadvantage, and 'Sanctuary' which aims to protect local habitats and wetlands. Their programmes are both about outreach and internal improvements to their own management. The global hotel chain supports outreach projects through funding and promotions and, where possible, art exhibitions and charity fundraising events to support these CSR endeavours. Guests of the hotel are invited to donate directly to the programmes, which are profiled on the hotel's website. The hotel has also joined the *Carbon Disclosure Project*, allowing them to disclose their responsible GHG management and disclose their GHG inventory (www.cdproject.net www.shangri-la.com/corporate/about-us/corporate-social-responsibility/sustainability/).

It Comes Down To You

All the (C)SR policies and agendas in the world won't mean much if the individuals inside the 'corporation' don't hold the values contained within the policies close to their hearts. If they don't have similar values, don't understand the concepts or don't understand what the organisation is trying to achieve or why, the whole thing may collapse. Delivering a sustainability vision into action is the responsibility of the individual, both professionally and personally.

Every person working within an organisation has their own morals, values and beliefs, and collectively will set the tone for the organisation. In most cases the workforce are representative of the society in which the organisation exists. Thus bringing values in from the community via your workforce is a great strategy.

As a side note, however, if it is known that corruption, for example, is common throughout society, and your organisation is working to address this within its policies, then perhaps simply reflecting community values is not the way to go!

The event industry is in a unique position, as our individual events are intense, with high impacts and short time periods, and quite often occur only once. This makes our impacts visible and our reporting periods short, and offers nowhere to hide that an ongoing business might enjoy. Conversely there is a risk that some in our industry may take the stance that they can hide, because their event is a quick in-and-out type of affair, with organising committees sometimes dissolving after the event.

As each event is often a temporary coming together of so many individuals and organisations in our industry, we don't have a continuous organisational culture as would a permanent business. It is therefore even more important that each of us is committed to it at an individual level and working together as an entire industry, to embrace the principles of social responsibility and ethical governance through one event and on to the next. Being part of an industry association that has a

---

Box 1.5

BONNAROO MUSIC & ARTS FESTIVAL WEATHERIZATION PROGRAMME

Giving Back to the Community

Bonnaroo Music & Arts Festival continues its long-standing commitment to the environment and community it calls home, Coffee Country, through a programme to help low-income homes reduce their power consumption and power bills, simultaneously reducing GHGs, called a 'weatherization program' in the USA.

The programme provides free energy retrofits to 100 low-income residents, including the installation of energy-efficient light bulbs and low-flow shower heads, and the education of residents about energy conservation. The programme is expected to save participating families an average of 20 per cent on their utility bills, and to provide long-term verifiable carbon offsets for *Bonnaroo*. Those will be tracked over a three-year period.

Bonnaroo already invests in verified offset green programmes and initiatives elsewhere; however, this project offers a chance to give back to the community in which the event is held, while simultaneously offsetting the event's GHG.

We Are Neutral, the project partner, recruits and trains local volunteers, identifies low-income housing complexes, provides energy audits for chosen complexes, coordinates residential retrofits, and tracks carbon reductions from retrofits. The offsetting company is also onsite at the festival, operating the *Carbon Shredders* booth, which works with patrons to reduce their carbon footprints at home.

This project, along with *Bonnaroo's* other greening initiatives, is a great compliment to the festival's commitment to social responsibility. *Bonnaroo's* charitable arm, the *Bonnaroo Works Fund* (BWF), was seeded by the festival, and today, $1 out of every ticket sold is diverted to the BWF for programmes invested in the arts, education and environmental sustainability with special emphasis on local reinvestment and asset building in the *Bonnaroo* communities. Through BWF, *Bonnaroo* also supports a number of regional and national environmental organisations, such as *We Are Neutral*, *Rock the Earth* and *A Change of Atmosphere*.

The *Bonnaroo Works Fund*, which began in 2009 with the help of the East Tennessee Foundation, identifies organisations seeking financial assistance and focuses its efforts on distributing funds where they will have the most impact. Over the past ten years, *Bonnaroo*, with the help of ticket proceeds, the generosity of fans, and vendors participating in fundraising opportunities, has donated over $5million to local, regional and national charities and organisations.

Over the past ten years, *Bonnaroo* has donated more than US$5 million to local, regional and national charitable organisations.

www.bonnaroo.com | weareneutral.com

sustainability focus is a good start. Some associations are listed at the end of this chapter.

It is the individuals working within our industry who will add to the value chain of social responsibility and ensure this continuum. Clients, event organising companies, individual meeting planners, sponsors, venues and suppliers all have a role to play to ensure that socially responsible practices are embedded throughout the industry.

A sustainable and genuine (C)SR programme goes beyond philanthropy and is closely tied up with corporate ethics and responsible governance. To be socially responsible, the organisation must be held accountable and be able to measure the actual or potential economic, social, cultural and environmental impacts it has on its stakeholder community. Measuring this performance is critical to its ability to continue to operate effectively.

Figure 1.3 Stand by your principles.
Source: Sunrise Festival.

SUSTAINABILITY POLICY

Putting together a Sustainability Management Policy for your event or organisation will be an important tool to focus your efforts, keeping you on the right path. It is a good document to have to disseminate publicly, make available for student enquiries, and provide to new contractors or staff. A Sustainability Management Policy can be either organisation-wide or event-specific.

You can go into as much detail as you like or make it more of a broad mission statement. It should indicate your commitment to sustainable development and describe your pathways to sustainability.

For an organisation that holds events but these events are not the organisation's primary purpose, there will likely be an overarching policy that covers all of the organisation's activities. In this situation the event department may find that it will wish to augment the policy to include event-specific content.

Alternatively, an event organiser whose primary purpose is to produce events for others may have a Sustainability Policy that guides the production of all events under its control. However, the client's policy on sustainability may also need to be taken into account in addition to the event organising company's policy.

Your policy should include the following:

- commitment to sustainable development principles, including a statement of purpose and values for the organisation as they relate to sustainability
- statement of goals or objectives regarding sustainability outcomes
- description of the indicators against which that performance will be measured
- information on the consultation process and training of staff and education of key stakeholders
- commitment to meeting the legal regulations
- commitment to adhere to international norms of behaviour with regard to sustainable development principles
- commitment to continual improvement
- commitment to excellence and leadership.

It should also include an overview on the key operational areas as they relate to the pillars of sustainability – environmental, social, cultural and economic.

This would include specific 'must-take' information that are a matter of policy. You could also include language such as 'we aspire to'.

The sustainability policy should then go on to detail how the following will be undertaken:

- compliance with targets
- monitoring and review.

General observations may also be included, such as government or industry policies or protocols you must meet, aim to exceed, or that may make an impact on your operations in the future. Make sure you keep abreast of any policy developments and technological advances which may be relevant to your work.

Be aware also of best practice standards or codes of practice relevant to event management and sustainability. Mention any certifications you are planning to achieve.

Having a policy in place is a requirement of international standard *ISO 20121 Event Sustainability Management Systems*. Read more about the standard in Chapter 11 and about the policy requirements in Clause 5.2 of the standard.

See a great example of a sustainability policy by *GOGO Events* on their website (www.gogoevents.com.au/sustainability-policy).

Sustainable Event Solutions has developed an easy-to-use policy wizard. The *SEMS Policy Wizard* guides you step-by-step through the process of identifying and documenting the level of your organisation's commitment to the principles of sustainable development and the practical requirements of implementing sustainable event production. Once you have completed the questionnaire the wizard generates a tailored policy based on your answers that is provided to you as a PDF or a text file. The final policy created by the tool gives you the core text you need to produce your policy. You would then decide to have a very detailed policy, or to carve the text up to have a succinct policy in addition to an annex or guidance document (www.semstoolkit.com).

NGOs and CHARITIES

Partnering with environmental or social justice non-governmental organisations (NGOs) or charities is a great way not only to learn more about sustainability but to raise the profile and credibility of your projects. By partnering with an NGO you can also potentially bring their volunteers on board and have them take charge of some of your greening action. The NGO can also have an information booth or their own creative activity to engage attendees in their message.

At *Glastonbury Festival, Greenpeace, WaterAid* and *Oxfam* are the main charitable causes for the event. These NGOs work around the world in very different ways, but are united in a common goal to make this world a safer, fairer, more sustainable place to live, for us and for future generations.

Figure 1.4 The SwissCityMarathon donation points.
Source: SwissCityMarathon Lucerne.

Greenpeace have an entire field they programme and run. They have eco showers, a children's play area, gardens, café and bar, FSC timber skate ramp (!), a carbon dating activity, and lots of other good Greenpeace information. Bob Wilson and his team do an extraordinary job.

WaterAid invite punters to help *Pump up the Volume!*, a petition delivered to world leaders to call on them to commit to achieving universal access to water and sanitation. *WaterAid* has also put in pit latrines onsite at the event similar to those they install in their projects across Africa and Asia.

Oxfam supply hundreds of volunteers to help in the camping grounds and pedestrian zones. Those people who wish to both support *Oxfam* and attend the festival volunteer their time.

All three NGOs are recipients of a proportion of the profits earned at the festival. They also work together to come up with the overall key campaign for the festival each year (www.glastonburyfestivals.co.uk).

The *SwissCityMarathon* – Lucerne arranges clothes donation points at the beginning of their marathon so that athletes can drop off their warm clothes before beginning the race.

MEASUREMENT AND REPORTING

To gauge the effectiveness of your sustainability management you will need to measure your performance and set goals for continual improvement. One of the cornerstones of sustainability management is disclosure of performance, and you should also have a protocol in place for how you will let your stakeholders know what your goals and objectives are, and what performance outcomes were achieved.

In various chapters there are details on how to measure and report on that chapter's subject. Coming up is a review of the *Global Reporting Initiative Event Organizers' Sector Supplement*. You are encouraged to download this supplement and delve into the suggested indicators to determine which you could report on.

In order to determine what performance you will measure, envisage the day you produce your sustainability performance report. Ask yourself the following questions:

- Who has an interest in what will be reported?
- What are they interested in finding out about?
- What are the sustainability issues specific to my circumstance that must be reported?
- What is best or accepted practice within my event industry sector or geographic region that should be reported on?

By going through this stakeholder interest process you will also uncover issues of importance that may need managing.

Through your diagnostic phase you will uncover the issues and impacts that need management, and the opportunities and legacies that may be possible.

Armed with this information, you will be in a good position to craft the skeleton of what will eventually be your sustainability performance report. You will know in advance what stakeholders will be interested in hearing about, what is expected to be reported on and what is relevant to report on. You will then be able to ensure that the appropriate processes are put in place to capture the data and information you will need to produce a comprehensive and informative sustainability performance report.

It is acceptable to produce several versions of your performance report. You may have the following:

- an executive summary or top management report with key recommendations and requests for approval for future initiatives
- a detailed performance report from which future sustainability management decisions may be informed
- a production stakeholder report going out to production partners, venues, key contractors, sponsors, government bodies, etc.
- a public performance report published online or distributed in printed form, and which highlights your commitments and outcomes
- a 'learning legacy' report which shares outcomes and learnings for the industry, future event producers and students.

Your performance report should be informative, illustrative and offer detailed metrics: words, pictures, numbers.

Describing the issue, the context surrounding it, barriers or challenges, and your management approach and lessons learned is just as, if not more important and informative, than the numbers. The numbers however are a necessary part of reporting and one which event producers should take seriously.

Common Reporting Metrics

Depending on your event type, the importance or relevance of certain issues and impacts and your level of control or ability to gather data, here are some suggested metrics on which to gather data.

It may also be relevant to report separately the various stages of the event's life cycle, such as the following:

- report pre-production
- event days
- pull-out.

Where events have distinct precincts, you may also report on these separately, such as the main park, an indoor venue and a closed-off street; or the campsite versus the entertainment arena; or the exhibition halls versus the conference centre.

Waste

- Total waste produced.
- Total waste sent to landfill.
- Total waste sent to incineration.
- Total waste recycled (by material stream if possible).
- Total biodegradable waste composted (sent to AD or other processing, such as chickens and pigs).
- Total waste salvaged and sent for reuse/repurposing.
- Total other waste (e.g. e-waste, hazardous).
- Total percentage of waste diverted from landfill and incineration.
- Reductions in waste created or waste diverted from landfill from waste initiatives.
- Waste per person per day or per event.
- Total biodegradable waste lost to landfill.
- GHG emissions from landfilled biodegradable waste.
- Total recyclable waste lost to landfill.
- GHG emissions from waste haulage (transport).

Energy

- Total kWh of mains and temporary power used.
- Percentage of renewable energy supply from mains/grid.
- Total fuel used in mobile generators by fuel type.
- Total number of generators and running hours.
- Total kVa of generators supplied.
- Total kWh from zero emissions power sources (solar, wind, pedal, hydrogen fuel cell, kinetic, etc.).
- Total bottled gas (kg).
- Total mains gas (kWh).
- Total percentage of event power from renewable energy supply.
- Total power and gas-related GHG emissions.
- Total renewable energy credits purchased.
- Total carbon offset credits purchased.
- Total investment in renewable energy technology or infrastructure for the event.
- Reductions in energy consumption and GHG emissions from initiatives (conservation or renewable energy supply on previous events or 'business-as-usual' scenarios).
- Total kg GHG per event attendee (per day or total event).

Water

- Total water consumed by source.
- Total wastewater produced.
- Total wastewater recycled and reused onsite.

For events needing temporary sanitation and water supply report on the following:

- Number of toilets (by type and number of seats).
- Total flush volume per toilet (by type).
- Number of water refill stations (and number of taps).
- Number of water-filled bollards (road blocks) and volume of each.
- Total wastewater removed by sullage hauler or disposed through sewer lines.

You may also choose to measure and report the GHG impacts of water supply and disposal, including the following:

- GHG emissions from water production.
- GHG emissions for sewage treatment.
- Transport impact of water cartage.
- Transport impact of sewage/wastewater cartage.

Travel and Transport

Attendees:

- Percentage of attendees travelling to event by mode of transport.
- Average distance travelled (return trip).
- Average occupancy for relevant modes of travel.
- Aggregate GHG emissions for each travel mode.
- Total GHG emissions for attendee travel.
- Average GHG emissions per attendee.
- Total carbon offset credits purchased for attendee travel (by organiser or attendee).

Production travel:

- Significant additional ground travel of event personnel (not including commuting) by mode, reported as GHG impact.

- Production-based air travel for personnel, total flights, destination, class of travel and resulting GHGs.
- Year-round event-related air travel for personnel.
- Total carbon offsets purchased for production air travel.

Production transport:

- Significant additional ground freight GHGs (infrastructure, materials, supplies, waste).
- Production-based air freight; distance/routes, volume/weight and resulting GHG emissions.
- Production-based sea freight; distance, volume/weight and resulting GHG emissions.
- Fuel use by site vehicles, site plant and runners during pre-production, event and pull-out, and resulting GHG emissions.
- Carbon offsets purchased for production transport.

Greenhouse gas emissions:

- Attendee travel: total GHG emissions and proportion of total event GHG emissions.
- Production travel: total GHG emissions and proportion of total event GHG emissions.
- Production transport: total GHG emissions and proportion of total event GHG emissions.
- Total event GHG emissions.
- Total carbon offsets purchased.
- Net GHG emissions.

Materials and Procurement

The key to procurement reporting is to measure the proportion of your procurement budget that met your declared sustainable procurement policies or goals. Examples of what these could be as follows:

- Percentage of expenditure on local manufacturers.
- Percentage of expenditure from local suppliers.
- Percentage of expenditure from companies with sustainability policies.
- Percentage of merchandise with sustainability certification.

- Percentage of hotels with sustainability certification.
- Number of venues or service providers compliant with *ISO 20121*.
- Proportion of suppliers that have been scruitinised for independent sustainability certification.
- Percentage of menu served with organic certification.
- Percentage of coffee and tea served that was Fairtrade certified.
- Percentage of produce served sourced from within 100 miles of the event location.
- Percentage of vendors at the event that are local.
- Percentage of workforce who live locally.

Key Sustainability Indicators

Accepted practice in sustainability reporting (and most reporting) is to establish indicators of performance. These indicators detail the topics and measures against which your performance will be assessed.

We are very lucky in the event industry to have produced for us an industry-specific set of performance indicators as part of the *Global Reporting Initiative* (GRI). In 2012 the *Event Organizers' Sector Supplement* (EOSS) was launched. Industry experts and sector-relevant NGOs came together to produce this supplement. I was on this working group representing *Live Earth* for whom I was Global Greening Director at the time.

The GRI produces guidelines which aim to help organisations prepare sustainability reports that matter, that contain valuable information about the organisation's most critical sustainability-related issues, and to make such sustainability reporting standard practice.

The key to GRI reporting is the concept of 'materiality'. This means reporting on what is important and relevant to the organisation and its stakeholders. It also includes the concepts of control or influence. The GRI recommends a sliding scale of sustainability reporting detail, depending on the level of control or significant influence an organisation has over the management of a certain issue. This means that sustainability reporting will focus on the issues critical to the organisation's management of its impact on and contribution to society and the planet.

The GRI's *Sustainability Reporting Guidelines* is now in its fourth edition. When the GRI EOSS was produced it was based on the GRI G3.1 guidelines. The GRI has recently produced the newest iteration of the guidelines, 'G4'. Keep up to date with the most recent edition of the GRI guidelines by downloading them for free on their website (www.globalreporting.org).

The GRI segregates sustainability reporting into the following categories and subcategories:

- Economic.
- Environmental.
- Social:

  - Labor Practices and Decent Work
  - Human Rights
  - Society
  - Product Responsibility.

The GRI produces almost 100 specific indicators and during the *Event Organizers' Sector Supplement's* development the working group went through each of the indicators and added event industry-relevant text. In some cases the actual title was adjusted to include additional text necessary to make it more applicable to our industry.

Also created were several new indicators needed for our sector to comprehensively report on them. The new indicators specific to our sector are as follows:

- **EO1** Direct economic impacts and value creation as a result of sustainability initiatives.
- **EO2** Modes of transport taken by attendees and participants as a percentage of total transportation, and initiatives to encourage the use of sustainable transport options.
- **EO3** Significant environmental and socio-economic impacts of transporting attendees and participants to and from the event.
- **EO4** Expressions of dissent by type, issue, scale and response.
- **EO5** Types and impacts of initiatives to create a socially inclusive event.
- **EO6** Types and impacts of initiatives to create an accessible environment.
- **EO7** Number and types of injuries, fatalities and notifiable incidents for attendees and other relevant stakeholders.

- **EO8** Percentage of and access to food and beverage that meets the organiser's policies, or local, national or international standards.

Also created were two new aspects: *Sourcing* and *Legacy*.

Sourcing indicators are as follows:

- **EO9** Type and sustainability performance of sourcing initiatives.
- **EO10** Type, amount and impact of benefits, financial and in kind, received by the event organiser from suppliers.

Legacy indicators are as follows:

- **EO11** Number, type and impact of sustainability initiatives designed to raise awareness, share knowledge and impact on behaviour change and results achieved.
- **EO12** Nature and extent of knowledge transfer of best practice and lessons learned.
- **EO13** Number, type and impact of physical and technological legacies.

The full supplement includes almost 100 indicators from which you can choose. Many of the indicators are aligned with sustainable development principles. Consider whether these are appropriate for your organisation to report to.

Remember also that you can use the GRI EOSS and its indicators as guidance only. You do not have to become an official GRI reporter. Certainly for smaller or one-off events, or those with limited resources, producing a formal GRI report will not be possible.

It is also acceptable not to produce a completely new GRI report, but to create an index whereby various aspects and indicators are already reported on within other reports. For example, your safety team, human resources, tourism impacts or procurement departments may all produce reports, and include many of the aspects and indicators suggested by the GRI EOSS. In this case you would produce an indexed report cross-referencing the location of the reporting to various indicators, rather than duplication of effort. See an

example by *London 2012 Olympics* and their GRI report index (learninglegacy.independent.gov.uk/publications/london-2012-post-games-sustainability-report-gri-content.php).

If you are staring at a blank screen wondering what to report on or where to start, I strongly suggest that you sit down with a cup of tea, read through the GRI EOSS and search out some information on how other events have reported using this framework. It really is beneficial.

EVENT PROFESSIONAL SUSTAINABILITY COMPETENCIES

To effectively implement best practice sustainability management at events, industry professionals should look to acquiring the following competencies. Much of this can be self-taught through reading, or you may wish to attend a professional development training course.

Check the *Sustainable Event Alliance* website for information on courses available worldwide both through private organisations and industry associations. Training is available in many formats, from self-paced through to live webinars or face-to-face classroom style. Check off which competencies you have. When you are ready, you may also enter the *Sustainable Event Alliance Accredited Professional Programme,* which has a peer-reviewed online examination, along with requisite career experience and contribution to growing knowledge to the sector. Read more on the SEA's website (www.sustainable-event-alliance.org).

EVENT SUSTAINABILITY INDUSTRY ORGANISATIONS

Since the first edition of this book was written, there has been a significant growth in organisations and programmes focusing on sustainability within our industry and subsectors. Here are some of the main ones.

In addition, look to your standard industry association to provide guidance and support in sustainability. If they're not talking about it, ask the question.

Box 1.6

EVENT PROFESSIONAL SUSTAINABILITY COMPETENCY CHECKLIST

Concepts

Sustainable Development Principles

Understand the principles of sustainable development, including:

- ❏ Inclusivity.
- ❏ Transparency.
- ❏ Stewardship.
- ❏ Integrity.
- ❏ Apply the principles of sustainable development to event planning and delivery.

Environmental

Understand environmental sustainability concepts within the context of event production, including:

- ❏ Resource utilisation.
- ❏ Resource conservation.
- ❏ Materials choice.
- ❏ Releases to land, air or water.
- ❏ Emissions reduction.

Economic

Understand economic sustainability within the context of event production, including:

- ❏ Local economy.
- ❏ Direct economic impacts.
- ❏ Indirect economic impacts.
- ❏ Legacy; innovation.

Social and Cultural

Understand social and cultural sustainability concepts within the context of event production, including:

- ❏ Fair trade and profit sharing.
- ❏ Equity.
- ❏ Role of labour standards.
- ❏ Health and safety.
- ❏ Social justice.
- ❏ Local community.
- ❏ Role of culture in sustainable development.
- ❏ Heritage and religious sensitivity.

Planning

Management System

- ❏ Create procedures, processes and documentation for the implementation of a management system for event sustainability.
- ❏ Undertake an internal audit of management system.

Policy

- ❏ Create an Event Sustainability Management Policy.

Stakeholders

- ❏ Identify stakeholders/interested parties.
- ❏ Establish the needs and expectations of stakeholders/interested parties.

Communication and Engagement

- ❏ Develop techniques to engage stakeholders in event sustainability.
- ❏ Create effective ways to communicate event sustainability objectives, messages and actions.
- ❏ Use communications and demonstration to convey sustainability concepts.

Box 1.6 (continued)

Issues

- ❑ Establish processes to identify event sustainability issues.
- ❑ Establish criteria to evaluate significance and relevance of sustainability issues.
- ❑ Establish criteria to prioritise issues management.

Legal and Regulatory Requirements

- ❑ Identify relevant legal or other regulations in the geographic area where the event is held.
- ❑ Ensure procedures and processes are in place to adhere to relevant legal or regulatory requirements.
- ❑ Awareness of and considerations for implementing best practice in the event industry internationally where legal or other regulatory requirements are not in place locally.

Destination, Venue, Accommodation

- ❑ Assess destination's sustainability credentials and potential for supporting sustainable event production.
- ❑ Assess venue sustainability credentials.
- ❑ Assess accommodation sustainability credentials.
- ❑ Create event-specific sustainability initiatives at venue and accommodation.

Supply Chain

Sourcing and Supply Chain Management

- ❑ Establish criteria to evaluate significance and relevance of sustainable sourcing issues.
- ❑ Create information for supplier tender or other documentation about sustainability requirements.
- ❑ Make sustainable sourcing assessments.
- ❑ Create a sustainable sourcing policy.

Operations

Waste

- ❑ Understand and identify waste issues.
- ❑ Waste impacts of procurement choices.
- ❑ Waste prevention techniques.
- ❑ Waste segregation techniques.
- ❑ Event attendee engagement in waste initiatives.
- ❑ At-event waste initiatives.
- ❑ Waste processing technologies.
- ❑ Waste auditing techniques.
- ❑ Waste measurement and reporting.
- ❑ Climate impact of waste.

Energy

- ❑ Understand and identify energy issues.
- ❑ Energy conservation techniques and initiatives.
- ❑ Renewable energy supply.
- ❑ Energy supply innovation.
- ❑ Energy measurement and reporting.
- ❑ GHG emissions factors of energy.

Transport

- ❑ Understand and identify transport issues.
- ❑ Reduce production transport impacts.
- ❑ Reduce attendee travel impacts.
- ❑ Sustainable transport options.
- ❑ Encourage sustainable transport uptake by attendees.
- ❑ Transport measurement and reporting.

Water

- ❑ Understand and identify water issues.
- ❑ Water conservation techniques.
- ❑ Water measurement and reporting.

Box 1.6 (continued)

Biodiversity and Nature Preservation

❑ Impacts that may occur onsite due to event activities.
❑ Indirect impacts that may occur away from the event site due to event activities.
❑ Issues that may occur during manufacture, use and disposal of product and materials.

Community and Society

❑ Impacts which may positively or negatively affect local communities.
❑ Practices to ensure an inclusive event.
❑ Issues regarding first nation, traditional owners, religious, cultural or heritage concerns.

Outcomes

Measurement and Reporting

❑ Setting performance objectives and targets.
❑ Setting performance indicators.
❑ Monitoring, measurement, analysis and reporting of performance.

Legacy and Innovation

❑ Understand role of legacy in event planning, policy and outcomes.
❑ Role of events to encourage innovation in supply chain and production solutions, and the economic legacy of such solutions.

Sustainable Event Alliance

This is a global not-for-profit incorporated industry association and affiliation of organisations, events and individuals who are focusing on improving the sustainability outcomes of event production and to harnessing the powerful opportunity to advance and promote sustainable development through events.

The SEA offers event professionals a pathway to understanding sustainability issues in event planning and delivery. It is a professional guild for individuals, an industry association for events and event organisations, and a network of like-minded organisations around the world all working in this space. The SEA website has a knowledge bank of resources and how-to guides, brings suppliers and event planners together through a growing database of sustainable solutions providers, and offers a portal for networking and discussion around sustainable event management issues.

The SEA sets competencies that event industry professionals should aim to achieve in event sustainability knowledge, and also lets the industry know what to expect from those who are advising, training or auditing

them in event sustainability (www.sustainable-event-alliance.org).

GO Group

Founded in early 2011 by *Bucks University, GreenEvents Europe Conference, Green Music Initiative (GMI)* and *Yourope* (the European Festival Association), *GO Group* (Green Operations) is an independent European and cross-industry association open to stakeholders interested in actively pushing the Green Agenda.

GO Group identifies, aggregates, communicates and shares international best practices to inspire people in the music festival and events industry to run their operations greener and smarter. Its aim is to establish working relationships between different industry groups.

GO Group carries out international workshops and provides major contributions on green issues to *GreenEvents Europe Conference*, Europe's leading conference for sustainability in the live music and event industry. It is offering support to festival organisers and is doing pioneering work for the festival and event industry. More than 100 festivals from 15 different countries, as well as experts, scientists, suppliers, etc., have been part of the project (go-group.org | www.green-events-germany.eu).

A Greener Festival

This is a not-for-profit company committed to helping music and arts events and festivals around the world adopt environmentally efficient practices. They provide information, education resources and facilitate the exchange of good ideas. Their website exists to provide information about how environmentally efficient methods are currently being employed at music and arts festivals, and to provide information about how the impact of festivals on the environment can be limited at future events. They facilitate the exchange of the best ideas from greener festivals around the world (www.agreenerfestival.com).

Green Meetings Industry Council

The *Green Meetings Industry Council* (GMIC) is dedicated to sustainability in the meetings and events industry, not only through education but also by spearheading research, policy and standards. The GMIC is a non-profit professional meetings association with member representation in over 20 countries. The GMIC is 100 per cent focused on advancing sustainability in the meetings industry and is a member of the Convention Industry Council (www.greenmeetings.info).

Julie's Bicycle

Julie's Bicycle is a not-for-profit organisation making sustainability intrinsic to the business, arts and ethics of the creative industries. Founded by the music industry, with expertise from the arts and sustainability, *Julie's Bicycle* bridges the gap between the creative industries and sustainability. Based on a foundation of peer-reviewed research, they sustain creativity, enabling the arts to create change. JB works with over 1000 arts organisations across the UK and internationally, large and small, to help them measure, manage and reduce their environmental impacts.

Their free online *IG Tools* allows organisations to monitor environmental impacts easily. Designed and developed by experts from within the sector, they are shaped specifically for the creative industries.

For those further along their sustainability journey, their *Industry Green Certification* is the leading mark of recognition for environmental achievement in the creative industries. An *Industry Green* star rating demonstrates to partners, suppliers, audiences and competitors a commitment to sustainability.

JB has a huge range of online resources available on its website (www.juliesbicycle.com).

Green Music Group

The *Green Music Group* (GMG) is a project set up by the non-profit organisation *Reverb*. GMG is a large-scale, high-profile environmental coalition of musicians, industry leaders and music fans using their collective power to bring about widespread environmental change within the music industry and around the globe (www.greenmusicgroup.org | www.reverb.org).

Council for Responsible Sport

The *Council for Responsible Sport* provides an independent, comprehensive certification for sustainable athletic events. By defining realistic objectives and providing a framework for achieving them, *ReSport* enables event directors to incorporate environmental responsibility into their events while informing consumers which events adhere to standards set down by the Council for Responsible Sport (www.resport.org).

Green Sports Alliance

The *Green Sports Alliance* is a non-profit organisation with a mission to help sports teams, venues and leagues enhance their environmental performance. Alliance members represent over 170 sports teams and venues from 15 different sports leagues.

Since February 2010, the Alliance has brought together venue operators, sports team executives and environmental scientists to exchange information about better practices and develop solutions to their environmental challenges that are cost-competitive and innovative. The information gathered from this collaboration is available to Alliance members in order that they may gain a better understanding of how sporting events can be performed in an environmentally sensitive manner (greensportsalliance.org).

Event Greening Forum, South Africa

The aim of the *Event Greening Forum* (EGF) is to promote and embrace sustainable and ethical business practices within the events industry in South Africa, with an initial focus on meetings, incentives, conferences, exhibitions and events. The EGF was established through the dedication and support of the industry associations who are recognised as founding members (eventgreening. co.za).

Green Your Festival Ireland

Greenyourfestival.ie has been set up to provide festivals, events and destinations with support materials and guidance to help them 'go green'. The experience and know-how already developed by participating events and local authorities is made available for free so that others can take the step towards more sustainable fun. The website also aims to support and promote the many festivals, events and destinations that have already gone down the green route, and to allow discerning participants to sustain these environmentally friendly celebrations of what it is to be Irish (greenyourfestival.ie).

Danish Sustainable Events Initiative

Set up as a legacy to the EU Presidency event held in Denmark, this project brings together those in the industry in this country working on event sustainability practice and to promote the concepts to the broader industry (www.sustainableeventsdenmark.org).

Powerful Thinking

A UK-based 'think-do' tank on sustainable energy at festivals and outdoor events. The *Powerful Thinking* campaign brings together festivals and suppliers to explore new ways of working which reduce costs and carbon through increased efficiency, and share findings to promote lower carbon energy supply.

It aims to drive a market for renewable energy supply at festivals, understanding and accounting for the business and cost restraints. It will support smaller renewable providers by raising their profile among promoters and suppliers that are using multiple power sources to strengthen their low carbon offer in a changing marketplace, and work with established suppliers and festivals to increase the efficiencies of existing relationships (www.powerful-thinking.org.uk).

Sounds For Nature

The Germany-based *Sounds For Nature Foundation e.V* pools experts from festival and concert organisations, communications and environmental protection.

The aim of *Sounds For Nature* is to raise the awareness of *'nature and environment'* in the context of live music events within the organisation teams of events and audience alike. It also promotes communication projects for a young target group to support a more sustainable lifestyle.

Sounds For Nature created guidelines for sustainable event organisation in 2004 and spearheaded the movement towards more environmentally friendly festivals in Germany by cooperation with driving forces such as the admission-free *RhEINKULTUR Festival* and the independent *Taubertal Festival* (www.soundsfornature.eu).

QUESTIONS

Definitions

Explain the meaning of the following terms, in your own words:

1   Sustainability
2   Social responsibility
3   Inclusivity
4   Transparency.

Simple answer

1   What does sustainable development mean to you?
2   What are the overarching principles of sustainable development?
3   Give an example of existing protocols or programmes that advocate globally accepted sustainable development principles.
4   What should be included in a Sustainability Management Policy for an event organisation?

Case studies

1   Provide four examples of applying the principles of sustainable development in action through an event.
2   Write an Events Sustainability Management Policy for an event or organisation.

3   Research and provide details on examples of different organisations that have undertaken CSR programmes from each of the ages and stages of CSR.

NOTES

1   Global Reporting Initiative's Event Organizers' Sector Supplement: www.globalreporting.org/reporting/sector guidance/sector-guidance/event-organizers.
2   ISO 20121: Events Sustainability Management Systems: www.iso.org.
3   UN Global Compact: www.unglobalcompact.org.
4   ISO 26000: Social Responsibility: www.iso.org/iso/home/standards/iso26000.
5   *Our Common Future* (1987), Oxford: Oxford University Press: www.un-documents.net/ocf-ov.htm#1.2.
6   United Cities and Local Governments: www.uclg.org.
7   '*Realizing the Future We Want for All*': www.un.org/en/development/desa/policy/untaskteam_undf/untt_report.pdf.
8   Transparency International: *Corruption and Sport: Building Integrity and Preventing Abuses*: www.transparency.org/whatwedo/pub/working_paper_no.03_2009_corruption_and_sport_building_integrity_and_preventing_abuses.
9   Transparency International 'Integrity Pact': www.transparency.org/whatwedo/tools/integrity_pacts.
10 ISO 26000: Social Responsibility: www.**iso**.org/sr.
11 Meetings Professionals International: *The Value of CSR in the Meeting Industry:* www.mpiweb.org (accessed October 2012).

We are trying not to force visitors to behave greener, we want to wake their interest as this is more sustainable. As visitors have a growing greener awareness we try to tie in this motivation and support it on site.

Ina Kahle, FKP Scorpio

Figure 2.1 Creative messaging letting attendees know what sustainability initiatives are in place. Sustainable Hospitality Summit, Cal State University, Monterey.

Source: Meegan Jones.

2

ENGAGEMENT AND COMMUNICATIONS

If you have been charged with the role of making your event or organisation more sustainable (by self-appointment or otherwise), you will need to create a toolkit of techniques to encourage all those who can make a positive impact to do just that.

Transitioning an event to a sustainably produced one will only work if all stakeholders and decision-makers are actively engaged, participating in change-making behaviour, and committed to reaching sustainability goals together.

You will need strategies to persuade people within your organisation and those who contract to you or provide products and services into the idea of sustainability, and to enlist their commitment.

Internal stakeholders include staff, the boss and temporary crew as well as external stakeholders such as contractors, and suppliers (e.g. waste, power, transport, catering and venue). Other external stakeholders having an influence on your outcomes include local municipal authorities and government regulators, community groups, local businesses, the general public, neighbours, NGOs, media, sponsors and funding bodies. Participants such as performers, athletes, speakers and exhibitors are also stakeholders to be engaged. Those who

'consume' your event – attendees, spectators, fans, audience, delegates – should also be the focus of your efforts.

Your engagement and communications plans are undertaken to influence these stakeholders to do a number of things:

1   To make pre-event decisions that will support your sustainability goals and expected outcomes.
2   To participate in your at-event sustainability initiatives.
3   To potentially make lasting changes in the way they go about activities which have similar sustainability impacts.

As you work through this book keep in mind the important people or groups who need to be on board. You will need to think who could buck the system, and what sneaky methods of engagement to use! Your role is as a

Box 2.1

STAKEHOLDER IDENTIFICATION CHECKLIST

Destination

- ❏ Event owner
- ❏ Client
- ❏ Sponsors
- ❏ Partners
- ❏ Funders
- ❏ Event management company
- ❏ Event staff

Staff

- ❏ Permanent staff
- ❏ Seasonal staff
- ❏ Contracted crew
- ❏ Workforce (cleaning, security, bar staff)
- ❏ Contractor's staff
- ❏ Volunteers

Suppliers

- ❏ Venues
- ❏ Accommodation/lodging
- ❏ Travel agents
- ❏ Transport providers
- ❏ Caterers
- ❏ Food and beverage serviceware
- ❏ Printing
- ❏ Signage
- ❏ Merchandise, gifts, awards
- ❏ Décor
- ❏ Food & Beverage
- ❏ Infrastructure
- ❏ Staging
- ❏ Light and Sound
- ❏ Cleaning, Paint, Timber
- ❏ General Supplies

Destination

- ❏ Fire
- ❏ Ambulance
- ❏ Medical
- ❏ Safety
- ❏ Security
- ❏ Waste
- ❏ Power
- ❏ Water

Regulatory Authorities

- ❏ Local government
- ❏ Environment protection agency
- ❏ State and Federal government
- ❏ Police
- ❏ Liquor agency
- ❏ Waterways agency
- ❏ Trade/workers' unions

Participants

- ❏ Speakers
- ❏ Performers
- ❏ Athletes and contestants
- ❏ Exhibitors and traders/stallholders
- ❏ Attendees/ticket holders/audience/spectators

Community

- ❏ Local residents
- ❏ Local businesses
- ❏ Indigenous communities
- ❏ Non-government organisations
- ❏ Media

change agent. Knowledge, inspiration and conversation are your most powerful tools.

Before you think of the best technique for each stakeholder, you will need to identify who in fact they are and whether or not they are going to be an easy nut to crack, especially old-timers stuck in their own way of doing things or who have 'tried the green way before and it didn't work'. This may have been the case previously, but solutions are different today than they were even five years ago.

Depending on your style of delivery and powers of persuasion, you may find that completely empowering people to make their own discoveries is the way to go. Rev them up, point them in the right direction and let them go for it. Drop in vital information at the right moment to keep them on the right track, but back out and don't get too in their face. This will work where you have highly experienced event professionals making daily decisions about operations and purchasing, and don't really need your help to do so. Get them inspired and interested in the issues and they should then take this knowledge on board when going about their job.

One of the best influencers we have right now is the fact that at every turn in daily life the topic of 'greening' is everywhere. Mainstream newspapers have pages on green living and environmental issues. Television schedules are full of documentaries on environmental and social justice issues. Supermarket shelves are flooded with new green/organic/eco products. And so on. Sometimes a single television show or report on a current affairs programme can switch people on.

The international standards *ISO 20121: Event Sustainability Management Systems* and *ISO 26000* both include sections on identifying stakeholders, or as they are known by ISO, 'interested parties'. Have a look at both of these standards.

Identifying Stakeholders

So who exactly are your stakeholders? How do we define and identify them?

Stakeholders are any individuals or organisations who have an interest in your activities, have needs or expectations around your activities, or who may be effected positively or negatively by your activities.

The first step when identifying stakeholders is to ask, with regard to your sustainability-related activities, impacts and outcomes, the following questions:

- Will they be affected?
- Can they contribute to the solution?
- Will they have an opinion or express concerns?
- Will they have an opinion that will be shared publicly?
- Do they regulate our actions?
- Do we have a legal obligation to them?
- Will they hinder us in meeting our goals?

It should be recognised that some stakeholders may have competing interests. There are also stakeholders who may have difficulty in voicing their opinions or actively engaging with your organisation, because they lack organisation or they may be from vulnerable communities. Some groups may not even realise they are stakeholders and it's your responsibility to reach out to them. Some stakeholders may also not yet exist! (i.e. future generations).

Figure 2.2 Enthusiastic waste volunteers at Splendour in the Grass.
Source: Meegan Jones.

INTERNAL STAKEHOLDERS

All internal stakeholders will have a role to play, some making managerial and planning decisions, and others participating in the initiatives devised for them.

Those making what I call 'buying and building' decisions need skills and knowledge in sustainability management to make informed, appropriate and effective decisions. They also need to be inspired and engaged in the topic of sustainability and to have an understanding of performance expectations for the event.

To categorise stakeholders, consider the following questions:

- Do they undertake sourcing and supply chain scrutiny?

- Do they make final purchasing decisions?
- Do they make operational decisions either before or at the event?
- Do they interact with attendees and therefore have the potential to influence their behaviour?
- Are they required to perform certain duties to effectively participate in sustainability initiatives?

For those previously not engaged or interested in sustainability management, you want a 'green penny' drops moment. When the eco light bulb switches on! I was working in a production company where we experienced what we called 'the green smile' when we talked about 'the environment'. This was an eyes-glazed-over, slightly perplexed and weak-cheeked smile which conveys 'that sounds good but I have absolutely no idea what you are talking about'. Then one morning one of the main guys doing the purchasing and contracting said to me, "Meegan, I was watching the television last night and I was so shocked to find out it takes *400 years* for a plastic bottle to break down." Even though I'd been talking to him about recycling every day for a month, the penny had finally dropped for him and we went on to make some great waste plans.

Depending on your event, internal stakeholders may just be one person, you, the person diligently reading this book. At larger events there will likely be a separation of roles with numerous people having either decision-making and purchasing power, or being involved in producing the various aspects of the event.

Whichever way the roles and responsibilities are allocated for your event, *people* are the common denominator. Working out the best way to get the ideas of sustainability into their hearts and minds will be one of your biggest challenges and, if done well, one of your great successes.

If left to their own devices, people will likely do what they have always done. You can connect these decision-makers with new options, or with contractors. You could also place a new topic on the table for discussion between contractors and event production staff.

For example, ask your sponsorship manager and your food service provider to talk through organic, fair trade and local supply issues, and to identify ways to change suppliers and potentially leverage sponsorship or product placement into the event.

Get your waste manager and recycling industry bodies, such as the aluminium recycling association or plastics recycling group, together, and look at ways to not only improve recycling separation and treatment, but also to use your event to promote the recycling organisation's aims.

A new green print company and your graphic designer, marketing or advertising staff could get together to discuss green printing practices, paper and ink choices.

Put yourself between the sustainability issues and the contractors and decision-makers, and encourage the key parties to discuss the issues and move solutions forward. A lot of your work will be done through one-on-one conversation, facilitating change by helping new processes get off the ground, and through constantly yet subtly pressuring change.

Internal stakeholders may include the following:

- Event director
- Artist liaison
- Event manager
- Backstage manager
- Programming manager
- Guest and VIP manager
- Production manager
- Stage managers
- Site manager
- Sound and lighting production
- Event assistant
- Site crew
- Infrastructure manager
- Signage
- Marshals and stewards
- Race officials
- Licensing manager
- Marketing, advertising, publicity
- Website
- Sponsorship
- Safety, medical, welfare, security
- Community liaison
- Traffic management.

EXTERNAL STAKEHOLDERS

Apart from your team of staff and crew involved with producing the event, you will also have many external people and organisations who can influence the success of your sustainability initiatives. These external stakeholders need to be identified and strategies put in place to bring them on board.

Let's drill down into some of these stakeholder groups to discuss how they can be engaged to play their part in your event's sustainability journey.

Contractors

Every contractor and service provider to your event is important to engage. They will either be playing key roles in the execution of the more practical sustainability initiatives, or their own activities at the event may have sustainability impacts.

Waste management contractors, amenities suppliers, power contractors and plumbers are all main service providers who contribute to the practical sustainability outcomes. Work with each of them during the contracting phase to establish the solutions they are able to bring to support the event's sustainability agenda. Do this through the following:

- Face-to-face meetings to discuss opportunities.
- Site visits and exploratory meetings.
- Providing them with the organisation or event Sustainability Policy.
- Enlightening them as to what they will be required to report on.
- Asking for their sustainability credentials, their sustainability ideas, and even their Sustainability Policy.
- Including requirements into their contracts.
- Offering bonuses for performance achieved.

Other contractors for events may include staging, marquees, sound and lighting production, portable building hire, fencing, roadways, barriers, signage, décor, furniture hire, security, welfare, medical, first aid, caterers, consumable suppliers, IT, phones, two-way radios, trucks, machinery, golf carts, transport, grounds workers, etc. The list goes on.

Every single one of these companies could green their offices, switch to a green energy supplier, put B20 biodiesel in their trucks, and make other general greening changes. They can then go a step further and actively change the way they source materials, manage waste, products they use, etc. By simply requesting to see their businesses' Sustainability Policy and a list of their sustainability initiatives could motivate them to review their current systems.

Regulating Authorities

Authorities who regulate your activities or grant licences for your event are very important stakeholders. These include local government, police, fire, ambulance, and environment agencies.

The local council and environment agencies may even be a step ahead and have tools or resources to help you. Work with them to seek out their targets for various environmental measures, and aim to better them.

For example, your local authority may already have a very active recycling and composting campaign. Seek out those in the Council responsible for rolling out these campaigns and enquire how your event can take on the concepts they are promoting.

They may have created a recycling 'brand' or bin tops, or signs you can use. They may even have mobile recycling displays and staff who can come and set up at your show.

Vendors

What you have for sale at your event is a signal to attendees as to the authenticity of your sustainability intentions. The sustainability credentials of items for sale by traders at the event should be managed. In many cases the event organiser will not be in direct control of the materials and products choices by these vendors, and so working with these food stalls and non-food traders on the 'greening' of their offer is essential.

Your vendors are likely to be one of the largest areas of waste creation and you must work closely with them regarding waste management. This is not only in managing how they deal with waste created as a result of their sales, but also putting controls on what they are allowed to bring in the first place – product packaging, plastic bags, take away food packaging, etc.

You may control what branded products you produce for your event or you may license out the rights for merchandising. Either way, sustainable sourcing needs to be considered.

If it's for sale at your event, it reflects upon your sustainability claims. You must get those involved in selling items to green their act.

Glastonbury Festival does just that through their '*Green Trader Award*'. During the event they judge vendors at the festival on a variety of topics from waste management through to product sourcing. Each year traders are awarded Gold, Silver and Bronze awards.

Figure 2.3 Made With Intent, a Gold Green Trader Award winner at Glastonbury Festival. This trader collected discarded tent material from Reading Festival in a project organised by the book's author and then set up a market stall selling items made from the tent material at Glastonbury Festival. Made With Intent is now an established merchandise business (www.withintent.co.uk).

Source: Meegan Jones.

Suppliers

Those who provide goods and services at your event are a major external stakeholder category who you need to engage to have them source and supply you with sustainable solutions or to modify their onsite production techniques to meet your requirements. Read more about supplier management in Chapter 8.

Competitors (Athletes)

If you are organising a big sporting competition your competitors are a separate group of stakeholders to engage. Inform them how they can minimise their impacts through their participation in the competition and how they can speak out to support aligned sustainable development messages being championed at the event.

Sport is a great equaliser, with nations at every stage of development competing on an even level. Sport is a great sector to align with social justice and community cohesion issues, and a natural issue to tackle as part of many sporting events.

At a more operational level, how teams are transported and accommodated is something that can be managed to reduce overall event impacts. Ensure that ways in which teams can get involved are promoted to clubs in advance.

Venue

Whether indoors or out, if you're hiring a venue, enlisting the venue manager's commitment to sustainability is vital.

Many sustainability impacts of an event held at a venue will be controlled by venue management. Your engagement with them will occur at the outset, when reviewing potential venues to host your event. Use the venue checklist in Chapter 4 as one of your engagement and communications tools.

NGOs and Campaigns

Regardless of the topic of your event, there are likely to be community, special interest or activist groups working in the area of sustainability you are managing or focusing on.

These may be NGOs, community activists, government programmes or industry bodies. Engaging them in the development of your sustainability projects will not only expand your workforce, but also increase the likelihood of your making the best decisions.

Groups exist to bring awareness to such issues as climate change, water conservation, biofuels, renewable energy, recycling and reuse, social justice, transparency, ethical governance, sustainable food sourcing, etc.

Look for local groups who may wish to participate in your sustainability schemes. For example, there may be action groups whose objectives are to rejuvenate a natural setting near your event that you are working to protect. There may be an upcoming 'Clean-up' campaign, or an activist campaign for non-GMO foods.

There may be community gardens or a group trying to create one. There may be an action group promoting organic vegetables or a local farmers' market. Aligning these groups with your food campaign can be a great fusion.

By inviting groups who are working these issues locally into your event, you get the benefit of their passion for sustainability issues, probably some very motivated volunteers, and also a chance to offer their causes some vital exposure to the attendees at your event.

Clients

Engaging the client in sustainability is absolutely necessary. It is possible that your client has actually asked for the event to be run sustainably. If you have to sell-in sustainability to the client, the triple bottom-line angle will do you some good. Depending on where your client is at, if they care about or understand sustainability issues, you should have enough in your toolbox to convince them that going green is good.

Volunteers

Getting your volunteers on board with your sustainability initiatives is essential. Your volunteer stewards are those people who are often on the front line, dealing directly with your attendees.

These are people who direct traffic in the car-parks, who run information booths, direct foot traffic, manage campsite hubs, show people to their seats, stand sentry over recycling bins, check wristbands and tickets, etc. Ensuring that the event's sustainability messages flowing to the attendees through these volunteers are clear and correct is really important. Engaging and motivating the stewards over various initiatives will filter through to the attendees. Make sure you have an effective communications programme in place to get the word out to event attendees through your coalface volunteers.

Participants

Those participating in the event through performing, speaking, hosting a workshop or panel, etc., must also be part of the sustainability process. They are prime talking heads who can promote the new sustainability initiatives both pre-event and on show day.

Make sure they know what's what before the event and brief them accurately throughout its duration. Pre-briefing may spark interest in a participant over

Figure 2.4 Calgary Folk Music Festival has volunteers at all bins to ensure attendees understand which bin to put their waste into.

Source: Calgary Folk Music Festival (calgaryfolkfest.com).

a particular element of sustainability, and they could become an ambassador or spokesperson for that project.

Artists and performers are role models, and are really effective as spokespeople for causes. History has shown this to be the case. Through song, performance, theatre and art, potent statements can be made on environmental and social justice issues.

They can entice and inspire crowds of people to take on issues, and with collective action invoke change.

- Target particular performers who align with your philosophy.
- Engage installation artists to produce thought-provoking artwork.
- Ask performance artists and roving performers to tackle green issues in their work.

- Set up a one-page information sheet in pdf and email which summarises all the sustainability activities you have going at your event.
- Ask programmers and artist-relations people in your team to make sure they get the word out that your event is 'green'.

Industry Sector Organisations

If there are industry associations connected to your suppliers and contractors who can help effect change across an entire industry, this is a good place to commence engagement. Waste is an obvious area that will have a lot of focus through industry associations for various recyclable materials and composting.

Event industry associations and tourism associations are also key stakeholders. Work with them to use your event as a showcase for others in the industry locally as to what is possible. When the *EU Presidency* was held in Denmark, the organising group worked with many event and tourism industry stakeholders and created the *Danish Sustainable Events Initiative* (www.sustainableevents denmark.org). Read more background on this on the book's website as well.

An unlikely industry changer was also found through *Shanghai Fashion Week*. Through some great sustainability work by *We Impact* and *MCI*, the event was an opportunity to open dialogue with the event industry and suppliers, and to demonstrate some best practice in action. Read more about this event's journey on the book's website.

Sponsors

Sponsors have the potential to dramatically affect the appearance if not the actual sustainability of an event. Choosing the correct sponsor and ensuring their product or company ethic aligns with your sustainability goals is essential. Image transfer is one of the prime benefits in a sponsorship relationship (apart from money and exposure). This is where the event benefits from the brand image or reputation of the sponsor, or the reverse.

Figure 2.5 ZIP water filters sponsored the water filter refill station at Sydney Festival.

Source: Meegan Jones.

Ensure that the sponsors include sustainable practices in their logistical operations of the activities they create, as well as through the message they are presenting to attendees. Encourage creative interpretation of sustainability ideas in their onsite activity. Their involvement should underscore your greening goals.

Sponsors' participation needs to be managed and guided to ensure they also add to the event's sustainability credentials. Rather than just a logo in the programme, sophisticated onsite activation is more effective.

Your event may be such that an association with it is hugely beneficial for the image and credibility of the brand. It is an important part of the sponsorship offer and something you can leverage where sustainability themes come in.

If you are OK to have commercial product alignment, getting sponsors on board which have a sustainability ethic is an excellent way to expand your potential sponsor income. A company that wants to demonstrate its commitment to sustainability could sponsor your recycling, or grey water management, or fund/subsidise the shuttle bus from the train station, thereby encouraging public transport use.

Other sponsorship alignment ideas include the following:

- Paying for and branding recycling volunteers' uniforms.
- Product logo on recycling bin signage.
- The sponsor constructing a venue, bar or installation from found and salvaged objects. The venue could be run on renewable energy, and offer mobile phone charging, for example.
- Bathroom home ware, range of cleaning products, or personal products, to sponsor amenities.
- Offer free product in return for attendees participating in initiatives such as recycling, car pooling or taking public transport.
- A bike shop to sponsor a pedal power stage or a bike valet parking station.
- Organic food brand to sponsor the creation of a permaculture garden onsite, including the composting programme for the event's wet waste that will be used to 'feed' the garden.

- 'Eco' paint company to supply all paints for the event's décor, in exchange for exposure.

Choose sponsors that also have a consumer line; for example, a brand of commercial cleaning products that may be used in bathrooms at the event, but also promoted for use by event attendees at home.

✓ Work out who will influence the success of your sustainability initiatives.
✓ Empower those who make purchasing and production decisions with the knowledge they need to make the best choices.
✓ Encourage all traders to be as sustainable as possible.
✓ Build into supplier and contractor agreements your expectations to meet sustainability goals, including materials choice, product use and waste management.

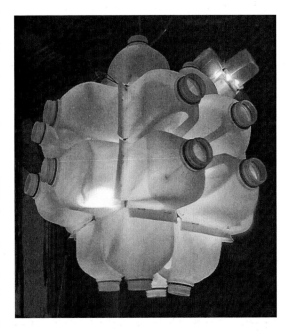

Figure 2.6 Milk bottle lampshade by Milkcrate Events, an event décor company based in Sydney, Australia that aims to actively change attitudes towards waste by reusing it to make events beautiful.

Source: Milkcrate Events (www.milkcrateevents.com).

✓ Work with regulating authorities, industry associations, interest groups and associations to be part of your green campaigns.

✓ Choose inspiring performers, speakers, artists and other participants who can champion your green goals.

✓ Use a variety of techniques to communicate with stakeholders, including face-to-face meetings, newsletters and emails, resource websites, summary sheets and info packs.

Local Community

The local community's acceptance of your event can contribute significantly to its success. If your event attracts a large number of people to an area, the day-to-day life in the area is likely to be disrupted.

Traffic and public transport, access, noise and waste are potential areas of contention. By consulting with the local community on greening your event and your sustainability policies, you may be able to pre-empt some potential complaints.

Many events are community-minded and have cultural cohesion at their core. These events will naturally reach out to and engage the participation of the local community as they are inherently for that community.

Business events (conferences, exhibitions, launches, etc.) may not naturally see community engagement as part of their remit, or even of importance. Likewise, at for-profit events (entertainment, sports or otherwise), while the 'community' may be the main attendee base, the idea of authentic community engagement may not be high on the agenda.

Meeting or communicating with people in the local community to discuss how the event could affect them or how they may benefit from it is an important aspect to sustainability performance. Certainly this is an aspect to report on if your event has positive economic or social legacies in place, and offers a positive and rewarding experience in the lead-up to the event, during the event and after the event has left the community.

• Enable access to community assets, if the event could take them out of action for the event period (e.g. an event fencing off a local park and cycle paths usually accessed by the local community).

• Offer compensation and alternatives if access to community assets is impeded.

• Invite local community groups to be part of event activities.

• Donate to local community groups in exchange for volunteer support.

• Allow a voice for local campaigns, causes or activities at the event to encourage participation.

• Allow community groups to organise catering outlets as a profit-making activity.

• Align community groups with various event activities or services, such as welcome desk, cloakroom, information stalls or programme sales.

• Offer discounted or VIP tickets/access for residents located adjacent to the event location.

• Offer 'local' event entry prices to those living in the same postcode as the event.

• Offer discount ticket prices for group purchases from community groups.

• Align with causes, campaigns or activities and set up donation of ticket price or event profit to these groups.

• Offer priority employment for event workforce to local residents.

• Engage with local contractors, product and service providers as a first priority.

• Set up a priority tender route for local providers.

• Offer discounted vendor pitches or exhibition spaces to local businesses.

• Identify and address any cultural or religious sensitivity pertinent to the event, or its activities, timing or location.

• Invite local businesses into the event's activities if the event will impinge on custom due to competition or access.

• Offer compensation or alternative profit-making opportunities.

Communications Techniques

Just plain old talking to your various stakeholders, in meetings, on the phone, via email, etc., is an opportunity to continually reinforce the event's commitment to sustainability. More formal communications tools may also be used to reinforce your goals, highlight issues, promote new ideas and successes, and to showcase results. Communications methods for internal and external stakeholders include the following:

- email
- newsletter
- meeting
- letter
- contract
- information sheets
- handbook
- intranet portal
- website
- signage
- programme
- media
- announcements
- onsite video
- advertising
- SMS/text/bluetooth access
- phone apps
- ticketing
- application.

If you're planning to implement *ISO 20212 Event Sustainability Management Systems*, you will need to have a process in place that documents how you have identified stakeholders and to log your communications methods (boring, I know). Read more about these requirements in Chapter 11.

Newsletters

A newsletter can be sent out to those whose operations and purchase decisions have an impact on the event's sustainability performance. They include good news stories, tips and ideas, resources, contacts and concepts. It may be emailed, or turned into a pdf document and attached to the email, or posted onto a website and a link emailed.

- Profile contractors who have 'gone green'.
- Introduce new initiatives at your event.
- Include 'how to green your business' information.

- Include information on how event activities can impact on the environment and society.
- Set out your event's sustainability goals.
- Explain your expectations for the stakeholder's participation in your sustainability plans.

You may wish to tailor the newsletter to suit each stakeholder group. For your infrastructure and equipment contractors you could send out a newsletter that speaks about your sustainability initiatives and offers resources and information on how companies can 'green' their business. For workforces and volunteers, your newsletter may include how they can travel sustainably to the event (e.g. your free shuttle bus for workers) or how they can participate in your sustainability initiatives – and to try and engage them in caring about sustainability and the role they have to play in its success.

Resource Website

For larger organisations with ongoing events throughout the year or with a major annual event with year-round pre-production, setting up a website full of resources which the event's production staff and key stakeholders can access may be a good way to go.

This becomes an archive of resources, and also makes it a one-stop shop for those needing to find a piece of information on a particular issue. For example, you may remind people in your newsletter if they are having any printing done for your event that they will need to follow your guidelines for sustainable printing. These guidelines, along with contacts for approved printers, can be placed on the resource website. This would be really useful for city-wide events like multi-arts festivals where many individual promoters put on shows across many venues. *Sydney Festival* has such a resource website which is available for staff, crew, major contractors, caterers, venues and artists to access information about the sustainability ambitions of the event, along with guidance information on the various issues.

Workforce Information Sheets/Booklets/Cards

For those organisations that supply a lot of front-line staff such as security or cleaners, or companies that recruit and manage your volunteers, you could prepare a newsletter that they can forward on to their staff and volunteers.

Rather than a newsletter as such, it could be a strategically timed information sheet summarising the sustainability initiatives both for the event and its attendees, but also your expectations for the involvement of the staff, crew and volunteer teams.

This could include information on staff travel options, expectations around their HQ waste management, letting them know that the food from catering will be organic and local, explaining the benefits of the compost loos in their compounds, etc.

At-event Workforce Inductions

Apart from pre-event communication, the event workforce (including volunteers) who only have event-day roles will likely also have team briefings and inductions. Ensure that the sustainability initiatives make it on to the agenda for these pre-event inductions and daily briefings. Or, if necessary, hold specific sustainability inductions.

Any staff or crew members whose daily activities come into contact with sustainability projects need to be reminded of how they can influence their success. For example, registration desk staff processing accreditation at a conference can remind delegates that at the close of the event they can deposit their lanyards in one of three boxes of their choice and by doing so they will be voting for one of three local community projects that will benefit from donations by the event.

Or: those staff members who direct foot traffic could also be charged with the responsibility, on the final day of a camping festival, to remind people to pack up their campsite and donate any unused items to charity rather than leaving them abandoned on the campsite.

Pull together a summary of your initiatives, tailored to each group of staff and volunteers, and supply the details to the person responsible for handling communication with these teams.

There will also possibly be handbooks or information kits handed out to the workforce. Ensure that you have a page or two included on sustainability policy, initiatives and expectations of staff behaviour, and how they can be involved in helping to achieve the event's sustainability ambitions.

Summarise key messages and issues you want your attendees to know about and projects you want them to participate in, and create a swing tag to go on a lanyard to hang around relevant workforce team members' necks. They will then have constant access to the correct information which they will hopefully pass on to your attendees.

If your volunteers have a HQ, put up a sign, reminders and messages about the sustainability ambitions, so that brief facts, a summary of the initiatives and what you want them to communicate to attendees is within sight. If the key messages change each day, put someone on the job of updating these messages.

ATTENDEE ENGAGEMENT

The way you communicate sustainability goals publicly will influence your event's reputation and also the effectiveness of your initiatives. At-event initiatives and attendee engagement programmes are great vehicles to encourage participation and facilitate lasting changed attitudes and behaviours.

Strategies are needed to engage those vital to the success of sustainability plans and thought must be put into the way you present sustainability credentials.

Think through how you want your event to be perceived from a sustainability viewpoint.

You may decide to push sustainability to the fore of all activities. This could be appropriate if it's the first time you are introducing sustainability, to give the focus it needs to gain traction.

Just because you run an event sustainably it isn't necessary for you to wave its 'green-ness' in attendees' faces at every turn. You may decide it isn't right for your event and you may not want to confuse the positioning, branding or image by over-emphasising this point. Events don't need to position themselves as 'Green-with-a-capital G' in order to be produced with social and environmental responsibility.

The way you approach the sustainability messaging and attempted lesson-learning and behaviour changing initiatives should be balanced or reflective of the context in which your event is held. Think very carefully about what is appropriate, possible, relevant and likely to be effective.

Figure 2.7 EnergyPlayground and DJ Energy FACTory getting attendees involved in renewable energy production.
Source: Global Inheritance (www.globalinheritance.org/energy-playground).

Brand Your Greening

If you decide to go down the green-theme road, a great way to get attendees' attention is to brand greening projects under the one banner or theme.

'*Ecobound*' is *Southbound Festival's* programme to brand all their sustainability activities. At *Roskilde Festival* they have introduced the '*Green Footsteps*' programme. *Electric Forest* call theirs *Electricology*.

Greenwash/Green Sheen

People can be cynical about companies promoting their 'green' credentials, their radars finely tuned to detect a greenwash. Make sure you walk the walk, rather than just talk the talk. Be prepared to be scrutinised. Don't over-stretch the truth of what you are doing. Read more about greenwashing in Chapter 8 (p. 183).

Think about whether more effort is put into promoting the green in your event than is actually committed to resourcing initiatives.

Influencing Attendee Behaviour

Event producers should have control over influencing back-of-house and internal operational activities such as reducing energy demand, using renewable resources, responsible purchasing, and resource recovery. Influencing the way attendees behave, particularly at a crowded event, is another story altogether.

When considering an attendee-dependent sustainability initiative, understanding the state of mind of attendees prior to and during the event will lead you to the best decisions and devices to motivate them to action. Bribery is a common and effective strategy!

Communications is the key. The way you explain your ideas before the event, and the way you convince people to act in a certain way at the event, is all influenced by the way you communicate with them and how convincing you turn out to be. Things to think about in your strategies to get attendees involved are as follows:

- attendee profile and predisposition to engaging with a sustainability theme
- event practicalities such as site layout, footfall, congestion, etc.
- pre-event communications opportunities
- at-event communications.

Before you dive into any ideas for managing at-event impacts, you will need to think carefully about the overall personality of event attendees as a collective group. Are they the type likely to respond enthusiastically to your greening efforts or will you need to coax them into participating? Some questions to ask yourself are as follows:

- Are attendees likely to respond to your onsite messaging of sustainability issues and requests to act in a certain way?
- Do they have the time/headspace/clarity of mind/ aptitude to take on the messages you are trying to impart?
- Will they object to being told how to behave?
- Are you preaching to the converted, thus making your job relatively simple and perhaps using energy and resources better allocated elsewhere?
- Are they likely to actively participate in initiatives where they must change their normal behaviour?
- If not given a choice and where participation is compulsory, will they take it on easily, or try to buck the system?
- Are you making it easy for them?
- Will behaviour-changing initiatives have a positive or negative effect on the event vibe?
- Do they need to be enticed or bribed into action?
- Will there be a penalty if they don't do it? Carrot or stick?

- Do you want to avoid a preaching tone? (The answer to this one should be yes.)

Remember: by the time show day comes, the horse may well have bolted. It is in the planning phase that you will be able to make the biggest changes, so do your homework. Talk to your people, and perhaps, if you are up to it, talk to your potential event attendees too.

Focus Groups and Discussion Forums

Getting feedback and ideas from event attendees is an obvious way to get a feel for what could work and also what they would like to see happen. Host a real-life focus group or conduct a discussion forum online. Just remember to have someone go into the forum to answer questions, give feedback, and glean the pearls of wisdom to distribute to the event planning staff for further consideration.

Pre-event Communications

In the lead-up to your event, there will be many opportunities to communicate with those considering attending. Start seeding sustainability ideas from the very first opportunities to communicate. Communications strategies may already be in place through the marketing team and, if that's so, integrate the sustainability messages into their content, or work with them on creating a specific campaign around sustainability initiatives. Communications methods may include the following:

- publicity and media releases
- website
- emailed newsletters
- posters and promotional flyers
- pre-event printed programmes or literature
- letters and invitations
- printed material accompanying tickets
- advertising.

Website

The event's website is one of the most powerful tools you have. It allows you to explain plans in detail, to use

Box 2.2

ROSKILDE FESTIVAL

Rethinking Trash, Trust and Eight Days

We're getting there, but a waste-free *Roskilde Festival* still has a long way to go. In the mist of an eight-day sensational ride, some of us still forget what happens when you leave something behind. How do we improve waste mentality?

Funny as it may seem, climbing out of your tent doesn't have to be a challenge trying to avoid a nest of beer cans. The smell of a new morning doesn't have to be an explosion of decay stepping on the can of fish you left two nights before. *Roskilde Festival* doesn't have to be that way with a little help from you and your friends. Despite numerous successful actions last year we are still struggling to create a healthy trash mentality. This year *Roskilde Festival* once again tightens effort against the trash issue. Introducing clean areas, putting up more bins and developing trash points making it even easier and more effortless for participants to keep the camping areas clean. Ultimately it will be up to everyone to see these actions through – hopefully changing the way we handle our cans and food wrappings for good. But that's not all you can do.

Sowing the seed of the 'Clean Areas': Common sense might become distant in a mix of green grass, alcohol and music, but sometimes the happy settings yield a flood of great ideas from creative souls. That was the case last year, when one very resourceful guy collected petitions to remove the silent part of the 'Silent & Clean' area, where he was situated. He felt too restricted – and decided to do something about it. Not only did he succeed in his mission, he made *Roskilde Festival* aware of the demand for 'Clean' areas only.

Rethink Roskilde on the web: When leaving this much trust and responsibility to you, developing the festival becomes a two-way street, which is why the festival invites you to share ideas and thoughts on not only environment and sustainability, but also co-creation, art, food, music and you keep filling in the need yourself.

On *Roskilde Festival*'s discussion forum for rethinking and developing *Roskilde Festival* (rethinkroskilde. com) everyone can upload ideas and participate in discussions on where to move *Roskilde Festival* in 2013, 2015 or 2020 – making the path from idea to action smooth and efficient. They can also read more about the many initiatives to overcome the trash challenges at *Roskilde Festival* and join the discussion.

rethinkroskilde.com

photos, put in context the way you will reduce the event's impacts, and show attendees how they can take part. The 'green pages' on your website may also be used to educate on various issues and offer links to further information.

If there's a news feature, use this to strategically drop in stories on various issues, particularly those that have relevance to decision-making timing by event attendees. Don't bury the sustainability information within the menu hierarchy. If possible put it at the top level so that it stands alone.

At-event Engagement and Communications

The following tools will reinforce the messages promoted to attendees at the event:

- key campaigns and 'green' themes
- signage
- waste stations and 'eco-booths'
- volunteer stewards
- green zones
- art installations.

Box 2.3

TOLLWOOD FESTIVAL

Leaving a Lasting Legacy

Since its very first festival in 1988, *Tollwood Festival* has embraced concern for environmental impacts into the event's production. What began with the demonstration of a small solar cell has grown over the years into an essential and extremely effective part of the festival.

In the early 1990s, *Tollwood* initiated an important innovation, contrary to accepted practice – that at festivals and similar events, food was only allowed to be served on disposables. *Tollwood* began serving food on porcelain, with a special dishwashing system set up by the organisers. It was this demonstration of what was possible, and a fantastic legacy to the industry in the region, which led to the City of Munich requiring the *Oktoberfest* to serve food in reusable dishes too.

Organic Catering

From the beginning, *Tollwood* has also served food and drinks that are as ecological as possible. Since 2003, their summer and winter *Tollwood Festivals* have been certified according to the EU Eco-Regulation. Today, the dishes constist of close to 100% organic ingredients. Furthermore, each food vendor must provide at least one vegetarian main dish. In addition to the organic label, tea, coffee, wine, rice, sugar, chocolate, bananas and mangos carry a fair trade label.

The project *'Bio für Kinder'* (*'Organic for Children'*) initiated at the beginning of 2006 together with the *Department of Health and the Environment* of the City of Munich has been one of *Tollwood*'s most successful campaigns. Thirty-one sponsors from Munich's business community helped to ensure that organic food is served at some 30 childcare institutions. As of today, close to 650 000 100% organic dishes have been served, with a mere surplus cost of 16.5% on average. The success of this project helped to foster a city council decision: from autumn 2013 on, 50% organic food will be served in all municipal kindergartens and schools – a model for Germany.

Renewable Energy

Since 2000, *Tollwood* sources green electricity from the Munich public utility company, this way avoiding 620t of CO^2 each year. Green event technology and saving energy programmes such as energy efficiency checks for vendors help to save large amounts of energy festival for festival.

Thought Leadership

In 2007, *Tollwood* initiated the *'Weltsalon'*. Here everything revolves around the major environmental and social issues of our time: Events about globalisation and equity, war and peace, environmental destruction and innovation, courageous people and forward-looking projects. In this fascinating tent, with light projections varying according to theme, people from all over the world – the 'leaders in their field' – come together on stage. The *Weltsalon* is a call to rethink. The focus is not only on becoming informed but on experiencing. Instead of theories, people. Instead of helplessness, encouragement to act. A place of both calm and movement.

www.tolwood.de

You can also hijack existing communications to include your green messages; for example:

- printed material and information kits
- information stalls
- video screen clips
- onstage announcements.

Gather together content to place into existing communications options and to supply for stage announcements and screen grabs. Produce a summary information sheet and a poster to place on the wall of your information stalls so that staff in these kiosks know what you have going on.

Installations and Interaction

Team up visual artists and performance artists with various issues and see the creative sparks fly. By twinning these natural bedfellows, namely environmental issues and the arts, you can creatively, humorously and inspirationally communicate key messages and provoke thought and action by attendees.

The Green Zone

If you're serious about using your event to promote sustainable living and giving a voice to environmental issues, set up a 'green zone'. Cluster activities, information booths, demonstrations, discussion forums, films

Figure 2.8 Energy stall by Magnificent Revolution educates attendees about energy creation.

Source: Magnificent Revolution (www.magrev.org.au).

and the like in one area. The type of event you're producing will direct the content, and this may not be appropriate at many events. But if you have large numbers of people and opportunities within your programme to fit such a space, it really is an opportunity not to be missed.

Get creative with your content and come up with ways to demonstrate and promote environmental conservation, sustainable living and the big issues affecting the earth today. Create activities in which people can get involved, be it hands-on, participating in discussions or watching films and listening to presentations. Invite NGOs, community groups, activist associations, single-issue campaigns, and everything in between.

The *High Five Program* strives to teach communities how to leave green spaces as they were, to divert waste from landfills, and it rewards people for their participation. The Michigan-based community organisation specialises in large-scale events, prevention of litter and significant reduction of waste streams. The program rewards attendees and volunteers for using sustainable practices and learning good green behaviours (www. facebook.com/thehighfiveprogram).

Volunteer Stewards

Face-to-face communication is probably going to be your most effective tool. Having people talk to attendees about green initiatives will cut through the clutter and get the message across. Recruit motivated people who have environmental issues under their skin. The free ticket to the event will be one of your main enticements, but you will want to make sure you have motivated people who really believe in the issues and who are also outgoing, friendly and OK to talk to strangers!

Give them a task to do, such as handing out bin bags or directing people around the site. Station them at sets of bins. Get them to walk around and hand out butt bins, or to help people set up camp. All the while, they should be charged with the role of promoting the sustainability messages you want conveyed to attendees.

Box 2.4

ENERGY FACTory

In 2007, *Global Inheritance* launched a new programme at *Coachella* called the *Energy FACTory*. This interactive energy museum was the first of its kind at a major music festival anywhere in the world. The mission of the *Energy FACTory* is to educate festival-goers on renewable energy and energy conservation via various entertaining and engaging programmes.

The *Energy FACTory* featured everything from 30 energy bikes that powered cell phones, live gas-to-electric car conversion, solar-powered sprinklers, wind-powered DJ sets, a DIY biodiesel exhibit plus much more. In 2009 it evolved into an *Energy FACTory* DJ Mixer. Festival-goers could win the chance to DJ at *Coachella*. The DJ stage was connected to an Energy Playground where fans could generate energy to power the concert. DJs had their fan base generate power by interacting with a re-engineered playground.

Thousands of festival-goers rode see-saws, swing sets, and bikes, ran on human hamster wheels and turned hand cranks among other things in support of their favorite DJ.

The energy that each piece of equipment produces went straight to an Energy Well – a large lithium ion battery prepared to both take-in and give-out stored energy.

The *Energy FACTory* DJ Mixer and Energy Playground are now staples at major festivals across the USA. Global Inheritance's Energy Playground not only has the capacity to power sound systems but in the past has also powered cell phone chargers, snow cone machines, televisions, and more.

www.globalinheritance.org/energy-playground

Box 2.5

REVERB ECO-VILLAGE

Every year *Reverb* works with hundreds of local and national non-profit organisations by providing an opportunity to present ideas and information at some of the season's most popular concerts and live music events.

They promote a message of environmental responsibility and action is via the onsite *Eco-Village* where they host environmentally focused organisations at each tour stop. Groups invited to participate free of charge include local and national environmental non-profit groups, green technology displays and exhibits, and eco-friendly product sampling. The organisations involved are able to interact with visitors during the show to provide a valuable educational experience that reaches millions of music fans every year. Most recently, *Reverb* had the pleasure of touring with artists such as Dave Matthews Band, John Mayer, Sheryl Crow, Jack Johnson, and many others, bringing environmental services and educational activations to their nationwide tours.

www.reverb.org

Figure 2.9 Reverb Eco-Village.

Source: Reverb.

Signage

Creative use of signage can be a great way of conveying environmental messages and information about sustainability activities. Depending on the tone you decide to take with the green messaging onsite, you can be subtle, or take a bolder stand and include it as part of your creative décor and display.

Bonnaroo Festival in the USA has created structures that are placed around the site letting people know what the recycling and composting successes have been and what they will be trying to achieve. *Glastonbury Festival* in the UK has an entire side of the event called *Greenfields*, where green crafts, alternative therapies, green

futures, *Greenpeace*, the permaculture garden, etc., are placed. There is a roadway called the 'Old Railway Track' that divides the festival in two. It acts as a natural barrier between Greenfields and the 'other side'. Along this road they have created *The Green Way*, photos of which have been reproduced throughout this book with the kind permission of the creator of the signs, Tracey Shough (picapicastuff.blogspot.com). As people walk along this roadway some fantastic use of signage has been created. The signs and images are mini-installations with an environmental theme. See other examples of at-event sign messaging throughout the book and on the book's website.

Figure 2.10 Creative messaging by Tracey Shough of picapica (picapicastuff.blogspot.com).

Box 2.6

ROSKILDE GREEN FOOTSTEPS

Green Footsteps to Roskilde

Green Footsteps is *Roskilde Festival*'s environmental campaign that gives festival-goers the opportunity to choose a more eco-friendly life and festival style. The campaign encourages festival guests to act with consideration for the environment by taking *Green Footsteps* before, during and after the festival. The overall idea is that individual actions have great significance when taking care of the environment.

The festival itself takes many green footsteps to take the event towards sustainability. This includes waste management, recycling and composting, container deposits for beer cups and energy management to source renewable energy options. And to encourage a greener footprint by their audience, the *Green Footsteps* programme has been implemented. It neatly communicates how the audience can be involved and *Green Footsteps* are found all over the festival site in which the audience can participate.

In the initial years of the campaign *Green Camps* were set up for campers who had taken their own *Green Footsteps* (e.g. taking public transport to the event) and allowed them to register to have a spot in these renewable energy-powered clean and green campsites. Now the programme has morphed and six *Green Camps* have been integrated throughout the entire campsite. Festival-goers were invited to host a green camp – and invited to submit an application which explains how they will:

- Minimise the waste.
- Have some fun green activities each day that involve and inspire other festival guests.
- Have some kind of original or unusual theme and a catchy slogan that reflects *Green Footsteps*' green feet. Everyone should be able to see immediately that it is a *Green Camp*.
- The green activities during the festival must be documented through photographs and video. The goal is to create a video that can inspire future festival guests to a green camp life.
- You must have fun in true Roskilde Festival style!

Festival-goers were then able to choose to camp inside these *Green Camps* and participate in the green fun the camp hosts had created.

At *Roskilde Festival* the guests can also participate in refund collection competitions where they receive cold beer in return, they can donate tents and sleeping bags to charity, and they are introduced to an extensive sale of organic and fair trade goods as well as a refund arrangement which makes sure that about 97 per cent of all sold plastic cups are recycled. They honour the national container refunds for all bottles and cans, even if the beverages were brought in from outside.

www.roskilde-festival.dk

PERFORMANCE REPORTING

Participation in initiatives and demonstrated behaviour change are the obvious outcomes to your communications and engagement efforts. Enduring or lasting changes in attitudes and behaviours are also excellent legacy outcomes for the event.

Report on successes such as the number or proportion of the following:

- Vendors signing and adhering to the vendor charter.
- Suppliers signing and adhering to the supplier charter.
- Artist and performers purchasing carbon offsets for their event-related flights.
- Conference delegates opting into the bundled ticket and offset offer.
- Food vendors offering organic meals.
- Bags of recycling returned to your recycling rewards station.
- Venues installing LED lighting permanently on stages.

Other reporting could include the enduring changes in operations or behaviour by stakeholders such as the following:

- Food vendors no longer using polystyrene.
- Artists switching their merchandise T-shirts to organic or rPET shirts.
- Venues which will now always meter event energy consumption.
- Caterers and venues which will now no longer serve seafood varieties which are on the *Greenpeace Red List*.
- Caterers and venues which now have in-kitchen compostable waste and waste oil collection services.
- Venues that now report event-specific waste to event organisers.
- Enduring sustainable solutions available in the supply chain locally and supplied to other event organisers.
- New ways of managing waste at venues and sites.
- New ways of planning and managing events sus-

tainability through the event workforce and supply chain.

The *Global Reporting Initiative Event Organizers' Sector Supplement* has created two new performance indicators specifically to cover these types of enduring behaviour changes. Organisers are encouraged to report on the following:

EO11: NUMBER, TYPE AND IMPACT OF SUSTAINABILITY INITIATIVES DESIGNED TO RAISE AWARENESS, SHARE KNOWLEDGE AND IMPACT ON BEHAVIOUR CHANGE AND RESULTS ACHIEVED.

EO12: NATURE AND EXTENT OF KNOWLEDGE TRANSFER OF BEST PRACTICE AND LESSONS LEARNED.

These indicators encourage organisers to report on the initiatives taken to raise awareness of sustainability issues and to encourage participation and behaviour change by stakeholders. This indicator gives examples of the types of activities that could be undertaken and reported on to achieve this raised awareness and potential changed behaviour:

- Number of briefing sessions for suppliers.
- Development of standards and local guidelines to improve the organisation of an event, and/or to improve other industries, with respect to sustainability.
- Webinars, conferences, seminars and workshops organised before, during and after the event.
- Number and type of reports published.
- Platforms for information sharing among event stakeholders.
- Initiatives to include all populations in the event and the provision of its products and services, in terms of legacy, specifically targeted at disadvantaged populations.

These indicators also encourage the organisation to report on the workforce capacity which has been lifted through knowledge and skills transfer.

QUESTIONS

Definitions

Define the following terms:

1   Internal stakeholder.
2   External stakeholder.
3   Greenwash.

Simple Answer

1   How does successful engagement and communication affect the outcome, in terms of sustainable practice, of an event?
2   Identify three types of event contractors and the main aspects of their sustainability impact.
3   How can greenwashing have a negative effect on a company, organisation or event?

Case Studies

1   Identify your event's economic and/or social legacy. What does the community and/or your clients expect from your event in terms of sustainable practices?
2   What are the cultural and/or religious sensitivities pertinent to your event? How do these influence the sustainable practices of your event?
3   Profile your event in terms of its internal stakeholders. What are the main priorities of each of these stakeholders? Identify areas of potential resistance to sustainable practice initiatives.
4   Research a festival or event considered at the forefront of event sustainability. What do you notice about how they project their event in the public arena? Are there any points that could be applicable to the promotion and presentation of your event?
5   What is the current culture of traders at your event? At what point along the road to sustainability are

they? Identify opportunities for improvement and barriers to change.
6   Using the list of questions on page 48, profile the attendees of your event.

Further Research

1   Draft an example of a communication piece for your event. Refer to the checklist on page 45 for examples. The document should aim to reinforce your goals, highlight issues, promote new ideas and successes, and to showcase past results.
2   Refer to the example of 'Made with Intent' on page 39. Brainstorm a visual initiative for attendees at your event. This presentation should take into consideration an issue that is poignant to the event and its participants, and also present suggestions or examples of ways in which attendees can change their behaviour to become active, ongoing participants in a sustainable solution.
3   Propose a sponsorship alignment suitable to your event. Consider not only how you would like to project your event as a brand but also companies that would work well with your market. What would the sponsor gain from such an alignment?
4   Compose a one-page information sheet summarising the sustainability credentials and activities of your event.
5   How can signage encouraging or demonstrating sustainable practice be integrated into your event? To what extent is it already? Can you identify opportunities for expansion and/or refining your message?
6   Develop the framework for a resource website or database for your event. This may be used as information go-to for all members of your team and should include all relevant information regarding sustainability and your event.

3

IDENTIFY ISSUES

By identifying your sustainability issues you are uncovering the event's potential impacts and legacies, and highlighting issues for management. You will need tools to establish the importance and scale of potential issues, and techniques to decide which issues to manage and when.

I call the issues identification process a 'diagnostic' or sometimes a 'green surgery'. This is where I lay the event on the table and look at it with several sustainability lenses; environmental, social, cultural; economic; and allow the quite often interrelated issues to reveal themselves.

You are looking at the impacts and legacies an event could have on community and on environment. These may be both positive and negative. They may be in your control, only partly influenced by you, or out of your direct control but viewed by others as definitely part of the event's responsibility.

Discussion of issues with stakeholders such as the event team, suppliers, venue management, catering contractors, service providers, performers or content providers, creative programmers, marketing, sponsorship includes all those who have a part to play in identifying and eventually managing event sustainability issues.

Undertaking the issues identifying process in concert with stakeholders is an opportunity to workshop solutions and get them engaged and committed to the event's sustainability journey.

Do a thorough analysis of your event's 'business as usual' performance in order to identify issues and opportunities for improvement. Consider the following:

* issues and impacts (positive and negative – risks and opportunities)
* challenges or barriers to improvement
* legalities and regulations that may impact on plans
* stakeholders' needs and expectations
* what you're already doing well.

Invariably, the key operational areas are the first things an event focuses on when identifying its sustainability issues. These include the following:

* destination, site and/or venue
* procurement/supply chain

- waste
- energy
- transport
- water and sanitation
- event workforce conditions
- engagement and communications.

Broadening the gaze beyond the obvious practical event production and logistics-related issues, we delve into areas where a little more thought and effort may be required to identify and manage issues. More information on these areas is given below.

Begin with the End in Sight

The backbone of strategic planning, and the catch-cry of my colleague and fantastic innovator in event sustainability-in-practice *Cameron Little*, is 'begin with the end in sight'. It makes sense to adopt this in so many aspects of event sustainability, let alone in life! It is something I adopt wholeheartedly when undertaking a diagnostic or identification process for event sustainability issues. Think of the final sustainability performance report you will produce, and map out what the readers of the report will be interested in finding out. Craft the report in your mind, or on paper/screen. Assess what to report on, and identify which issues in fact need to be managed.

Taking the report writing as an issues identification tool further, I use the *Global Reporting Initiative Event Organizers' Sector Supplement (GRI EOSS)* to guide me in what may be important to report on. This is also guided by who will be reading it and what they care about.

The *GRI EOSS* was launched in 2012 as an industry supplement, tailoring the generic indicators to make them relevant for the event industry. The guidelines map out almost 100 sustainability performance indicators across seven aspects, which have been specifically edited to make sense to the event industry. Download the *GRI EOSS* for free, and read more on the reporting protocol and the new aspect 'legacy' in upcoming chapters of this book.

Additional guidance on what could be included in a sustainability performance report for your event or organ-

isation, and therefore will influence issues identification, prioritisation and management, are the *United Nations Global Compact*'s ten principles. If your organisation or event has established sustainable development principles, it is possible that either of these two programmes has guided them.

Broadening the Issues Horizon

Issues that are broader than the obvious move past just the event site and production logistics to include the proposed event destination as a whole, the event venue and the supply chain – in factories as well as right back to the mining, growing or production of raw materials. Considerations may include the following.

Workforce, Labour and Human Rights

- the right to freedom of association, collective bargaining and membership to trade unions
- working conditions
- workplace health and safety
- discrimination and ensuring a representative workforce
- fair wages and wage disparity
- local employment
- supply chain human rights screening expenditure supports fair and safe work conditions
- how the event's expenditure does not make it complicit in human rights abuses.

Fair Trade Practices and Anti-corruption

- fair trading practices in the supply chain, including a fair proportion of profits from the sale of products going back to growers and producers
- transparency and anti-corruption within event tenders and contracts
- transparency and anti-corruption issues where winners at events are chosen or assessed
- anti-competitive or monopoly-based trading practices
- compliance with regulations and reporting instances of fines or other non-conformities
- corruption or fair trade issues in the event industry

- how the event's expenditure supports fair trade practices and anti-corruption
- anti-doping in sports events.

Community and Society

- management of perceived (or actual) impacts on the local community
- impact of event activities on the local community, such as noise, nuisance, and on local business trade
- ensuring an inclusive event
- physical accessibility
- expressions of dissent for the event or its content and the event's response to this dissent
- complaints and communications channels for making and handling complaints
- indigenous or first peoples rights
- religious and cultural sensitivities
- heritage and archeological preservation.

Environmental Stewardship

- impacts on natural environment
- protection of biodiversity
- local environment protected or restored
- solid, gaseous and liquid wastes as a result of procurement choices
- toxicity, chemical use and irradiation
- proliferation of genetically modified organisms
- natural resource depletion, use of non-renewable resources, and result of sourcing choices
- animal welfare and unsustainable harvesting practices as a result of sourcing practices
- impacts on water scarcity and fair distribution of access to water.

Economic Benefits and Legacies

- physical legacies left by the event
- knowledge transfer and lessons learned
- establishment of enduring programmes or processes in a destination or supply chain as a result of event activities and sourcing practices
- event activities or production practices which raise awareness about sustainability issues and solutions

- direct and indirect economic benefits of the event to the destination, industry and supply chain
- return on investment
- building capacity within the supply chain or event destination to support the industry and its growth
- encouraging innovation through sustainable sourcing.

Thus you can see that the range of potential event sustainability issues goes way beyond recycling, banning packaged water bottles or counting greenhouse gas emissions from mains electricity supply.

PRIORITISING ISSUES

Working out what should be focused on, what is relevant, where the biggest gains will be and where the 'must-takes' are, no matter the size of the potential impact, are the next steps.

One of the most common questions I am asked by students and clients is: "What issues do I focus on? I can't do everything at once!"

To avoid being overwhelmed to inaction, working out which issues to tackle is a skill in itself. The international standard in event sustainability management systems *ISO 20121* suggests looking at the *relevance* and *significance* of issues in order to prioritise action.

There isn't a plug-and-play methodology I can provide you to enable issues identification, nor for determining the priorities or level of importance to act on an issue. Each organisation and its events will have a unique set of circumstances and influencing factors. I can, however, suggest ways to help guide the issues identification journey and in determining which issues to manage.

The context that surrounds the event will influence the importance of various issues to be addressed and in fact what can be effectively managed.

The organisational context will influence what is important to manage. This includes the organisation's primary reason for being and the cultural or societal context in which the event takes place or the organisation operates.

Where the event is held, the ability of the local event industry to service expectations and the likely results also have a part to play in the prioritisation of event sustainability issues for management. The size, complexity and nature of the event are also considerations and will play a role in highlighting the types of issues that should be managed.

Consider external or internal issues that may limit the ability to do all that is necessary to manage sustainability issues at a best practice level. These may include things issues as:

- the non-existence of solutions in the region
- a head office corporate policy under which you must operate
- a climate of unrest in an area which makes some aspects impossible to achieve
- a requirement to have sponsors which may conflict with some of the operational sustainability ambitions
- a cultural aspect which may impinge on best practice in other regions
- safety concerns.

Control or Influence

The concepts of control and significant influence are explored in the *Global Reporting Initiative Event Organizers' Sector Supplement* when defining the boundary of sustainability performance reporting.

It makes sense that after identifying issues, you will probably only be able to take action in those areas that you have a level of control or influence over. The *GRI* defines 'control' and 'significant influence' as follows:

- *Control: the power to govern the financial and operating policies of an enterprise so as to obtain benefits from its activities.*
- *Significant influence: the power to participate in the financial and operating policy decisions of the entity but not the power to control those policies.*

Taking this approach and applying it to event sustainability issues management, 'control' would be those activities, issues and impacts where the event organisation has the power to manage the decision-making and operational control. This is where staff or contracted

teams are acting under the direct authority and delegation of the event organisation.

For example, the production activities on an outdoor event site, or the decisions being made around destination, venue or merchandise choice by a professional conference organiser.

'Significant influence' would be where the event organisation has the power to have some say in the decision-making and operational control of the activity, issue or impact. For example, where an arts festival is held in multiple venues across a city, the organising body may not be able to control what happens operationally within the venue (e.g. the waste procedures or the source of mains electricity supply) but they can significantly influence in many cases the choice of lighting equipment used on stages.

The inclusion of the word 'financial' in the *GRI EOSS* definition of control and influence infers the fact that money is changing hands, and adds to the level of control, certainly in a situation where the organiser will be in a position of influence; for example, the decision to buy or not to buy a product, to contract or not to contract a service, or to hire or not to hire a venue. The organiser can make decisions based on certain sustainability requirements being met, and therefore definitely increase the influence they have over managing a certain issue.

I would also suggest extracting the word 'significant' from the GRI definition and looking again at just 'influence'. What can you influence, significantly or otherwise? If an issue is deemed important by the organisation or its stakeholders, or is significantly large in scale, whether you can control or influence it or not does not necessarily mean you can ignore it.

This is where we put the next lens over the issues identification and prioritisation process, and that is determining just how big the impacts are, what would happen if you didn't act to manage them, and of course just how important the issues and their resulting impacts are to those who have an opinion about what your organisation or event does. And finally, what's the risk of not acting at all?

Figure 3.1 shows a decision tree for assessing issues management and reporting.

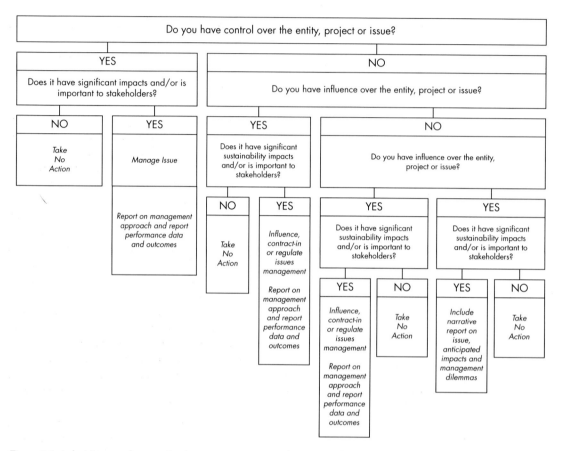

Figure 3.1 A decision tree for assessing issues management and reporting, based on the decision tree created by the GRI.

Sustainable Development Principles

As mentioned in the previous chapter, an initial step for any organisation, event or venue starting their sustainability journey is a declaration of and commitment to sustainable development principles.

Certainly referring back to the organisation's guiding sustainable development principles would help when assessing an issue for management.

Are any event activities and potential issues or impacts likely to cross-cut with the sustainable development principles the organisation holds close?

For example, if forced or child labour have been highlighted as aspects the organisation absolutely will not tolerate, then the back story of products purchased by the

organisation must be scrutinised. To make this practical, the organisation would establish criteria for assessing procurement choices. An option may be to place a dollar figure over which the full chain of custody investigation needs to take place to ensure the products being procured don't conflict with the organisation's sustainable development principles. Alternatively, a percentage of total event procurement budget expenditure could be the measure that triggers deeper scrutiny. Or, the directive could be for certain sectors of the supply chain such as merchandise, timber or coffee to be 'must-takes' for further investigation into any conflicts with the principles by which the organisation stands.

Significance and Relevance

Determining the significance of issues and their relevance to stakeholders is a methodology recommended by the international standard *ISO 20121: Event Sustainability Management Systems* in its Annex C.2.

Determining Relevance

The biggest test of relevance is considering how important an issue is to the event's stakeholders, or 'interested parties' as they are known in *ISO 20121*. It may be expected, on a societal level, that an event organiser would address certain issues and impacts.

For example, it would be a fairly common expectation that recycling be in place by an event held in a destination where its citizens are active and passionate recyclers. On a broader level, it would be expected by most societies that events at least clean up after themselves or arrange for someone else to do so.

Moving from broad societal expectations to more individual concerns, those attending the event would also have expectations such as for the event to be safe, acceptably comfortable, and to deliver on what is promised. This last point crosses over with the 'Product Responsibility' aspect in *GRI EOSS*. Look at the indicators under this aspect in the *GRI EOSS*.

Included in assessing relevance is how often an issue comes up, regardless of the size of the impact compared with other issues and impacts. If you have an issue that is recurring, it is likely to be quite a relevant aspect to address. Noise complaints are an obvious one. Actually any complaints would be addressed if you get a lot of them!

Identifying regulations that apply to the event activities and sustainability impacts is also a measure of relevance of an issue. If it is regulated, it has been done so as to be seen as a frequent or high-risk impact that society expects to be managed.

Determining Significance

Once you have determined the relevance of issues through the lens of the organisation's SD principles, stakeholder and societal expectations, frequency, and regulations that apply, it is time to decide which issues have the greatest significance.

In order to do this, further criteria should be set up to estimate the size of the issue and impact relative to others, so that issues management may be prioritised.

The extent of the impact of the issue on stakeholders or on sustainability outcomes is the first consideration. What will be the actual impact and just how big will it be? What would occur if no action were taken at all?

Closely tied to relevance to stakeholders is the scale of concern those stakeholders have for a particular issue or impact, regardless of the actual size of the impact. It is about the perception of size of impact that matters here.

The old adage 'bang for your buck' is another measure that may be applied: how many resources are required to manage an issue and its related impacts, relative to the outcomes achieved?

ISO 20121's guidance annex advises that *"The criteria for the evaluation of significance shall be based on sound arguments and/or science. They shall include a consideration of feedback from interested parties, including the identification of new emerging issues. The outputs of the procedure shall be documented, kept up-to-date and shared with relevant interested parties."*

Basically you will want to make sure you're going on more than a hunch, and that you have diligently researched the potential issues, regulations, likely impacts and stakeholders' points of view.

Keeping abreast of issues that are on the horizon for future consideration should also be flagged for future focus.

Understanding the relative scale of impacts in comparison to others, while also blending in the relevance to stakeholders, may be demonstrated in the following example.

In year one of the analysis and diagnosis of various sustainability issues at a major event I determined that some real numbers were needed to fully understand the extent of impacts in comparison to each other to help me work out where our limited resources would be focused to maximum effect in the following year's event. I meticulously measured the transport impacts of attendee travel to an event through a rigorous onsite car occupancy survey, cross-matched with ticket sales postcode analysis, car park counts, coach and rail occupancy reports and shuttle bus movements. Likewise, the fuel used in mobile generators was reported, along with mains electricity demand. I wanted to match each of these factors against each other to understand the relative scale of impact compared to each other. The analysis showed that coach, bus and rail uptake was at maximum occupancy and potential, and that the only area which needed improvement was in the occupancy of private vehicles. Comparing the GHG emissions of attendee travel compared with power use, I came up with the startling fact that if we were able to get one-third more of a person (!) into each car that would wipe out the GHG emissions from mobile power supply.

On the flip side of this, we realised that things were just about at capacity level in the private vehicles due to the camping equipment the festival-goers brought with them, and that in order to achieve increased occupancy this would be closely tied to attendee campaigning around bringing a lot less camping equipment – and that

---

Box 3.1

SYDNEY FESTIVAL – ISSUES IDENTIFICATION

Sydney Festival is an iconic multi-arts festival held annually over three weeks in January in Australia. With an estimated audience of 500,000 at over 30 venues by more than 1000 artists from Australia and abroad, the sustainability issues and impacts, including resource consumption, waste creation, transportation and greenhouse gas emissions, could be considerable.

Sydney Festival undertook a detailed diagnostic of its event planning activities including events directly produced by them and events and performances held at partner venues. This was done to identify and understand potential sustainability issues.

The first decision was to determine over which venues *Sydney Festival* could have some influence and additionally which venues would stakeholders view as *Sydney Festival* 'controlled'. Looking at the breadth of venues and performances, it was decided that those with a total audience of at least 2000 (cumulative across all shows) would be included in the diagnostic and issues management. Of course *Sydney Festival* aimed to have influence over all venues and activities that came under the event's umbrella.

Those areas over which *Sydney Festival* had direct control or significant influence:

- direct procurement by SF
- *Day One, Parramatta Opening Night Party, Parramatta Festival Garden, Paradiso Festival Bar, Honda Festival Garden and The Domain* operational logistics, including waste, water and energy
- travel; artist and crew travel
- artist and crew accommodation bookings
- engagement with local community, biodiversity protection, health and safety, accessibility and labour practices
- communications and marketing
- sponsorship choice and at-event sponsor activation.

Areas over which *Sydney Festival* only has influence:

- Food and beverage stallholder procurement
- Show freighting.

Those areas over which they had little influence but whose impacts were significant in size and in stakeholder expectation:

- Ground travel choices by audience
- Venues: policies, procurement, waste, energy and water.

www.sydneyfestival.org

challenge directly related to probably the largest issue at this event, namely the abandonment of camping equipment at the end of the event! Thus complex and co-dependent themes started to be unpacked.

Converse to all of this was the fact that once through the festival gates, the attendees forget their cars and have several days in amongst event production with huffing and puffing generators, and simultaneously being suggested, via a sponsor, that they should switch to green energy!

So you can see that all these issues were intimately linked, but the relatively small scale of the GHG emissions from event power increased in importance when societal expectations, the profile of the issue at the event and our degree of control in being able to reduce impacts was included in the equation.

Timing

Once you have determined the context in which your organisation and event is operating, who the interested parties are and their needs and expectations, what you can control and influence, and how significant and relevant issues are, the next step is to work out an order of proceedings. Consider whether you will:

- do it now,
- do it soon, or
- do it later.

Box 3.2

ISSUES IDENTIFICATION CHECKLIST

Destination

❑ The location requires many attendees to travel considerable distances.
❑ The destination does not have many sustainable solutions available to event production.
❑ The destination has questionable sustainability credentials (e.g. human rights, environmental responsibility, corruption).
❑ The location requires many attendees to travel considerable distances.

Heritage/Indigenous/Cultural/ Archaeological

❑ The event must acknowledge and include first peoples or indigenous communities.
❑ The event must manage issues concerning heritage sensitivity.
❑ The destination has questionable sustainability credentials (e.g. human rights, environmental responsibility, corruption).

❑ The event must manage issues concerning archaeological sensitivity.
❑ The event must manage issues concerning cultural or religious sensitivity.

Inclusivity

❑ The event must manage physical accessibility for those with sensory impairment.
❑ The event must manage accessibility by those who may not usually have access.
❑ The event must manage accessibility to the event by marginalised communities.
❑ The event must ensure that ticketing is fair and accessible to all who wish to attend.

Transparency and Integrity

❑ The event must investigate if it is complicit in human rights abuses through its procurement choices.

Box 3.2 (continued)

❏ The event must manage issues of discrimination.
❏ The event must manage issues of corruption.
❏ The event must put practices in place to ensure transparency of information.
❏ The event must manage issues of privacy and information protection.

Local Environment/Local Community

❏ The event's activities may disrupt local wildlife.
❏ The event's activities may impact on the local ecological environment.
❏ The event's traffic impacts may affect the local community.
❏ The event's lighting and/or sound may affect the local community.
❏ The event may disrupt trade to local businesses.
❏ The event may disrupt access to local services and facilities by the community.

Economic

❏ Direct economic value will be generated and distributed.
❏ Indirect economic value will be generated and distributed.
❏ The event offers employment opportunities.
❏ The event encourages development of innovation in the supply chain and in event logistics.
❏ The event plays a role in building market capacity for events in the region.
❏ The event contributes to increased demand for sustainable solutions.

Stakeholder Engagement

❏ The event must encourage the supply chain to offer sustainable solutions.
❏ The event must work with contractors to offer sustainable solutions and operating practices.

❏ The event must engage with attendees to encourage uptake and participation in sustainability initiatives.
❏ The event must identify communications channels and opportunities for engaging with stakeholders on sustainability issues.
❏ The event must identify all stakeholders who may be interested in sustainability issues or whose involvement may impact on its success.

Energy

❏ Mobile energy is used and sustainable energy supply needs to be sourced.
❏ Mains energy is used and sustainable energy supply needs to be sourced.
❏ Energy-efficient equipment needs to be sourced.
❏ Efficiencies in use of energy need to be identified.

Waste

❏ Total volume of waste is minimised.
❏ Biodegradable waste is created and managed onsite to ensure optimal recovery.
❏ Recyclable waste is created and managed onsite to ensure optimal recovery.
❏ Recovery of resources is ensured, through onsite segregation and processing options.

Safety and Legals

❏ The event has issues of worker or attendee safety to manage.
❏ The event has sustainability-based legal requirements to meet.

Sourcing/Procurement

❏ The event reviews all procurement to ensure the most sustainable options are chosen.

Box 3.2 (continued)

❏ The event balances the financial bottom line with responsible procurement practices, to ensure that company profit is not the only consideration in sustainable sourcing.

❏ Venue – the event venue has sustainable operations and sourcing in place.

❏ Accommodation – sustainably operated hotels and lodgings are chosen in preference.

❏ Printing – the volume of printed material is reduced.

❏ Printing – sustainable paper stock and sustainable printing companies are sourced.

❏ Merchandise/collateral – sustainable options for branded event merchandise are sourced.

❏ Signage – sustainable options for event signage are used.

❏ Décor – sustainable options for event dressing/décor are designed-in.

❏ Timber – sustainable/certified timber is sourced, and also used by subcontractors purchasing on our behalf.

❏ Cleaning products – non-toxic, environmentally sound cleaning products are used by the event, caterers, venue and subcontractors (e.g. cleaning companies).

❏ Food and beverages – sustainable options are sourced by the event and by subcontractors such as caterers, food stallholders and venues with in-house catering.

❏ Fair trade – fair trade coffee, tea and other products are sourced where relevant and the optimally sustainable choice given the event location and circumstances.

❏ Fair labour – scrutinise the labour conditions of all products procured and require contractors procuring on behalf of the event to do the same.

❏ Reuse – reduce consumption and disposal by reusing and renting items.

❏ Office and event supplies – source sustainable supplies and reduce the amount of single-use stuff purchased.

Transport

❏ Production transport impacts could be reduced.
❏ Attendee transport impacts could be reduced.
❏ Procurement transport impacts could be reduced.
❏ Site transport impacts could be reduced.
❏ Initiatives to reduce event-related travel and transport impacts will be planned and implemented.
❏ A communications and engagement programme will be established to influence travel and transport decisions by stakeholders.

Greenhouse Gas Emissions

❏ Potential event-related greenhouse gas emissions need to be identified.
❏ A scope of measurement of greenhouse gas emissions will be determined.
❏ Likely greenhouse gas emissions can be estimated pre-event.
❏ Reduction opportunities will be identified pre-event.
❏ Initiatives to reduce greenhouse gas emissions will be planned and implemented.
❏ Greenhouse gases produced by the event will be measured and disclosed.
❏ Opportunities to compensate greenhouse gas emissions through internal reinvestment in reduction technology and infrastructure will be explored.
❏ Offsetting residual greenhouse gas emissions will be planned, including offering offsetting opportunities to stakeholders.

Performance Measurement

❏ The event will set performance objectives.
❏ The event will identify key performance indicators for sustainability.

Box 3.2 (continued)

❏ The event will put systems in place to capture performance results.

❏ The event will produce a sustainability performance report.

❏ The event will disclose sustainability performance results to interested parties.

Legacy

❏ The event has an opportunity to transfer knowledge into the community and/or industry.

❏ The event has an opportunity to offer employment opportunities to the local workforce.

❏ The event has an opportunity to offer commercial opportunities to local businesses.

❏ The event will attract tourism attention to the destination, venue or other event-related components.

❏ The event has an opportunity to rehabilitate the natural environment as part of its production activities.

QUESTIONS

Definitions

Define the following in relation to event sustainability:

1 Issue
2 Impact
3 Risk
4 Opportunity

Simple Answer

1 What tools and steps would you take to undertake an issues identification process?
2 What techniques can you use to evaluate and prioritise issues for management?

Case Studies

1 Define your event's sustainable development principles.
2 Conduct a thorough analysis of your event's business-as-usual performance in order to identify issues and opportunities for improvement.
3 Using the checklist in Box 3.2, undertake the initial process of identifying the potential sustainability issues of your event or an event with which you are familiar.

4 Prioritise the results. What are the issues that should be focused on, where could the biggest gains be and what are the 'must-takes'?
5 What is the *context* of your chosen event and how does this influence your prioritisation of issues?
6 In what areas does your event exert direct control or significant influence, merely exert some influence, or exert little influence?
7 Given the results of (2) through (6), how do you see your sustainable development principles being enacted over time? What are you able to achieve now, what can be achieved soon and what must wait until a later date?

Further Research

1 Design a simple questionnaire/feedback form for discussing sustainability issues with the event's stakeholders. These may be the event team, supply chain, venue management, catering contractors, service providers, performers or content providers, creative programmers, marketing, sponsorship people, etc.
2 Watch the SEMS demonstration video at www.sems toolkit.com. How do you see a reporting system such as this benefiting your event?

4

DESTINATION AND VENUE

The event destination – host city, region or country, and the event setting – and the venue or site have significant parts to play in the eventual sustainability performance of an event. Those destinations with a high level of engagement with sustainable development principles and sustainably operated venues will mean a fertile ground from which to stage your event sustainability goals.

Whether choosing a destination or venue in which to hold your event, or being stuck with the one you're given, their sustainability credentials will impact on your ability to run your event sustainability as well.

When planning an event, often the first thing to consider for many types of events is where to hold it. Event owners may put their events out to tender and have destinations bid to host them.

For events such as conventions, industry summits, international sporting competitions and exhibitions, the choice of where to hold the event is one of the first things to establish.

In the world of mega-events, such as the Olympics and World Cup events in various sports, the bid process is integral, and happily, many bodies controlling these events are placing sustainability into the bid book requirements and bidding nations are responding.

For those organising events held within venues managed by others, the organiser may have little control over many of the typical sustainability issues and impacts. In this case, organisers seeking to produce their event as sustainably as possible should seek out venues that are operated sustainably.

This chapter looks first at the sustainability aspects of destinations (city, region, country) and second at the role the venue plays.

There are many considerations that influence the decision of where to hold an event, including the following:

- bids, promises or compensations offered by the bidding or tendering destination
- a progression of locations from year to year
- cost to organiser and attendees
- availability of suitable venues and accommodation
- relevance or proximity to the event's subject

- proximity to likely attendees
- overall suitability of the event destination considering its purpose.

DESTINATIONS

Reviewing the potential event destination's engagement with sustainable development will give you a good insight into the likelihood of the region being able to support your efforts to produce your event sustainably. There are organisations that can help you, specifically called 'destination managers', to navigate the industry locally, and they can certainly be given the duty of understanding the 'sustainability profile' of a specific destination. The local convention bureau, chamber of commerce or tourism authority will also be keen to let you know what their destination's sustainability credentials are. This will also highlight some aspects or issues that are unavoidable and that may need to be addressed in your event planning and delivery.

At the end of this chapter is a checklist produced by my company GreenShoot Pacific,[1] which you can use to self-assess the sustainability profile of a proposed event destination. In summary the following are the key aspects:

- Resource management
- Agriculture and food
- Environmental stewardship
- Waste management
- Energy source
- Climate change and greenhouse gas emissions policies
- Transport infrastructure and urban connectivity
- Walkable and cycleable city
- Nuclear policy
- Ethics and governance
- Community involvement and engagement
- Existence of eco-labelling
- Sustainable building practices
- Working conditions
- Welfare practices
- Labour rights
- Diversity and discrimination policy
- Innovation.

In addition, the way the event industry interacts with sustainability is something to look at. Indicators of potential sustainable good practice locally include the following:

- Sustainable venues, hotels and lodging
- Event industry competency in sustainability
- Conformity with standards and certifications
- Availability of sustainable solutions, services and suppliers
- Industry network and sharing of sustainability knowledge
- Local government commitment to sustainable event production.

Consider these aspects when assessing the destination as having the potential to support your event's sustainability performance outcomes.

We will now delve into detail for some of these aspects.

Environmental Stewardship

The use and protection of natural resources is an obvious indicator of the destination's adherence to the sustainable development principle of environmental stewardship.

Consider whether the destination carries out responsible and sustainable resource exploitation. This includes renewable and non-renewable resource use, and protection of natural habitat and ecosystems.

Energy Source

Investigate where the destination's primary energy supply comes from. Is it mainly non-renewable fossil fuel based? Does it rely on importing coal? Has the destination optimised the potential for renewable energy supply given its natural resources (e.g. sun, wind, geothermal)? Will the event be able to readily access renewable energy mains/grid electricity supply? Has the destination set targets on renewable energy creation, demonstrating its commitment?

Indicators to look for include the following:

- the GHG 'emissions factor'[2] for mains/grid electricity supply

- total percentage of renewable energy supply to the mains electricity grid
- renewable energy tariffs available
- renewable energy certificates or some other programme that allows energy users to buy equivalent kWh of renewable energy
- renewable energy creation on buildings
- feed-in tariffs which support the proliferation of micro-generation.

Another consideration is whether the destination's buildings require continual heating or cooling to make human habitation comfortable – meaning potentially high energy consumption, adding to your event's greenhouse gas emissions inventory.

So which destinations are performing well when it comes to energy supply? When looking at the GHG emissions factor for mains electricity, a smattering of countries come in at close to 0.00kg of GHGs per kWh of electricity, which is a fantastic figure to achieve, though some are getting this from nuclear power which is a debatable alternative. With 16 per cent[3] of the world's energy supply coming from hydro, countries such as Norway, Switzerland, New Zealand, Paraguay and Laos are the winners.

Canada has many provinces in the top 25 lowest GHGs per kWh, and seems to come out the winner on a pure numbers game. A very special mention goes to Greenland for tapping into its geothermal energy resources.

When looking at countries that don't have enormous energy-creating natural assets such as pounding mountainous rivers or hot bubbling earth underfoot, we should be rewarding those countries or destinations that are at least taking advantage of their natural potential renewable energy assets, rather than those that have those assets but just continue to use non-renewable GHG-creating energy sources.

Countries that are actively committed to and encouraging diversification of renewable energy provision need to be rewarded as awesome. Many countries, particularly in Europe, have incentives to help proliferate the creation of renewable energy production by big investors and by individual property owners. There are varying models and incentives, but the most successful are seen when there is a strong commitment at governmental level. For this, Germany comes out the winner, with more than 20 per cent[4] of its energy coming from renewable energy supply.

Within Germany the *City of Freiburg* is located on the edge of the Black Forest, and is known as Germany's 'green capital'. The *City of Freiburg* adopted a vision that embraced long-term energy supply options, giving birth to the *SolarRegion* vision. Thanks to those progressive decisions, Freiburg can now boast over 500 solar energy projects, ranging from residential houses, office buildings, institutions and clubs, public buildings to hotels and department stores.

Natural Resource Use

The sustainable and responsible extraction of natural resources such as timber, minerals, fossil fuels, even fisheries, is an indicator of a destination's approach to the principle of *environmental stewardship*.

Does the destination protect its natural assets and ensure sustainable natural resource use? Does the destination manage natural resources so that they are not unduly depleted, allowing ecosystems to remain in balance? Indicators would include the following:

- the existence of protected fisheries and wilderness
- controls on logging and the forestry industry
- public ownership of mines (rather than selling off a nation's mineral and fossil fuel resources to private ownership and uncontrolled exploitation)
- appropriate management of river systems, watersheds and the use of dams.

A great measure of any country's extraction (also called exploitation) of its natural resources is custodianship at a governmental level, ensuring that the resources exist for future generations to benefit from, which in turn infers conservation measures.

When it comes to thinking about responsible natural resource extraction, Canada has traditionally been a winner. It has vast natural resources and is concerned for the equitable and responsible extraction of those resources. Current policy changes may affect its reputation in this area, but let's wait and see.

Look for independent watch-dog organisations which monitor resource extraction – if they are embraced by a region's natural resource industries, you are likely to see some good green brownie points there.

Environmental Protection

How a destination manages its urbanisation and industrialisation and its protection of biodiversity and the natural environment from encroachment by development and human activity is a great indicator of the sustainability profile of a region. This shows how much they care about the natural environment and the health of its inhabitants, both human and non-human.

Are waterways littered or polluted from industrial and residential wastewater or solid waste? Are there parks and wilderness areas where nature can be enjoyed or where wildlife is protected? Does the destination have an active and effective Environment Protection Agency to monitor societal impacts on the natural environment? Are there NGOs campaigning for protection of the region's natural assets?

Australia certainly has a large number of natural reserves, national parks and protected marine zones. I would say that on a broad level we are doing well. On a region-by-region basis however there are some serious concerns, such as putting in major shipping ports through the Great Barrier Reef, and continuing logging in old growth pristine forest land in Tasmania, just to mention a couple of examples.

Transport

Transport to an event destination has a major potential impact, especially when considering the GHG emissions impacts of air travel. The transport available on the ground to the proposed destination also has a part to play.

Is there a well-developed and well-used public transport system in the proposed destination that your event attendees can use, helping to reduce the travel-related greenhouse gas emissions of your event?

Is cycling and walking safe and easy? Are there dedicated bike lanes and walking paths and promenades? Will your event attendees be inspired to get around on two legs rather than four wheels?

So where are the world's best destinations when it comes to urban connectivity? I would have to say that Europe wins on this one. And although Londoners complain bitterly about the tube and the cost of train travel they have no idea how fantastic it is compared to Australia. We have huge distances and hardly any people, and such convenient transport is just not possible. You have to time your bus and train trips, as they come at very sparse intervals, and sometimes not even every day. So London, I am sorry to say, you win in my book. Thanks for the bikes too.

Copenhagen is famous for being one of the most cycle-friendly cities. The website (www.cyclecopenhagen.dk) is a cycle-route navigator, with route mapping by the shortest, quietest, safest, greenest or the most dedicated cycle-route routes. Fantastic! Sydney in Australia is a more modest example, but the level of commitment of making the inner city as cycle-friendly as possible is impressive (sydneycycleways.net/the-network/the-routes). Boston should also be given its due for its great campaigns and real action by the city. Have a look at www.bostonbikes.org. And the world's number one cycle-friendly city is Groningen. With 180,000 residents and 300,000 bikes it is testament to great urban planning. (Or a bike-buying fetish!)

The use of electric vehicles (EVs) by residents and businesses and the availability of charging infrastructure in a city is also a good indicator. San Francisco seems to win in this department. The city has installed almost 100 free charging stations and there are many more privately placed charge points in service stations and parking garages. Visit www.sfenvironment.org to read more great things going on in the city.

If you want to know how many EV charging points there are in a North American city, go to the *Chargepoint* website or app (www.chargepoint.com).

London is also upping the ante in the EV charging station ranks, with 1300 charging points. Their aspiration is to have 100,000 EVs on the road. *Source London* is the programme and charging point search and trip planning website (www.sourcelondon.net). Anyone who has driven in inner London will know about the congestion charge. Electric vehicles are exempt from this hefty daily fee. plugsurfing.co.uk and ev-charging.com are also good websites for searching charge points if you're interested in how into EVs your potential event destination is.

We want all of these EVs to be charging on renewable energy, so double check the sources of electricity in these cities too – otherwise they're just replacing oil with coal or gas.

Waste

Understanding how waste is managed in the proposed destination will give you valuable insight into the heart and pulse of sustainability in that destination.

Is recycling possible? Are systems in place at a municipal and householder level? Is there evidence in place that shows it is important to the community and government? For example, look for on-street 'recycling on the go' bins. Are households provided with recycling bins? Are businesses recycling and are services set up to collect commercial and industrial recyclable material? Are there community-level recycling programmes, advocacy groups or a local *Zero Waste International Alliance (ZWIA)*[5] group?

Are there salvage yards and programmes to establish second lives for materials?

How does the destination manage biodegradable waste? Are there commercial-scale composting facilities within the destination? Does the destination encourage householders to compost at home? Is there concern in the destination for sending biodegradable materials to landfill, thus creating methane and contributing to the country's GHG emissions?

Does all waste just get sent to landfill or incineration? Or are there no formal municipal waste services at all?

Are labour and safety issues concerning the way waste is handled addressed? If the event destination is in a developing nation, what controls are in place to ensure the safe and appropriate disposal of your event's waste while not impinging on the rights of all people to safely earn a living?

In Mumbai, the *Dharavi Slum* is the recycling heart of the city. The working conditions are hazardous to health, and the monies paid to rag pickers and all those along the recycling chain are neither guaranteed nor fairly distributed. Stop and think, though – if a mechanised MRF is installed in Mumbai, what would that mean for the potentially millions of people whose livelihoods are dependent on the recycling ecosystem?

So what is a winning destination? I would have to say that the State of California in the USA is right up there in the running. At a governmental level there are requirements in place (specifically for events too) that have filtered all the way down through industry to ensure that systems exist to service waste recovery goals. Northern European and Scandinavian countries are also over-achievers when it comes to waste. See Chapter 9 for some of the statistical results of their waste efforts.

An encouragement award must go to the UK, which has recently realised how poorly it performs in relation to its neighbours across the pond, and many awesome projects to reduce waste creation and maximise diversion are being promoted by the government bodies DEFRA and WRAP. Even my own state of NSW has co-opted the terrific *Love Food Hate Waste*[6] programme from the UK.

You should also conduct your own research into what systems the potential venues have in place, even if the country does not apparently have its house in order. For example, a five-star hotel that is part of an international chain may have its own systems in place that meet its corporate policy for hotel waste handling, the standards of which could be way ahead of local best practice.

Water

Water's a big issue, and the way a destination treats its water resources is a major indicator. Considerations for water in a destination are where the water comes from, if there are scarcity issues, and where wastewater ends up.

As water is a fundamental need for any human civilisation to exist, most destinations will take their water provision seriously. Tied closely with water provision is energy consumption – if you are considering a destination in which water is scarce and it uses desalination to provide water, you will also need to consider the energy impacts of your event's water demand.

Closely tied to a destination's water provision, and relevant for environmental protection, is how a destination protects the watershed, the use of damming and downstream consequences, and the disposal of wastewater and watercourse protection.

Destinations should also have adequate water quality testing regulation and processes, which will enable confident consumption of water by your event attendees. In destinations with finite water resources, the amount of water per person available (and used) is closely tied to population.

The amount of water available (and used) is also influenced by the actual access to water – is it delivered through mains supply, is it trucked in and stored in tanks (and paid for at a hefty rate), is rain-water captured, or is it pumped from ground or surface water bodies?

Another important area is agriculture and industry. Has a destination been smart about the types of activity it allows to occur in its region, considering the water supply? I grew up in an inland rural area in Australia, which is dry and hot. Irrigation systems have been put in place that were, looking at them retrospectively, a stop-gap idea. The river that the irrigation is sourced from is being sucked dry and several years ago it stopped actually reaching the coast. At a local level, the irrigation of land that was not meant for soaking has now caused salinity, rendering a massive area of land infertile. Crops such as cotton and rice should not be grown in dry lands where the water is being taken from local rivers.

If there are water scarcity issues in a proposed destination, it really is up to you to decide if your event will require more than its fair share of water, considering the numbers of people in attendance.

Figure 4.1 Visitors to Te Punanga Nui market on Rarotonga are able to compost and recycle waste from the weekly event.

Source: Shawna McKinley (eventcellany.com).

Consider if the other benefits of bringing a large number of people to a destination will outweigh or be outweighed by the impacts of demand on local water supply. What are the impacts on water security once your event leaves town?

The *Meredith Music Festival,* held in a water-scarce rural destination in Australia, have approached this in a clever way. They have set up rain-water harvesting and store water year round in tanks so that they have sufficient for their event needs without drawing on the precious water resources needed by the local farming community.

Local Sourcing

Does the proposed destination have the raw materials, supplies, products, contractors, service providers, talent, staff and specialists necessary to provide the event with the goods and services it will need?

Will you have to transport everything in, further increasing transport-related greenhouse gas emissions attributable to your event? Or can you get everything you need in the host destination, having the added benefit of supporting the local economy?

Knowing if there is produce available locally, and if sustainable agricultural practices are embraced, will mean you are able to source sustainably farmed produce locally

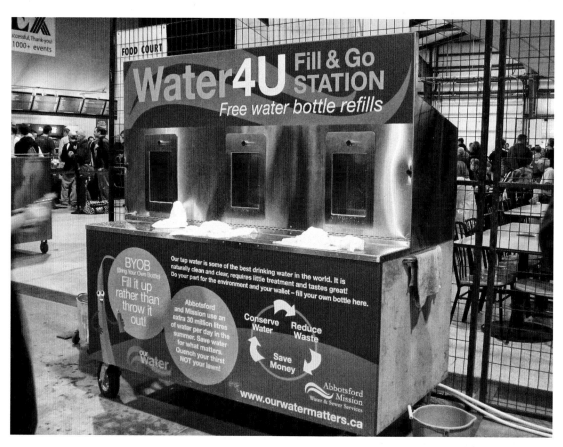

Figure 4.2 California takes its water conservation seriously (www.ourwatermatters.ca). Event refill station.

Source: Shawna McKinley (eventcellany.com).

– healthier for your attendees, supporting the local economy and reducing food miles for catering.

A good indicator of the embracing of sustainability within the supply chain is the existence of sustainability or environmental programmes, standards or eco-labels to independently assess the performance of products, services, processes and buildings. So who's the winner of this one? Let's look at a regional, city or even neighbourhood level.

Destinations that are close to food-growing zones will definitely be winners. For example, I spoke at a conference in Monterey, California, and the lunchtime buffet was awash with local produce. So impressive was the spread that every item had a little story to tell where it came from and what the sustainability credentials were. The region has a great vegetable-growing district and it would be a glaring omission by any event producer, caterer or hotel hosting a conference not to be sourcing produce locally and telling everyone about it. Well done Beverly Oviedo and her team at Cal State Monterey.

Tasmania is another great example. You can't turn around for bumping into yet another farm gate produce market, stall, sourced restaurant or local artisan outlet. Newcastle, my home town, also has a fantastic programme called *ReNew*[7] whereby local artisans and designers have the opportunity to rent retail outlets for free, to both revitalise the city centre and offer a direct line of contact between buyer and seller.

Any event organiser looking for the bespoke production of gifts or awards should be sourcing them through these producers.

On a larger scale, looking at a destination and figuring out whether you have to bring everything in from ten towns over is something to consider. Bigger towns will have more stuff available. The trick is to look at a destination and work out if they actually have, right there, in the town, the stuff you will need.

Labour and Human Rights

Moving past environmental issues, we should start to think about the social and human aspects of sustainability and sustainable development. Judging a destination by the working conditions and the state of human rights and inclusivity, freedom of speech and the right to dissent will be very powerful indicators of a destination's commitment to sustainable development.

Health, Safety and Welfare

How a destination looks after its own people's safety, welfare and health is a great indicator of sustainable development principles held by the region.

Does the destination have acceptable health and safety, labour rights and working condition standards?

Does the destination have acceptable social welfare, including provision of health services, and pensions for the old and infirm? Are controls in place to regulate safe working conditions, including the existence of risk assessment requirements and workplace health and safety legislation?

Are fair wages and the concepts of a living wage embraced, with no disparity of rates of pay between groups of people?

Human Rights

Upholding basic human rights is fundamental, and as far as I am concerned a deal-breaker when it comes to a destination's sustainability credentials. They can 'green' things as much as they want, but if they don't take care for the welfare and dignity of their citizens and visitors, then they don't get any points from me.

Considerations may include whether the destination is a party to international human rights treaties. The foundation of international human rights law is the UN's *Universal Declaration of Human Rights.*[8] Consider whether there are human rights abuses such as child or forced labour in the supply chain of the potential event destination. Are anti-discrimination laws in effect? Are the rights of minorities protected?

Any country signed up to international protocols which actually enacts these with vigour gets my vote. To see how the country you're considering as an event destination fares with regards to international human rights, use the search function on Amnesty International's website (www.amnesty.org/en/human-rights).

Figure 4.3 When hosting an event near Monterey, California, you cannot help but avail yourself of local produce. Sustainable Hospitality Symposium at Cal State University.

Source: Meegan Jones.

Inclusivity

Looking at the spirit of human rights and bringing them to a more localised level is the way a destination includes all of its citizens. How are minority communities and subsectors of society included? Are people of different ethnic backgrounds and diverse religious or cultural heritage embraced as part of the community's rich fabric? What is the level of social acceptance of the gay, lesbian, bisexual and transgender community? How are the elderly cared for at a national level? Single parents? People with mental or physical impairment? Are women treated equally in society?

At the time of writing there was controversy over the laws in Russia that criminalised advocacy for gay rights. This is a major issue that organisers of the Winter Olympics 2014, will need to have considered.

Transparency and Corruption

Knowing whether dealings within government and businesses are carried out with integrity, transparency and anti-corruption procedures in place is important in assessing a destination's sustainability credentials. These aspects are key sustainable development principles.

By having this knowledge you will be able to assess whether you are going to be treated fairly, and if money from your local expenditure is flowing where it should. Do you want to support corrupt businesses or government with your event's income? How can you be sure the economic benefits from your event will flow to the local economy and be fairly distributed?

I'm not going to name names here, but countries, and indeed cities and towns with responsible governance, will be the destinations that tick this box.

Community

This one's about the vibe. How does the destination engage with and support community? Is the citizenship engaged with community matters? Is there a sense of civic pride? Is there evidence of the community embracing sustainable development principles? Good indicators, which have relevance for the eventual support of event sustainability ambitions, may include the following:

- the existence of community gardens
- a community-run environment centre
- well-attended farmers' markets
- lots of NGO- and community-supported social programmes
- destination-wide (government- or NGO-led) waste programmes and active participation in recycling by the citizenship
- people using the public transport system, and if relevant, cycling and walking.

National Vision

It would also be useful to review what the national or city-wide vision is with regard to sustainable development and how the people have embraced it, or how communities and organisations have translated it to create their own programmes.

Greenest City 2020 is an initiative aimed at addressing Vancouver's environmental challenges. It has put the city on the path to fulfilling the ambition of becoming 'the greenest city in the world by 2020'. The Council has developed the *Greenest City 2020 Action Plan* that challenges citizens, businesses and governments to help make Vancouver a better place. The Action Plan is divided into ten smaller plans, each with a long-term goal and 2020 targets. Combined, these ten plans address three overarching areas of focus: carbon, waste and ecosystems. Vancouver has one of the lowest GHG emissions per capita in North America.[9] They're capturing steam heat for energy, offering city-side food waste collection, have a terrific public transport and cycle infrastructure, and the majority of electricity in the province is provided by hydro.

Qatar, a country with a reputation as a fossil-fuelled country of wealth and excess, with limited water resources, is constantly coming out on top with the highest per capita GHG emissions, along with a reputation for dubious working conditions for migrant construction workers. Qatar must be congratulated for their vision to tackle these perceptions (and in some cases real issues) head-on. The *Qatar National Vision 2030* addresses four key pillars – human, social, environmental and economic. It details how working together with the government, private sector, NGOs and individuals can reduce environmental impacts, move the nation's economy past fossil fuel reliance, address workers' and human rights issues, and ensure food security for the nation. This vision has likewise been embraced, adopted and interpreted by many private sector organisations, and working together it will be exciting over the next 15 years to see where Qatar will go. Certainly the inspiration, ambition, dedication and resources are in place to make huge progress towards true sustainable development.

Event sustainability specialist Shawna McKinley travelled to China to undertake supply chain scrutiny for one of her US-based client's events, to understand how the event sustainability ambitions for the event could be realised in this country. In her blog, Shawna poses some thought-provoking questions about event destination choices on her old blog, greendestinations. blogspot.com. Her new blog is eventcellany.com, and it's great reading.

Tyranny of Distance

The impacts of large numbers of people travelling to your event destination by air will likely be the largest environmental impact your event has. Therefore location of the event in proximity to the likely attendance base is a major component of destination choice and eventual GHG impacts created by the event.

The fundamental question with the biggest line on the GHG balance sheet will be: Does the event location require a large proportion of attendees to travel by air and, if so, are direct flights available?

Choosing a destination that minimises air travel is simple to say; the reality is that many event destinations cannot be changed, or are in fact chosen in order to have people travel to the destination; for example, for tourism purposes, or for a conference to focus on an issue unique to that destination. Or perhaps an event needs to be in a different location each year in order to give fair access to all potential attendees.

For events where the destination requires the bulk of attendees to fly in, the GHG emissions as a result of the event will be substantial.

One way to counter this is to support and encourage the uptake of carbon offsetting by those who will fly to your event. It really is your responsibility, as event organiser, to ensure maximum uptake of carbon off-setting by air travellers, as without your encouragement and leadership it is possible they will not offset.

Lead by example by purchasing carbon offsets for all talent and crew air travel, and then require/request your attendees to do the same.

Read more about carbon offsetting and other compensating strategies for your event's GHG inventory throughout the book.

Box 4.1

SUSTAINABLE DESTINATION REFLECTIONS BY SHAWNA MCKINLEY

Sustainable Destination Reflections – China

Event sustainability specialist Shawna McKinley travelled to China to undertake supply chain scrutiny for Oracle, one of her US-based client's events, to understand how their event sustainability ambitions for *Oracle OpenWorld* could be realised in this country. In her blog, Shawna poses some thought-provoking questions about event destination choices.

What did I learn?

That China does indeed have its fair share of sustainability challenges, from severe air pollution to cancer villages[10] *and human rights*[11] *concerns. These are problems that are outside of our ability in the event industry to immediately solve.*

Should these problems cause us to boycott China as a meeting destination, or embrace our buying power to make situations better where we have the ability to influence change?

One thing is clear based on my recent visit: we in North America have our own share of sustainability issues, and it may not be correct to assume that China is trailing in terms of sustainable hospitality and event potential. But don't take my word for it, check out the following postcards from our trip, ask your own questions and sound off on your conclusions.

- *Site inspections of host hotels revealed that 100 per cent use key card-activated rooms to minimise energy use. All properties were also participating in some type of proprietary or government-endorsed energy benchmarking programme. While the power mix in China remains dominantly non-renewable, green building upgrades like this reflect recent Chinese government mandates to increase energy efficiency.*
- *The Intercontinental Shanghai Expo displays its IHG 'Green Engage' credentials prominently to staff back of house, whose community service activities supporting children's charity 'Mifan Mama' (www.*

mifanmama.com) are also prominently celebrated in photos along service corridors. Where government programmes may be lacking, proprietary environmental management systems like 'Green Engage' can fill a gap by structuring and promoting improvement at the property level.

- *Intercontinental Values – including 'Responsible Business' – are affirmed in staff areas back of house. These are translated into daily practices for employees to build awareness of how they impact on all operations areas, such as housekeeping and food and beverage.*
- *Linen and towel reuse was offered at 100 per cent of properties visited. Seventy-five per cent of hotels required guests to opt out of standard linen reuse. Twenty-five per cent required guests to opt into the programme.*
- *While not necessarily administered by large companies, recycling is practised by residents and commercial businesses in Shanghai. China has recently claimed increased investment of US$320 billion in recycling programmes.*
- *The Sheraton Shanghai Pudong encourages guests to reduce waste by practising portion control at buffets . . . and minimising use of paper towels in public restrooms.*
- *Restaurant menus at the Sheraton Shanghai Pudong clearly identify certified organic options. While China does have its own organic label, many hospitality companies rely on external organic standards in order to address food safety issues.*
- *The Sheraton Shanghai Pudong practises comprehensive recycling, including providing recycling bins in all guest rooms. The property is taking part in a pilot programme supported by the Shanghai municipal government to encourage hotels to be 'green'. The programme audits hotels in terms of design and architecture, energy management, food and beverage, customer service, and community and*

Box 4.1 (continued)

economic benefits. In addition, it requires properties to set and meet energy and water conservation and waste reduction targets.

- Staff engagement and interest by property management was evident and it is worth noting that general managers accompanied our team throughout the entire 'green' tour of each property and were able to communicate detailed knowledge of sustainability programmes. This was a first for me, in any city.

- In spite of asking for and receiving environmental information about venues before our site visit, it was an unexpected and happy surprise to learn the Shanghai Expo Centre is LEED® Gold certified. Suffice it to say that face-to-face discussion about sustainability is critical to improving trust, communication and collaboration across cultures when it comes to planning sustainable events. Don't expect you will be told or shown everything in advance. Also anticipate it will take longer to develop good relationships in order to be invited back of house to verify practices.

- Green building features of the Shanghai Expo Centre are communicated through onsite signage and include grey water reuse, a solar array and geothermal heating and cooling. During sunny periods the building can draw as much as 32 per cent of its power from solar panels that cover 70 per cent of its roof. Approximately 50 per cent of heating and cooling needs are met by a water pump system that recirculates river water through the building.

- Onsite digital signage throughout the Shanghai Expo Centre would eliminate a significant amount of temporary event signage for Oracle OpenWorld, a financial and environmental gain.

- Separated kitchen organics await pick-up at the Intercontinental Pudong, a practice mirrored by several venues visited. While we're still trying to determine where organics are taken and how they are used, the separation of wet food waste is promising. All properties are required to use recycling and waste haulers who are permitted by the Shanghai government in order to ensure materials are properly recycled.

- Upon arrival and departure, Shanghai travellers are reminded "Water is precious, so start conserving it now".

In spite of efforts by government, hospitality businesses and event planners like you, I and Oracle, it is indeed the choices of individual Chinese consumers and the country's growing environmental movement who will determine if the future of their country and the planet can indeed be sustainable.

Shawna McKinley's observations on more event sustainability topics may be read at eventcellany.com.

SUSTAINABLE DESTINATION CHECKLIST

Box 4.2

SUSTAINABLE DESTINATION CHECKLIST

This checklist includes the 30 indicators *GreenShoot Pacific* recommends to review when assessing an event destination. Consider the following sustainable development aspects for the city, region or country:

❑ **Resource management:** Ensures sustainable resource management, including water, forests, minerals/mining, and fossil fuel extraction.
❑ **Agriculture and food:** Encourages and demonstrates leadership in sustainable agricultural practices, including availability of locally grown food.
❑ **Environmental stewardship:** Demonstrates stewardship principles in biodiversity and environmental protection.
❑ **Waste:** Has outstanding performance in recycling and biodegradable waste diversion from landfill and incineration.
❑ **Energy source:** Has, or is working towards, increasing, renewable energy supply to the main electricity grid.
❑ **Renewable energy certificates:** Encourages microgeneration of electricity, adoption of feed-in tariffs, or RECs.
❑ **Climate change and GHGs:** Has an effective Climate Change Policy that includes holding the major industrial polluters to account along with GHG reduction incentives.
❑ **Transport:** Has effective and well-used public transport infrastructure.
❑ **Walking/cycling:** Encourages walking and cycling, both through communications and engagement campaigns to its citizens, and suitable infrastructure.
❑ **Nuclear:** Holds a Nuclear Non-proliferation Treaty or similar protocol.

❑ **Ethical:** Upholds the principles of ethical business practices and democratic governance, including transparency and anti-corruption measures.
❑ **Community:** Has a sense of community support and involvement, and engaged citizens.
❑ **Eco-labelling:** Has established eco-labels or other programmes to recognise best practice in sustainability performance across the supply chain.
❑ **Buildings:** Recognises, encourages and supports sustainable building practices along with sustainable operating practices.
❑ **Working conditions:** Has safe and fair working conditions for its citizens, including fair working wages and acceptable minimum wages.
❑ **Welfare:** Has social welfare programmes, including acceptable provision of health, education and policing.
❑ **Labour:** Ensures child, forced, unfair or unsafe labour practices are not supported through products and materials created or sold in the destination.
❑ **Diversity and discrimination:** Encourages diversity and has a generous and empathetic immigration and refugee policy. Has anti-discrimination policies and laws. Recognises and respects traditional or first owners and indigenous peoples.
❑ **Innovation:** Has policies that encourage and reward innovation in sustainable solutions and practices.
❑ **Engagement:** Has programmes to engage citizens and businesses in sustainable development, sustainable living and sustainable business practices.

Box 4.3

SUSTAINABLE DESTINATION – EVENT INDUSTRY CAPACITY CHECKLIST

Also developed by *GreenShoot Pacific*, this next set of questions concerns the capacity of the event industry within the proposed destination to support the organiser's event sustainability goals. What is available in the event industry supply chain locally along with the ability of the event industry to understand sustainability issues and to have solutions on hand will inherently impact on the sustainability performance of your event? Consider the following aspects:

❏ **Venues:** Sustainably built and operated venues are available in the destination for event use.
❏ **Hotels and lodging:** Sustainably built and operated accommodation/hotels/lodging are available.
❏ **Industry competency:** Event industry practitioners and event contractors in the supply chain have an understanding of event sustainability issues and their management.
❏ **Conformity:** Events and organisers in the desti-

nation have achieved conformity with *ISO 20121* or relevant national standard or certification.
❏ **Suppliers:** Suppliers with sustainable materials and products are available (printing, signage, décor, merchandise, etc.).
❏ **Services:** Service providers with ability to provide sustainable solutions are available.
❏ **Catering:** Sustainably farmed food is available locally to service event catering requirements.
❏ **Equipment:** Equipment and infrastructure with sustainability credentials is available for hire.
❏ **Industry network:** Local business chamber, tourism body and/or the convention bureau supports the proliferation of sustainable event production practice.
❏ **Local government:** Local government has policies, programmes and resources which can support the proliferation of sustainable solutions in the event industry and its supply chain.

VENUE AND ACCOMMODATION CHOICE

For those organisers holding events in venues and sites owned and managed by others, choice of venue is a key decision that frames the event, the experience of attendees and the potential for sustainable event outcomes.

Venues can be 'dry hires' with access only to the space and basic amenities (power, toilets, loading dock, etc.) with all other components overlaid by the organisers. Other venues will be full-service, with everything available from concierge and electronic signage to in-house catering kitchens. For those held in the conference rooms of large hotels, facilities also come with accommodation for delegates.

Outdoor events also don't need to be just greenfield sites (where nothing but grass and the gate keys are

given). Many outdoor event sites are in parks and reserves, closed-off streets, piazzas or sports fields. These sites may come with access to mains power, contracted waste services, mains water and sewer lines, permanent toilets and showers, office buildings and sheds, stadium seating and outdoor stages.

When choosing an event venue or site some aspects that will support your event's sustainability performance outcomes include the following:

- access to public transport, distance from services
- provision of mains (renewable power)
- availability of water (mains or rain-water tanks)
- availability of amenities and direct to sewer line or septic black water disposal
- other permanent infrastructure and equipment
- ecologically sensitive areas.

Figure 4.4 Vancouver Convention Centre's living roof. Read more about the initiatives at this venue in Box 4.5.

Source: Vancouver Convention Centre.

For indoor events, you may also wish to delve into the details of the building's efficiency, operation, and perhaps whether it was designed and built with sustainability in mind. Chapter 5 includes more details on energy efficiency in buildings. There is a massive amount of information available published elsewhere on this subject which I won't attempt to replicate here in detail. A summary of considerations of sustainably built and operated buildings includes the following:

- built using sustainable materials
- designed and operated to be responsive to the local climate
- energy efficiency considerations, including insulation, passive heating, cooling and natural light
- water management includes rain-water capture and grey water recycling and reuse

- waste minimisation and diversion, potentially with onsite compostable waste processing
- considerate to the natural environment and sensitive to biodiversity
- has consideration for indoor environment quality issues such as ventilation, clean air, low VOC, natural light, etc.

When reading through the other chapters in this book, consider what is the responsibility of the venue and what is your responsibility.

The Venue and Lodging Checklist (Box 4.5) is created from the point of view of an event manager hiring an indoor venue or lodging. Use the information in this checklist to add the relevant sustainability aspects to your own venue assessment checklist.

Don't forget to tell your attendees why you have

VENUE AND LODGING CHECKLIST

Box 4.4

VENUE AND LODGING CHECKLIST

Building and Certification

❏ Has 'Green Building' or sustainable building rating.
❏ Has been retrofitted to ensure resource efficiencies.
❏ Has achieved independent certification for efficient building operations and sustainable operating practices.
❏ Has *ISO 14001* or *ISO 20121* conformity.

Policy, Planning, Staff Engagement

❏ Venue has a sustainability management policy.
❏ Venue has a 'greening committee', dedicated sustainability staff member or programme.
❏ Venue has a training programme to educate venue staff about sustainable operations.
❏ Venue staff induct venue hirers into sustainability initiatives.
❏ Venue discloses its sustainability performance.

Location

❏ Located close to public transport hubs.
❏ Accessible by foot and bicycle, with bicycle parking onsite.
❏ Venue is located close to hotels where delegates will be staying.
❏ Hotels are located close to event venue.

Procurement

❏ Uses environmentally sound cleaning supplies.
❏ Uses 'green' cleaning techniques.
❏ Uses washable/reusable cups, crockery and cutlery.
❏ Sustainable catering policy is in place (see Catering Checklist in Chapter 8 for more details).

Water

❏ Has water conservation initiatives in place.
❏ Captures rain-water for reuse onsite.
❏ Has grey water capture and recycling in place.
❏ Water-wise grounds maintenance is used.

Energy

❏ Is on a renewable energy supply.
❏ Is willing to switch to renewable energy supply.
❏ Has its own sustainable micro-generation such as solar or wind.
❏ Has energy-saving operations in place.
❏ Venue rooms have access to natural light.
❏ Venue rooms have windows that can be opened for ventilation.
❏ Lighting can be controlled within the venue room, with various modes available.
❏ Room heating and cooling can be controlled in the room.
❏ Venue sound and lighting equipment used is energy efficient.
❏ Venue is able to report energy use to the hirer.

Waste

❏ Paper, cardboard, plastics, metals and glass are recycled.
❏ Salvage bays are available for donation of materials for repurposing.
❏ Compostable waste is collected separately for composting.
❏ Food donation systems are in place.
❏ E-waste, hazardous waste and waste oil collections are in place.
❏ Caterers use reusable produce delivery boxes.
❏ Venue is able to report waste performance to the hirer.

Box 4.4 (continued)

Guest Rooms

❑ Have access to natural light.
❑ Windows can be opened for ventilation.
❑ Venue has energy-saving operations in place.
❑ Heating and cooling can be controlled.
❑ In-room waste segregation.

❑ Water conservation messaging, including short showers, towel and linen replacement.
❑ Have in-room communications on sustainability initiatives.
❑ Smoking is not allowed indoors or covered areas, or within 20 metres of doorways.

---

chosen a particular venue or lodging, what the great sustainability attributes are and how they can play their part.

When looking for a venue, you don't have to do your own inspection with clipboard and pen in hand to identify the venue's sustainability credentials or attributes. There are energy efficiency, green building and eco-label ratings programmes, standards and certifications which will do this work for you.

First, look for any independent certification which is based on the original design and construction of the building, such as the *Green Building Council of Australia*[12] or the *US Green Building Council's LEED programme.*[13]

If the building is old and not likely to have been built with concern for energy efficiency, then retro-fitted intervention, appliances and operations could be put in place to achieve efficiencies. They may be recognised by a scheme or certification for energy efficiency in buildings, such as *NABERS*[14] in Australia or *Energy Star* rating in the USA.

In the EU, there is a directive for all new builds, along with all commercial buildings being rented or sold to disclose energy performance (*Energy Performance of Buildings – EPBD*[15]). In the UK this means having an *Energy Performance Certificate.*[16] So look for disclosure by venues of their energy performance rating.

There are also sector-specific programmes such as *Industry Green*[17] for music and theatre venues, or regional programmes such as the *Michigan Green Venues*[18] certification run by the state government there. Within the hotel, tourism and convention sector there is also the independent certification scheme *EarthCheck.*[19] Access the links at the end of the chapter to read more about these programmes and look for a programme local to you or specific to your sector.

Box 4.5

VANCOUVER CONVENTION CENTRE

The *Vancouver Convention Centre,* situated on the waterfront in downtown Vancouver, is a stand-out conferencing and exhibition centre with a unique building featuring countless green technologies and operating techniques.

Just some of the highlights include the following:

• Recycling an average 50 per cent of all waste created, which amounts to 180 tonnes annually. They also collect 150kg of organic waste weekly.

• They use fresh and local ingredients, reducing transport impacts, avoiding additives and prepackaged canned goods.
• Washable crockery, glass and cloth napkins are used, with no disposables, and nearly all condiments are served in bulk or reusable containers.
• 'Happy Earth' menus offer certified organic and free-range options, and they encourage purveyors to deliver their goods in reusable containers.
• With their commitment to advanced energy

Box 4.5 (continued)

management they received one of Canada's first 'Go Green' certificates from the *Building Owners and Managers Association* (BOMA) for environmental best practices.

- As part of the design of the building, energy and resource use is monitored in real time throughout the facility.
- The West Building has LEED Platinum certification. This makes them the first convention centre in the world to earn the highest LEED rating.
- A restored marine habitat is built into the foundation of the West Building. Water quality in the area has improved dramatically, with the growth of a large variety of sea life.
- The West Building features a sophisticated drainage water and recovery system, and a seawater heating and cooling system.
- The West Building's six-acre living roof – the largest in Canada and the largest non-industrial living roof in North America – features more than 400,000 indigenous plants and grasses as well as four beehives. The bees help pollinate the plants and grasses on the living roof while supplying honey for the venue's kitchen.
- The unique roof has been designed to act as an insulator – reducing heat gains in the summer and heat losses in the winter. Drainage and recovery systems are designed to collect and use rain-water for irrigation during the summer months.
- The sophisticated black water treatment plant provides toilet flushing water and rooftop irrigation during warmer weather. They have successfully reduced potable water use by 72.6 per cent.
- Local DC wood products from sustainably managed forests are used throughout the facility.

vancouverconventioncentre.com

NOTES

1 GreenShoot Pacific: www.greenshootpacific.com.
2 This is generally reported as the kilograms (or grams) of GHG emissions per kWh of electricity produced.
3 Worldwatch Institute: www.worldwatch.org/node/9527, accessed May 2013.
4 German Association of Energy and Water Industries: www.bdew.de/internet.nsf/id/EN_press-release, accessed May 2013.
5 Zero Waste International Alliance (ZWIA): zwia.org.
6 Love Food Hate Waste: www.lovefoodhatewaste.com and www.lovefoodhatewaste.nsw.gov.au.
7 ReNew Newcastle: renewnewcastle.org.
8 The Universal Declaration of Human Rights: www.un.org/en/documents/udhr/index.shtml.
9 Live Smart BC: www.livesmartbc.ca/learn/emissions.html, accessed June 2013.
10 China takes steps to clean up 'cancer villages': www.newscientist.com/article/dn23212-china-takes-steps-to-clean-up-cancer-villages.html.
11 Human Rights Watch – China: www.hrw.org/world-report/2013/country-chapters/china.
12 Green Building Council of Australia: www.gbca.org.au.
13 US Green Building Council LEED: www.usgbc.org.
14 NABERS: www.nabers.com.au.
15 Energy Performance of Buildings – EPBD: ec.europa.eu/energy/efficiency/buildings/buildings_en.htm.
16 UK Energy Performance Certificate: www.gov.uk/government/policies/improving-the-energy-efficiency-of-buildings-and-using-planning-to-protect-the-environment.
17 Industry Green: www.juliesbicycle.com/**industry-green.**
18 Michigan Green Venues: www.michigan.gov.
19 EarthCheck: www.earthcheck.org.

If festivals are to play their role in the wider context of carbon reductions, and mitigate for potentially significant cost increases, we must actively work together across the industry to embrace new practices, technology and business models which reduce energy consumption. The technology has arrived, and we can look to existing pioneering events and companies which already act as a litmus for what can be easily achieved with a culture shift toward smarter thinking.

Chris Johnson, Chair, Powerful Thinking; Co-Founder and Director Shambala Festival; Sustainable Event consultant, Kambe Events; Associate for Festivals and Events, Julies Bicycle

Figure 5.1 Dancing up your own power with Energy Floors.

Source: Energy Floors (www.energy-floors.com).

5

ENERGY

Sustainable energy management is a complex topic; however, the solutions to minimising the impact of energy use at events are relatively simple: reduce demand and use renewable energy supply.

No matter the type of venue or event, its location, size, or if it sources power from mains or temporary supply, organisers have the opportunity to make sourcing and operational decisions that may reduce the demand for energy and related greenhouse gas emissions.

Our thirst for power is causing greater and greater demand for fossil fuel extraction and combustion. And it's the combustion of these fossil fuels (coal, gas, oil) for electricity and heating that is contributing significantly to escalating greenhouse gas emissions, which in turn is affecting our climate to undeniable negative effect.

It is important that all industry, societies, governments and citizens work together to both reduce energy demand and support innovation and expansion of renewable energy supply.

The event industry has a part to play in this story. We certainly use energy; to operate our venues, to light our stages and stadiums, meeting rooms and concert halls, and chill our drinks. Our caterers use gas to feed attendees, and gas is used to heat water and rooms. And our mobile power generators gulp down gallons of fuel and puff out plumes of GHGs right there onsite and in view.

This chapter addresses what you can do right now to reduce the impacts of powering and lighting your event. We will look at where your energy comes from and delve into the detail of how to actually achieve power reductions, through both mains and temporary power supply.

It is important to understand that reduction in power impacts at your event can be achieved through either **technological intervention** or through **human interaction** with the way in which equipment is used or buildings are operated.

Innovation in sustainable ways of powering our lives is moving rapidly, and in this chapter we will discuss how events can take advantage of this burgeoning field. We also focus on lighting and how to adjust it to a greener level.

Be the Change

Moving away from a reliance on fossil fuel-based energy supply to renewables, ensuring energy efficiency in equipment use and building operations, and engaging commitment by energy users are the ways forward. Consider the following aspects:

1. Stop Fossil Fuel Addiction

Fossil fuels extraction and their impacts on biodiversity, agriculture, community and health, GHG emissions, and climate change must be addressed. Venues can install their own renewable energy generation or source a renewable energy tariff from the mains. Organisers using mains power at hired venues can purchase *Renewable Energy Certificates*[1] to source green power for their indoor event. Temporary generators can run on renewable fuels, or zero emissions options such as solar, wind or pedal, or demonstrate renewable energy innovations such as hydrogen fuel cell or kinetic energy.

2. Reduce Energy Demand

Planning an energy-free event gets top marks. For those that do need power, reductions can be realised through using energy-efficient equipment, smart power planning, power-down policies, and thoughtful distribution of temporary generators to optimise their efficient running and ultimate fuel efficiency.

Those making power-planning decisions need the knowledge to make accurate power demand estimations and to ensure energy-efficient equipment sourcing, distribution and operating plans.

3. Change Usage Habits

Key to success is changing energy-use habits. You need engagement and buy-in by those planning sound and lighting design, catering and other equipment, or those who will be operating or using equipment at the event. Without their effective implementation of your energy-saving plans, savings may not be achieved.

What does this mean for events?

Entwining energy efficiency, renewable energy and shining a light on the issues surrounding climate change in the context of your event and perhaps influencing the attendees to consider doing the same is a good place to start.

The Business Case

The business case for sustainable energy management at events comes down again to cost reductions, meeting stakeholder expectations and enhancing your organisation's reputation.

Reduced Costs

Using less energy will mean that in many cases your power invoice will be reduced. At indoor events this will occur if the venue charges for power use. Ensure accurate metering is in place so you can see the efforts you put into reducing power demand are realised in reduced power charges.

When using temporary power generators, if you use less fuel you will receive a smaller fuel invoice. This can be achieved through switching off generators when not needed, or through using fewer or smaller generators.

When moving to renewable energy supply, you may experience some cost increases. Biodiesel may be more expensive than mineral diesel, depending on global oil prices and subsidies offered or taxes imposed by your government for various fuel types. I have however bought biodiesel at a cheaper rate than mineral diesel. If you couple reducing demand on generators through efficient equipment, planning and operating, this may result in smaller or fewer generators. Costs saved here may counter any increased price of biofuels, making the switch cost neutral.

Reputation

Using sustainably sourced, renewable, zero-emissions and innovative energy supply and equipment will see your event being positioned as an industry leader. How high on the agenda renewable energy is in the region your event is held, and therefore what expectations are held by event stakeholders for your renewable energy use, will impact on the reputational benefits received.

Offering your event as a showcase for renewable power innovations and as a vehicle to promote energy conservation in action at your event will also enhance your reputation.

Compliance

The business case for energy efficiency actions and sourcing renewable energy supply may come down to expected practice in the industry or requirements by sponsors, funding partners, venues or attendees.

Independent recognition of your energy management and sourcing may also be a motivation to put certain solutions in place, in order to achieve the certification, awards or recognition.

POWER PLANNING STAKEHOLDERS

Achieving reduced GHGs from event power demand and supply includes a tangled web of people, opinion, fact, Chinese whispers, technology, promises, plans, expectations and realities that need to be navigated. Apart from this need for clarity and decisive action, and those that play an active part in outcomes, stakeholder communications should include those who may have an opinion on your power sourcing and GHG emissions production.

Key to the plans are venue management, technical producer, lighting designer, AV supplier and operators, talent, talent/artist liaison and overall creative controller of the event's programme. And that's just for what's on stage.

Next you will need to involve all those additional areas that require power, including traders/vendors, bars, caterers, offices, general site or front-of-house lighting and other back-of-house production aspects.

Production Management

The team planning the power requirements, along with planning and procuring infrastructure and equipment for your event, are key stakeholders to engage. This also includes the technical production manager (or other similar role) who wrangles the actual on-stage or on-site power requirements of the various participants.

These staff/crew members need to understand power efficiencies and the technicalities involved to achieve them given your power supply situation. They also need to know what types of renewable energy options to look for, along with being inspired or incentivised to actually plan for and achieve GHG reductions.

✓ **Provide energy efficiency training**
Those planning and making final decisions on power provision and distribution need to know how to achieve efficiencies when using both mains and temporary power supply. The team doesn't need an electrician's qualification, but if team members can demonstrate a basic understanding of the principles behind supplying power to an event, they can hold a decent conversation about options and solutions.

✓ **Obtain external support**
If the skills don't exist in the team and formal training isn't an option, look to where you can gain this knowledge. If starting from scratch, there's no one better than your friendly power contractor to ask for this education. Get them talking amps and kilowatts, kVA and loadings, and the team will become more equipped to investigate energy-saving options.

✓ **Incentivise reductions**
Set reduction goals and offer rewards for achieving them. Pit various departments, stages, venues or teams against each other to achieve the biggest savings.

ENERGY PLANNING STEPS

Consider the following steps when investigating the best
energy strategy for almost any type of event:

Table 5.1 Energy Planning Steps

---

1 Get go-ahead. Get resources.

Gain support internally and externally. Find out what resources and knowledge exist and what's needed. Look to your organisation, supply chain, production staff, power providers and energy programmes.

2 Establish team. Delegate duties.

Whose responsibility is it to research, plan, implement and report energy management? Assign tasks. Include production designers, venue managers, artist liaison, sound/light/visuals suppliers and operators.

3 Research energy demand.

Evaluate what needs to be powered. What does business as usual look like? Identify activities and behaviours that will cause energy demand and look for savings. Will the operating hours, location or content/programme aspects influence energy demand?

4 Identify solutions.

Which venues offer renewable energy supply or energy-efficient operations? Investigate what options there are for achieving reduced energy demand. What equipment is available? Can renewable energy sources be used?

5 Engagement and commitment.

Who needs to be engaged? Will there be resistance? Is there a clear communication flow between technical production, stage management, artist management, AV providers, power providers, power and AV staff? Can energy use habits be changed?

6 Evaluate feasibility.

Estimate efficiencies and savings. Compare the costs of hiring more efficient equipment, hiring energy-efficient venues, using renewable energy, or changing event timing so that energy demand reductions can be realised.

7 Set objectives and plans.

Estimate litres, kWh and resulting GHGs and establish reduction targets. Confirm where reductions can be made and put plans in place. Reconfirm tasks and engage all those who have a part to play. Identify what you will measure and how you will capture data.

8 Event production.

Implement operational plans for achieving reductions. Continue communications with relevant crew and contractors. Monitor compliance with plans at the event and adjust in real time if adherence is not achieved. Measure energy consumption.

9 Compliance and reporting.

Collect energy consumption data and report it, including kWh, litres of fuel by type, percentage of event energy from renewable sources and total GHGs. Interpret results and set objectives for the future.

10 Celebrate success.

Inform all those involved of your results against objectives and plans for the future.

Generator Suppliers

One of the biggest players in the complex planning and operating web that must be successfully navigated to actually achieve efficiencies are the suppliers of the kit themselves.

Your generator suppliers are experts in power provision and often the event organiser won't have an expert in their team to really be able to get to grips with the technicalities of what sized generators are required, where they should be placed and, when looking at efficiencies, how reductions can be achieved successfully without fear of under-supply and cut-outs.

If you trust them, in that they won't just supply you with the largest kit to get the big payment, then it may be better to leave it to them to plan efficiencies and alternatives. However, a fresh set of eyes (yours) that aren't too narrowly focused may come up with options to reduce demand for generators and other innovative solutions to reduce energy consumption.

Perhaps working a bonus into their contract to reduce kVA (generator size) or fuel volume would be an incentive.

Consider striking a deal that includes you paying for the fuel bill separately, so that generator providers are not getting a kick-back for every litre of fuel that goes through the generators and therefore their profit margin being tied to fuel consumption.

Be aware that sometimes the generator hire company may supply kit that is well above the size needed for the specific job. Ask for an assurance that the requested kVA for the generator ordered will be the kVA supplied.

One power contractor confessed to me that on a regular basis up to 50 per cent of fuel goes up in smoke, a lot of which is due to oversized generators being delivered because of poor planning on behalf of the hiring company.

Talent/Artists

Performers and other talent who have specific creative requirements for stage sound or lighting will also need to be engaged. Lighting and visuals use the largest amount of power on stage, and opportunities exist to reduce energy demand if performing talent is willing to switch to energy-efficient lighting and equipment.

Convincing performers and their teams to design stage lighting with consideration for energy efficiency is essential to achieve reduced power demand on stage.

✓ **Pre-event engagement**
Inform talent when they are contracted that the event is trying to reduce energy demand and GHG creation, and that you need them to play their part by considering the power demand of the lighting and visual design of their show.

✓ **Require equipment specifications**
In order to have talent reflect on the energy consumption and GHG impacts of their planned lighting/visuals design, ask them to calculate the potential kWh to be used for all equipment, including anticipated peak loads for specific equipment.

✓ **Encourage harmonisation**
The trick to maximising the efficiency of temporary power generators is to keep a power demand of 70 to 80 per cent of capacity. To achieve this you will need to harmonise the power demand across all users. This means that if a particular performer needs a power-hungry effect to occur at a particular point during their show, this peak will be the marker for the generator size. If this peak is dramatically higher than all the other artists' demand then inefficiencies will occur. This is because a larger-sized generator will be required in order to have enough capacity for that one special effect, but it will run at under the optimal load for most of the time. Highlight to 'offending' talent what consequences their requirement for that special big effect to be powered has on the generator size and consequent GHG increase. See if you can get them to change their design (without adversely damaging creative execution of their show).

✓ **Monitor demand**
Keep an eye on power consumption and report back results to talent.

Site/Stage Operators

The team that run the sound and lighting equipment on stage are also key stakeholders to engage in the realisation of efficiency plans into actual savings.

The best plans can be set but, without those who actually operate the equipment being personally invested in achieving efficiencies, all may be lost.

✓ **Include operators in planning**
Those who actually operate equipment at the event are likely to have the most realistic ideas on what may be done to achieve efficiencies and how various equipment may be optimally used.

✓ **Pre-event training/briefings**
Ensure that all staff operating equipment have been trained or briefed pre-event on the event's efficiency goals, plans to achieve them and the role they are expected to play.

✓ **Onsite inductions**
Organise inductions into the plans and operating processes that must be undertaken to achieve energy reduction goals.

✓ **Onsite auditing of compliance**
Undertake audits of planned equipment operation during the event to ensure that efficiencies are being achieved and plans are being adhered to by staff and users.

✓ **Incentivise reductions**
Set reduction goals and offer rewards for achieving them. Pit various departments, stages, venues or teams against each other to achieve the biggest savings.

Power Users

Many event participants use equipment plugged into power, such as exhibitors, caterers, temporary food traders, merchandise stalls and activities providers. Just as site and stage operators need to be engaged, so too do these participants need to be informed of the event's energy-reduction goals and to be motivated or incentivised to play their part.

✓ **Pre-event engagement**
Those who use power at your event, but who cannot be directed as can staff, will need to be involved in the event's energy-reduction ambitions. Let them know from the outset why there are plans in place to reduce energy, if it will mean any cost savings to them, and what the options are for them to help achieve reductions.

✓ **Inform users of power diets and reduction goals**
As part of your event's energy-reduction goals, you may be setting consumption limits on various users. If this is the case then all users need to be conscripted into the idea of reductions and be pre-informed of what this will mean to their own power and equipment planning.

✓ **Onsite inductions**
Remember to remind all power users at the beginning of the event of energy conservation goals and what they should do to help achieve these reductions. Ensure that this information is included in general inductions, or brief someone to speak to users as they are setting up.

✓ **Incentivise reductions**
Just as with the other internal stakeholders, these external power-using stakeholders can also be incentivised or rewarded for achieving planned power consumption reductions.

✓ **Onsite auditing of compliance**
Undertake audits of participants' power use during the event to ensure efficiencies are being achieved and plans adhered to.

POWER PLANNING PATHWAY

Figure 5.2 maps interacting communications flows among the many stakeholders in establishing power provision for an outdoor event, using temporary generators. You will see that there is the potential for much 'rounding-up' of requirements, which may mean oversupply of generator capacity. This in turn will lead to inefficiencies and unnecessary GHG creation.

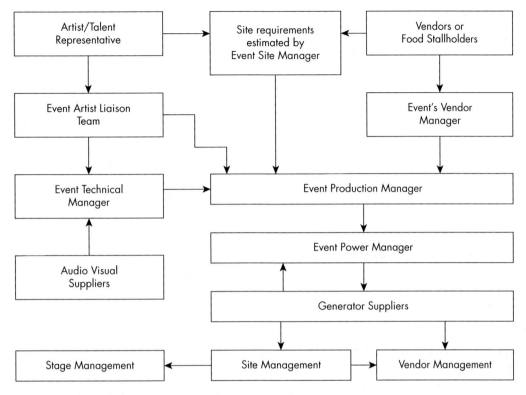

Figure 5.2 Power demand planning communications map —outdoor events.

Understand the role played by each person in the power-planning pathway in contributing to energy-efficiency success or in adding to the complication of why efficiency is difficult to achieve. Some examples of considerations include the following:

- **Artists/vendors:** They should provide information on what their AV specs or requirements are. How do you currently get this information from them? Is it accurate?
- **Artist liaison:** Does the person communicating with performers collect the requirements/AV tech specs, and do they do any aggregating of information? Do they understand what the event is trying to achieve with energy efficiency and can they adequately communicate the concepts to artists?
- **Generator suppliers:** Are they interested in helping you achieve an energy-/fuel-efficient event? Will they happily downsize generators if information shows you could manage with a smaller one? Do they have control over what generators are actually assigned to your event?

VENUE OWNER'S ENERGY CHECKLIST

Box 5.1

VENUE OWNER'S ENERGY CHECKLIST

Planning and Commitment

❑ The venue has made a public statement of its commitment to energy efficiency and reductions.
❑ The venue has an energy management plan.
❑ The venue has a staff communications and engagement strategy in place.
❑ The venue has undertaken an energy audit and understands where efficiencies can be made.
❑ The venue has comprehensive metering and analysis in place.
❑ The venue discloses its energy consumption data.
❑ Feedback channels for users and guests are in place.

Energy Source

❑ Mains electricity is from a renewable energy source.
❑ Where only fossil fuel-based mains is available, Renewable Energy Certificates are purchased for total kWh used to effectively source renewable energy.
❑ Power is supplied from decentralised combined heat and power/co-generation.
❑ Power is supplied from permanent renewable micro-energy supply.

Energy Efficiency: Equipment

❑ Building and surrounds have been designed to optimise passive heating, cooling and lighting, and to be responsive to the local environment.
❑ Thermal energy storage is used.
❑ Building has adequate insulation, ventilation, glazing, tinting and draft seals.
❑ Light colours (walls and floors) are used to optimise daylighting effect.

❑ Building has sensors and timers installed for lighting, heating, cooling and escalators.
❑ Solar or gas hot water heating is installed.
❑ Hot water pipes are insulated.
❑ Gas is used for cooking and heating.
❑ Fans are available in addition to air conditioners.
❑ Internal and external lighting is energy efficient.
❑ Refrigeration equipment is energy efficient.
❑ Laundry appliances are energy efficient.
❑ Air drying is used in preference to tumble drying.
❑ Stage AV equipment is energy efficient.
❑ Catering equipment is energy efficient.
❑ Office equipment is energy efficient and set to energy-efficient modes.
❑ Equipment is maintained to ensure efficiency.

Energy Efficiency: Venue Operations

❑ Room temperature set points are adjusted seasonally.
❑ Daylight is used in preference to powered lights.
❑ Heating and cooling simultaneously is not occurring (!) and switched off when large dock doors are open for extended periods of time.
❑ Power diets are placed on users or energy-efficient operating guidance is provided.
❑ A 'power-down' policy is in place, including opening and closing procedures.
❑ Windows can be opened by room user.
❑ Conference room AV can be controlled by user and powered down easily in breaks.
❑ Room heating and cooling can be controlled from within the room by the user and guidance is given for optimal temperature.
❑ Lighting can be controlled within the room, with various modes available.
❑ Staff know how to use heating and lighting controls.

EVENT ORGANISER'S ENERGY CHECKLIST

Box 5.2

EVENT ORGANISER'S ENERGY CHECKLIST

Venue Choice

- ❏ Choose a venue that has been designed and built for maximum energy efficiency.
- ❏ Choose a venue that has sources of power from renewable energy supply. Alternatively, purchase RECs equivalent to kWh power consumed.
- ❏ If event-specific energy consumption cannot be provided, choose a venue that has undertaken an energy audit and can provide accurate energy consumption estimates for your event.
- ❏ Choose a venue that has an energy management plan in place and ensures energy efficiency in venue operations.
- ❏ Choose a venue that has energy-efficient equipment and lighting.
- ❏ Choose a venue that has comprehensive metering in place.
- ❏ Choose a venue that can report on your event's energy consumption.

Temporary Energy Source and Planning

- ❏ Power generators use biofuels.
- ❏ Use variable speed temporary power generators.
- ❏ Mobile solar power is used.
- ❏ Mobile wind power is used.
- ❏ Pedal power or people power is used.
- ❏ Kinetic energy is used.
- ❏ Hydrogen fuel cell power is used.
- ❏ Power demand is accurately estimated.
- ❏ Generator distribution is planned to optimise loads and efficiencies, including isolating overnight loads to separate generators.
- ❏ Lighting, sound and visuals design is planned with concern for energy consumption.
- ❏ Energy-efficient equipment is used.
- ❏ Efficiency planning leads to smaller, fewer or short running time for generators.

Energy Efficiency

- ❏ Use stage lighting, sound and visuals with energy consumption in mind.
- ❏ Equipment is maintained to ensure maximum efficiency, including cleaning filters in ventilation systems and cleaning house lighting bulbs.
- ❏ Daylight is used in preference to powered lights.
- ❏ Windows are opened and fans are used over powered cooling.
- ❏ Power diets are placed on users or energy-efficient operating guidance is provided.
- ❏ A 'switch-off' or 'power-down' policy is in place.
- ❏ Turn off PAs, including the desk, and if powered, the speakers, when they are not being used.
- ❏ Consider if you really need as much stage lighting during the day as you would at night.
- ❏ Turn off stage lighting when it is not being used.
- ❏ Don't leave battery chargers (for phones, two-way radios and other equipment) on all day long.
- ❏ Third-party users such as exhibitors are required to 'opt in' to inefficient booth lighting, with energy-efficient lighting provided as the norm.

Communications and Engagement

- ❏ Policy is formally communicated.
- ❏ Energy initiatives are communicated to attendees.
- ❏ Energy initiatives are communicated to event crew and they are engaged in reductions goals.
- ❏ Innovative renewable energy sources are used.
- ❏ Staff (venue or organiser) are allocated to ensure energy-efficiency planning is actually implemented.
- ❏ Third-party users are audited at the event to make sure they are using what they said they would use.
- ❏ Power usage during the event is audited to assess consumption patterns for future planning.
- ❏ Event energy consumption and GHGs are measured and reported.

Figure 5.3 Getting onto the grid in Koh Tao.

Source: Tara Jones.

ENERGY SOURCE

To set the scene, first here's an overview of energy supply through the grid from renewable and non-renewable sources.

Electricity is commonly created at centralised locations (power stations) and delivered to users through the electricity grid. Power stations are optimally located close to the source of fuel supply and their customers.

The mains electricity grid is also added to by myriad small energy producers, usually renewable energy creators. This provision is called 'decentralised power'.

At coal-, oil- and gas-fired power stations, the fossil fuel is combusted and the heat energy is converted to mechanical energy which in turn drives turbines to create electricity. Carbon dioxide (CO_2) is the most famous of the greenhouse gases emitted by burning fossil fuels, and is a major player in the energy production debate.

Read more about CO_2 and other greenhouse gases in Chapter 7.

The alternative to electricity generated by fossil fuels, nuclear or major hydro schemes, is nice, clean, green, renewable and non-polluting energy such as wind, solar, geothermal and biomass. Which of these alternatives makes sense to you?

It is interesting to discover where mains electricity comes from in your city or country – what proportion from which energy source. When I ask in training courses where power comes from in the cities where the students live, I often receive vague and unsure answers. Some are not even sure if renewable energy is available locally. Do a little research to understand what the energy mix is on your local mains power grid.

The majority of the world's energy supply comes from fossil fuels (67.4%),[2] namely from coal and peat, natural gas and oil. The remaining comes from hydro, nuclear and 'other'. The 'other' is solar, wind, geothermal, biofuels and waste, and accounts for 3.7 per cent of the world's energy supply. It puts renewables into perspective, doesn't it?

Apart from understanding where power is sourced in your country, it is also interesting to know what the GHG 'emissions factor' is per kWh of power. Do this by accessing the *International Energy Agency's* 'CO2 Highlights' document.[3]

Non-renewable Resources

The creation of electricity from non-renewable sources leaves a legacy of greenhouse gas emissions and hazardous waste. It uses up precious fossil fuels and releases 'ancient carbon' into our system that was previously locked out. Resource extraction can potentially displace people and affect biodiversity. Additional impacts to be considered are those from transporting raw materials and also inefficiencies from heat losses in generation and transmission by centralised power stations.

Coal

Coal is a major player in global electricity production, with 42 per cent of the world's electricity derived from coal, with China, USA, India and Australia being the top coal producers.[4] Indonesia and Australia vie for the spot as largest exporter in the world.[5] Coal is the least efficient of the fossil fuels.

I have the dubious honour of living a few blocks from the world's largest coal port, in Newcastle, NSW. Well, when I was writing the first edition of this book this was the case. During the writing of that book, the capacity of the port doubled, with a second coal loader being installed, much to the chagrin of local campaigners. Newcastle went from the largest coal port in the world to still being the largest, instead a factor of 2.

Since the publication of the first edition of this book, a third coal loader has been installed. At the time of writing this chapter for the revised edition, there was a protest rally in my city against the about-to-be-approved-but-not-if-we-the-citizens-can-stop-it fourth coal loader.

The concerns are for the amount of coal our region is sending out into the world, shipping off climate change-in-waiting. Coupled with this are the health concerns of mountains of uncovered coal and the inevitable coal dust making its way across the city and into its residents' lungs.

Natural Gas

Natural gas consists primarily of methane. It is found deep underground and is often associated with coal beds or petroleum deposits. Natural gas is processed to remove impurities and then delivered by pipeline.

Gas may be used 'as is' with its ignition creating heat to be used for cooking, hot water or heating rooms. This is delivered through pipes or compressed and stored in tanks. (CNG = compressed natural gas, or LPG = liquid petroleum gas).

Gas is also used as a major source of electricity generation. It's a more efficient source of energy creation than its fossil fuel siblings, coal and oil, and is therefore the 'cleanest' with the lowest GHGs per equivalent unit of energy created (see Table 5.4 for comparisons with other fossil fuels.)

The new kid on the block is 'coal seam gas' (CSG) exploration and extraction. The methodology for extraction is known as 'fracking' (fracturing) rock bed to access the coal gas seams. The potentially devastating impacts on the natural environment, including waterways, and the health of those living in the region (humans and non-humans) are much debated. The proponents of coal seam gas, and the governments that approve exploration licences, maintain that there is no dangerous impact, but that is hotly contested by the anti-CSG camp. To learn more about the issues, watch the film *Gasland* (www.gaslandthemovie.com).

Oil

Oil (petroleum) is a fossil fuel also used for electricity generation. It is comparatively more expensive than gas or coal, and had its heyday twenty years ago. The total share of electricity produced by all non-renewables has dropped since the 1970s, due primarily to oil use being reduced from 20.9 to 4.6 per cent.[6]

Nuclear Energy

Nuclear is a controversial energy source, due to the radioactivity of the raw material used and the resulting hazardous waste produced. Recent events in Japan further support those who see nuclear as a problematic solution to energy supply.

The nuclear energy debate has been taking place since nuclear energy first raised its head as an alternative to fossil fuels.

However, proponents of nuclear energy promote its effectiveness in producing energy for its relative 'minor' negative environmental impacts. It is touted as GHG free, with no harmful emissions to air.

Greenpeace list what they see as some potent problems with nuclear energy.[7] First, it is 'too little too late' with regard to its halting climate change. They claim that nuclear power stations couldn't possibly be built quickly enough to have an assured GHG-reducing impact. Radioactive waste, the risk of accident and targets for terrorism are also listed as concerns. The potential for plutonium (part of nuclear waste) to be used in dirty bombs is also a major issue.

Combined Heat and Power

In a combined heat and power (CHP) system, both heat and power are produced from a single process. Losses of energy through unused heat and transmitting electricity out to the customer via the grid make traditional centralised power plants inefficient in comparison to CHP.

In a CHP system the recovered heat is distributed to the immediate surrounding areas and used for hot water, space heating, or the steam may be used for industrial purposes. CHP systems are highly efficient in comparison to centralised power generations. 'Waste' heat from the production process is captured and used, and no energy is lost through transmission.

Renewable Energy Sources

Rather than combusting 'ancient carbon' (fossil fuels – oil, coal and gas) or using nuclear power, it is possible to generate mains electricity from combusting or harnessing 'recent' carbon, or from the power of sun, wind and water.

Large-scale Hydro

Viewed as renewable energy supply, and certainly zero emissions, this option uses gravity to force water from dams through turbines to create electricity.

Figure 5.4 Lock the Gate action. The ingenious Lock the Gate[8] campaign has joined those previously at opposite ends of the environmental debate: farmers and 'greenies'. Farmers lock their gates in a peaceful protest action, effectively preventing entry onto private property. The mission of the Lock the Gate Alliance is to "protect Australia's natural, environmental, cultural and agricultural resources from inappropriate mining and to educate and empower all Australians to demand sustainable solutions to food and energy production." If you want to know more about the campaign, go to www.lockthegate.org.au.

Source: Kate Ausburn.

Hydroelectricity causes controversy when biodiversity/habitat/ecological issues arise from reclamation of land for dams. There may also be downstream impacts on waterways and ecosystems.

Wind Power

Harnessing the power of wind is a truly zero emissions source of energy supply. The *Global Wind Energy Council* reports that wind provides electricity in over 100 countries, 23 of which now have at least 1000 megawatts installed. The largest creators of wind power are China, the USA, Germany, Spain and India. A clutch of other countries are giving it a real go too. Their data shows that in 2012 the global capacity increased by 20 per cent to a grand total of 282,482 megawatts.[9] When the first edition of this book was published it was 158,000 megawatts. Great stuff indeed!

Some communities may put up resistance to installations of wind turbines if views are interrupted or if there are concerns of turbines being hazardous to bird life. There are also studies underway about the health impacts of the low-level noise made by wind turbines. Watch this space for issues and as research is completed.

Solar

Harnessing the power of the sun is also a truly zero emissions source of energy supply. The energy of the sun is captured and turned into electricity through two technologies – photovoltaic (PV) cells or concentrating solar power (CSP). PV panels directly convert solar energy (sunlight) into electricity. In CSP, mirrors or lenses concentrate energy from the sun's rays to heat a receiver to high temperatures, which is transformed to mechanical energy and then into electricity. Both options are being enthusiastically taken up by governments and private ventures across the world.

The *International Energy Agency* (IEA) reports that during the decade to 2011 the cumulative installed capacity of solar PV reached 65 gigawatts. This was up from 1.5 gigawatts in 2000.[10] Germany and Italy are the largest producers, accounting for more than half the global cumulative capacity. Other major PV solar producers are Japan, Spain, the USA and China. The USA

and Spain are the main players when it comes to CSP. The first commercial plants were built in the 1980s in California. CSP is now re-emerging as an energy option[11]

With 'feed-in tariffs' offered in many countries, venue owners are incentivised to install permanent solar arrays, reducing their reliance on fossil fuel-based energy.

Many venues are investing in solar power, especially in those countries where installation is incentivised through feed-in tariffs. The *City of Sydney* has taken a proactive approach to its GHG emissions inventory management.

Rather than purchasing renewable energy credits, they are reinvesting in renewable energy infrastructure. *Sydney Town Hall*, a popular venue for special events and single-day conferences, and located right in the centre of the city, is completely solar powered and is the largest solar power installation in the CBD. It generates enough energy to supply the council chambers and the Town Hall offices next door.

Outdoor music event *Bonnaroo Music & Arts Festival* in the USA has also invested in a 50kW solar photovoltaic system that supports 20 per cent of the festival's energy needs.

In its quest to be a carbon-neutral event, the *FIFA World Cup 2022* to be held in Qatar is planning vast solar installations to provide power requirements for the 30-day football tournament while also leaving a lasting legacy of ongoing renewable power generation for the country.

Geothermal

This is harnessing the energy from heat generated naturally from within the earth. Some of the heat is from the formation of the planet, while other heat is created from the decay of naturally radioactive materials.[12] The *Geothermal Energy Association* reports as of May 2012 that there were approximately 11,224MW of installed geothermal capacity online globally.[13] In 2010, geothermal energy generated twice the amount of electricity as solar energy did worldwide. The USA leads world geothermal electricity production.

Box 5.3

BLACK ROCK SOLAR AT BURNING MAN

Black Rock Solar began as a volunteer crew installing a 30kW solar array at the Burning Man festival in 2007, which was promoting the Green Man theme. But things grew from then on.

After the 2007 event, the solar array was donated to the school in the nearby town of Gerlach, Nevada, and *Black Rock Solar* began its mission of building low-cost solar for organisations and communities which use it the most.

Now a 501©3 non-profit in its sixth year of business, *Black Rock Solar* has installed over 2 Megawatts of solar in Northern Nevada to other non-profits, schools, hospitals and tribes who would not otherwise be able to afford it.

Black Rock Solar hosts a solar tour each year at the *Burning Man* event showcasing all the many camps and art installations utilising solar and other alternative power on the playa, which is increasing every year. In 2011, the solar tour visited about ten different solar or alternative energy camps or art installations. Highlights from the tour were:

* The *Alternative Energy Zone*[14] village is 500 people in 70 camps that use NO generators. Only solar/wind/bats and conservation/efficiency.
* *Snow Koan Solar*[15] brings the largest solar array to the playa each year, providing over 27kW of power to *Nectar Village*.[16]. They also provide an electric vehicle recharging station and snow cones each afternoon. Estimated population of *Nectar Village* was about 350 people. *Snow Koan Solar* also powered 26 art projects on the playa, including the 22 CORE projects that circled the man.

www.blackrocksolar.org
www.burningman.com

Biomass

Recovering the energy stored in biological material to be converted directly or indirectly to electricity is seen as a renewable form of energy (waste to energy or energy from waste). Greenhouse gases are still emitted during combustion, but it is the combustion of 'recent' carbon rather than 'ancient' carbon (fossil fuels) that were previously locked out of our carbon cycle. Biomass to electricity can be achieved through thermal conversion such as incineration and pyrolysis. In incineration the biomass is burned and the heat created is used to turn water into steam to drive electricity turbines. In pyrolysis (gasification) biomass is turned into gas through burning at an intense heat in the absence of oxygen. This gas is then used to fuel power generation. The by-product of pyrolysis is 'biochar' which is also receiving a lot of attention as it may be added to soil, both sequestering carbon and improving fertility.

Anaerobic Digestion

Anaerobic digestion (AD) is the decomposition of biodegradable material in the absence of oxygen. The result is biogas (a mixture of methane and CO_2) used to generate electricity and provide heat. Digestate also results, which is the solids/liquids left at the end of the decomposition process. This digestate may be used as agricultural fertiliser or additionally treated in a traditional composting operation.

Landfill Gas

Methane extraction from landfills is also a form of renewable energy. Biological matter, as it breaks down, creates gas (primarily methane but also CO_2). At many landfill sites this gas is actually burnt off to avoid the landfill igniting, but increasingly landfill sites are capturing this gas for conversion to electricity. Existing landfills are retrofitted with the technology required, and some landfills are being purpose-built for methane extraction. Sending biodegradable material to landfill for methane harvesting is discussed in more detail in Chapter 9.

Green onto the grid?

So how does the 'green' electricity get to those who want it via the mains electricity grid? Renewable energy producers send their electricity to the electricity grid where it is mixed with all the other electricity. Power retailers buy the renewable energy delivered to the grid from the producers and then on-sell it as a 'green' or 'renewable' energy tariff to consumers. In some cases, such as *Good Energy*[17] in the UK, the retailer is the producer of the actual renewable energy.

What does this mean for events?

Through switching to a 'green' energy tariff you are supporting the development of renewable energy pro-duction. By adding to this development and also to the overall demand, governments will be encouraged to increase their targets for total renewable energy reaching the grid.

Certainly the great increase in solar photovoltaic production in the past few years is evidence of this in action. If you own your venue, or are advising your event's venue to switch to green energy, check for an accreditation scheme for renewable energy in your country to make sure you're switching to a good green energy source.

Most venues should be able to sign straight up or choose the green energy tariff from a conventional power company. You will need to check if your country actually has green energy options available for purchase as they

Figure 5.5 Salt Palace Convention Center in Utah installed one of the USA's largest rooftop solar array projects featuring project 6 006 solar panels. It provides 18 per cent of the venue's power demand. In terms of scale, imagine five football fields of solar panels!

Photo: Salt Palace Convention Centre.

Box 5.4

BONNAROO MUSIC AND ARTS FESTIVAL SOLAR ARRAY

In a groundbreaking effort to actively reduce its energy consumption, Bonnaroo Music and Arts Festival has installed the USA's first permanent solar array for a major music festival. The 50kW solar photovoltaic system supports 20 per cent of the festival's energy needs.

The solar project was fully funded by 'opt-in' contributions from fans selected during the ticket-buying process. In 2012, in order to generate guaranteed resources, a US$1 fee was added to every ticket sold to enable the financing for the wonderful additional green initiatives at the event. Bonnaroo fans can take full credit for helping the event to expand its environmental commitment. Past dollars have been used to fund the compost pad, the garden and the *Mobile Tower of Power*.

The solar system installed at the permanent event site comprises 196 American-made *SolarWorld* solar panels along with micro-inverters and related components mounted to the roof of a metal structure in the festival's back stage area. It generates more than 61,000kWh per year.

As a certified participant in the local power authority's *Green Power Provider Program*, Bonnaroo sells the energy produced by the solar system back to the local utility distribution network.

www.bonnaroo.com

Figure 5.6 Solar array installed at Bonnaroo Music and Arts Festival.

Source: Bonnaroo Festival.

are not available everywhere. Examples are *WindMade Event Certification* in the USA and *GreenPower* in Australia (www.windmade.org, www.greenpower.gov. au). Read more about these on the book's website.

✓ Ask venues if mains power is from renewables.
✓ Ask venues if they create any renewable energy.

✓ Ask venues if they can meter your event's power consumption.
✓ Investigate if you can independently purchase renewable energy certificates for your event.
✓ Consider installing renewable energy onsite and providing it to the national grid through your country's feed-in tariff.

Figure 5.7 'Sunny Bin' solar sound systems by www.wheely binsoundsystems.

Source: Wheely Bin Sound Systems.

TEMPORARY POWER

Many outdoor events will use mobile power generators to supply electricity. The majority of generators run on mineral diesel, a non-renewable and -polluting fuel. By transitioning to sustainable fuels or to zero emissions options such as solar, wind, pedal, hydrogen fuel cell or kinetic energy, you will be getting off fossil fuels, demonstrating a commitment to renewable energy, and reducing your event's greenhouse gas emissions.

Diesel Motor Generators

For those events held outdoors with insufficient or no access to mains power supply, mobile power generators

are the go-to solution. Mobile power generators are a ubiquitous sight at concerts in parks, festivals in fields, starting lines at marathons or community fairs on local streets. They generally run on fossil fuels –mineral diesel or petrol. Generators are also able to run on renewable fuels such as 100 per cent or a blend of biodiesel, ethanol or even pure vegetable oil.

We'll now track through the options for fuelling temporary/mobile power generators.

Fossil Fuels

Diesel and petrol are the two most popular fossil fuels used in temporary power generators. However, some generators do run on gas. GHGs, other gases and particulates (commonly known as 'air pollution') are emitted by temporary power generators using these fuels, as a result of the combustion of the fuel.

The issues with using non-renewable resources for temporary power generators are the same as those outlined earlier in the mains power energy source section of this chapter.

Biofuels

As opposed to fossil fuels, which are made from non-renewable resources taking millions of years to create and until we extract them, and were locked out of the carbon cycle, biofuels are made from renewable materials such as oil seed, wheat and sugar. There are two basic types of biofuel: ethanol (alcohol) and biodiesel (methyl ester).

Biofuels are used for creating electricity via power generators, or used as a transport fuel. Biofuels are beneficial, as they replace fossil fuels and are seen as having zero GHGs, since they use 'recent' carbon rather than unlocking the 'ancient' carbon embodied in fossil fuels.

For biofuels to be truly beneficial, they need to produce relatively fewer GHGs across the product life cycle, and to offer no negative and hopefully positive socio-economic benefits in comparison to using fossil fuels. Full life cycle analyses have been undertaken to compare fossil fuels to biofuels. There is no one answer for all biofuels. The relatively lower GHG outputs of using biofuel over fossil fuel will depend on factors such as the feedstock, manufacture process and proximity to market.

GHGs are created through the entire life cycle of biofuel production, including carbon stored in trees and soil being released into the carbon cycle as forests are cleared and soils tilled. Fuel is also used to run equipment for the sowing, harvesting and transporting of feedstock. Fertilisers are used, with its own back story of fossil fuel use in the raw material, its manufacture and transport. Processing into biodiesel also uses energy, as does transport of the final fuel product. (Hopefully the fuel used for transport or to run machinery is actually biofuel!)

There is much campaigning against using arable land for the production of crops for fuel not food. It is believed that only so much land can be set aside to grow biofuels before food supplies and biodiversity are threatened. In addition, the insatiable demand for fuel crops can push up grain prices.

Social concerns are also at play, including the loss of farmland and displacement of farmers, or loss of natural habitat on which a community's livelihood may rely.

There has been a strong backlash against biofuel crops grown in Malaysia and Indonesia where palm oil plantations and the consequential destruction of forests has occurred on a grand scale. Where multinational biofuel companies are sourcing existing agricultural land for their fuel crops, including previously smallholding farmland, displacement of farmers is an issue.

The race to produce biofuels has in large part been started through mandates by some governments to require fuels to contain a certain percentage of biofuel. Rather than just prescribing the percentage of biofuels, responsible governments also dictate sustainability credentials of the growing and manufacture of the fuel, localised socio-economic factors and proximity to markets to reduce transport impacts.

An example of taking a responsible attitude towards biofuel sourcing is the UK's *Renewable Fuels Agency,*[18] which is an independent sustainable fuels regulator. Many countries also have renewable fuel standards, imposed by the government to assure the sustainable sourcing of biofuels.

To address the concerns of the cropped fuel, in 2011 the *UN Food and Agriculture Organization (UN FAO)*[19] published its framework to help governments evaluate bioenergy potential and assess its possible food security impacts. In the same year the *Global BioEnergy Partnership*[20] launched sustainability indicators for biofuel production, intended to help countries assess and develop sustainable production and use of bioenergy.

The debate and analysis continue. Keep your eye on this if you are looking to move to biofuels as the pros and cons continue to be deliberated and life cycle analyses are undertaken. Nonetheless, using biofuels builds demand for renewable fuels, encouraging a market for and making potentially viable advancement in second- and third-generation biofuel technologies.

These next-generation biofuels include BioHydrogen Diesel, Biomethanol and Algae Oils.

Non-food oils are the way ahead but, without a proven market, bringing these new technologies to commercial viability may not be possible. Next-generation biofuels could be more sustainable in production, cheaper, have greater environmental benefits and, significantly, not upset world food production, price stability, or threaten biodiversity or livelihoods.

Looking to the past is a way to a bright green future . . . Henry Ford's first car was run on hemp oil (and panels were built from hemp plastic), and Rudolph Diesel, the man after whom diesel technology is named, ran his first engine on peanut oil. But it was soon discovered that getting oil from the ground was a cheaper and more effective fuel source.

Biodiesel

We are lucky in the event industry to be using a piece of machinery (the mobile power generator) that is currently well suited to a fuel available at a commercial scale, namely biodiesel. Biodiesel is created from vegetable oil or animal fat. It's made by chemically reacting the oil with alcohol to form a methyl ester, which is the biodiesel. As discussed above, the vegetable oil can come from crops grown specifically for fuel, or as an alternative with no ethical dilemma to consider: waste vegetable oil (WVO).

In either case, cropped or waste, the greenhouse gas emissions from the ignition of biodiesel are considered as zero. This is because it is 'recent carbon' rather than 'ancient carbon'. The carbon contained in the fuel was recently taken up by the growth of the plant or animal already existing in our carbon cycle, rather than being entered into the cycle by fossil fuel extraction. It should be noted, however, that there are still actual greenhouse gas emissions created from the combustion of biofuels to convert to energy (for transport or electricity), but it's counted as zero.

Biodiesel is in ready supply in many countries, and often at a competitive price. It's a renewable resource, thus eliminating fossil fuel use. The price of biodiesel (WVO or cropped) fluctuates and reacts to world oil prices and levies, taxes, and subsidies placed on biofuels in various countries.

If waste vegetable oil (WVO) is the raw material, then it has even more sustainability credentials, having already been used once before and is a waste product. It is the ultimate in up-cycling – closing the loop by taking a waste product and transforming it into a fuel with so many excellent benefits.

Suppliers of this WVO biodiesel source their raw material from commercial cooking operations, such as frozen food factories. Tallow comes from abattoirs. There are also many backyard producers and boutique commercial operators who source their biodiesel from local takeaway shops and businesses.

Even *McDonald's* are using their WVO to turn into biodiesel to fuel their trucks. In their European stores, more than 80 per cent of used oil is currently being converted into biodiesel, and in the UK the figure stands at 100 per cent.[21] There you have it. . . .

Little is required to be done to a mineral diesel power generator using biodiesel except for a tank clean and filter changes. There is usually no reduction in performance and no reliability problems with using generators fuelled by biodiesel – assuming that high-grade biodiesel meeting the European standard *EN 14214* is used.

To avoid filter changes and tank cleans, generator suppliers need to switch and commit their fleet or part of it to permanently running on biodiesel.

If your supplier resists your request, seek out a supplier with biodiesel kit available and an eye on the future. You don't want to force a diesel generator supplier to constantly switch back and forth between fuel, as this is when problems with the generator's performance will occur. Apart from hesitation by contractors, the avail-

ability of a supply of good-quality sustainably produced biodiesel will be your main hurdle. If there is an ongoing supply of sustainably produced biodiesel, do all you can to coax your generator provider into committing their kit to it full time.

It is sometimes difficult to find where to source biodiesel. If you are small scale and are located in the UK, USA or Australia, you may wish to look at *Find Biodiesel* (findbiodiesel.org).

Pure Plant Oil

Rather than converting oil into biodiesel, it's possible to use straight plant oil. 'Pure Plant Oil' is the term and there are mobile generators that can run on this fuel. Conventional diesel generators may also be converted to run on pure plant oil.

The benefit of using this over biodiesel is that less energy is used in the fuel's production. Large processing facilities and associated environmental and financial overheads are not needed in the production of pure plant oil.

The use of pure plant oil comes with the same concerns for all cropped biofuels – land being used for fuel not food. The pure plant oil business is meeting this head-on and sustainably sourcing its fuel feedstock. One of the major things to look for is that no palm oil is used by your pure plant oil supplier and any rapeseed or soya seed oil is sourced from certified sustainable producers.

Algae Oil

Let us take a moment to reflect on the future potential of algae oils. Algae grows in waste water, it is high yielding and may be used to create oil or processed into ethanol. The benefits of algae as a feedstock for oils include not needing potable water or using land to grow. Keep an eye on the future of algae oils.

An innovator of algae oil is Australian made, and I am happy to promote them (algaetec.com.au).

Figure 5.8 Magnificent Revolution Australia, pedal-powered cinema.

Photo: Conor Ashleigh (www.conorashleigh.com).

Zero Emissions Mobile Energy

Relying solely on fossil fuels is not a sustainable long-term solution to energy supply. Look for alternatives to power your event and mimic developments in zero emissions solutions to not only power your event, but also to demonstrate what is possible for the future.

Zero emissions energy is growing rapidly with large-scale investment and the development of big wind and solar. Apart from the need for global GHG emissions reductions being at crisis point, no one can predict with certainty what will happen to global oil and coal supplies, and the relative costs necessary to extract them.

There isn't just one solution to energy production. The answer is in variety and harnessing the natural resources in the immediate geographic area – wind, sun, tidal, rivers, etc.

The current reality is that green energy isn't the solution to 100 per cent of the world's energy needs, but maximising every renewable energy and zero emissions option is surely the best and most immediate action we can take.

Scientific advancements in solar technology, energy efficiency, hydrogen fuel cells and as yet undiscovered solutions will bring us closer to a sustainable and more stable energy future.

Rather than simply replacing mineral with waste vegetable oil biodiesel or other sustainable fuels, it is possible to do without diesel generators altogether. This is where we move to truly green energy sources for your event such as solar, wind, pedal, hydrogen fuel cell and kinetic energy.

Solar Power

Mobile solar set-ups are readily available to power events, and are proven and reliable – assuming you have some sun. There is no need to take you on a detailed lesson on the science of converting solar energy into electricity. A crash course is best. Here goes:

1 There's the sun.
2 It shines on solar panels (photovoltaic cells).
3 This is captured and goes through a technical process that includes capacitors, regulators, inverters and batteries.
4 It comes out the other end as a steady stream of electricity (AC and/or DC).
5 A distribution board is set up.
6 You plug in your appliances and they work!

But . . . you must put your event on a 'power diet' in order to achieve reliable results. What you do need to know in order to successfully run solar at your event is the following:

* What power various equipment pulls.
* How long the equipment will be running and at what time of day. Which leads to . . .
* Wattage and amp hours requirements.
* Is there a spot, facing North in the southern hemisphere, and South in the northern hemisphere, where the solar panels can be set up without shade being cast on them?
* Do you have a back-up if the sun doesn't shine?
* Do you have steps in place to stop someone plugging in unplanned energy-intensive equipment and using up all the available power?

Solar power providers are emerging who supply mobile kit specifically for the events industry. Mobile solar panels pop up out of trailers, or swing out from the sides of trucks. Some are stand-alone units; others form part of the staging infrastructure and display.

The most effective outcome will be when they also provide their own PA, lighting, projectors and backline. They will know exactly how much power everything uses rather than having a separate company supply sound and lights and the potential for miscommunication (or lack of understanding) by the AV provider.

Usually, the solar rig will come with a fully charged set of batteries. The power stored in these batteries will have been charged by the sun in the lead-up to the event. Over the first day, these batteries will run down. The PV panels present on the day will trickle charge back to the batteries so that you can run it on the following day.

As compared to diesel generators that produce power no matter whether it is being drawn, a solar power generator will store unused capacity in batteries. It is also very reliable and not prone to breakdowns, as there are no motors or engines involved.

If you have a one-day event, solar power is a hassle-free option. If you are running a multi-day event, things become a little trickier. You need the sun to shine so that the batteries are topped up ready for the next day. If the sun doesn't shine, then you will need a back-up – such as a biodiesel-fuelled generator on standby to recharge batteries or take over the power job.

Demonstrating what it is possible to power using the sun is a major benefit. If you've powered your show resulting in no GHG emissions and your attendees leave inspired, then you've won.

There are other solar power solutions for events not based around performance stages, solar-powered ice-cream carts being a lovely example. What could be greener than buying an ice-cream which has been frozen using energy from the sun? Brilliant. Installations are also a great way to combine energy production with décor, art and eco-education.

At *Glastonbury Festival* all the power in the '*Green Fields*' (the side of the event dedicated to all things natural, green, environmental and handmade) comes from micro-generation. Individual stalls bring their own solar set-ups. In 2010 the farm where the event is held invested in the UK's largest privately owned solar array. This provides year-round power for the farm and event offices (www.glastonburyfestivals.co.uk).

The team at UK-based *Croissant Neuf* have developed a solar power system to run PA and lights in their own circus tent. The venue is hired to festivals, either programmed or as a dry hire. It comes complete with seating, carpets, staging, lighting (solar powered) and a studio-quality, 10Kw, 16-channel, solar/wind-powered PA (www.croissantneuf.co.uk).

Students from the RMIT collaborated with Melbourne-based event sustainability solutions providers *Creative Environment Enterprises* to design and build a mobile solar-powered audiovisual production system. The RMIT 'work-integrated learning project' (named *The Germinate Project*) involves undergraduate students working together to develop a design for *Germinate*, a highly efficient, 5kw audiovisual production system.

Germinate features the latest in efficient audio amplification technology and an LED lighting array using less than a quarter of the energy of a single standard stage spotlight. The system can power a small- to medium-sized music festival stage for musicians using standard 240-volt music amplification equipment. The aim of *The*

Figure 5.9 Germinate solar rig (www.thegerminateproject. com).

Germinate Project is to develop a 'think green' ethos within the Australian music industry and to promote best practice in solar power generation and efficient audio technology (www.thegerminateproject.com).

Sunny Bins is a mobile solar-powered sound system that utilises the humble wheelie bin. These are used for playing music or facilitating live performance and talks at events. The bins have a battery attached to the solar panel lid. The sound is high quality and is hooked up to an amp powered by a car-sized battery. *Sunny Bins* are a regular fixture in Sydney and are often used for many outdoor events from street parades to community festivals and they are popular with local councils (www.wheelybinsoundsystems).

In fact it's not just 'green' events wanting solar power; the first-ever sustainably powered sheep-shearing event was held at the *Balmoral Royal Show*, Ireland's largest agricultural and food event! *Firefly* provided a *Cygnus HPG 12kVA* generator charged by 8 × 540Wp *FoldArrays* to provide power for the sheep-shearing equipment, LED displays and PA system over the three-day event (www.fireflysolar.net).

Wind Power

Wind power is not the sole domain of massive wind farms. I am sure you have seen off-grid systems where home owners or even boat owners have modest-sized wind turbines providing power. It is possible to have mobile wind power set-ups for your event.

Although there is not likely to be a purpose-built for-hire-for-events turbine available at your convenience, local providers of wind power equipment at a domestic or modest scale may be able to set up demonstration kit to power aspects of your event. Match power requirements at your event with those suitable for powering by wind. For example, an information kiosk that just needs some lights for four hours at night could be perfect.

A little LED light set-up, a stash of batteries, and you are good to go. The additional benefit of this kind of power option is showing the attendees micro-generation in action. Get the wind turbine provider to leverage promotion from their participation to increase awareness about the availability and ease of use of this excellent zero-emissions technology.

Hybrid Systems

Many mobile solar power suppliers come with hybrid systems. Check with your solar provider if they have this set-up or if they can create one for your event. The best hybrid system is where there is solar, topped up by wind, connected to a variable speed drive WVO biodiesel generator which kicks in only when required and with the motor running only at the speed needed to produce the amount of power required.

As portable solar, wind and kinetic energy moves to scale, it is likely that more traditional diesel generator power providers will offer this facility. Certainly traditional generator hire companies offer solar- and wind-powered roadwork kits (e.g. tower lights, traffic-lights and traffic information signs).

Hydrogen Fuel Cell

The commercial viability of power supplied by a hydrogen fuel cell generator is increasing rapidly. A hydrogen fuel cell is an efficient form of power supply with no GHG emissions and only water vapour emitted from the exhaust. It's a clean and efficient alternative to diesel generators. A fuel cell is an electrochemical device that converts hydrogen and oxygen into water, and produces electricity in the process. A battery is also an electrochemical device. It has the chemicals stored inside it and converts those chemicals to electricity, but the charge eventually dies out. With a fuel cell, the chemicals are constantly flowing into the cell so that it never runs flat. As long as there's a flow of chemicals into the cell, out comes the electricity. The technology is being developed to power motor vehicles; however, it has also been set up to provide electricity as a generator alternative. Keep your eyes open for when this option becomes available.

Arcola Theatre in London have taken power matters into their own hands and have innovated and installed a 5kW hydrogen fuel cell power system at their theatre. What's more it's mobile, and when they perform at outdoor festivals, such as *Latitude Festival*, they bring their fantastic power system with them. It's a great example of demonstrating renewable energy innovation in action, while also providing a real solution to the theatre's power needs. Off the back of its innovative and successfully installed and operated 5kW hydrogen fuel cell energy system at their Hackney-based facility, *Arcola Theatre* have now launched *Arcola Energy*, where they design, integrate and deploy hydrogen fuel cell power systems. *Arcola Energy* is the UK agent and distributor for *Horizon Fuel Cell Technologies*. The development of *Arcola*'s mass-customisation manufacturing approach is supported by the *UK Technology Strategy Board* (www.arcolaenergy.com).

People Power

People power is harnessing kinetic energy – movement-based energy. Some other examples of kinetic energy being harnessed into electricity are wind and hydro. However, matters have been getting a little creative in the event space, as it has been realised that we have the perfect raw ingredient – masses of people needing to move about.

For the past five years or so, kinetic energy has been used for demonstration purposes at events; for example, a phone sponsor at *Glastonbury Festival* having kinetic energy phone chargers strapped onto people's arms, and who were then made to dance to charge up their phones! Have a look at *nPower® PEG*, the human-powered charger for hand-held electronics (www.npowerpeg.com).

Pedal power is one of the first examples of kinetic energy, using legs and motion to move parts to propel a bike. But pedal power's revving up power at events too. The attendees, or dedicated volunteers, sit on stationary bikes and pedal their hearts out to produce power. Eight bikes daisy-chained can power a PA big enough for around 200 people. *Magnificent Revolution* in the UK and Australia is such an example (www.magrev.org.au). In Canada, hire in *People Power Productions* (www.peoplepowerproductions.com).

There are also novelty set-ups where the pedalling is directly attached to a sound system using vinyl records. I have also seen a pedal-powered washing machine. My personal favourite is a pedal-powered juice bar at *The Channon Markets* in northern NSW, innovated by Peter Pedals, founder of the *Rainbow Power Company*. A mechanical set-up attaches bikes, through a series of cogs and wheels, to food blenders. This juice stall has staff pedal to power the blenders (www.rpc.com.au).

Taking the concept of pedal power one step further is to create an entire people-powered zone. *Global Inheritance's EnergyFACTory, EcoCharge Live* and *Firefly Solar's Kinetrics Playground* are some of the initiatives designed to harness the power of event attendees' arms and legs. Read more on the book's website about these great initiatives and see if you can reserve them for your event.

The next steps in people-powered events have literally been steps with energy-generating floors being innovated by the clever Rotterdam-based team *Energy Floors.* This portable or permanent dance floor is installed in museums, or makes an appearance at exhibitions, for product launches and has been seen to pop up at festivals all across the world, with people dancing on its specially embedded panels which capture the energy from the dance moves of festival-goers. This terrific Dutch company has innovated human-powered interactive dance floors for events, exhibitions and public spaces. Starting with their *Sustainable Dance Club* back in 2006, by the end of 2012 they had 17 permanent SDF installations, and had toured their SDF to events in 69 different cities in 18 countries on five continents. All this dancing has resulted in approximately 950,000 visitors who generated 2 billion Joules of energy in 2012 alone! One of Energy Floor's biggest projects so far was an interactive installation at the EDF Sponsor Pavilion at Olympic Park as part of the London Olympics and Paralympics.

Box 5.5

MAGNIFICENT REVOLUTION AUSTRALIA

Magnificent Revolution (Mag Rev) has pedal power headquarters in London and Melbourne, with an ever-expanding network of side projects across Europe and Australia. It was started up in 2007 in Cambridge, UK by a group of enthusiastic cyclists with an idea to create a drive-in cinema with bikes instead of cars.

Magnificent Revolution pulls on the collective skills of educators, artists, event organisers and engineers, and in 2011 a partner project was started on the other side of the globe in Australia. *Magnificent Revolution* also run pedal power stages, educational workshops, art installations, and pedal-powered smoothie stalls.

With its strong emphasis on education through experience, *Magnificent Revolution* demonstrates how energy innovation can be better understood and accepted through creativity. By encouraging audiences to become an integral part of the performance, *Magnificent Revolution* presents pedal power as an interactive and tangible experience of sustainability for audiences young and old.

Participants can feel directly the energy being consumed by the show, and need to work together to share the load. Mag Rev's event's production equipment is designed to be extremely energy efficient in order for the cyclists to directly power the show, often without the use of batteries. Generally, each cyclist produces 50 to 100 watts of energy, so an eight-bike system has about 400 watts of continuous power with an 800-watt peak. This shows that even on an energy diet, we can still have a good time! The flow-on effects of pedal power are an event manager's delight, providing much more than just green energy, but also having the potential to impact upon transport, education and other sustainability indicators.

Magnificent Revolution has designed its pedal power systems to fit almost any road bike, which provides encouragement for the audience to cycle to the event and hook up their own bike to power the show. When was the last time you went to the cinema and everyone clapped at the end? At the Cycle In Cinema this is a regular occurrence, with everyone congratulating each other on a job well done.

www.magrev.org.au |
www.magnificentrevolution.org

Their suite of exciting event-specific solutions includes the mini-dance floor set up which can hold up to eight people with a virtual DJ creating a great clubbing atmosphere, and powering it all themselves (sustainable dancefloor.com).

PaveGen's installation of kinetic energy pavers at West Ham tube station during the *London Olympics* is also an interesting example (www.pavegen.com).

Electric Picnic wanted to have a people-powered dance tent, and in 2012 they got their wish. *Electric Ireland* was the official energy partner of the festival 2012. They set up 'Dancergy' which included 64 sustainable dance floor modules by *Energy Floors*. To get the most energy out of the huge dance floor, Mr Motivator was hired to heat up the crowd with a grooving fitness programme. Daily retro dancing sessions for the festival-goers contributed to the *Electric Picnic* energy requirements of the festival.

Romande Energie, a Swiss power supplier, wanted to create an activity at the *Paléo Festival* in Nyon, Switzerland. *Family Déco*, together with the communication agency *Parenthèse*, came up with a game concept about generating as much energy as possible when dancing for two-and-a-half minutes in a customised MiniClub along with image uploads online. Entering the tent, the visitors selected a pair of headphones, each playing a different song, and started dancing. The DJ booth was situated in front of a large screen with a digital energy meter – another great installation by *Energy Floors*.

Gas

Compressed gas such as butane, propane or LPG is used for cooking or heating at events. This will either be supplied bottled, or via the mains. There are also compressed natural gas mobile power generators available. You should include gas in your GHG emissions calculations. Encourage food traders and caterers to use gas cookers and bains-marie rather than electricity-powered equipment. Pieces of equipment which have heating elements are extremely power hungry and generally a gas-powered alternative will be far more efficient when it comes to GHG produced for the same amount of heating/cooking delivered. Remember to report on the volume of gas used for cooking or heating purposes.

Micro-generation

Solar, wind, combined heat and power, anaerobic digesters and run-of-river-hydro are all examples of micro-generation: permanent energy generation delivered locally and off the mains grid.

We all know about massive dam-based hydroelectric schemes. Micro hydro or run-of-river hydro is an alternative for small power requirements. Riverside mills converted into boutique function centres own this space. These historic buildings, which were purpose-built to take advantage of the water power running past them, are being refitted with micro hydro systems to provide GHG-free weddings and events.

Mains versus Temporary

Running your event on mains power supply will likely be more cost-effective than temporary generators. To determine which is likely to produce more GHGs, however, depends on the source of the mains and your temporary power options.

Planning time is also a consideration, with temporary power again likely to take more staff planning time than just plugging into the mains. If you're holding an event with a single generator, things are obviously less complex than if you have multi-generator requirements.

If you have a permanent site with mains power supply but it is not sufficient to service your requirements, rather than continually augmenting with temporary power generators, it may be optimal to install a sub-station.

Alternatively on such sites, permanent power distribution can be put in place so that fewer temporary generators are used, with cabling servicing outlying areas that previously had their own generators.

INDOOR EVENTS

Most indoor events will use mains power provided by the venue. However, the power coming down the line is not the only consideration in reducing energy impacts at indoor venues. Improvements to your event's power performance can be achieved through the following:

1   choosing a sustainable venue
2   achieving energy efficiency
3   changing power use habits
4   using renewable energy supply.

In the following pages we look at techniques to reduce demand for power and encourage changing behaviours by those involved with your event making planning, sourcing and operating decisions affecting power demand and resulting GHG emissions.

Choose a Sustainable Venue

Choosing a venue that has been designed with energy efficiency in mind, which has energy-efficient equipment, lighting and appliances and which is operated with regard for reducing energy demand, will help towards reducing the energy impacts of the event you hold there.

The way a building was initially built – to be reactive to the local climate, to allow natural daylight in, to ventilate hot air out, to keep warm air in, to have shade-giving trees or sun-facing aspects – will all reduce demand for electricity or gas. Likewise the efficient running of equipment and the energy intensity of the equipment itself have a part to play in the overall energy consumed by the venue, and therefore by your event.

Where the venue sources its energy from is also a massive part of the picture. Look for venues on a 100 per cent renewable energy tariff, or which, better still, produce their own renewable energy. Also look for venues that disclose their energy initiatives and results and have staff engagement programmes.

As demand for information about energy performance and efficiency increases within society and is specifically asked of venue owners by event organisers, more venues will have this information readily available, and, what's more, may actually instigate changes to their facilities management to improve their energy performance.

Energy Efficiency

Energy efficiency is a much-touted phrase. When you break it down, it can be achieved in two ways at indoor events – through building design and operations, and through using energy-efficient equipment.

Energy efficiency is about getting the same result for less energy – kilowatt hours. You will have seen on your own electricity bill at home or at work the electricity usage figure expressed as 'kWh'; this is the number of watts (divided by 1000) of electricity consumed per hour. This is the number we are trying to reduce, and to reduce it you are either conserving energy or becoming more energy efficient.

Power demand is not constant, and understanding how your power-hungry equipment works and how efficiencies may be achieved is a key to achieving efficiency. You may have heard of 'peak demand'. This means either when everyone is turning everything on all at once (e.g. in a domestic situation at dinner and bath time) or at an event when catering or entertainment commences. Peaks may also occur when a particular piece of equipment is first turned on; for example, a data projector, whirring at the beginning as the bulb 'warms up' before settling down into its normal running mode.

Power pull by a piece of equipment is not constant either. If something is running harder, louder, hotter, brighter, you will also be drawing more power. That big flashy ending to a stage show? You're hitting some peaks there.

You may also be surprised to know that music with a lot of bass can pull more power than music with a higher register. I have experienced this first-hand when on a bike in a pedal power set-up. Music was playing, a lovely classical piece – easy pedalling. Then a track came on with lots of beats and bass, and all of a sudden the pedalling became very heavy as more power was being demanded in order for the speakers to push out a greater volume of air – and sucked out of our rotating legs!

When looking to achieve energy efficiency at indoor events, consider the following. Venue managers should:

✓   Conduct an energy audit to identify where wastage may be occurring and put an energy management plan in place.
✓   Use energy-efficient stage/theatre lighting, sound and visuals.
✓   Ensure switches on power boards or power points on walls are easily accessible by staff and are clearly labelled.

✓ Plan lighting and power distribution around the venue so that users can easily switch off specific equipment without everything else being turned off. (One switch for all is convenient at the close of the night; however, users will not require all the equipment you have set up, so enable isolation.)

✓ Use energy-efficient (e.g. Energy Smart-rated) equipment and appliances – in kitchens, laundries, foyers, dressing-rooms and bathrooms.

Event managers using venues should carry out the following:

✓ Request an induction into the venue on how to adjust temperature and lighting. If not available indoors, request a visit from staff a couple of hours before the event starts.

✓ Understand which equipment can be powered down and ensure that it is (either by the organiser or by AV/venue staff).

✓ Design stage lighting, sound and visuals with energy consumption in mind.

✓ Request energy-efficient lighting and visual effects such as from LEDs by venue or AV hire company.

✓ Book energy-efficient lighting for exhibitor stands and require exhibitors to opt into energy-intensive lighting options (and charge more).

✓ Use power boards with on/off switches so that people don't have to crawl under tables or behind equipment to unplug at the wall in order to switch off.

✓ Include people-powered interactive elements to both entertain and invigorate attendees and to provide power elements to your indoor event.

Venue managers or venue users should carry out the following:

✓ If feasible, coordinate rehearsal and tech run-throughs with bump-in time, so that double power is not being used.

✓ Reduce bump-in/load-in times. Rather than allow a ten-hour bump-in, if practicalities allow, reduce the load-in window.

✓ Keep to lighting and climate control rations during load-in and load-out. Don't light areas that don't need lighting! If back docks and doors are open, consider switching off the HVAC during load-in.

✓ Open windows and doors to achieve airflow rather than defaulting to air conditioning.

✓ Use fans rather than air conditioners where possible.

✓ Use daylight rather than electric lights.

✓ Embrace light colours in your overlay design and décor to optimise the daylight effect.

✓ Consider if you really need as much stage lighting during the day as you would at night.

✓ Turn off PAs, including the desk, and if powered, the speakers when they are not being used.

✓ Don't leave anything on overnight such as battery chargers or equipment on standby. If the equipment is charged, take it out of the charging pod and put it into a basket labelled 'charged'.

✓ If dressing-rooms are used infrequently (e.g. once a week rather than daily), switch off all power-pulling equipment such as fridges until they need to be used. Turning them on a few hours before arrival of talent is enough to cool down the contents.

✓ Run a power-down check across all aspects of your event, including exhibitors, stallholders, bars, kitchens, amenities and break-out rooms.

✓ Venues should create a close-down routine that includes powering down all equipment not needed overnight.

Changing Behaviours

The successful implementation of an energy-efficient event is dependent on staff, crew, contractors and exhibitors being involved and actively committed to the event's power reduction goals.

Pre-event communications and engagement, site inductions, at-event reminders and real-time monitoring are all needed to encourage, entice or demand that crew, vendors, exhibitors, caterers and contractors power-down.

At many indoor events, such as trade shows and exhibitions, stallholders will be plugging in en masse. To get everyone to kick the power-board habit, communicating the reasons why reductions are important, along with incentives and penalties, is key.

To ensure that power plans are not forgotten in the cut and thrust of event day, focused understanding and commitment to new ways of operating must be embraced by the event production team and power users.

Encouraging the production team to consider power-reducing behaviour is essential. They are the ones who are likely to leave PAs humming, unnecessary lighting on, fans blowing, etc.

Some ways to ensure that the team is engaged and your plans come to fruition through their active involvement are listed below. This may be from both a venue management point of view or from the venue user/event organiser's.

✔ Formalise an energy management policy and reduction action list.
✔ Communicate the policy and specific actions pre-event to the relevant people.
✔ Put up reminder signage around the venue during the event.
✔ Delegate a team member to check that the policy and planned actions are happening.
✔ Induct venue users into the ways to operate the venue/room for maximum energy efficiency.
✔ Offer incentives or rewards for reduced power usage.
✔ Put users on power diets and charge them for more power supply.
✔ Require a list of equipment to be powered and estimated run times, providing worksheets to allow users to calculate and understand the GHG impacts of their equipment and operating choices.
✔ Place energy reduction and power-down/switch-off notices at relevant locations around the venue.
✔ Make an announcement about powering down at the close of each day of a multi-day exhibition.

YouPower is the UK's first renewable energy power generation and management system designed for the business event markets. Created by *Pebble Productions*, the adapted gym equipment includes recumbent and hand bike generators, together with a portfolio of fun adult playground rides. As delegates use this equipment, their energy is transformed into electricity, which is then stored in batteries and used to power the audio-visual equipment at their conferences and meetings. The

Kinetrics products are linked to a software display system, which can be customised with client or venue branding. The display screens provide real-time feedback on the power generated, both individually and as a cumulative session total. Reports on the event's power consumption are logged and a breakdown of the system's output is also provided (www.pebbleproductions.net).

OUTDOOR EVENTS

The go-to option for events needing power where mains are not available or supply is insufficient is the huffing puffing diesel-fuelled generator. Hiring-in generator kit and the cost of fuel are significant line items in any outdoor event's site infrastructure budget.

With fuel costs ever rising and an imperative for responsibly operated businesses to reduce their greenhouse gas emissions, focusing attention on energy demand, fuel consumption, number and size of generators, and renewable fuelling options are the pathways forward for outdoor events.

Alternatives to traditional diesel generators are possible. Innovations are continuing to present themselves and outdoor events are a great opportunity for demonstrating new directions in renewable energy supply. From solar to wind, pedal, fuel cell, real-time biogas and kinetic energy – all are options to power your outdoor event, replacing diesel generators and showcasing innovative renewable energy in action.

Using mineral diesel in temporary power generators may also create more greenhouse gas emissions than the equivalent power sourced from mains. This calculation is dependent upon the mains GHG emissions factor per kWh, and the kWh your generator produces per litre of fuel: good number crunching to do if you're so inclined.

Considerations in moving to more sustainable temporary power supply at outdoor events include the following:

• Available data on costs and impacts to inform decisions.
• Technical knowledge required to navigate concepts of power production, direct savings, and simply understanding the language and terms used.

- Availability of power solutions locally that suit your purpose.
- Engagement by and communications among the key stakeholders – artists and their representation, vendors, caterers, AV/lighting/equipment providers, event technical production, generator suppliers and their ground staff, and stage/lighting/sound staff.
- Resistance by crew who have 'always done it this way'.
- Uncertainty by crew that alternative power solutions will get the job done.
- Cost of alternatives to diesel-fuelled temporary power generators.

When planning your distribution of power, keep GHG emissions reductions and minimising fuel use in mind through equipment choices and power source options.

You can reduce the impact of mobile generated power through the following:

1   reducing demand for power, leading to
2   fewer or smaller generators, or running time;
3   using sustainable biofuels in generators;
4   using innovative renewable energy sources.

Temporary Generators

Unlike on mains power, where using energy-efficient equipment or just switching it off leads to reduced power consumption and therefore GHG emission, with temporary generators, achieving reductions is a little trickier. There are complex and interlinking effects that must be considered when planning power supply from temporary generators to achieve reduced fuel consumption and therefore reduced GHGs.

Rather than reducing GHGs, often the prime concern of an event's technical production team is that power is always available and no outages are experienced – especially at events that have a live entertainment component; more so if it's televised!

Reduce Demand

There is no substitute for cutting emissions at the source. By reducing the number of generators you need and using fewer more efficiently, you can reduce fuel consumption and resulting GHG emissions, no matter if they are from mineral diesel or a sustainable biofuel. Undertake a thorough assessment of likely power requirements for your event in collaboration with production staff and the power contractor. **Plan, plan, plan, plan, plan . . .** for the following:

- placement of generators;
- loads and usage patterns;
- distribution of cabling;
- usage peaks and troughs.

Adding a requirement to reduce GHGs makes this already complex job just that much harder. Thus an engaged and enlightened power-planning team is needed to actually achieve reduced GHGs at an event when using traditional temporary power generators on mineral diesel.

Practical considerations and issues which may go against the reduction imperative include the following:

- A requirement for convenient, trouble-free, time-saving sourcing of reliable power solutions.
- Ensuring the generator provided is fit for purpose (i.e. that it will meet power demand, including start-up peaks or one-off peaks).
- Logistical aspects such as access, availability, generator noise, and a reliable and reputable supplier.
- Accurate estimate of power requirements.
- Ensuring generator capacity will cover peak load/s.
- Provision of correct sized gensets, rather than 'upsizing' offered by the supplier due to lack of availability and hiring mix-ups.
- Contracts that require dedicated generators (e.g. by artists, bars, sponsors).
- Distance between the locations of generators is required, leading to stand-alone generators that are oversized for the power demanded.
- Cost, which is impacted by the number and size of generators and duration running (and therefore fuel costs).

When we include the GHG reduction goal into the planning process more issues start to unpack. Issues to consider or be aware of are the following:

- Simply switching off equipment while the generator still runs does not necessarily mean reduced fuel consumption and GHGs.
- Potential lack of knowledge by those planning power to be able to estimate potential demand, generator sizing and how to realise efficiencies.
- Lack of information or understanding on concepts such as peak generator load, optimal running loads and diminishing efficiencies.
- Many generators are running at less than optimal loads and they become increasingly less efficient the lower the power load.
- Lower demand during the site build and bump-out means super-sized generators in place for event days may be used by default, leading to considerable fuel wastage during the lighter demand times.
- Considerations for overnight load, and isolating equipment which must be switched on overnight (such as chillers and cool-rooms) from equipment which is just run during the day.
- Planning distribution for maximum efficiency.

Matching Power Demand

A consideration when using mobile power generators is that unless they have 'variable speed' or 'load-adjusting' features they output a constant amount of power. If you don't draw that potential power through equipment that is plugged in, the energy created is lost – which in essence is a massive and very direct inefficiency.

If reductions in GHGs are to be achieved on standard temporary power generators, rather than running more efficient equipment on the same-sized generator, you must actually reduce the size of the generator, the number of generators you use, or the amount of time they are running.

Thus you will need to plan your demand to keep the generator running in the 'sweet spot' – the optimal efficiency range is between 70 and 80 per cent of its power capacity being drawn by the equipment plugged in. As you get below 60 per cent you're losing efficiency, with unused fuel effectively being burnt off.

You may remember seeing huffing and puffing generators at events. This is often not a sick piece of machinery; it's your money going up in smoke as the equipment is under-used and burning off fuel. You need to allow for spikes in demand to ensure no power cut-outs, but consistently running a generator at well below the optimum range will lead to burn-off of fuel which is wasteful financially, a waste of non-renewable resources and causes unnecessary GHG emissions. It will also lead to damage of the generator.

A diesel generator's efficiency is rated by the number of kWh it achieves per litre of fuel consumed – just like a car. At low loads, inefficiencies start to kick in, with ever-diminishing loads meaning ever-diminishing efficiencies.

If a generator runs at a low load, what this effectively means is that you're using a generator that is too big. Generally, the bigger the generator, the higher the fuel consumption. Again, just like a car – you've hired a 5-litre V8 touring sedan, when a 1.3L 4-cylinder hatchback would have done the trick.

Powerful Thinking – a UK think-do tank on sustainable energy at festivals and outdoor events – produced the report *The Power Behind Events*. The report found that 60 per cent of generators studied at UK music festivals were more than double the capacity really required. Of the generators monitored at eight events, every single system had periods of working below 25 per cent load. Some of them operated entirely below 25 per cent.[22]

Sizing and Distribution

The event site manager or production manager and the power contractor will work together to plan numbers and placement of generators. Often power distribution planning has to come after site layout factors such as footfall patterns, creative production and aesthetics, access routes, and lay of the land, etc., have been considered. With careful planning of generator placement, efficiencies can be made.

Usually generators will be sited at the centre of a 'hub' with distribution fanning out from it.

If you don't have the benefit of a power contractor based onsite to do your planning and it's up to you, the following points need to be considered:

- number of outlets requiring power;
- maximum load for each outlet;

- estimate of peak usage times;
- distribution and cabling planning.

Production staff not worried about minimising the energy used will carry out rough estimates and then use a generator a couple of sizes up to make sure there are no power cut-outs. If you want to be diligent in your energy planning, you will need to gather as much information about potential power pull and usage patterns as possible. Overlay this onto your site plan, do some calculations and you should come up with a good estimate on the power required in each area.

Look for areas where a generator is used for a single purpose and whether there are other ways to power that piece of equipment. In remote locations at large events, oversized generators are often located for a single use, which leads to wastage, the reasoning being that a small generator, which could do the job, is vulnerable to theft. If you have some equipment which needs to stay on overnight (e.g. chillers at bars), ensure that this equipment is isolated to its own appropriately sized generator.

You may have generator-powered tower lights in car parks, remote entry points and any areas that need security lighting at night. Ensure these are switched off during the day. A simple thing, but it is often overlooked. Mobile solar-powered lights could be an alternative solution. If they don't exist in your region, talk to a solar power supplier and see if they are interested in putting together a prototype, trialling it at your event with a view to future development.

In addition, be aware of possible overstating of power requirements by production staff on music stages for sound, and particularly for lighting. There tends to be a snowball effect, with more power requirements added as the word passes from band to tour manager, to production manager, to site manager, to power contractor.

Energy-efficient Equipment

Power at outdoor events is used for stages (sound, light, visuals), for stallholders (food, merchandise, catering), for general site lighting, to run cabins and offices, for amenities, and for other entertainment-based equipment (e.g. amusement rides). A stand-out user at large music

festivals is the power demand from tour buses – particularly to keep the AC running.

Dr Ben Marchini, a Ph.D. graduate at the Institute of Energy and Sustainable Development, *De Montfort University* in the UK, measured energy data for over 70 different event activities across 18 festival events between 2009 and 2012. Based on these measurements, he has found that the total electricity consumption at a festival can be roughly broken down by thirds:

- stage-related electricity consumption (lighting, audio and video);
- trader-related activity (food traders, non-food traders, bars);
- site infrastructure (production areas, performers' tour buses, festival lighting, etc.).

His research also found that main stage lighting takes up more than half of the main stage-related power demand. Main stage sound and main stage video took up about 15 per cent each of total main stage power demand.[23]

There has been a noticeable increase in the amount of energy-efficient sound and lighting equipment coming onto stages in recent years. For the efficiency presented by this equipment to impact upon fuel used and GHGs emitted, the efficiencies must accumulate sufficiently to enable a reduction in generator size or numbers.

It has been a common misunderstanding by those using power generators that running energy-efficient equipment means actual energy efficiency. The reality is almost the opposite. The reason for this is what's known as 'power factor' correction. Low wattage or equipment with a high energy efficiency rating used on generators may cause a power imbalance which actually leads to the generator running less efficiently, effectively causing more GHGs to be emitted due to higher fuel consumption. (This is quite a technical concept concerning resistive and inductive loads, watt and volt amperes!)

For site lighting, catering equipment and anything else needing to be plugged into the generator, the same situation with regard to energy-efficient equipment is at play.

None the less, in order to take advantage of the reduction in wattage offered through energy-efficient equipment, power factor correction devices have to be installed in generators. If power factor correction is not

Figure 5.10 Firefly Solar's Kinectrics 'HamGen' at Electric Picnic, Ireland (www.fireflysolar.net).
Source: Firefly Solar.

addressed, production staff and power contractors will keep using larger generators than are really required, leading to wasted fuel and increased GHG emissions.

Install Permanent Cabling

If your event is on a permanent site and you have a fairly stable site plan, you may make huge energy savings by putting in permanent distribution. Often stand-alone generators are required in the far reaches of your site, as running temporary cabling is not possible or efficient. Installing permanent underground cabling in these key areas will mean a reduction in the number of generator units you need and therefore create efficiencies by optimising consumption of power output.

Power Usage Monitoring and Event Day Auditing

Asking how much the end users require is all well and good, but if you don't put quotas on them up front and actually police usage, you could end up with some problems.

Ensure continual monitoring during the event so that the pledges made by power users are kept or, if increases are needed, you know what to expect next time around.

An audit of load and usage patterns will give you solid data for future planning. Most generators will produce readouts which can be tracked manually or automatically. Monitors can be attached to the generators and the data then transferred to computer. This is similar to doing an energy audit at home. By measuring the power consumption over the time of the event you will see if you are oversupplying an area or where other savings could be made.

The results of your energy audit may highlight potential efficiencies where you could do the following:

- Reduce the generator size.
- Have secondary generators connected to switch on only at peak times.
- Reduce generator numbers by extending distribution.

Providing oversized generators (in terms of kVA size) when a specific size is requested is common. Check whether what was planned for and ordered was actually delivered, so that all your planning isn't wasted because of an administrative or booking challenge at the generator hire company's depot.

LIGHTING

Lighting is a way of illuminating your sustainability. Lights left on during the day, use of old technology, grunting and puffing lighting towers . . . are these the best way to shine a light on your green credentials?

Let us now look at the best way forward for lighting your event. We will look at the role of energy-efficient bulbs at events, in venue, general site and stage lighting.

Old-fashioned incandescent light bulbs waste as much as 95 per cent of the energy they use. Compact fluorescent lamps (CFLs) have been put forward as the answer and have been enthusiastically taken up across the world.

I am proud to say that Australia was the first country to place an outright ban on incandescent light bulbs. In order to reduce greenhouse emissions by approximately 800·000 tonnes, incandescent light bulbs had been phased out by 2010. From November 2009 the retail sale of non-compliant lighting was banned.

Greenpeace calculated that if only energy-efficient light bulbs were sold in the UK, over five million tonnes of CO_2 emissions could be saved across a year.[24] The UK phased out the sale of incandescent light bulbs in 2009. Most of the countries with new laws ban the sale and production, but not the *use* of incandescent bulbs. In tandem with the laws come tight controls on the disposal of CFL bulbs. Mercury is in every CFL and is a safety concern, as is their eventual disposal.

The use of CFLs indoors is becoming standard practice and many venues with an eye on energy efficiency will likely have CFLs installed in at least some of their light fittings.

Outdoor events, with festoon lighting that has always used incandescent bulbs, are finding it a challenge, financially and operationally, to switch from these bulbs. CFLs are limited in their practicality for outdoor and temporary use. The use of CFLs at an outdoor event is discussed below, as are the other brilliant solutions for low-energy lighting, LEDs. But before we do, let us focus on a simple truth your dad has been telling you since childhood:

TURN THE LIGHTS OFF!

No matter which light bulbs you choose, you should ensure that they are not left on during the day or when not needed, in order to demonstrate a responsible attitude towards power conservation.

For those events using mobile power generators, be aware that turning them off will generally not reduce power, fuel use and resulting GHG emissions. This is a broad statement and may not apply to every set-up, as it depends on what appliances are plugged into each generator. Generally, though, where a generator is running events such as market stalls, stage sound and lighting, plus strands of festoon lighting, turning the lights off is not going to result in much of a drop in overall load. The generator needs to run at the optimal load range in order to run efficiently anyway.

All of this may be too difficult to explain to your audience and it is best just to make sure you remember to turn the lights off! But just to complicate the situation a little more it may not be a simple case of flicking a switch to turn off the lights, given how the distribution may be set up. If it's impossible to turn the lights off, then you have some messaging you need to roll out to explain the whys and wherefores to your attendees about the lights being left on.

CFLs and LEDs

Using energy-efficient light bulbs (CFLs and LEDs) is a popular way of reducing energy consumption indoors. However, at an outdoor event using mobile power generators, there are not the same savings when using CFLs. Bear with me as I try and explain some technicalities described to me by those in the know. . . .

CFLs, while having lower wattage (e.g. 11 versus 60 watts), have a poor power factor. This means that the current is not reduced proportionately with the power. CFLs are heavily 'inductive' in their power use and thus need power factor correcting or this may cause damage to a generator or, at the very least, lead to poor efficiency. The current is the determining factor in sizing a generator. Therefore, by replacing large numbers of incandescent bulbs with CFLs, a reduction in power demand and therefore the ability to reduce generator size is not necessarily going to occur. As generator engines are normally sized to match the maximum output of the alternators, this poor power factor may lead to inefficient running of the engine and therefore higher GHG emissions per kW generated. Phew!

I have included this information so you don't automatically assume that changing to CFLs when powered by mobile generators is a beneficial step. (Courtesy of the lovely Bill Egan from *Aggreko* who did the power at *Glastonbury Festival* when I worked there.)

CFLs are designed for long-term use, and the financial returns come back through the reduction in energy bills along with the fact that they last longer and therefore you don't need to outlay for new bulbs every year or so. These savings don't translate at a temporary event.

CFLs are also difficult to handle. This is not a problem when you only have to change them once in five or ten years indoors. They're fragile, not really suited to handling in bulk, and not designed for outdoor use. The kinds of bulbs that look like little curled tubes are particularly unsuitable, but there are bulbs that come with a traditional outer casing which are probably more practical. None the less, your crew must be committed to minimising breakages. Each bulb contains mercury and, if broken, it is recommended that you don't breathe in the dust! In fact, it is recommended that you open the windows and leave a room for 15 minutes before clearing up a broken bulb. Broken bulbs also cannot be placed in landfill because of their mercury content. They must go to an authorised WEEE (electronic) recycling facility. This will add to the inconvenience of using CFLs at a temporary event. It is unlikely that your crew will adhere to these warnings due to the realities and pressures of event logistics. So unless you're a boutique event with time and space for careful handling, CFLs probably aren't for you.

Great information on disposal of CFLs in the US may be found on the EPA website (www.epa.gov/cfl). You may find similar guides in your country's environmental agency (e.g. www.climatechange.gov.au). If not, take a look at those links above for guidance on disposal safety.

Developments in LEDs are coming thick and fast. *Philips* seem to be leading in innovation and commercial viability, with some of their large-scale LED lighting projects being absolutely stunning, and their range of domestic and office solutions attractive and functional. The fast growth in the development of LED lighting is being fuelled by both environmental concerns for energy efficiency and the technological advances around the lighting effects that can now be achieved. The reliability and maintenance costs are also considerations, with life cycle costs of the product now being competitive. LED lighting is particularly useful when using zero emission energy supply. The low loads pulled by LED set-ups make it the perfect partner to solar, wind or hydrogen fuel cell power. The development of technology and application of LED is moving quickly, and you are encouraged to keep your eye on it as this excellent lighting solution gains traction.

Low-energy equipment and lighting is available off-the-shelf and innovative new solutions are continually being developed. Requesting participants to use low-wattage lighting should be part of their agreement to attend. Using energy-efficient lights such as CFLs or LEDs is becoming standard practice across the world, both commercially and privately. However, you will need to make it a matter of policy for those at your event.

At an exhibition I was consulting to we decided that all exhibitors should automatically be supplied with low-energy booth lighting and be required to 'opt-in' to high-wattage lights, with an additional fee. This intervention, along with reducing load-in times and having HVAC off during load-in, reduced total energy by one-third.

Figure 5.11 Ecolite hydrogen fuel cell lighting tower.
Source: Ecolite.

Lighting Towers

Many events require stand-alone lighting towers in remote areas of the event, car parks, walkways, etc. These often come with their own power source, such as a small diesel generator as part of the rig. Some great advances are occurring in this area of temporary lighting, even with both fully solar lighting towers and hybrid sets being available.

TCP Ecolite, produced by the *Youngman Group*, is the world's first supplier of low-energy LED hydrogen fuel cell-powered lighting towers. The towers are noiseless and their only exhaust emission is water vapour. There are no

Box 5.6

LED LIGHTING RESEARCH

RADIOHEAD LEDs

At *Leeds Festival* in 2009 in partnership with the Institute of Energy and Sustainable Development at *De Montfort University* in the UK, we undertook a study of stage lighting, visuals and audio power draw on the main stage.

The energy demand on generators was recorded at regular intervals, and mapped against video footage of the stage lighting and visuals. This cross-logging of when lights/visuals were used, along with information on the energy requirements of specific equipment, enabled analysis of the proportion of power demand for each.

Each band on stage was logged, and a remarkable difference was noted in energy demand between acts. In stark comparison was the drastic reduction in energy demand for *Radiohead*'s set, who had their LED lighting rig on stage, in comparison to other bands performing.

This was the beginning of a four-year study of event power from temporary power generators across many events in the UK.

For more information on research into electricity use at outdoor events, contact Professor Paul Fleming, Institute of Energy and Sustainable Development at De Montfort University (pfleming@dmu.ac.uk).

carbon or particulate emissions and as a result the process is virtually silent. This is the first time that fuel cells have been integrated into a low-energy, low-voltage LED system and using only 150W of energy. Using *Ecolite* towers can reduce running costs and GHG emissions but up to 80 per cent over traditional diesel-fuelled 1000W lighting towers (www.tcp.eu.com).

PERFORMANCE REPORTING

Reporting event energy used is an important addition to event reporting. The proportion of energy from renewable supply should also be measured and reported. Some aspects measured are also useful for management and future planning purposes, such as total number of generators and total kVA.

In summary, measure the following.

Permanent mains/grid power supply:

- Total kilowatt hours (kWh) consumed from mains/grid/permanent power supply.
- Proportion from renewable energy.

Gas:

- Total bottled gas (kg).
- Total mains gas (kWh).

Temporary power generators:

- Total kWh from zero emissions mobile supply (solar, pedal, kinetic, hydrogen fuel cell, wind).
- Total litres of fuel used in generators by fuel type.
- Total number of fuelled generators and total kVA.

Renewable energy:

- Total percentage of event power from renewable energy supply.

Greenhouse gas emissions:

- Total power- and gas-related greenhouse gas emissions.
- Reductions in energy consumption and GHG emissions from initiatives (conservation or renewable energy supply on previous events or 'business as usual' scenarios).
- Total kg GHG per event attendee (per day or total event).
- Total renewable energy credits purchased.

- Total carbon offset credits purchased.
- Total investment in renewable energy technology or infrastructure for the event.

Calculating Event-renewable Energy Proportion

A useful reportable figure to have is the proportion of total event power from all sources from renewable supply. To do this accurately, you must get all sources back to the same measure. The best measure for this is kilowatt-hours.

What is a Kilowatt-hour?

But first, what is a kilowatt-hour? It is the amount of electricity in units of 1000 watts, consumed every hour.

For example, if you have a piece of equipment marked '300W' then running this piece of equipment for five hours a day for a month uses 45kWh.

300 watts $\times$ 5 hours $\times$ 30 days = 45,000; divided by 1000 it is 45 kWh.

This is a simplistic equation, but you get the picture.

Mains Monitoring

For mains electricity, it should theoretically be a simple case of either reading the meter or looking at your electricity invoice. There will hopefully be a kWh figure written conveniently for you.

Things become a little more complex if your event is only taking up part of the venue and does not have individual rooms or spaces sub-metered. Many buildings are like this, but more venues are installing sub-meters, especially as the price of electricity is going up drastically in some regions and because event organisers are asking (awesomely) for their energy consumption readings.

As these twin pressures move venues to sub-metering, we will see more venues billing energy separately rather than as part of the booking fee. This is a great incentiviser for event organisers to address power consumption and efficiencies.

If sub-metering is not in place, or if the venue cannot offer a meter reading, the next option will be for an estimation of kWh for your allocated amount of space to be calculated. This is not an impossible task. The venue, however, must be willing to participate in this exercise. If you're from a venue and if you're not able to provide event-specific power metering, then undertake the following exercise so that you can provide useful usage information to your clients.

Venues that are unable to sub-meter to offer daily or event-long power consumption readings should audit their venue's power over a certain sample period of time to provide, room by room, space by space, activity style or attendee-based kWh estimates. To get this information you will need to take your quarterly power bill, which will have kWh on it, and undertake a mapping audit which looks retrospectively at the activities that occurred in each of the spaces. This would be mapped against the square metres of each of the spaces, enabling you to allocate a proportion of total venue energy consumption to each. Included should be common areas such as reception, toilets, kitchens, hallways, loading bays and car parks, which are attributable across all events proportionately.

In summary, gather together the following information to make an accurate estimate of average kWh demand by event space, event capacity or event activities over the sample period:

- total kWh
- total square metres of the venue
- square metres of all common areas
- square metres of all hireable spaces
- total people/attendees
- whether kitchens are fully operational at all times or only for specific events
- seasonality, heating and cooling.

Next you will need to find out if the mains power is on any renewable energy supply. For our example we will say it is on a 30 per cent tariff and 500kWh was used for the event.

Mobile Power Generators

Diesel, petrol or bio-fuelled generators will use fuel, measured in litres. This should be reported. The total kVA of the generators should also be reported – this is effectively the 'engine size'. The engine size, as with a car, dictates the fuel consumption per kWh of fuel. Bigger generators will possibly use more fuel per kWh of energy produced; however, poorly maintained equipment, poorly engineered equipment, old equipment or even generators that are oversized for the power being demanded of them will all run at lower efficiencies (i.e. they use more fuel for every kWh of power they produce).

The best way to find out the kWh output per litre of fuel is to ask the generator supplier what that figure is on average, and to ask them to meter the equipment and formally report the results to you. But remember to tell them in advance that you want this monitoring done.

The average figure you could go on, if you have no way of knowing the power output of the generators you are using, is 3.5kWh per litre of diesel. Biodiesel is reported to run less efficiently than mineral diesel, but again it depends on the generator and fuel quality and size.

Zero emissions energy providers such as pedal, solar, wind, kinetic energy or hydrogen fuel cells will be able to provide you with total kWh of energy produced. Simply remember to ask them in advance.

In our example let us have the following:

400 litre of diesel = 1000kWh
400 litres of biodiesel = 1000kWh
200kWh from pedal power

Therefore, for mobile power generators we have the following:

45 per cent from non-renewable energy supply
55 per cent from renewable energy supply

Gas

Mains and bottled gas will come in two different measures. Mains gas – gas which is delivered to buildings through permanent piping – will be reported in kWh, so that's a simple figure to get hold of from the venue's meter or from gas bills. Bottled gas will come in kgs. Use the average figure of 12kWh per kg of LPG. For our example we will be using 300kWh of mains gas and 100kg of LPG, which is 1200kWh.

Total Renewable Energy Supply

For our example of the amount of power being used, with a final result of 32 per cent of power from renewable energy sources, see Table 5.2.

Table 5.2 Example of renewable energy percentage calculation

	kWh Non-renewables	kWh Renewables
Mains	350	150
Generators	1000	1000
Pedal		200
Mains gas	300	
Bottled gas	1200	
Total	**2850**	**1350**
Percentage	**68%**	**32%**

Converting Usage to Greenhouse Gas Emissions

The next step in energy reporting is to convert the kWh, litres of fuel or kg of gas into greenhouse gas emissions. To do this you will need to find out the 'emissions factor' for each type of energy source. These are constantly being updated and adjusted, so check with your national greenhouse gas office what is relevant for you. At the time of publication I had the following for emissions factors for CO_{2e}:

Natural gas – mains: 0.1852kg CO_2e per kWh
LPG – bottled: 1.4920kg CO_2e per kg
Diesel: 2.672kg CO_2e per litre
Petrol/gasoline: 2.322kg CO_2e per litre

A credible foundation source for energy-based greenhouse gas emissions is the *International Energy Agency* (www.iea.org).

Continuing our example further we will have the calculations for energy-related greenhouse gas emissions as shown in Table 5.3. We will use the UK average mains electricity greenhouse gas emissions factor of 0.4869kg CO_2e per kWh. We end up with 1.426 tonnes of greenhouse gas emissions!

Table 5.3 Example of energy GHG calculation

	Non-renewable energy supply	Kg CO_2e
Mains	350kWh	170.42
Generators	400 litres	1052
Pedal	–	0
Mains gas	300kWh	55.56
Bottled gas	100kg	149
Total	**1426.98**	

Global Reporting Initiative Performance Indicators

The *Global Reporting Initiative Event Organizers' Sector Supplement* has several indicators relevant for energy reporting.

EN3 DIRECT ENERGY CONSUMPTION BY PRIMARY ENERGY SOURCE

This indicator is straightforward and aligns with the accepted definition of direct energy when reporting Scope 1 greenhouse gas emissions. For event organisers this means that fuel is combusted to create energy while under the control of the organisation. This isn't that clear, so I'll put it another way; it's:

- fuel used in power generators to create event electricity;
- mains or bottled gas which is ignited onsite at the event/venue for cooking, heating or even electricity generation;
- energy consumed from temporary or permanent onsite renewable energy sources such as solar, pedal,

wind, run of river hydro, kinetic, anaerobic digestion, hydrogen fuel cell or other sources;

- fuel combusted in vehicles plant and equipment onsite at the event or venue, or under the organisation's control (e.g. in hire vehicles or shuttle buses used exclusively to move people to and from the event).

The *GRI EOSS* suggests that this should be reported in kWh, along with their mix of energy sources.

EN4 INDIRECT ENERGY BY PRIMARY SOURCE

This is purchased electricity, heat, cooling or steam, and is aligned to Scope 2 greenhouse gas emissions. This is where you will report on the total kWh of electricity supplied from the mains/grid. In regions of the world where district heating or cooling is supplied, this would also be reported here.

Reporting would include the 'fuel mix' of the mains/grid energy supply – which means if the electricity was produced using coal, gas, oil, hydro, nuclear, wind, solar, biomass, etc.

EN5 ENERGY SAVED DUE TO CONSERVATION AND EFFICIENCY IMPROVEMENTS

EN7 INITIATIVES TO REDUCE INDIRECT ENERGY CONSUMPTION AND REDUCTIONS ACHIEVED

These indicators are great because it gives you a chance to report on your energy conservation and improvement initiatives. When we created the *Event Organizers' Sector Supplement* we realised that indicator sets for other topics such as waste, water and transport did not have this component, either built into existing indicators or as separate indicators, to the depth it is treated within the energy indicators. Thus you will notice that we have included the words 'conservation and improvement initiatives and results' or similar to the waste and water indicators and created two additional indicators for transport.

But back to *EN5* and *EN7*. These indicators suggest that you report on the initiatives or activities designed to conserve energy and improve efficiency of both direct and indirect energy consumption.

This may be through technological intervention using more efficient equipment, through passive conservation methods (particularly relevant in the built environment) or through achieving behavioural changes by energy users.

Goals and Targets

When setting energy-related goals and targets, the first thing to do is to establish a baseline, as without this reduction targets cannot really be set or areas to achieve reductions identified.

Estimating Energy Consumption

Estimating energy consumption may be a relatively painless exercise if you are holding your event in an existing venue. The venue should have data for various styles of events previously held there, including length of time and number of attendees. This will give you a business-as-usual estimate from which to start.

For events on temporary power, by working with technical production and power providers you will be able to estimate 'business-as-usual' energy consumption, assuming 'normal' practices. (These stakeholders will have their previous experience to draw upon and potentially also have insight into conservation techniques that have been successful.)

Once a baseline or business-as-usual estimation of likely energy consumption has been established, you will be able to look for ways in which you can achieve reductions. As mentioned earlier in the exhibition example, we recognised that by switching all exhibitor lighting to low energy among other actions we would reduce energy consumption. We actually worked out a calculation to estimate the likely reductions we could achieve through this initiative (Table 5.4).

Set Goals and Targets

Energy goals may include the following:

- reduce total energy consumed;
- increase proportion of renewable energy supply;
- demonstrate innovative renewable energy supply;

Table 5.4 Estimating GHG reductions

	Flood lights	Halogen lights
Wattage	150	23
Bulbs	2	2
Total kW	0.3	0.046
Hours	20	21
kWh	6	0.966
Exhibitors	**80**	**80**
Total kWh	480	77.28
CO$_2$e (kg)*	**510**	**80**

Note: * Emissions factor 1.0625kg CO$_2$e/kWh

- encourage energy-efficient behaviour by energy users;
- use energy-efficient sound and lighting equipment;
- facilitate energy metering at the event venue;
- promote energy-efficient behaviour and new technologies to event attendees.

Next you will need to write down objectives and targets. This is where the numbers come in. Examples could be as follows:

- reduce total mains electricity consumption by 15 per cent upon business as usual at the event venue;
- reduce the number and size of generators used to achieve a total reduction of 250kVa;
- increase proportion of biodiesel used to 20 per cent of entire fuel used;
- increase percentage of LED lighting to 50 per cent.

QUESTIONS

Definitions

Define the following concepts:

1 Renewable Energy Certificate
2 Heat and power co-generation (CHP)
3 Power diet
4 Communication map

Simple Answer

1 Suggest three specific ways of better engaging stage production crew in energy-saving initiatives. Ensure you understand the specific stresses placed on these personnel.
2 Draw a table in which to list the three different light bulb technologies. In separate columns compare them in terms of working lifespan, energy efficiency and disposal requirements.
3 (a) What is the difference between 'cropped' and 'WVO' biofuel?
   (b) Outline three pros and three cons of 'cropped' biofuel.
4 Using the information on pages 126–30, design a checklist measuring energy usage and breakdown at an event.

Case Studies

1 Complete the checklist on pages 98 and 99 as it applies to your event scenario or a venue with which you are familiar. Suggest other items that could or should be added to the list.
2 Research the design (sustainable or otherwise) along with the power provisions in venues in which you have, or have considered, holding or attending an event. How do they compare?
3 Research a festival or event considered at the forefront of event sustainability. What are some of the significant systems they have in place for power usage, saving and/or generation? Could you implement any of these systems in your event? What would be required to make them work? What are some of the challenges to progress in this aspect of your festival?
4 Analyse your event, breaking it down into its relevant departments and contractors. Identify the main sources of energy used in all aspects of the running of the event. Where are the particular demands for power consumption, both in terms of department and different times of the day?
5 The energy footprint of an event begins long before and continues long after the actual day(s) of the event. How is the significant and day-to-day power consumption in the lead-up to, and clean-up of, your event constituted? How could it be reduced, made more efficient or less reliant on non-renewable sources?

Further Research

1 Research a 'green energy' accreditation scheme. What are its defining points? How does the scheme work?
2 Design a 'tech rider' worksheet (a document made up of a list of technical requirements that forms part of the contract between artist and event) for artists which can serve as a questionnaire concerning their show's energy requirements. This document would also serve to raise awareness of energy consumption in this context.
3 Investigate where power comes from in your part of the world. What renewable sources are available, what percentage of power consumed is from these sources and which providers offer renewable options?
4 Research an energy-saving or renewable energy initiative active in your region or country. How could it benefit your event in the future? Identify the impediments to this initiative being applied to your event.
5 Investigate an emerging form of energy production such as those mentioned on page 109. What are its advantages and disadvantages? What do you forecast for its future?

NOTES

1 Renewable Energy Certificates: also known as Green tags, Renewable Energy Credits, or Tradable Renewable Certificates (TRCs), are tradable, non-tangible energy commodities that represent proof that 1 megawatt-hour (MWh) of electricity was generated from an eligible renewable energy resource.

2 OECD (2013), 'Electricity generation', in *OECD Factbook 2013: Economic, Environmental and Social Statistics*, OECD Publishing. dx.doi.org/10.1787/factbook-2013-43-en.

3 *CO2 Emissions from Fuel Combustion* (2012 Edition), IEA, Paris (www.iea.org/co2highlights).

4 World Coal Association: www.worldcoal.org/resources/coal-statistics/ Accessed 2 March 2013.

5 World Coal: www.worldcoal.org/coal/market-amp-transportation/ Accessed 2 March 2013.

6 OECD (2013), 'Electricity generation', in *OECD Factbook 2013: Economic, Environmental and Social Statistics*, OECD Publishing. dx.doi.org/10.1787/factbook-2013-43-en Accessed 2 March 2013.

7 Greenpeace – Nuclear Power – The Problems: www.greenpeace.org.uk/nuclear/problems Accessed 4 March 2013.

8 Lock The Gate: www.lockthegate.org.au.

9 Global Wind Energy Council – Global Wind Statistics 2012 Report: www.gwec.net/wp-content/uploads/2013/02/GWEC-PRstats-2012_english.pdf Accessed 5 March 2013.

10 International Energy Agency: www.iea.org/topics/solarpvandcsp/ Accessed 7 March 2013.

11 International Energy Agency: www.iea.org/topics/solarpvandcsp/ Accessed 7 March 2013.

12 Union of Concerned Scientists: www.ucsusa.org/clean_energy/our-energy-choices/renewable-energy/how-geothermal-energy-works.html.

13 Geothermal: International Market Overview Report, May 2012. geo-energy.org/pdf/reports/2012-GEA_International_Overview.pdf Geothermal Energy Association. Accessed 3 March 2013.

14 Alternative Energy Zone at Burning Man: ae-zone.org.

15 Snow Koan Solar at Burning Man: www.snowkoansolar.org.

16 Nectar Village at Burning Man: www.nectarvillage.com.

17 Good Energy: www.goodenergy.co.uk.

18 Renewable Fuels Agency: www.renewablefuelsagency.org.

19 UN FAO – Bioenergy and Food Security (BEFS) Analytical Framework: www.ethanolrfa.org/page/-/rfa-association-site/position%20papers/UN%20FAO.pdf?nocdn=1 Accessed 8 March 2013.

20 GBEP Sustainability Indicators for Bioenergy: www.globalbioenergy.org/fileadmin/user_upload/gbep/docs/Indicators/The_GBEP_Sustainability_Indicators_for_Bioenergy_FINAL.pdf Accessed 8 March 2013.

21 McDonald's – waste vegetable oil biodiesel: www.aboutmcdonalds.com/mcd/sustainability/library/policies_programs/environmental_responsibility/biodiesel_and_recycling_cooking_oil.html.

22 Powerful Thinking: www.powerful-thinking.org.uk Accessed April 2013.

23 Festivals and sustainability: reducing energy related greenhouse gas emissions at music festivals:www.dora.dmu.ac.uk/handle/2086/8840. For more information on research into electricity use at outdoor events contact Professor Paul Fleming, Institute of Energy and Sustainable Development at De Montfort University (pfleming@dmu.ac.uk).

24 Greenpeace UK: www.greenpeace.org.uk/blog/climate/how-many-retailers-does-it-take-to-change-a-lightbulb Accessed September 2008.

Figure 6.1 Event attendees arriving by rail and shuttle bus at Glastonbury Festival.

Source: Meegan Jones.

6

TRANSPORT

Transport is the largest GHG contributor for most events. Moving people, goods and equipment is necessary, since without these commodities you would have no event. The cost of fuel and pressures on organisations to take responsibility for their climate change impacts are helping to reduce these GHGs. Convenience rather than cost or social obligation still largely influences attendee travel decisions, and strategies are needed to get people to become responsible event travellers.

Unless we all stop throwing events, people will still need to travel to our shows. The equipment, food, infrastructure, participants, staff, goods and crew do too. The waste has to be transported away, as does sewage, and everything else that was taken to the event that needs to be returned.

The key transport-related issues for events are as follows:

- congestion
- traffic noise
- localised pollution
- safety
- surface protection
- availability or suitability of sustainable transport options
- use of fossil fuels and resulting GHG emissions.

Most transport is fossil fuel reliant. It functions through sucking up oil or gas and belching out GHG and other emissions, getting us where we need to be in the process. The result of our reliance on this transport technology is obvious. The knock-on economic, social and environmental effects of this are well documented.

Transport is a necessary part of the current model of modern living and economic growth. Following the assumption that for the foreseeable future the way we currently live will be the status quo, our ultimate goal should be a model where transport has a minimum or even zero impact on the environment and a positive effect on communities. A truly sustainable transport system.

Innovations in sustainable transport solutions are revving up around the corner and we will hopefully soon see technology offering drastic emissions reductions, fuel efficiency improvements and sustainable solutions for alternative fuels. Advances in vehicle technology such as hybrids, electric vehicles and hydrogen fuel cells are all part of the picture.

Towns and cities need to be geared towards ensuring convenient urban connectivity, with the use of public transport, bike riding and walking. As we see technological, social and community aspects of sustainable transport develop, events will be able to benefit from this growth.

Agriculture, mining, manufacturing, retail and construction are transport super-users and they are the main players in encouraging sustainable transport develop-

ment. The events industry really is a small part of the market, but as we are creative and experimental types, perhaps we can push some greener alternatives into the limelight.

While we wait for these innovations to present themselves we need to look to the here and now. This includes looking at ways of changing people's transportation behaviour to be more sustainable.

This chapter looks at immediate steps, innovations, strategies and programmes you can undertake to reduce the transport impact of your events.

Figure 6.2 Event attendees arriving by train at Glastonbury Festival.

Source: Meegan Jones.

TRAVEL AND TRANSPORT CHECKLIST

Box 6.1

TRAVEL AND TRANSPORT CHECKLIST

Production Travel/Year-round Travel

- ❑ Low emission, hybrid, electric or alternative fuel vehicles are used and promoted for product ground travel requirements.
- ❑ Cycle couriers are used year-round and for the event.
- ❑ Event production runner's trips are scheduled to reduce number of trips.
- ❑ Video conferencing/virtual conferencing is used in event planning to reduce travel impacts.

Venue/Site

- ❑ The venue/site is located within walking distance from public transport hubs.
- ❑ The venue/site is accessible by bike and bike parking is available.
- ❑ Priority parking is available for those cars arriving at full capacity.
- ❑ A parking fee is applied in order to dampen enthusiasm for driving.
- ❑ Electric vehicle charging stations are available at the venue.
- ❑ Anti-idling policy in place.

Offsetting

- ❑ A project is chosen as the recipient for event carbon offsetting.
- ❑ Attendees are encouraged to opt-in to carbon offsetting programme.
- ❑ Carbon offsetting for flights is bundled into the ticketing.
- ❑ Carbon offsetting is purchased for event production air travel.
- ❑ Talent/artists are encouraged to offset their event-related air travel.

Attendee Travel

- ❑ A programme to encourage cycling and walking to the event is in place (if possible and practical).
- ❑ Shuttles are arranged to transport attendees from hotels, satellite locations, surrounding suburbs and public transport hubs to the event.
- ❑ A car pool/car-share programme is in place and promoted to attendees.
- ❑ Attendees are rewarded or incentivised to walk, cycle, use public transport or car pool.
- ❑ Airport transfers are arranged using shuttles or car share rather than single taxi trips.
- ❑ Shuttles are arranged to transport delegates from hotels to venue.
- ❑ Shuttles are arranged to transport delegates to offsite activities.
- ❑ If no shuttles are provided, a car pool/car-share programme is in place.
- ❑ Sustainable travel options are communicated pre-event.
- ❑ Travel agents are engaged in promoting sustainable travel options.
- ❑ Anti-idling policy in place.

Exhibitors and Vendors

- ❑ Encouraged to source local staff supplies.
- ❑ Encouraged to consider load-sharing.
- ❑ Storage of exhibit packaging is provided to reduce transport runs.
- ❑ Anti-idling policy in place.

Reporting

- ❑ Production travel is measured and reported.
- ❑ Attendee travel is measured and reported.
- ❑ Carbon offsetting (production and attendee) is logged and reported.

Sponsor Opportunities

Travel and transport is a major part of event logistics and there are some great opportunities to align sponsors and partners. These can be to support the actual event logistics, to add value to your event's programming, or as a sponsorship money-spinner.

Here are some partner and sponsor ideas:

- Align with a sustainable freighting or courier company. This may include a business that uses sustainable vehicles, or with a bike courier or other green transporter.
- Match up branded biodiesel suppliers with plant and machinery suppliers to have a high-profile roll-out of the fleet in conjunction with your show (generators, tractors, etc.).
- Get a bike brand to supply site bikes for your crew to move about on.
- Approach 'green' vehicle manufacturers – of hybrid cars, electric vehicles or biofuel vehicles – to sponsor your event. Use their vehicles in conjunction with the event, to transport participants, staff, or for onsite movement.
- Create a brand around public transport to your event. Align with a coach company and big-up your coach travel.
- Establish a partnership with one car pool scheme, and invite them to be part of your onsite activities.
- Schedule a special train to your event and align a sponsor with it, and include on-board brand activation.
- Align with an offsetting project and have an example of the project in action at your event so that your audience understands where their money is going. Set up a booth to allow people to offset their emissions then and there.
- Offer shuttle bus 'real estate' to sponsors, including adding on-bus entertainment to make the event fun start early!

PRODUCTION TRANSPORT

Achieving efficient and yet sustainable transport of infrastructure, equipment and supplies is a challenge facing the events industry. Events are reliant on the efficient movement of goods and equipment in order to deliver the event on time and on budget.

Production assets may be moved by contracted freight, consolidated shipping or couriering companies, or through supplier-owned transport. If you're a small event it's possible that many runs to and fro in privately owned vehicles will fulfil your transport needs. Contractors bringing in big infrastructure items such as staging, generators, fencing, etc., will likely arrange their own transport, which they may own or they may use freighting companies to move. Some simple steps to look at include the following:

- establish procurement policies focusing on local sourcing
- identify and use sustainable transport companies
- encourage sustainable choices by staff, contractors and suppliers when freighting decisions are made.

Sustainable Road Transport

Road transport is the largest, most convenient, popular and polluting surface transport mode. It is also popular because it is convenient and accessible.

Road freight companies looking to be more sustainable reduce their impacts through planning, technology, driving techniques and fuel choices.

Moving more equipment on large fuel-efficient vehicles is a primary solution, as opposed to lots of smaller vehicles. However, using larger vehicles is problematic in congested urban areas. The solutions to this include the location of delivery depots, fuel-efficiency advancement and vehicle engineering, allowing greater and safer manoeuvrability of these large vehicles.

Freighting industries are working with government and industry associations to make sustainable trucking a reality. The *Centre of Sustainable Road Freight Transport* was recently launched in the UK. It is a collaboration between *Heriot-Watt University Logistics Research Centre* and the *University of Cambridge Engineering Department*. The road freight vehicle engineering expertise from *Cambridge* and logistics expertise from *Heriot-Watt* will together explore ways of making road freight economically, socially and environmentally sustainable.

Emissions control is being researched and regulated by government and this will benefit all freight users as the findings make their way into production. Truck manufacturers are working at a fast pace to minimise their vehicles' emissions and maximise fuel efficiency. Greenhouse gas emissions of the sector are top of the list for those researching sustainable transport.

To jump-start sustainable road freight, government or voluntary sector-led standards will be developed which will enable road freight companies to comply with a series of sustainable fleet operating requirements ranging from vehicle engineering, to driver and driving policies and fuel use.

Initiatives in sustainable road transport are being created all over the world. *Green Freight Europe* is an independent voluntary programme for improving environmental performance of road freight transport in Europe. It is establishing a platform for monitoring and reporting carbon emissions and promotes collaboration between carriers and shippers in driving improvement actions. It is also establishing a certification system to reward shippers and carriers who participate fully in the programme (www.greenfreighteurope.eu).

Wider government controls, scientific research and infrastructure development are the answers to sustainable transport.

Looking at the here and now, transport companies can provide sustainable solutions through alternative fuel choice, engine efficiency and planning logistics.

You may be surprised at the number of trucks running around roads empty, having failed to secure return trip loads. It's an obvious place to start and one that is being tackled as an immediate solution. With a commitment to change and the implementation of systems, including load sharing and minimising '*Less Than Loadfull*' freighting, the road transport industry could make a genuine move towards impact reductions.

Onsite Transport

If your event hires vehicles and plant to use onsite, consider having vehicles that can run on either 100 per cent waste vegetable oil biodiesel or a diesel/biodiesel blend. Any vehicles that can run on mineral diesel will be able to run on this fuel. Note that you will probably need to use biodiesel that meets the *EN 14214* standard in order to maintain vehicle warranties.

Plant and machinery, such as tele-handlers, forklifts, trucks, tractors, diggers, etc., should all be able to run on a biodiesel blend.

Electric golf carts are easily available to hire and are a wonderful silent and calming alternative to petrol-run carts. They do of course need recharging by electricity, but if you are hooked up to renewable energy on your mains or running generators on sustainable biofuels, then you are on to a winner.

An excellent sustainable option for onsite transport is bikes. Supply site bikes to crew so that they can get around quickly without being tempted to jump into a vehicle or cart. If you have an office car, consider using a hybrid or an electric vehicle. A great example of innovative site transport solutions is by the *Calgary Folk Music Festival*. They have been moving away from petrol/diesel-powered vehicles to electric vehicles, including two electric cargo bikes co-owned by the event and *Big Bike*. The environment crew uses the Big Bikes to move

---

Box 6.2

TNT ELECTRIC VEHICLES AT LONDON MARATHON

Electric Fleet

With a 26-mile-long event site, getting things from start to finish for a marathon is a logistical challenge. *London Marathon* enlisted the help of *TNT* for event freight logistics.

Marathon competitors offloaded warm clothes and other belongings they arrive with which need to be safely transported to the finish line where they can conveniently collect them.

At the 2013 event three of the trucks used by TNT were zero emissions electric vehicles. TNT is the London Marathon's transport partner and they are rolling out the largest fleet of zero emissions vehicles in the world, with 100 electric lorries in London.

www.london-marathon.co.uk

recyclables around the site, primarily using pedal power but with a back-up boost of electric power for the heavier loads, up inclines or negotiating large bumps. The battery cell is charged with solar power.

Reducing Transport Miles

Trailing behind the transport of raw materials and manufactured products is a significant GHG legacy. Food, materials and supplies criss-cross the planet in a never-ending journey from farm gate to plate, mine to manufacturer, ship to shop. Product miles are a common consideration when looking at the environmental impact of consumption. The same concept applies for freighting kit and goods to your event. By reducing the distance travelled of everything you need at your event, you will also be reducing your event's GHG emissions inventory. In addition, consider where your contractors are based.

Including local sourcing as part of your procurement policy will immediately reduce event-related GHG emissions. Require the sourcing of all products and hiring of contractors locally as a first choice.

Not only should goods be purchased from suppliers as close to the event as possible, but you should also consider where these products originated. Were they manufactured in the same country using raw materials also originating from there? This concept is discussed in more detail in Chapter 8.

Figure 6.3 Production site transport by bike at Calgary Folk Music Festival.
Source: Calgary Folk Music Festival.

Contractors and suppliers should be encouraged to also have a Sustainable Transport Policy. If they own their own fleet, this should include the areas discussed earlier, namely efficiency and planning, renewable fuels, and choosing low emissions vehicles.

✓ use transport companies that use sustainable biofuels, efficiency training for drivers and low emissions vehicles;
✓ use local contractors, hire local equipment and buy from local suppliers;
✓ schedule 'runner' times to reduce short trips;
✓ communicate the environmental impacts of transport to contractors to encourage their use of sustainable transport solutions;
✓ assist in coordinating load sharing.

CREW AND PARTICIPANT TRANSPORT

The greenhouse gas emissions produced as a result of transporting performers, participants and crew to your event are likely to tally to a considerable figure. As you have some control over these groups and how they travel to your event, you have the opportunity to streamline their travel impact.

Provide performers, participants, crew and volunteers with information on transport options and comparisons of the various impacts.

The contractors that supply large numbers of staffing such as security, bars, volunteers, etc., should be encouraged to transport their crews to your event by bus. Ask these operators to provide you with transport impact statements of their involvement in your event.

Performers

Performers are probably the most difficult to manage in terms of sustainable transport. Appeal to their green conscience and ask them to consider how they travel to your event. If you arrange ground transport, transferring from airports or hotels to the event, look for the most sustainable solution. Options include people movers, low emission vehicles, electric vehicles and biofuelled buses.

Ensure that someone within your team has the responsibility of coordinating ground transport for artists so that there are no unnecessary trips with half-empty vehicles or single people going back and forth in taxis.

Volunteers

Volunteers are often sourced from charities and community organisations. Encourage them to promote car pooling. You can also put on coaches or shuttle buses specifically for volunteers. Pre-allocate car-parking spaces to volunteer groups, rationing out how many each can have, which will also encourage car pooling.

Crew

Crew and staff will be working hard and long hours. Interruptions to their work plan to include sustainable transport options may not be so welcome. Rather than annoy individual crew members, work with major contractors who bring in large numbers of crew to devise the best transport solutions for their teams. Crews may include cleaning, stage and marquee erection, security, medical and welfare. Limit car-parking spaces allocated for each team to encourage car pooling.

Participants

These may include market stallholders, caterers, bars and their staff. Participants may also be speakers, workshop leaders and competitors in sporting events. Put together information for participants so that they can understand the transport impacts of their attendance and limit the number of car-parking spaces allocated to each group.

✓ Place car-parking quotas on each group of participants.
✓ Provide shuttle buses for crew arriving early from key transport hubs linking public transport to your event.
✓ Promote the impacts of transport and promote sustainable options.
✓ Set up lift share schemes specifically for crew, staff and volunteer stewards.

Figure 6.4 Provide bicycles so that event crew can get around the site quickly rather than being tempted to drive.
Source: Meegan Jones.

✓ Ensure that ground transport for performers, participants and VIPs is well coordinated to maximise occupancy rates in vehicles and minimise unnecessary runs.
✓ Lay on shuttle bus transport to event locations for participants, so avoiding taxi use.
✓ Hire low emission, hybrid and biofuelled vehicles.
✓ Supply site bikes to get people around the event.

ATTENDEE TRAVEL

The common ingredient in most events is the presence of large numbers of people. Getting them to and from the event sustainably will prove to be one of your biggest challenges. The options you have right now are to persuade attendees to use public or mass transport, getting them to walk or cycle, or to fill up every seat in their cars.

Events exist to attract people, and the travel impact of attendees is often the largest contributor to GHG emissions. When choosing a venue, access to public transport is essential for the event's sustainability performance, to minimise attendee-related travel GHGs.

In the long term the largest reductions will be achieved through vehicle and fuel technology innovations, and through city- and country-wide transport infrastructure and connectivity developments. While we wait it out for these to come, the following options are available to reduce attendee travel impacts:

• get more people to use mass transport;
• encourage walking and cycling;
• increase car occupancy rates;
• site the event close to where the attendees are.

Traffic Management and Congestion

When preparing the event licence, application or approval document to hold a one-off event of significant size, you will need to have addressed likely transport impacts.

Licensing, traffic and police authorities are interested in congestion, parking, road closures, etc.

As your assigned team member is analysing the traffic impact from these perspectives and developing the traffic plan, they could also be given the responsibility of considering the environmental impact of transporting attendees to the event. They should produce a sustainable attendee travel plan and potential initiatives to encourage uptake of sustainable modes.

In many situations congestion and car-parking space will be a problem, making public transport an attractive part of your overall plan. This plan may include using existing public transport services, or running extra coaches and shuttles specifically for the event. Whether indoors or out, you need to analyse the most efficient and low-impact way to transport attendees.

Many local municipalities are giving preference to planning submissions, or are insisting that developments encourage travel by walking, cycling and public transport. To meet their sustainable transport goals, some councils don't grant planning permission for developments or initiatives that would be dependent on travel by private motor vehicles. This is relevant for new events where development applications and licence approvals must be sought, so ensuring that large numbers of people travelling by car to your event is avoided may be integral to your event approval.

Depending on where your event is located, you may find that your city, town or region is actively promoting sustainable transport for its citizens. Rather than going from a standing start, it would be wise to work with these existing programmes and leverage the exposure they already have from these programmes, along with their resources and knowledge.

Urban Connectivity

This term is often used when discussing revitalisation of cities, especially when there is a disconnect between the urban centre and suburbs. Cities that are serious about sustainable development are also serious about how their citizens can move around. This includes linking modes of transport such as walking, cycling, buses, trams, ferries, rail and underground, along with having well-located and functioning interchanges. Having frequent and conveniently located embarkation points, easily available timetables and route maps, along with being clean, safe and affordable, are all musts. Sometimes it can be as simple as connecting footpaths so that you don't have to jump kerbs or scale walls to get to the sandwich shop from the office (as was experienced by me recently when working in a city with little foot traffic connectivity).

Chapter 4 highlights some cities with great connectivity.

An example is the many European cities which have banks of identical bikes parked around the city, available for hire. They work on a credit card and passcode system. These are implemented in coordination with a city's transport plan, with city-wide cycle ways and special bike lanes on roads, along with shared bike and pedestrian zones. With access to thousands of bikes across hundreds of parking zones, cycling in the city is highly attractive.

With more cities moving towards sustainable transport you will find event attendees becoming less car dependent. You can then leverage these sustainable transport trends for your event.

Influencing Attendee Transport

Recognising the practical reasons why people prefer to take their cars must also be understood if you are to come up with strategies to influence them otherwise. These include the following:

- Inflexible departure times of buses and trains.
- Inflexible route.
- Preplanning or booking of tickets necessary for long-distance locations.
- Possibly cheaper in a full car with fuel costs shared among all passengers.
- Difficult to coordinate a group of friends or colleagues to travel together and depart at the same time.
- Walking or cycling is too far, too difficult or will take too long.

However, there are also some great benefits which can be promoted to attendees about travelling by public transport, walking, cycling or car pooling, including the following:

✓ Skip traffic jams and congestion at car park entrances if on buses.
✓ Delivered right to the event doors rather than to outer car parks.
✓ Environmentally friendly.
✓ Can be cheaper than driving alone.

Overarching all of this is the need to achieve a change in travel behaviour by attendees so that they will consider car pooling, travelling by public transport, cycling or walking to your event.

It may be that your current plan makes it easy for attendees to drive to the event, with plenty of parking and no penalties in place if they drive. If this is the case you will need to create situations to encourage them to use public transport and discourage driving. A car-parking fee could be charged, with a price point chosen to discourage driving or single occupancy. If doing this, ensure it doesn't backfire. Attendees could buck the system by parking in every nook and cranny in the surrounding streets outside the car park, which will lead to neighbourhood complaints.

Other tactics to consider are pre-purchased car passes and limiting the number of cars that can park up, even if you have the space.

Packaged coach or train travel with event tickets can be bundled at a cheaper price than if purchased separately. If your event sells out quickly, allocating these bundled tickets may be effective.

If you discourage driving, you will need to ensure that you have the capacity available on public transport to cater for demand. You will need to meet with public transport providers to assess likely volume of trains and public buses, to see whether more services need to be

Figure 6.5 Cyclists arriving at Boom in Portugal.
Source: Jakob Kolar.

added. If you are considerably increasing the number of coaches arriving at your event, you will need also to have the capacity for drop-off and pick-up points, and well-thought-through and laid-out bus lanes and bus stops on your site. This will all be part of your traffic plan.

When encouraging attendees to travel by public transport, you will need to meet their requirements for timing, accessibility, reliability and, most importantly, to have a successfully functioning system so as not to discourage its use in future years. If public transport hubs are more than a quick walk away from your venue, shuttle buses will be needed to make using public transport a seamless ride from home all the way to the event.

To reduce audience travel impact, you could also encourage carbon offsetting by attendees against their travel emissions. More information on this is available in Chapter 7.

Car Travel

Travelling to an event by car will be necessary for some attendees. Encourage them to fill up all the seats in their car. You can also provide information on the transport impact of travelling alone by car, to encourage single drivers to bring friends along for the ride. If your event is prone to causing traffic congestion and delays in entering the car parks, promote quick entry and easing of congestion through reduced car numbers and possibly allocate preferential parking to those arriving with full cars.

If driving an average-sized petrol-run car, carrying four passengers will bring the impact down to less than travelling by train. Offering information can be quite effective.

Incentives such as free parking, vouchers to use onsite, discounts or other rewards can be put in place to encourage attendees to fill up every seat in their car. Alternatively, you can include penalties for those who drive with only one or two people in their car. Charge a green tax, of a significant amount, for those cars that arrive less than full. Make it double the cost of a single driver, half for two people, and free for three people or more.

The *Big Green Gathering* in the UK charged £30 for car parking. This reduced significantly the potential car

numbers. They also had convenient shuttle buses running to and from the closest town, so that people could jump on the buses if they needed to get cash, top up their mobiles, pick up supplies, etc., rather than getting into their cars.

Download Festival in the UK have a programme to encourage people to fill up every seat in their cars. Car park attendants identify those cars that arrive filled to capacity, and give them an entry form to win an upgrade to VIP passes which gets them into the special guest area. A winner is drawn every day.

In addition, as we will hear from *Coachella Festival*, they have a long-standing programme to encourage people to car pool. If not with friends, then encourage attendees to join a lift-share programme.

✓ charge for car parking;
✓ reward those who arrive in full cars;
✓ charge a green tax to all those drivers who arrive in a less than full car;
✓ offer premium parking spots to full cars, including fast-tracked exit at the end of the event;
✓ promote lift-share schemes.

Car Pooling and Lift Share

Lift share is a concept which can be promoted if you have a destination-based event where driving will be a popular option for your attendees. Lift-share programmes match drivers with those needing a lift. They work particularly well for multi-day festivals where the attendees are accustomed to making friends with strangers during the event, and that spirit can translate into camaraderie en route.

Drivers and passengers enter details of where they want to go (which event) and use the search tool on the website to match lifts. There are great options online, and there is likely to be one close to you. Choose a programme that is well used by the types of people attending your event, is suited to your event style and well used in your area. Some programmes integrate payment into their systems, others recommend cash payment between passengers and drivers to cover petrol costs, and others leave the finances up to the participants.

The best option for an event is to partner with one programme and arrange to set up a special page or 'event' for your event, to focus the matches, rather than leave it to the 'open market'.

Participants may be concerned about safety. As an event organiser, you should put together tips for safe car pooling on your website. Look at the tips on www.agreenerfestival.com. Here are some great lift-share programmes that are event-focused and embrace social networking log-ins, smart phone apps or real-time matching.

Zimride is a car pooling website used by *Coachella, Bonnaroo* and *Lollapalooza* festivals in the USA (www.zimride.com). *goCarShare* is primarily UK based and also Facebook integrated (gocarshare.com). *BlaBlaCar* is the largest car pooling website in Europe and is supported by a smart phone app (www.blablacar.com). *Kangaride* is a Canadian car pooling website which operates on an annual fee basis (www.kangaride.com). *Jayride* is an Australian car pooling website and is free to use, but the price can be set by the driver, with an option of a 'free ride' if the passenger shares the driving (www.jayride. com.au). *PickupPal* is mainly USA based, is a free service and is easily customisable for any event (www.pickuppal. com). *Liftshare* is mainly UK based but has international application, and is integrated with Facebook (www. liftshare.com).

Coach and Train Travel

Coach travel has the lowest GHG impact per person, followed by rail and then car (depending on how full the car is). Setting up convenient coach or train travel from handy geographical centres, and bundling it with ticket sales, is essential in order to reduce the attendee transport impacts. Promote coach and train travel to attendees as enjoyable and convenient, as well as appealing to their inner greenness by promoting its positive environmental aspects.

There may be perceived and real barriers to getting people into buses and trains rather than the convenience of a car. Coach and train travel tickets will usually need to be booked in advance. In research I have conducted for music festivals, people don't start thinking about the way they will travel until one month before the event, whereas they may purchase the ticket to the festival more than six months before.

You need to make public transport easy to plan, easy to commit to, and more convenient than driving. Think through the departure times from various locations if you are scheduling coaches. Make sure people can get to the coach without having to take too much time off work. Consider when they would need to get back in order to start work after your show.

Put the bus stop close to the event entry. This is a major selling point for travelling to the event by coach or shuttle bus. Having to walk a long way from the car parks can be a deterrent to driving. Keeping buses out of the car parks also means that they won't get caught up in traffic jams.

My research has also shown that the cost of transport isn't a major factor in transport decisions. Of course this is research for music festivals with a certain demographic and based in the UK, but it is worth noting in case you feel it may be a similar situation for your attendees. The respondents in the research preferred the flexibility and convenience of their chosen transport mode (even if it was coach or train) as compared with concerns over cost.

If the cost of travelling by train or coach is considerably more than, say, two or three people in a car for a similar distance, it's not going to stack up. Make sure you consider fuel versus coach or train ticket costs when planning public transport services. The ultimate solution could be to have free public transport, and charge heavily for car parking.

To encourage taking public transport, walking or cycling to your event, offer incentives, bonuses or rewards. Ticket upgrades, special camping, free drinks, etc., are all ways to promote sustainable travel.

For those events that have camping grounds, a great idea is to have a special 'car-free camp' – reserved camping for those who travel to the event by public transport. The campers get special privileges and rewards, and are located in the best areas of the camping grounds. A similar idea is to have dedicated campsites for people who have cycled to the event.

Les Trans Musicales is an indoor event, held in several venues in Rennes, France across five days with more than 100 bands and 60,000 attendees. The event encourages the use of public transport and offers a shuttle bus from Rennes to the train station (10km), running every three to four minutes. The frequency and convenience of this

Box 6.3

CARPOOLCHELLA CAR POOL PROGRAMME

Coachella Valley Music and Arts Festival is a three-day annual music festival held in the USA. Its capacity is 100,000 people, and it is held in an urban area with up to 50,000 cars driving to the event each day. To alleviate traffic congestion and cut down emissions from the transport of its audience, Coachella has created Carpoolchella!

Carpoolchella is a car-pooling initiative created by *Coachella + Global Inheritance* that rewards people for driving to the venue with four or more people in a car. Festival attendees have the opportunity to win a range of prizes by advertising their environmentally conscious decision with a sign on their car that says 'Carpoolchella'. Attendees often decorate their cars

more elaborately to raise the profile of their entry. *Carpoolchella* has transformed into an opportunity for car poolers to boast their individuality, their Coachella spirit, their hometowns, their favourite bands and more. Several times a day, a representative walks around the parking lot and chooses a car at random to reward with special prizes.   Some of these prizes include VIP tickets for life, wristband upgrades, tickets to the following year's *Coachella Festival,* as well as merchandise and attraction vouchers. Beyond congestion and emissions reductions, *Carpoolchella* generates excitement about the festival before people even enter the grounds.
www.globalinheritance.org | www.coachella.com

Figure 6.6 Coachella Valley Music and Arts Festival, brands its lift-share programme as Carpoolchella.

Source: Coachella Valley Music and Arts Festival (www.coachella.com).

service result in it being used by almost 40,000 people. The event also provides shuttle buses to 25 surrounding cities in partnership with five separate bus lines. Return trip by train from any station in Brittany or Pays de Loire for just €10/12 is also in place in partnership with the national railways SNCF (www.lestrans.com).

Glastonbury Festival commits a significant percentage of available tickets bundled with coach travel. With the sheer size of this event, every step must be taken to encourage people to travel to the event by bus and train to reduce congestion on the small countryside roads leading to the event site. In 2011 the *Green Traveller* initiative was introduced to encourage sustainable travel by attendees and further reduce the significant attendee travel impacts of the festival. Every person arriving at the festival by public transport or bicycle is given a special

Figure 6.7 Bike riders have secure parking at Glastonbury Festival.

Source: Meegan Jones.

Green Traveller pass/lanyard when they walk from the coach to the entrance gate or once they have locked up their bike. The lanyard's pouch contains vouchers to obtain discounts at food stalls and the official festival T-shirt. The *Green Traveller* team also patrols the Festival grounds randomly handing out prizes to people proudly wearing their *Green Traveller* lanyard (www.glastonbury festivals.co.uk/information/green-glastonbury/green-traveller-initiative).

Melt! Festival in Germany puts on the *Melt! MiXery Beds On Wheels Hotel Train.* Providing a train ride from Cologne to Ferropolis as part of the M!Eco environmental project, and the *Melt! Train* stops in many cities in between. Stopping right in front of the festival grounds, the train provides beds and bathrooms for the four days. The train has accommodation on board for 400 people (www.meltfestival.de).

Air Travel

Air travel has increased remarkably in recent years and shows no signs of slowing. Public demand is rising exponentially. and the aviation industry is quickly standing to attention and servicing our demands. The aviation industry and government are working towards solutions to make air travel more sustainable.[1]

Assuming we are all going to keep flying around the world, fuel efficiency and renewable fuels are where progress towards more sustainable air travel will be made. *Virgin* is keen to see its entire fleet running on clean burning fuels by 2020.[2]

Events such as specialist conferences, international sport and destination event tourism are all likely to rely on air travel. So too will destination locations such as Singapore and Hong Kong for business conferences, and island resorts around the world for professional conferences. Without air travel, these events couldn't take place. If your event relies heavily on air travel for attendance, then establishing the facility for offsetting is something that should be seriously considered. Read more about this subject in Chapter 7.

Whether the biggest steps towards a sustainable future for air travel occur in the technology of aircrafts, the fuels they run on, or the choices we make in needing to travel remains to be seen. The challenge of sustainable air travel faces us all: the event industry, tourism, business and the airline industry. We will need to look at multiple solutions to combat the environmental impacts of air travel.

Cycling

Riding bikes to your event is probably the ultimate in sustainable transport. If your event is located in an area with safe bike routes, and if bike riding is popular, you should really promote cycling to your event.

If there are organisations promoting cycling in the region, bring them on board to help increase the number of people cycling to your event. In addition, look at setting up a partnership with a bike shop or bike brand to sponsor your cycling activities onsite. Support cyclists by having a bike repair shop at your event which the bike shop or brand can host. You could also create a 'bike bus'

Box 6.4

BLACK ROCK CITY YELLOW BIKE PROJECT AT BURNING MAN

There's a thriving bike culture at *Burning Man* sponsored by Black Rock City's Department of Public Works, which maintains the *Yellow Bike Project*, providing bikes for participants to use. They also operate a lost and found for bikes that have been misplaced during the event.

So, how do you move 53,000 people around a city where driving is prohibited? The answer is bicycles, bicycles and more bicycles! *Black Rock City's Yellow Bike Project* was launched in 2006, and has been growing each year. The Yellow Bikes are community property at *Burning Man*, and are designated to be shared within the community and available for all to enjoy.

Gifting is part of the philosophy of the event and in 2007 the programme got an unexpected major kick in the pants when an anonymous donor gifted 1000 bikes to the *Yellow Bike Project*. The shipment of unassembled bikes hit Black Rock Station just a couple of weeks before the event. After a mammoth assembly operation, the bikes were transported to *Black Rock City* by truck, except the last load, which came via a pedal-powered armada of bike enthusiasts riding from the *Burning Man* ranch to the playa on an historical ride that's now repeated each year. Like all new programmes in *Black Rock City*, it takes a couple of years to educate everyone about community bike etiquette. Bike volunteers inspected parked bikes to ensure that community bikes were not being locked or hoarded. Bolt cutters helped educate a couple of participants that community

bikes are owned by, well, the community. About 80 per cent of the Yellow Bikes were recovered after the event, meaning that about 20 per cent were taken from the playa either as outright theft or perhaps because people thought they were MOOP (Matter Out Of Place) and were trying to do their part to Leave No Trace!

Since 2006 the *Yellow Bike Project* has had a staggering 2000 per cent growth. One of the most important aspects of the cycling projects at *Burning Man* is the community gifting that happens each year after the event. Approximately 1000 bikes are left/lost/abandoned/donated and these make their way to charity and community projects.

Volunteer cycling groups such as the *Bike Guild* and the *Black Label Bike Club* have supported the bicycle metropolis in numerous ways over the years. The *Bike Guild* taught participants how to maintain bikes, and in 2003 it began matching lost bikes with happy riders. In 2007, the Reno-based *Black Label Bike Club* took over lost and found duties and also staffed the Yellow Bike Project.

Burning Man occurs in the desert near Reno, Nevada, USA. Biking around the temporary city at *Burning Man – Black Rock City –* is the main mode of transport.

To read more about the core principles of this unique gathering, see Box 1.2 in Chapter 1.

www.burningman.com

whereby you organise specific time/s and location/s when riders meet and cycle to the event together. A support vehicle can be offered to carry additional belongings if the event is a multi-day one and everything cannot be carried in panniers (though usually keen cyclers are kitted out with all the stuff they need). Or simply set up safe bike parking!

The *Bicycle Music Festival* is the largest 100 per cent bicycle-powered music festival in the world. The free, all-day (and into the night) event takes place annually in San Francisco, California on the Saturday closest to the summer solstice. The *Bicycle Music Festival* features: a 14,000-watt pedal-powered PA system, as many as 15 bands, multiple festival stops, outrageous critical mass-style bicycle party caravans between festival stops, and zero use of cars or trucks. With its completely bike-haulable stage, the event is packed up and deployed numerous times: staged sequentially at different public parks and also on a moving *Live On Bike* stage which rolls down city streets (bicyclemusicfestival.com).

Video/Virtual Conferencing

Seminar-based events may be able to grow their attendance through offering online real-time video conferencing or holding several smaller events in various geographical markets, to reduce air travel demand.

Each year the *Bioneers Conference* is held in California. It convenes leading social and scientific innovators to share stories, present model solutions and network with each other. They also have the *Beaming Bioneers* programme where partners receive a simultaneous broadcast of the conference plenary talks and complement them with locally produced workshops, tours and activities tailored to the needs of specific bioregions. Beaming all across the USA and around the world, this enables the conference to expand its horizons without expanding its footprint unnecessarily (www.bioneers.com). Read the great paper on hybrid and virtual events by *Sonic Foundry* at www.sonicfoundry.com/white-paper/hybrid-meetings-and-events-toolkit.

You can also hold events completely online with all attending virtually. A great example – and the obvious sector to be early adopters – social media is the virtual conference *Social PLM*. It includes Visio Conferencing with Geolocation, based on *Google's Hangouts* technology and *Altadyn*'s apps. Attendees can interact with expert speakers and vendors, in a format close to face-to-face, which favours social collaboration. They can also network in real time with other attendees from around the world. Attendees just log into the Virtual Conference with their social media profile (LinkedIn, Facebook, Google+) at social-plm.com. Get your virtual conferencing solutions with *Altadyn* at altadyn.com/solutions/for-what/virtual-events/.

Box 6.5

VIRTUAL CONFERENCING

A Blog Post by Shawna McKinley

On television they're the evil Visitors. In the graphic novel and film he's scorned as a terrorist. For meetings the letter 'V' might assume the same degree of loathing and dread: the Virtual Meeting! Striking fear in the hearts of many an event professional, the virtual meeting is something we cannot deny but at the same time find it impossible to fully embrace given how counter it is to the destination-driven business model for meetings.

Yet for event sustainability, the model presents significant benefits, as proven by a recent analysis of a hybrid meeting.

The Event

An invitation-only business meeting, hosting attendees from around the world, 1600 executive attendees attending in person, 5700 technical specialists attending virtually.

The Scope

Carbon footprint analysis completed for the in-person meeting, including venue, hotels, ground transport and air travel. Additional analysis of the virtual meeting, including estimated electricity used while in the virtual environment.

The Result:

An estimated 2355 metric tons of carbon emissions were produced by the in-person meeting for 1600 participants. The 5700-person virtual event produced an estimated 5.6 metric tons of carbon dioxide; 10,054 metric tons of emissions were avoided by inviting technical experts to participate virtually: the equivalent of taking 2000 cars off the road for a year.

The Reality Check:

Would all of the virtual attendees have attended in person if afforded the opportunity? Probably not. However, the question remains: as a specific audience whose event participation needs are fulfilled by attending virtually, *should* they attend in person? In the case of this event it would seem that the traditional model of more heads in beds might not apply, and another business model is at work to meet attendee expectations.

What does the trend towards hybrid meetings that integrate technology to enable participation mean for event sustainability and destination managers? Are we denying what seems to be an inevitable march towards an increasingly virtual meeting experience? Or are we creating a proactive strategy to deliver the best experience using the most effective medium for the audience?

Shawna McKinley is an event sustainability consultant, auditor and blogger. Read more of her event sustainability observations and experiences on her blog.

eventcellany.com

Box 6.6

SUSTAINABLE ATTENDEE TRAVEL CHECKLIST

❏ Create a project to encourage or reward public transport use by attendees.

❏ Link public transport hubs with shuttle buses to your event.

❏ Take advantage of existing sustainable transport initiatives within the destination.

❏ Hold your event close to accessible transport networks.

❏ Identify and communicate to attendees the modes of transport, routes and timetables.

❏ Assess capacity if your event adds significantly to public transport demand. Can it cope?

❏ Meet with local public transport authorities to establish a transport plan.

❏ Arrange additional public transport, such as shuttle buses, to link between transport hubs to the event.

Encourage sustainable travel options by attendees:

❏ Charge for car parking, with a price point chosen to dampen demand for driving, but not to alienate.

❏ Sell pre-purchased car passes.

❏ Reward those who arrive in full cars.

❏ Charge a 'green tax' to all car drivers or those drivers who arrive with less than full cars.

❏ Offer premium parking spots to drivers of full cars, including fast-tracked exit at the end of the event.

❏ Promote the benefits of coach travel, including reducing congestion, the bus stop being very close to the event gates as opposed to car parks, and of course the environmental benefits.

❏ Promote public transport access before event tickets go on sale and ensure all options to get to the event are available on your website so that attendees can plan before they purchase.

❏ If you have group registration, work with group organisers to ensure coach travel is also arranged.

❏ Bundle ticket sales with coach or rail travel.

❏ If your event sells out quickly and these bundled tickets are the only option available, put other elements in place so that the audience doesn't buy these tickets and then drive anyway.

❏ Offer incentives or rewards for those who cycle or walk.

❏ Create a special walk or cycle campaign to promote this to attendees.

❏ Create partnerships with walking and cycling clubs.

❏ Organise a 'bike bus' with a support vehicle for cyclists' belongings.

❏ Offer secure bike parking, and a bike workshop for puncture repairs and tune-ups.

❏ If camping is at your event, offer premium camping to those who cycle or walk.

Encourage carbon offsetting for attendee travel:

❏ Identify the best carbon-offsetting scheme for your event and develop a partnership with them.

❏ Promote it online and make the purchase of it an add-on to ticket sales.

❏ Alternatively add it into all tickets as a green tax.

❏ Put a carbon calculator on your website if appropriate, so that attendees can calculate their emissions based on their mode of transport and the distance they will travel.

❏ Ensure you also offset event production travel.

PERFORMANCE REPORTING

Reporting event travel and transport impacts is an important inclusion in your overall event sustainability performance measurement and reporting. Analysing transport impacts is an important measurement tool, since it allows you to understand where reductions can be made. Measuring impacts and disclosing results is also an important part of sustainability reporting, as it allows stakeholder review of the impacts of the event, especially with such a focus on greenhouse gas emissions.

Measuring travel (people) and transport (things) impacts is one of the areas of reporting where you will need to get your hands dirty. Whereas waste or water measurements can be offloaded to the venue or contractor, for travel and transport reporting you will need to do the data wrangling. Attendee travel in particular is an area where you will often not have complete control – and therefore obtaining accurate information will need some forethought. This may include setting up ticketing systems that capture transport data, conducting simple surveys at entry gates, or doing more complex surveys with attendees during the event to obtain accurate samples. We will delve into some methodology below.

For production travel and transport over which you have direct control, it will be an administrative task to bring together the data you need. For third-party travel and transport (e.g. artist travel or merchandise transport), you will need to engage stakeholders to gather data.

When measuring transport and travel impacts you will be reporting on the following.

Attendee Travel

• Percentage of attendees travelling to event by mode of transport.
• Average distance travelled (return trip).
• Average occupancy for relevant modes of travel.
• Aggregate GHG emissions for each travel mode.
• Total GHG emissions for attendee travel.
• Average GHG emissions per attendee.
• Total carbon offset credits purchased for attendee travel (by organiser or attendee).

Production Travel

• Significant additional ground travel of event personnel (not including commuting) by mode, reported as GHG impact.
• Production-based air travel for personnel, total flights, destination, class of travel and resulting GHGs.
• Year-round event-related air travel for personnel.
• Total carbon offsets purchased for production air travel.

Production Transport

• Significant additional ground freight GHGs (infrastructure, materials, supplies, waste).
• Production-based air freight; distance/routes, volume/weight and resulting GHG emissions.
• Production-based sea freight; distance, volume/weight and resulting GHG emissions.
• Fuel use by site vehicles, site plant and runners during pre-production, event and pull-out, and resulting GHG emissions.
• Carbon offsets purchased for production transport.

Overall

• Attendee travel: total GHG emissions and proportion of total event GHG emissions.
• Production travel: total GHG emissions and proportion of total event GHG emissions.
• Production transport: total GHG emissions and proportion of total event GHG emissions.
• Total event GHG emissions.
• Total carbon offsets purchased.
• Net GHG emissions.

Measuring Attendee Travel

When collecting data for attendee travel you will need to access the following information:

• mode of travel
• distance travelled
• occupancy rates (for cars and chartered mass transport)

- greenhouse gas emission factor per km or mile or per passenger km or mile.

Assessing Mode of Travel

Measuring and reporting mode of travel is useful for making management decisions on travel logistics, to make informed decisions on reductions initiatives, to assess the success of your campaigns, and to publicly disclose your event's impacts.

This information may be gathered through the following:

- Collect ticketing geographic data (requesting postcode upon sale of ticket).
- Gather bundled ticket sales data and include this in calculations (e.g. event ticket + train).
- Conduct attendee survey at event, or online/via email (asking mode of travel, distance travelled and if attendees shared cars).
- Obtain car-parking figures and cross-tabulate these figures with occupancy rate survey figures to gain estimated number of people in total number of cars.
- Exit audits of car occupancy rates.
- Request a report on coach numbers and occupancy rate, to get total passengers travelling by coach.
- Obtain similar information from your shuttle buses. Ensure you have told the driver or company organising it in advance that you want this information captured. You will need it by day so that you can analyse usage patterns for future years, along with uptake of the service.
- Ask your local train station, ferry terminal or other transport interchange if they have automatic traffic counters on gates and see if they can provide figures for the day on which your event is held.
- If you have a certain entry gate that feeds from car parks versus from bus stops or train stations, position people counters at these gates if you have no other way of counting entrants.
- Position manual counters at bus stops and train stations.
- Count the number of bikes in your bike-parking station.

Use all this information to come up with the total percentage of people who have travelled by each mode of travel.

If you don't have all the required information you can also work backward. For example, if you have figures from the shuttle buses taking people from the local train station to your event, a car-park count of the number of cars, and those entering through the special bike/foot entry door/gate, you can calculate the number of people who arrived by car and therefore the car occupancy rate. The following is an example:

Total attendance: 10,000
Total arriving by shuttle bus: 4,000
Total arriving on foot/by bike: 1,000
Total cars in car park: 2000
Arriving by car: 10,000 − 4000 − 1000 = 5000
Car occupancy rate: 5000/2000 = 2.5.

Coach and Bus Travel

If attendees are travelling by standard scheduled national coach or local bus to your event, you will need to report their GHG impact in terms of 'passenger mile' or 'passenger km'. The GHG emissions factor for scheduled buses and coaches is calculated based on average occupancy rates. You will need to access the average figure for your country; however, the problem is that many countries don't have such data to hand. The other challenge is that the national average occupancy rate for these vehicles may be quite low and not reflective of your event's impact on these vehicles. For example, I have viewed national coach per passenger mile figures that have been as low as nine people on average in each coach.

If a significant proportion of attendees travel by coach or bus and every single vehicle is full, or if you have chartered these vehicles, then you should use the 'vehicle mile' or 'vehicle km' figure. This is also relevant if you charter the bus or coach and it is not full, as the vehicle is running anyway and would not have run if you didn't hold your event.

If there is mainly urban bus transport rather than chartered coaches, use the per passenger mile figure published by your country's GHG office or transport department.

Box 6.7

SEMS TRANSPORT TOOL

When you purchase the *SEMS Tool* (US$350) you will receive free access to the travel and transport tool, which has embedded into it the greenhouse gas emissions for various modes of transport.

This is a spreadsheet-based tool which runs in Microsoft Excel, and is available in kilometres or miles. It has separate tabs for production travel and transport, stakeholder, talent and attendee travel.

You enter the total numbers for each mode, along with distance travelled, and for cars, occupancy rate. You then select the subcategory for each mode; for example, business class flights, hybrid vehicles, or road freight by truck size and per km or per tonne/ km. The tool then calculates totals for each mode of travel across the various categories and gives you totals and percentages. There is also a field to input any carbon offsetting done, and it will adjust total GHGs accordingly.

www.semstoolkit.com

Because of lack of available data across all countries for per passenger mile figures, the *SEMS Travel Tool* uses the UK national average figures published by *DEFRA*.

Train Travel

Passenger miles (or km) are the standard way to measure train travel GHG emissions. As trains used by attendees are likely to be regular scheduled services, this is the only option for measurement. Events which attract huge numbers of people in many cases will also have a lot of attendees travelling by train (e.g. sports matches, huge concerts and festivals, etc.). The peaks in usage attributable to these events are fed into the calculations that are used to come up with national occupancy rates and passenger mile emissions factors. Therefore it is acceptable to use the national averages in this case.

As the trains used by attendees are likely to be regular services it may be difficult to assess accurately the actual numbers travelling to the event by train, unless you have presold bundled tickets. Even so, some people may purchase event tickets and then buy a separate train ticket. If you provide a shuttle bus from the station to your event, use the shuttle bus figures to estimate the number of train travellers (unless, of course, people being dropped off by car at the station or who arrive there on foot or bike can also use the shuttles; then you will need to do some on-bus surveys to work out the proportion coming by train versus other modes).

If the venue is within walking distance of the train station, you will need to use another means, probably train passengers. Ask the train station to do a turnstile count, which they can then compare against their usual average traffic figures. Make sure you set up all this data capture in advance.

Car Travel

You will need to know the total number of cars and the average occupancy to come up with final GHG emissions attributable to car travel.

As mentioned earlier, you will need to assess the number of people coming by car, the distance they have travelled, and potentially, if relevant, the type of vehicle travelled in. This may be done through a combination of ticket sales geo-data, attendee surveys, car-park counts and visual audits of vehicles upon exit from the car parks.

I have managed many exit surveys for car parks and the information one can gather from them is really valuable. I would suggest that if you are going to arrange such a survey, and it is you who will be analysing the data, you should take a shift out on the car-park gates so that you get an understanding of the context. By visibly observing the types of people travelling by car, and the amount of belongings they bring with them, you will be better placed to combine the final data you crunch with observational audit to come up with practical and effective initiatives to try to reduce car travel impacts.

When undertaking such a car-park exit survey at *Latitude Festival* in the UK, I engaged *DeMontfort University* to be the data collectors and crunchers. This was before the advent of iPads or apps! We used a hand-drawn table and clipboard. They have since developed an ingenious iPad app to automate the collection process, called *Carbon Tally*. Data is entered on your device and stored locally, then when collected it is uploaded to the server where data is analysed for you. I'm very proud of this innovation (www.carbontally.org).

To measure the impact of production car travel you will need to collect information on the following:

TAXI TRIPS

As taxis charge by distance, you can find out what that rate is and divide the total taxi cost by it to reveal the total distance travelled by taxis. Taxis are either paid through 'cabcharge' dockets with a monthly account or via petty cash. Either way you will be able to collect the total amount paid on taxis and convert it back to total distance travelled. Use an average vehicle size emissions factor, unless you know the specific emissions factor such as London Black Cabs, which is published by DEFRA. Remember to clue up the accounts department or the person responsible for petty cash reimbursements so that they know to collect that information separately.

Petrol will also be paid out directly for personal cars, runners' cars or hire cars. Just as with taxis, collect the total cost of fuel, and take an average car size to estimate distance travelled. You will also need to know the total GHGs for production car travel. This may be done by simply multiplying the litres of fuel by the vehicle type's GHG emissions factor, or use an average vehicle size GHG emissions factor.[3]

Here is an example:

Total petrol receipts: $1000
Cost of fuel per litre locally: $1.20
Total litres of fuel used: $1000/$1.20 = 833 litres
Average litres per vehicle: 6.1 litres per 100km

Total distance travelled:

833 litres / 6.1 = 136.55 × 100 = 13 655 km

Total GHGs:

833 litres × 0.33477kg = 4584.94 kg CO_2e
(average petrol car CO_2e per litre is 0.33577kg)

Air Travel

Air travel will be a significant GHG contributor for many events, especially for conventions and international sporting events. Even though you cannot control all of the travel decisions made by every attendee, the travel would not have occurred if you didn't put on your event. It is your responsibility to measure and disclose the event's air travel impacts. It is also incumbent on the organiser to promote carbon offsetting, making it an attractive and convenient process for attendees to contribute. Certainly, if you're promoting offsetting to your attendees, you should be offsetting your production-related air travel too.

Calculating air travel GHGs is a simple task of gathering the required data from your staff, travel department, accounts department, travel agent, or the attendees and participants themselves.

Where participants such as exhibitors, speakers, VIPs, sponsors or performers arrange their own air travel, you will need to put processes in place to capture this data.

Freight

At the beginning of this section I used the term 'significant additional'. This is to exclude what I call 'production commuting'. Any infrastructure, equipment, materials and products being delivered from local suppliers would need to be included in your GHG inventory. The reason I suggest this is that, just as with local staff, this is 'commuting', and the collection of this level of data is potentially problematic to accurately gather, requires a massive amount of data collection, and is possibly quite inaccurate, as suppliers make their own estimations. It is also very difficult to track every delivery, especially when you scope in third-party activities, such as caterers and exhibitors.

There is definitely a great research job to be undertaken to benchmark the industry across various types of events, locations and budgets, to get some industry data that everyone could use. However, I view the event industry as similar to a supermarket. Every aisle or section of the supermarket could be an event industry sector, and every product on the shelf is a different event.

Every one of those products/events has its own ingredients/materials and transport and energy back stories. It is really hard to create accurate averages, and doing what would be a full product life cycle on a single event is not as practical as it would be, say, for a specific brand of baked beans.

So, back to freight. I say log, measure and report significant additional freight impacts. This may be if the event is based in a regional centre and there aren't enough portable toilets, so that these will need to be transported from the closest city. Or you may be bringing in a special installation from halfway across the world. Or you may even be producing a significant number of branded T-shirts and other merchandise which are coming from India or China and you're in the UK or Canada – then I would be tracking the freight-related GHGs.

Freight may be air, ship, road or train. There are published GHG emissions factors for freight, by vehicle or by vessel type, and may be reported by km or mile, or by volume or weight.

Consider the production-related freighting impacts of your event and decide what should be included in your GHG reporting and accounting. and then start calculating!

Additional Reporting

The *Global Reporting Initiative Event Organizers' Sector Supplement* has created two event industry-specific performance indicators and also includes several other indicators appropriate for travel impact reporting.

EO2 MODES OF TRANSPORT TAKEN BY ATTENDEES AND PARTICIPANTS AS A PERCENTAGE OF TOTAL TRANSPORTATION, AND INITIATIVES TO ENCOURAGE THE USE OF SUSTAINABLE TRANSPORT OPTIONS.

This indicator was written specifically for the event sector supplement and encourages the organiser to report on the proportion of transport by various modes along with initiatives undertaken to encourage participants to take up sustainable transport options. This indicator includes a very useful term, 'access point', which means the participant's travel up to the point where the event organiser takes control of their travel options.

EO3 SIGNIFICANT ENVIRONMENTAL AND SOCIO-ECONOMIC IMPACTS OF TRANSPORTING ATTENDEES AND PARTICIPANTS TO AND FROM THE EVENT AND INITIATIVES TAKEN TO ADDRESS THE IMPACTS.

This indicator offers the opportunity to report non-GHG-related impacts of event travel. This may include fuel consumption, localised pollution, disruption of access (road or availability of space on public transport), congestion, safety, noise, and damage to local transport modes through intense use. In the planning phase many of these impacts will have been anticipated, and this indicator offers the opportunity to report on the initiatives undertaken to reduce these impacts and the results achieved.

EN29 SIGNIFICANT ENVIRONMENTAL AND SOCIO-ECONOMIC IMPACTS OF TRANSPORTING PRODUCTS AND OTHER GOODS AND MATERIALS USED FOR THE ORGANISATION'S OPERATIONS, AND TRANSPORTING MEMBERS OF THE WORKFORCE.

As with EO3, this indicator encourages the organiser to report on the impacts of transporting materials, supplies, infrastructure and equipment. As with attendee transport, impacts may include disruption to traffic and neighbourhood amenity through many large lorries entering the event site, along with noise and localised pollution. Note that the GHG emissions resulting from production transport will be reported via EN17.

EN17 OTHER RELEVANT INDIRECT GREENHOUSE GAS EMISSIONS BY WEIGHT.

This indicator suggests reporting of all 'other' relevant GHG emissions and included in this would be all travel- and transport-related GHGs as detailed earlier in this section.

EO6 TYPE AND IMPACTS OF INITIATIVES TO CREATE AN ACCESSIBLE ENVIRONMENT.

Where an event has initiatives in place to facilitate accessible transport (for example, for those with a physical impairment) this would be reported under EO6. Other examples of offering accessible transport would be preferential parking for those with disabilities or parents with prams and small children.

Goals and Targets

When setting transport-related goals or targets, you may first need to establish a baseline to understand exactly how people are travelling to your event, to gauge the scale of the impacts in comparison to other areas of concern and to assess where in fact improvements could be made.

If you have a recurring event, and have never previously conducted any travel and transport measurement, you should take the next event as your baselining year. You should still put initiatives to improve performance in place, as you will then be able to gauge where improvements could be made. However, obtaining the hard data will be very enlightening.

Once you undertake your first baselining audit you can make an informed judgement about where you could make improvements. Understanding the scale of the event's transport impacts compared to other impacts will also assist in determining which issues to manage. For example, you may determine that there are huge gains to be made through a car-pooling programme, having realised that there is a massive proportion of people arriving alone in cars. Conversely, you may see that all the cars are quite full, and what's more they are full of families with young children and solo parents, making public transport an unattractive or impractical option. Your analysis may also make you realise that

there are only incremental improvements possible, which would take a great deal of resources and time to achieve, in comparison to other initiatives where much less time or resources are required for significantly better results.

Set Goals and Targets

Once this analysis is undertaken you can set goals and targets, such as:

- reducing year-round production travel;
- reducing number of lorries entering the event site;
- increasing sustainable travel modes by attendees;
- increasing opt-in by artists and attendees to the carbon offsetting programme;
- promoting cycling in the event destination through establishing a cycle-to-the-event programme.

Next you will need to write down objectives and targets. This is where the numbers come in. Examples could be as follows:

- achieve 50 per cent of attendees travelling to the event by train;
- achieve 25 per cent of delegates voluntarily opting into carbon offsetting schemes;
- reduce air travel GHGs by 10 per cent through local programming.

QUESTIONS

Simple Answer

1 List five key transport-related issues for events.
2 Identify four deterrents for attendees considering using public transport to travel to events.
3 How can you encourage and facilitate sustainable travel for event attendees? Refer to Box 6.1 Travel and Transport Checklist.
4 Identify three potential negative impacts of crop-grown biofuels and strategies to avoid them.
5 List four measures to report on for production transport.

Case Studies

1 Identify the transport and travel requirements of an event with which you are currently or have recently been involved. Develop sustainable transport initiatives to reduce transport and travel impacts.
2 Brainstorm sponsorship proposals to align with your transport initiatives. Suggest suitable companies and consider how the proposal would benefit them.

Further Research

1 Draft an in-house communication piece for engaging the production workforce in your sustainable transport initiatives.
2 Calculate the GHG impact of your production-related freighting.
3 Conduct an attendee survey, car-park exit audit and/or ticketing analysis to assess the mode of travel for attendees to an event.

NOTES

1 IATA: www.iata.org/whatwedo/environment. Accessed July 2013.
2 Clean burning fuels at Virgin: www.virgin.com/people-and-planet/blog/richard-branson-on-biofuels. Accessed July 2013.
3 Average fuel consumption per litre UK figures: www.gov.uk/government/uploads/system/uploads/attachment_data/file/48913/env0103.xls. Accessed July 2013.

7

GREENHOUSE GAS EMISSIONS

Greenhouse gases occur at every turn within our industry and come from many sources: electricity from the grid, burning up fuel in our portable generators, gas in our kitchens, fuel in vehicles, and the big one – air travel. They're hidden in our materials and supplies, in the food we serve, the water we use and processing of the waste we create.

Some event managers place GHGs out front and work backwards, doing everything with a GHG reduction focus. Others manage their activities with regard to sustainability, with GHGs as one of the impacts they measure for management, reduction and disclosure.

Both viewpoints are valid and both are getting us to the same end point – a responsible attitude to GHG management by our industry, with a focus on measurement and disclosure of our GHG inventory. The motivations behind GHG measurement by our industry are as follows:

• to enable reduction management;
• to prove that reduction management has been effective;
• an obligation or requirement to disclose impacts;
• voluntary disclosure of impacts as we are a responsible member of society.

However, measurement is a complex issue and is made more so by the fact that there is no clear directive or agreement on how far down the line a GHG emissions calculation should go for our industry.

Each event will have a certain set of circumstances and access to resources which makes it unique, and that makes creating a one-size-fits-all directive or methodology difficult.

Before we delve into what should and shouldn't be measured, establishing baselines and looking for ways to reduce GHG emissions, let us look at what those GHGs in fact are.

Gases such as carbon dioxide, methane, ozone and water vapour act as insulators, trapping heat in our atmosphere and keeping the planet to the temperature to which we (and it) are accustomed. This is the greenhouse effect and thus the collective term for the gases performing this role is 'greenhouse gases'.

GHGs occur naturally in the earth's system, but because of human activity, the amount of GHGs being released into the atmosphere has risen dramatically since the beginning of the industrial age.

Greenhouse gases are now reaching artificially high levels because of the burning of fossil fuels needed to power all the stuff we are building and producing. Methane produced due to the decomposition of our biodegradable waste, such as food and sewage, is another contributor to GHGs in our atmosphere. All of this is consequently producing the famous effects of global warming and climate change.

In early 2007 the *International Panel on Climate Change* (IPCC) concluded that irrefutable evidence exists that human activity is the main driver behind the big GW. This announcement was contained in its fourth *Climate Change Synthesis Report*.[1] At the time of writing, the fifth edition of this report was under production, due to be released in late 2014. These reports published by the IPCC synthesise and integrate material contained within IPCC Assessment Reports and Special Reports, which are the work of more than 800 authors. The purpose of these reports is to provide information suitable for policy-makers. The report will provide an update of knowledge on the scientific, technical and socio-economic aspects of climate change.

Each nation, or in fact state, territory and even city, that has a concern for, or policy on, climate change will also have research and publications on climate change, GHGs and the relevance of these for their context.

An Australian example of this is *A Critical Decade*, produced by *The Climate Commission*. This publication has reviewed what science was saying about the need to act on climate change and the risks of a changing climate to Australia.[2]

A Note on Methane

Methane (CH_4) is an effective GHG, which is produced, in basic terms, when things rot. It's over 20 times more effective in trapping heat in the atmosphere than CO_2 over a 100-year period. It's emitted from both natural and human sources.

Discarding biodegradable waste to landfill is the event industry's biggest methane crime.

Biodegradable waste is dumped in landfills all over our planet, and GHG gases are created and emitted into the atmosphere. The UK's DEFRA reports that in the UK methane from landfills accounts for 40 per cent of the country's methane emissions.[3]

Landfill gas (made up of approximately 50 per cent methane and 50 per cent CO_2) is created from the decomposition of organic materials, through both aerobic and anaerobic processes in landfill.

We discuss landfill gas and incineration emissions in further detail in Chapter 9.

Every event is going to have the ultimate by-product of all that eating and drinking . . . sewage. The by-product of this by-product is indeed a greenhouse gas – methane. Newer sewerage treatment plants are harvesting methane to power the plants, rather than bubbling, gurgling and fluffing it off into the atmosphere.

MEASUREMENT SCOPE

There is no debate to be had as to whether the GHG impacts of an event should be measured. That is a given. Measuring impact is necessary for so many reasons; from our responsibility to society to disclose our impacts, through to measurements to enable effective management. Where the controversy lies is in the question of what should in fact be included in the scope of measurement.

There is no straightforward, clearly defined, industry-wide, accepted scope of inclusion for the GHG impacts of events. Measurement of event industry GHGs is fraught with controversy and confusion, as there is no clear direction or agreement regarding how far down the line a GHG emissions calculation should progress.

Therefore, there can be no authentic, widely understood and globally accepted definition for what could be included in an event's 'carbon footprint', which renders that term misleading when used in isolation.

It follows that claiming a 'carbon-neutral event' also has the likelihood of misinterpretation and misuse.

The problem is that we do not have common measurement protocols, we don't have a system to accurately and independently assess claims and there is no one to whom our industry needs to report.

In measuring GHGs there is international guidance to follow – with clear definitions for Scope 1, Scope 2 and Scope 3 greenhouse gas emissions. Our common factors are Scope 1 and Scope 2 emissions – that is straightforward. Where things become a little unstuck is Scope 3. I will explain what each of these mean for our industry below.

The reason it all becomes unstuck is that while Scope 1 and Scope 2 are very valid and necessary inclusions, they are inadequate to authentically cover what common sense would say should be within an event's actual GHG impacts. Each event will have a certain set of circumstances which make it unique and that makes creating a one-size-fits-all directive or methodology quite impractical (and almost impossible) for our industry.

With that in mind, let me introduce you to Scope 1, 2 and 3 emissions and explain their significance in the context of the event industry.

What could be measured?

The *Greenhouse Gas Protocol*[4] categorises GHGs into direct or indirect emissions and further categorises them into Scope 1, 2 and 3 emissions.

Direct GHG emissions are those from sources owned or controlled by the reporting entity. Indirect GHG emissions are those that are a consequence of the activities of the reporting entity, but which occur at sources owned or controlled by another entity.

- **Scope 1**: All direct GHG emissions.
- **Scope 2**: Indirect GHG emissions from the consumption of purchased electricity, heat, steam or cooling.
- **Scope 3**: Other indirect emissions, such as the extraction and production of purchased materials and fuels, transport-related activities in vehicles not owned or controlled by the reporting entity, electricity-related activities (e.g. T&D losses) not covered in Scope 2, outsourced activities, waste disposal, etc.

Scope 1 GHGs for Events

Scope 1 emissions are those from sources that are owned or controlled by the event – 'direct' emissions. These would include the following:

- fuel used in mobile power generators;
- bottled gas and mains gas;
- fuel used in site plant, equipment and vehicles;
- vehicles owned by the company and used offsite;
- if waste is disposed of at the event site and emissions are estimated to be generated (i.e. methane from buried waste) these are also included in Scope 1.

Scope 2 GHGs for Events

Scope 2 emissions are those from 'indirect' sources – purchased heat, steam or electricity used by the event. The most relevant to most events is the following:

- mains/grid electricity supply.

For events held in very hot or very cold locations, district heating and cooling could be included in Scope 2.

As a note, the location of the 'ignition' of the fuel into energy is a determining factor in whether it is Scope 1 or Scope 2. This is important for mains gas supply. It may feel as though mains gas should be in Scope 2 along with mains electricity, but as the fossil fuel is ignited and turned into energy under the reporting entity's control, it is Scope 1, direct emissions.

As previously mentioned, the event industry as a whole does not have a determination as to what should be included in emissions calculations over and above Scope 1 and Scope 2 emissions. This leads us to the big one for our industry: Scope 3 emissions.

Scope 3 GHGs for Events

Scope 3 emissions are 'other indirect' emissions – these are emissions that occur as a result of an event's activities but occur at sources owned by others. This includes the following:

- transport of employees (including all paid contractors, talent, crew);
- hotel nights for event production (crew, talent, staff, contractors);
- significant additional freight impact of equipment, goods and services required by the event or waste produced by the event;

- hired transportation (shuttle buses, taxis, limos, boats, aircraft).

And then, going deeper:

- emissions embodied in the products and materials purchased for the event;
- transport of products and equipment for the event;
- energy used or emissions created in processing waste (liquid and solid);
- transport of waste (liquid and solid);
- energy and transport to produce and supply water.

In addition:

- attendee travel – the single GHG contributor for many events;
- hotel nights of attendees (e.g. delegates at a conference/convention).

How to Determine What Goes into Scope?

We can make a start by following guidance developed by such protocols and standards as *Greenhouse Gas Protocol* (international), *ISO 14064*[5] (international), *PAS 2060*[6] (UK) and the *National Carbon Offset Standard*[7] (Australia) among others.

The first step should be to identify and estimate likely GHG emissions, next to make measurable reductions through our own actions, and only then to head for carbon neutrality via carbon offsetting.

The *National Carbon Offset Standard* (Australia) sets the following principles to consider in the calculation of a 'footprint':

- **Relevance:** ensure that the GHG inventory appropriately reflects the GHG emissions attributed to the event.
- **Completeness:** account for all GHG emissions within the defined boundary. Disclose and justify exclusions.
- **Consistency:** ensure that methodologies from event to event are consistent to allow for meaningful comparisons.
- **Transparency:** ensure that the collation of GHG emissions data can be evaluated by auditors. Disclose assumptions, reference methodologies and data sources.
- **Accuracy:** Ensure that quantification is accurate.

Setting a Boundary

The boundary defines event venues/sites/activities that should be included in the calculation.

- events (venues, locations, activities) that are under the direct control of the organising body;
- events (venues, locations, activities) that are not under the direct control of the organising body but which are perceived to be 'part of the event'.

For example, the boundary for a single event is easy to determine, but a city-wide festival which has a concert series in a park produced by the event organising body as well as satellite events and venues throughout the city under the event's banner (e.g. many city-based performing arts and fringe festivals) would find determining the boundary a very important step.

Operational control is usually the deciding factor; however, stakeholder perception is also a contributor to deciding what would be included within the boundary of reporting. Operational control is defined as being where the event has the authority to introduce or implement operating policies, health and safety policies or environmental policies.

The *National Carbon Offset Standard* (Australia) prescribes that at a minimum, organisations (which may or may not be events) should report Scope 3 emissions from the following:

- business travel of employees;
- disposal of waste generated (landfill emissions);
- use of paper in the course of its business.

The recording of emissions from landfill is problematic for countries that have not published a national or statewide GHG emissions factor. In addition, there is controversy around the accuracy of landfill emissions factors in the first place. A national figure does not really work, especially if you are sending your general waste to an effective landfill methane extraction facility.

The *GHG Protocol* guides Scope 3 emissions calculations by first determining relevance to the organisation (event). Determining relevance is guided by the following:

- including them if particular Scope 3 emissions are large or relatively large compared with the event's Scope 1 and Scope 2 emissions;
- including them if particular Scope 3 emissions are deemed critical by key stakeholders;
- including them if the organisation (event) could undertake or influence the potential reduction.

The event must transparently document and disclose which Scope 3 emissions have been included in its calculations when making any assertions about emissions reductions.

We need to decide how wide we cast our net in terms of what to include in Scope 3 emissions calculations. For example:

- Do we include audience/attendee travel? If we use the premise of 'direct control or significant influence' then, in some cases, audience travel would be included.
- What about emissions from the processing and transport of waste, water and/or sewage?
- What about embedded energy in materials, food and/or supplies?
- Do we include freighting of materials and products, equipment, infrastructure, etc.?
- How do we separate what would be considered staff commuting from crew event transport?
- Do we include only air travel for talent/performers/speakers/VIPs, or their ground transport as well?

Some events measure electricity only; others go into extravagant detail and measure everything that has a whiff of GHG emissions about it.

In the UK, the British Standards Institution (BSI) has published *BSI PAS 2060 – Specification for the Demonstration of Carbon Neutrality*. This standard offers guidance to organisations on quantifying, reducing and offsetting GHG emissions. It guides us to include all emissions resulting from **core activities** to the **production of the event**. This is still not a cut-and-dried directive as to what would be considered *core*.

The event industry needs to discuss what is appropriate to include in Scope 3 emissions as 'core' emissions and what 'non-core' emissions, which the event takes responsibility for, could also be voluntarily reported.

Guidance on when to include attendee travel needs to be developed. In addition, guidance and agreement are needed on what circumstances would be when it becomes too resource-heavy to gather primary emissions data for other Scope 3 emissions versus perhaps 'secondary' data provided by consolidating benchmarked figures from industry research.

Carbon Footprint

There are hundreds of footprint measurement tools available online and, while the results do vary, simple personal and simple business footprint measurement is possible.

This is not the case currently for events. Tools do exist claiming that they can measure an event's footprint, but investigation shows that there are wildly variable methods of measurement and indeed they are measuring different things. Until the areas to be measured, methods and emissions factors are determined, agreed upon and accepted by the majority of the industry, the footprint of an event is not really a valid or robust measurement tool to use in making public claims or comparisons against other events, or for using as a performance indicator.

Where most of these services fall short is in offering either too basic a scope or an inappropriately complex one. Both instances ignore the peculiarities of live event production. Auditors can include a report with a certain figure on the front page which you should take as your 'footprint'. Perhaps they may also leave you with the promise of a convenient offsetting solution.

Measurement of emissions is a fantastic management tool, but how you actually use this data to sustainably manage your event going forward is the key. Taking steps to reduce your event's impact is the challenge we all need to take on.

Rather than attempting to measure a 'carbon footprint', which infers total emissions, one should instead measure the areas where robust data can be gathered and actual change effected as a result of having this information.

The following areas can be measured to assess your performance, set goals for future reductions and, if you choose to, offset the emissions created.

Easy to measure: Energy and Transport

Calculating GHG emissions of energy use at your event is simple. So is transport of attendees if you know the postcode or town where they travelled from (ticket sales information), attendee numbers, percentage by transport mode, such as coach and shuttle bus figures and car-park figures, car occupancy rates, etc. How to do this is explained in Chapters 5 and 6.

Difficult to measure: Food and Beverage

I would not suggest trying to measure the embedded energy in food sold at an event. People would have eaten, no matter where they are, and the main way you can reduce the GHG impacts of food eaten at your event is through ensuring local sourcing of produce to reduce transport impact, offering organic and vegetarian, etc. For an event to be managed sustainably, these should be part of the plan anyway.

Even more difficult: Freight and Products

Attempting to calculate freight is particularly troublesome. Consider such things as what percentage your load took up on the truck, where it went en route to your event, what sized truck, open road or city congestion, did it come from the courier's depot, direct from supplier, or did it come from a central warehouse? Before this, were the products you're moving manufactured locally, at the other end of the country or overseas? Where do you stop? And how do you track every delivery?

You can of course employ averages, but how accurate is that going to be? The standard GHG emission factor for freight is split into vehicle sizes and may be calculated on a tonne of goods per kilometre rate or just per kilometre. But what do you do with the information at the end?

Trying to calculate the embedded energy in products used at your event will be effectively impossible until there is universal carbon emission product labelling.

The Key Sustainability Indicators outlined in this book do not include such things as the embedded energy in food and beverage, materials and goods. This is because the methodologies required to accurately measure these are currently wide and varied. As was discussed in Chapter 8, the measurement of the climate impact of products and materials is becoming increasingly standardised. We are seeing carbon footprints being included on products but it will be some time before all products are so labelled, enabling easy calculation of the GHG emissions resulting from one's purchasing habits.

'Carbon neutrality'

PAS 2060 requires the following to calculate emissions and then make carbon neutrality claims:

- Identify and define what will be included in a carbon emissions calculation.
- Define, clearly communicate and adequately justify what is included, the methodologies undertaken and emissions factors used.
- Measure and disclose what the emissions for an event were, or are (in advance) anticipated to be.
- Take action to make measurable reductions in carbon emissions.
- Report/disclose performance indicating what reductions were made and how they were achieved.

Reducing GHGs

It is widely accepted that the best way to reduce GHG emissions is to:

- reduce energy demand;
- reduce transport demand;
- replace fossil fuels with renewable sources of energy;
- reduce consumption of items with high carbon footprints;
- reduce consumption;

- reduce waste created, and keep biodegradables out of landfill;
- reduce water use;
- reduce waste water created;
- don't chop down trees.

Mitigation options for unavoidable emissions include the following:

- Internal investment in GHG-reducing technologies or techniques (also called Carbon Compensation).
- External investment in GHG-reducing technologies or techniques (also called Carbon Offsetting).

CARBON COMPENSATION AND OFFSETTING

Measuring GHG emissions and then mitigating them through internal reinvestment in reducing technologies or techniques, or through investing in projects by others (offsetting), is the final way to deal with unavoidable emissions from your event.

Offsetting works, in simple terms, by awarding 'carbon credits' to projects which have been certified to be GHG reducing. Those organisations that are required to, or who voluntarily wish to offset their own GHG emissions, in turn purchase these credits, thus supplying funding to support the reduction projects.

A carbon credit represents the removal of one tonne of carbon dioxide, or its greenhouse gas equivalent, from the environment. Carbon offset schemes set a price on the amount it costs to mitigate the harm from emissions. These vary from scheme to scheme according to how the carbon credits are traded. Trading is subject to the influence of supply-and-demand economics.

Many fantastic projects are being developed and new retailers of offsets are being established every other day. These retailers are the websites and companies which sit between the buyers and sellers; that is, between the projects and the purchasers of offsets.

While a great tool to get funds flowing to renewable energy and other GHG-reducing projects, voluntary offsetting is the final option an individual, business, organisation or event should look to use.

Voluntary carbon offsetting is not a cure for climate change but it may be seen as a tool to help raise awareness of the issues of consumption and reduce the impact of our actions on the environment.

In the early days of offsetting schemes there was little regulation and few codes of practice or controls in place. Most projects take place outside the country where the emissions are created and the offset paid, and it was with a leap of faith that voluntary offsets were purchased by consumers. However, as we will discuss shortly, the voluntary offsetting market is now regulated.

There is still some discussion being held on the appropriateness of carbon offsetting as a concept. One side of the debate is the view that buying offsets is akin to paying for the right to pollute; on the other side is the view that through funnelling money to support development of solutions, new zero-carbon and GHG-reducing technologies will be more quickly developed.

Also available are projects that simultaneously reduce GHGs while protecting biodiversity and community. More information on these projects is given below.

To tackle climate change, developed nations need to cut GHG emissions as well as assist developing nations in cutting theirs. Offsetting can help redistribute wealth, gained from exploiting the earth's resources and polluting it in the process, to emerging nations to make sure they don't become a carbon copy of the developed world.

To put things in context and to provide a quick and basic précis of the offsetting market, let us look at both types of offsetting: voluntary and mandatory.

Mandatory offsetting is where the big carbon emitters – oil, power and car manufacturers, etc. – offset the emissions resulting from their operations in order to meet their country's obligations to the *Kyoto Protocol*.[8]

Those countries that have ratified the *Kyoto Protocol* and agreed to meet certain GHG reductions goals pass this requirement along to their country's big emitters. Regulation has swiftly entered the mandatory offsetting market, as those organisations required to reduce emissions can only have their reductions taken into account if they purchase carbon credits from certified projects.

Under the *Kyoto Protocol* there are two programmes through which emissions reductions projects can be certified: the *Clean Development Mechanism* (CDM) and *Joint Implementation* (JI). Once projects meet these standards they are certified through various schemes. The *Gold Standard* is one of the optimal certifications and more information on this may be found on their website if you are inclined to investigate further (www.cdm goldstandard.org).

The projects that meet the standards are awarded carbon credits or *Certified Emissions Reductions* (CERs). These are then sold to companies whose governments have mandated that they must reduce their emissions. CERs are registered and issued by the Executive Board of the *Clean Development Mechanism* (CDM) of the *United Nations Framework Convention on Climate Change*.[9]

Carbon offsetting allows those that emit planet-warming gases to pay for carbon cuts in developing countries as a cheaper alternative to cutting their own.

The first step to managing emissions is to cut them at the source, rather than proceed with business as usual by exporting carbon responsibility offshore along with a payment cheque.

As the event industry is unregulated and we have yet to establish a firm boundary around what GHG emissions are our responsibility and what aren't, we need to maintain the conversation and establish an industry-wide agreement as to what those measures should be.

If we decide to apply carbon offsetting to our events, we must consider the following questions:

- Has action been taken to make measurable reductions in GHG emissions?
- Has the scope of GHG emissions metrics for the event, and what is included in it, been defined, clearly communicated and adequately justified?
- If the decision has been made to offset, have we applied no more than 49 per cent of our total GHG emissions to carbon offsets?

Additionality

For a project to be a valid form of carbon offsetting, it must be demonstrated that the project faces barriers that would have made it unfeasible without revenues from carbon offsets. It also cannot be a project that is already widely employed or mandated by regulation or expected in business as usual. It must be 'additional' to what would have happened anyway. Barriers may be financial, technological or institutional.

So at what point do the 'financial' or 'institutional' barriers stop being real and start really being about a company not wanting to take its own responsibility and write its own cheques for GHG emissions-reducing activities?

If you are considering offsetting, scrutinise the projects that are being funded, and actively choose the ones that work for you. Actively seek out some of the wonderful projects that have ongoing and broad sustainability benefits.

I firmly believe that carbon offsetting in the traditional sense should be primarily attached to air travel and significant additional ground travel. If you don't have the option to purchase a renewable energy tariff in your country, and if no biofuels or mobile renewable energy supply is available for temporary power, then you could prescribe offsets to these emissions.

For methane emissions from waste, however, if you *have* to offset them because your biodegradable waste is going into landfill, please look again at how you can change waste management processes onsite or influence the industry locally to create composting or anaerobic digestion opportunities for this waste.

If you're baulking at offsetting against your event as a whole, I still encourage you not to ignore all the wonderful projects around the world innovating ways to reduce GHG emissions. These are particularly important in developing countries where the benefits are also social and economic, and are empowering to local people and the rural poor, improving standards of living and reducing the need to move to cities to earn an income.

View your financial support of the projects as part of your organisation's social responsibilities, and not as a way to excuse yourself for the GHGs your event has chugged up into the atmosphere.

Seek out the project that fits your ideology, and actively support it. If you choose to go down the carbon-offsetting route be careful about calling it an offset against a 'footprint' unless you have played out every possible emissions-reduction solution at your event. Otherwise your offsetting may scream of a greenwash.

If you want to learn a little more about offsetting, have a look at the glossary (www.carbonoffsetguide.com.au/glossary).

Let us now look at voluntary offsetting as it applies to the event industry, how the offsetting market is regulated and what project options there are for your offsetting dollars to support.

Voluntary Offsetting

Businesses and individuals can offset their emissions on a voluntary basis. This is done through verified projects rather than certified projects. Verified emissions reductions (VERs) are the cornerstone of the voluntary carbon offsetting market. These are virtually 'over-the-counter' sales of voluntary offset carbon credits, facilitated through online offset retailers.

As compared with the big solar and big wind projects supported by CERs, the voluntary offsetting market mostly supports projects with strong sustainable development benefits, improving the quality of life for local communities as well as reducing GHG emissions. These projects have climate, community and biodiversity in mind. They ensure that the economic and social benefits of the GHG emissions-reducing projects are transferred back to the communities involved in the projects.

The voluntary offsetting market is not yet regulated by law, so it is a case of buyer beware. However, there are many certification systems and standards that ensure rigorous auditing of projects selling voluntary offsets. This allows transparency, and those purchasing voluntary offsets can be confident that their money is going to a project that will have an effect. With thorough investigation into the offsetting project you're considering, you can make an informed choice and support a scheme which is beneficial to conservation and biodiversity, sequesters carbon, encourages the development of new technologies, and does so without the need to displace people or damage ecosystems.

Above all else the scheme you choose should be independently verified. The following are some of the main voluntary offset standards or certifications.

Voluntary Carbon Standard (VCS) is the world's most widely used voluntary GHG reduction programme. Almost 1000 registered projects have collectively removed more than 120 million tons of emissions from the atmosphere through VCS (www.v-c-s.org).

SOCIALCARBON® is a standard developed by the *Instituto Ecológica* in Brazil. The standard certifies emissions reduction projects for their contributions to sustainable development (www.socialcarbon.org).

The *CarbonFix Standard* has set a quality benchmark for worldwide climate forestation projects. It was developed in 2007 by experts in the fields of forestry, climate change and development aid (www.carbonfix.info).

Plan Vivo is a framework for supporting communities to manage their natural resources more sustainably, with a view to generating climate, livelihood and ecosystem benefits. Quantifying ecosystem services enables projects to generate 'Plan Vivo Certificates', which can be sold to generate funds for activities and payments for ecosystem services, for example, through the voluntary carbon market. The Plan Vivo Standard may also be used to apply CSR, development or other sources of funding, to demonstrate good project design, governance and monitoring of performance (www.planvivo.org).

The *Woodland Carbon Code* is a new voluntary standard for woodland creation projects in the UK, which makes claims about the carbon dioxide they sequester. Independent certification to this standard provides assurance and clarity about the carbon savings of these sustainably managed woodlands (www.forestry.gov.uk/carboncode).

Climate Action Reserve ensures the environmental integrity and financial benefit of emissions-reduction projects in North America. The Reserve establishes high-quality standards for carbon offset projects, oversees independent third-party verification bodies, issues carbon credits generated from such projects and tracks the transaction of credits over time in a transparent, publicly accessible system (www.climateactionreserve.org).

Green-e Climate is a voluntary certification programme launched in 2008 that sets consumer protection and environmental integrity standards for greenhouse gas (GHG) emission reductions sold in the voluntary market (www.green-e.org).

The *Climate, Community and Biodiversity Alliance* (CCBA) has developed voluntary standards to encourage land management projects to additionally meet goals of conserving biodiversity and protecting and developing communities. Carbon project developers will aspire to this triple agenda so that community and biodiversity impacts are included in their carbon mitigation projects (www.climate-standards.org).

The *American Climate Registry* provides an electronic registry system to register offset projects and record the ownership and retirement of serialised verified emission reductions (VERs) branded as emission reduction tons (americancarbonregistry.org).

ISO 14064 standard provides governments, businesses, regions and other organisations with a complementary set of tools for programmes to quantify, monitor, report and verify GHG emissions (www.iso.org).

There are also country-specific offset standards such as the *Pacific Carbon Trust*. This corporation under the Government of British Columbia in Canada has been created to deliver 'made-in-BC' GHG offsets and drive the growth of BC's low-carbon economy (www.pacific carbontrust.com).

Investigate within your country to see if such a project also exists. You will need to make a fundamental decision, however, as to whether (if you live in a developed and seemingly wealthy country) you believe it is the responsibility of your country to look after its own environmental restoration or if offsetting funds could credibly be spent domestically. The test of 'additionality' is essential in offsetting, and at its core is the question of whether the project would have occurred if the offsetting funds were not provided. For me, this means a developed nation 'deciding' to allocate the funds as compared to a developing nation where much more urgent issues of human welfare are at stake, or in fact, if the money just does not exist.

Offset Projects

If you decide to offset your production transport or to offer an offsetting opt-in for attendees, you will first need to decide to which projects you want your offset money channelled. You are not constrained to just 'tick a box' on the airline's website or go with whatever projects an offsetting retailer is offering. You can alternatively search through offsetting project directories to look for projects that resonate with you, and then look at who retails their offset credits.

Carbon Catalog is a free and independent directory of carbon credits, listing carbon providers and projects worldwide (www.carboncatalog.org).

Ends Carbon Offsets is an independent guide to the voluntary carbon market and directory of offset providers (www.endscarbonoffsets.com).

Carbon Offset Guide Australia is an independent directory of Australian carbon offset providers (www.carbonoffsetguide.com.au).

Carbonify is a directory of carbon offset retailers in the USA, Canada, the UK, Europe and Australia (www.carbonify.com).

The project you choose in which to invest your offsetting money should adhere to the voluntary offset standards, and to have been independently verified so that you know the project is doing what it says it will.

It is worth doing your own research to see exactly what the offsetting money is supporting, and how the projects are rolled out to make sure this aligns with your event's ideals. Ask questions of the retailer and look at how much money is held by them for administration as compared to the percentage that makes it to the project.

To conduct a detailed check on the project, its verification and its progress reports, visit *MarkIt*.[10]

You will also need to decide whether you want your project to be in your own country or offshore, most likely in developing regions such as South Asia, Africa and South America.

Carbon offsetting projects will usually fall under one of the following categories:

*   renewable energy
*   sequestration
*   energy efficiency
*   methane capture.

Solar

Solar offsetting projects range from providing lighting, or solar cookers, to solar hot water and electricity for homes and businesses.

Selco India provide sustainable energy solutions and services to underserved households and businesses in India. Their projects are also recipients of offset funding (www.selco-india.com/carbon.html).

Non-profit organisation *Energetica* in Bolivia is distributing solar water-heating systems to urban and semi-urban areas. In perfect conditions in the Andes, the power of the sun heats the water, replacing the need for electricity in water heating. The ambition is to provide 10,000 units. The project is funded through the off-setting company *myclimate* (www.myclimate.org www.energetica.org.bo).

Wind

Wind-generated energy is growing very fast; however, building and installing turbines is expensive. Carbon offsetting funding offers the added finance needed to make these projects viable. Wind projects are generally profit-making ventures and sell electricity on to the national grid.

Foot-Powered Water Pumps

International Development Enterprises India (IDEI) has developed the treadle pump, a foot-operated water-lifting device that can irrigate the plots of land of smallholders in regions that have a high water table. A low-cost system, simple in design and easily manageable, it is perfect as an irrigation solution for small farmers. The pumps replace diesel-driven pumps needed in the dry season, saving CO_2 emission, improving agricultural yields and empowering the rural poor. With the installation of treadle pumps come environmental, financial and social benefits. IDEI adopted the *Voluntary Carbon Standard* (VCS) for its programme and is aiming to upgrade from VCS to *Gold Standard* (www.ide-india.org).

Cooking Stoves

In many developing countries the main source of fuel is wood, which is used for cooking on an open fire. Apart from the GHG emissions from burning wood, if used inside, the kitchen fills with smoke, resulting in health problems for occupants. Cooking on an open fire is inefficient, with much of the heat lost meaning that more wood is used than needed. In addition, in areas where firewood is scare, deforestation is an issue.

Many options have been developed to combat this issue and have become the targets of offset programmes. The 'rocket elbow' stove is one such design: it reduces wood use by 50 per cent or more, and eliminates smoke

from indoor areas. Zero-emissions cookers, *Scheffler Solar Concentrators*, have been developed for domestic and large-scale use. Large-scale adaptations include where large volumes of rice need to be cooked such as in hospitals and schools.

In order to reduce GHGs and counter the deforestation on Madagascar, *myclimate* supports the manufacture and distribution of climate-friendly solar and efficient cookers (www.myclimate.org).

The *Shimoni* efficient wood stove offsets is a beautiful project that has many benefits apart from slowing deforestation and protecting health. Deforestation occurring because of harvesting timber for burning is causing coastal erosion and sedimentation, which affects the delicate mangrove and coral reef ecosystems. This in turn has negative effects on marine life which depends on these habitats, including a rare species of dolphin which is also one of the area's top tourism attractions. This simple but effective and multi-beneficial project is retailed by *CO2 Balance* and is a great example of the type of project to look out for, especially if your event has a coastal or tourism element to it (www.co2balance.co.uk

Hydroelectricity

Micro-hydro or 'run-of-river' hydro projects are the ones to look for when searching out a voluntary offset project to support. Full-scale hydro with dams and the requisite infrastructure are too controversial in their creation and impact on biodiversity and livelihoods, so I would suggest leaving them alone. *Climate Friendly* offer voluntary offsetting for a run-of-river hydro project that has 95 small individual power plants which use the flow of rivers to generate clean electricity. The hydropower plants are spread across four provinces, in some of the most disadvantaged and least developed areas of China. Many of the projects are located in remote mountain regions, isolated from the rest of China (www.climatefriendly.com).

Compost

There are measurable greenhouse gas reductions from using compost over chemical fertilisers and from preventing biodegradable waste from creating methane when it is sent to landfill. The use of energy and fuel in mining and transport of the non-renewable raw ingredients for chemical fertilisers (petroleum and minerals), along with the energy needed to manufacture the final product, all adds up to a much weightier carbon debt than the natural alternative: compost. Read about the project funded by travel company *Kuoni* in a brilliantly aligned offset project in Box 7.1.

Biogas

Anaerobic digestion is a commonly used treatment for waste. This is taking green waste, agricultural waste, food scraps, animal manure or sewage, and processing it in the absence of oxygen to produce biogas (methane). This is then burnt to generate electricity or used as a fuel for cooking, etc. This prevents methane from being naturally produced and expelled into the atmosphere, and by using the methane created it avoids other sources of fuel and electricity being used such as burning wood or coal.

In 2012, *Shambala Festival* in the UK encouraged car and van pass buyers to offset their travel GHGs. Almost 1000 took up the offer and raised more than £4000. *Shambala* asked attendees to vote between various offsetting projects to support. The most popular were *Tree Flights*, which received 38 per cent (£1594) of the carbon vote, which was used to sponsor a dedicated forest area in Kenya. This project will save carbon by protecting existing rainforest. *Tree Flights* also work with the local community to plant productive trees to further prevent deforestation, improve communities' self-reliance, and encourage stewardship of the forests (www.treeflights. com). *Converging World* received 42 per cent (£1762). This money will support a new community and medical centre in the sprawling slums of Mumbai to install a solar panel for light and to run a medical fridge. This pioneering community project is employing street children to develop a network of people to find those who are unwell and bring them to the centre for affordable or free treatment. Those children involved also engage with a

---

Box 7.1

COMPOST OFFSETS

The *Gianyar Waste Recovery* **carbon offset project on Bali composts organic waste that previously had to be dumped. In this way, methane emissions from the tip can be avoided and high-value compost is being produced.**

Bali, the most important tourism destination in Indonesia, has a growing waste problem which is already having an impact on the tourism sector. In the so far untouched landscape, waste is being illegally disposed of in rivers and lakes, canals, and along the streets. The small amount of gathered waste from the project region Gianyar, in the southeast of the island, is disposed of on a tip in the vicinity of the village Temesi. The methane developing from such a tip is neither collected nor burned and therefore rises unhindered into the atmosphere.

In the face of the deterioration of the situation onsite, the Rotary Club of Bali Ubud decided to counteract this problem and planned and implemented a composting plant. Eighty-five per cent of waste in the region is from organic material, which can be composted. Another 5 per cent, mainly plastics, can be recycled so that after the implementation of the project only 10 per cent is dumped on the tip. Since aerobic composting does not cause methane emissions, a considerable reduction of GHGs can be achieved.

The local population also benefits, in that the air pollution from the tip is reduced, the waste volume is reduced by around 90 per cent, and jobs are created.

This project is supported exclusively by luxury travel company *Kuoni* and retailed by *My Climate*.

www.myclimate.org www.kuoni.co.uk

programme reconnecting them with human impact on the natural environment, and urban food-growing skills. This project saves carbon through renewable energy installation, and will prevent diesel generators from being used in this already polluted environment (www .theconvergingworld.org).

Planting Trees/Reforestation

In the early tree-planting days the carbon cowboys created tree 'farms' through wide-scale planting of a single species with no regard for biodiversity issues, appropriateness of the species for the area, and no ongoing maintenance to ensure the trees actually grow to maturity and therefore sequestering the carbon that was claimed they would.

Things have now moved on from that scenario. Considerations include the local population who live in or depend on forests being involved in projects to ensure they are not displaced. Land that has been farmed but is no longer arable is being converted into managed forests and the farmers who originally worked the land are paid to protect and nurture the newly established forests, offering them a much-needed income.

Biodiversity issues and conservation concerns are embedded into greening projects, so that the restoration of forests and habitats and the flow-on benefits of this are just as important as the sequestration of carbon.

Avoided Deforestation

A cousin of the tree-planting option is *Avoided Deforestation* – and that is exactly what it sounds like – preventing GHGs from entering the atmosphere by keep the carbon exactly where it is: in the forest. According to the *Stern Review on the Economics of Climate Change*, deforestation causes 24 per cent of GHG emissions and 18 per cent of greenhouse gas emissions globally.[11] The premise of avoided deforestation (also known as REDD – reducing emissions from deforestation and forest degradation) is that communities are paid to conserve the forests, rather than clear them for their timber or to make room for agriculture or mining. Avoided deforestation as a carbon offsetting vehicle is hugely controversial and is in hot debate. If you wish to know more about this issue

visit both sides of the debate (www.reed-monitor.org and www.un-redd.org).

Integrated Projects

Other projects can be a combination of beneficial technologies and outcomes.

For example, the project by French development organisation GERES in Ladakh has offset credits sold through *My Climate*. In this project, through the construction of 500 hothouses, the vegetation period is extended in the Himalayan region of Ladakh. At the same time the living conditions of the rural population in the Himalayas are improved. Through the hothouses, imports of foodstuffs by airfreight are also reduced. In addition to the hothouses, 20 small 10kW water power plants have been constructed which replace diesel generators and reduce additional CO_2 emissions. (www.geres. eu and www.myclimate.org).

Internal Offset

Rather than sending money offshore to projects you can look to your own event and reinvest in projects that will either result in reductions in your emissions or through educating attendees which will in turn help them in reducing theirs.

Consider investing in, funding or supporting an area at your event where attendees can learn about the consequences of GHG emissions and climate change, their personal contribution to creating emissions, and the best ways for them to reduce their impact. This is a way of leveraging the power you have in putting on the event to talk to people about these issues.

If you feel it inappropriate to have such an area at your event due to its nature, look at other ways whereby you can include these ideas. Perhaps you could invite activist groups to manage recycling points or property lock-ups/ cloakrooms, where they can also promote their messages in a less intrusive way.

If there are extra costs involved in hiring in solar kit, composting toilets, running a dual or triple waste management programme to purchase biodiesel, or to have all your signs hand painted, look at these extra costs as an internal offset.

Calculate how much energy and GHG emissions you're saving, the volume of toxic chemicals not produced, and the volume of waste you're preventing from hitting the landfill through your initiatives, etc.

Convert this to GHG equivalent tonnes. Then cost that out at standard offsetting rates for purchasing voluntary emissions reduction certificates. This is your budget for upscaling and costing out your sustainability initiatives.

QUESTIONS

Definitions

1   What are greenhouse gas emissions?
2   What is an 'emissions factor'?
3   What are Scope 1 emissions?
4   What are Scope 2 emissions?
5   What are Scope 3 emissions?

Short Answer

1   Explain the concept of a carbon footprint and why this may or may not be an appropriate term of measurement for events.
2   In the context of an outdoor event, give examples of Scope 1, 2 and 3 emissions.
3   What proof exists that elevated GHGs are causing climate change?
4   If an event claims to be 'carbon neutral' what would you look for in order to scrutinise this claim?

Case Study

1   At a conference run by a company for its employees and held in a conference centre, what GHGs would you include in the scope of measurement for the event, which is the responsibility of the event owner? How does this differ from a conference owned by an event promoter that sells tickets to the general public?
2   Choose an event (location, size, type, attendance), and define what would be Scope 1, 2 and 3 greenhouse gas emissions. Explain the techniques you could use to estimate the greenhouse gas emissions likely to occur at this event. For one of these techniques, do the calculations to determine likely GHGs. Identify what intervention could be put in place to reduce the estimated GHGs.

3   Find a carbon offsetting project online and review the benefits of the project and the assurances given that this project is valid and effective.
4   Create communications techniques, ideas or initiatives that would be effective in encouraging the purchasing of carbon offsetting by:

a)   delegates at a conference;
b)   professional musicians playing at a music festival;
c)   sporting teams participating in an international sports final.

NOTES

1   Climate Change 2007– Synthesis Report: www.ipcc.ch/pdf/assessment-report/ar4/syr/ar4_syr_spm.pdf
2   Climate Commission – A Critical Decade Report: climatecommission.gov.au/topics/the-critical-decade/
3   DEFRA – Waste Strategy for England 2007: archive.defra.gov.uk/environment/waste/strategy/strategy07/documents/waste07-strategy.pdf, accessed June 2013.
4   Greenhouse Gas Protocol: www.ghgprotocol.org.
5   ISO 14064-1:2006 Greenhouse gases – Part 1: Specification with guidance at the organization level for quantification and reporting of greenhouse gas emissions and removals: www.iso.org/iso/catalogue_detail?csnumber=38381.
6   PAS 2060 Specification for the demonstration of carbon neutrality: www.bsigroup.com/en-GB/PAS-2060-Carbon-Neutrality/.
7   National Carbon Offset Standard: www.climatechange.gov.au/government/initiatives/national-carbon-offset-standard.aspx.
8   Kyoto Protocol: unfccc.int/kyoto_protocol/items/2830.php, www.kyotoprotocol.com
9   Executive Board of the Clean Development Mechanism of United Nations Framework Convention on Climate Change: unfccc.int
10   Markit: mer.markit.com/br-reg/public/index.jsp?s=cpmer.markit.com/br-reg/public/index.jsp?s=cp.
11   The Stern Review: www.hm-treasury.gov.uk/sternreview_index.htm accessed October 2008.

9 billion people live well, and within the limits of the planet.

World Business Council for Sustainable Development: Vision 2050
(www.wbcsd.org/vision2050.aspx)

Figure 8.1 Enough! One of the great installations at events by Tracey Shough of picapica (picapicastuff.blogspot.com). If you want thought-provoking installations about a huge range of sustainability topics, contact Tracey. Her work is seen at many events, including 'The Greenway' at Glastonbury Festival.

Photo by Meegan Jones.

8

PURCHASING AND RESOURCE USE

Purchasing and materials use are two powerful players in the overall and eventual sustainability of an event. A mountain of 'stuff' is needed to run most events, much with a once-only use. Purchase decisions are made throughout the event's entire life cycle and the right choices need to be made to reduce the impacts of consumption.

Events can play their part in resource conservation, reducing consumption, and product redesign, and I hope to inspire you to take these issues on board at your event.

Most events are for enjoyment, for entertainment, for celebration. And without celebration, an opportunity for release, expression and creativity, to share ideas, participate in sporting achievements or promote new concepts, what would we have?

No matter the reason for your event, there is a responsibility for event managers to purchase with sustainability in mind. Using recyclable materials, reuse, closing the loop and buying low-carbon products are all ways to reduce your purchasing. Choosing organic, buying Fairtrade, buying locally and ensuring workers' welfare are all steps along the sustainable procurement path.

Let us choose to use these products. Let us also redesign with end of life in mind. Let us close production

and disposal loops, and reduce the pressure on the earth to endlessly feed our appetite for more and more.

Products made sustainably and from renewable and sustainable materials are available for many event needs. Choose them and you push demand and encourage their continued development. Products with recyclable components, made from sustainable materials and whose processes close loops, are the end goal. Use timber from sustainably managed forests. Avoid PVC and non-organic cotton. Your paper can even be tree-free. Cleaning products shouldn't poison waterways.

This chapter discusses the way in which your purchasing decisions can be adjusted to produce more sustainable outcomes for your event, for the planet and for its inhabitants. We will delve into the detail of the impacts of consumption, including the concept of full life cycle analysis, and reveal some answers for environmental, ethical and socially responsible purchasing.

We will look at the environmental impacts of purchasing, including eco-labelling, organics, local procurement, sustainable agriculture and the climate impact of purchasing. We will also discuss supply chain management and how you can coax your existing suppliers towards more sustainable sourcing and operations.

The overarching considerations in purchasing should include asking the following questions:

1   Where did the product come from?
2   Who made the product?
3   What is it made of?
4   What does it come packaged in?
5   How will it be disposed of or could it be used again?

Event Purchasing Needs

So what materials, supplies and products do events use? Many are single use, disposed (or recycled) at the end of the event, and others are optimally reused, hired in or, if single use at the event, sent for salvage for others to use as-is or for repurposing. See Chapter 9 for more details on end-of-life alternatives than landfill for your single-use items. Event supplies include the following:

- event merchandise
- signage, décor, props and dressing
- paper and printing
- ticketing and wristbands
- timber, paint, cleaning products
- promo items, gifts, awards, giveaways
- food, beverage, drinking water
- food and beverage serviceware
- AV, infrastructure, staging
- fencing, barriers, scrim, masking.

Additional sourcing comes through the following:

- venues
- caterers
- stallholders/vendors
- service providers (security, cleaning)

PROCUREMENT HEALTH CHECK

1 Do you need it?

2 Can it be hired instead?

Can existing items be used? Can you hire or share instead of purchasing? With some extra organisation and people power, can you salvage, store and reuse materials from your event breakdown?

3 What sustainability credentials?

What is it made from? What are the labour conditions, toxicity, waste management, resource use, manufacturing process, raw material extraction? Is the product water intensive? Is the product energy intensive? Is the product independently eco-labelled? Does the product meet expected standards of manufacture, human rights, and responsible business practice? Is the product manufactured locally and made from local materials? Can the product be recycled? Is the product made from recycled materials?

4 Are you just creating waste-in-waiting?

Do you need to hand out thousands of promotional flyers, thereby creating more litter, when different advertising opportunities are available? Can you influence participants, delegates, exhibitors and traders to bring less disposable material to the event, thus both reducing consumption of resources and producing less waste? Are your activities buying into the one-way flow of resource use, consumption and disposal?

5 Encouraging consumerism?

Do you need to have vendors selling useless items? Are the event activities promoting needless consumption to your audience? Does product placement or sponsorship promote less than responsible brands?

6 Can you come up with a better way?

IMPACTS OF CONSUMPTION

The materials and supplies we use to organise events, especially those products with a one-way and short-lived lifespan, have the potential to contribute to resource depletion, toxicity, displacement of communities, being complicit in forced or child labour, or endorsing unsafe working conditions for those mining, harvesting or making your products.

Conversely, we have the opportunity through our purchasing decisions to support the proliferation of fairly traded products, great working conditions and fair pay. We can help reduce the use of toxic chemicals which persist and accumulate in nature, to support innovation in sustainable materials, help close the loop by using products designed for disassembly, repair or recycling, and to support communities through purchasing locally.

We're using more than our planet can give us, we're eating into our capital investment, earning no interest, and our nest egg is shrinking. The amount of products we personally buy in our lives, let alone in association with putting on events, is causing depleted resources, polluted waterways, and contributing to climate change.

The by-product of all of this consumption is waste. And waste equals climate change. The climate change potential of a one-way system of resource use, manufacture, transport, product consumption and disposal is immense. Every step along the way is potentially causing greenhouse gas emissions and the depletion of non-renewable resources. The demand for more products means more mining, more transport and more land clearing, all of which are contributors to climate change.

The backstory of every material or product can be a history of resource extraction, toxic waste, energy consumed and fuel burnt, snowballing waste at every step, and possibly a large number of underpaid workers, displaced communities and destroyed ecosystems.

Unless you dig into this shady history of the lovely fresh box of treats you've ordered for your event, you can very easily close your eyes to the likely consequences of your purchase decisions. It is hidden from you, hidden from view, and unless you question their origin and impacts, you'll never know.

Would you like to watch the backbreaking work of indentured labour in cocoa plantations, while snacking on a chocolate bar made from the product produced from their hard labour? If you went to the river and watched the toxic chemicals flow from a manufacturing plant, causing chaos downstream to ecosystems and human health, would you still buy their products? Could you stand in a factory among underpaid workers watching them produce the products for which you screwed your supplier down to their 'best price'?

Buying cheap and dirty is often a budget imperative of many event producers. Budgets are always tight and the lowest quote is often sought. But buying with consideration for protecting and sustaining natural resources and the people involved in the product's backstory means buying responsibly and buying well.

Do you want to vote with your dollars and help be the change or do you want to keep being cheap and dirty?

In summary the impacts of consumption and materials production are as follows:

* extraction/mining or growing raw materials
* water use
* energy use
* toxicity
* transport for every step
* consequences of disposal.

Life Cycle Impact

The bedrock of any sustainable purchasing decision has to be consideration for the full life cycle impact of the products used to produce the event, or indeed products sold, provided or promoted to attendees.

Every product leaves its mark on the environment from extraction of raw materials and their transport and processing, to the manufacturing, distribution, sale and use of the product, and its ultimate disposal or return to the manufacturing system through recycling. Every product also makes its mark on the community in which it was grown, mined or manufactured and on the workforce necessary for it to come into creation.

In these pioneering days of sustainable event management, the questioning and consideration of the full life cycle impact of products and materials, by event producers, is essential. Looking at the products you use or sell, the materials they're made from, the impact of their manufacture and the welfare of those who grow and manufacture them is necessary to make informed and responsible purchasing decisions.

By doing so you will be helping to green the event industry supply chain. You will also be helping to grow the market for sustainable alternatives and hopefully pushing out those products that are not doing so.

A Life Cycle Assessment (LCA) is a technique used to assess the environmental aspects and potential impacts associated with a material or product through all inter-linked stages, including the following:

- raw material extraction
- production of materials
- manufacture of parts and final products
- transport and distribution at each step
- product use
- materials recovery, reuse, recycling
- energy recovery and final disposal.

From an event procurement point of view, when making a judgement as to the best product to buy, you need to be looking out for the major issues and impacts with that area of the supply chain. Later in this chapter we will delve into the event industry's supply chain so that you will know what to look out for.

Footprinting

Footprinting is a popular concept. It allows you to visualise in physical proportions the impact of a particular product or activity by a given measure. When evaluating products and materials to purchase, you may wish to include the footprint lens so that you can assess competing products on their impacts. There are several common footprint types:

- **The Water Footprint:** the amount of water a material or product requires. Consider the thirstiness of various products and materials when making purchasing decisions;
- **The Carbon Footprint:** the total GHGs from power used and transport needed;
- **The Ecological Footprint:** the total equivalent bio-capacity a material or product needs to be created.

Read more about ecological footprinting in *WWF* and *Global Footprint Network*'s *Living Planet Report*.[1]

Water Footprint Network (www.waterfootprint.org) has published the water footprint of lots of products. The following calculation shows the litres of water needed to create some of your favourite things:

1 cup of tea = 30 litres of water
1 glass of beer = 74 litres of water
1 glass of wine = 110 litres of water
1 cup of coffee = 140 litres of water
1kg cane sugar = 210 litres of water
1 cotton shirt = 2500 litres of water
1kg rice = 2500 litres of water
1kg beef = 15,500 litres of water.

Figure 8.2 Buy less crap! Installation by Tracey Shough of picapica.

Source: Meegan Jones.

BUY LESS, BUY BETTER

Buying the most environmentally and socially responsible products for your event is all well and good, but we must also review just how much stuff is needed.

To achieve your budget goals and not enter into the cheap and dirty buying vortex you should consider the volume of stuff you need and work out ways in which you can reduce that hefty overhead. Using fewer resources creates impact reductions all along the lifecycle of a product.

There are many items at events that with a little forethought could be designed and handled in such a way as to prevent their re-purchase at the next event.

Many outdoor events, for example, put up temporary fencing and screen those fences off with 'scrim'. I constantly see this material ripped off fences and thrown into rubbish skips headed for landfill. It is true that at some types of events this stuff becomes the back wall of a urinal, and these areas should be identified, but across every outdoor event in every country of the world, just how many miles of eight-foot-high plastic fencing covering is being discarded? I think we could circumnavigate the globe with it!

Signage is a similar story. Design way-finding signage without logos, date or sponsor details, which otherwise renders the signs disposable after a single use. Design branded signage so that dates and sponsor logos are replaceable each year.

In lean times, most event managers would be looking at their line items and working out how they can make savings, and where expenditure on printed materials becomes a focus we can see a positive sustainability outcome as well (as long as the solution isn't to go cheap and dirty). But how many events have you been involved where litter-producing promotional flyers have been handed out, or where boxes of programmes and posters are left over at the end of the event?

Think seriously about the volume of printed materials you order, or you allow to be distributed.

Vendors selling (or sponsors giving away) silly, useless, gimmicky and single-use items have to be stopped. Are you just encouraging mindless consumption by allowing this waste-in-waiting to be sold or handed out? At exhibitions, this is at crisis point. Exhibition organisers need to work with exhibitors to encourage more experiential or entertaining brand demonstration or activation. Certainly, if things must be given away, it should be a sample of the product (in minimal packaging) rather than a gimmicky item with a logo printed on it, or huge amounts of printed material when an email can mean information provided electronically.

Look seriously at your purchasing habits. It is very easy to detach from the reality of purchasing when you are using someone else's money, and the only thing between you and the production of thousands of dollars' worth of materials is a purchase order.

Understand that every 'OK' on a purchase order means the mining of resources, transport and manufacture, energy consumed, greenhouse gas emissions and waste created.

Reducing the amount of stuff means great sustainability benefits. Consider the following outcomes if you use less:

✓ money saved;
✓ renewable and non-renewable resources conserved;
✓ water and energy use reduced during the extracting, growing and manufacturing of the material or product;
✓ less toxic substances used or released, such as chemical fertiliser, toxic additives, chlorine (bleaching), inks or dyes, and less toxic substances released upon disposal where they may leach into ground water through landfills;
✓ fewer emissions to air and water from manufacturing processes;
✓ reduced waste to landfill.

There are some great sustainable procurement resources available online. Look in your country or even your specific city to find supplier databases. The *Sustainable Event Alliance* has a growing database of event-specific sustainable solutions – it is crowd-sourced, so if you find a good solution and want to share it with the industry, suggest it for listing.

The *Australian Green Procurement Database* is a free resource of environmentally preferable products and services available in Australia (www.greenprocurement.org.au). *GoodGuide* provides authoritative information about the health, environmental and social performance of products and companies. Search or browse over 145,000 foods, toys, personal care and household products to learn about the best and worst products in a category (www.goodguide.com).

Conscious Consumption

Making conscious purchasing decisions is extremely important. Take time to think through and investigate the upstream impacts of your intended purchases, along with the consequential end-of-life disposal.

Ask the following questions when making a procurement decision (for your event or in everyday life!):

- Is this item produced in line with the sustainability principles and values of the organisation?
- Will our purchase decision support the local economy?
- Are the people who produce the item treated and compensated fairly?
- Is this item built to last, can we reuse it, or is there an end-of-life strategy for it which is not disposal?
- Are there better alternatives to this item?

Boom Festival in Portugal is a logo-free consumption environment. This encourages a culture of change, conscience and responsibility. The food establishments at the festival are rigorously selected in order to provide the best quality and diversity, but, above all, healthy choices. A great part of the Boom economy is based on human creativity and the concept of bioregionalism, which also strengthens the local economy (www.boom festival.org).

Burning Man is money free. The *Burning Man* event advocates gifting and decommodification as essential aspects of the community experience. Everyone comes armed with the 'stuff' they are willing to gift. Strangers are invited to share food, and no money exchanges hands. You give to someone and another person gives to you. Food, jewellery, bikes. Beautiful. "*In order to preserve the spirit of gifting, our community seeks to create social environments that are unmediated by commercial sponsorships, transactions, or advertising. We stand ready to protect our culture from such exploitation. We resist the substitution of consumption for participatory experience*" (www.burningman.com).

Evaluating Options

In order to make informed, fair and justifiable sourcing decisions, you must create an evaluation process and establish tools which your team can use. Your sourcing choices must in the first place be as follows:

- fit for purpose (the item must do what you need it to do, and be of the quality or standard you require);
- be delivered on time, from reliable suppliers;
- be budget appropriate.

And then we bring in sustainability requirements.

To make sourcing decisions that reflect your organisation's sustainability principles and policy, evaluation tools should be developed to act as decision filters and justification devices for event purchasing decisions.

These tools can include aspects which are mandatory for specific areas of the supply chain, or a set of requirements from which just some must be in place.

In addition, you could impose a dollar value or proportion of total budget, over which a specific level of detailed supply chain scrutiny must be instigated.

Tools to make the best sourcing decisions and through which to establish tender specifications may include the following:

- life cycle analysis impacts of materials and products;
- a scoring system which weights various requirements, such as local, certified, specific material, etc.;
- establishing a supplier code of conduct for your organisation against which many aspects of the potential product or supplier is evaluated.

PROCUREMENT CHECKLIST

Box 8.1

PROCUREMENT CHECKLIST

Reducing Consumption

- ❏ Do you need it?
- ❏ Can it be hired instead?
- ❏ Are you just creating waste-in-waiting?
- ❏ Are your activities buying into the one-way flow of resource use, consumption and disposal?
- ❏ Do your purchase decisions add to the depletion of resources and creation of pollution?
- ❏ Is the product reusable or more durable?
- ❏ Are the activities/giveaways/merchandise promoting thoughtless consumption?
- ❏ Do the product placement or sponsorship deals you have promote less than responsible brands?
- ❏ Strategies to avoid unnecessary consumption and manage demand are in place.
- ❏ The purchase of single-use promotional items is reduced or eliminated.

Product/Supplier Scrutiny

- ❏ A budgetary figure over which scrutiny of sustainability credentials of all materials and supplies procured is undertaken.
- ❏ Companies/products with sustainability policies are chosen.
- ❏ Products chosen have achieved relevant eco-label certification.
- ❏ Where no eco-label is available, suppliers chosen have sustainability credentials and claims.
- ❏ Tenders include sustainability requirements in specifications.

Product Footprints

- ❏ What distance do raw materials and products have to travel from point of extraction or harvesting, to production facilities, to distribution networks and to the end user?
- ❏ Does the product have a large carbon, water or chemical footprint (from its manufacture)?
- ❏ Does the product contribute to energy or water efficiency through its use?

Materials

- ❏ What are the product's sustainability credentials?
- ❏ Does the product meet the relevant eco-labelling certification?
- ❏ What is the product's life cycle impact from the extraction or growing of raw materials through to disposal?
- ❏ Is it made from recycled materials or sustainably produced materials?

Disposal Planning

- ❏ What is the end-of-life plan for the product? Can it be recycled, reused, composted or returned to the manufacturer, closing the loop?
- ❏ Is any special handling in its disposal necessary?

Socio-economic Impacts

- ❏ What is the impact on community and neighbours of the mining, growing or manufacture of materials and products?
- ❏ How are workers treated and producers paid?
- ❏ A waste audit is undertaken to establish the waste streams present and any contamination and non-compliance with initiatives.
- ❏ Total waste diverted from landfill or incineration is reported.
- ❏ Total waste per person per day is reported.

Box 8.1 (continued)

Reporting

❏ Percentage of local procurement.
❏ Percentage of procurement from companies with sustainability policies.
❏ Percentage of procurement from companies/products with sustainability certification (eco-labels).
❏ Percentage of printing from companies with *ISO 14001* or green printing eco-label.

❏ Percentage of paper from sustainable sources.
❏ Percentage of total timber used with FSC or similar chain of custody certification.
❏ Percentage of environmentally preferable cleaning products used with eco-labels.
❏ Total hotel nights and percentage with sustainability credentials.

Greenwashing

When deciding to 'go green' in your purchasing you will need to be aware of 'greenwashing'. This is where companies appropriate terms such as 'eco', 'natural', 'green', 'biological', but don't have any evidence to back up their claims. Scrutinise the claims and ask questions if companies are vague or have no apparent certification.

In an effort to describe, understand and quantify the growth of greenwashing, in 2007 *UL Environment* conducted research into product labelling claims, and as a result created the *Six (now Seven!) Sins of Greenwashing*.

To create this great set of sins, they surveyed a sample of US and Canadian consumer retail stores in 2007 and again in 2009 to assess the number of products making environmental claims and committing sins! In the 2010 report they identified that a whopping 95 per cent were committing at least one of the sins of greenwashing.

The number of actual products making environmental claims also increased by 73 per cent for each of their surveys. The final survey in 2010 noted a total of 4,744 products making 'green' claims.

They also discovered that legitimate eco-labelling was on the rise with almost a quarter of all products making 'green' claims being independently certified (up from 13.7 per cent in the 2007 research). In addition, and encouragingly, products that are actually 'sin-free' in their claims had risen to almost 4.5 per cent.[2]

There's still a long way to go, but consumers are voting with their dollars. They are demanding 'green' products and they are becoming more astute in scrutinising claims and sniffing out a greenwash.

UL Environment's goal of putting practical tools in the hands of consumers and companies to scrutinise claims and to encourage and reward genuine efforts towards sustainable innovation is clearly being achieved.

LABELLING AND CERTIFICATION

Looking for products or services with independent product labelling or certification will help ensure your procurement decisions are as environmentally and socially responsible as possible.

Certification, or labelling, identifies the sustainability attributes or credentials of a product or service. It is voluntary and includes independent assessment and confirmation against criteria specified by the certification programme.

As discussed in the earlier section on greenwashing, certifications and labelling are more than just a self-claim or statement of credentials; they are a rigorous programme of independent scrutiny and performance disclosure. Certification and labelling programmes can be environmentally focused, look at fair labour practices, fair prices paid to producers, or holistic sustainability performance. The challenge with certification and labelling programmes is that there are so many of them. In the following pages I hope to clarify the types of programmes and how to sort out which ones are reputable.

Box 8.2

SEVEN SINS OF GREENWASHING

Sin of the Hidden Trade-off

For example: Paper from sustainably managed forests which is still chlorine bleached or organic produce yet flown halfway across the world.

Sin of No Proof

For example: Cleaning claiming to be 'eco-friendly', but with no verifiable information, or 'recycled' paper with no evidence of source or content of material.

Sin of Vagueness

For example: Products claiming to be 100 per cent natural when many naturally occurring substances are hazardous, such as arsenic and formaldehyde.

Sin of Worshipping False Labels

Products that have images of 'nature' or whales and such, giving an impression of certification.

Sin of Irrelevance

Claims that are truthful but irrelevant. For example: Products claiming to be CFC-free, but CFCs are banned already.

Sin of Lesser of Two Evils

For example: Organic cigarettes or 'environmentally friendly' pesticides.

Sin of Fibbing

For example: Products falsely claiming to be certified by internationally recognised environmental standards.

sinsofgreenwashing.org/
findings/the-seven-sins

© 2009 UL LLC Reprinted with permission.

Eco-labelling

Eco-labelling is the generic term given to certification programmes, focused primarily on environmental sustainability. There are three types of eco-labels:

1   **Type I** eco-labels are voluntary third-party certifications based on multiple environmental criteria. Type 1 eco-labels should be in compliance with *ISO 14024*.
2   **Type II** eco-labels are informative self-declarations such as biodegradability claims. Type 2 eco-labels are informed by *ISO 14021*. Governments may also regulate what is allowed to be claimed. For example, in Australia the Trade Practices Act regulates this.
3   **Type III** eco-labels are voluntary product information labels that provide environmental data on a product, and which are independently verified and based on life cycle assessments (the process of which would adhere to *ISO 14040*).

Type I eco-labels are often nation-based, covering a range of products, and the country concerned will most likely have just one pre-eminent programme. There are also sector-specific or issue-specific certification programmes, such as for chemical use, rainforest protection, timber, paper, energy efficiency or carbon labelling. Food-based eco-labels include organic or sustainable farming practices.

The common goal of eco-labelling organisations based in each country is to establish third-party environmental performance recognition, certification and labelling.

Many products have 'green' symbols or 'claim statements' developed by the manufacturers themselves, often misleading consumers. In contrast, third-party certifying processes award eco-labels, so making buying environmentally preferable products all the easier.

Check that the Type I eco-label is a member of the *Global Ecolabelling Network (GEN)*, the association of certifying organisations from various countries. The range of product categories that are covered by eco-labelling includes batteries, burners/boilers, cleaning, clothing/textiles, construction/building, home appliances, home care products, lights, office equipment/furniture, office supplies, packaging/containers, paper products, inks, personal care products, services, solar energy, vehicles, fuels, water-saving, food, plants, and adhesives (www.globalecolabelling.net).

Moving from these general nationwide cross-sector eco-labels to sector-specific certifications, we see eco-labels on items such as timber, rainforest products, food, seafood and chemicals.

To review the full breadth of eco-labels possible, visit the *Ecolabel Index* to search for programmes relevant to your region and area of the supply chain you are interested in (www.ecolabelindex.com).

Shortly we will be delving into the detail of sustainable procurement for various areas of the event industry supply chain and may also mention relevant certification programmes or labels there as well.

As well as an environmental focus, ensure ethically and socially responsible purchasing in association with your event. For broader sustainability certifications and labelling programmes, check to see if they are members of the *International Social and Environmental Accreditation and Labelling Alliance* (ISEAL) (www.isealalliance.org).

Carbon Labelling

It is useful to understand the GHG impacts of the materials and products you are considering procuring, so look out for those whose carbon footprint measurement has been independently assessed and that offers transparent information on their energy and transport impacts.

The *Carbon Reduction Label* is an initiative of the *Carbon* Trust (UK). It allows businesses to communicate with consumers that they have made a commitment to reduce their product's carbon footprint and how their product's carbon footprint compares with other products within the same category. This label is also found in Australia and is in partnership with *Planet Ark* (www.carbon-label.com).

Fair Trade

It is likely that you will have heard of the fair trade concept, and have seen various symbols on products on the supermarket shelf. Goods such as tea, coffee, sugar, bananas, honey, cotton and rice are the prominent product ranges that are part of fair trade producer schemes. The concept of fair trade expands further than primary agricultural production and also includes handicrafts, clothing and goods made by artisans in the developing world.

The guarantee of a fair price paid creates opportunities for economically disadvantaged producers or those marginalised by the conventional trading system, and empowers them to achieve economic self-sufficiency, becoming stakeholders in their own enterprises. Apart from these economic considerations the movement promotes sustainability and environmental sensitivity, fair work conditions, ensures that women's work is properly valued and rewarded, and makes sure that participating organisations respect the *UN Convention on the Rights of the Child*.[3]

Fairtrade International owns the *Fairtrade Mark*, which certifies that products meet the Fairtrade Standards. Its member organisations promote *Fairtrade* in their countries on a national basis (www.fairtrade.net).

World Fair Trade Association's (WFTO) mission is to enable producers to improve their livelihoods and communities through fair trade. In order to receive the WFTO Mark, organisations must pass through their monitoring system which embeds the '*10 Standards of Fair Trade*' (www.wfto.com).

The *Ethical Trading Initiative* is a leading alliance of companies, trade unions and non-governmental organisations (NGOs) that work together to improve the lives of workers around the world (www.ethicaltrade.org).

Fair Labour

Integral to sustainable production is concern for the labour conditions of those working in the world's factories and on farms. Fair labour certifications, programmes and associations exist to regulate and monitor working conditions.

The *Fair Labor Organisation* creates lasting solutions to abusive labour practices by offering tools and resources to companies, delivering training to factory workers and management, conducting due diligence through independent assessments, and advocating for greater accountability and transparency from companies, manufacturers, factories and others involved in global supply chains (www.fairlabor.org).

The *International Labour Organisation (ILO)* is devoted to advancing opportunities for people to obtain decent and productive work in conditions of freedom, equity, security and human dignity. Its main aims are to promote rights at work, encourage decent employment opportunities, enhance social protection and strengthen dialogue in handling work-related issues (www.ilo.org).

Worldwide Responsible Accredited Production (WRAP) is the world's largest facility certification programme focused mainly on the apparel, footwear and sewn products sectors. It is dedicated to the certification of lawful, humane and ethical manufacturing throughout the world (www.wrapapparel.org).

The *Fair Wear Foundation* supports and promotes good labour conditions in garment production. The foundation was set up by various organisations, NGOs and trade unions related to the fashion industry. The *Fair Wear Foundation* verifies whether companies comply with its *Code of Labour Practices* (www.fairwear.org).

The *Clean Clothes Campaign* (CCC) takes action on specific issues related to unfair labour conditions. The CCC brings together consumers, trade unions, campaign groups and other diverse organisations to exert pressure at all levels of supply chains, calling on those with the power in global supply chains to take responsibility for workers' rights (www.cleanclothes.org).

TIMBER PRODUCTS

Events use timber for building and construction, set design, décor, fencing, staging, signage and outdoor furniture, right down to woodchip on the ground. We also use a massive amount of paper and cardboard for promotional and communications material, packaging and displays.

The challenge with timber is that once logged and moved from its original forest, it is very difficult to identify not only whether it has been sustainably produced, but whether it was legally logged at all.

Chain of custody is key in timber and paper sourcing, to have an unbroken line of assurance that the timber or paper was indeed sustainably harvested and produced. Other issues include the toxic substances used in making composite timber products. For paper, additional issues include how the paper was bleached (with or without chlorine). The amount of travel involved from tree to mill to manufacture to distributor to you is also a factor to consider in your timber and paper product purchasing choices.

The only way to be sure that the timber or timber products aren't from old growth virgin forests and possibly logged illegally is to purchase certified forest products. Illegal or poorly managed forests ruin ecosystems, deplete biodiversity and displace communities, preventing the self-sufficiency of indigenous people depending on the forest for their survival.

Forest depletion and degradation also has a climate change impact with the conversion of forests to agricultural land, illegal logging and forest fires accounting for nearly 20 per cent of global greenhouse gas emissions – more than the entire global transportation sector.[4]

Greenpeace reports that an estimated 80 per cent of the world's forests have already been either destroyed or degraded, and half of that has occurred in the past 30 years.[5] The world needs forests to survive. Its lungs are being chopped out by our insatiable desire for timber products, copy paper, toilet paper and new furniture.

The demands for timber and paper are not the only motivators for forest destruction. Our thirst for palm oil (in products and in biofuels) is also fuelling the destruction of forests with palm oil plantations going up in their place. Soya bean farms are also replacing forests to churn out the feed for chickens that in turn feed our fast food appetite.

The reality is that the human race does need the products that forests can provide, and sustainable forestry management is the solution. This ensures that forests are managed in such a way that natural resources are extracted without negative environmental, societal, economic or cultural impacts.

In 1993, *Forest Europe*, the pan-European political process for the sustainable management of the continent's forests, created the term which is commonly accepted as the definition of sustainable forestry management and which many independent certifications take as their core principles. Their definition is: *"The stewardship and use of forests and forest lands in a way, and at a rate, that maintains their biodiversity, productivity, regeneration capacity, vitality and their potential to fulfil, now and in the future, relevant ecological, economic and social functions, at local, national, and global levels, and that does not cause damage to other ecosystems"* (www.foresteurope.org).

If you use timber or timber products, make sure that they originate from forests that have been sustainably managed. Better still, use reclaimed timber. *Greenpeace* in Australia has produced a guide to help consumers find Good Wood coming from ethical and ecologically sustainable sources (www.goodwoodguide.org.au).

MDF and Particleboard

Medium Density Fibreboard (MDF) is a wood-based sheet material which is versatile and considerably cheaper than plywood, making it a very popular product. MDF is what I call the 'devon' of the timber world. Those of you who grew up in Australia will know what I mean: 'devon' is a pressed meat made with goodness knows what, mushed together to form a vaguely pale represen-tation of meat. So it is with MDF: it is a combination of soft and hard timber particles blended with synthetic adhesive resins, including formaldehyde.

A coarser version is particleboard. Its versatility also makes it a popular material for quick turnaround, and for relatively cheap timber props and sets. The issues with particleboard are the chain of custody of the timber used to make the board – it needs to be from sustainable forests or preferably from post-industrial recycled timber.

The opposing issues with these materials is that they are great for temporary set and prop construction, and MDF is particularly good for cutting intricate shapes; however, through the cutting process, tiny formaldehyde and synthetic resin-laden wood dust particles are released. This is extremely hazardous to human health, both through contact with skin and inhalation. For this reason strict controls are placed around acceptable levels of formaldehyde in MDF and particleboard, and in the materials handling and dust extraction procedures in workshops. This is great for those countries that have systems allowing for such controls to be implemented and monitored. This is mainly confined to carpentry and woodworking shops. On event sites it is possible that extraction fans and personal protective equipment may not be used. In addition, as soon as the material is used for a second purpose, often by non-professionals, knowl-edge about the hazards of safely handling and cutting this material will be quickly lost.

If you have to use MDF or particleboard, look for products with no added formaldehyde and that are made from 100 per cent post-industry recycled timber. *Medex®*[6] is such an example for MDF. In the USA, the *Composite Panel Association* has a 'green' standard, so look for materials meeting their requirements. Search for similar certifications or standards for these composite materials in your country (www.compositepanel.org/standards/).

X-Board

With approximately 2.5 million × 40ft shipping containers of resin-bonded MDF and particleboard consumed globally each year, much of which ends up in landfill within 10 to 15 years, looking to more sustainable options is important.[7] X-board is a brilliant temporary construction material and signage option all in one. It's a natural fibre-based sandwich board with an internal core made from post-consumer recycled kraft paper and agricultural waste. This innovative product may be used instead of MDF or particleboard, and is a super-lightweight, energy-efficient and formaldehyde-free. These panels are coated with thin decorative surface skins. Perfect for mobile displays, if handled well it may be used many times before being completely recyclable (www.xanita.com).

Timber Certification

Certification programmes enable you to have confidence in the chain of custody of timber and paper products you purchase. There are many sustainable forest programmes, with *Programme for the Endorsement of Forest Certification* (PEFC) and *Forest Stewardship Council* (FSC) being two independent globally recognised programmes.

Rather than being a certification, PEFC is a standard that verifies the quality of national forestry certification schemes. With about 30 national forest certification systems endorsed by PEFC and a total of more than 240 million hectares of certified forests globally, PEFC is the world's largest forest certification system (www.pefc.org).

The FSC certificate scheme offers chain-of-custody certification of timber, from forests to mills and final sale (ic.fsc.org).

Other sustainable forestry programmes include the *Sustainable Forestry Initiative* (www.sfiprogram.org) and national programmes such as the *Australian Forestry Standard* (www.forestrystandard.org.au). A country's national standards body may also have a sustainable forestry standard such as the *Canadian Standards Association's National Sustainable Forest Management Standard*.[8]

The *Rainforest Alliance* also works in sustainable forestry certification, as one of the founders of the Forest Stewardship Council and currently the world's

Figure 8.3 FSC timber used for onsite construction of the Greenpeace installation at Glastonbury Festival.
Source: Meegan Jones.

PAPER

A few major players control the retail paper market; cheaper paper is demanded by customers, and in order to keep the competitive edge, retailers pressure paper manufacturers to supply cheap paper. Cheap paper means the cheapest form of fibre (trees), and cheap processing means using chlorine or chlorine derivative bleaching (bad) as opposed to oxygen bleaching (good).

Most people think of 'recycled' paper being made from the paper you use, place in the recycling bin, and then it makes its way back into the recycling system as a secondary raw material. When choosing recycled paper you should be careful of 'recycled' claims, as there are actually three categories of paper that may be used as feedstock for making recycled paper:

1   **Post-consumer recycled:** The optimal recycled paper, it is made from paper discarded after being used in the home or office. It is what most people think of when talking about paper recycling.
2   **Pre-consumer recycled:** This is produced from paper discarded before it reaches homes and offices, such as print overruns, misprints, damaged or unsold stock, etc.
3   **Mill broke:** This is paper trimmings and scrap from the actual manufacture of paper, and is recycled internally within the mill, but sometimes branded as 'recycled'.

Many papers are blends of virgin paper and recycled content, and that's OK, as paper cannot be recycled indefinitely. The general thinking is that virgin paper can be recycled four to seven times, as the fibres are weakened and shortened with each reprocessing. Make sure the virgin pulp used in your mixed recycle and virgin paper is sustainably sourced, and choosing *Forest Stewardship Council* certified paper is a way of doing this.

Does Recycling Save Trees?

It is difficult to quantify the 'number of trees saved due to recycling', as demand for paper is growing with population growth and trees are used for many non-paper purposes. So a figure of 'this many trees were cut down

Figure 8.4 Forest destruction in Weld Valley, Tasmania.
Source: Danny Kennedy.

leading FSC certifier of forestlands. When consumers see the *Forest Stewardship Council* logo coupled with the *Rainforest Alliance Certified*™ seal on products and packaging, they know that the timber or product they are buying comes from forests that have met rigorous standards for protecting forestlands, communities and wildlife (www.rainforest-alliance.org/work/forestry).

✓   Use reclaimed timber rather than new timber.
✓   Use timber with the most credible independent sustainable forestry certification relevant to your region.
✓   Upon completion of your event, if you cannot deconstruct and store for reuse, de-nail and send to a timber salvage yard for reclamation.
✓   If timber cannot be salvaged, send it for recycling.
✓   Ensure pallets are reclaimed rather than disposed of.

to produce that amount of paper' is an impossible figure to confirm. Recycling does extend the life of the total yield of each tree, and that's a good thing. It takes some of the pressure off forests.

One of the main benefits of recycling and using recycled paper is to reduce volume of waste sent to landfill or for incineration, thus reducing greenhouse gas emissions potential. By reducing the demand for virgin pulp, recycling also reduces the energy and fossil fuels needed in planting and maintaining forests, harvesting, transport and milling.

LCA of Virgin vs. Recycled

What about the life cycle assessment comparison between virgin and 100 per cent post-consumer waste paper? There are many factors to consider when looking at this, as the location of the plantation, mill, recycling processing facilities, distribution centre, end user and waste channels all need to be considered and will be different for every single brand of paper.

The *Environmental Paper Network*, a coalition of over 100 non-profit organisations, have created the *Paper Calculator* which uses industry averages to calculate life cycle assessments (c.environmentalpaper.org). The main figures it drills down to are timber used, water used and GHGs emitted. When entering 1 tonne of virgin paper versus 1 tonne of 100 per cent post-consumer waste paper into the calculator, these are the resulting figures:

- virgin paper uses 4 tonnes of wood to produce 1 tonne of paper, whereas 100 per cent recycled uses none;
- virgin paper production uses over 50 per cent more water than 100 per cent recycled paper does;
- virgin paper production creates 1197kg more GHGs than 100 per cent recycled does.

Paper Tissue Issues!

According to the WWF, every day about 270,000 trees are flushed down the drain or end up as garbage all over the world.[9] At events we have quite a few 'tissue issues' – toilet paper, paper hand towels, serviettes and kitchen paper towels. If you scrutinise your paper tissue product's backstory, you will likely find that tissues are made from virgin paper stock, possibly from unknown forest sources, and unless requested specifically, are likely to have no recycled content, and chlorine bleached to the whitest of white.

In March 2012, the WWF launched a campaign asking 20 US grocery chains believed to be the top buyers of toilet paper connected to tiger forest destruction to remove a specific brand of toilet paper from their shelves. The brand in question was known to be made from fibre supplied by a paper-pulping company causing rain forest destruction in Sumatra. The WWF reports that this company and its affiliates have pulped more than five million acres of natural forests in Sumatra, land that is essential to the survival of tigers and other species.[10]

Thousands of WWF supporters spoke up and took action in support of this campaign, and as a result 17 of the 20 companies removed the brand from their shelves. This was followed by a decision by the manufacturer to stop selling the toilet paper brand across the United States. Win. If you're looking for the right toilet tissue for your event, check out the great guide on the WWF website (wwf.panda.org/how_you_can_help/live_green/fsc/tissue_issues/tissue_brands/).

What does this mean for events?

Consider whether your event has tissue issues! Can you track and declare the sustainable origins of the toilet paper, hand towels and serviettes you provide? If not, consider the bad PR that could occur if a motivated event attendee questions your tissue sourcing. Don't stop at sustainable sourcing for your printed promotional materials – consider your tissue issues too!

Tree-free Papers

Trees are not the only material that paper can be made from. The relatively lower fibre content and higher lignin content of wood pulp is reputed to make this a less efficient option than many other quick-growing crops.

Until the mid-1800s all paper was produced with agricultural fibres, not wood. This included rags and fabric scraps along with purpose-grown crops and agricultural waste by-products. Even today, much of the paper produced in China and India is made from crops such as wheat straw, rice straw and sugar cane bagasse.

Paper may be made from cotton, a plant similar to cotton called kenaf, from hemp, recycled sugar cane fibre, and myriad other fibres used in the specialty paper market such as tobacco, coffee, and even elephant poo!

As some tree-free alternatives are cropped and need land allocated for their growth, the environmentally preferable option may be to use agricultural waste and residues as source fibre. These pulps may be combined with recycled paper fibres or with sustainable virgin wood pulp to make conventional papers such as photocopying paper, coated papers for magazines and programmes, as well as newsprint or high-end specialty papers.

A tree's longer growth cycle creates biodiversity, sequesters carbon and uses fewer chemical fertilisers. Deciding on which is the most environmentally preferable option is a difficult decision. It is one of those grey areas and one to keep an eye on as the industry progresses.

Sugar Cane/Bagasse Paper

Bagasse is the fibrous residue left over after sugar cane has been crushed and the sugar removed. It is an agricultural by-product that would otherwise most likely be burnt (sometimes for energy). It is used widely and is the world's most popular non-tree fibre.

In fact in India, the nation's largest paper producer *Tamil Nadu Newsprint and Paper Company* makes paper primarily from bagasse using as little wood as possible (www.tnpl.com).

Look out for the bagasse copy paper brands *Canefields* (www.canefields.asia) and *Eco-Paper* (www.ecopaper. com). *Eco-Paper* also produces paper made from 10 per cent banana or mango fibre mixed with post-consumer waste paper.

Enquire of your printing company if sugar cane fibre/bagasse paper stock is available for your printing requirements, as several paper companies supply 100 per cent or blends.

Cotton Fibre Paper

The benefit of using cotton for paper is that the fibres are almost pure cellulose, compared with trees, which are almost half. Fewer chemicals are needed to produce cotton paper; however, cotton is a chemical and water-intensive agricultural process, and that needs to be considered when looking at full-life cycle impact.

Kenaf Paper

Kenaf is a plant related to cotton and okra and originated in Africa. Its fibres are similar to wood fibres. It is fast growing, pulping requires less energy, heat and time than wood pulp, and it's easily bleached with chlorine-free processes. Keep an eye out for this as a non-tree paper alternative.

Hemp and Flax Papers

Hemp is fast growing, has a natural resistance to pests and out-competes weeds, so there is the dual reduction in necessity for herbicides and pesticides, which is a very good thing. Its high fibre yield as compared to wood means that its pulping is less energy intensive. The length and strength of flax fibres also make it an optimal paper source.

Hemp Heritage paper, by *Greenfield Paper Company*, may be purchased by the ream as copy paper. It is made in the USA by pulping Canadian-grown hemp fibre blended with post-consumer waste (www.greenfield paper.com).

Ask your printing company if hemp or flax fibre papers are available for your print job.

Bamboo Paper

Bamboo is a sustainable and renewable resource. It's fast growing, doesn't use pesticides or fertilisers, and needs little water for growth. It is still a speciality paper and not widely available, but one to watch.

Wheat Sheet

Paper made from wheat straw pulp is produced primarily in China and India, and now in Canada. Any country that produces massive amounts of wheat straw waste could be creating this paper. Look out for *Nature's Paper*, 100 per cent wheat paper (natureintl.com) and Canada's *Step Forward Paper*™ (stepforwardpaper.com).

Paper Bleaching

Another consideration in choosing your paper stock is the process through which it is bleached. Wide-scale bleaching using chlorine decreased in the 1980s and 1990s when it was discovered that a by-product of this bleaching was the production of dioxin, a highly toxic and carcinogenic substance. There are several bleaching options to look out for.

Elemental Chlorine Free (ECF)

ECF papers are made from pulp that has been bleached using derivatives of chlorine such as chlorine dioxide or other chemicals, but in the absence of pure chlorine. The chlorine derivatives used in ECF papers, while less harmful than elemental chlorine, still produce toxic compounds such as chloroform, and these may be released into waterways to do their damage.

Totally Chlorine Free (TCF)

If using a virgin pulp paper, TCF is what you want your paper to be, with it either oxygen bleached or not bleached at all.

Processed Chlorine Free (PCF)

Recycled papers from mixed sources, bleached in the absence of chlorine or its derivatives, are known as PCF. As recycled paper is produced from all types of recycled content, some of which could have originally been chlorine or ECF bleached papers, they cannot be totally chlorine free.

TCF or PCF are the most environmentally preferable alternative for paper bleaching, and what you should look out for when choosing a paper, depending on whether you are buying paper made from virgin or recycled pulp.

Unbleached

You can also make a strong point through your communications material and use unbleached stock. *Ecocern* has a fantastic unbleached 100 per cent post-consumer waste paper with a natural brown colour. It is available in Australia but there will be similar products in your country (www.ecocern.com.au).

Paper Certification

To make the best paper decision, you should refer to independent certification. As for timber, chain of custody is important. Paper certification comes in several varieties:

- sustainable forestry/origin of timber
- percentage of recycled content
- chlorine free.

The *Forest Stewardship Council* (FSC) certificate scheme offers chain-of-custody certification of timber and paper pulp, from forests, to mills and factories, printing companies and final paper products (ic.fsc.org). Certification labelling includes the following:

- 100 per cent from 'well-managed forests';
- a percentage content from post-consumer recycled paper and well-managed forests;
- 'mixed sources', which includes the previous two plus 'controlled sources', meaning forests which have been screened as not having harmful impacts but which have not received full FSC certification.

In the absence of formal regulation, some countries' paper associations have developed 'recycled marks' which inform the consumer about the percentage of recycled paper content. In the UK the *National Association of Paper Merchants* (NAPM) has a recycled mark that informs the purchaser of 50 per cent, 75 per cent or 100 per cent recycled content. Look for the recycled mark in your country and choose to use 100 per cent. The *Chlorine Free Products Association* offers certification for paper bleached without the use of chlorine.

PRINTING

Printing for an event can include promotional posters and flyers, event programme booklets, tickets, vehicle passes, onsite newspapers and publications, plus various forms and documents.

Many participants such as exhibitors and sponsors may also print specific items in association with the event.

The production of printed material has potential sustainability issues that need to be considered and the best choices made. Apart from the choice of paper (discussed earlier), printing issues include inks and varnishes used, print company processes and policies, plus the location of the print company and consequential transport impacts.

Vegetable Inks

Printing inks are made up of pigment for colour, liquid that carries the pigment and which evaporates, and other resins and polymers that make it stick to the paper. The problem with traditional inks is the emission of 'volatile organic compounds' (VOCs) and potential toxicity of the residue in the clean-up process.

The liquid used in traditional inks (mineral oil) is petroleum based, a non-renewable resource, and in the drying process the petroleum and alcohol components evaporate releasing VOCs. In addition, traditional inks need solvents in the clean-up process that cause a further release of VOCs.

VOCs are harmful to humans if inhaled excessively or trapped indoors. The clean-up process needed when using traditional mineral inks also requires solvents.

'Vegetable inks' instead use vegetable oil, which creates significantly lower VOCs, and the clean-up process may be done with water rather than with more solvents.

It is also a good idea to avoid metallic colours as they contain metallic particles that upon disposal of the waste ink cannot be recycled. Also avoid fluorescent colours, as they comprise toxic compounds and, if they eventually end up in landfill, may add to the creation of toxic releases from landfill into the water table.

Biodegradable Laminate

Many printed items have a gloss finish. This is called 'Gloss OPP' (oriented polypropylene) lamination. Traditionally, this gloss finish is made from petrochemicals, and as it is a 'plastic' it will not readily biodegrade or be able to be recycled with the paper.

The use of a gloss finish is often an important part of the finished job, but there are gloss 'laminate' finishes that may be recycled with the rest of the paper, and also will biodegrade if sent for composting.

The benefit of this is the production of printed material without using non-renewable resources, and you can be confident when ready to be disposed of that your posters, flyers and programmes will be composted or recycled effectively.

The benefit to your printing company is that any trim which comes off finished jobs can be kept with the rest of the paper scraps and not contaminate their in-house recycling systems. *CelloGreen*, a wood-based laminate, is a great example (www.celloglas.co.uk).

Low VOC Varnish

Varnishes also offer a gloss or matt finish and are usually applied to print jobs that need extra durability or longevity. They coat the paper and protect it from scratches, finger prints, scuff marks, etc.

Varnishes are applied during the printing process just like ink, and are generally solvent based and thus emit VOCs. The most environmentally friendly option is to use a vegetable-based or water-based varnish, or in fact no varnish at all. If you've found a printer who will use vegetable inks, asking for a vegetable- or water-based varnish should be no problem.

Printing Certification

Printing certification comes in several forms:

- **ISO 14001** – this is where the print company has conformed to the requirements of this international standard on environmental management systems. This means that the printing company has procedures and processes in place to identify and manage potential environmental impacts of its printing operations. This should be a minimum requirement to look for in any printing company you use.
- **FSC certified** – this is where a printing company has been certified to provide FSC certified paper. It means you can be assured that the FSC certified

---

Box 8.3

PAPER AND PRINTING CHECKLIST

- ❏ Paper stock is 100 per cent post-consumer waste paper.
- ❏ Tree-free paper alternatives are used.
- ❏ Paper is from sustainably managed forests.
- ❏ Paper is a blend of the above three options.
- ❏ Paper is 'totally' or 'processed' chlorine-free bleached.
- ❏ Paper has independent and reputable certification for sustainable forestry, recycling content and chlorine free.
- ❏ Paper with vague recycling or chain or custody claims is not used.

The printing company:

- ❏ Has a sustainability or environmental policy.
- ❏ Preferentially uses and/or recommends the use of paper stock from 100 per cent post-consumer waste paper, from certified sustainably managed forests or tree-free alternatives.
- ❏ Uses vegetable-based inks and varnishes.
- ❏ Uses biodegradable laminates.
- ❏ Has waste management processes in place to recycle or reuse paper offcuts, ink containers, cartridges, pallets, packaging, die cut patterns and waste inks.
- ❏ Uses computer to plate technology to avoid film use.
- ❏ Offers job sharing to maximise use of paper and reduce energy and paper offcuts.
- ❏ Has water conservation techniques in place.
- ❏ Has energy-saving equipment and operations in place.
- ❏ Sources electricity from renewable energy.
- ❏ Has *ISO 14001* management system in place.

---

paper you request actually is the paper stock used by the printing company.

- **National/industry certifications** – this is where the printing industry in a country (usually via an industry association) has created a 'green printing' certification programme. An example of this is *Sustainable Green Print* in Australia.

SIGNAGE

From branded overlay to way-finding, event signage is a common consumable for just about every event. Signage can be simple A4 sheets of paper stuck to a wall, or elaborate full-colour stickers, banners, flags, fence screening or main stage coverings. The issues for consideration when planning signage are as follows:

- What materials are used?
- Can they be recycled?
- Are signs and scrim able to be reused?
- Is printing on signs low or VOC-free inks?
- Does the signage company have sustainability initiatives in place?
- Does the signage company have a sustainability policy?
- Is the signage company independently certified?
- Where is the signage company located and what are the transport impacts?

PVC Banners and Overlay

Vinyl has traditionally played a major part in the stable of signage for many events – as banners or as adhesive stickers offering branding overlay. They are convenient, easy to handle, durable, weather resistant, relatively inexpensive and quick to produce. It is the go-to quick fix of many event organisers when they need to produce a sign. But what of the costs to the environment? Vinyl banners are made from PVC

Figure 8.5 Most of the signage at Glastonbury Festival is hand painted onto timber and reused each year.

Photo: Meegan Jones.

(polyvinyl chloride), a material many describe as a 'poison plastic'.

US-based *Center for Health, Environment and Justice* has a campaign specifically around consumer awareness of the hazards of PVC manufacture and use. It describes PVC as *'one of the most hazardous consumer products ever created'*.[11] *Greenpeace* campaigned hard against PVC in the 1990s, including being involved in ensuring that the *Sydney Olympics 2000* was a PVC-free games. Read more about PVC at *PVC Free* (www.pvcfree.org).

Smells can ignite memories, and one of my earliest memories is triggered by the smell of PVC! We used to go on weekend excursions to the 'rubber' and outdoors store where my dad would pick up bits and pieces for the fishing boat or for our latest camping expedition. The store's intoxicating (how true) smell reminded me of exciting Christmas mornings unwrapping presents and breathing in deeply the delightful smell of new blow-up toys to take to the beach. Now a whiff of PVC brings me back to those days picking out my new blow-up toy, or unwrapping it on Christmas morning and running to try it out in the backyard pool at 6 a.m. I am sure you have similar memories. To me, the smell of PVC means Christmas. That is a little worrisome. Rather than the smell of summer and the smell of Christmas, I was breathing in PVC's process of off-gassing. Off-gassing is the evaporation of volatile chemicals at normal atmospheric pressure. Think of all those products which have a lingering 'smell': the interior of a new car, paints, varnishes, stains, carpet, insulation, linoleum flooring, kitchen countertops, paint strippers. These products are all off-gassing volatile organic compounds (VOCs), and you're breathing them in, and if you don't catch them up your nostrils, off they go, up into the atmosphere, playing their part in our man-made atmospheric delights.

PVC is purported to be dangerous during its entire product lifecycle. Its production process is chemical heavy, toxin rich and dioxin emitting. When in use, as described above, it continues to 'off-gas'. You're breathing in all its lovely chemical toxins. When disposed of, burning causes dioxins and toxic gases to be released, and if landfilled its eventual breakdown will cause the cocktail of nasties from which it was made to potentially leach into the ground and waterways.

PVC cannot be recycled easily or cost effectively. This is due to the many different toxic additives used to soften or stabilise PVC. If mixed with other plastics it's going to contaminate the recyclate. *Vancouver Winter Olympics* did come up with a special programme to collect all their vinyl signage for recycling by a local carpet company. Read more on the book's website.

Interestingly, bottles or other hardened PVC products are sometimes printed with the universal recycling symbol showing the three arrows and a '3' inside. This symbol was developed by the plastics industry to identify each type of plastic, not to indicate if it is recyclable. So, if you see the '3' in a 'recycle symbol' on any product, don't automatically include it with the other plastics recycling, as your MRF may not be able to handle it. Certainly, PVC banners cannot readily be recycled. The best option is to turn them into other items, such as the wonderful bags pioneered by *Freitag* (www.freitag.ch) and now copied by companies salvaging vinyl advertising banners around the world. They may also be repurposed for waterproofing and temporary covers, or just turned over and used for another sign.

At events, the main use for PVC is for banners and adhesive stickers overlay branding. But PVC may also be used in many construction materials, household products and office supplies. All are likely to make an appearance, such as plumbers' water and wastewater piping, cables, floor coverings, shower curtains, furniture, binders, folders and pens. So what we're really saying here is that PVC isn't the most environmentally preferable product and, if you can find alternatives, you are encouraged to use them.

Beware of PVC claiming to be biodegradable. The scientists on each side of the argument are in hot debate about this product. When considering this product at an event I was working on, the technical people from the product manufacturer were in direct contact with technical experts from anti-PVC groups. I still didn't get a final decision and so I used the precautionary principle – if the effects are not fully known or in debate, then don't touch it. I will continue to keep an eye on this material and if answers become clearer I will post it on my book's website.

Timber Signage

Timber, particularly recycled or reclaimed timber, is a great option for signage. It is the ultimate reusable sign. Store for reuse and if the signs aren't right next time, paint over them. If you're using new timber, make sure you use timber that has been sustainably forested.

Fabric Signage

An alternative to all that PVC is fabric, albeit some fabric is made from plastic. The options for fabric-based signage include the following:

- fabric made from recycled bottles
- virgin, but recyclable, polyester
- cotton or canvas (preferably organic).

FortiBanner™ is an example of the new generation of PVC alternative banner materials. It's made from LDPE coated polypropylene and is 100 per cent recyclable (of

course, that's 'where facilities exist'). A great thing about fabric signs is that they can be readily repurposed into colourful bunting and décor for community events.

Ecophab™ is a PVC alternative material for banners. It is made from 100 per cent post-consumer soda pop bottles. A fine example of up-cycling, the plastic bottles are taken through the recycling process, and spun into fibre which is then woven into fabric. This process produces the *Ecophab*™ fabric. *Banner Creations* in the USA uses *Ecophab*™ to produce a huge range of products, including banners, table covers, table runners, point-of-purchase displays, backdrops, flags and a range of bags (www.bannercreations.com).

Corrugated Plastic Board

Way-finding and informational signage is often produced on dual-wall corrugated polypropylene board. In Australia the common brand name and generic term for this material is '*corflute*'. This product is used extensively in the event industry and is also the signboard of choice for the real estate industry.

Way-finding and event-specific signage is often single use and therefore massive amounts of this material are discarded every year. The company that produces corflute, *Corex*, recognised its responsibility in the full life cycle of the product and has created a dedicated recycling programme and facility for reprocessing used corflute signs. The material is recycled into new corflute board, under the brand name '*Encore*': brilliant producer responsibility in action. Well done *Corex* (www.corex. net.au).

MERCHANDISE, GIFTS AND GIVEAWAYS

Events, especially exhibitions and trade fairs, are a 'giveaway' nirvana. People are used to attending events and coming away with a hoard of freebies. Lots of this 'stuff' is single-use promotional items, made cheap and dirty and destined for landfill.

Along with giveaways, other items such as branded event T-shirts, jackets, hoodies, caps and bags are produced. For sports events such as marathons or triathlons, racer 'bibs' are made by the thousand. At conferences,

Box 8.4

SIGNAGE CHECKLIST

Enhancing Reusability

❏ Choose a venue that's easy to move around and that has existing permanent direction signage in place.

❏ Consider using staff to direct attendees upon arrival, to reduce the amount of single-use signage needed.

❏ If there are options at the venue for digital signage, use them.

❏ Plan signage artwork without dates so that they are reusable at the next event.

❏ Plan signage artwork with removable or replaceable pieces where sponsor or partner logos go, so that you can use it again at the next event.

❏ Use wording in such a way that signs may be used across multiple events.

❏ Don't change your colour schemes every year so that reusable signs don't become dated.

❏ Consider whether the printed surface is removable from the main sign board. If it is removable, you may be able to reuse the substrate.

❏ Alternatively, print directly onto the surface of the primary sign board, to facilitate easy recycling.

❏ Ensure that the entire sign is made from the same material type. This includes no eyelets, adhesives, stickers or attachments.

Materials and Printing

❏ Signs are made from sustainably produced renewable materials.

❏ Signs are made from materials that may and will be recycled.

❏ For plastic signage, include the relevant number plastic symbol on sign artwork so that if they end up at waste facilities they may be selected for recycling

❏ Inks are preferentially vegetable/soy based (VOC free).

❏ The use of vinyl (PVC) banners is avoided.

❏ Signs are sent for reuse/repurposing to relevant salvage organisations.

❏ Branded banner roll and fence scrim is stored and reused. It is only discarded if it is degraded or contaminated.

Signage Company

❏ Signage companies have sustainability practices in place.

❏ Signage companies have a company sustainability policy.

❏ Signage companies are *ISO 14001* compliant.

conventions, gala nights and presentations, gifts, trophies, medals, awards, and take-home table centre pieces are given away.

Many participants also bring merchandise items – exhibitors and sponsors touting their brands, artists promoting their tour, or campaigns promoting their message.

When sourcing garments or merchandise there are several sustainability issues that must be considered when making sourcing decisions. You should also promote these issues to those external parties producing items that will be used, given away or sold.

Issues for consideration when sourcing merchandise and gifts include the following:

• Are products made locally, supporting the local economy?

• Are the product's raw materials grown or produced with environmental responsibility?

• Does raw material production have decent and safe working conditions?

• Are fair trade principles included in the production of raw materials?

- Are the raw materials and final product free of toxic substances?
- What manufacturing processes are undertaken? Do they ensure no pollution to air, land and water, and are they resource efficient?
- Is manufacture undertaken with safe and fair working and labour conditions?
- Do manufacturing operations have relevant independent certifications such as ILO, *Fairwear* or *ISO 14001*?
- What is the transport impact of the product all along the supply chain?

As textile-based merchandise is such a major category of items purchased by events, we will go into more detail on the various material types available below. For now, let us look at some other categories of merchandise items that could be produced for your event and some clever alternatives which events have created to reduce the impacts of these (sometimes) single-use items.

Lanyards and Name Tags

The name tag is a potentially wasteful and highly visible event item. Ensuring they are not just disposed of after the event is something to design in.

Don't print the 'year' on the lanyard, as this will render it unable to be reused. If you offer the lanyard as sponsor real estate, see if you can think up another way to get those sponsorship dollars rather than printing on a disposable item.

If you do have to print on the lanyard, design the graphics in such a way that the lanyard will not date. In addition, the less printed area, the less ink used. This is a minor point but one worth mentioning.

You can also make the lanyards multi-purpose. For example, provide the conference notes on a USB that is also attached to the lanyard.

For the name tag section of the lanyard, you can have a plastic pouch for either a recyclable delegate name tag, or somewhere for them to place their business card. This will depend on your event accreditation processes. Alternatively, you could do away with the plastic pouch and print onto card, and clip these directly to the lanyard.

There are purpose-made cards with holes and clips that prevent them from easily tearing off.

The lanyards themselves are available in sustainable materials such as rPET, organic cotton, bamboo fibre, hemp linen, corn based, and *TENCEL®*. In addition, printing with vegetable/soy inks is possible, so enquire of your lanyard supplier what materials are available and what printing methods are used.

Avoid fluorescent colours, as the dyes used to achieve these colours are toxic.

And Sew On in Canada has a great range of rPET and organic cotton lanyards (www.andsewon.ca). So does *Fairware* (www.fairware.com) and *R3volved* (www.r3volved.com). If available, preferentially buy rPET lanyards made from recycled bottles sourced from and manufactured in your country, rather than from factories overseas where your country's waste has been shipped. We're trying to close loops here, people, not extend them across the globe.

Figure 8.6 Merchandise ready for conference delegates.
Photo: GreenShoot Pacific.

Collecting lanyards and name tags after the event's conclusion for reuse, recycling or repurposing is also part of the story. A great way of doing this is to set up collection boxes at entrances/exits with each box allocated to a local charity or community programme, and delegates are asked to deposit their lanyard to the project of choice. Then, depending on the proportion of lanyards in each box, donation funds are allocated out.

Lanyards may be reused for the next event. You may wish to sanitise them. This can be done by bundling the lanyards up in lots of a hundred and placing the bundle in a sealable mesh wash bag and putting them in the washing machine. If they're not actually dirty but you still wish to sanitise them, you can also freeze them.

If you don't want to reuse them for your event, you could donate them to a reuse or salvage shop.

Delegate Packs

Anyone who has attended a conference (or produced one) will know that getting a goody bag of lovely conference-related (and unrelated) items is part of the fun. Before sustainability impacts of purchasing were a consideration, these bags were jam packed with pamphlets, individually wrapped sample-sized items, gifts, single-sided printed-out conference notes, pens, notepads and special offers.

But things have progressed a little now and smart conference organisers are reducing the impacts on their bottom line as well as the planet through considerate and responsible conference pack planning.

Delegate packs now come in bags made from last year's banners, packed with just the right amount of environmentally and socially responsible items, such as 100 per cent post-consumer recycled unbleached notepads, pens made from recycled plastic, sustainably harvested bamboo USB drives with conference notes, and biodegradable bags full of locally sourced sample products.

Gifts and Awards

For those events that offer gifts, trophies and awards, the ideas for sustainable options are as endless as there are local artisans. These items are usually fewer in number and larger in value, and so there is generally no reason

why you cannot find some fantastic locally sourced item, handcrafted or produced locally. Look for local arts organisations that can link you to artisans locally.

In the city where I live, there are two great avenues to find such producers. First is *ReNew Newcastle,* which connects artisans and small creative production groups with empty retail space (www.renewnewcastle.org). The second is *CultureHunter,* an online resource where artists can promote their products (www.culturehunter.org). *Etsy* is a great online eBay-style website where artisans can place their items for sale. You will find the most brilliant range of potential designers of your gifts and awards here (www.esty.com).

Trophies are just asking to get creative. Who wants a boring trophy from a trophy shop, or an engraved plaque mounted on timber, when you can have a fantastic

Figure 8.7 A Greener Festival Award is made out of old tent fabric by www.idressmyself.co.uk.

Source: Hel Innes, A Greener Festival.

handmade creation from reclaimed materials? *A Greener Festival* came up with a brilliant and very appropriate award by using old tent material made to look like festival décor flags for their annual awards. *Fairware* again come up with the goods by offering beautiful recycled glass trophies and plaques made out of recycled bike chains. Awesome!

Promotional Products

If your event, or participants at it (such as exhibitors or sponsors), must have logo-ed items to give away to event attendees, then the responsible thing to do is to come up with a clever, relevant, useful item which is designed in such a way that attendees will want to continue using it (rather than feel as if they are an advertising medium for you, and discard it post-event). Design in the longevity and usefulness of the item. Source sustainability with consideration for materials choice, labour conditions, manufacturing impacts, transport impacts and end of life (e.g. recyclable).

Fairware, based in North America, is a good place to start looking for ethically sourced and environmentally responsible merchandise items (www.fairware.com).

GARMENTS

The first consideration is the material from which the item is made. Traditionally, cotton is the most popular material used for manufacturing the types of garments used in the event industry. There are alternatives to this pesticide- and fertiliser-hungry and very thirsty crop. We will now trawl through a range of material choices for your garment-based event merchandise or other cotton-type products such as tote bags.

Cotton

Cotton is one of the world's most important natural fibres used in a huge range of products from clothing to bedding and medical supplies. Cotton is a renewable resource but its sustainability challenges are widely reported – environmental impacts of chemical insecticides and fertilisers, water use and waterways protection from chemical run-

---

Box 8.5

MERCHANDISE CHECKLIST

- ❏ Don't overproduce numbers of products.
- ❏ Don't produce unnecessary or frivolous items.
- ❏ Commission creatively produced items from salvaged and recycled materials.
- ❏ Merchandise is sourced locally to reduce transport impact and support the local economy.
- ❏ Packaging is reduced.
- ❏ Merchandise and giveaways are designed with consideration for at least two more uses.
- ❏ Giveaways or samples are only provided where they are necessary.
- ❏ Incentives/giveaways are only given to those participants who 'opt in' to receive them.
- ❏ The product's raw materials are grown or produced with environmental responsibility, fair trade and fair labour practices.
- ❏ Products are made from alternative and sustainable materials such as bamboo, recycled PET and hemp.
- ❏ The product's raw materials are free from toxic substances.
- ❏ The products are made in factories with fair labour certification (e.g. WRAP, ILO, Fairware).

---

off, safe and fair working conditions on farms and in factories, and fair prices paid to producers.

There are many reports that have researched and analysed the impacts of cotton production and many programmes have been developed to reduce the environmental impacts and enhance welfare for workers and benefits to local communities. These include organic cotton production, Fairtrade cotton, and cotton production that reduces chemical use and enhances worker welfare. We will look at some of these programmes below, which are ways to help you assess your cotton-based event procurement.

Cotton production is incredibly chemical intensive and is considered to be one of the world's dirtiest crops. In its 2007 report *The Deadly Chemicals in Cotton*, the

Environmental Justice Foundation and the *Pesticide Action Network* report that cotton covers 2.5 per cent of the world's cultivated land, yet uses 16 per cent of the world's insecticides, more than any other single major crop. They also report that a single drop of the pesticide *aldicarb,'* absorbed through the skin, can kill an adult. Aldicarb is a commonly used pesticide in cotton production.[12]

Apart from the health risks to workers and the chemicals remaining with the cotton all the way along the manufacturing chain until they are the clothes on your back, a major problem is that these chemicals will make their way back into the ecosystem. They wash down off the plants into the soil, into the water table and go on their merry way to our streams and rivers, wreaking havoc as they travel. These chemicals are also doing damage to the health of workers on the farms and those who are dependent on the surrounding natural environment, let alone the fish in the rivers. (Let us pay homage to Rachel Carson's work at this moment.)[13]

Cotton needs water, and responsible and sustainable cotton production ensures that water sources are not depleted and natural waterways are not polluted from this potential chemical run-off. To illustrate the water consumption of various products, *Water Footprint* has tracked the water consumption of lots of products and reports that it takes 2700 litres of water to produce a single T-shirt![14]

While there are alternatives to cotton production, an obvious move is towards organic cotton production – chemical free and healthy for workers, the environment and wearers. Moving to organic cotton eliminates most of the bad elements of cotton production – chemical (fossil fuel-based) pesticides and fertilisers. No chemicals means better health for workers in the field, no pollution of toxins to the land and waterways, and an end product you'd feel safer wearing.

The *Textile Exchange* produces the *Organic Cotton Farm and Fibre Report* which records the amount of organic cotton grown and analyses reasons for trending increases or declines. If you are interested in more information, access their reports.[15]

Organic cotton is not the only answer, and sometimes the lower yields and therefore relatively higher cost of the final product render it a niche or top-end product. 'Responsible' rather than organic, cotton production has grown in popularity to include the *Cleaner Cotton™* campaign in the USA and the *Better Cotton Initiative* internationally.

Cleaner Cotton™ is an initiative of the *Sustainable Cotton Project,* the group which helps farmers develop a working knowledge of practices which reduce chemical use that can be successfully and economically applied to cotton. *Cleaner Cotton™* is grown without using the 13 most toxic chemicals identified as used in conventional cotton production in California. Farmers growing this cotton use non-genetically modified seed and biologically based pest management practices (www.sustainable cotton.org).

The *Better Cotton Initiative* (BCI) works to *"promote measurable and continuing improvements for the environment, farming communities and the economies of cotton-producing areas"*. Production practice is based on six principles with participating farmers: minimising the harmful impact of crop protection practices; using water efficiently and caring for the availability of water; caring for the health of the soil; conserving natural habitats; preserving the quality of the fibre; and promoting decent work practices (bettercotton.org).

Cotton producers in developing nations who are at the whim of global commodity prices are protected through the *Fairtrade Cotton* programme by being paid a fair price. By selling to the *Fairtrade* market, cotton farmers have the security that they will receive a minimum price which aims to cover their average costs of sustainable production. They also receive a *Fairtrade Premium* that allows them to invest in community projects, such as schools, roads or health care facilities.

Because of the high use of chemical insecticides and fertilisers in cotton, and the chemical substances in the colouring and treatment of materials, there is a demand from consumers for textiles that pose no risk to health.

This has led to the creation of the *Oeko-Tex®* standards. This label allows consumers to assess the human ecological quality of textiles and it gives a uniform safety standard for textile and clothing companies (www.oeko-tex.com).

- *OEKO-TEX® Standard 100* is for textile raw materials, intermediate and end products at all stages of production.

- *OEKO-TEX® Standard 1000* is for environmentally friendly operations along the textile chain.
- *Sustainable Textile Production (STeP)* is for brands, retail companies and manufacturers from the textile chain to communicate their achievements to the public.

rPET Bottle Fabrics

A great end product for recycled plastic (PET) bottles is as a fabric, either a 'polar-fleece' or a T-shirt material. The material is generically known as rPET (the 'r' obviously being for 'recycled'). The official name of the polar-fleece fabric is *Fortrel EcoSpun™*, a polyester fibre made out of the recycled plastic bottles, which is then made into fleece.

The process for turning bottles into T-shirts is relatively simple. Bottles are collected for recycling and separated by colour, then sent for processing where they are ground and cleaned, and turned into PET flakes. These flakes are then extruded (melted and remoulded into lengths). The extruded polyester fibre is then spun into yards and woven into fabric (including colouring). The fabric is then cut and sewn into garments. The final product looks and feels just like virgin polyester, but uses 90 per cent less water in the manufacturing process.

The entire process saves energy and uses a waste recourse rather than creating new petroleum-based fibres. Plastic bottles in landfill take hundreds of years to begin decomposing. As such, rPET clothing not only minimises waste now, but potentially reduces waste problems for future generations. rPET's carbon footprint has been calculated to be 75 per cent lower than virgin polyester, making it one of the more environmentally sustainable clothing options on the market.[16]

Given the sheer amount of plastic bottles in existence this makes this fabric a no brainer. Ask your merchandise supplier to source rPET shirts – there are many suppliers worldwide.

Rethink offer a range of shirts and other apparel made from 100 per cent rPET. Rethink's rPET clothing is also recyclable: at the end of their life T-shirts can be reclaimed and the fibres used to create new clothing, reducing waste in the manufacturing process and completing the cradle-to-cradle life cycle. Based in the US, *Rethink* support local fibre and yarn mills, and maintain strict control over the manufacturing process. They also provide an index to help customers measure and track their reduced environmental impact by purchasing rPET products (rethinkfabrics.com).

R3volved in the USA has a great range of rPET products – they're changing the 'supply curve one bottle at a time' (www.r3volved.com).

Hemp

Hemp is one of the longest, strongest natural fibres on earth, said to have double or triple the strength of cotton. It grows in just about any climate and, with the proper cultivation and rotation practices, without the need for chemical pesticides, herbicides, fungicides and fertilisers. Your merchandise supplier will likely be able to source a 100 per cent or hemp blend. If not, search directly for the manufacturer, as it seems that at this stage (sadly), hemp T-shirts are more of a specialty item.

Bamboo Fabric

Bamboo is fast growing and its cultivation is sustainable using no pesticides or fertilisers. In addition, it doesn't need replanting after harvesting due to its established root system. Bamboo fabrics are promoted as moisture wicking, and claim to be antibacterial and UV resistant.

As with all agricultural and forest products, sustainable plantation methods must be used. Currently there are no certifications that independently assess bamboo cultivation to ensure sustainable agricultural practices. This is something to look out for.

The production of bamboo fibre into fabric can be done mechanically or chemically. The mechanical way, namely by crushing pulp in a similar way to making linen from hemp or flax, is the most environmentally friendly production of bamboo fabric – often called bamboo linen. The most common bamboo fabric available to consumers (and definitely to event producers looking for promotional T-shirts) is the chemical-intensive one. The leaves and inner pith of bamboo are chemically treated to break the fibre down to a state where it can be extruded and spun.

Bamboo fabric is promoted as a sustainable fabric, primarily due to its quick growth and low use of pesticides or fertilisers, but little is mentioned about the high chemical uses to create fabric from bamboo fibre.

Wool

Wool, like cotton, is a hugely popular, useful, effective, natural and renewable material. It is difficult to make a broad-brush statement about the 'sustainability' of wool production, as so many factors come into play. Wool is grown in many countries in the world and some regions are certainly more suitable than others for the agricultural processes required to raise and keep sheep. Considerations when choosing wool products are as follows:

✓ Ensure your wool is sourced from farms that aren't contributing to desertification. Sheep farming is hard on the land, with sheep eating grass down to the roots, causing a loss of topsoil, triggering erosion.

✓ Ensure your wool is sourced from growers who do not practise 'mulesing' (Google it for the gory details!).

✓ Source wool from countries where water scarcity is not an issue and grazing sheep is an appropriate use of agricultural land.

✓ Source wool garments that have reduced the impacts of chemicals, dye and bleach use in yarn and garment production.

PAINTS AND VARNISHES

Many events (and venues) will use paint for signage, sets, décor and to preserve permanent infrastructure. To purchase the most 'environmentally friendly' products, you need to look for paints and varnishes which are:

1 Volatile Organic Compound free (VOCs)
2 Water based
3 Use non-toxic pigments
4 Safe for waterways.

Box 8.6

GARMENT CHECKLIST

❏ Garments are made from materials with sustainable production methods.
❏ Garments are made from renewable resources.
❏ Garments are made from recycled materials.
❏ Ensure fair prices are paid to materials producers.
❏ Ensure fair labour practices in manufacturing facilities.
❏ Source locally to support local economies.
❏ Source locally to reduce transport impacts.
❏ Promote sustainability credentials of garments.
❏ Only provide giveaways to those participants who opt in.

Figure 8.8 Hand painting signs onsite.

Source: Meegan Jones.

You remember that lovely freshly painted smell? That's the paint off-gassing. In most cases the painting occurs outdoors so you won't have the problems of indoor air pollution. Those VOCs are still setting sail off into the atmosphere. In indoor painting (either of permanent structures or in workshops), air quality and worker health are concerns.

The VOCs come from the chemical and solvent mix from which paint is made. As paint dries, evaporation causes the off-gassing of these VOCs. The carcinogens and neurotoxins in paints include benzene, formaldehyde, kerosene, ammonia, toluene and xylene. (The latter two are solvents.) Using water-based paints and varnishes means you aren't using further solvents for clean-up and you aren't using up even more precious mineral oil. Paints that are water based will still contain pigments and chemicals, and you will need to consider the wash-up and wastewater disposal. Consider going a step further than just water-based VOC-free paint to truly 'eco' paints – those which contain non-toxic pigments. Search for or request 'eco paints'; there are many on the market and they're easy to find.

Disposal of paint is also an issue. If you have paint tins with not enough in them to warrant saving or donating, tip the paint out onto newspaper and allow it to dry before putting into the general waste bin. Tins can usually go into metal recycling. Check locally to see the recommended disposal of unused paint and tins as conditions alter. For tins that contain a large amount of paint, donate it! Check out *Community RePaint* in the UK (www.communityrepaint.org.uk).

✓ Use zero or low VOC paint and varnish.
✓ Use paint with non-toxic pigment.
✓ Donate unused paint for reuse.
✓ Use reclaimed paint in the first place.
✓ Manage water run-off in the wash-up process, including using paint wastewater collection and removal so that it doesn't run down the drains.

CLEANING PRODUCTS

As you would imagine, conventional cleaning products are a fantastic cocktail of chemical compounds, solvents, bleach, artificial fragrances and the like. They may cut through grease, decontaminate and leave a room lemon fresh, but at what cost?

We clean to protect our health; however, ironically, while conventional cleaning products may kill germs they are also adding toxins and poisons into our environment and into our bodies.

Apart from the direct health impact on people, the black marks also against conventional cleaning products include the following:

- **They use non-renewable resources:** The bulk of raw materials are made from petroleum. As we know, this is a non-renewable resource, and the impact on our planet through its extraction and processing is considerable.
- **They contain chemicals:** There is a danger to human health through inhalation, skin contact and also the buildup of these chemicals in our environment.
- **They emit greenhouse gases:** Due to the solvents and other chemical compounds, there are abundant VOC emissions from conventional cleaning products.
- **They poison waterways and aquatic life:** The final black mark is that the cocktail of nasties are flushed away down sinks and drains, onto land and into streams and oceans, poisoning waterways and wreaking havoc on aquatic life.

Green cleaning should protect health without harming the environment. What should you look for in a green cleaning product?

1   They use renewable resources

Environmentally sound cleaning products contain raw materials sourced from vegetable and mineral resources. They are renewable, able to be grown again or replenished.

2   They are 100 per cent biodegradable

Certified environmentally sound cleaning products will be 100 per cent biodegradable. This means that all components of the product will biodegrade, with all that remains being water, CO_2 and minerals.

3   Non-toxic

Green cleaning products are non-toxic to aquatic life, and are safe for septic systems (and therefore your sewerage treatment plant). They are free from chlorine bleach, synthetic dyes and artificial fragrances.

4   Solvent-free

By not containing solvents you are likely also looking at a VOC-free product. This means that it's not off-gassing harmful greenhouse gases.

5   Phosphate-free

Phosphates were once a popular cleaning product ingredient as they remove dirt and grease. Many countries have banned or limited phosphates in most cleaning products but it's still a prime ingredient in dishwashing powder. When phosphates hit the waterways they disrupt the natural balance in lakes and streams, allowing abnormally high algae growth.

If your existing cleaning company hasn't considered these issues get them on the case and ask them to report back to you on the state of environmentally sound cleaning products and practices.

At *Glastonbury Festival* we did just that. The *GreenClean* product range was developed after a specific request to the event's consumables supplier, *Concept Products*, for an environmentally sound cleaning product that met the government requirements in the UK for public hygiene and cleaning standards. It was consequentially developed with the specific cleaning needs of outdoor events. *Concept Products* now market it directly to UK festival cleaning contractors and have found festival organisers requesting that their cleaning contractors use this product.

Meeting Government Standards

In applying environmentally sound cleaning products to commercial cleaning you should look into your country's standards for cleaning products and the actual product performance. Federal, state and local government may place controls on products used for cleaning public places. These are generally based around food-handling and washroom hygiene concerns. Historically these regulations have been to the exclusion of 'green' products, with only chemical-heavy products meeting stringent demands.

We are seeing environmentally sound cleaning products benefiting from Environmental Preferential Purchasing (EPP) policies being implemented on a wide scale through government.

Where this isn't the case, *'green'* cleaning products are finding work-arounds by using science to ensure that their products meet the exacting standards of the likes of local council food safety inspectors. Products are being developed which tick all the boxes of bureaucracy, while also meeting the goals of environmental sensitivity.

Your cleaners may insist on using certain products under the assumption that these are the only ones that can be used. Old habits die hard, and you may need to put some strategies in place to coax them into using a different product. Instead of forcing them to change, work with them on a trial of a cleaning product with a view to rolling it out full scale in the future. What you want to aim for is to encourage your cleaning contractors to permanently switch to environmentally sound cleaning products.

In addition, check out the *Environmental Working Group*'s guide to green household cleaning products (www.ewg.org/guides/cleaners).

✓   Identify the cleaning products used at your event and seek out the most environmentally sound options.
✓   Engage your cleaners, staff, food stalls, caterers, and any other person who may have a mop and bucket or spray bottle and cloth and get them committed to cleaning green.
✓   Ensure that all cleaning staff are inducted into how to use the products effectively and what processes they should use.

Figure 8.9 Mediterranean-style share platters at the Women In Green Forum facilitate cross-table networking.
Source: Three Squares Inc, Genivieve McCormick.

✓ Have a system in place to check that staff are using the products as intended and that processes used are as instructed.

✓ Contract into cleaning agreements the use of your chosen cleaning products or that meet the same specifications.

✓ Supply handwash, bodywash, shampoo, etc., for your participants.

✓ Work with hotels (for conferences) to have them review their use of cleaning products and what products they supply in guest-rooms.

FOOD AND BEVERAGE

Those serving or selling food at events are increasingly being required by event organisers to consider the sustainability aspects of their sourcing, kitchen and service operations. Customers are expecting it and our planet needs it!

From paddock to plate, caterers and food stallholders at events can play a part in supporting a sustainable food system and the sustainability credentials of the event, by providing healthy, fresh, seasonal, local, fair, culturally appropriate, dietary diverse and naturally grown food.

You may have noticed other caterers and food stallholders at events you have attended on the journey already . . . organic wood-fired pizzas, Fairtrade coffee stalls, caterers using local produce, or bars selling locally brewed beers.

On supermarket shelves there are more ethical food choices, organic produce, gluten-free products, Fairtrade tea/coffee/chocolate and even supermarket brand organic baked beans than ever before.

Sustainable food sourcing includes many considerations, and there will never be one right way to the 'most sustainable' solution. You must consider the various issues and impacts that apply to your own situation such as where you are located, what produce is available locally, what is of priority to your event attendees, and what your organisation's core sustainability principles are.

This section will unpack the issues for consideration in scrutinising your food and beverage sourcing.

Food is a terrific way of exploring sustainability issues. From showing where food comes from and the impacts of unsustainable agricultural practices and the benefits of chemical-free food, to using food to unite communities, events are a perfect platform.

Jaime Nack of Three Squares Inc thoughtfully crafts meal-moments to encourage interaction by delegates at her events. *"Since time eternal, food has always provided an outlet to bring people together and build community. When creating the menu for the Women In Green Forum, we looked at seasonal produce from the local farmer's market and realized that a Mediterranean-themed lunch would allow us not only to serve fresh, vegetarian fare but in a family style format. The appetizer platter was a delicious display of Mediterranean salads served on a palm leaf plate."*

Global + Fair

Going local does not always win out when you broaden the scope of your sustainability considerations to include more than just your own backyard.

Is it, for instance, more sustainable to serve local yet chemical-laden food than serving organic produce from a farm 2000 miles away?

Or is it more sustainable to purchase products that have been grown on the other side of the world but where they are part of schemes to ensure fair prices paid to producers and workers in developing nations?

If you wish to support sustainable development, fair labour and fair trade practices, and wish to ensure that profits stay in these communities, then sourcing through the *Fairtrade* programme may be for you.

You may also have a concern for the working conditions of farm labourers in your home region. Look out for programmes that protect the rights of workers and ensure fair pay and conditions – especially if you are based in a region where immigrant workers make up a significant proportion of farm workforces.

Local + Seasonal

Buying local, seasonal and fresh products are usually the first things to look for. This approach to food sourcing means you are supplying food that is supporting the local economy. It's short travelled, or has low 'food miles' – meaning its carbon footprint is lower than that which has taken a world tour before hitting the kitchen.

Planning menus around what is seasonal inherently means that you are sourcing locally and fresh, ticking all the boxes.

Fresh produce (rather than processed food) means (hopefully) that it is short travelled and seasonal, and has not been in cold storage, further reducing greenhouse gas emissions from the energy needed to power refrigeration.

Seasonal and fresh produce is also likely to taste a whole lot better. It won't have been irradiated to ensure longevity, and it hasn't travelled around the world to get to you.

Buying locally may also ensure that profits are going into the hands of the producers and their workers, supporting your local economy.

Look for a seasonal food guide in your region.

Australia: www.seasonafoodguide.com
USA: www.fieldtoplate.com/guide.php
UK: eatseasonably.co.uk

One of the best seasonal food guides for a local region I have seen has been produced by *Gosford City Council* in Australia. They produce four downloadable PDFs for their region for each season, letting residents and caterers know what is in season. Have a look at their brilliant work (www.gosford.nsw.gov.au/environment/sustainability/food-drink/buy-local-and-seasonal-food).

Box 8.7

LOCAL MENU SOURCING AND PLANNING

When planning the 2012 *Sustainable Meetings Conference* in Montreal, Quebec, Jaime Nack and her team at Three Squares Inc were challenged with the potential frost on the ground in April, limiting the variety of local produce available for menu selection. Because they were planning the event to meet three international standards – ISO 20121, APEX/ASTM and the Quebec BNQ sustainable event standard – they were eager to find a solution that would allow us to source local and organic items.

During the site visit in February (with snow heavy on the ground), discussions with the chef and catering team about sourcing local produce seemed hopeless. They predicted that given the extreme winter weather, frost would continue to hold through the months of March and April, making it difficult to design a menu featuring local produce. After just a few days in Montreal, it became apparent that the people of Quebec are extremely proud of locally made products and all that the beautiful city of Montreal has to offer. Realising that the menu-planning conversation had reached an impasse, they focused on Quebec-quiz-made products most often – from cheeses to wine to maple syrup. They were able to develop a wine and cheese reception featuring a wide variety of products from local purveyors.

One of the reasons why this experience was so memorable was that it served as a reminder of the importance of framing when implementing sustainability initiatives. *"Focusing on the positive emotions related to national pride allowed us to reach our desired outcome."*

www.threesquaresinc.com

Healthy + Appropriate

'You are what you eat.' 'A moment on the lips a lifetime on the hips.' 'Have your five a day.' We all know that eating healthily is important and that good health is stimulated by good food.

Consider the food offerings you are providing to your event attendees, and what you're saying about your care for them through the meals you offer. This may include healthy eating options such as fruit and vegetables, low in trans fats and low GI, dietary considerations such as vegetarian, vegan, lactose free, gluten free, or religious or cultural-based food requirements.

Obviously food at events needs to be 'fit for purpose', looking at aspects such as the event setting, whether it is a stationary audience or a moving crowd – finger food or seated at tables. The type of event, congestion, access and timing will also contribute to menu-planning decisions.

Providing food that is not over-processed and is fresh and chemical free should be possible for most events. Certainly having a range of food that meets the expectations or requirements of your event attendees should be given high priority, as should food that will enhance the event experience – avoid foods which are too rich and heavy at conferences!

- ✓ Serve unprocessed and fresh meals.
- ✓ Serve low calorie and low GI meals.
- ✓ Restrict foods with trans fats.
- ✓ Have gluten-free, coeliac options.
- ✓ Offer lactose-free options.
- ✓ Offer vegetarian and vegan options.
- ✓ Offer Halal, Kosher or Jain appropriate meals.
- ✓ Offer culturally appropriate food (consider tastes of attendees, acknowledging regional preferences).

Sustainable Farming

Farming on an industrial scale can cause soil erosion, pollution to waterways, land degradation, pests of plague proportions, and cause damage to natural habitats.

On the positive side a new way of doing things is being embraced by farmers around the world – whether due to the cost of agricultural chemicals, a realisation that farming in harmony with the environment is more efficient, through awareness programmes such as *Landcare* (www.

Figure 8.10 Food at the Sustainable Hospitality Symposium, held at the Monterey campus of California State University, was sourced as locally and organically as possible. All food at the buffet was tagged to inform the attendees exactly where the food was sourced and what its sustainability credentials were.

Source: Meegan Jones.

landcareonline.com) groups, through market demands, or even younger farmers with a progressive eye – the principles of sustainable agricultural practices are being embraced.

Industrial-Scale Farming

The creation of factory farms and highly intensive single-crop production can lead to a disproportionate need for chemical pest control and fertilisers. Intensive practices such as feedlots for cattle, caged hens, or pigs in pens have animal welfare issues.

Irrigation demands can disrupt natural water systems and cause land salination. Chemical-laden water run-off or treatment of huge volumes of sullage from feedlots are also issues to be managed.

Industrial scale agriculture also has social impacts as smaller farmers are pushed out and agricultural land is taken over by corporations.

Humane Animal Treatment

The welfare of animals during their lives and during transport and slaughter is a major issue, and a hotly debated and often emotional subject. Ensuring you know the food you serve has come from animals which have been treated humanely is a critical aspect to sustainable sourcing. Read more about animal treatment issues in the upcoming section on meat, eggs and dairy products.

Chemical Free

Organic food production means that the produce or animals have been grown (or fed on produce) that is free from chemicals – fertilisers or pesticides. It also means that produce has not been irradiated, or has not been genetically modified. There are hundreds of organic certifying organisations around the world. The barometer against which to test the validity of an organic certification's programme is to check whether it is a member of the *International Federation of Organic Agricultural Movements* (IFOAM). This body has 750 member organisations and it ensures equivalency of standards in over 100 countries. IFOAM doesn't undertake certification activities but the standards it sets form the basis for many nations' organic standards (www.ifoam.org).

Producers in 'transition' to organic should not be neglected, however – these are producers who, for example, do not use chemical fertilisers and pesticides but have not (or cannot due to costs) achieve independent organic certification. In addition, there are other programmes such as produce that has been grown to biodynamic specifications and have reached *Demeter* (www.demeter.org.au) certification. You may also choose to source produce that has been grown using the principles of *permaculture*. The principles of sustainable development dovetail perfectly with the founding tenants of permaculture: to take care of the earth, take care of the people, set limits to consumption and reproduction, and redistribute surplus.

Low GHG Emissions

From a greenhouse gas emissions viewpoint, consider the energy and GHG consequences of highly intensive agricultural practices – fertilisers and pesticides need to be manufactured (electricity) and transported (fuel), as well as applied to crops (more fuel).

Aspects of food production that will increase its carbon footprint include the following:

- Animal production with a high demand for grown stock feed – fodder crops may need fertilisers, pesticides and transport.
- Out-of-season produce will need to be put into long-term cold storage (electricity).
- Food produced in large volumes at single locations will have major transport impacts to get to their end-user markets (fuel).

Look for options that offer competitive carbon footprints. Weigh up the various GHG impacts. Consider sourcing products that, although they may have travelled some distance by air, land or sea, have been produced through low-intensity (and low-GHG) agricultural practices.

Fruit and Vegetables

The growth of farmers' markets, community supported agriculture, and the availability of organic produce in supermarkets is testament to the signals that consumers are pushing through the supply chain.

People are increasingly demanding the fruit and vegetables they eat to be free from genetic modification, not to be grown with chemical fertilisers or pesticides, not to have been irradiated, and they want to be confident that the farmers growing the produce are using sustainable agricultural practices.

Consumers also want to know where their food comes from, how far it has travelled, what the working conditions are on the farms, and where the profits flow.

Farm to Table or *Farm to Fork* is a highly popular concept with a direct line between farm-sourced produce and menu offerings.

Box 8.8

WAY OUT WEST GOES VEGETARIAN

WAY OUT VEGGIE. . .!

Music festival *Way Out West* (WOW) in Sweden take their sustainability performance seriously and catering has been taken one step further with a requirement for seasonal and local sourcing, under the responsibility of *Restaurant Wasa Allé* and Mats Nordström who have won multiple rewards for their organic cuisine.

All vendors at Way Out West must work with an ecological approach and be 'environmentally smart'. That means organic, fair and eco-labelled. Way Out West is the first festival in Sweden to be *KRAV-certified*.

In 2012, WOW took the next step to reduce the event's GHG emissions. Studies have shown that food was the biggest environmental thief, with meat by far the worst. The big decision of making WOW a full vegetarian festival was taken and announced through social media, creating lots of reactions, debates and articles.

The ecological footprint of the festival was reduced by 23.9 per cent, although visitor numbers increased by 19 per cent. The impact from the catering reduced from 62 per cent to 37 per cent of the total ecological footprint. The environmental impact per visitor was reduced by 40 per cent. To calculate the ecological footprint, the online *EPA Event Calculator*[17] was used. Data was collected from the festival organiser and through a survey of visitors across five categories of resource use: energy use, transport, waste, consumption of food and lodging and total surface of the festival used.

www.wayoutwest.se

Community supported agriculture is a network or association of people who have pledged to support one or more local farms, with growers and consumers sharing the risks and benefits of food production.

The same principle may be seen within the catering industry with *Restaurant Supported Agriculture.* Some restaurants and caterers are going as far as having their own market garden farms.

You will find more on community or restaurant supported agriculture in the following:

> www.localharvest.org/csa/
> www.organicfooddirectory.com.au
> www.slowfoodusa.org
> www.makinglocalfoodwork.co.uk

Organic Certifications

There are hundreds of organic labelling systems around the world. Some are nationwide, while others are limited to smaller geographic areas or agricultural regions.

Organic certification requirements are strict and include such things as no irradiation, no GM, no sewer sludge fertilisers, no synthetic pesticides or fertilisers, and no antibiotics or hormones in meat. Here are some of the main certifiers:

USA: *USDA Organic, Farm Verified Organic, Organic Crop Improvement Association*
UK: *Soil Association, Organic Farmers and Growers Ltd*
CANADA: *Organic Agriculture Centre of Canada, Certified Organic Associations of British Columbia, Alberta Organic Producers Association*
AUSTRALIA: *Australian Certified Organic, Biological Farmers of Australia*
EUROPE/SCANDINAVIA: Denmark: *Stats-kontrolleret okologisk logo;* France*: 'AB' logo;* Italy: *bio agri cert;* The Netherlands: *SKAL;* Sweden: *KRAV;* Switzerland: *'bud'* or *'knopse'*
ASIA: China: *Ecocert;* India: *Indian National Programme for Organic Production;* Japan: *Organic Natural Foods Association;* Nepal: *Himalayan Bio-Organic;* Thailand: *ACT Organic*
Middle East/Africa: South Africa: *AFRISCO, EcoCert South Africa;* Saudi Arabia: *Organic Standard Kingdom of Saudi Arabia*

Tea, Coffee, Cacao

The coffee industry began its sustainability journey more than two decades ago, embracing the principles of fair and responsible production and trade. *Fairtrade* coffee is now a ubiquitous and somewhat expected attribute for coffee, from the world's largest brands to boutique specialty providers. Environmentally sustainable agricultural practices have been embraced with organic, chemical-free and eco-labelled coffee. Shade-grown and single-origin coffees are sought and consumers now select their coffee with as much passion as wine connoisseurs.

The issues around coffee production and trade are common to tea and cacao industries as well, with these industries also embracing the principles of fair trade and sustainable agricultural practices:

- use of land and impingement on forests
- production in harmony with the local environment
- soil degradation from chemical use
- pollution of natural environment from chemical use
- fair and safe labour conditions for farm workers
- indentured, forced or child labour.

The coffee, tea and cacao industries also have broader sustainability issues, such as:

- fair prices paid to producers for these commodity crops
- transport impact all along the supply chain
- energy intensity of production
- energy intensity of final coffee product (espresso machines are highly energy intensive).

UTZ Certified, Fairtrade Certified and *Rainforest Alliance* are the main eco-labels in these industries.

UTZ Certified is one of the leading sustainability programmes in the world for coffee, cocoa, tea and rooibos. Through the UTZ programme farmers grow better crops, generate more income and create better opportunities while safeguarding the environment and securing the earth's natural resources. The cooperation with companies all over the world enables *UTZ Certified* to increase the availability of sustainably produced commodities on a large scale (www.utzcertified.org).

The Rainforest Alliance has recognised that current agricultural practices will only continue to accelerate the cycle of poverty experienced by most farmers, especially in and around our planet's most sensitive and unique ecosystems which are under threat from the continuing march of the fields into the forests. In response they have introduced a certification system for farms in the tropics. Their little green frog certification mark is the symbol to look for on products that have been produced on *Rainforest Alliance Certified* farms. Food products receiving certification include bananas, coffee, cocoa (in chocolate), grapes, juice, mangoes, pineapples and tea. The Rainforest Alliance also certifies timber, flowers and plants, wine corks, paper products, and items that include timber from guitars to shovels, toilet seats and skateboards (www.rainforest-alliance.org).

Look also for locally produced products to reduce the transport impacts of these products, as this may be more appropriate than importing.

Meat, Dairy, Poultry

Sourcing sustainably produced beef, lamb, pork, chicken, turkey, veal and other animal-based food products is a hot topic and one that has many aspects to consider. Many of the sustainability considerations in sourcing animal food products stem from the intensity of farming at an industrial scale.

The use of feedlots, cages, crates and pens, plus the general welfare of animals and their humane treatment, are concerns. The uses of growth hormones and of genetically modified feeds are also considerations.

Meat

The use of gestation crates in pork farming is highly controversial – and something to avoid. This is where breeding sows are kept in pens only as large as their bodies where piglets can access their milk.

Veal (calves) is also traditionally raised in individual crates, but it has been banned in many countries but persists in the USA. Look for pasture-raised veal and gestation crate-free pork.

The agricultural impacts of fodder crops provided to animals not fed on natural pastures include the ongoing land clearing needed for these crops, the use of chemical fertilisers and pesticides, water use and disposal, and transport and greenhouse gas emissions from these aspects.

Extended live transportation of animals and their treatment during slaughter are also issues that need addressing.

Sourcing sustainably means purchasing animal products where the animals have been treated humanely during life and during slaughter, where the farming practices used to raise them are not damaging to the environment, where the animals are fed from chemical-free pastures and feed, and where they are not treated with growth hormones.

Dairy

The production of milk and dairy products, the use of antibiotics, and treatment of male calves and cows being kept in the pregnancy cycle are all highly debated topics.

Keeping a female dairy cow lactating is of course the aim, and to do this, of course, the cow needs to have a calf but not feed it. Female calves are kept so that they will become milk-producing cows, but male calves are the by-product of this process. Called 'bobby calves', these young animals are slaughtered as vealers. There are concerns for the welfare of these young animals, including them being 'crated' as well as the time between their last feed and slaughter.

Crating calves for veal has stopped in Australia, the UK and the European Union; however, many countries still practise it, including the USA – where it is due to end in 2017.

Additional concerns for sustainable sourcing in the dairy industry include the health and welfare of dairy cows – mastitis and lameness from standing on concrete during milking are common problems. The use of antibiotics in dairy herds to treat disease is part of an ongoing and controversial debate.

Organic certification in the dairy industry is designed to promote good health and limit stress for farmed animals. It addresses the substances used in health care and feeding of dairy herds, as well as herd management and housing. It also requires that any fodder supplied must have organic certification.

Depending on your own ethics, standards or those of your customers, you may wish to delve also into the way that a particular dairy manages bobby calves – what the chain of custody is in their treatment. In addition, to make cheese, enzymes are required and traditionally 'rennet' is used, which is obtained from calf stomachs. Imported cheeses will not be subject to the same controls as those of your own country, and the welfare of calves/vealers to extract rennet cannot be assured. So think about the issues involved before sourcing imported cheese.

Milk and cheese products from goats and sheep tend to be from boutique producers with less likelihood of factory farm intensity of main dairy farms. However, you are advised to investigate the welfare of animals and farming methods used.

Poultry and Eggs

The welfare of caged hens has long been a topical and emotional issue, with free-range and/or organic chicken meat and eggs the most sought after solutions.

Foraging is a natural act for the humble chicken and being able to scratch and peck a happy chicken makes, so this is one of the top must-takes for friendly chicken farming. Growth hormones and antibiotics are reputed to remain in meat, and so organic production does not allow the inclusion of these. Likewise, organic production does not allow the chickens to be fed genetically modified feedstock. The age of slaughter is an issue, as chickens would usually live to the age of about seven, but they are often slaughtered at between two and three months of age. Beak trimming, stock density in barns and the ease of access to outdoors from barns are also issues that are regulated in certified free-range and organic chicken farming.

Figure 8.11 The author's chickens waiting to be fed.
Source: Harmony Shire, Morrow Park Bowling Club.

Figure 8.12 Mermaid Sculpture created by Gaby Jung for Sustainable Table's work at the Melbourne Food and Wine Festival. It's made from disposable soy sauce packs!

Source: Gaby Jung.

Seafood

Our insatiable demand for seafood is causing the unnatural depletion of essential, protected and much loved marine life. Fish stocks will recover and the millions of people who rely on seafood for food and livelihoods will be protected if we only source sustainably caught seafood.

Sustainability issues in seafood production include the following:

1   Overfishing of oceans and depleting stock of popular fish species.
2   'Bycatch', where other species are unintentionally caught through net and 'longline' fishing techniques – particularly hazardous for sharks and turtles.

3   Threatened and endangered species caught through 'bycatch'.
4   Threatened and endangered species being intentionally caught, sold, served and eaten.
5   Animal cruelty, especially when marine mammals are caught.
6   Accumulation of toxins in fish, perpetuated through human pollution of waterways, particularly plastic waste.

An emotional issue in seafood consumption is 'dolphin-friendly' tuna (apart from actually sourcing threatened tuna species). The danger to dolphins comes through the intentional herding and encircling of dolphins on the surface – done as tuna follow and school underneath dolphins. This awful practice has killed millions of dolphins, and while most brands claim they do not use this practice, there are still some 'dolphin-deadly' tuna brands on the shelves.

The *Earth Island Institute* monitors tuna companies around the world to ensure that tuna fish are caught by methods that do not harm dolphins and which protect the marine ecosystem. Look for *Dolphin-Safe* certifications on any tuna sourced (www.earthisland.org).

Sustainable seafood certification programmes exist in most nations and there are also international programmes. Underlying all such programmes should be the *UN Food and Agriculture Organization of the United Nations' Guidelines for the Ecolabelling of Fish and Fishery Products from Marine Capture Fisheries*.[18]

The *Marine Stewardship Council* produces fantastic resources, from a certification programme, to a mobile app, to help identify sustainable seafood, and also a great online search function (www.msc.org).

Access the terrific resource *Greenpeace Red List* that Greenpeace has created on threatened/endangered species. It identifies the top species to avoid in your menu planning (www.greenpeace.org/usa/en/campaigns/oceans/seafood/red-fish/).

Good Catch provides practical information and events for chefs, caterers and restaurateurs, making it easier for them to serve more sustainable seafood (www.goodcatch.org.uk).

The *Sustainable Seafood Guide* is an online sustainability guide for seafood consumers in Australia. It is

Box 8.9

SUSTAINABLE TABLE AND MELBOURNE FOOD AND WINE FESTIVAL

Sustainable Table uses food as an entrée to explore sustainability issues.

They work to build an engaged community of people who want to learn about sustainable food production and how they can support a fair food system for all.

Sustainable Table was approached by the organisers of the *Melbourne Food and Wine Festival* to invigorate a space at their opening weekend event at the historic Como House in South Yarra, Melbourne.

A *Sustainable Seafood Square* was developed, which engaged local fishermen and seafood producers in a space that generated awareness around the issues we are facing in terms of the sustainability of our oceans, waterways and fish populations.

A number of free cooking classes were hosted by Oliver Edwards, Founder of *GoodFishBadFish*, who demonstrated how to cook with more sustainable, yet sometimes less popular fish species such as mullet. The event space was plastic free and was enlivened with posters and sea sculptures made from discarded soy sauce containers and plastic salvaged from the ocean, created by artist Gaby Jung.

An informational *Fishy Business* video was created by Sustainable Table and played throughout the weekend, whilst visitors were also given take-home information that included a wallet fish guide.

sustainabletable.org.au
melbournefoodandwine.com.au

designed to help make informed seafood choices and play a part in swelling the tide for sustainable seafood in Australia (www.sustainableseafood.org.au).

SeaChoice is Canada's sustainable seafood programme, created to help Canadian businesses and shoppers play an active role in supporting sustainable fisheries and aquaculture at all levels of the seafood supply chain. Based on scientific assessments, *SeaChoice* has created easy-to-use tools that help you make the best seafood choices (www.seachoice.org).

What does this mean for events?

One of the challenges for event organisers is ensuring that sustainable seafood is served, and is communicating with, gaining commitment to and an understanding of, the issues by those planning menus – venues, caterers and food stallholders.

Identify the possible non-sustainable seafood choices which may be available locally, and create a list to alert menu planners of what not to serve. Review menus well in advance to ensure that no risky options sneak through.

Vancouver Aquarium is taking sustainable seafood provision into its own hands with the *Ocean Wise* programme. They work directly with restaurants, markets and caterers to ensure they have the most current scientific information regarding seafood and helping them make ocean-friendly buying decisions. The *Ocean Wise* symbol appears on menus, display cases and products, making it easier for consumers to make environmentally friendly seafood choices. They also have a search tool, so that event planners can search for caterers tuned into sustainable seafood sourcing (www.oceanwise.ca).

Look for a similar programme locally and then preferentially contract venues, caterers and food stallholders that meet sustainable seafood standards.

Drinking Water

If you have any doubt over whether you should sell bottled water, have a quick look at Annie Leonard's *The Story of Bottled Water*.[19] If that doesn't convince you, watch the feature films *Trashed*[20] or *Tapped*.[21] Still not convinced? Watch *Captain Charles Moore's TED Talk*[22] on plastics in our oceans. Or visit one of the many websites or campaigns dedicated to keeping plastics out of our oceans. I have included a few details on plastics in our oceans in Chapter 9.

Now that we are on the same page, let's talk about what you can do to minimise or completely get rid of

Figure 8.13 City of Malmö, installed water refill stations at the recent Eurovision Song Contest.

Source: Daniel Skog and City of Malmo.

packaged water in single-use disposable plastic bottles. The first and obvious solution is to work out how you can provide drinking water in reusable containers – be they cups or refillable bottles. It will depend on your event type – a conference or static indoor event really has no excuse for handing out bottled water – unless there is no tap or bulk water supply that is drinkable. Event organisers will come up with lots of excuses as to why they 'must' have bottled water. The weakest one is that their profit is tied to the sale of bottled water. There may be operational or practical reasons why bottled water is needed, such as if you have a huge site and it's a long way back to a tap for a work crew – but then again they'll be in a vehicle and they could take a big cooler, all iced up, for the day.

For events where attendees are moving about and if it is the type of crowd and event style that you could encourage attendees to bring their own water bottles, then you really should get a lovely campaign going to promote them to bring their bottles. You could augment this by having a sponsor or event-branded water bottles to give away or sell.

If you are up against bottled water converts saying that tap water is not drinkable, and you're located in the USA, draw on this awesome piece of research. Laboratory tests conducted for the *Environmental Working Group* found that ten popular brands of bottled water, purchased from grocery stores and other retailers in nine states and the *District of Columbia*, contained 38 chemical pollutants altogether, with an average of eight contaminants in each brand. More than one-third of the chemicals found are not regulated in bottled water.[23] You can also pull out of the bag that bottled water costs more than 1500 times the cost of water from a tap – yes, the organisers need to pay for the water refill station infrastructure, but they also have to pay for all waste removal if they use bottled water. Bottled water is also a big old GHG producer, when you factor in the oil used in the production of the bottle itself along with the energy needed in the manufacture of the bottle and the bottling process, along with the transport of the finished product. There is no exact bottled water carbon footprint, as each brand has varying production methods and locations, but suffice it to say that the total GHGs created by bottled water far exceed that of water from your tap.

To help maximise uptake of people 'remembering' to bring their refillable water bottles, tie your messaging to a water or waste campaign, such as one of the clean ocean projects, or a drinking water programme. Great programmes are out there which bring safe drinking water to communities that need it. Take a look at *The Water Project* (thewaterproject.org), *Frank* (www.frankwater.com) and *Wateraid* (www.wateraid.org).

By aligning with an environmentally or socially beneficial campaign, you will hopefully elicit an emotional connection from your event attendees and encourage 100 per cent participation, as they will be socially shunned if they're seen to be drinking from a disposable water bottle!

In 2013 *Shambala Festival* was the first music festival of its type in the UK to go completely disposable water bottle free. Absolutely no bottled water was available onsite. They aligned with Frank water charity, which sold branded refillable water bottles.

At *Sydney Festival* in 2012, the naming rights sponsor was *ZIP*, the water filter company. They set up great water refill stations, using the in-home water filters they promote, as well as giving away branded water bottles. A waste audit was conducted to assess whether the water bottles given away were actually discarded as well, but the results were very encouraging, with few of the reusable bottles being thrown away.

Set up a refill station

There are many ways in which a water refill station can be set up. Your local water authority is the first port of call. Their promotions department will always be keen to promote drinking their tap water, as it is a testament to their great product delivery! It is possible that they will already have a water refill station that just needs to be booked.

The local government/council will possibly also have a refill station for events. The amenities provider you use for toilet hire will most likely have something available to put together a refill station. In addition, as mentioned earlier, getting a water filter sponsor on board is a fast track to having very flash water refill points.

If you're lucky, there will be a water refill station on wheels that is for hire by events such as by *Tranquil Water* in Australia (www.tranquilwater.com.au) or *Water on Wheels* in Canada (www.wateronwheels.ca).

If you're organising a marathon, triathlon or similar, and require hydration stations, look at whether you can use the local fire hydrant or mains water supply. Read about how the *Medtronic Twin Cities Marathon* started using water hydrants for fluid stations for competitors in place of bottled water on the book's website.

What does this mean for events?

✓ Ban prepackaged bottled water and use refillable cups and bottles only. Bring back the tap!

✓ Ensure that the water is 'potable' (suitable for drinking). Have it tested and promote the results of the test to reassure your patrons that what they are drinking is healthy. Put water filters on taps if there is any doubt or psychological barriers to drinking water on behalf of the audience.

✓ Pre-promote to the audience that they should bring their own bottles for refilling.

✓ Double-check the health and safety regulations with regard to the aforementioned 'spit transfer' from tap nozzle to bottle opening.

✓ Offer refillable bottles for sale.

✓ Adequately signpost the water points, including them on site maps and other relevant communications material.

✓ You could offer a partnership with your local water authority. They are likely to want to promote their water and its consumption.

Food and Beverage Serviceware

Serving food and drinks is a major activity at many events. The most sustainable option is of course washable and reusable serviceware, but at many events this may not be practical and disposable solutions are the alternative.

This section of the chapter will look at the myriad sustainable disposable food packaging options available to the event industry, some of which are made specifically with our sector in mind.

First, I need to make a point, and that point is: *there is absolutely no reason why polystyrene products need be used, as there are fantastic sustainable options available.* If you do one thing . . . BAN POLYSTYRENE. Let's take a moment. Breathe. And let's repeat:

BAN POLYSTYRENE AT YOUR EVENTS

I would prefer to go hungry than accept a meal served on this horrible product. And I've done so many times, leaving a perplexed and confused kebab seller after an anti-polystyrene rave by me. It hurts every time I see one of those foamy evil things sitting atop a counter or lying in the gutter.

Polystyrene is a plastic, made from petroleum, which we know is a non-renewable resource. It may look like 'normal' plastic, such as inside CD jewel cases or the trays that contain meat at the supermarket, or be 'foamy', like the ubiquitous coffee cup or hamburger container (called expanded polystyrene). This foamy material is a big

Box 8.10

FOOD AND BEVERAGE CHECKLIST

❏ Food sourced from producers using sustainable farming practices.

❏ Food with relevant independent certification is sourced.

❏ Transport impacts/food miles are considered.

❏ Waste impact of service is managed.

❏ Unopened or unserved food is donated to charity.

❏ Locally and seasonally sourced ingredients.

❏ Consideration for seasonally available produce found locally is included in menu planning.

❏ Local sustainable food programmes, campaigns and messages are included in the event.

❏ Food is chemical and growth hormone free.

❏ Food has not been irradiated.

❏ Food has not been genetically modified or treated with nano-technology.

❏ Healthy and fresh options are available.

❏ Cultural or religious requirements are catered for.

❏ Diverse dietary requirements are catered for.

❏ Food service is used as a vehicle to promote healthy eating and sustainable sourcing.

❏ Humane animal treatment during life, transport and slaughter.

❏ Food with fair labour practices is sourced.

❏ Food with fair prices paid to producers is sourced.

❏ Workers on farms that produce our fresh fruit and vegetables receive a decent living wage.

❏ Fruit and vegetables with independent organic certification are sourced.

❏ Local growers that are 'transitioning' to organic are supported.

❏ Local growers that are using sustainable farming methods and are not using chemicals but are unable to afford national organic certification are supported.

❏ Fresh produce with biodynamic/demeter and other independent recognition of sustainable growing practices is sourced.

❏ Fairtrade produce is sourced.

❏ Fresh fruit and vegetables are used in preference to frozen or canned.

❏ Communications material is included on tables to explain food providence.

❏ That which is not sourced locally has a comparably low carbon footprint – in terms of farming practices and transport impacts.

❏ Pasture-fed rather than grain-fed feedlot beef is sourced.

❏ Pig products are sourced from free-range farms.

❏ Pig products are sourced from farms that do not use gestation crates.

❏ Veal is pasture-raised.

❏ Poultry and eggs sourced are free range.

❏ Halal and Kosher meat and poultry is sourced where applicable.

❏ Dairy products use non-animal non-GMO enzymes in place of rennet if vegetarian menus are promoted or if rennet sourcing is a concern.

❏ No threatened or endangered species are sourced.

❏ Seafood is sourced from sustainable fisheries.

pollution problem, as it's light and blows around in the wind and floats on water. It's also difficult to recycle, and not all kerbside recycling pickups take it. It's unlikely that recycling facilities will exist in your area to process it and you really shouldn't be using a product made of non-renewable resources that is made for a moment on the lips and a lifetime in the tip!

There are some manufacturers of this product that are taking on the responsibility of recycling it. At an industrial level, polystyrene is a plastic that has some value, and so advances are being made in its recapture and recycling. This isn't likely to make its way to the disposable food container any time soon.

You may already have a ban on polystyrene food

Figure 8.14 Compostable food serviceware made from bulrush.

Photo: Be Green Packaging.

packaging in your state or city. Many across the USA are passing laws at local or state government level to this effect.

So no to plastic or polystyrene: what are the alternatives? You want your food packaging to be made from sustainably produced materials and, if you are able to collect food and food serviceware for composting, for it to be compostable. Here are some options for you to consider.

Bagasse

Bagasse or sugar cane fibre is a renewable material and makes a great disposable food container. Bagasse is a by-product of sugar cane production – the fibrous pulp left after the juice has been extracted from the cane. It is used to make paper products, including copy and printing paper, as discussed earlier in this chapter.

The food service products made out of bagasse include plates, bowls, cups, boxes, trays and lunch boxes. They're heat resistant and chlorine-free bleached. They are made

in just about every country where sugar cane is manufactured. Your food serviceware supplier should be able to source the product for you, or do your own research and purchase directly from the manufacturer. Just make sure that you check the product's origin in case it's done several trips around the globe before reaching you! If your only option is to use imported stock, look for a product that has offset the transport GHG emissions.

BioPak manufacture and distribute 100 per cent carbon-neutral bagasse food serviceware, which is certified as compostable by the *Biodegradable Products Institute* (*BPI*)[24] and meets the requirements of *EN 13432*. Their products are available in Australia. Visit their website (www.biopak.com.au). In the USA *Stalkmarket* and *Ecoguardian*. both have great ranges of bagasse products and are certified by BPI (www.stalkmarketproducts.com; www.ecoguardian.com).

Bulrush

Bulrush is a unique material source for producing disposable packaging. Bulrush is robust and grows rapidly, making it a great raw material fibre for producing paper-like products. It grows wild in the low mountain areas and marshlands in southeastern China and is harvested sustainably once a year from wild crops rather than from cultivated plants. When sourcing serviceware made from bulrush, request assurances that the harvesting has been undertaken sustainably.

Be Green Packaging manufactures disposable serviceware and food/take-out packaging from natural plant fibres including bulrush, along with bamboo and wheatstraw. Their line of products is compostable and biodegradable, and is also microwave, oven and freezer safe.

The packaging is unbleached, meaning that it retains its natural colour (tan) and is highly durable for a range of uses. The packaging has received *Cradle to Cradle* certification. Visit their website (begreenpackagingstore. com).

Palm Fibre

Palm fibre is another great source of renewable (and in this case waste) material to create serviceware. Palm fibre is discarded when the fruit from the palm husk is harvested throughout the year for its oil.

This leftover palm fibre would traditionally be incinerated or landfilled, but now, with the smart design concept of *Earthcycle*, the fibre continues its useful life in the form of disposable packaging and, once finished, is able to be composted. The products are certified as compostable to standards *ASTM D6400* and *ASTM D6868*[25] and are free from bleach, dyes and chemicals. *Earthcycle* products are available in North America, Australia and New Zealand. Check their website for more information (www.earthcycle.com).

Palm Leaf Plates

These wonderful plates are usually made in India but have found markets far and wide around the globe. They are made simply from fallen palm leaves. The areca palm is the tree of choice and the manufacturing process uses no chemicals or bleaches, no glues or resins. It is manufactured by soaking the leaf in water and pressing it into shape.

It is a truly sustainable product that uses a waste stream that would otherwise be burnt or left to degrade. I encourage you to use them. Again ask your food service packaging supplier to source them, or go directly to the companies set up in just about every country that import this terrific product.

The knock-on social benefits are also wonderful, with the reputable companies that manufacture and supply areca palm plates also integrating fair trade concepts in the sourcing and manufacturing of the products. Drill in the backstory of your chosen product and make sure the palm plates you choose also benefit the communities from which they are sourced.

Asapana are manufacturers, traders and distributors of areca palm leaf plate products made from fallen palm leaves. Their plates have been used at events such as the *Kumbh Mela*, one of the largest religious gatherings in the world, the *Big Chill Music Festival* in Goa and the UK, along with *Glastonbury Festival* and *Womad Festival* in the UK (www.asapana.com).

Potato Starch

Potatoes are a great source of starch, which may be used to make packaging. Potatoes, on their journey from farm to dinner plate, are blasted with water – washed, scrubbed, and then pushed through knives to cut wedges or chips. The water, which is now full of starch from the cut surfaces, is processed through a starch extractor. What comes out is potato starch, a valuable by-product, and after being filtered leaves another valuable resource: clean, reusable water. *Earthpac Ltd* in New Zealand produce serviceware made from potato starch, and their products are compostable in both home and industrial compost facilities. They are certified to meet composting standards *EN 13432*,[26] *ASTM D6400*,[27] *EN 14995*[28] and *ISO 17088*.[29] Visit their website to purchase directly or find a distributor near you (www.earth-pac. com).

Tapioca Starch

Tapioca is another great source of starch, and this starch is being mixed with grass or wood fibres to create an innovative non-tree and non-plastic compostable container option.

Biosphere® produce packaging made from renewable materials, designed to be home as well as commercially compostable. They are primarily made from annual renewable resources, with some additional renewable ingredients coming from materials with more than an annual growth cycle.

Biosphere® use a unique process to transform the product from raw material into serviceware – baking plant starch into rigid shapes, similar to the process of making waffles or ice-cream cones.

Their *Blueware®* range is designed to be marine safe, so if their products do reach the ocean, they will degrade in about three weeks with no toxicity produced. All products are GMO free and human non-allergenic. They have been approved by the US Navy and certified by the *US Army Natick Soldier Research Development and Engineering Center* to be marine degradable per *ASTM D7081.*[30]

With more than 20 per cent of marine plastic debris estimated to come from ocean-going vessels and platforms, the US Navy endorsement is hugely relevant and a great achievement for this supplier of fantastic serviceware made from renewable resources. Products may be purchased directly through *Biosphere*'s online store, or contact them to find a distributor near you (www.biosphereindustries.com).

Bio Plastics

Bio plastics are a new class of polymers derived from organic (i.e. carbon-based) sources. In most cases this is crop waste, with the majority being the by-products of corn farming.

Polylactic acid (PLA) is a resin developed by *Cargill and Teijin Limited* of Japan under the banner of *Natureworks LLC* (www.natureworksllc.com). PLA uses the carbon stored in starch plants such as corn, which break down into sugars. A fermentation process changes these natural sugars into a plastic look-alike material. Its popular use is for cups and straws, but it is also used as a coating for paper products. PLA biodegrades in four to six months. According to *Natureworks LLC* it uses 65 per cent less fossil fuel resources to produce, and reduces greenhouse gas emissions by 80 to 90 per cent compared to traditional petroleum-based polymers (plastic to you and I).

Unlike regular plastics, bio plastics are not petroleum based, and are *technically* compostable in industrial scale facilities. Many industrial composting facilities will still not accept bio plastics, as their processes usually turn out the end product in a week or two, and PLA just cannot decompose in that time, no matter the intensity of the process. So if you use PLA and intend to send it for composting at an industrial facility, check first that they will accept PLA and at what volume or proportion of your total organic waste.

The big problem with this seemingly sustainable product is that it can corrupt existing recycling systems, since the user may see the product as 'normal plastic' and place it in the recycling bin. This then disrupts recycling processes, as few MRFs have the technology (or the time and enough people if manually sorted) to separate PLA from plastic. The industry is tackling this problem and technology is available to accurately separate PLA bottles from plastics. Every region's MRFs operate in slightly different ways and you will need to check if your MRF can separate PLA from other plastics.

Of great concern is the emergence of PLA packaged bottled water being marketed to the event industry as a 'green' solution. The challenge is that any responsible event producer will have efficient recycling systems in place already and if they want to sell/provide these PLA-based single-use water bottles they will need to create a separate waste system for them, further complicating waste management at the event. It then becomes a convoluted messaging issue as you can no longer simply say 'bottles' or 'recycling' with a picture of a bottle on your bin signs, since soft drinks and other beverages would be made from normal plastic. And if you are successful at segregation, what to do with all the PLA cups and bottles? Do you have industrial composting facilities that will take them?

The benefits of PLA are that they don't use fossil fuels as a source material, and they are in fact biodegradable – they will break down naturally over time. Some brands

Figure 8.15 Promoting the fact that serviceware is compostable.

Source: Meegan Jones.

SERVICEWARE CHECKLIST

❏ Reusable and washable serviceware is used.

❏ If disposable serviceware is used, minimal packaging is provided.

❏ If disposable serviceware is used, choice of type is based on the waste-processing facilities available and venue separation systems.

❏ If disposable is used, optimally, compostable materials are chosen.

❏ A system is in place to collect food scraps and serviceware for composting.

❏ Recyclable serviceware is used if 'dirty recyclables' can be recycled.

❏ Single-serve sachets are not used (e.g. for condiments). Rather, bulk dispensing is used.

❏ Prepackaged bottled water is not provided or sold, and water refill stations are available.

❏ 'Compostable' materials are promoted as 'green options' to event attendees only if they are actually collected for composting.

❏ 'Biodegradable' materials, if chosen, are not promoted as 'green options' if they are only ending up in landfill.

Figure 8.16 Food vendors impact upon purchasing.
Photo: GreenShoot Pacific.

will also conduct a life cycle assessment and provide you with a comparison of the total carbon footprint of the product so that you can make an informed choice.

If you have been converted to the use of PLA cups, bottles or food containers, have an appropriate disposal plan in place. They must be collected separately and composted, and plans in place to avoid accidental confusion for recyclables or just ending up in landfill.

VENDORS, EXHIBITORS AND SPONSORS

Everything sold or provided at your event, whether or not directly by you, will still be viewed as being part of your event's final offering. The event's reputation, green or otherwise, hinges in part on the behaviour of these vendors and exhibitors, sponsors and catering experienced by event attendees.

Choosing, contracting or approving the participation of caterers, food vendors, exhibitors, sponsors and non-food traders may be viewed as one of the event organiser's sourcing decisions. You will have varying levels of control or influence over vendors' consequential sourcing decisions or at-event production behaviour; however, you will, in most cases, have control over their actual participation. Their sourcing and at-event production logistics may be either controlled or significantly influenced through your contracting agreements, and through engaging their interest and participation in your sustainability goals.

For those events where permanent retailers, restaurants and cafés put temporary outlets into an event, such as a street fair, things do get a little trickier in terms of being able to put controls on these participants. In the case of a street fair, it is likely a main street committee, tourism association or Chamber of Commerce to which the traders belong that will be putting on the event, and through this organisation the vendors' sourcing and production logistics as part of the fair could be influenced.

Certainly, street fairs of this type are a great opportunity to permanently change sourcing and operational behaviours of permanent traders. What better way to get an entire street of cafés to stop using polystyrene burger containers permanently, than through a focused campaign aligned with the annual street fair?

Caterers and Food Vendors

Those providing food services are major stakeholders in your sustainable sourcing successes. Caterers will be contracted by you via the venue or directly, and will undertake food sourcing on your behalf. Your control comes in the actual sourcing of the caterer or venue in the first place.

For food vendors, if you're in a position to approve those that attend your event, then you can place requirements on them concerning their participation. Some events will have food vendors on waiting lists, while others (often new or one-off events) may be trying hard to persuade any food vendors they can find to be involved. In the latter case it will be more a situation of engagement and buy-in as well as targeted recruitment of vendors already operating sustainably than placing restrictions up front, which may deter likely participants.

If you're in a position to choose the venue and/or the caterer, include requirements in the request for tender. Contract it in and have a system in place to pre-check plans and adherence to requirements, and double-check that all is going according to plan at the event.

If you have to go with one particular venue and the caterer is already contracted to that venue, things get a little trickier. In this case you will be using your best influencing techniques to persuade the caterer to potentially change their behaviour. You will need to understand what the motivation could be for the caterer or venue to wish to change. Make sure you suggest things they will be able to keep doing, rather than a quirky one-off idea exclusively for your event. The lasting legacy will be for your event to have left a positive change in the way a venue undertakes food sourcing into the future.

The trick in any of these scenarios is not to leave the food service decisions until the last minute, as caterers and food vendors need advance warning to be able to source sustainably on your behalf. Look for a caterer, venue or food vendor that:

- Has a sustainable food sourcing policy.
- Confirms that only sustainable seafood sourcing is undertaken.
- Is able to meet your sourcing requirements, including local, certified, dietary and culturally appropriate food.
- Has in-kitchen operations that ensure biodegradable waste is collected for composting, biogas, worm farms or animal feed.
- Has in-kitchen operations that ensure recyclable materials are segregated and recycled.
- Has a used vegetable oil pick-up service.
- Is able to meet your serviceware requirements (reusable or compostable).
- Minimises the use of waxed or polystyrene boxes for produce deliveries.
- Is able to meet your at-event waste management requirements.
- Has initiatives of their own which enhance the sustainability aspects of your event.

Exhibitors and Non-food Vendors

At trade fairs and exhibitions the vendors are there specifically to promote their wares (products, services, ideas). When sponsors set up shop at your event they are there to either blatantly hand out or promote their products, or they will create (usually) fun activities for attendees to 'interact' with their brand. Non-food vendors setting up stalls to sell market-style items are also a popular choice for events.

Whether indoors or out, exhibitors, sponsors and vendors setting up at events will create temporary installations, booths and activities, all of which will use power, create waste and consume resources.

Influencing the behaviours and sourcing decisions of the exhibitors will drastically affect the sustainability outcomes of your event, especially where waste, energy and overall consumption of materials is concerned.

Consider the following list when choosing, accepting, setting up application forms or trying to influence the behaviour of exhibitors, vendors and sponsors. Encourage them to take on the following in their own design and operations of their at-event activities.

DISPLAY/BOOTH DESIGN

✓ Reduce the amount of materials needed to produce the display – this saves resources (materials and money).
✓ Hire rather than buy if only single use is needed.
✓ Hire furniture and decorative items locally, rather than transporting items that could be sourced at the event destination.
✓ Reduce the amount of new materials used.
✓ Consider reuse – does the design allow relatively easy disassembly, packing, transport and storage for future use?
✓ Design for durability – reuse is only going to be possible if the display materials are kept presentable. Consider how to prevent scratching, scuffing and denting so that reuse is assured.
✓ Flat pack – design flat packs to minimise transport requirements and facilitate easy storage.
✓ Design for deconstruction – design the booth construction with end of show in mind. No glue. Pulls down into component parts for storage and reuse, recycling or salvage/repurposing.
✓ Inks – consideration for non-toxic ink use is included in the design of display materials requiring printing (panels, stickers, signage).
✓ 'Brand Roadkill' is considered – ensuring that no brand activation will end up as litter!
✓ Use display materials from recycled content such as X-Board.
✓ Timber used is from sustainably managed forests with appropriate certification.

✓ Use renewable rapid-growing natural materials (e.g. bamboo).

DÉCOR, FURNITURE, DRESSING AND SUPPLIES

✓ Use paints, varnishes, finishes, etc., with appropriate certification – VOC free/low VOC, non-toxic.
✓ Do not use PVC.
✓ Do not use polystyrene/Styrofoam.
✓ Use carpets made from recycled materials and/or are able to be recycled at end of life. Carpet squares are best; hired is great.
✓ Don't include any single-use decorative items, and avoid any 'booth bling' that is likely to create litter.

PROMOTIONAL ACTIVITY

✓ Avoid waste-creating giveaways.
✓ Do not hand out plastic bags.
✓ Do not hand out pamphlets which are redundant when electronic transmission of promotional material is effective.
✓ Do not produce single-use gimmick giveaways unrelated to the company's core purpose.
✓ Use electronic means to capture delegate/visitor information, including lanyard swipe technology.
✓ Use electronic promotional materials such as screens, ipads and displays.
✓ Any items produced for sale or distribution adhere to the event's sustainable procurement guidelines.

SUSTAINABLE PROCUREMENT POLICY

A written Sustainable Procurement Policy highlighting all the likely purchasing categories and impact areas is a useful document to have. It will set the foundation for tender requirements and for evaluating and justifying final sourcing decisions.

The policy may be prescriptive, with 'must takes', or only guiding in nature, with 'where possible', 'where feasible' or 'where available' language used. In addition, it may be appropriate to include a dollar value over which full backstory scrutiny of the product's material supply chain is undertaken. It is not going to be practical for everything to be scrutinised in such detail; for example, to drill right down to the one roll of tape you are using in the office. Here are things to consider including in your policy.

Preamble

Include the following at the beginning of the policy:

- state your commitment to sustainable purchasing, and list the stakeholders and decision makers;
- detail any specific elements peculiar to your situation;
- include your intentions on buying reusable, refillable, durable and repairable goods.

Energy and GHG Emissions

The policy should include specific aims regarding materials and products with low carbon footprints and energy efficient. Included in the policy would be the following:

- position on purchasing RECs (e.g. *GreenPower*);
- technology and appliances to be energy efficient and have good energy star ratings (or similar programme);
- lighting (interior, exterior and theatrical);
- heating, cooling and ventilation;
- vehicle choices – purchasing and hire;
- travel policy;
- carbon offsetting policy.

Recycling and Reuse

The policy should include mention of recycled materials and recyclability of materials. Examples of considerations to include in your sustainable procurement policy include the following:

- products and packaging made from recycled materials;
- products which can be recycled at end of life;
- to actively source salvaged products for creative reuse;
- to send your used products for reuse or repurposing.

Biodegradability

If your events have waste management that has a composting stream or other non-landfill way of managing biodegradable waste, you will want to include specific materials requirements in your procurement policy:

- beverage containers;
- food serviceware;
- cutlery;
- serviettes (e.g. low ink);
- use of pizza boxes (e.g. don't use or ensure low inked).

Toxins and Pollutants

Materials and products to be free of or low in toxins, chemicals and pollutants. Items to specify would include the following:

- cleaning products (solvents, VOCs, marine safe);
- paints and varnishes (solvents, VOCs);
- printing inks (chemicals and VOCs);
- pest control (chemicals, toxins);
- garments (chemical use in cotton);
- paper (bleaching);
- buy products with relevant eco-label certification.

Forest Conservation

Many products used at events can be traced back to being sourced from forests, or where forests once existed. If forest conservation and protection is a concern, include details in your policy for the following:

- timber;
- paper products;
- coffee, tea, and other rainforest crops;
- palm oil.

Local Supply and Product Miles

Supporting local suppliers is an important aspect of any procurement policy. Include considerations such as the following; however, you may wish to be very specific about products, especially if the local region is renowned for a particular item.

- buy locally;
- buy products made in your country from materials grown, mined or created in your country;
- preferentially plan for the inclusion of materials or products which are grown or manufactured locally;
- give preference or reduced rates to local traders to participate in the event;
- give preference to local contractors;
- give preference to local recruitment of the work-force.

Fair Trade and Fair Production

Your policy should also consider the welfare of those producing the products you require, along with fair payment to producers and workers. Included in the policy could be the following:

- buy products which pay a fair wage to labourers;
- buy products which have a fair price paid to primary producers;
- buy products which are part of the Fairtrade system, protecting producers from market fluctuations in commodity crops such as coffee and tea;
- buy products manufactured under fair labour conditions with independent certification.

Water

The policy should include consideration for water conservation, and could include details on the following:

- low water footprint in the creation of raw materials;
- low water footprint in the manufacture of the product;
- low-flow and water-efficient products being used.

Sustainable Food Sourcing

As for many events, food sourcing is a major activity, and it may warrant its own section within your policy. Include relevant food sourcing considerations you wish to adhere to, such as the following:

- sustainable seafood;
- sustainable agriculture practices;
- humane animal products;
- use of organic, Fairtrade or other certifications;
- use of local produce (specify items relevant to the region);
- dietary, cultural and religiously appropriate foods;
- provision of drinking water;
- food and beverage serviceware sourcing.

Performance Measurement

The policy should include how the performance will be measured against the policy. See more details on procurement performance reporting below.

SUPPLIER MANAGEMENT

In the event industry, many production aspects are delivered by service providers (e.g. contracted crew, cleaning workforce) and much of the sourcing of materials and supplies is indirect (e.g. by venues, caterers and participating vendors).

The organising team for many events is modest in size compared with the venues and contractors providing infrastructure, cleaning, security, and other services. The organisers will have direct control over the choice of the following:

- venue;
- caterers and bars (unless incumbent to venue);
- sponsors and vendors;
- performers/talent, programme content;
- marketing material;
- merchandise and gifts;
- event-specific signage and décor.

These last three services may be subcontracted out to a marketing or design agency making materials sourcing on your behalf.

Depending on the venue, the organiser may also have control over choice of the following:

- lighting and sound;
- staging and temporary infrastructure;
- signage and décor;
- furniture.

In addition to the above, for outdoor events the production team will also have direct control (in most cases) over the choice of the following:

- temporary staging and infrastructure, including fencing, barriers, marquees;
- temporary power providers;
- waste infrastructure and cleaners;
- security, welfare, safety, medical;
- amenities.

As you can see, the bulk of the physical materials procurement is often carried out by third parties contracted to the event organiser. Therefore processes must be put in place to strictly control or significantly influence the materials sourcing decisions being made on behalf of the event.

Most of the supplier management process is a case of managing those third parties making sourcing decisions impacting upon the event, rather than directly liaising with product providers.

It is advisable that you be fully informed of the specific materials and product sustainability issues, and conduct supply chain research to understand what solutions are possible so that you can include these requirements in contracts with third parties.

The supplier management processes set up must reflect your sustainable procurement policies and be effective in communicating these requirements to those suppliers purchasing materials on your behalf, along with any suppliers with whom you deal directly. Your supplier management process should also include searching out solutions, and have a structure around evaluating sourcing choices.

The *ISO 20121 Event Sustainability Management Systems* standard includes a requirement to undertake supply chain management. Refer to Clause 8.3 in the standard.

You will want to get to the point where your suppliers and contractors are presenting you with the most sustainable choices as a matter of standard business practice. With enough continual reinforcement of what you want them to supply, eventually you'll be batting them off with a stick!

Included in your supply chain management process will be the following tasks:

- Identifying direct and indirect materials and products to be procured or hired.
- Identifying sustainability issues relating to each.
- Identifying the optimal sustainability solutions.
- Identifying which solutions are available locally and engaging in dialogue with suppliers regarding potential provision of products and services meeting sustainability requirements.
- Identifying the level of control of sourcing decisions and establishing techniques or controls to influence those procuring on your behalf.
- Setting and communicating tender sustainability specifications.
- Setting and communicating the evaluation process.
- Quality delivery and supplier management process.
- Inclusion of supplier support and guidance to deliver to specifications.
- Supplier performance review specifications and process.
- Supply performance feedback process.

Rather than simply swapping to a new supplier, work with your existing contacts. For example, get them to investigate organic cotton, to report to you on the welfare of the workers in garment factories, and to understand the climate impact of transporting goods around the world.

Roskilde Festival in Denmark does just this. For the past few years they have been working with their merchandise partner to make a shift towards fair trade and environmentally friendly products. Instead of changing to another partner, they encouraged their current supplier to alter their collection. After checking the supply chain, they succeeded in having a certified Fairtrade crew T-shirt and official festival T-shirt. They also changed to Fairtrade wine. Needing to be glass free, they collaborated with *Tetrapak* and their wine merchant to produce custom-made Fairtrade wine. This also allowed them to print the logo and the refund instructions, ensuring the cartons were returned for recycling.

Suppliers may include providers of materials and goods as well as services, and also include those making sourcing decisions on your behalf. A list of example supplier categories is included at the beginning of the chapter.

PERFORMANCE REPORTING

When reporting on the performance of sustainable procurement initiatives, you should include the following:

- Sustainable sourcing initiatives undertaken.
- Quantitative outcomes of sourcing initiatives.

Measuring this in metric terms may seem a difficult or even tedious task to undertake. All events (should) require the following to enable effective and informative sustainable procurement reporting:

- a budget, segregated by expenditure category;
- a sustainable procurement policy.

Using these two tools you can cross-calculate the amount of money spent on certain line items with what you said you were going to do within your policy. It really is that simple.

For example, you state in your policy that you will use 100 per cent post-consumer recycled paper. In your budget you have logged that you have spent £X on printing. Analyse how much of your spend on printing was actually on 100 per cent post-consumer recycled paper. And so on for all your pledges within your policy.

If your organisation has various departments or divisions responsible for different areas of the budget, set them up with spread sheets or online interfaces whereby they can log what they spend and whether it meets the requirements you have stipulated.

What you report on will be determined by what you have specified in your sustainable procurement policy as mandatory or preferential. Examples include the following:

- percentage of expenditure on local manufacturers;
- percentage of expenditure from local suppliers;
- percentage of expenditure from companies with sustainability policies;
- percentage of merchandise with sustainability certification;
- percentage of hotels with sustainability certification;
- number of venues or service providers compliant with *ISO 20121*;
- proportion of suppliers scruitinised for independent sustainability certification;
- percentage of menu served with organic certification;
- percentage of Fairtrade certified coffee and tea served;
- percentage of produce served sourced from within 100 miles of the event location;
- percentage of vendors at the event that are local;
- percentage of workforce that live locally.

GRI Reporting Indicators

The *Global Reporting Initiative Event Organizers' Sector Supplement* (GRI EOSS) has several reporting indicators which are relevant to sourcing. When we produced the GRI EOSS we created three additional indicators and a new aspect: 'Sourcing'.

EO8 PERCENTAGE OF AND ACCESS TO FOOD AND BEVERAGE THAT MEETS THE ORGANISER'S POLICIES, OR LOCAL, NATIONAL OR INTERNATIONAL STANDARD.

As food and beverage provision at events is such a major activity and area of sourcing, it deserves its own indicator.

This indicator suggests you report on the provision of food and beverage that:

- meets your sustainable sourcing policy;
- meets recognised international standards (such as eco-labels and certifications).

These would be reported as a percentage of total food and beverage expenditure. For example, if your policy states that you must only provide sustainably caught seafood from certified suppliers, then the report would be the percentage of total expenditure of seafood meeting this requirement.

This indicator also suggests reporting on the initiatives undertaken to ensure food and beverage health and safety.

In a final recommendation, this indicator suggests reporting on the communications techniques used to inform participants (e.g. caterers and vendors) and attendees of the sustainable food and beverage sourcing policy and initiatives.

EO9 TYPE AND SUSTAINABILITY PERFORMANCE OF SOURCING INITIATIVES.

This indicator suggests disclosure on approach to sustainable sourcing. This would include discussion on the level of control or influence an organiser has on various components of the supply chain. The initiatives undertaken or planned for should be disclosed, along with the performance outcomes.

EO10 TYPE, AMOUNT AND IMPACT OF BENEFITS, FINANCIAL AND IN KIND, RECEIVED BY THE EVENT ORGANISER FROM SUPPLIERS.

This indicator is most relevant for professional event organisers planning events on behalf of clients. It is often common practice to receive commissions, incentives or rewards for using certain suppliers or venues and encouraging clients to do so, or in fact just using suppliers without telling clients.

This indicator offers an opportunity to authentically disclose any such commissions or incentives. Financial or in-kind benefits to event organisers are part of standard industry practice and are acceptable, as this is how many organisers are paid for their services. Excessive commissions or incentives may result in undue influence by the supplier on the organiser and it is this that the performance indicator is primarily addressing.

The indicator requests that processes to manage supplier influence through commissions are in place.

These could be various policies held by the event organiser preventing staff from taking personal benefits. It may also include a conflict of interest policy.

The indicator suggests that the organiser report the total commissions received and the proportion of the organiser's workforce receiving additional commissions or rewards.

EC6 POLICY, PRACTICES, AND PROPORTION OF SPENDING ON LOCALLY BASED SUPPLIERS AT SIGNIFICANT LOCATIONS OF OPERATION.

This indicator gives the organiser an opportunity to formally report on the proportion of the event budget spent locally. The first thing to do is to define what is 'local'. This will be unique to each event and it is acceptable to define 'local' within the destination's context.

The indicator suggests reporting on whether the organiser's procurement policy has stated a preference for or commitment to local procurement. The tender evaluation process, including 'local' as a decision filter, should be explained. This would include an explanation of how other factors in supplier evaluation such as cost and other sustainability factors are balanced.

During the creation of the *Event Organizers' Sector Supplement* an additional indictor was devised which allows the reporter to disclose the economic impacts and value creation as a direct result of sustainability initiatives.

EO1 DIRECT ECONOMIC IMPACTS AND VALUE CREATION AS A RESULT OF SUSTAINABILITY INITIATIVES.

This indicator could sit within any chapter of this book, as it is relevant to all sustainability initiatives.

The business case is something that most top managers wish to understand before making any significant financial investment or resource allocation (staff, time, materials) to a specific sustainability initiative. In some cases the business benefits will be immediate and obvious (e.g. save energy = pay a lower electricity bill, or create less waste = lower cleaning and waste disposal fees). Other initiatives may result in increased revenue (more people want to come to the event or more sponsors want to be involved), and in enhanced reputation and brand value.

This indicator suggests that organisations report on the direct economic impacts (cost savings, revenue received, additional expenditure/investment) resulting from sustainability initiatives. It also suggests reporting on value created for the organisation as a result of sustainability initiatives. 'Value' is defined by the GRI EOSS as *additional or increased benefit delivered by an organisation's activities, including brand value and employee satisfaction, among others.*

The impacts may be to save money or earn revenue, or in fact require an investment of funds and resources. Both should be reported on. The latter is especially important if intangible benefits and value such as reputational enhancement are achieved. To prove the added value qualitative evidence or empirical research may be undertaken.

Report on direct financial impacts from initiatives such as the following:

- Energy conservation.
- Water conservation.
- Responsible printing practices.
- Waste management initiatives.
- Community engagement programmes.
- Safety and security programmes.
- Sustainable and/or responsible sourcing initiatives and solutions.

The value created for the organisation, as a result of sustainability initiatives, should also be reported and the GRI EOSS suggests the following:

- Increased amount and scale of sponsorship.
- Increased media reach and impact.
- Enhanced brand value.
- Product and service innovation.

EC9 UNDERSTANDING AND DESCRIBING SIGNIFICANT INDIRECT ECONOMIC IMPACTS, INCLUDING THE EXTENT OF IMPACTS.

Whereas the direct economic impacts of financial expenditure of an event locally are reported through indicator EC6, indicator EC9 allows the organisation to report on the enduring economic impacts occurring as the financial benefits circulate throughout the economy. Whereas the direct economic impacts are the amount of money transacted between the event and supply chain, the indirect impacts are the outcomes or benefits of that financial injection into the economy. The indirect benefit can also be to the reporting organisation, such as giving it competitive advantage locally, enhancing reputation and involvement by the community with the event, or just giving it a 'social licence to operate'. This means that the community supports the event's existence as the organisers have proven they are committed to supporting the local economy. The opposite of this would be the local community actively obstructing or boycotting the event planning and delivery.

Indirect economic impacts to the local community and supply chain may include the following:

- enhancing or enabling increased productivity;
- creation of jobs;
- creation of business opportunities which endure;
- knowledge transfer into the region or supply chain which builds capacity and enables the ongoing delivery of goods and services;
- enhanced awareness of the region through alignment with the event, which may result in increased tourism;
- increased foreign investment through exposure offered by the event;
- increased business opportunities and networking offered by events such as trade shows, conventions and exhibitions.

PR8 TOTAL NUMBER OF SUBSTANTIATED COMPLAINTS REGARDING BREACHES OF CUSTOMER PRIVACY AND LOSSES OF CUSTOMER DATA.

Through the ticketing and registration process at events, much personal information is provided. This indicator allows an organisation to report on the processes it has in place to assure customer privacy as it relates to their interaction with the event.

This indicator is core to the *Event Organizers' Sector Supplement* which means that all formal reporters to the GRI must report on this indicator.

If no breaches of customer privacy, complaints or losses of customer data have been experienced, then a simple statement to that effect is acceptable.

If any of these issues have occurred, included in reporting should be fines or other action taken against the organisation as a result.

EN26 INITIATIVES TO MITIGATE ENVIRONMENTAL IMPACTS OF EVENTS, PRODUCTS AND SERVICES, AND EXTENT OF IMPACT MITIGATION.

Reporting to this indicator could include explanation of the sourcing decisions made to significantly reduce the upstream impacts of specific materials choices (e.g. signage materials, or food and beverage serviceware). The indicator suggests reporting on the environmental impacts such as energy, waste, water and GHGs specifically related to materials choices and the sourcing decisions made by the organisation to mitigate these choices (e.g. the decision to move from plastic cups and food serviceware to compostable). Reporting would include justification for this based on full life cycle impacts from manufacture through to waste.

EN27 PERCENTAGE OF PRODUCTS SOLD OR PROVIDED AND THEIR PACKAGING MATERIALS THAT ARE RECLAIMED BY CATEGORY.

This indicator is relevant for events specifically designed around food and beverage service. If you have an initiative requiring food vendors and caterers to use reusable produce crates rather than single-use polystyrene boxes for product deliveries, this could be reported under this indicator. As per the example in EN26, if you choose compostable food and beverage serviceware, then the next step is to actually collect the material for composting. This initiative and the resulting outcomes would be reported under this indicator.

EN1 MATERIALS USED BY WEIGHT OR VOLUME.

This indicator is relevant to report on for those organisations making significant raw material purchases. This could be, for example, road base, woodchip or building materials. For those events undertaking significant construction, such as mega sports events, reporting to this indicator would be important.

EN2 PERCENTAGE OF MATERIALS USED THAT ARE RECYCLED INPUT MATERIALS.

This indicator is also relevant for those organisers making significant raw materials purchases. For example, woodchip could be made from damaged pallets or construction timber reclaimed from other jobs. Those events involved in construction may also be able to reclaim materials onsite during earthmoving, for example, and use this material as fill for other uses.

QUESTIONS

Definitions

Explain the following terms or concepts:

a) Life cycle assessment
b) Ecological footprint
c) Greenwashing
d) Fairtrade
e) Fair labour.

Simple Answer

1 Choose a product in the event industry supply chain and research its water footprint (look for published data).

2 Look for an eco-label in the region in which you work or live. Describe its aspects, whether it is a type 1, 2 or 3 eco-label. Describe the features of a product that has been eco-labelled under this programme.

3 What are the main sustainability issues for timber and paper production and what are the ways to ensure sustainable sourcing?

4 What are the main sustainability issues for producing printed products and how can you ensure sustainable print sourcing?

5 What are the main sustainability issues for signage production? Research a sustainable signage material and explain its benefits.

6 Describe ideas for sustainable merchandise, gifts and awards. Research and describe a product that has good sustainability credentials.

7 Research the closest reuse centre in the area in which you reside or work. What do they reclaim and how could an event use this facility?

8 What are the main sustainability issues for cleaning products or paint? Research a sustainable solution (e.g. brand of commercial cleaning product or paint) and describe its sustainability attributes.

9 What are the main sustainability issues for food and beverage sourcing? Choose one area and describe in detail the issues. Research a product that has excellent sustainability credentials, and explain why.

10 When selecting food and beverage serviceware, what are the issues to consider?

11 What role do vendors, exhibitors and sponsors play in supporting your event's sustainable sourcing outcomes?

12 Describe the supplier management process and produce an example of communications material that could be used to ensure suppliers meet your requirements.

13 Produce a sustainable sourcing policy.

14 Choose (and describe) an event scenario and then detail how you would report on sustainable sourcing outcomes.

NOTES

1 Living Planet Report, www.panda.org/about_our_earth/all_publications/living_planet_report, accessed April 2012.

2 UL Environment: Greenwashing Report 2009: sinsofgreenwashing.org/findings/greenwashing-report-2009/index.html.

3 UN Convention on the Rights of the Child: www.unicef.org/crc/.

4 REDD+: www.un-redd.org/aboutredd/tabid/582/default.aspx.

5 Greenpeace: www.greenpeace.org.uk/forests, accessed November 2008.

6 Medex®: www.metrohardwoodsjackson.com/jk/mdf/medex-moisture-resistant-mdf.

7 Xanita: www.xanita.com.

8 Canadian Standards Association: www.csa-international.org/product_areas/forest_products_marking.

9 WWF: wwf.panda.org/how_you_can_help/live_green/fsc/tissue_issues/, accessed April 2013.

10 Don't Flush Tiger Forests: WWF Report – worldwildlife.org/pages/don-t-flush-tiger-forests-report.

11 Center for Health, Environment and Justice, www.besafenet.com/pvc, accessed December 2008.

12 The deadly chemicals in cotton. Environmental Justice Foundation in collaboration with Pesticide Action Network UK. ejfoundation.org/sites/default/files/public/the_deadly_chemicals_in_cotton.pdf.

14 Water Footprint: www.waterfootprint.org.

15 Textile Exchange, *Organic Cotton Farm and Fibre Report:* textileexchange.org/2011-farm-fiber-report.

16 National Association for PET Container Resources: www.napcor.com/pdf/FinalReport_LCI_Postconsumer_PET andHDPE.pdf www.napcor.com/pdf/v411_NAPCOR_PET_Interactive.pdf.

17 EPA Event Calculator: www.epa.vic.gov.au/ecological footprint/calculators/event/introduction.asp.

18 UN Food and Agriculture Organization of the United Nation's *Guidelines for the Ecolabelling of Fish and Fishery Products from Marine Capture Fisheries*:www.fao.org/docrep/012/i1119t/i1119t00.htm.

19 Story of Bottled Water: www.storyofstuff.org/movies-all/story-of-bottled-water/.

20 *Trashed* (movie): www.trashedfilm.com.

21 *Tapped* (movie): www.tappedthemovie.com.

22 Captain Charles Moore's TED Talk: www.ted.com/talks/capt_charles_moore_on_the_seas_of_plastic.html.

23 Environmental Working Group: www.ewg.org/research/bottled-water-quality-investigation.

24 Biodegradable Products Institute: www.bpiworld.org/Certified-Biodegradable-Foodservice-Items-Plates-Cups-Utensils.

25 ASTM D6868 – *11 Standard Specification for Labeling of End Items that Incorporate Plastics and Polymers as Coatings or Additives with Paper and Other Substrates Designed to be Aerobically Composted in Municipal or Industrial Facilities*: www.astm.org/Standards/D6868.htm.

26 EN 13432:2000 Packaging requirements for packaging recoverable through composting and biodegradation. Test scheme and evaluation criteria for the final acceptance of packaging: shop.bsigroup.com.

27 ASTM D6400 – *12 Standard Specification for Labeling of Plastics Designed to be Aerobically Composted in Municipal or Industrial Facilities*: www.astm.org/Standards/D6400.htm.

28 DIN EN 14995:2007: Plastics. Evaluation of compostability. Test scheme and specifications: shop.bsigroup.com.

29 ISO 17088:2008 Specifications for compostable plastics: www.iso.org.

30 ASTM D7081 – *05 Standard Specification for Non-Floating Biodegradable Plastics in the Marine Environment.*

Only we humans make waste that nature can't digest.

Captain Charles J. Moore

Figure 9.1 Can recycling.

Source: Meegan Jones.

9

WASTE

Most events produce mountains of waste, with eating, drinking, site build, décor and staging all playing a part in event waste creation. Designing in ways to prevent waste, and viewing waste as a resource to be recovered, are essential to managing waste and contribute to the overall sustainability performance of your event.

In the following pages we will consider the creation of waste and how to limit the valuable resources that might be sent to landfill or for incineration at the end of your event.

No matter the event size, type or location, there are common themes for event waste management at all events. Moving your event *Towards Zero Waste* should be a goal for all organisers.

So why should you care about minimising waste created and maximising the diversion of waste from landfill or incineration?

Your attendees, the community, local government, venue or site owner, sponsors or talent may expect it. Meeting stakeholder and societal expectations for responsible waste management is a major motivation. This ties in very tightly with your reputation, which may impact upon future attendance and sponsorship attraction.

1 Conserve Resources

Saving the earth's precious natural resources is a major benefit. By putting recyclable and compostable materials to work as inputs to make new materials, we are preventing new resources from being mined up, chopped down or grown.

2 Save Money

It usually costs less to haul and dispose of recyclable materials than it does for garbage. Reducing waste in the first place means shorter cleaning times, fewer staff, bins, skips, trucks and transport, all leading to lower cleaning and waste disposal costs.

3 Climate Change Impacts

There is also the climate change imperative – the impact that resource consumption and disposal has on the creation of greenhouse gases (GHGs) is immense. Sending biodegradable waste to landfill is a major contributor to methane creation. Read more about the climate impact of waste at the end of this chapter.

If you have a large event you will invariably have a waste management company on board to plan and conduct waste operations. You will need to know your way around rubbish so you can talk trash with them and design ways to achieve the best result. You may have one company that supplies staff (cleaners), another that supplies the 'binfrastructure', another that hauls waste away, and another who is the actual waste processor. Or you may have various combinations of the above.

This chapter gives you a tune-up on waste management know-how. It will take you through each type of recyclable material likely to be found at your event, logistics on waste separation and pre-treatment at the event, plus the low-down on the different types of waste processers your waste may end up in. If you're managing the event waste in-house, you'll find the content of this section most helpful. Also included are examples and initiatives from events around the world of all shapes and sizes – how they have tackled waste challenges and also engaged their attendees in their waste campaigns.

Before we forge ahead and get into the dirty detail, I want to impress on you how important it is to match the waste-processing options available within the event destination with your event or venue waste management systems, and importantly the type of waste you create in the first place. It is no use sourcing a 'recyclable' item and feeling great about it if you cannot actually find anywhere to recycle it locally.

Many items used at an event will quickly be turned into waste, so the type of material the item is made from should be considered, as well as its disposal options. Sometimes there will not be appropriate disposal options available locally, so ensuring the disposable items you procure are at least made from recycled or sustainable materials in the first place is a great approach. Ensure you understand the difference between 'recycled' and 'recy-clable', as these terms are often confused. Recycled is something made from recycled raw materials; recyclable is an item that is able to be recycled.

THE WASTE BACKSTORY

It is important to remember that waste occurs at every step along a one-way road of resource consumption, production, use and eventual disposal.

To manufacture the products which events use and dispose of, a constant flow of resources needs to be dug up, manufactured, transported, distributed, purchased, used, and then if not responsibly recycled, composted, reused or repurposed, finally being buried or incinerated at the local garbage facility.

As you read the following pages and continue to develop solutions for your event, keep in mind this additional volume of waste produced resulting from the creation of the single-use products you have chosen, rather than just what goes in the bins at the end of your event.

For every tonne of end-of-life-cycle waste, approximately 71 tonnes of waste are produced during the original product's journey from raw material to manufacturing, distribution and sale.[1] By reducing the amount we use and responsibly sourcing the products we sell at or use for events, we also reduce waste back through the supply chain.

Of course consumption is what keeps the money wheel ticking over at many events. You don't want to reduce the sale of stuff so much that your event is no longer financially viable. You want your attendees to eat and drink, buy a programme, get a souvenir T-shirt, spend money at the market stalls, participate, and enjoy themselves.

But remember the waste backstory – make decisions about what you sell, what 'waste-in-waiting' stuff is given away for free, how things are packaged and so on. Considerations such as ethical purchasing, product miles, and buying products made from recycled and sustainable materials are just some of the ways you can help reduce waste production. These are discussed in greater detail in Chapter 8.

WASTE HIERARCHY

Reduce/Refuse
Prevent waste in the first place.
Plan for less. Design out waste-in-waiting.
Design for durability. Hire don't buy. Reduce packaging.
Replace disposable with re-usable.

Repair
Repair what you can.
Purchase materials that have replacement
parts and can be repaired.

Re-use/Re-purpose
Using 'as-is' or repurposing into new stuff.
Design for re-use. Design for re-purposing.
Plan for disassembly/deconstruction.
Plan salvage systems. Organise recipients.

Recycle/Compost
Using waste as ingredients for new materials.
Assess local markets for recyclable material.
Assess local facilities for segregation.
Match procurement with recycling options.
Plan resource capture and segregation.

Recovery
Extracting energy from waste resources.
Waste to energy through incineration or pyrolysis.
Convert biodegradable materials through anaerobic digestion.

Disposal
Disposal without material or energy recovery.
Send waste to landfill. Send waste for incineration.

Figure 9.2 Waste hierarchy

WASTE TIMELINE

Design
When the event is being conceived.
How can waste avoidance and recovery be included in event
design - location, activities, venue choice, caterers, vendors,
and contractors. What are the 'must takes' now,
which should be included in design?

Planning
Procedures, processes, requirements.
Establish objectives. Assess what resources and facilities are
available locally. Who needs to be engaged and influenced?
Set requirements or make plans to meet requirements.
Establish budget.

Implementation
Contracting, procuring, pre-event.
Include waste requirements in all tenders and contracts.
Source all resources, delegate tasks; establish measurement and
monitoring systems. Train or induct staff. Bump-in event.

Delivery
Event is carried out.
Put plans into action. Ensure compliance with planned
systems and that awareness has led to action. Correct
departure from plans in real time. Monitor performance;
gather feedback; collect data.

Completion
Bump-out of event and post-event review.
Undergo debrief. Analyse results. Calculate savings or return
on investment. Set plans for improvement.

Figure 9.3 Waste timeline

business case for responsible waste management is a
necessity.

The Business Case

Like all decisions, there needs to be a business case
to support change. Motivation may be financial,
reputational or regulation based. For organisations
who have a profit motivation, or not-for-profits who
have a budget-stretching imperative, establishing the

1 Reduced Costs and Increased Earnings

Using fewer materials, being more efficient with the
materials you do use and reducing the volume of waste
to be cleaned up and disposed of will all lead to reduced
operating costs.

The 'cost to throw' is also becoming more expensive in many regions, with landfills reaching capacity and a growing concern about the greenhouse gas impact of sending biodegradable waste to landfill, where it creates methane. Putting controls in place to reduce total waste and diverting biodegradable waste from landfill will benefit the planet and your financial bottom line.

Direct savings can be made through the following:

✓ Reduced cleaning staff numbers or hours.
✓ Reduced number of bins and waste supplies.
✓ Reduced removal costs.
✓ Reduced disposal or landfill tax costs.
✓ Earnings from sales of recyclable materials.

2 Reputation and Competitive Advantage

Those who attend events, along with talent and performers, sponsors, government and the wider community, increasingly expect events and the venues which host them to be operated sustainably. By thoroughly, thoughtfully and sustainably addressing waste management, your event will stand out as industry-leading (temporarily at least – until everyone else catches up).

This will enhance the reputation of your event or organisation. Reduced costs will mean a stronger financial position, allowing other elements such as enhanced attendee experience to be focused upon or an increased budget for promotion to be put in place, in turn making your event more successful.

3 Compliance

The business case for exceptional waste management at your event may simply come down to a need to meet government, venue or industry regulations and requirements.

Regulation may be in the form of local government by-laws requiring certain behaviour or performance results by events. State or federal legislation may be in place, dictating certain criteria under which events of a certain type or scale must operate.

Requirements may be put in place by venues, particularly those that are publicly owned. Without adhering to requirements the venue simply cannot be used.

Exposure to fines and penalties (if in place) may be reduced by events meeting minimum requirements and in some cases bonuses may be achieved.

Industry associations, codes of conduct, membership charters and the like may also place expected best practice and principles upon its constituents.

Independent recognition of your waste management processes and performance may be a motivation to put certain solutions in place also.

WASTE PLANNING STEPS

When planning event activities, production logistics, and making procurement decisions, keep an eye on the waste consequences of your decisions. Think of the waste impact of the materials you choose, the activities you plan, or the production logistics you devise. This may include the waste created in making the product in the first place, the waste created through using the product, and the consequences of its disposal. Think through how waste will be generated by the performance components of your event. Do you really need the confetti bomb to go off at the end of the night? Consider the steps to follow when investigating the best waste strategy for your event (Table 9.1).

STAKEHOLDERS

So who has a part to play in waste management decisions and processes? Who will have an opinion on your planning, the actual waste management at your event, or an interest in your outcomes?

The event workforce, waste or cleaning management contractor, government waste programmes, traders (food, bars and non-food), venue, and general suppliers and contractors all have a part to play.

Consider ways to involve them in waste planning at the outset, involve them in waste operations at the event, or inform them of performance outcomes.

Key to the plans is the client, if you're an event organiser wanting to do great waste management on their behalf. Conversely, if you are the event owner and wish to show great waste performance, a key stakeholder will be the event organising company you engage.

Table 9.1 Waste Planning Steps

1 Get go-ahead. Get resources.

Gain support internally and externally. Find out what resources and knowledge exists and what is needed. Look to your organisation, supply chain, local government, venue and waste-related programmes.

2 Establish team. Delegate duties.

Whose responsibility is it to research, plan, implement and report waste management?
Assign tasks.

3 What waste at your event?

Evaluate what waste streams could look like.
Identify activities and behaviours that will cause waste to be created. Will the size, location or attendee profile influence waste creation?

4 Identify barriers.

Investigate what is needed and who needs to be engaged. Will there be resistance? Are solutions available and possible? Will attendees participate?

5 Waste facilities?

What types of waste facilities are available in your region and what processes do they use? Is there a market locally for recycled materials? If so, which materials?

6 Evaluate feasibility.

Compare the cost of disposal of compostable and recyclable waste versus sending to landfill.
Set the business case for your planned initiatives.

7 Set objectives and plans.

Establish what you want to achieve and how you will achieve it. Re-assign tasks to the team and engage all those who have a part to play.
Identify what you will measure and how you will capture required data.

8 Waste avoidance and creation.

How can you prevent or minimise waste from being created in the first place? How can you influence or regulate the types of waste created to match available facilities, and optimise recovery?

9 At-event segregation.

What at-event waste segregation and 'binfrastructure' is needed to optimise waste-processing options? How will segregation work? What is needed for success?

10 Communications.

How will you communicate and engage event participants to support your efforts? Signage, announcements, staff, materials.

11 Compliance and reporting.

Audit compliance onsite with segregation and initiatives. Collect waste data, including volumes or weights, percentages per material type by disposal method, weight per person per day and total waste diverted from landfill (volume, weight, percentage). Interpret results and set objectives for the future.

12 Celebrate success.

Inform all those involved of your results.

Vendors

Vendors, stallholders, caterers, traders – call them what you will. Those selling food or goods to attendees play a central role in the eventual waste created and the success in segregation. Packaging, ordering decisions, kitchen operations, and food and beverage serviceware (cups, plates, bowls, cutlery, etc.) choices are all critical factors that must be managed to both reduce waste and divert that which is created.

It's the eating and drinking at events that create most waste, most of the time, and you must have vendors engaged and enthused about your waste plans and be willing to participate in your initiatives.

Creating event-specific communications for all vendors is essential. Get them interested, explain why, show pretty pictures, and tell them how you can help.

It will most likely be necessary to mandate specific food and beverage serviceware. Contract it in.

Here are some ways to go about engaging this critical stakeholder group.

✓ Include information on enquiry forms, websites and any other communication where the vendor enquires about participating in your event. Let them know from the outset what your expectations are.

✓ Include information about waste avoidance in vendor kits. This may include buying in bulk or using providers that supply goods in reusable or exchangeable boxes.

✓ Include information about mandatory food and beverage serviceware to be used. This needs to have been worked out by you already, and matched with waste processing facilities, onsite segregation and bin systems.

✓ Provide the actual serviceware to the vendor at no cost or considerably discounted if you feel compliance may be difficult. In this case there's no excuse (assuming you have ensured the serviceware you provide is suitable to the meals they are serving).

✓ Consider printing messages ("I'm Recyclable" or "I'm Compostable") on event-specific serviceware.

✓ If you don't provide serviceware at no charge, but recommend specific products to be used, arrange for a wholesaler to be at the event to enable restocking,

so that the vendors are not nervous about over- or under-ordering mandatory serviceware.

✓ Provide pre-event training for food vendors. Make it worth their while to attend by including other educational elements in the training, for example, local sourcing, signage and stall layout.

✓ Provide all in-kitchen bins, bags and signs they will need, or provide guidance on the best way an in-kitchen system should be set up.

✓ Provide all back-of-house bins, liquid waste and waste oil barrels in clusters at convenient locations behind vendors. Don't make them walk too far.

✓ Always have all options available. Ensure signs are clear and simple.

✓ Induct all vendors into the waste system and ensure they have a process to transfer the knowledge to their entire team.

✓ Assign a staff member from the event team to vendor liaison, specifically for waste management and systems control.

✓ Continually monitor onsite compliance with systems both in kitchens and back of house.

✓ Put incentives in place to entice vendors to comply with regulations, or put penalties in place if they do not.

✓ Place site bonds on vendors that are refundable if they meet all their requirements.

✓ Require all vendors to be 'signed out' and sign off on their 'clean pitch' so that bonds can be refunded. Take photos for evidence.

✓ Give 'green vendor' awards or rewards for the best operating stalls.

Workforce

Without question, apart from vendors, the most common reason for things not going to plan is the lack of engagement, interest or concern by event staff. You need their participation to ensure your systems keep functioning.

Your best-laid plans, as made perfect by you upon setup, may come unstuck as soon as your back is turned. Bins will go missing or be moved to the wrong location. Signs will fall off or be hung upside down. Carefully stored stacks of extra materials, signs, bins and bags will

Table 9.2 Stakeholder engagement methods

Venue/site: The owner or management of the location in which your event is held will either be instrumental in the waste management processes or will have a strong opinion, interest or place requirements on you. (e.g. local government allowing you use of a city street or park, or the owner of a property where your outdoor event is held).

- Meetings to determine existing at-venue/onsite waste services.
- Meetings to discuss specific plans.
- Waste management planning documents prepared and exchanged.
- Exchange of information regarding signage and messaging at the event.
- Provision of performance data.

Regulatory authorities: Local government, waterways authorities, national parks departments, environmental protection agency, authorities, departments, agencies and bureaux may have a voice to either regulate, put requirements on, or provide licences based on waste plans and outcomes.

- Contact to establish relevant requirements.
- Filling in required paperwork.
- Meetings to discuss waste aims of the event.
- Provision of policy, plans and waste campaigns.
- Onsite visits for compliance auditing.
- Provision of performance data/report.

Sponsors/funders/partners: Those providing money, resources or aligning their brand with your event will be interested in all aspects of your event production, to ensure no risk to reputation.

- Discussion of event waste goals at outset.
- Provision of policy, plans and campaign ideas.
- Discussion of their involvement and support.
- Identification of unique sponsor-related waste.

Waste contractor/cleaners: Those providing cleaning services, bins and other at-event waste-related services are key, as are removal/haulers, materials dealers and recyclers.

- Discussion of event waste goals, and roles.
- Discussion of at-event segregation and logistics.
- Discussion of bulk storage removal options.
- Discussion with waste processors.

Participants/workforce: Staff, crew, contracted workforce and volunteers will have a part to play in ensuring that your waste plans work. You need their interest, engagement, and active and accurate participation to achieve your waste objectives.

- Inclusion of clauses in engagement contracts.
- Provision of policy, plans and campaigns
- Workshops and discussions to identify issues.
- Onsite induction and auditing of compliance.
- Provision of performance results.

Vendors/caterers/exhibitors: Those who have displays, retail, sampling or other information, product or experiential aspect that has a physical set-up and interfaces with attendees have a major part to play in waste prevention and segregation.

- Discussion to identify likely waste streams.
- Information for serviceware requirements.
- Information explaining at-event waste systems.
- Requirements in contracts and agreements.
- Onsite induction and auditing.
- Provision of performance results.

Attendees: Those who attend the event will have an expectation about how waste will be managed, and have a part to play, at many types of events, in doing the right thing and putting their waste in the right bin.

- Pre-event promotion of waste initiatives.
- Engagement through event programme and signage.
- Provision of stewards to assist in segregation.
- Performance reported in real time at the event.

Community: Those residents or businesses affected by the event will have expectations of performance around waste management.

- Meetings to discuss concerns.
- Provision of policy, plans and campaigns.
- Provision of performance results.

go missing. Staff will change over and no one will brief new people. Wrong bags will go in the bin and then different cleaners will change the full bags over, placing them in the wrong skip out at the back. Overnight crews will turn your perfectly managed skip of cardboard into a rubbish skip, because site crew forgot to install lights in the waste compound.

Every single one of these mishaps (and more) has happened to me on an event site. Oh, I forgot about the 'someone drives over your pallet of wooden signs with a forklift, when you had spent a month having signs hand painted by the décor team' example. I think you get my point.

Here are some ideas to consider when engaging your workforce in the event's waste plans:

✓ Include information about performance expectations around participation in and support of waste efforts at the event in all engagement contracts and staff communications.
✓ Hold pre-event training to the critical event production or site management team.
✓ Ensure all site staff, such as production coordinators, décor teams, site management and others who are running around doing their thing at the event site, understand the importance of the waste system and that it is their participation and oversight that will ensure success.

✓ Include information about the waste system in inductions to the event site for the entire workforce.
✓ For those with a hands-on role in waste management (cleaners, volunteers), ensure they understand exactly what goes in each bin.
✓ In addition to having stewards on bins to assist the event attendees with waste segregation, place stewards at the bulk waste storage compound to ensure cleaners put the right items in the right skips.
✓ Supervisors of cleaning teams are especially critical. They must be highly engaged, informed and motivated to get their teams to do the right thing. Set up competitions between supervisors and their teams. Offer awards and prizes.
✓ Make the cleaning staff feel very special. Get them great uniforms (T-shirts, hats, etc.). Keep them fed and watered – remember: salt and sugar are a cleaning team's friend! Ensure they are not understaffed and overworked. Give them the resources they need to do a great job for you.

Offer prizes for various departments' participation in the event waste plans. This could be the best segregated office waste, or one-off green champion awards for things being done and initiative being taken onsite by the event team.

Box 9.1

WASTE CHECKLIST

Leave No Trace and Zero Waste

❏ The event embraces a *Leave No Trace* ethic.
❏ The *Leave No Trace* ethic is communicated to all relevant participants and stakeholders.
❏ The *Leave No Trace* ethic is enacted in the event's operational logistics planning and delivery.
❏ The event has adopted a *Towards Zero Waste* philosophy.

❏ The end-life of everything you purchase to produce the event and all the items provided is envisaged.
❏ The event sees waste as a resource and at-event waste management as a resource recovery exercise.

Box 9.1 (continued)

Waste Evaluation and Planning

- ❑ Event destination has outstanding performance record in recycling and biodegradable waste diversion from landfill and incineration.
- ❑ Venue chosen offers relevant waste segregation options, bins, signage and other resources and processes to ensure optimal diversion of waste from landfill.
- ❑ Areas and activities of the event that are likely to produce waste are identified.
- ❑ Likely items and materials that could become waste are identified.
- ❑ Local methods of waste collection, segregation and processing are understood.
- ❑ Potential local waste-processing facilities are identified.
- ❑ Waste streams that can be processed locally, rather than exported, are identified.
- ❑ The practicalities of the event type, attendee type, venue location and facilities are identified and included in waste planning.

Waste Reduction

- ❑ Only necessary material is printed in order to avoid wastage.
- ❑ Water refill stations, rather than packaged bottled water, are used.
- ❑ Single-serve sachets, straws, stirrers and small disposables are not used to reduce 'micro-litter' potential.
- ❑ Caterers are requested to use reusable produce delivery boxes.
- ❑ Advertising flyer handouts or sample giveaways are not permitted.
- ❑ Attendee packs (giveaways) are designed to ensure minimal waste creation.
- ❑ Attendees are able to 'give back' packs for onward donation if they are of no use to them.
- ❑ Lanyards are reusable, collected and/or recycled.

- ❑ Plastic bags are not permitted to be handed out by stallholders.
- ❑ Polystyrene/Styrofoam is not permitted at the event.
- ❑ Smoking is prohibited, or in designated areas only, to prevent cigarette butt litter.

Waste Reporting

- ❑ Total waste created is measured and reported.
- ❑ Recycled, composted and salvaged waste is measured and reported.
- ❑ A waste audit is undertaken to establish the waste streams present, as well as any contamination and non-compliance with initiatives.
- ❑ Total waste diverted from landfill or incineration is reported.
- ❑ Total waste per person per day is reported.

Waste Streams

The following materials are recycled:

❑ Cardboard and paper	❑ Glass
❑ Metal	❑ Timber
❑ PET	❑ PP
❑ HDPE	❑ LDPE
❑ LLDPE	❑ PS
❑ Oil	❑ Serviceware

The following materials are composted or anaerobically digested:

❑ Food waste	❑ Food serviceware
❑ Green waste	❑ Other

The following materials are sent to landfill for gas extraction:

❑ Food waste	❑ Food serviceware
❑ Green waste	❑ Other

Box 9.1 (continued)

The following materials are sent for incineration or gasification to create electricity:

- ❏ Food waste
- ❏ Green waste
- ❏ Food serviceware
- ❏ Other

The following materials are collected separately and disposed of responsibly:

- ❏ E-waste
- ❏ Clinical waste
- ❏ Hazardous waste

The following materials are salvaged:

- ❏ Event supplies
- ❏ Unserved food
- ❏ Décor/signage

Waste Segregation

- ❏ Segregated bins or skips are in place during event/site build/bump-in.
- ❏ Segregated bins/skips/compounds are set up back of house for collection of recyclable materials (single stream or mixed).
- ❏ Caterers and food stallholders have bins in kitchens and back of house for collection of food waste for composting.
- ❏ Front-of-house (FOH) bins are in sets of two (recycling and general), or
- ❏ FOH bins are in sets of three (recycling, compost, general), or
- ❏ FOH bins are segregated into multiple waste streams.
- ❏ Segregated bins are placed in artists' dressing-rooms.
- ❏ Segregated bins are placed in artist/crew catering zones.
- ❏ Segregated bins are placed in hospitality zones.
- ❏ Micro-waste systems in place to collect discarded materials from giveaways.
- ❏ Segregated bins are in place post-event/pull-out.

Bin Signage

- ❏ Bin signage is at eye level.
- ❏ Bin caps or toppers are used to reduce 'copycat contamination' by being able to see inside the open top of the bin.
- ❏ Bin signage is specific and relevant to materials created at the event.
- ❏ Bin signage has colour-coding which is logical and consistent.
- ❏ Bin signage includes images of the materials.
- ❏ Bins are always in 'sets' with all segregation options always present.

Initiatives

- ❏ Set up at-source separation and get attendees involved in actively separating waste.
- ❏ A container deposit system is in place to give out refunds for returned cups, bottles, cans, etc.
- ❏ 'Recycling stations' or 'resource recovery stations' are set up.
- ❏ Waste as art or other waste-based installations or interactive elements are included.
- ❏ Colour-coded or printed bin bags are distributed to picnickers and campers for waste segregation.
- ❏ Incentives encourage participation in waste segregation activities.
- ❏ Attendees are encouraged to bring shopping bags and water bottles.
- ❏ 'Litter-free' camping/picnics are encouraged of attendees.
- ❏ Stewards or volunteers are placed at bins to assist and instruct attendees on accurate segregation.
- ❏ Onsite mini-MRF is set up to segregate mixed recycling in the single material streams.
- ❏ Biodegradable waste is composted onsite.
- ❏ A salvage yard is set up and a team works towards collecting everything salvageable.

Box 9.1 (continued)

Adventure Races and Sports Events

❑ All waste created on tracks in nature races and events must be carried out by participants, support crew, production staff and/or deposited at checkpoints.

❑ Participants sign a litter-free race agreement and commit to a *Leave No Trace* ethic.

❑ If water cups are used at hydration stations, they are collected for recycling.

❑ Polystyrene/Styrofoam is not permitted.

Exhibitions

❑ Exhibitors design-in waste reduction in booth construction and operation.

❑ Exhibitors do not use disposable stand packing material.

❑ If disposable packing material is used, it is recycled.

❑ Back-of-house storage for packing boxes and road cases is provided.

❑ Exhibitions have own small waste bin in-stall with appropriate recycling/food segregation to capture at-stall waste creation.

❑ Staff bring refillable water bottles and cups.

❑ During bump-out/pull-down, exhibitor leaves a clean pitch with waste segregated and/or placed in appropriate waste bays.

❑ Exhibition materials are designed for durability, deconstruction and flat packing.

❑ 'Brand roadkill' is considered – ensuring no brand activation will end up as litter.

❑ Exhibitors do not use polystyrene/Styrofoam.

❑ Exhibitors do not include single-use decorative items, and avoid 'booth bling' that may create litter.

Catering and Bars

❑ Food is provided fresh rather than individually packaged.

❑ Uneaten food/food scraps are collected for composting.

❑ Food salvage programmes are in place to send unserved food for charitable use.

❑ Caterers and stallholders are incentivised or penalised to ensure participation in waste segregation and 'clean pitches' at the end of the event.

❑ In-kitchen and in-bar bin systems match back-of-house venue/event waste segregation systems.

❑ Pouring of individual bottled or canned drinks into disposable cups is avoided.

WASTE MANAGEMENT IN THE EVENT DESTINATION

To make the best decisions for your event, you need to identify which waste treatment processes are available within the event destination. The frustrating thing about managing waste from event to event is that in each location, town, city, municipal government area, etc., waste is handled differently and in some cases less than optimal services are available.

The decisions regarding at-venue or onsite waste segregation need to be made in concert with consideration for what types of facilities are available to receive your event's waste.

You may find that the venue you choose, or the waste management service you engage, already has contracts with a particular waste haulage firm, which in turn may be connected to a specific treatment facility. Events held in public spaces with the support of the local municipality may find that they are locked into using the local government waste services.

You need to know these details to effectively influence the type of waste generated and to plan how you will manage it onsite to optimise the offsite processing.

Figure 9.4 Municipal waste management in Mumbai.
Source: Meegan Jones.

It may be possible to segregate your waste into single recycling streams at the event, and to send it directly to the recycling reprocessors, bypassing the materials recovery facility (MRF; see explanation below). Most recyclable material is worth money, and depending on volumes, you could be looking at a profit or conversely your haulage fees may bring you to break-even, rather than paying someone to haul your waste away.

Every event destination manages waste differently. In some countries waste segregation is common practice in homes, in businesses and in public places. In other destinations waste is barely managed by local authorities and whole communities make a living off the leavings of others.

There are a huge number of examples of community-led or government-imposed programmes to keep biodegradable waste, or more specifically, food waste, out of landfill and diverted to other uses such as compost and waste to energy treatment.

Europe is leading the way in formalised waste management, and the way is away from landfill. Across Europe countries are recognising landfill as the last resort for waste and as a result have introduced restrictions on the landfilling of biodegradable waste and recyclable materials. Everything must go through treatment to minimise waste going to landfill. The European Union's *Landfill Directive* obliges member states to reduce the amount of biodegradable municipal waste sent to landfill to 35 per cent of 1995 levels by 2016 (for some countries by 2020). A recast of goals is currently being addressed.[2]

Germany, The Netherlands and Denmark all have impressive waste performance with figures unheard of in other Western and developed nations. So if you're putting on an event in a European country, chances are that the mind-sets of attendees, the resources available to put your systems in place and the treatment facilities available to send your waste to will be fantastic.

Norway has also introduced a ban on biodegradable waste to landfill. This has resulted in increased biological treatment (e.g. composting) at 40 per cent of total waste and 'waste to energy' at 30 per cent of total waste.[3]

Scotland is the most active in the UK with its *Zero Waste Plan*[4] aiming to eliminate food waste from landfill by 2020. This is anticipated to give a boost to demand for anaerobic digestion plants. (These produce biogas, which in turn is used to make electricity – reducing the need for burning fossil fuels. The residual 'digestate' may be used for fertiliser, further reducing demand for chemical or phosphate fertilisers.)

In Australia the price on carbon, known as the 'carbon tax', includes landfill gas. It will be interesting to see how this plays out as the 'cost to throw' increases, and to see what processes will be put in place to keep biodegradable waste out of landfill.

Fundamental to the direction you take will be the overall waste strategy of your country and the waste habits of its citizens. What is your country's recycling habits?

Government Policy

One of the most effective tools for controlling food serviceware and compliance by vendors and events is for local government, which allows events to occur in public places, to put strict controls in place.

However, they often don't provide guidance or resources to help the organiser meet their requirements, leaving them to do research from a standing start on the waste-processing options, appropriate food and beverage packaging, bin signs and waste segregation at the event, and collection services.

California has a state law that requires events with more than 2000 people, that charge admission, or that are funded by a public agency, to recycle.[5] Rather than just enforcing the state law, municipal governments have realised that their role is to support event waste management through working out what best practice could be, and offering specific information for event organisers in their counties.

Alameda County in California have created a great resource through their *'Stop Waste'* (www.stopwaste.org/docs/specialevents-swp.pdf). Also in California, the *City of Oakland* has created a fantastic guide for organisers, *'Oakland Recycles'* (www.oaklandrecycles.com).

The *San Francisco Bay Area* tops the list. With the assistance and drive of local zero waste guru *Green Mary* (www.green-mary.com) they've got down into the dirty detail, by area, to let vendors and event managers know what materials may be used where. Styrofoam is completely banned at all Bay Area public events. All San Francisco public events require composting as well as recycling. They have full systems for food vendors and attendees to put food scraps and food-related service items in the appropriate containers, and sorting behind the scenes ensures maximum diversion.

The Americans are again showing best practice and this time it's in the city of *Boulder, Colorado*. They incentivise events to perform by offering a US$250 rebate to those events that meet the waste performance prescribed by the City. Read more in Box 9.2.

In Australia, many local councils receive state government funding for waste and sustainability improvement programmes. This funding is attached to requirements for an Event Sustainability Management Policy to be in place. This has been further interpreted and enacted by some councils to place requirements on event organisers, particularly around waste. Some have gone the next step,

---

Box 9.2

CITY OF BOULDER WASTE INCENTIVE

Waste Incentive

The *City of Boulder*, Colorado's *Local Environmental Action Division* (LEAD), has developed the *Zero Waste Incentive* to assist event organisers source compostable and recyclable containers, collection services or educational materials that facilitate zero waste.

This is an example of a municipality not just telling event organisers what they must do, but taking an active role in enabling them to do it – both through financial incentives and through offering guidance, services and doing some of the groundwork research.

Event organisers can claim a maximum US$250 rebate for expenses relating to supplying compostable and/or recyclable serviceware, waste collection services for same, and educational materials and services.[6]

In addition, the city supplies the event with a small three-bin container system (compost, recyclables, landfill). This is designed to go above and beyond the regular waste disposal services of the city.

Event approval requires the event organisers to ensure that vendors remove from the event site any items that are both non-compostable and non-recyclable, and provide only recyclable or compostable serviceware (examples of local sources are provided by the city on their website).

LEAD states that its mission is to engage and assist the community to reduce waste and energy use through education, services and economic assistance.

www.bouldercolorado.gov

such as *Hawkesbury Shire Council* and *Warringah Shire Council*, and have produced checklists and guidance for event organisers.

WASTE AND CLIMATE CHANGE

From the production of waste-in-waiting (stuff), through to its ultimate disposal in landfill or by incineration, waste, my friends, equals climate change.

In mining, manufacturing, distribution and retail of goods, at every step along the way, energy is used and greenhouse gases are created. How we manage the eventual volume of waste created at our events plays a part in our contribution to climate change impacts.

As discussed in Chapter 8, if we send our end-of-life products on a one-way trip to landfill rather than their being composted or recycled, we must continually extract new resources to replace those materials that are buried or burned.

Recycling and composting reduces the use of non-renewable primary resources, putting secondary materials back into the manufacturing cycle rather than using virgin materials.

Through creating compost you are displacing the need for fossil fuel-based fertilisers along with the GHG impacts of the manufacture of these products.

Landfill makes a direct contribution to GHGs through methane creation where biodegradable waste 'rots' in the absence of oxygen. Read more on this in the section on landfill gas extraction below.

Figure 9.5 Plastic waste washed up on Kamilo Beach, Hawaii. This destination has to deal with the plastic from all around the world washing ashore.

Source: Tim Silverwood (www.timsilverwood.com).

MATERIAL TYPES

If reuse or repurposing is not an option, then reprocessing rather than disposal is the optimal outcome. No matter what the item was in its original form, if it is to be recycled or biodegraded (composted or turned into biogas), you will need to identify the material type.

Again – begin with the end in mind. Understanding what the items you will need to dispose of are made from will not only direct your waste management decisions, but also (hopefully) guide your purchase decisions in the first place. Let us now look at the different types of materials that event items and eventual event waste will be made from, and what the disposal options are for them.

Metals

Metals will appear in event waste streams through beverage cans (aluminium and steel), catering waste (steel cans and drums), and production waste (metal offcuts and scrap from construction and infrastructure).

Steel

Steel will be produced at events through beer cans (yes, some still come in steel), catering (from canned food items) and production-based waste.

Recylability: Steel can be continuously recycled, and a good price is often paid by metal recyclers.

Recycled into: More steel!

At events: You can put metal beverage and food containers into mixed recycling; however, odd-sized items such as tent poles or damaged fencing would need to go directly to a scrap-metal merchant. It is easy to arrange a skip for metal-only items if you feel you will produce a volume worthy of this single-stream collection. At a minimum, a scrap-metal merchant should supply you with a waste skip and its delivery and removal, in exchange for the metal you put into it. Just make sure your crew only put metal in the skip. One motivator for ensuring that you get the maximum metal in the skip is to come up with a deal with your site crew that they will receive the proceeds of the metal recycling money to use for beer at their end-of-show party.

Aluminium

The most obvious item that will be made from aluminium at events is the beverage can. However, other production-based aluminium waste may be created from bespoke construction or from damaged items such as gazebos or fencing.

Recyclability: Aluminium has the potential for indefinite closed-loop recycling. The high cost and energy needed to create aluminium from scratch as compared with the efficiency of recycling it makes aluminium an excellent target for events' recycling programmes. The recycling of aluminium yields excellent greenhouse gas benefits, as to create an aluminium can from recycled material takes just 5 per cent of the energy used to create it from scratch.[7] Recycling 1 kilogram of aluminium can save about 8 kilograms of bauxite, 4 kilograms of chemical products and 14 kilowatt hours of electricity. An aluminium can recycled today could be back on the shelf within six weeks, doing its job as a can again.

Recycled into: More aluminium!

At events: Beverage cans and tins from catering will in most cases be a straightforward material to recycle. For other aluminium items, check whether you can put them in the mixed recycling (with paper, glass, plastic, metal cans and tins), or whether you need to collect them separately for direct recycling with the scrap-metal dealer or recycler.

The price paid for aluminium for recycling is usually pretty good, and income can be made through selling it directly to the recycler or re-processor. Why pay a MRF to take away your waste when you can earn money from it?

Plastics

The thing about plastic is that it takes an anticipated 450 years for a piece of plastic to 'decompose'. Every piece of plastic ever produced, since it was first developed in the 1950s, is still with us today – in landfill, in oceans, in the bellies of sea birds.

Plastics are an obvious material to target for recycling at events. Plastic bottles will be used for water, soft drinks and possibly for alcoholic drinks, and are made of a popular type of plastic. However, there are many other

Figure 9.6 Alupro Can Man, a great example of recycled can art.

Source: Alupro.

materials used at events which are made of various types of plastic and which can also be recycled. Here's an explanation on different types of plastics and items made from them.

Plastics are 'hard' (such as bottles and containers), or 'soft' (such as bubble wrap, plastic bags, cling/pallet wrap, shade cloth, builders' sacks and plastic sheeting).

Materials recovery facilities exist to separate and sell on plastics to reprocessors, and as businesses they are looking for plastics that have enough value to resell at a profit.

There are many types of plastics that may be recycled. PET, HDPE, LDPE, LLDPE and PP are the plastics to look out for. See explanations on each of these types of plastics below. Make sure you check that your recycling facility can take all the plastics you intend to collect and send their way; otherwise it will end up in landfill. Plastic bags and other 'film' plastic or soft plastics are sometimes a problem to handle at recycling facilities which segregate different types of materials, so check first what they will take.

If, for whatever reason, your MRF won't take a certain type of plastic, and you'll produce a lot of it, search out a reprocessor or dealer to whom you can send it directly. You may have transport costs to pay, but this shouldn't be more than the landfill-per-tonne fee you would pay anyway. What's more, depending on the market at the time of your event, for plastics you may be paid for your recyclable material.

The demand for plastics does fluctuate, since much of it is shipped to China for reprocessing, and demand and supply fluctuate, influencing prices.

Polyethylene terephthalate (PET)

Polyethylene terephthalate is a very common plastic, and is used for synthetic fabrics (polyester) or beverage bottles and food-grade containers (generally called PET).

Recyclability: PET is probably the most commonly collected plastic for recycling in communities through business, residential and public place recycling schemes. The sheer volume of PET being manufactured primarily for disposable packaging makes its collection for recycling an imperative.

Recycled into: PET is readily recyclable, and many products, including carpets, polar fleece, T-shirts and bottles, are made from recycled PET.

At events: You will mainly see PET in your waste as beverage containers but other items such as containers and bottles from catering may also appear. The best way forward is to consider how you can reduce the volume of PET in the first place (usually through the reduction or elimination of disposable beverage bottles – most often bottled water). For the PET that does make it into your event, ensure it is effectively managed and collected for recycling.

An obvious thing to consider is the use of materials made from recycled PET from your T-shirts to the beverage brands you sell.

High Density Polyethylene (HDPE)

Items made from HDPE include milk and juice bottles, cleaning bottles, shampoo bottles, yoghurt and butter tubs, and some rubbish and shopping bags.

Recyclability: HDPE is a common plastic and the majority of recycling facilities will accept it. In most cases it is acceptable to put HDPE into mixed ('commingled') recycling bins, as the recycling facility is able to identify HDPE from other plastics effectively.

Recycled into: HDPE is also readily recyclable, and items such as more bottles, floor tiles, pens, benches, picnic tables, fencing or drainage pipes are made from recycled HDPE.

At events: Apart from bottles, you may have leftover plumbers' piping or hose from bars and damaged plastic furniture, etc. It's possible you could put any item made from HDPE in with your mixed ('commingled') recycling to be picked out at the MRF. But do check before you put this material in the mixed recycling. If you're using a MRF that is primarily dealing with household waste, the 'odd-shaped' items from HDPE may not be accepted in mixed recycling, but may be accepted if delivered in bulk pre-sorted. If not, contact a plastics recycler or dealer directly to arrange the recycling of your pre-sorted HDPE material.

PVC

Polyvinyl chloride (PVC) is one of the most commonly used plastics and comes as a rigid or flexible material, as flexible sheeting and as fabric (e.g. vinyl banners).

Rigid PVC is most often used for building materials and piping. PVC is 'plasticised' to make it flexible through the use of additives (phthalate). Packaging, handled bottles and cabling are made from this flexible PVC. Sheeted and flexible PVC is used for stickers, labels, and wrapping overlay such as event or sponsor branding on walls. We also have PVC fabric, which is used for signs (vinyl banners), billboard ads, marquees, roofs, etc.

PVC has been the focus of environmental concern for some time, and is called the 'poison plastic' by some. For more about the material and its impacts, see Chapter 8.

Recyclability: Apart from the bad press it gets from the environmental impacts of manufacture, use and disposal through landfill or incineration, PVC is, surprisingly, quite recyclable. The challenge is the availability, consistency and quality of volume of PVC material to recycle. Unlike PET, PE and PP, which are often used for single-use 'disposable' items such as beverage bottles and packaging, PVC is built (and used) to last.

Recycled into: If PVC is successfully collected for recycling, it can be made into flooring, mats and panelling.

At events: You will have vinyl sticker sheeting to brand your event (overlay) which needs to be disposed of, and possibly vinyl banners, which, once they have been used over and over again, eventually need to be disposed of.

The challenge is to find a MRF, recycling dealer or processor that will take your PVC material for recycling. A solution may be to purchase signage and overlay branding (stickers) from a sign-making company that has a take-back programme, and who arranges onward bulk disposal of used PVC material to recycling.

To find out the options, the first place to enquire is your country or region's plastics industry association. This type of organisation was involved in brokering the collection and recycling of all vinyl overlay at the *2010 Vancouver Winter Olympics* which was then recycled by a local carpet company along with its other PVC recycling. Read more in Box 9.3.

If you must use PVC for banners, ensure that the artwork is designed for reuse each year. Once vinyl banners must be disposed of, an alternative to recycling is repurposing. Look for a reuse centre that will take them or a company that turns banners into bags and other items. You could even arrange for this year's banners to be made into next year's merchandise, as they did at *Cherry Creek Arts Festival* in association with *Billboard Ecology*. Read more in Box 9.4.

Low Density Polyethylene (LDPE)

LDPE is a flexible plastic with many applications. Shopping bags (the ones that make a loud scratchy noise), squeezable detergent bottles and plastic containers, and even clothing, furniture and carpets are often made from LDPE. Items such as big one-tonne white builders' bags and shade cloths are also made from LDPE and may be recycled.

Many events, especially mega-events like the Olympic Games, take over venues and need to rebrand these venues. Often this is called 'overlay' when it comes to signage and branding. They need to be wrapped, signed and rebranded, often with huge vinyl stickers.

At the *2010 Olympic Winter Games* in Vancouver, approximately 200,000 square feet of vinyl graphics were used on Olympic buildings such as the *Richmond Olympic Oval* and the *Pacific Coliseum*, outdoor venue grandstands, 4600 vehicles, 500 buses and eight resurfacing machines.

3M Canada was the official supplier of building and vehicle vinyl wraps for the 2010 Olympic Winter Games, and they were charged with the task by organisers of ensuring that all vinyl materials they supplied would be reused. With assistance from the *Vinyl Council of Canada*, they partnered with *Mannington Commercial*, a vinyl flooring company with a long track record of vinyl recycling projects.

This great industry collaboration resulted in all of 3M's vinyl graphic material from the 2010 Olympics being diverted from landfill and remanufactured into Mannington high recycled content flooring.

Recyclability: LDPE is not often collected for recycling through municipal recycling programmes. However, it is definitely a recyclable plastic, and plastics recyclers will accept it.

Recycled into: Rubbish bin liners, rubbish and compost bins, panelling, lumber, and floor tiles.

At events: Shopping bags and bin liners are probably your biggest offenders at events. Those events that involve lots of cleaning (of people or items) may also create LDPE waste streams. You may be able to send containers made from LDPE to mixed recycling; however, shopping bags and odd-sized items will need

single-stream separation and confirmation from the MRF that they can take the items. If not, and if you have a large volume, contact a plastics recycler or dealer directly.

Linear Low Density Polyethylene (LLDPE)

The 'cling wrap' plastic encasing virtually every pallet of goods delivered to an event and which is designed to stretch and stick is LLDPE. Bubble wrap is also LLDPE.

Recyclability: LLDPE may be recycled; however, finding a MRF that will take it can be a challenge. There is absolutely no problem in recycling it; the hassle comes in when it is mixed up with other items, making it troublesome to separate. Often a MRF won't take it due to handling issues.

At events: Check if the MRF your recycling will go to can take film plastic, and how they want it presented. The best thing you can do is to ensure that all LLDPE is bundled up together and bagged if necessary, so that it is easily handled.

If you have a massive amount (e.g. at events with a lot of materials or products delivered on pallets wrapped in this plastic), and if the MRF won't accept it, look directly for a plastics dealer or re-processor that will.

A Note on 'Film Plastic'

One thing to watch out for when separating out LDPE or LLDPE from other plastics is to not mix in shopping bags, which are often made from HDPE. HDPE is usually not see-through and has a more crinkly feel (less soft than LDPE).

Don't mix these plastic bags in with your LDPE or LLDPE. Keep them separate. The reason for this is that the different types of plastics undergo recycling processing separately rather than altogether.

Polypropylene (PP)

Polypropylene is another commonly found plastic – wherever there's a need for a bag, bottle, container or box, you are likely to find PP. It can be soft and pliable, or rigid. Some yoghurt containers and bottles such as for sauces or syrups, bottle caps and straws are made from

Box 9.4

BAGS FROM BANNERS BY BILLBOARD ECOLOGY AT CHERRY CREEK ARTS FESTIVAL

Taking the initiative to store materials from last year's event is providing organisations with an opportunity to upcycle and resell unique products at their next event.

Billboard Ecology are a company aiming to bring this vision to life by salvaging advertising billboards and creating individually styled tote bags along with other unique products.

The *Cherry Creek Arts Festival,* one of the USA's top arts festivals held every year in Denver, has embraced this initiative. Over the years the event coordinator has collected banners and, through *Billboard Ecology*, these have been repurposed into beach bags, shopping totes

and unique Kindle covers. These were all sold at the festival in the merchandise stands alongside the usual T-shirts, water bottles, posters and other items.

An added advantage of this repurposing of products is that sponsors of the events get another chance for their logo to be displayed on one of these creatively inspired new products.

Other festivals embracing the idea of repurposing their event banners include *Belmar Italian Festival* and *Starz Film Festival* which have each created custom-made tote bags and wine bottle bags to distribute as gifts at VIP events.

www.billboardecology.com

Figure 9.7 Bags from Banners.
Source: Billboard Ecology.

PP. It has a high melting point so is used for containers that will tolerate hot liquid.

Recyclability: PP plastics have traditionally not been accepted by municipal recycling programmes, but this is changing. Check whether your MRF can take PP.

Caps On! The most common message that has gone out there is to take off bottle caps, as they 'cannot' be recycled. The reality is that PP is recyclable, but until recently the technology or ability of workers has not existed at MRFs for them to be able to either take off the bottle caps or separate them out. What happens now, at those facilities that accept PP bottle caps left on bottles, is that the bottles and caps are ground down to flakes together, and then separated out through the washing process, as PP floats and PET sinks. So check whether you can leave caps on and promote that to your attendees.

Recycled into: PP can be recycled into all sorts of other plastic products, from cables to brooms, bike racks, rakes, pallets and trays.

At events: Elimination from the front-of-house waste streams is difficult to achieve, since bottle caps are made from PP as are straws. One trick could be to not sell straws and to take lids off bottles. But the latter would be inconvenient. Find out if your MRF can accept 'Caps On' and promote heavily to your attendees to screw the caps on before putting in the recycling bin.

If you are baling your plastic waste, this won't work. Review onsite waste-handling plans to create the best messaging and practical solution to ensuring that both PET and PP are recycled.

Polystyrene

Polystyrene can be made into rigid products such as disposable trays and containers or 'expanded' into a foam for products such as food serviceware. This expanded polystyrene is often referred to as Styrofoam. Polystyrene is light, with it mainly being air. This enables it to escape from waste receptacles and even landfill in windy conditions. In its packaging form it is bulky, and when it does make it to landfill, it takes up lots of space and does not break down. It's also brittle and breaks down into tiny pieces very easily, making it difficult to clean up. It floats, and is a major component of marine debris, also being ingested by marine life and birds. It almost never breaks down, as it is resistant to degradation through sunlight.

Recyclability: Polystyrene is generally not accepted by municipal recycling services. Some commercial services may accept this material. The industry has take-back programmes, so search for one in your country.

Expanded Polystyrene Australia has a database of collection services. The most commonly recycled polystyrene products are foam produce boxes and so collection services are often found at produce markets (www.epsa.org.au).

Recycled into: Polystyrene can be recycled into insulation, egg cartons, rulers and foam packing.

At events: The best option at events is to ban all polystyrene food packaging and requiring take-back services to be in place for produce boxes. Don't think you're doing the right thing by asking caterers to take their polystyrene boxes away with them, as you will probably just be delaying (very shortly) its journey to the landfill. Sure, you don't have to deal with it, but you're not being a responsible event producer by diverting this waste to another landfill site.

Polycarbonate

All 'other' plastics come under the symbol number 7, including polycarbonate. This is the type of plastic that is almost unbreakable and is a 'glass replacement'. Those beer cups you drink from after 11 p.m. at the rowdy pub? Polycarbonate. Champagne flutes in your picnic set? Polycarbonate. Water cooler refill containers? Polycarbonate. Sunglass plastic and headlight covers are also polycarbonate. Basically, where you want the strength of glass without the shatter potential, polycarbonate's your man.

You may have heard of BPA (Bisphenol A) and BPA-free plastics. Polycarbonate is BPA-full; it is the plastic that contains BPA. The main controversy centres around the use of polycarbonate in babies' bottles. However, the effects of BPA are hotly debated. Although events won't be serving warmed-up beverages in babies' bottles, this is an issue to watch if it applies to you personally. Government health departments have information on the ingestion of BPA and the internet is full of information.

Recyclability: Polycarbonate is recyclable; however, it is not something that will go in your commingled recycling service. At a municipal level, polycarbonate will either be incinerated or landfilled. Single-stream collection is necessary for polycarbonate if you have a significant volume and want it recycled. Finding someone to recycle it will also be the next challenge.

Recycled into: 'Recycle' grade polycarbonate to be used to make more polycarbonate items.

At events: Polycarbonate is built to last, and so it is likely that you will have minimal volumes at an event. The most likely place you will see polycarbonate is in reusable cups. As these are designed for reuse, it is unlikely that you will be disposing of them.

Plastics in Our Oceans

Plastic debris in our oceans is a huge environmental issue, causing the deaths of seabirds and sea mammals when mistakenly ingested, or through entanglement. What is more, the plastic breaks down into tiny fragments of its former self, and becomes a toxin magnet. Being water-repelling and oil-attracting, marine plastic debris attracts toxins. Apart from the toxins already floating around in the ocean (put there by us), toxins from the manufacture of the plastic are also released as the plastic breaks down into tiny pieces.

The next disturbing fact is that these tiny poisoned plastic pills are ingested by marine life at the bottom of the food chain, and are passed up the chain, ever accumulating.

You will likely have heard about the 'ocean garbage patch' or 'gyres', where massive accumulation of marine plastic pollution is occurring. These were first documented by Captain Charles J. Moore. Read more about his work in Box 9.5.

There are numerous organisations around the world combating or building awareness of the growing issue of plastics in our oceans. From grass-roots campaigns like *Take 3* (www.take3.org.au) to large, well-funded multinationals like *Greenpeace*, all have a common purpose: to tackle this complex and growing problem.

Attempts to address this issue vary from fundraising for research and documentary film-making (www.plasticoceans.net) to designing large plastic retrieval systems for removing plastic from the oceans (www.boyanslat.com). Others concern themselves with education campaigns for ocean awareness (www.plasticfreeocean.org) and lobbying lawmakers for policy reform (www.biologicaldiversity.org).

Many of these organisations are multi-faceted in their approach and focus on numerous methods for addressing the rapidly growing problem of plastic in our oceans. One of the most well recognised of these is the not-for-profit *Surfrider Foundation,* based in California, with 80 active chapters and over 50,000 members worldwide. Closely aligned with surf culture, the *Surfrider Foundation* establishes custodianship of the world's oceans with *CARE: Conservation, Activism, Research and Education.* As such, *Surfrider* actively opposes inappropriate coastal development, seeks to raise awareness around the impacts of climate change, and advocates for increased pedestrian access and biodiversity in all coastal areas. One of their key programmes is the *Rise Above Plastics* initiative, raising awareness and funds to help clean up and prevent plastic going into the ocean. In so doing, the *Rise Above Plastics* initiative advocates for a reduction of single-use plastics and recycling of all plastics with ten easy tips for everyone to take on board (www.surfrider.org).

The diving industry is also taking a positive stance with *Project Aware*, which focuses on marine debris (along with sharks in peril). If you're holding an event in a destination known for diving and delegates or attendees are likely to dive, ensure you support *Project Aware* (www.projectaware.org).

What does this mean for events?

The best thing you can do is to join the global movement to reduce plastic use, to ensure that all plastic is recovered for recycling and to make the public aware of this urgent issue.

Choose one of the fantastic plastic-in-oceans campaigns and offer them a platform for exposure via your event.

Make a stand and ban disposable plastic items at your event. Connect the dots between this action and the critical environmental issues that are occurring as a result of our disposable plastic habits.

WHAT GOES IN THE OCEAN GOES IN YOU.

A RECENT STUDY FOUND THAT 35% OF FISH SAMPLED OFF
THE WEST COAST HAD INGESTED PLASTIC. FIND OUT HOW
YOU CAN HELP. VISIT WWW.SURFRIDER.ORG/RAP
MAKE THE PLEDGE. BAN THE BAG.

SURFRIDER and the SURFRIDER LOGO are registered service marks of Surfrider Foundation.
Copyright © 2011 Surfrider Foundation. All rights reserved.
Source: http://www.algalita.org/research/blspap-ingestion-update-9-09.html

Figure 9.8 Surfrider Foundation Rise Above Plastics campaign message.

Source: Surfrider Foundation.

Box 9.5

CAPTAIN CHARLES J. MOORE AND THE GREAT PACIFIC GARBAGE PATCH

Captain Charles J. Moore is an oceanographer known for bringing the world's attention to the *Great Pacific Garbage Patch*, a remote area of ocean twice the size of Texas and strewn with floating plastic debris.

Described as a 'toxic soup', this area of ocean is replete with plastic pellets floating on or near the surface, causing untold damage to the marine ecosystem. The area, known as the *North Pacific Gyre*, is the destination point for numerous ocean currents, which spiral in this location and deposit their toxic cargo.

Moore founded the non-profit *Algalita Marine Research Institute* (AMRI) in 1994 as his concern for ocean health grew, but it wasn't until 1997, on a return trip from a yacht race in Hawaii, that he discovered the extraordinary amount of plastic detritus floating in the area of open ocean known as the North Pacific Gyre. *"Every time I came on deck to survey the horizon, I saw a soap bottle, bottle cap or a shard of plastic waste bobbing by. Here I was in the middle of the ocean and there was nowhere I could go to avoid the plastic"* (Charles Moore).[8]

Ever since, Captain Moore has been conducting research on the distribution, quantity and fate of plastic pollution in the world's oceans. His studies have examined oceanic toxicity, the effects on marine life and the impacts on human health. With the data collected from each research voyage, AMRI provides educational findings to students, scientists, the general public, government and the private sector, and collaborations

Figure 9.9 Captain Charles J. Moore with plastic from an ocean trawl.

Source: Algalita Marine Research Institute.

are actively sought with organisations working towards oceanic restoration.

A large part of the work conducted by AMRI centres on awareness and education. The *Ship-2-Shore* education campaign links students with research vessels investigating plastic pollution in the oceans.

In this way, students can share questions, answers and ideas about the current research voyage and plastic pollution in real time with crew on board.

www.algalita.org

Recycling Symbol and Plastic Codes

Back in the twentieth century (around 1970), a paper company ran a competition to create a symbol to promote the recycled content in their products. A university student won the competition, the company did some slight alterations and the resulting three chasing-arrows recycle logo was born.

This symbol has been appropriated by many since then and has become a universal, if somewhat overused,

design. The plastics industry put their system of numbers inside the recycle symbol to identify the type of plastic.

Unfortunately, many people take the chasing-arrows symbol with a number inside to mean that the item is recyclable. It still depends on what your local facilities will accept.

The recycle symbol is not trademarked and may be used by anyone. In various countries and states, government has put restrictions on its use to ensure that misrepresentation of recycled content does not occur.

In the UK, a per cent sign can be placed inside the symbol to indicate the percentage of recycled content.

1   PET Polyethylene
2   HDPE High Density Polyethylene
3   PVC Polyvinyl Chloride
4   LDPE Low Density Polyethylene
5   PP Polypropylene
6   PS Polystyrene
7   OTHER
20, 21, 22, 23 Cardboard, mixed paper, paper, paper-board
40, 41 Steel, aluminium
50, 51 Wood, cork
60, 61, 62 to 69 Cotton, jute, other textiles
70, 71, 72, 73 to 79 Mixed glass, clear glass, green glass

Tetrapak

Tetrapak produce beverage cartons, most popularly used to hold juice and milk. The cartons are made of cardboard, coated with polyethylene and lined with aluminium.

Recyclability: They are completely recyclable; however, not all MRFs have the technology to sort them from other materials.

Recycled into: The reprocessing takes the cardboard back out as pulp, which can then go for onward recycling into paper and cardboard products. The plastic coating, polyethylene, and the aluminium can then be combined to form a composite product. This may be used for roofing or wall cladding. A further option is to end up with separated polyethylene and aluminium that can be individually recycled.

At events: Ask your waste company to find out if the MRF your recycling will hit will take *Tetrapak*. If not, restrict the use of beverages provided in *Tetrapak*, or alternatively arrange separate collection and send it to a MRF that can recycle it.

Timber

Timber is used at many events, much of it being reused as part of hired-in infrastructure. At many events, though, timber is used for bespoke construction and inevitably, upon the build and breakdown of the event, scrap timber will be created and will need to be disposed of.

Recyclability: Timber is certainly one material that you cannot put in your commingled recycling bin. It needs to be collected separately.

Untreated soft and hard timber (that which has not been painted, varnished or chemically treated) is often turned into woodchips for use as mulch. Check whether timber needs to be de-nailed first. Chipboard can also be recycled, but you will need to check if your recycler accepts it.

Some timbers can be salvaged for reuse, being sent to a recycled timber yard.

Timber which has been chemically treated for termites with Copper Chrome Arsenate (CCA) is hazardous waste in many countries and cannot be disposed of in landfill. Check what the situation is in your country.

Recycled into: Timber can be recycled into mulch or used for what I call the 'devon' of timber: MDF. Recycled timber can also be turned into paper.

At events: Timber waste will most likely be created through the construction/build of an event and during the take-down. Certainly not many event attendees will have timber to dispose of while they are enjoying your event. Timber recyclers will provide you with a skip bin, and you may need to separate the various types of timber from each other. Work with your production team to ensure that during the build and breakdown of your event all scrap timber makes its way into the skip/s for recycling. You may wish to further segregate timber for use as scrap by a reclaimed timber merchant, or send for chipping to be turned into mulch.

The biggest hurdle will be getting your crew to be diligent in putting all scrap timber in the right skip, and in fact not contaminating that skip with other materials. Work with them to make sure they understand what you are trying to do – to prevent valuable resources from going into landfill or incineration.

If you have a need for woodchip, and you produce a large quantity of scrap timber, you may wish to hire a woodchipper and turn all your scrap timber into a resource for your event. Alternatively, you could use your own scrap timber for décor, set design and construction in ensuing years.

Figure 9.10 Scrap timber is used to construct the bars at Latitude Festival.

Source: Meegan Jones.

Glass

Glass is an obviously popular material and one that makes its way to events via beverages and glass cups, along with bottles and jars from catering. Some events will have disposable glass bottles, and others that have returnable bottle programmes will be managing the reclamation and refunds of glass bottles. In countries such as India, there is no deposit on a bottle, but it is accepted behaviour to return the bottle rather than dispose of it.

Recyclability: Glass is continuously recyclable, losing no quality with each recycling circuit. Glass bottles and jars are first separated by colour and then ground into what is known as 'cullet'. This is then melted down and formed back into other glass products. Contamination from other materials is a problem in glass recycling, so this is why you see single-stream glass collection.

It must also be noted that only glass bottles and jars are accepted for recycling rather than other items of glass, as the types of glass used to manufacture items such as light bulbs, windows, etc., contain different ingredients and are not suitable for recycling into container glass.

Less energy is required to make glass with a recycled content than 100 per cent virgin materials. *FEVE*, the *European Container Glass Federation*, has found that 30 per cent less energy is required to melt down cullet compared with virgin raw materials. Visit FEVE for their life cycle assessments on glass.[9] Some organisations report that more than 70 per cent less energy is used. No matter which report you read, apart from energy savings there are the obvious environmental benefits of less mining of raw materials, including land degradation, and the energy needed for mining and transport of raw materials.

Recycled into: More glass!

At events: Many high-energy events ban glass from their shows for safety reasons. Even when banned, it is likely that glass will still make its way into your front-of-house bins. Many events will confiscate glass bottles before entry into certain parts of an event site. This gives a great opportunity to collect glass separately for onward recycling.

Ensure all production staff understand that only glass bottles and jars can be placed in the recycling bin and any other glass, such as broken cups or windows, should be placed in general waste. It is important that glass is clean, so tell your caterers.

Cardboard and Paper

Cardboard is invariably produced wherever foods and beverages are provided. The massive stash of cardboard that accrues behind food traders at events is a ubiquitous scene.

Recyclability: Paper and cardboard are readily recyclable; however, virgin materials do need to be introduced into the mix, as the cellulose content degrades with recycling. This is needed to give paper its form.

Recycled into: More paper and cardboard!

At events: Collecting cardboard and paper back-of-house can be done separately, and sent for recycling, rather than mixed in with front-of-house recycling of, for example, beverage containers. If you have enough volume, collect cardboard separately, keep it in a compacting skip or bale it, and send it directly for recycling. As anyone who has worked at a supermarket during their high school years knows, flattening boxes first makes the whole process a lot easier.

Office paper is also a likely material that you will create in your production office. You can also place this in with mixed recycling, you can put it in with cardboard recycling, or collect it separately for high-quality paper recycling if the volume warrants it.

'Degradable' Waste

The endgame for waste that is suitable for decomposing under biological conditions is that it should be kept out of landfill. This waste will be anything made from plant or animal material. Thus, for events this includes food waste, certain disposable food and beverage packaging, paper, and possibly cardboard. Some fabrics are also suitable for composting if they are not dyed.

The reason you will want to keep this waste out of landfill is that it will potentially decompose in the absence of oxygen deep down in the landfill, and create methane. Methane is a greenhouse gas and it's many more times as strong a greenhouse gas than carbon dioxide (some say 25 times, some say 60).

Processing options for this waste stream are composting or anaerobic digestion (AD). If you have a lot of green waste it could also be mulched, which will eventually naturally break down when used on garden beds. Methane harvesting from landfill sites is also an option. Read more on this below.

The main consideration in planning for this waste stream from your event is whether it will end up in a landfill site to create greenhouse gas emissions, be converted into biogas for electricity generation, or be turned into life-giving compost.

You will come across the words 'biodegradable', 'degradable' or 'compostable' on food and beverage containers and other materials. It is important to understand what these terms mean, so that you can make the best decision for your materials, as well as the appropriate disposal route.

Figure 9.11 Compostable waste.

Source: Meegan Jones.

Biodegradable

Biodegradable means that in the fullness of time (probably within six months by most definitions) the material will decompose through natural processes (involving bacteria or fungi). Various countries have different requirements for what may be officially claimed as a 'biodegradable' material. Common themes are the time it takes to be converted from carbon into carbon dioxide, that the material is broken down to a certain size (e.g. 2mm) by a given time, and that the resulting material is non-toxic (i.e. it does not contain heavy metals and chemicals).

Being biodegradable does not necessarily mean that it is compostable.

Compostable

Compostable means that the material will decompose quickly in one compost cycle (generally 10 to 14 days). There is a further difference between 'controlled compost conditions' such as in a commercial composting facility and your average backyard compost heap. Different countries have different standards for what is officially 'compostable'.

Claims of 'compostable' and 'biodegradable' are regulated by standards such as the *US Standard ASTM D6400, European Standard EN13432* and *Australian Standard AS4736-2006*.

The Australian standard adds a worm eco-toxicity test. There are also other requirements, such as the pH, salinity, and other elements' existence (potassium, magnesium, etc.).

At events: Don't take the label or the manufacturer's claims as true. If you are purchasing items you intend to send for composting after their use at the end of the event, ensure they meet the standards for compostable material in your country. If there is no such standard, check that the intended composting facility or process you plan to use can actually successfully compost the materials.

The massive impact that waste has on climate change potential is discussed on page 250.

For more information on biodegradable products, visit the *Biodegradable Products Institute* website (www. bpiworld.org) and their terrific site www.findacomposter. com.

Oxo- or Photo-Degradable

Degradable, oxo-degradable or photo-degradable means that the material will disintegrate into small pieces of the same material in the presence of sunlight or oxygen (fragmentation).

If these items are left as litter (e.g. a 'degradable' plastic bag or bottle), they will eventually disintegrate or fragment. However, there is controversy over the question of how long these tiny fragments will persist in soil or marine environments.

If you use these 'degradable' materials and you put them in the general waste bin to go to landfill, you are not doing anything different than if you had used non-degradable normal old plastic materials, as they are inert in the absence of sunlight or oxygen (e.g., when they are buried in a landfill).

If you use items made from this material, don't promote it as one of your 'green' credentials. You're not leaving litter, are you? So its 'degradable' nature is irrelevant to your circumstances and not a 'green' action you can promote.

Bioplastics

Bioplastics are products that perform as plastics (e.g. bottles, cups, packaging) but are made from renewable plant-based resources, rather than the fossil fuels that conventional plastic is made from. Not all bioplastics are biodegradable. Bioplastics are either starch based or cellulose based. Often bioplastics are called nature-based plastics. Read more in Chapter 8.

Polylactic Acid (PLA)

This cornstarch-based material is used to make products which resemble oil-based plastics. In the event industry this will appear most often as beverage cups or clear salad containers with lids. PLA cutlery and coffee cup lids are also available.

Benefits: Using PLA as opposed to oil-based plastics will save on the use of non-renewable resources, and some PLA brands report reduced energy used in the manufacturing process.[10]

Challenges: Some PLA products are promoted as being compostable; however, this is only possible in commercial composting facilities, and only if the facility confirm they can take PLA. Not all can. PLA will not degrade readily in landfill. Genetically modified corn is often used in the manufacture of PLA. This is a moral challenge for many.

Hazardous Waste

Hazardous waste is waste that is harmful to human health or the natural environment either immediately or over an extended period of time. Managing hazardous waste will be regulated by your local government or the relevant governmental environmental agency.

The following are some examples of hazardous materials:

- asbestos
- chemicals
- electrical equipment containing components from potentially harmful substances
- components such as cathode ray tubes (e.g. old TVs)
- fluorescent light tubes and energy-saving lights
- bulbs
- lead-acid batteries
- non-edible oils
- refrigeration units with ozone-depleting substances
- solvents and dyes.

Ensure you have protocols for collection of any likely hazardous waste created by your event.

Clinical Waste

Any events with first aid stations or catering to those with diabetes or others needing to dispose of syringes will need to manage clinical waste. Again contact the local council for collection and disposal regulations.

WASTE PROCESSING

It is important to understand what processing facilities are available in the event destination. What there is, what materials they will take and in what condition is a very important piece of the event waste puzzle.

We will now look at the various options for processing recyclable, compostable and general waste.

It is likely that in each destination in which you hold your event there will be different waste-processing options in place. In fact, within one city there will be many options. For those events that have the freedom to choose the end processor, this makes for a much more tailored approach.

For example, in my city there may be access to a fully automated MRF where 'commingled' recyclable waste is sent and then an automated system segregates each type of material from the others. There may also be a mechanical biological treatment (MBT) facility where all waste is mixed together (including general waste and food waste) and the processing includes a composting component. In this case, I could, if I wished, send all my waste in one bin to be 'sorted' after the event offsite at this facility.

There may also be a landfill which has purpose-built landfill gas extraction, meaning that any biodegradable waste sent to it will decompose and turn into gas (methane and CO_2) which will then be used to produce 'green' electricity.

There may also be a traditional windrow composting facility on the outskirts of the city where farms are located. Closer to town there may be a commercial-sized worm farm. Or there may be a commercial-sized in-vessel composting facility turning compostable waste into high-grade compost in about a week.

An alternative for food waste may also be an anaerobic digestion facility, serving the food waste needs of the catering industry.

There may be glass, cardboard and metal recyclers and dealers. And certainly any city worth its salt which has all its waste bases covered should have a 'tip shop', salvage yards and a waste-as-art resource reclamation centre.

We will now look at the different types of processing facilities in more detail so that you can understand how these facilities, if available close to your event, may be used, and you can start to think about how to manage procurement and at-event waste operations to match these facilities.

Figure 9.12 Metal and aluminium cans compacted and baled onsite and sent directly to the processor, rather than being sent 'loose' to a MRF. This photo is of baled cans and bottles that have come out of Closed Loop Recycling's onsite mobile MRF (www.closedloop.com.au).

Source: Meegan Jones.

Recycling

Recycling paper, cardboard, plastic, glass, metals, timber and aluminium is common practice. Residential and commercial recycling services are available in most developed nations and, through necessity, developing nations seem to do a good job of taking anything of value and recycling or reusing it.

The best place for any recyclable material is the recycling plant or being reused or repurposed, and not in a landfill site or incinerator.

Material Recovery Facility

In most circumstances mixed or 'commingled' recycled materials will be taken to what is known as a MRF (pronounced MERF). MRFs are ingenious places and you are encouraged to find out how the MRF, to which your waste will go, operates. There are suckers and blowers, magnets and conveyor belts, lines of people, and machines that whiz and whir. Each type of recyclable material is sent shooting off in a different direction, contaminants being extracted at each step along the way.

Figure 9.13 Recycling cooperative in São Paulo, Brazil receives recyclable event waste hauled from the Transamerica Expo Center by waste management company Multilixo.

Source: Shawna McKinley.

Some MRFs are council run, others are private concerns, and the technology and investment in infrastructure varies, which impacts on what can and cannot be recycled at each facility. Some will take plastic drink bottles, but not milk bottles. Only some can take *Tetrapak* (cardboard cartons lined with aluminium).

Some need glass separated by colour. Some MRFs are able to take a wide range of plastics and others just clean plastic bottles of one type, such as PET.

They may need the plastic bottles to be uncrushed, as the technology used may look for cylindrical objects when separating plastic bottles and crushed ones could get missed.

Most MRFs don't want plastic bags, and what is more require all their waste loose rather than bagged – so if your system is to bag and tie all your recyclable waste,

you may need to put an additional process in to slash and empty bags into skips or trucks.

What does this mean for events?

Your waste manager will need to know what the MRF will accept and how they want it presented to optimise the final recycling results. Don't just collect the waste, think you're doing an awesome job, close your eyes, hold your breath and hope everything will be OK once you wave goodbye to the recycling truck at the back gate. Consider the following questions:

✓ Does the MRF take 'dirty plastics' (e.g. food containers with food residue on them)?
✓ Does the MRF take cardboard such as pizza boxes with oil and food residue on them?
✓ What plastics does the MRF take? Get a list of the types of plastic by plastics code (see details later in this chapter) and also a description of the types of items.
✓ Can the MRF take 'film plastic' and does this need to be all collected into big transparent plastic bags, or can the film plastic be intermingled with the bottles, cans and cardboard?
✓ Does the MRF need flat lids on or off containers? (Some MRFS identify flat, light objects as paper, and so a lid off a plastic container that is separated from its container could be missed and not recycled.)
✓ Does the MRF want bottle lids off the bottles and, if they are left on, what degree of tolerance does the MRF have and will they reject your load of bottles with lids on? (A very important thing to know for events where lots of bottled drinks are consumed.)
✓ Can bottles be crushed or do they need to remain in their original cylindrical shape?
✓ What other tricky things does the MRF have in its processing that may influence how you manage your waste at the event to optimise the effective segregation of your waste at the MRF?

Transfer Stations

Ask the MRF, recycling processor, local council, waste contractor or waste manager to supply you with a list of

Box 9.6

TRASHed BY GLOBAL INHERITANCE AT COACHELLA MUSIC AND ARTS FESTIVAL

Since 2003, *Global Inheritance* and *Coachella* have been working together to make a sustainable and environmentally friendly festival for all to enjoy. Creative campaigns have led to improved recycling, reducing the festival's impacts and educating the public on recycling through interactive means.

In the past seven years, *Coachella* has seen thousands of festival attendees prowling the grounds in search of discarded plastic bottles and empty cans. In order to encourage not only the recycling of plastic waste but also a healthy level of hydration (an important concept for a music festival 50 miles into the California deserts), *Global Inheritance* allows attendees to trade in 10 recyclable water bottles for one fresh bottle of water. People get excited about the prospect of turning their trash into items of value; *Global Inheritance* and *Coachella* work together to make the festival more sustainable and to keep the site clean.

Global Inheritance has breathed life into waste collection at festivals by introducing the *TRASHed Recycling Store*, a one-stop recycling incentive shop. Starting in 2004 at *Warp Tour, Global Inheritance* has implemented the *TRASHed Recycling Store* as an interactive recycling centre powered by motivated people who recycle their empty plastic bottles, cups and even compostable items in exchange for cool, free merchandise. The more recyclable items attendees bring to the *TRASHed Recycling Store*, the better the prizes become, ranging from autographed festival merchandise, to backpacks and headphones, to festival tickets. By offering an enjoyable and rewarding experience, the simplicity of recycling and how to play a part in solving the problem of excess waste is easily learned.

As a bonus, event grounds are picked clean of empties.

Global Inheritance has brought this incentivised recycling programme to festivals, including *Coachella, Outside Lands, X-Games, Sasquatch, Virgin Festival, Warp Tour,* and many more.

In addition to the recycling store, *Global Inheritance* developed *TRASHed: Art of Recycling* campaign. Launched at *Coachella* in 2003, *TRASHed* brings artistic expression into the greater picture of recycling, recruiting hundreds of artists to redesign recycling bins that are integrated at major festivals/events. These bins become eye-catching art pieces as well as safe homes for rogue bottles and cans. The *TRASHed: Art of Recycling* campaign has been an integral component of the *Coachella* environment for the past eight years. The customised bins not only provide a creative canvas to re-imagine the common icon of a standard recycling bin, but also make it a lot easier for attendees to differentiate between waste and recycling.

Another initiative for recycling and brainchild of *Global Inheritance* and *Coachella* would be **Recyclosaurus Rex**, a 25-foot-tall/40-foot-long robotic dinosaur that eats recyclable bottles and cans, and compacts them into small cubes. **Recyclosaurus Rex** is not only an environmentally conscious and resourceful aid to the recycling process but it has been a large attraction and visual icon for many festival-goers in the past two years.

Global Inheritance has worked with *Coachella* to merge such unconventional and original concepts into fruitful and exciting recycling programmes, successfully saving millions of bottles from landfills over the past several years.

www.globalinheritance.org/ trashed-art-of-recycling

items they will recycle so that you can work backwards in making your purchasing decisions and managing what waste will be generated in the first place. You can then put in the most appropriate requirements to traders and participants, prepare the best way to present bin stations and signage, and work out the onsite treatment and separation of waste.

Sometimes your recyclable waste will first stop off at a transfer station to be mixed with other recyclable waste, and then be transported en masse to the MRF for segregation and onward processing. In these transfer stations, your waste will sometimes be 'tipped' onto a large sorting floor and a worker, using a grabber machine, will decide on where the good 'batches' of recyclables are in the lot on the floor.

What does this mean for events?

Be aware of the way in which the transfer station operates and understand the best way to present your waste to ensure it is chosen for the onward journey to the MRF. Think about the way in which you will be measuring waste. It is also possible that the truck picking up your waste up may also go to other places and mix theirs in with yours. Establish how you will be measuring the volume or weight of your waste.

Mixed-Waste Recycling

You may discover that the local waste-processing facility asks for all waste to be placed in one bin, and that they will sort everything at their facility. If you have a 'one-bin system' processor it is likely a 'dirty MRF' or a mechanical biological treatment (MBT) facility.

Figure 9.14 Recyclosaurus by Global Inheritance. Toss those cans in that gob!

Source: Global Inheritance (www.globalinheritance.org/trashed-art-of-recycling).

In a standard MRF the expectation is that the bulk of waste received is recyclable and the main task the MRF undertakes is to remove contaminants (non-recyclables) and to separate each type of recyclable material into single streams (i.e. glass, plastics, metals, paper). At a 'dirty MRF' they take waste they know is going to be full of non-recyclables, and their main task is to harvest the recyclables from the main waste, letting all waste they don't 'pick' continue to landfill.

At an MBT, mixed waste from a single bin (often they are also receiving municipal/householder waste) is sorted, with recyclables being separated from the general, biodegradable and liquid waste. The facility then composts this residual mixed general and biodegradable waste in tunnels or 'in vessel', and through a series of sieves and other processes, the biodegraded matter is separated from general waste. The challenge in this style of processing is that any toxic substances (e.g. solvents, chemicals, paint, even battery acid) makes its way into the residual composted material, rendering it unsuitable for human contact use. These facilities often have more than one 'line' and so uncontaminated material could potentially make more user-friendly compost. More information on managing biodegradable waste is given below.

What does this mean for events?

The primary issue with sending recyclable materials to a dirty MRF or an MBT is what this means for your at-event separation, considering attendee expectations.

It is a confusing decision sometimes, as you want to demonstrate responsible waste handling, and attendees (especially those not local and used to a one-bin system) expect that there will be recycling bins, and possibly compostables collection as well.

I have placed front-of-house recycling separation at events where the waste was going to a MBT because of the expectation by attendees that 'proper' waste segregation would be available onsite at the event. We also realised that by delivering pre-segregated waste to the MBT, the likelihood of successful final segregation at their end would be increased.

Conversely, I have also made the decision to go over to a one-bin system, where a twin system (general and recycle) would have a high degree of contamination and the logistics of truck access meant that the twin bins would be hard to manage. This was at a busy event where city streets were closed off, pedestrian traffic congested and vehicle access difficult and possibly a safety risk. What we did, though, was to explain (on the bins via signage) that the single-bin system was in place and that the waste would be sorted offsite. We also put this information on the website. And yes, we still had emails asking why there was only one bin. . . .

MRF Recycling Rate Claims

A little note needs to go in here about the recycling rate claims made by recycling facilities. You may be told that the recycling rate is, for example, '80 per cent'. Don't be confused into thinking that this is the result you will get for your recycling.

This figure is the recycling rate of the MRF, generally as a year-round rate. But does that mean they have an 80 per cent success rate of extracting recyclable materials, or does it mean that 80 per cent of the materials which go through the MRF are recyclable and they are successful in capturing all 100 per cent of recyclables?

Either way, the annual recycling rate for a MRF doesn't really reflect your recycling results. If you are measuring recycling rates for your event, ensure you have a measurement system in place that allows you to know your real recycling results, not the percentage quoted by the MRF. For more on measuring waste see the end of this chapter.

Single Stream

Waste can be pre-treated and sorted at your event before it goes off in the trucks or skips, and sent directly to the re-processor or materials reseller, rather than through MRF.

This may be done through having bins set out into single streams (e.g. glass, plastics (by type), steel, aluminium, paper, cardboard, food waste, food packaging waste, etc.). Alternatively a 'mini-MRF' could be set up on tarps, tables or conveyor belts with staff manually sorting the waste into similar items.

Or you could go to the mother of all mini MRFs, and bring in *Turnstile 21*, a purpose-built onsite MRF for events. Read more about this on page 301.

Once segregated into 'single streams', the materials would be delivered directly to the relevant re-processor or reseller. Glass, paper, cardboard and metal recycling directly with the processor is commonplace in many countries. Waste materials are a valuable resource, and industries are created around the extraction and resale of these valuable materials.

Depending on your event location, logistics and likely volume of each type of material, you may be able to separate onsite and sell your materials directly to the re-processor, or at the least to a materials reseller (if available locally).

To facilitate the logistics of this, you could bring in a community group to facilitate staffing the onsite MRF, and offer them the profits from the sale of the materials reclaimed. They would need appropriate personal protective equipment and waste-handling training.

What if There's no MRF?

In countries such as India where there is a massive population and massive rubbish problem, waste is big business. There aren't many automated MRFs and, to the casual observer, the streets may seem dirty and there may appear to be no organised waste system. But if you take a closer look, you will discover a magical world of recycling and resource recovery.

Anything of value is quickly snapped up and taken on

Figure 9.15 Waste picker in India.

Source: Meegan Jones.

a journey from a pile on the street, into a rag picker's' sack, through a network of scrap dealers and brokers, and eventually to a recycling processor.

As well as waste pickers scavenging recyclable material, in place of mechanised MRFs India has the 'Kabadi Walla' system. These collectors move through the streets calling for cardboard and other recycling. Caretakers and cleaners at housing estates collect anything of value and sell them to these dealers. Anything with a recycling or reuse value makes its way through many pairs of hands, but rather than a concern for the environment, this system occurs through financial necessity. In *Dharavi Slum* in Mumbai, India lays the recycling lungs of this huge city. Completely unofficial and practically unrecognised by the municipal council, millions of people make their living, often in terrible working conditions, from the recycling precinct in the slum. They scrape a living by scouring the streets, bins, rubbish trucks and rubbish dumps and collecting every last thing of value, which is then processed by hand in a labyrinth of micro-processing plants in the slums. I recommend a visit to see it in action if you are ever in Mumbai; it is at once amazing, inspiring and heart-breaking. To find out more about how this system works go to www.dharavi project.org.

An example is the fantastic organisation *Stree Mukti Sanghatana*. They train women waste pickers to use safe handling practices, assist in the transport of collected items, and help broker a good price and guaranteed outlet for the recycling they collect (www.streemukti sanghatana.org).

What does this mean for events?

If you're running an event in a country that has no mechanised MRF or any formal recycling separation facilities but has an 'underground' recycling industry, seek out organisations which work with and support people who earn their existence from the stuff other people throw away.

Include waste separation at your event so that attendees will appreciate the value of recycling and gain an understanding of the importance of what they throw away. Then ask organisations which support waste pickers to come and collect your recycling, offering them

a valuable income stream and helping to improve the working conditions of the people who provide cities throughout the developing world with this essential yet unrecognised sanitation service.

BIODEGRADABLE WASTE

Any event that serves or sells food will likely have biodegradable waste. Those events that use disposable food and beverage serviceware have the potential for large volumes of biodegradable waste.

At *Latitude Festival* in the UK, an audit of waste created in the arena showed ten bags of compostables to two bags of recycling to one bag of landfill. The majority of waste produced was takeaway food packaging and food

Figure 9.16 The event team checks back of house to ensure food waste is being properly separated for pick-up at a hotel venue in Shanghai.

Source: Shawna McKinley.

scraps. By capturing this waste separately, the event was able to divert a major proportion of waste from landfill.

Now that you have all this biodegradable waste, what are you going to do with it? You may be feeling quite happy that you have no plastic food packaging going into landfill, and that you're not using up fossil fuels to produce this plastic.

Unless you put in a third set of bins to capture it, all that compostable food packaging, food scraps and catering waste could end up in landfill, rot down and create methane, a potent greenhouse gas. It is your responsibility to ensure that you track the cradle-to-grave journey of what is potentially one of your biggest waste streams.

Once your biodegradable waste is collected, you can send it offsite for processing into compost or biogas, or keep it and compost it onsite. Alternatively, you may be sending your waste to a methane extraction landfill site or a mechanical biological treatment facility, where in either case you could opt for a single-bin system.

Don't just leave it to your waste contractor to work out where your compostable waste will end up, especially if they're a little rough and ready with the details. Insist on knowing where your compostable waste will be processed, what level of contamination is acceptable, what the actual process is that the waste will go through, and what will be done with the compost on completion.

Composting

Collecting compostable waste separately and sending it to the closest processing facility, whether an in-vessel composting site, windrow setup or even composting on the land where your event is held, is an important step towards reducing the landfill footprint and consequential production of methane emissions.

Commercial composting facilities use fast processing in-vessel systems or traditional windrows or heaps located outdoors. Uncontaminated compostable waste can enter an in-vessel compost system and come out the other side as usable life-giving compost within a week or two.

If you're sending your waste to a commercial in-vessel composting facility a near-perfect level of uncontaminated compostable waste needs to be achieved. Sending waste contaminated with plastics, metals or other non-

compostable material will result in the entire load being rejected. Ensure you have done what you can to prevent the wrong thing from mixing in with the biodegradable waste.

Depending on the size of your event and the volume of compostable waste it creates, you may be able to adopt a more DIY approach. Some events such as *Bonnaroo* in the USA have set up systems to compost their own waste onsite. Composting all of its cutlery and serviceware is one of *Bonnaroo*'s proudest accomplishments. In the past five years they have sent almost 120 tonnes of compostable serviceware provided by *Eco Products* to their purpose-built onsite compost pile. They are lucky enough to either own their own property in a rural setting, or to have very obliging landowners. If you find yourself in this situation, what better way than to completely close the loop by feeding the land compost from materials generated through the land-use activities (i.e. your event)? Read more about Bonnaroo compost efforts on the book's website.

For smaller events you may be able to team up with the local community gardens to take your compostable waste. They may also be interested, in exchange for tickets, promotion or a donation, to staff the bins, do up beautifully decorated bins, and to remove the waste, along with composting it. This could be a great greening story for both of you. *Stomp Festival* in Newcastle, NSW did just this. Bins were given to *Figtree Community Garden* whose volunteers painted them up. They were then brought to the event, filled with biodegradable waste, and returned to the gardens for composting and use there.

At a few events I have even heard of the food waste being gathered and sent to the stallholder's pigs or chooks. A great solution. And if you have your own compost heap at home that can take a modest quantity of food waste, why not take it home? Sure, there are some minor council rules being violated, but I won't tell anyone if you don't.

So what of compost itself? What is it good for? Compost adds organic matter to soil, improving plant growth and offering a natural fertiliser. Modern agricultural techniques deplete organic carbon levels in soil, making it less stable, less able to hold water and contributing to erosion and salinity. Compost also has a wonderful benefit of sequestering carbon, keeping it in the soil, where eventually it will be taken up by plants and returned to the natural carbon cycle.

Anaerobic Digestion and Biogas

Anaerobic digestion (AD) is used all over the world, particularly on a small scale in agriculture in nations such as India and Thailand, and it is also used widely in Europe. AD is composting biodegradable material in the absence of oxygen. The result is biogas (a mixture of methane and CO_2) used to generate electricity and heat, and digestate (the solids/liquids left at the end of the decomposition process). This digestate may be used as agricultural fertiliser or additionally treated in a traditional composting operation.

DEFRA's 'Waste Strategy for England' published in 2007 strongly supports AD to treat food waste.[11] The UK government is now encouraging local authorities and businesses to use AD. Keep an eye on whether there are AD facilities in your local area towards which your compostable waste or sewerage could be directed.

Worm Farms

Another great solution for compostable waste is the humble worm. If you are lucky enough to have a commercial-sized worm farm in your vicinity, arrange for your compostable waste to go to them. Broken Hill, New South Wales houses Australia's largest worm farm, *Australian Vermiculture* (australianvermiculture.com.au). If you happen to have a similar facility in your town there is absolutely no excuse not to collect your food waste and send it to the worms. I wonder how many events there are in Broken Hill? Do a quick google and see where the worms are near you.

Or you can take *ExCel* in London's lead and install your own in-house worm farm! Read more about this terrific project in Box 9.8.

What does this mean for events?

The only real way to prevent the negative impacts of sending biodegradable waste to landfill (methane emissions) is to prevent it from entering in the first place.

Box 9.7

ONSITE COMPOSTING AT WOODFORDIA, AUSTRALIA

Woodfordia

Woodford Folk Festival in Queensland, Australia is held on land owned by the Queensland Folk Federation, who also run the event. It has continuing sustainable development of the land as an underlying feature of the event and site operations, and composting its biodegradable waste is part of this.

Organic waste is collected from the Festival Village and camping areas in 120-litre bins and transported to the onsite processing location. An effort is made to manually remove non-organic contaminants from the collected waste. The level of this contamination is the weakest point in the process. The site where the composting takes place is graded hardstand, and has its own leachate dam. This is where rainwater run-off goes.

The dam is mechanically drained to onsite 'black water'. The raw festival waste is blended with a carbon-rich waste stream and placed in a windrow on the hardstand. The windrow dimensions are governed by the composition of the two waste streams.

Post festival, the heap is covered with waste hessian to deter animal interference and aid moisture retention. The heap is left to the elements and natural life forms to break it down to compost that will be less than 10 per cent the volume of the original material. After stick picking the remnants of biodegradable cutlery and shredding them for mulch or discarding them, this product is used on the festival grounds and some is used to activate the fresh waste collected at the next Festival.

www.woodfordfolkfestival.com

Box 9.8

ONSITE WORMERY, EXCEL LONDON

ExCeL

ExCeL London is an international exhibition and conference centre situated on the Thames in the heart of London's Royal Docks. They have also installed the UK's largest and only commercial wormery.

The venue is part of a 100-acre campus, including three onsite train stations, easy access to the London underground tube line, five onsite hotels and numerous bars and restaurants.

The wormery holds 300,000 worms capable of eating at least two times their body weight a day. Earthworms are the ultimate recycling machine. All types of food waste can naturally be recycled into productive, nutrient-rich soil. Food waste is collected from the kitchens and preparation areas and delivered to the wormery. It is processed through a macerator into a pulp that is fed to the worms. The pulping makes the food easily consumable for the worms, removing the need for rotting to break it down. The worms digest the waste and convert it into rich worm cast.

There has been a 90 per cent reduction of waste volume to landfill which includes great GHG avoidance benefits – both from methane created by biodegradable material in landfills, and through transport of waste reductions.

ExCel has also installed an onsite MRF to process paper, cardboard, plastic, wood and glass. There are colour-coded bins for all events, the campus, onsite partners and hotels.

www.excel-london.co.uk

If you choose to use disposable food and beverage serviceware which is compostable, ensure that you actually collect these materials and send them for composting. If you choose not to do so, and prefer to send these materials for general disposal (see options below), do not promote your event as using compostable serviceware, as you will be caught out if questioned about whether you are in fact composting. The same goes for recycling. If you use materials that are promoted as 'recyclable' then you will actually need to recycle them for the claim to mean anything. Bear in mind the following:

✓ Estimate the likely volume of compostable materials that will be part of your waste stream and determine if collecting it separately is warranted.

✓ Investigate the claims of materials to understand the difference between 'degradable', 'biodegradable' and 'compostable'.

✓ Determine if processing facilities are available.

✓ Determine if at-event logistics will allow the successful collection of compostable materials.

GENERAL WASTE

An event's waste that ends up in 'general' waste should be anything that is not salvageable, recyclable or compostable.

Unfortunately, the event industry has a long history of producing mountain ranges of waste, often from single-use 'disposable' items. The 'too hard basket' is also often an excuse for not doing anything other than a single-bin, all-in, straight to landfill or incineration as a waste solution. Waste is seen as a problem to be dealt with, with no litter left lying around and an event site or venue restored to its original condition as quickly as possible being the main aim.

Most event logistics mean that there will always be time and budget pressures to get the site or venue cleared and clean. However, great waste management, segregation and diversion from landfill results have been achieved by many, many events. Yes, there are some cases where a single-bin system is the way you have to go; however, I have heard every excuse from event producers on why they cannot manage at least a twin-bin system with 'the people won't put the right thing in the right bin' being pretty much the weakest. If you have the will to do it, you will come up with a way to make it work.

Nonetheless, at many events, despite a zero waste-to-landfill aim, there will still be residual waste that cannot be recycled, salvaged or composted, and will need to be disposed of (given access to available technologies). The options include landfill and incineration.

Landfill

Landfill is the end of a one-way road for our habit of buying, using and discarding. The by-product of consumption, our dirty little secret. Well, perhaps not so secret, and definitely not so little, and definitely dirty. Shall we just call it dirty? Massive lost opportunities lie in the heart of a landfill.

Tonnes of valuable recyclable material sit buried while new resources are extracted from the ground or created in factories to replace what we have discarded. Tonnes of biodegradable waste lie rotting, sending up methane, when it could have become fertiliser if processed through a composting facility, or energy if used as feedstock for biogas plants.

Beyond methane emissions and lost opportunities through burying recyclables and compostables, landfill holds the potential for the escape of leachates that cause soil and groundwater pollution. In some areas we are simply running out of landfill space.

Enter stage right landfill mining. Sites are being upturned to pull out recyclables, deal with toxicity issues, take out the soil which has now combined with rotting biodegradable waste, and also to free up landfill space to accommodate more stuff.

Methane Extraction Landfill

Landfill owners, waste treatment companies and the like are rolling out investment–heavy technology and infrastructure to capture the energy potential of methane generation from landfill – energy from waste (EfW). This is then used to create electricity.

In the United States there are EfW landfill gas harvesting landfill sites in every state. But, and this is a BUT-with-a-capital B, having EfW sites can also encourage guilt-free trashing and destruction of resources.

Some landfills are either purpose-built or retrofitted to extract the methane which has been created by biodegradable waste in the landfill site.

Sending all waste to these sites may be regarded as a better option than a traditional landfill site; however, it is not optimal if there is the potential and ability to collect compostable material and actually compost it.

Gas created by biodegradable material in landfill is a major target for those countries looking to reduce their greenhouse gas emissions. In Australia, the top 500 polluters (of greenhouse gases) are taxed for the GHGs they create (generically called the 'Carbon Tax'). Some local government councils are in the top 500 because of the landfill sites they own and the GHGs these sites emit. It will be interesting to see how this eventually flows down the cost to throw waste in general, and biodegradable waste specifically, into landfill.

Methane is generally accepted to be between 23 and 27 times more potent a greenhouse gas than CO_2, but there is some debate over this figure. In order to come up with a standard set of measures to place the various greenhouse gases on an even keel, CO_2 is used as the base, with a 100-year life span. But methane's average lifespan is just 12 years. When you consider the actual short-term potency of methane, it's far more than 23 times that of CO_2.

We're dealing with a very effective greenhouse gas here, and every time we throw something biodegradable into the bin to make its way to landfill, we're contributing to the problem in quite a big way.

In the UK, *DEFRA* reports that 40 per cent of methane emissions in the country come from landfill alone.[12] Combine this with a report from the UK's Waste and Resources Action Programme, *WRAP Household Food and Drink Waste in the UK Nov 2009*, that 6.7 million tonnes of food in the UK is thrown out annually, costing consumers £12 billion.[13] How much uneaten food ends up in the bins at your event?

Waste to Energy

Incineration (and creating energy from the process) should be the final method of waste disposal chosen, only after the maximum amount of recycling and compostables has been extracted from the waste stream.

However, some countries have leapfrogged recycling and send stuff straight for incineration, opting for 'energy from waste' or 'waste to energy' processing. Waste is 'burnt' in the absence of oxygen through a process called pyrolysis, and 'syngas' is produced. This gas then fuels energy generation.

Most European countries have moved to the point of maximising recycling opportunities and send to incineration only the waste that cannot be used as a secondary raw material.

This option of waste processing can however undermine recycling projects in nations where citizens are not predisposed towards the recycling habit.

The resulting energy is labelled 'green' or 'renewable' energy, as it is either using materials that would otherwise have ended up in landfills, or because the carbon which is embodied in the waste material is 'recent carbon' currently in the carbon cycle, rather than 'ancient carbon' (fossil fuel).

I personally have a problem with waste to energy because it does not do anything to encourage the reduction of waste created. In fact it requires feedstock, and for-profit facilities need a certain amount of volume through to make their businesses financially viable. If they have agreements of waste 'supply' by householders within municipal councils, the council would have an obligation to ensure waste volumes to maintain the contracted agreement, and this flies in the face of any waste-reduction campaigns that could be in place. There will be many types of agreements in place and we can only hope that those cities with waste to energy have structure in their agreements to allow waste reduction campaigns to be effective. If I know my energy is coming from 'green' sources, I don't have such a moral pressure to conserve energy. So, for me, using waste to create energy means the following:

*   resources are lost, causing demand for more virgin materials to be created, rather than using recyclable materials;
*   no incentive to reduce waste volumes;
*   no imperative to reduce energy consumption.

You will need to inform yourself of the issues, do further research into where your own country sits with the various options, and make a decision on whether or not to support waste to energy.

What does this mean for events?

To avoid creating GHG emissions from waste disposal and to support the avoidance of more virgin materials being produced, I would say no to sending compostable or recyclable waste to landfill. Consider the following:

✓   Paper, timber, green waste from grounds maintenance, food scraps or anything else that can rot down should be either composted, mulched or recycled.
✓   Do all you can to manage recyclable materials at your event to maximise the effectiveness of recycling processing offsite.
✓   Don't send any waste to incineration if it could have been recycled or composted.

Imagine the impact, both immediate and from an educational point of view, if all the events in the world were to start separating food and other compostable waste. Imagine if all events get their recycling sorted to such a degree that just about everything that can be recycled, is. By playing our part in keeping compostable and recyclable materials out of landfill and incinerators, events can help to drastically reduce methane emissions from landfill and CO_2 from incineration and the knock-on climate impacts of consequential production. Move your event towards zero waste, reduce the pressure of resource extraction and reduce the climate change impacts.

WHAT WASTE AT YOUR EVENT?

When you go step by step through your event, you will be able to identify what rubbish will be created and where. You will then be able to plan for recycling, composting, salvage, reuse and disposal.

Waste will probably be created in every area and phase of your event. This includes the pre-production phase,

Figure 9.17 Once people get into the swing of separating their waste, they would prefer to overfill the correct bin rather than put their waste in the wrong one. Can you see what doesn't belong?

Source: Meegan Jones.

the build or creation of your event site or bump-in to the venue, where everything is unwrapped, unpacked, set up or built. During the event waste will obviously be created through activities that the attendees participate in (front of house) and through what goes on behind the scenes to service these activities (back of house). The breakdown, bump-out, pull-out, exit or 'the out' is also a major waste-creating part of an event's life cycle. 'You're only as good as your out', a production manager I know always says. Stuff discarded by everyone who has either attended or been part of the creation of the event is often a trouble-some and high-volume waste stream.

In the following pages we will look at waste that is produced throughout the life cycle of your event and how to reduce it and manage what it left.

Back-of-House Waste

Back-of-house production areas will generate many of the everyday recyclable and compostable waste items as staff, crew and other people go about their work. However, there may also be unique waste streams as a result of that work. As each event is different the list could be endless, but here are examples of some of the waste that could be created:

- timber offcuts
- metal strips from pallet deliveries
- cling wrap from pallet deliveries
- cardboard boxes
- scrap metal
- plastic piping from plumbing
- electrical cabling offcuts
- batteries and electrical equipment
- plastic and cardboard packaging
- plastic sheeting/scrim for fences
- fabric drops used to mask backstage areas
- light bulbs and fluorescent tubes
- packaging material such as polystyrene balls (aaagghh!)
- plastic film wrap (e.g. bubble wrap or pallet wrap)
- waste cooking oil
- paint tins, fuel tins and other liquid receptacles
- compostable catering waste
- damaged equipment and goods.

Don't put all your energy into designing the perfect systems for front-of-house/attendee waste. Remember to arrange the best waste disposal options for your production team as they create the event site, during the event and for pull-down.

Front-of-House Waste

Most waste at events is created by the attendees – often from eating and drinking. By controlling what foods and beverages are sold at your event, restricting what people can bring in, and managing the interface between exhibitors/stallholders and attendees will allow you to also manage the creation of waste. At many events, waste streams from attendee participation could be as follows:

- aluminium cans
- plastic bottles
- glass bottles
- newspapers, magazines, flyers, printed programmes
- plastic bags
- uneaten food
- food and beverage serviceware
- packaging from merchandise purchases

- stuff which attendees bring to the event
- cigarette packets and butts
- unwanted giveaways
- lanyards and name tags.

You should also identify any areas of waste creation specific to your event. For example, are sponsors bringing in unique items to give away? Is a particular planned activity likely to produce more waste of a certain type than others? Are promotional flyers handed out, only to be dropped moments later? Is there a free drinks station, creating loads of disposable cups or bottles?

WASTE PREVENTION

The best place to start when tackling waste management at your event is at the beginning. What waste will be created and can you influence its creation? If you are in a position to restrict what attendees bring inside your gates or doors and to control what is sold or served at your event or inside the venue, you have a massive head-start over those who have no control over what wanders into their event in the attendees' hands.

Design-In Waste Prevention

Plan your event activities and the materials you use in such a way as to prevent waste from occurring in the first place. This could include the way signage is made so it can be used every year, rather than the placement of a date or sponsor on it, rendering it disposable after one use. Mindful procurement is the key.

Identify Waste Streams

Understand the type of waste you are dealing with. Undergo an audit to identify what is in your waste or conduct pre-event analysis to identify all the types of waste that could be created.

Engage and Communicate

Working out who will be involved with creating the waste is an important step as without buy-in by these people and departments, you're sure to struggle. You need the potential waste creators to be inspired to devise solutions to prevent that waste from occurring. Tools to use may be guidance and encouragement towards the inclusion of contract clauses and requirements, and inclusion in tender documents.

Zero Waste

In nature, systems are cyclical, producing no waste, one thing feeding into the next. Earth, water, air and sun energy continually exchange, create, regenerate. As Captain Charles Moore says, "Only we humans make waste that nature can't digest."

The 'Zero Waste' movement has an overall vision for the future where we are working within closed loops, producing no waste at all. The idea is to see any waste as a residual product or potential resource and to develop systems to optimise this.

The goal is to design-in waste prevention through processing techniques, component design, materials choice, minimising packaging, eliminating hazardous processes and materials, and forward planning uses for residual products.

The entire life cycle of a product's journey from extraction of resources, through manufacturing, transport, use and disposal is a one-way trip for many products.

We need to imitate nature and close our loops, creating continuous cycles of resource creation and use, so that our waste re-enters the manufacturing system as valuable secondary materials. A product, its components, packaging and manufacturing by-products all have the potential to become the materials from which new products are made.

Zero Waste International Alliance (ZWIA)[14] defines 'Zero Waste' as follows:

> Zero Waste is a goal that is ethical, economical, efficient and visionary, to guide people in changing their lifestyles and practices to emulate sustainable natural cycles, where all discarded materials are designed to become resources for others to use.
>
> Zero Waste means designing and managing products and processes to systematically avoid and eliminate the volume and toxicity of waste and materials, conserve and recover all resources, and not burn or bury them.
>
> Implementing Zero Waste will eliminate all discharges to land, water or air that are a threat to planetary, human, animal or plant health.

ZWIA's *Recognition Program for Zero Waste Businesses* provides a framework to recognise businesses that have reduced their waste to landfill, incineration or the environment by 90 per cent or more. Read more on the ZWIA website (zwia.org).

In the ultimate recycling, we are looking to 'up-cycle', where new and valuable products are made, keeping the resources out of landfill or incinerators, rather than 'down-cycling', where lower and lower grade products are made from recycled materials, only putting off for a little while longer its eventual role as waste in landfill.

Up-cycling and keeping materials in a constant flow of being a manufacturing ingredient, being used in or as a product, and being recycled to be used again is the 'closed loop'. Paper recycling is virtually a closed-loop system, though virgin pulp does need to be introduced into the cycle as paper can only be recycled four to seven times before its fibre length is too short to be useful. Plastic recycling has traditionally down-cycled, with each cycle of reuse producing lower grade material. However, technological advancements are seeing plastics being reused for their original purpose. Aluminium and glass both have near-perfect closed-loop recycling potential. Aluminium recycling has the additional benefit of just a fraction of the energy needed to recycle it than to make it from scratch.

The *London 2012 Olympics* created the *London 2012 Zero Waste Events Protocol*[15] to support and encourage best practice for managing waste at events associated with the Games. The programme was supported by Olympic partner *Coca-Cola*. In legacy *Coca-Cola* has created the *Zero Waste Events*[16] website and programme (zerowasteevents.org).

WRAP in the UK has great programmes for 'working together for a world without waste', including *RecycleNow.com* and *Lovefoodhatewaste.com*. It has now established a vision for zero waste events. *Zero waste events: a 2020 vision* sets both a challenge – to develop and stage successful events, reducing the amount of waste produced along the way – and a roadmap to help deliver and exploit the potential for more sustainable events. If you're in the UK and looking for great waste resources specific to your area, access their website. Split into 'Getting Ready', 'Showtime' and 'Packing Up' it has loads of links to resources and tools to help get you towards a zero waste event (www.wrap.org.uk/zero wasteevents).

The London Olympics and WRAP partnership have also produced an online waste planning tool for events (rmp.wrap.org.uk)

What does this mean for events?

The goal of moving an event towards *Zero Waste* is to identify every type of waste that could be generated, and plan in advance to eliminate its creation. By doing this we will be reducing waste management costs, reducing purchasing, and potentially moving to profit-making from the sale or reuse of 'waste'. Consider the following:

✓ Make your procurement decisions with an eye on the endgame – the clean-up of the event. What are you purchasing to produce the event that is just waste-in-waiting, with its final destination a rubbish tip?

✓ Consider using the phrase 'Towards Zero Waste' when communicating your intention for waste to be avoided or diverted at your event.

✓ Plan procurement in such a way that the residual 'waste' materials can be resources for other things. This may be as obvious as recycling and composting, or get a little cleverer and look at salvage and materials repurposing.

✓ Look for a zero waste-inspired initiative in the event destination and see how your waste avoidance and diversion ambitions can be supported by their programmes.

✓ Identify waste that will be created, and set up the right bins or skips with good signage at convenient locations, to collect waste, recyclables and those materials that are identified for reuse.

Circular Economy

The concepts of zero waste and resource recovery tie in tightly with the idea of a circular economy. In what we have previously seen, industry and consumption is the one-way or linear system of extraction, manufacture and disposal or 'take, make, throw'. A circular economy recognises that each material, function, process, product and user has a part to play in keeping resources from being discarded and lost, but rather to be part of an ongoing interacting system. The circular economy eco system designates a role for designers, manufacturers, retailers, consumers, repairers and recyclers. Go to the *Blue Economy* website for great video explanation of this concept (www.blueeconomy.eu).

Production Waste

During the build of the event site, the bump into the venue, the setting up of booths and stands, lots of waste will be created. All of the stuff that happens behind the scenes, out at the back to make the show run, is just as waste-creating as what happens front of house.

Wave Rock Weekender Festival in Western Australia issue a challenge to their staff – the no gaffa tape and no cable ties challenge! This is so that all their production materials are either compostable or reusable. Even the roadies enjoy the challenge and prior to the event they share ideas about different ways to hang or stick things around the site. The answer ends up being a good stock of clamps, clips, twine and u-bolts (www.soulhighway. com.au/menu/events/wave-rock-weekender/).

RAI, an exhibition centre in Amsterdam, requires all exhibitors to sort their waste into designated streams but to leave all waste at their exhibition stand location upon pull-out. RAI staff then travel around to the stands and weigh each lot of waste, and transport it to the back-of-house bulk waste area. Each exhibitor is allowed to produce a certain amount of waste as part of their exhibitor fee. Those who produce more or do not segregate as directed are given a charge-back fee (www.rai.nl).

Consider setting up a visible 'salvage yard' and encourage exhibitors, stallholders and contractors to bring to the yard stuff that they think might be suitable for reuse. Assign a motivated volunteer who knows their scrap to be the salvage yard monitor.

The *Sydney Convention and Exhibition Centre* has a fantastic multi-stream waste service that includes setting up a compound on the day of the exhibition pull-out for all salvageable materials to go into (www.scec.com.au). *Reverse Garbage*, a reclamation, reuse and repurposing centre and service, will pick up the materials and resell them at their facility. They 'mine the urban landscape' for industrial and commercial waste, which is then used by others to use 'as is' or to repurpose into other things. It's a treasure trove for visual artists and community organisations looking for affordable décor materials (reversegarbage.org.au).

RREUSE is a European umbrella for social enterprises with activities in reuse, repair and recycling. Check out the members' page to find a centre near you to arrange event salvage (www.rreuse.org). Consider the following:

- **Get the bins there first:** It's important that before any kind of installation at the event site or in the venue room/s the bins are there first, in the right place, with the right signs on them.
- **Do inductions:** Include in existing inductions or hold special inductions on how the waste needs to be managed, separated and stored by production staff during the build, running and breakdown of the event.
- **Monitor them:** Keep a close eye on how the system is working at the beginning. If it doesn't work then, it won't work during the heat of the event and in the fast-paced pull-out.
- **Set up temporary systems:** You may need a temporary system set up to service unique waste streams that occur during the build or the bump-out of the event. Place bins in front of stalls or areas. Set up compounds for participants to put waste in right in the middle of the event space.
- **Service them directly:** Have staff go around continually to exhibitors or stallholders as they set up and collect unique waste streams (such as film plastic) as everything gets unwrapped and unpacked, before the stallholder or exhibitor throws it in the wrong bin or skip.
- **Temporary storage:** encourage participants to bring reusable storage containers and provide a temporary storage location for these containers. Many exhibitors will hire trucks for delivering stand materials and won't have a truck sitting in a car park for four days just to store boxes.
- **Encourage and promote reusable décor:** In communicating with stallholders and exhibitors encourage the use of reusable materials for stands and stalls' construction and décor. Reward or incentivise those that have a completely reusable exhibit.
- **Service dressing-rooms:** For those events with talent and dressing-rooms or greenrooms, don't forget to also service these areas with the full complement of waste disposal options. The same goes for VIP or guest hospitality areas.
- **Flatten cardboard:** Contract into agreements with major cardboard waste producers that they must flatten cardboard and place it in the designated area/container.
- **Recycle film plastic:** Food traders, bars and caterers will be the big producers of film plastic. Create a campaign among these stakeholders to help make them understand that film plastic can be recycled, to allow them to identify what sorts of film plastic to separate out, and to set up systems to make it easy to do so.
- **Metal:** Set up a scrap metal zone or skip. Encourage your crew to separate and save all scrap metal. Offer them the proceeds of the scrap payment to encourage them to do this.
- **Timber:** Set up a scrap timber zone or skip. Send for recycling or woodchip it and reuse it onsite.
- **Signage:** Design signs so that the dates and sponsors are changeable for the following year, or as a separate smaller sign so you can keep the main event brand signs for each year.

Printing and Paper

By reducing the amount of printed material you produce you will save resources, money, and the eventual waste when it is inevitably all thrown away. This may be at your event (such as ticket stubs) or on the streets (when you have distribution companies handing out your flyers or doing letterbox drops). Consider the following:

✓ **Paperless ticketing:** Establish a system with your ticketing provider to go paperless rather than printing and mailing out tickets or registrations.

✓ **Electronic, Bluetooth and Apps:** Supply conference materials on a thumb drive, rather than printed. Send programmes via Bluetooth and Apps.

✓ **Agenda/programme:** Print onto signs placed around the event or venue, rather than printing them out separately.

✓ **Reduce:** The volume of promotional flyers and posters printed and distributed. Be frugal in producing your printed programme and other material.

✓ **Printing:** Print or copy on both sides of the paper, and use lighter-weight paper.

✓ **Social media:** Use social media to generate awareness and a buzz about your event. Don't be so old school as to mail out stuff via snail mail.

✓ **Databases:** Avoid mailing hard copies. Go virtual! If you must use mail, ensure that there are no duplicates in the database.

✓ **Scanners:** Use bar scanners for exhibitors to collect visitor information.

Giveaways

Many events give away samples, gift bags and other promotional items by the event, sponsors, exhibitors, etc. Promotional flyers and brochures are also given away. Many of these items are 'waste-in-waiting'. Put controls in place to either prevent giveaways that are likely to be waste-creating, or put systems in place to collect up the items, once discarded, into the appropriate bins.

Who hasn't been to a travel expo or 'sustainable living fair' only to be weighed down under all the stuff that's thrown at you? Encourage your exhibitors to come up with creative ways of 'activating' their brand or business at your event, rather than blindly handing out samples and promotional leaflets, all neatly wrapped in plastic and then popped in a plastic bag. Experiential promotion is the name of the game. Get those who want to 'hand things out' to create an interactive setup at your event that will offer both entertainment and a chance for them to spruik their message or product. Consider the following:

✓ **Limit hand-outs and freebies:** Restrict hand-outs of brochures, show bags, sample sizes and freebie promotional items that will be quickly discarded.

✓ **Flyer wall:** Set up a flyer wall. Let conference delegates take the stuff they think they will use.

✓ **Merchandise:** Don't over-order, or purchase one-off gimmicky items. Put a policy in place that any branded event merchandise must be designed to last and likely to be used at least three more times.

✓ **Merchandise:** Request that merchandise is not over-packaged, such as individually wrapped items, unless this is necessary for product protection. Request that no polystyrene pellets are used as filler.

✓ **Virtual gift bag:** Create virtual gift bags where information and offers are hosted online, and delegates/attendees can access the offers.

✓ **Opt in:** Have delegates opt into gift bags, newspapers in their hotel rooms or for branded merchandise, create limited editions and have pre-ordering only, so that no surplus remains.

Beverage Containers

The bottles, cans and cups that drinks are sold and consumed in may make up a huge proportion of event waste. Coming up with a way to serve drinks that will produce the least amount of waste is the first place to start. If you control the sale of beverages, then you can control the waste.

If you have control you may be able to make a decision to serve in reusable cups, for drinks to be bulk dispensed into cups, or if they are sold in individual packaged bottles or cans.

The best option

The obvious way to reduce waste volume from bars is to sell beverages from bulk supply (kegs, post-mix, etc.), which eliminates single beverage packaging waste, into reusable cups. At conferences and events with table service and waiters, this is standard catering practice. At outdoor festivals and entertainment or sports events things get logistically trickier but not impossible. Solutions such as Europe's *Cup Concept* or Australia's *One Green Cup* are ways that have been devised to

Figure 9.18 Cup concept at Latitude Festival.

Source: Meegan Jones.

provide reusable cups to large-scale events. The cups generally have a deposit on them, which entices attendees to bring them back for a refund, or keep them for a souvenir (www.cupconcept.de www.onegreencup.com).

If mobile washing facilities are available, you have adequate wastewater disposal options, staff to service the set-up, and willing caterers and/or bar operators, using washable cups is something that could put a massive dent in your overall waste volumes. As every event, attendee, site or venue is different, this will not be a solution for all.

The next best

If a reusable option is not possible, then bulk supply into disposable cups that are collected for recycling or composting is your next best option. Choosing between paper or plastic, compostable or recyclable, is an issue to deal with under this option.

The third choice

If bulk supply of the beverages is not possible, then selling or serving prepackaged drinks in single servings (i.e. in bottles and cans) is going to be the next option for you. This will create significant waste volumes proportionate to other waste streams at most events. Make sure you have systems in place to collect all of the individual bottles or cans handed out.

Last and certainly least

Pouring single-serve drinks from bottles and cans into disposable cups is the most prolific waste-creating option and the least preferable. Avoid this at all costs!

Bottled Water

A good way to reduce the amount of plastic bottles used is to ban bottled water (or at least not sell or provide it).

If you have water stand-pipes (taps) available and the water is of good drinking quality, consider giving up the profit you may earn from selling bottled water and give it away for free.

It is possible that the amount of money you lose on water sales profits may end up being similar to the cleaning and waste removal costs of all those empty plastic bottles.

Refillable Bottles

Reusing glass bottles is the most environmentally preferable option for single-serve beverages. Refillable bottles are used in many European countries, North America, Latin America and India. It was also something that was part of my childhood memories in Australia, but sadly now only an option in South Australia.

Norway has pioneered the reverse vending machine. The bottles are taken to vending machines where the customer puts in the empty can or bottle and receives a token or coin refund.

Laws on container deposit, or 'Bottle Bills' as they are known by the lobby group of the same name, are what drive these programmes.[17] If your country doesn't have this in place, there's nothing to stop you running your own container deposit system, as illustrated by the examples in this chapter.

You could also team up with Bottle Bill activists in your region to help push the example of how effective bottle deposits can be in getting maximum recycled bottles collected. If you are holding an event in a country or state that is on the verge of implementing container deposit laws, you could help the cause by publicly demonstrating how a container deposit can work and share the results on how your event performed. To learn more, go to the Bottle Bill website (www.bottlebill.org).

Extended Producer Responsibility

For some time now there has been pressure on companies such as beverage bottlers to take responsibility for the packaging that their products come in. We can see this taken in hand in countries where bottle deposits are the norm. You will notice, however, as you move from country to country that the same multinational companies have different systems in different countries. It is not so much their heartfelt environmentalism that leads them to recycling and reusing bottles, but the laws of that country.

The concept of *Extended Producer Responsibility* is something we are seeing written increasingly into laws. It is designed to promote the integration of environmental costs associated with full product life cycle impact. Manufacturers must guarantee physical or financial responsibility for final disposal. It is particularly relevant for packaging, as this is the part of the product that has almost immediate redundancy built into its design.

An excellent example is that of *Tetrapak*'s work in India. They have teamed up with an NGO to get waste pickers allocated to schools, working with the children to recycle the thousands of milk cartons drunk every day across the city. The children flatten their packs after drinking and these are then picked up and taken to a central recycling plant. The waste pickers who collect the *Tetrapak* containers are given a guaranteed price per kilogram.

What does this mean for events?

When you are negotiating your beverage sponsorship or product placement deals, discuss the contribution to the responsible collection of containers by the beverage companies.

There are no better potential sponsors of the recycling activities at your event than the companies that are responsible for the waste stream in the first place.

Stallholders and Exhibitors

Most of the aspects relevant to stallholders (food and non-food) and exhibitors is covered in many of the other sections in this chapter. Of particular relevance to them are the following:

✓ **No polystyrene:** Ban polystyrene packaging or require all such material to be taken away by the traders and contractors at the end of the event.
✓ **No plastic bags:** Put a 'No Plastic Bag' policy in place and encourage traders to sell or give away reusable shopping bags.
✓ **Reduce giveaways:** Encourage the reduction of samples that are waste creating and tacky branded promo giveaways.

Food Service

Food waste and loss is not just an event problem. The *Food and Agriculture Organization of the United Nations (FAO)* estimates that one-third of all food produced in the world was lost or wasted in each year. The biggest wasters per capita are Europe and North America,

food waste

coming in at 280- to 300kg ... ...ut unfortunately also lots of
and South/Southeast Asia t... ...ostable waste, including food
170kg/year.[18] ...cessfully segregated onsite due

There are lessons to b... ...d interest, the effectiveness of
industry in this global revi... ...ng bin stewards on the bins.
loss can occur at events ... ...d in putting the right thing in
food in temporary premis... ...d the *Love Food Hate Waste*
undereating. You would ... ...lent at the time in the com-
concern for this major int... ...sistency to messaging and made
the food service at your ev... ...efoodhatewaste.com).

The main reasons for fo... ...ow skilled you are, events will
or overestimation of the ....se a food rescue service is your
leading to: friend. They are set up in just about any city that has
social programmes and charitable works.

- oversupply of food by caterers;
- too many food stallholders being booked;
- stallholders stocking up on too much food.

Many local governments will have a finding service,
like the fantastic one that Metro in Portland have
through their *Fork It Over Food Donation*[19] have a food
rescue service on their website. In Australia *Oz Harvest*[20]
and *Second Bite*[21] are both fantastic food salvage programmes that service events. The UK has *Fare Share*[22]
and *FoodCycle*[23] and in Canada you can use the *Find A
Food Bank* service at *Food Banks Canada*.[24] The *Green
Restaurant Association*[25] has been working with restaurants in Massachusetts to collect and divert food waste
from landfill to composting. This is now being up-scaled
with a region-wide programme with the *Massachusetts
Department of Environment Protection* committing to a
goal of food waste diversion increased by 350,000 tons
per year by 2020. [26]

In addition, attendees may just not be hungry (e.g. conferences where by day two everyone is full, not doing any
exercise and not interested in eating), or possibly because
the wrong food has been served at the wrong time.

To ensure there are no mountains of served yet
uneaten food, don't over-cater, match with event activities and bring the food out at times when people will be
actually hungry.

Using reusable washable crockery is an effective way
to reduce waste in food and beverage service. This again
is a no-brainer for catered events indoors with restaurant
or buffet service, waiters, permanent kitchen facilities,
etc. For those events which must use disposable food
serviceware for logistical reasons, the biggest lesson in
managing this waste stream is to ensure that you match
the material the serviceware is made from with the venue
waste management options, onsite waste logistics and
eventual waste-processing facilities where waste will end
up. While you will still be creating waste, you will be
creating a waste resource that can potentially be reclaimed
and used as a secondary material.

We should all know by now that sending biodegradable (e.g. food) waste to landfill is a bad thing. It rots
down in landfill, creating GHGs (primarily methane).
Segregation of food waste is key.

At one festival I worked on, 80 per cent of the waste in
the arena was compostable, and 13 tonnes were collected

Food serviceware should also be made from renewable
or recycled materials, rather than virgin or non-
renewable. Compostable food packaging can be made
from paper/cardboard, or may be made from some of the
wonderful non-paper options such as palm leaves and
sugar cane waste. Cutlery can be made from potato starch
or timber. Look at the options for sustainable food
packaging in Chapter 8. Whichever type of material you
choose for your food serviceware, ensure you have
systems in place to keep it out of landfill – whether
through reuse, recycling or composting.

Food waste streams:

- Kitchen prep scraps.
- Prepared food that is unsold or unserved – but
  presented for consumption.

- Prepared food that is unsold or unserved – but still covered and not presented.
- Served or sold food uneaten by attendees – i.e. plate scraps.
- Attendees bringing their own food, not eating it and discarding it.
- Disposable food packaging (that is compostable).
- Non-compostable food (e.g. meat in some composting facilities).

Reduce food waste:

✓ Serve less food.
✓ Accurately estimate the volume of food required, considering the number of attendees, the event type and timing of activities or breaks.
✓ Communicate honestly these volumes to third-party traders.
✓ Understand if attendees may bring their own food and adjust communications and logistics accordingly.
✓ Ensure you don't book too many food stallholders considering the likely event attendance.
✓ Accurately and honestly advise food stallholders of the expected or actually known numbers of attendees.
✓ Ensure an even spread of types of food options that are likely to appeal to your attendees, so that no individual food stallholders are less well attended than others, leading to food waste.
✓ Ensure pricing of food does not lead to lower sales volumes than anticipated.
✓ Inform attendees what food will be available and at what price.
✓ Ask for dietary requirements in advance to reduce wastage and satisfy attendees.
✓ Request that caterers do not uncover/open/serve all food at once, so that if oversupply has occurred, the perishable food has been handled correctly for donation to food salvage programmes (organise the programmes in advance and ensure your system meets their health and handling regulations).

Reduce service-related waste:

✓ **Reusable, not disposable:** Use washable and reusable crockery and cutlery rather than single-use disposables.
✓ **Reduce serviceware size:** Rather than extravagantly packaged food, if it must be in disposables, go for less waste options such as a serviette rather than paper plate for 'finger foods', serve pizzas on trays and not in pizza boxes, and don't put lids on coffee cups and take-out if they are to be consumed immediately.
✓ **No single-serve sachets:** Ban single-serve sachets and straws, and discourage individually pre-wrapped food items (muffins in plastic wraps, pre-made sandwiches in plastic wedges, etc.).
✓ **Order in bulk:** Encourage caterers and food vendors to purchase their ingredients in bulk. Use large 2-litre cans rather than lots of small cans, for example.
✓ **Reusable packaging:** Encourage caterers and food vendors to receive their fresh produce in reusable boxes, rather than single-use disposables such as foam boxes. There are many services available that have take-back/exchange for delivery boxes.
✓ **Cleaning:** Use washable cleaning cloths rather than paper towel disposables.

Compost waste:

✓ Identify whether food waste collection for separate treatment (e.g. composting or anaerobic digestion) is possible. Is there a service locally?
✓ Identify whether onsite at-event segregation of food waste can occur from a practical perspective. Will attendees participate? Can food service or waste operations adjust to collect the food waste separately?

Donate unserved food:

✓ Identify if a local food rescue service exists and discuss the logistics with them.
✓ Plan menus and service so that unserved food can be donated to charity and arrange logistics.

✓ Set up a food donation programme for attendees to donate unopened non-perishable food (e.g. picnickers and campers).

✓ Arrange for food to be collected and redistributed with a local food rescue programme.

✓ Put 'binfrastructure' and systems in place to collect food waste both in kitchens (back of house) and attendee side (front of house).

✓ Ensure systems are effective – considerations for placement of bins, appropriate signage, etc.

✓ If disposable food serviceware must be used, use compostable.

✓ Collect food waste and compostable food serviceware for composting.

✓ Ensure bin signage accurately communicates what food and serviceware can be composted.

Communications and engagement:

✓ Get creative with communications (e.g. signage, bin toppers, campaigns).

✓ Have waste stewards/volunteers at the bins.

✓ Have onsite auditing of the system's effectiveness and adjust in real time.

✓ Engage catering or food stallholder manager on the event production team.

✓ Engage food service contractors (venue, caterers, food stallholders). This includes both the owner/manager and the staff who will be conducting the onsite operations.

✓ Induct onsite/at-venue cleaning and waste services.

✓ Inform waste removal and processors.

✓ Work with event marketing and communications (to assist in communications).

✓ Work with sponsorship (sometimes sponsors have food-based activation).

✓ Communicate with and engage attendees.

Décor and Materials

Any party needs decorations, and special events and launches are the big culprits of the event world when it comes to bling! Much of the pizazz of events comes from the look and feel, and that look and feel is quite often disposable. Be mindful when you are thinking up what

bells and whistles you will augment your event with, to reduce the disposability factor down as low as you can go. Here are some tips:

✓ **Balloons and confetti:** Don't release balloons or confetti, especially foil confetti. Use bubbles instead.

✓ **Flowers/plants:** Any cut flowers or living plants should be donated after the event or allowed to be taken home by attendees. Don't leave it to chance; have a disposal plan.

✓ **Table centrepieces:** Plan for table centrepieces to be taken away by attendees – put notices on them indicating that they are gifts to be taken home by attendees. Or make your centrepieces the dessert tray or snacks tray. Edible decorations!

✓ **Signage:** Design signage and sponsor branding so that dates or sponsor details can be updated and signage reused.

Lanyards and Name Tags

Name tags and lanyards are a common tool used at conferences and exhibitions, and one that is (obviously) visible to delegates and needs to be dealt with responsibly at the close of the event. By 'lanyard' I mean the part that goes around the neck, and by 'laminate' I mean the piece that dangles off the bottom. By 'name tag' I mean something that is pinned or clipped onto you. Consider the following tips to reduce waste relating to lanyards, laminates and name tags. This can be upstream waste (in using a virgin material in the first place) or downstream (what you do with them after the event).

✓ Use stickers, printed from the computer or even handwritten. Stick them straight on the shirt.

✓ Use a slip-in pouch and ask delegates to place business cards or specially printed cards in the pouch.

✓ Avoid the plastic pouch and go for a printed version with a clip to attach to the lanyard/shirt.

✓ Don't print a 'year' on the lanyard, and, if possible, don't include it as sponsor real estate unless you know you have a multi-year sponsorship.

✓ Use lanyards made from recycled or renewable sources. Collect lanyards, name tags and laminates at the end of the event for reuse, recycling or donation. Locate collection boxes and/or staff at exits to encourage depositing.

✓ Lanyards may be washed in a sealable mesh-washing bag to sanitise for reuse if necessary. Make the lanyard and laminate multipurpose, and include details of where delegates can get lunch at local cafés (if you're not having catering in-house). Or provide information about the event on a USB thumb drive which is attached to the lanyard and which also has the laminate dangling from it.

✓ For smaller meetings, ditch name tags or laminates altogether and put people's names on their coffee mugs!

Attendee 'Stuff'

Events where you don't have control over either the sale of products or what people turn up with in their bags will need to use psychology and persuasion as their main tools to influence their attendees' waste disposal habits. The best-case scenario for an event is either through necessity, through convenience or through persuasion that people walk into your event with little more than their wallet and a reusable bag. We're not assuming all events are shopping expeditions, but it is likely that most people will consume something at the event. So get them to bring minimal stuff, and ensure they don't bring stuff they will then dispose of through non-use (uneaten prepackaged food), or because they can't be bothered to take it away with them (chairs, umbrellas, event-shade marquees). Consider the following:

✓ Encourage attendees to bring reusable bags, water bottles and coffee cups.
✓ Encourage attendees to refuse handouts if they will only quickly become waste.

Camping Equipment

This is an odd one to think about for events such as conferences, exhibitions or sporting matches, but for

Figure 9.19 Trashed campsite.
Source: Meegan Jones.

those readers who are involved in managing multi-day events, be they music festivals, sporting carnivals, huge gatherings for any reason out in the countryside somewhere, or even the local show or agricultural field day that runs for a few days, people often set up camp. These types of events will usually include campsites managed by the organiser (or a designated third party), on the event site, adjacent to it or offsite within walking or shuttle bus range.

I have worked on quite a few of these events in the music festival sector, and I can tell you, the camping ground rubbish includes mountains of tents, chairs, eskies (coolers), sleeping bags, pillows, gazebos (which blow down at the first gust of wind), uneaten food, cookers, gas cylinders, blankets, gum boots (wellies), tarps, lanterns, torches, and tent pegs by the million being left behind. In the UK there is the unfortunate trend of young people trashing their campsites on the last night as some sort of rite of passage, or at best just abandoning all of their camping equipment.

I have even seen trashed camping grounds and abandoned gear in what I thought was a very neat and tidy Norway! There's a lot of work being done in trying to at least salvage the stuff that's left. To make any kind of impact though it's a cultural change that has to happen. The *Love Your Tent* campaign in the UK is trying to tackle this very issue (www.loveyourtent.com).

✓ Encourage attendees to 'camp light' and discourage the 'disposable campsite' in your communications.
✓ Incentivise attendees to take their gear home or to pack it up and hand it in.
✓ Set up zones in your campsites. If you cluster all the people that are likely to party hard and make a mess together, and the people that are likely to be clean and green together, that will make your job afterwards easier.
✓ Hand out colour-coded rubbish bags to campers upon arrival.
✓ Set up food donation bins for unopened non-perishable food that people shopped hard for and brought but didn't eat because they went for cheesy chips instead!
✓ Set up salvage points in the campsites for campers to deposit/donate unwanted camping gear.

✓ Arrange community groups to salvage the grounds ahead of your waste team. (Ensure they have the proper safety induction and personal protection equipment.)

Leave No Trace

Many events, especially adventure races, triathlons and outdoor festivals, occur in nature, wilderness, the bush, forest, outdoors, and the principle of taking only photos and leaving only footprints (if that!) should be embraced. One thing that can bind all these events to the spirit of environmental stewardship is the *Leave No Trace* philosophy (www.lnt.org). The *Seven Leave No Trace Principles* are as follows:

1 Plan ahead.
2 Travel and camp on durable surfaces.
3 Dispose of waste properly.
4 Leave what you find.
5 Minimise campfire impacts.
6 Respect wildlife.
7 Be considerate of other visitors.

Despite its reputation for burning down large-scale art, *Burning Man* is proud to be the largest practising *Leave No Trace* event in the world. Read more about *Burning Man*'s leave no trace philosophy on the book's website.

WASTE SEGREGATION

To get the most effective recycling and composting results and to ensure that none of your waste is rejected by the MRF or waste processor, you will need to have strategies in place to achieve clean waste separation at your event.

There are many practicalities to bear in mind when going for front-of-house waste separation. Just because you plan to put two bins next to each other, with the word 'recycle' on one and 'waste' on the other, doesn't mean you will have effective and successful waste separation at your event.

Ensuring that attendees put the right thing in the right bin is the first step you need to take. Minimising

Box 9.9

LOVE YOUR TENT

Love Your Tent is a campaign in response to the vast amounts of tents and rubbish left behind by people after attending events, and it was inspired by Eco Action Partnership's work as Sustainability Consultants to the *Isle of Wight Music Festival.*

The aim: To make the process of getting up and leaving everything behind you after an event has finished, in order for somebody else to have to clear it all up, completely socially unacceptable. This campaign is about behaviour change and we want to encourage people to have more respect, both for their environment and definitely for themselves.

So, what's the problem? We work on a conservative estimate of one to two in every six tents being left behind, depending on the size of event, the audience demographic, and the all-important weather conditions. Add into this all of the other waste such as chairs, sleeping bags, marquees, pillows, cookers, etc., and it means that there is a significant tonnage that is just simply collected and sent to landfill. We acknowledge the great work that individual event producers are doing to salvage as much as possible from abandoned campsites. But there is only so much demand for second-hand camping equipment, and the salvage programmes don't do much to change attitudes to trashing tents.

The campaign: Our hope is that at every camping event people attend they will see the same actions, the same logo, the same coordinated support and the same message. We have made a short film and gathered support from festivals, social media sites, press and campers. We're setting up an industry recognised standard, with both UK and EU government recognition, helping to guide and drive events towards a more sustainable and waste-aware strategy. This takes the form of a checklist to help and advise events on best practice, and different grades will be awarded relative to size of event, green credentials, and ability and commitment.

We are spreading this one simple message to every festival and to everyone: Love Your Tent and take it home.

The benefits: It doesn't make financial sense to organisers having to pay to clean up camping waste and landfill charges. Surely it cannot make much sense to the punters either, buying a new tent and all the associated equipment every time they go to another festival. And it makes no sense to the environment. We hope to show people, organisers and campers, how much waste there is – how much it costs them each year – what happens to this waste. To show them there is an alternative to the present situation – organisers save money – punters save money – less waste – less landfill – less damage to the environment – less resources being used up.

www.loveyourtent.com

---

contamination at the coal-face is important to the success of the whole waste operation. Waste stewards, volunteers or staff standing by the bins is always a great way of minimising the contamination levels. Your considerations will include the following:

1   binfrastructure
2   pre-treatment or a mini-MRF onsite
3   planning volume, quantity and placement of bins
4   volunteer bin stewards
5   audience incentives.

Event Personality

A common and often the most fundamental element of successful event waste management implementation is the participant's engagement in your plans, and the effectiveness of your communications.

Figure 9.20 Bin segregation at Glastonbury Festival.

Source: Meegan Jones.

An important thing to think about is the attendee and event 'personality' and what will best suit your situation. This includes the type of event, the location, congestion, demographic of attendees, and the level of likely engagement or interest in waste and what they do with it.

Think about the vibe your event will have and ask the following questions:

- Will the event be congested and busy, hustling and bustling, or will it be more like a relaxed day in the park?
- Will people be able to get to the bins and have a moment to sort their rubbish into the right bin?
- Will people be seated when they eat and drink, or will they be walking around?
- What *shade of green* are they and how into getting it right will they be?
- Will your event attendees be distracted and likely to throw their rubbish into whichever bin is closest, or will they have the head space to put some thought into their rubbish disposal?
- Will your attendees throw litter on the ground, or hold onto waste until they come across the next bin?
- Do they need to be rewarded, bribed or penalised to encourage them to participate?

Some of the answers to these questions will inform the waste segregation decisions you need to make, the style of signage on your bins, and also give insight into the overall waste management system you should operate.

Binfrastructure

This is a great term that I learned from one of the attendees at the training course I teach on event sustainability. I've taken it on as my own, and use it constantly. I hope you're as delighted with the word as I am.

Binfrastructure covers the items you will need to get the waste collection, storage and transport happening, including the following:

- the actual bins
- signage, lids, toppers
- skips and bulk storage bins
- trucks

- bin bags
- compactors and balers
- handy hoops and litter-picking sticks
- builders' sacks or wool packs (for cardboard)
- frames into which massive clear bags go.

How you set up your binfrastructure will depend of course on many details, and the logistical realities, staffing levels and budget all need to be taken into account when working out what will work for your event.

For the bins which attendees will use front of house, you will go for either a single, twin or at least a triple separation system to keep compostable waste away from recyclables and rubbish that goes to landfill. This needs to be clearly signed with a description of what may go in each bin.

Here are some combinations.

Single-bin System

- **General waste:** all rubbish in the one bin, all going to landfill, incineration or a mechanical biological treatment facility.

Twin-bin System

- **General waste:** rubbish, including food and packaging, going to landfill, incineration or a mechanical biological treatment facility.
- **Recycling:** usually commingled, to include paper, cardboard, plastics, glass and metals (i.e. bottles, cans and papers).

Triple-bin System

- **General waste:** rubbish going to landfill or incineration.
- **Recycling:** usually commingled, to include paper, cardboard, plastics, glass and metals (i.e. bottles, cans and papers).
- **Compost:** food waste or food waste plus compostable packaging, to be sent for composting or processing to a worm farm or anaerobic digestion facility.

Multi-bin System

- **General waste:** rubbish going to landfill or incineration.
- **Recycling:** usually commingled, to include plastics, glass and metals (i.e. bottles, cans and papers).
- **Paper and cardboard:** for paper recycling. Sent directly to a paper recycler.
- **Food waste:** food waste to be sent for composting or processing to a worm farm or anaerobic digestion facility.
- **Food packaging:** compostable packaging to send for composting.

Single-stream System

- **General waste:** rubbish going to landfill or incineration.
- **Metal:** aluminium and steel cans. Sent directly to a metal recycler.
- **Glass:** bottles and jars, front and back of house. Sent directly to a glass recycler.
- **Paper and cardboard:** for paper recycling, sent directly to a paper recycler.
- **Plastics:** possibly separated into hard plastics and soft plastics, or by plastic type. Sent directly to plastics dealer or recycler.

Figure 9.21 Zero Hero Tent Bin.

Source: Zero Hero (www.zerohero.org).

- **Food waste:** food waste to be sent for composting or processing to a worm farm or anaerobic digestion facility.
- **Food packaging:** compostable packaging to send for composting.

Salvage System

- **Food:** collected for redistribution.
- **Products:** to be reused 'as is' and sent to a reuse centre, salvage facility or programme.
- **Materials:** for repurposing and sent to a reuse centre, salvage centre or programme.

Planning

Once you have completed your investigation into the types of waste facilities available, what the local market is for recyclable material, if composting can be accepted, and how you can match procurement and processes to optimise landfill diversion and resource recovery, the next step is to plan the actual roll-out of your waste systems.

Things to think about are as follows:

- Bulk storage onsite – skips or trucks?
- Who will provide the bins and skips?
- Bin quantity and placement.
- Segregation streams (e.g. mixed recycling or single stream?).
- Who is responsible for putting the bins in place?
- When do the bins go out? Remember that waste is generated as soon as the event begins to be created.
- Where will the waste consolidation site be (for bulk waste temporary storage before removal)?
- Will bins be wheeled to the bulk storage site, will bin bags be used and removed by hand, will vehicles come around to the bin locations for emptying?
- What waste signage will be used for both front-of-house and back-of-house bins?
- Do additional bins, bags and signage need to be provided for vendors, bars, catering?
- Are staff or volunteers used for front of house to assist with attendee segregation?
- Are staff or volunteers used for back of house to

Figure 9.22 Back-of-house waste separation may include sullage and waste oil bins.

Source: Meegan Jones.

ensure that the waste consolidation goes according to plan?

- How often (and when) will waste be removed (from bins and offsite)?
- Do you have all the necessary supplies to ensure segregation can occur effectively (gloves, litter-picking sticks, bin bags, trollies)?
- Are the waste workforce and supervisors well informed and motivated to do the tasks required?
- Where will waste go once it leaves the site?
- Will measurement or auditing need to be done at the event site, or is measurement occurring offsite?

Bin Quantity and Placement

We will assume that you have decided to, at a minimum, separate waste into recycling, compostables and general waste.

Once defining things such as attendee profile, event personality, attendee congestion, access to bins and other logistical concerns, you will be able to make some basic waste management decisions. These would include volume of bins on the event site or floor, the number of bin pickups/empties, and the number of staff to manage bin cleaning. The site layout and access will be major factors in these decisions, along with budget for waste staff and roving cleaners. Accurately plan the following:

1 number of bins
2 volume/size of bins
3 placement of bins
4 access for emptying
5 frequency of emptying.

Be mindful that a full-to-overflowing bin may lead to the immediate disintegration of your well-thought-out recycling plan. As soon as a bin starts to overflow, bin etiquette seems to go out of the window.

If you have to do the waste planning yourself, the quantity of bins and their size or volume capacity is really just a numbers game. You will need to include in the calculation attendee numbers, types and size of waste, size and layout of your event site or venue, entry and exit points, etc. Consider the following:

- Can your waste team access the bins continuously to empty them? Is this done by hand or by vehicle?
- Where are the pinch points where foot traffic will converge?
- Where are the high-impact areas of waste generation such as around bars or eating areas?

Walk your event site or venue, either in your mind, or on the ground with a site map in hand, and work out what bins will be necessary. Despite the best-laid plans, be ready to be flexible and to react to the need for rearranging the location of your bins once show day's here and the event takes on a life of its own.

To Bag or Not to Bag?

You will need to consider whether you can actually move bins during the event, and if not this means you will need bin bags, which cleaners will change out. But remember to use clear bin bags for everything other than general waste, because once they've been taken out of the bin and tied in a knot, what's inside will be forgotten by the time it's walked back of house.

If you have a small venue, you should be able to do all your collections by hand, and if outdoors with the assistance of a wheelbarrow or trolley.

However, at large outdoor events or those with many venues on a campus such as at an expo centre, waste will need to be moved with some mechanical assistance: golf buggies, horse and cart, pushbikes with trailers, lorries or pickup trucks, vans and trailers or rubbish trucks.

Depending on how your other waste streams are collected, you could either empty and collect the contents of your biodegradables bin at the same time as the other waste or separately.

One thing is for sure: you are going to need to use bin liners if you have lots of small bins. A bin liner is essential so that you don't get smelly and fly-attracting bins.

You don't always need to use a liner for recycling and general waste, but for food waste it is the best option.

Depending on whether there will be a lot of wet waste in your compost bin, or whether it will be mainly empty biodegradable food containers and cups, will make a difference to the style of bin liner you use. Wet waste is quite heavy and will need sturdy, strong bags to move the waste around. You will also need to think about the size of the bin, since removing bags from 240L or more wheelie bins will be very difficult if filled with wet waste.

If you feel you will get minimal or zero contamination in the bins at audience level, then using a biodegradable bin liner is a good option. These are generally opaque. The top can be tied shut and the whole neat package put in a skip or truck. However, if you need to do a visual contamination check, then a sturdy clear bag will be the best option.

Think about reusing bags also, if they don't get too dirty. If not, consider using bags that will be able to go for onward recycling, as you will probably go through quite a lot of them.

If you end up putting your bin liners in the landfill, make sure they have been made from recycled plastic in the first place. At least that helps. Beware of bin liners that promote themselves as 'degradable'.

This actually means photo-degradable, not biodegradable. They need sunlight to break down, which is not going to happen in a compost heap or in-vessel composting facility or landfill.

All your waste will need to make its way back to a central storage location. Rubbish can get quite smelly if left in an open skip for more than a few days.

Plan the skip size and removal timing so that this doesn't occur. It may also attract vermin and birds. Over the course of a few days you may also get eruptions of

Figure 9.23 Andy's 'Handy Hoops' as used by UK waste contractor Leisure Support Services. These handy hoops work where there is a lot of crowd congestion leading to difficulty of access to bins and roving litter-picking staff are necessary.

Source: Leisure Support Services.

previously unseen insect numbers as they find a juicy home to reproduce in your skip.

It may seem obvious that the waste staff know what is a bag of compostable waste and what is a bag of recycling or landfill, but this is not necessarily so. Remember you are likely dealing with large numbers of staff or volunteers and they won't all be as motivated as you are to see an uncontaminated skip full of precious compostables leave your event. You may need to put some dumb-arse signage on your bulk collection bins, or actually roster someone to stand guard over them. One or two bags of general waste or recycling thrown up and over the top of a skip can destroy all your good work.

You will get a lot more into a skip if you empty the bags out rather than throw them in whole (even if you are using biodegradable bags). This second stage of handling will offer an opportunity to pick out any cans, bottles or other foreign objects.

Sign it Right

Achieving the right look for your bins will go a long way towards encouraging participation in your waste efforts by your attendees. You may find in your state, territory, country or council district that pre-existing colour coding or symbols are used to identify various waste streams and

Figure 9.24 Extreme at-event waste separation by GreenSweep in the Greenfields at Glastonbury Festival.
Source: Meegan Jones.

bins. Don't re-invent the wheel if recognition among your attendees already exists for this waste branding. Research your area's government waste board, as they're likely to have resources you can use.

If there's no local branding, make sure you create your own easy-to-understand theme. Colour coding is a good way to go, as are images or photos of the items that should go in each bin. Use simple but accurate language. Consider those who may speak other languages. Consider multilingual signs.

Signs need to be at eye level or on top of the bin if the lid remains closed and there's an entry hole for the rubbish. You can even put overhead signs up nice and high so that the location of bins may be seen from a distance.

Ask other people to look at your proposed signs before you commit, as you may miss the obvious. This was evident at a very green fair I went to in a park in London that really does have excellent recycling separation, including stewards at some of the bins. However, one small word, 'FOOD', caused their recycling bins to become terribly contaminated. The bin they had for drink cans had 'Food Tins and Drink Cans' written on the sign. The idea was for metal cans (drink cans) to be collected, but at this event, a one-day fair in a park, no one would be opening up a can of baked beans. The inclusion of the word 'Food' in the first line of the sign resulted in food plates in the bin meant for aluminium drink cans. The logo was taken straight from the *WRAP* artwork toolbox, and if they had used the one that just said 'Aluminium Cans' it may have been a better result.

One way to place signage at your bins is to use the very effective 'bin topper', rather than a sticker on the front (not at eye level) or a flat sign standing behind the bin. The bin topper is a cap that goes on the top of the bin. It restricts the size of the hole into the bin (preventing traders from putting in cardboard boxes), as well as offering an excellent eye-level signage location. It also reduces copycat contamination – where, rather than reading any signs, a person peers into the bin and follows the lead of what has already been thrown in. Thus, if the previous people have contaminated the bin, more contamination is likely to occur in an open-topped bin.

Without someone standing guard over your bins to make sure everything is put in the correct bin, copycat contamination is likely to be one of your biggest obstacles. Contamination may not be too big a problem for recycling bins if you're running your waste through a MRF after the event, or if you have your own mini-MRF back of house; however, if you're trying to collect compostables separately, contamination is your enemy. Too much plastic or metal (or possibly any at all) may result in your composting load being rejected. Every biodegradable item placed in the wrong bin will add to your landfill figure. In some MRFs, too many food plates and food scraps in with your plastic bottles, cans and cardboard, and your load of recycling could be rejected.

If you control the sourcing of all food serviceware, and you are sure that it is all compostable with no random polystyrene burger clams likely to turn up, then having a bin with a sign 'Food and Packaging for Compost' may work. But if you are not going to have control over the packaging used by caterers or stallholders, or if you have an event where food from outside could make its way in, then this will be a problem. In the latter case, you will definitely need to have stewards on the bins, or have cleaners collect up the compostable waste directly off tables.

A great way to ensure that the right item goes into the right bin where food serviceware is concerned is to create a diorama to display the packaging used by a trader to serve food in, right there at the trader's stall, along with a sign labelled 'I'm Compostable' matching the signage you have on your bins. Consider the following:

✓ **Group your bins:** If you have waste separation make sure you always have each bin option available, and in the same order, left to right.

✓ **Use bin toppers:** Cover the top of the bin with a lid, plastic shroud with a hole, or a bin cap. This offers a spot for signs and also reduces copycat contamination.

✓ **Eye-level and overhead signs:** Place signs at eye level and/or overhead so that they may be seen from afar and over the crowd.

✓ **Colour code bins/signs:** Match the colour scheme of your bins or bin signs with the way the local bins or bin signs are colour coded.

✓ **Use clear language:** Make it as simple as possible but not so simple that it's not effective. Having 'Compost' or 'Recycle' as your only words may lead to contamination. Add 'Food and Plates' and 'Bottles and Cans' to the signs.

✓ **Use pictures or dioramas**: Posting clear line drawings of the items that go into each bin is often effective. If it suits the style of your event, post an example of the item on the sign or the bin too.

At the *Rally to Restore Sanity*, Jaime Nack and her team at *Three Squares Inc* worked hard to get the signage just right; this was based on understanding just what the waste haulers and processers would and would not take in the various waste streams for this 500,000-person-strong event at the *National Mall Park* in Washington, DC. The signs visually portrayed the 'yes' items and the 'no' items. Each set of three bins was staffed by a *Comedy Central* volunteer Green Team member. At the end of the event volunteers formed a line sweep with segregated bags to pick up after the attendees. The volunteers were given a comprehensive briefing onsite for what was to go into each bag or bin. This information was also given to them pre-event via a website page. The results were outstanding. Not only did the event break all previous mass transit records for the day, but the Park Service reported that they had never seen a cleaner event for one of this scale. Right signs. Right bins. Right Research. Right on, Green Event Guru Jaime Nack!

Footfall, Congestion and Event Layout

You will be familiar with the sheep mentality, namely people blindly following the crowd at large events. You have probably been one of them at an event when you're not working! When people are in a crowd moving around an event, you will need to put strategies in place to influence their behaviour, and guide them to where you want them to be and what you want them to do. This needs to be considered when planning green schemes too.

For example, all your best plans may come undone if you have beautifully presented sets of bins, but the crowd density is such that either you couldn't possibly keep up with the volume of rubbish produced, or attendees just cannot see the bins because of the human tide and everything ends up on the ground anyway.

In this case, one solution may be to employ a team of roving litter pickers rather than stationary bins. Kit them out with bin bag hoops so that that they become mobile bin stations, and send them off into the crowd. The separation of recycling from general waste may go out of the window, and you would need to have a mini-sorting centre to go through the rubbish. Or you could send them out in teams of two, with separation occurring on the spot.

Remember to be ready to react to change also, as sometimes the event will take on a life of its own.

If there are starting lines, entry gates, meeting points, eating zones, bars, or other areas that have specific purposes which will attract a crowd, you will need to think through how your proposed initiatives will play out in that circumstance. What you have in mind may work where people have the time and space to think things through, but in the excitement of the particular activities it may all come unstuck.

Put yourself in the attendees' shoes and think through the journey they will go on while attending your event, from arrival, through to getting settled in, purchasing stuff, getting to where they need to be at your event, eating and drinking, disposing of rubbish, participating, and anything else you can think of.

Make sure you don't set things up against the flow. For example, when doing a recycling incentive where

Figure 9.25 Waste stations with volunteers at the Rally to Restore Sanity.

Source: Three Squares Inc.

people need to bring their bags of recycling, cups, cans, bottles, etc., back to a recycling centre, the location of these centres will be key to their success.

Waste Overlay

Events held in venues where venue management has control of the waste and binfrastructure is sometimes a difficult situation for organisers – if the venue doesn't have the waste set-up you want. Of course, you would have considered this in choosing the venue in the first place, but if you have a venue that suits your purpose in every way except for detail on the waste, you can look to 'overlay' your own system.

Many venues will have their day-to-day waste systems and then special-event waste systems that require more bins, extra signage, and back-of-house and staffing processes. A good example of this is where a venue is both a convention and an exhibition centre. When lots of small conferences are happening in their smaller rooms, standard waste systems will be in play. At a large conference, say, with 2000 delegates or more, waste services will go into overdrive.

If the venue doesn't have, for example, recycling separation in your meeting room, there is nothing to stop you setting up your own set of bins, or working with the venue to adjust their system to service your requirements – more so for exhibitions. Many exhibition centres these days have terrific waste systems in place both back of house or front of house for attendees. There are still centres out there with the old one-bin/one-pile system, and whoosh, it all goes to landfill. In this case you should absolutely set up your own system.

Think about the type of waste that will be created front of house by attendees and install binfrastructure to suit. You may either need to arrange collection and removal separately, the venue may arrange it for you, or it may already work with the venue's existing removal services, just not their usual front-of-house segregation and collection.

The reason the perfect service may not exist in venues already is that every event held there may have unique waste streams. Venues can really only plan for commonly created waste. You may wish to set up waste systems for the following:

✓ a lanyard or name badge return point;

✓ a set of bins for returning unwanted hand-outs which will either go back to the exhibitor or be donated to charity;

✓ small bins provided for each exhibitor suited to the waste they will be creating, for example, sample-serve spoons or cups for at-stall taste tests;

✓ bins next to water refill points if disposable cups are offered;

✓ bins next to coffee carts scattered throughout your exhibition, where bar stools and tables are provided for quick coffee breaks;

✓ separate bins to capture waste from food and beverage brought in by delegates/attendees if they are likely to go offsite for food or to deposit morning takeaway coffee cups they used en route to the conference;

✓ remember that all the little spots where bins may be needed that the venue may not think about – break-out rooms, within the exhibition floor and not just on the periphery, in hospitality areas, at registration desks/lobby, along walkways between conference room-break-out room-exhibition hall.

Back-of-House Bins

Some events will have skips back of house into which all the waste is placed. These skips could be compacting skips, to allow maximum volume of waste to be stored onsite. If this system is used, ask the question of the cleaning company or contractor what is proposed to be placed into the compacting skip and what that means for effectiveness of recycling and further separation offsite. If it's being proposed for anything but general waste for landfill to go into the compacting skip, question it. Most MRFs will have a hard time separating out recyclables from each other that have been fused together under pressure.

The theory is that food traders should organise themselves so that they are throwing out minimal food scraps during and at the end of the show. Food stalls that are doing a lot of preparation at the event such as chopping up vegetables will produce compostable waste during the show. Fruit juice stalls are also prime targets. Caterers for staff and crew, guests and performers will also be doing a lot of kitchen prep. Pre-identify which vendors will need to have bins allocated to them for the collection of biodegradable waste. The clincher in getting this system to work will be what they do inside their food units, tents and kitchens at their prep benches. They will need their own bin system inside their operation so that their staff can easily separate food scraps into a bin that is then tipped into the larger bin that the event will provide.

It is a good idea to have a dedicated member of the waste team to act as a communications, service and quality control coordinator for food stalls' compost waste collection, particularly if you have a large number of vendors.

Post-event is another matter altogether. The best-case scenario is that your food operators will slide into home plate with little more than a bread roll and a carrot in their kitchens, but this is not likely. The weather and other reasons for unexpected drops in audience numbers, or over-inflated estimates on behalf of the organisers, may mean that traders with perishable stock will need to throw food out at the end of the event. Be prepared for this potential. Work out when they will pack up, and ensure you have a clearly communicated process in place for them to leave out their perishable food waste.

Although cardboard is also biodegradable it is best to just keep it to food scraps only. If you feel they won't empty boxes of bread rolls and bags of chopped onions into compost bins without a fuss, ask food operators to put it all out in one pile still packaged and have a team of your people go around and unpack the cartons and bags.

Kitchen Binfrastructure

If you want food vendors, caterers and kitchens to collect prep scraps and unsold/unserved food for composting, do they have the correct bin systems in kitchens to collect up the waste? Do you need to provide them with clearly labelled bins? Do you need to check on them or even walk through with them the best way to collect compostable waste given their usual kitchen operations? Don't send anyone into a kitchen to discuss waste collection who has not worked in a kitchen before. It's a special place in there, and anyone who has worked for a 'chef' will know what I am talking about. If not, well, just don't. . . .

If you have an event with lots of temporary food traders all lined up next to each other, make sure there is a set of all the waste options they need, right behind their stalls.

Onsite MRF

Waste may be pre-treated and re-sorted before it goes off in the trucks or skips. This may be done through setting up a conveyer belt system where bins are tipped out and either recyclate or food packaging is picked out or contaminants picked out, depending on which bin the waste is coming from.

If you don't hire in conveyor belts you can also set up large tables where waste is tipped and sorted. Alternatively you could put a very simple pre-sort in

Figure 9.26 Closed Loop Recycling's onsite MRF being demonstrated at their launch at the Sydney Festival. Pictured is my colleague Jane Fullerton-Smith showing how it's done!
Source: Meegan Jones.

place. As vehicles arrive with either bins or bin bags, staff are armed with a litter-picking stick (or hands and gloves) and contaminants or recyclate are picked out before or as it's tipped into the skip.

Turnstile 21 is a purpose-built sorting system that can separate up to eight waste streams, including compostables, and comes with compacting balers built in. The entire system is built into a shipping container. Waste is tipped in one end onto a conveyor belt and up to 16 staff stand along the belt segregating their allocated material into compacting bays. These compactors then release bales of compacted single-stream materials. It can also include compostable waste and glass. It is available for use in Australia and the UK and was pioneered by the wonderful Steve Hunter (let's call him *Captain Shunter*!) of *Douglas Site Services* (www.closedloop.com.au).

The *Shire of Dowerin* in Western Australia have invested in their own event recycling trailer, along with the *Dowerin Recycling Centre* to facilitate the recovery of recyclable waste in the region. Recyclables are sorted at the centre and packaged for transportation. All profits made through the recycling centre go back into the Dowerin local community. Read more about it on the book's website.

Sunrise Celebration in the UK has taken sorting onsite to a whole new level by having waste bins front of house segregated into more than a dozen material streams. Each morning, teams of volunteers hand-sort the waste in front of attendees, correcting any placement of waste into the wrong bin. This demonstration quickly adjusted the attention event-goers placed on making sure they placed their waste into the right bin. Read more about this on the book's website (www.sunrisecelebration.co.uk) and see also Figure 9.24.

SALVAGE

The purchase and use of 'stuff' to produce your event creates volumes of waste, greenhouse gas emissions, and uses up fossil fuels and non-renewable resources. Introduce salvage, reuse and repurposing into your event planning, and make a positive impact on your event's sustainability performance as well as on the environment. Fewer new materials will need to be purchased and produced, along with less waste, both of which are money

savers and earth savers. Go through each section of potential waste and identify what could be reused.

1   Identify salvageable items.
2   Find a home for salvaged stuff to end up in.
3   Build a salvage yard.
4   Put the salvage programme in place.

Behind the scenes there is likely to be a goldmine of quirky items that can be reused rather than being thrown into the rubbish skip and sent to landfill. These may include the following:

*   banners and signs
*   flags, bunting, fabric, table cloths, shade cloth
*   printed cups and containers
*   stage flats, props and design pieces
*   left-over paint
*   carpet offcuts
*   plumbers' piping (makes great props)
*   cabling and tubing from bars
*   electrical cabling
*   timber and metal offcuts
*   cable wheels (make great tables)
*   catering buckets and lids
*   plastic and wooden crates (bread, fruit and veg)
*   hessian and fabric sacks (potatoes, rice, flour)
*   cooking oil (to make biodiesel)
*   event-specific stock, merchandise, giveaways, promo items, printed materials.

The most important thing, apart from identifying what can be salvaged, is establishing a home for these goods to end up in. You will need to have worked out who could possibly use the ice-cream containers or bread crates left before you start gathering them up. The first place to look is for creative reuse centres. These marvellous facilities accept industrial waste to be used for arts, commercial, décor and design use. Look around your local area to find a scrap store or reuse centre. If there's no reuse centre or scrap store in your region, investigate whether there is a recycling organisation, community organisation or theatre group that may need a particular item you feel you will have in excess, such as banners, set design pieces, décor, light bulbs, etc. You may even find you could kick

Figure 9.27 Salvage yard for craft materials.

Source: Meegan Jones.

start a salvage or reuse centre business. Other groups that love to get hold of stuff are charity shops, school flea markets, scouts and guides, pre-schools and holiday camps (for craft). I have even had a dog's home come and collect blankets. Get creative in thinking about who can get creative with your salvage.

If you have a multi-day event with camping, it is likely that there will be some really good items left by your audience which can be reused for their original purpose. Salvageable stuff from the production or event activity areas are also likely to be abundant and these may be harvested and reused creatively by someone else.

But music festivals aren't the only place where beautiful treasures may be found. Think of all those special events, conferences, opening nights, product launches and fashion extravaganzas that create bespoke staging and décor which may need decontstructing and rehoming. Things are starting to formalise around this with event salvage services popping up. In the USA, we have *Used Event Stuff*, an online store which works like a clearing house, similar to eBay (www.usedeventstuff.com). In the UK *Event Surplus* is starting up (www.event-surplus.com). Back in the USA the terrific team at *Repurpose America* salvage materials and rehome them from exhibitions all across the country (www.repurpose america.com). And in Australia the wonderful team at *Reverse Garbage* in Sydney mine the 'urban landscape' for lots of goodies and will come to an event and take anything that can be used as-is or materials that can be creatively repurposed (reversegarbage.org.au).

WASTE INITIATIVES

Alongside putting out your bins, having lovely signs, setting your segregation in play and letting everyone know about it, you may also wish to be a little more creative with the way to get your waste out of people's hands or off the floor, and into the right bins.

In creating waste initiatives or campaigns for your event, again consider the personality of both the attendees and the event as a whole. Can you get the event attendees involved in your initiatives in a creative or fun way, or does everything have to be handled by staff or dealt with back of house?

Will incentives work, can you place deposits on items sold (e.g. cups and bottles) to ensure they are returned? Can you get people to bring their own serviceware? Would loading in a waste bond work, to be redeemed when they return waste? What art and theatre can you include to make the whole thing a bit of fun? Previously in this chapter I offered examples of waste initiatives that you may wish to put in place at your event. The following pages suggest some examples that previously haven't had a mention.

Container Deposit

A great way to ensure that your recyclables cups, bottles and cans are returned rather than them ending up on the floor or in the wrong bin is to have an incentive to encourage drinkers to be bothered handing them in. You can do this by charging a deposit on bottles, cans and cups of drinks sold, the 'incentive' being for attendees to have their deposit returned.

Reading Festival in the UK charge a 10p deposit on all drinks sold in cups over the bars, along with beer cup trays. They report a 94 per cent redemption rate. Anyone who has been to this festival over the past 20 years will know that the norm was previously ankle-deep beer cups in the arena. The festival also has an incentive to bring back a bagful of cans in exchange for a free beer. This results in tonnes of cans being returned.

Splendour in the Grass in Australia have a recycling initiative where they give away a $3 drink voucher for every five empty cans or bottles returned to their recycling centres. They received 180,000 cans and bottles at the 2008 event. For a show with just 17,500 people, that's some serious recycling statistics. It also means 36,000 drinks being given away. However, all drinks are sold onsite and profits flow through the festival. So if you run your bars and control the wholesale sales of soft drinks and water to your traders, an increase

Figure 9.28 Recycling rewards at Bonnaroo Festival by Global Inheritance.

Source: Global Inheritance.

Figure 9.29 Can return machine at Hurricane Festival.
Source: FKP Scorpio.

in price along the chain should cover the cost of this campaign.

Among many other creative ways, *Hurricane Festival* has devised a system to collect up all the empty bottles and cans from the Trash Mob to money return systems; they have also brought Germany's nation *'Pfand'* bottle and can return machines to the event. Anyone who has lived in Germany will know that there is a unique recycling system set up for bottles and cans. You save up all your bottles and cans, and feed them one by one into machines set up at supermarkets. You then get a printed-out receipt which you take inside the supermarket to get your money back or the equivalent amount off your grocery bill.

Recycling Incentives

Another option is to offer rewards such as vouchers or merchandise in return for bags of recycling. Set up recycle 'exchanges' or stations throughout your event's site for people to bring back their booty to collect their bounty.

Electric Forest Festival in the USA have their recycling efforts wrapped under the wonderful name of *Electricology*. Supported by the team from *Zero Hero* and *High Five*, festival-goers are encouraged to bring their recycling to the *EcoZones* in the campgrounds or to properly dispose of their waste inside the venue. When they do, they earn *EcoPoints* to redeem at the *Electricology Store* for rewards such as signed artist merchandise, festival vendor prizes, tickets to the next Electric Forest,

private shows and more (electricforestfestival.com, www.zerohero.org, facebook.com/thehighfiveprogram).

TRASHed Recycling Store has given away everything from autographed Beastie Boys skateboard decks and Smith Sunglasses to Motorola RAZR phones and DJ kits. By offering an enjoyable recycling experience, the simplicity of recycling and how to play a part in solving the problem of excess waste is easily learned, and as a bonus, event grounds are picked clean of empties (www.globalinheritance.org).

Southbound Festival in Western Australia has introduced Green Money, a DIY recycling programme that rewards recycling. Patrons are given recycling bags which are filled with crushed empty cans or bottles, and in return receive a clear conscience and a AU$5 green money voucher to spend at the festival. The cost of these green money vouchers is covered by the event (www.sunsetevents.com.au). Figure 9.30 is a brilliant example of *Southbound Festival* demonstrating recycling in action while also beautifying the event. This structure is colourfully lit, which looks amazing. See a colour version of this on the book's website.

Waste Stewards

A great way to both reduce contamination and offer a point of interaction and eco-education is having waste stewards stationed at sets of bins. This will work wonders in minimising contamination rates. If you have access to a labour force (volunteer or paid), you should consider this, as you will immediately increase the quality of your separation and almost guarantee no contamination of the various waste streams.

Armed with gloves and a litter-picking stick, these stewards can pull out anything that gets thrown into the wrong bin, offering a quick pre-treatment solution at the coal-face. They can also work as a back-up to your waste team. If bins start to get close to full, the stewards can replace the bin liners.

Stewards may be volunteers, recruited and managed internally, or you could use a green volunteer/steward recruitment service. Volunteers usually pay a bond (the ticket price) so that they are guaranteed to do their hours. Be aware that if you have an event that sells out, this is a sneaky way of getting into the festival. They will sign up, pay the bond and then not show up for their shift. I always over-subscribe to my requirements, usually about 20 per cent, as there is always attrition through conniving or through honest reasons such as illness. There is also self-inflicted illness that happens when the partying becomes all too much and a four-hour shift in front of some bins just cannot be faced.

There are also some services where you can pay to provide stewards. Certainly any workforce provider for cleaners could do it, but I would strongly recommend a specialist service. Cleaning staff are usually not that personally motivated to interface effectively with your event attendees. You are really looking for a communications service here, and people doing the job need to be friendly people-people.

There are organisations set up to supply waste stewards for events – either as paid staff or volunteers. See the book's website for a list of such organisations.

Personal Waste Kits

If you have an event where people will be camping or picnicking, or creating rubbish without really wanting to get up and walk to the nearest bin straight away (e.g. an outdoor cinema or a concert in a park), providing patrons with their own set of bin bags is a good option. Be aware that people are often excited about getting to an event, so the entrance may not be the best place to hand out the bags. Have people roving around the campsites or approaching those seated with their picnics, and hand out the bin bags.

The bags should match your waste system. For example, a black bin bag for general rubbish (make it a small one), a nice big green bag for recycling, and a clear compostable bag or paper bag for compostables.

You can print the instructions on them too if you have a huge event and can justify the budget and trouble.

Sydney Festival in Australia hand out colour-coded bags to audience members at their concerts in *The Domain* in the *Royal Botanic Gardens*. Rather than have the audience bring their bags to bins at the end of the concert, people are asked to pack their waste up into the correct bag and leave it on the ground. Waste staff then have a comparatively easy task of picking up the pre-separated bags. The audience are asked not to tie the bags up, which makes for a much happier waste processor, as bags can be tipped out for recycling and compostables.

The ubiquitous and troublesome plastic shopping bag is often a problem for anyone wanting to manage waste at camping and picnicking events. Sure, more people are using reusable bags, but plastic bags are still used a lot, especially in regions or within demographics of people not tuned into using reusable bags. I would like to see a project where rather than handing out yet another plastic bag we encourage attendees to use the plastic shopping bags to collect up waste. I've come up with 'Three Bags Full'. Bring back three bags full and you'll get XYZ rewards. (a beer, a meal voucher, festival dollars, what have you).

Figure 9.30 Southbound Festival can cage.

Source: Sunset Events.

BoomTown Festival in the UK have created the 'BoomTown Eco-Bond' – £10 loaded into every ticket price, which is redeemable when a 'citizen' brings a bag full of waste or recycling (one or the other to avoid contamination). When people enter *BoomTown* they are given a bag and voucher for their £10 refund. Then during the event they can take their bag of waste or recycling back to the exchange depot. The event in 2012 saw around 60 per cent of attendees returning a bag of waste by the end of the festival and for 2013 the aim is to increase participation to 80 per cent by bringing in extra depots and staff around site to reduce queuing and speed up the processing time (www.boomtownfair. co.uk).

There are many other examples of this rubbish bond occurring at events, especially those music festivals with camping facilities. In Slovenia at *Punk Rock Holiday* (5,000) and *Metal Holiday* (11,000) campers are given a general waste bag, a bag for recyclables and a bag for compostables. Each bag has a €10 deposit. They receive 90 per cent of the bags back, and of all the waste created in the campsite, 70 to 80 per cent is collected through the bag system (www.punkrockholiday.com and www. metalholiday.com). *Shambala* in the UK also have a bond and they have provided some details and questions on the book's website.

Reusables and BYO

Many events are steering away from disposables and either investing in their own reusable serviceware, forming or using lending collectives, or encouraging attendees to bring their own plates, bowls and cutlery. At many events this may not work due to logistics or the 'tone' of the event, but if you think it has legs, go for it! The transference between the kitchen serving equipment and the customer's serviceware is a health and safety issue when encouraging BYO plates, cups and cutlery. A trick to get around this is to have waxed/greaseproof paper to place on/in a plate or bowl so that no transference can occur and you will definitely keep the food safety officers happy.

Waste In Their Face

At big events that produce a lot of waste, don't hide away the rubbish. Put the waste-processing area in a visible location (though not in a place that's going to make your event look ugly and smelly!).

If you have waste separation happening in a sorting area at the event, locate this in a spot where the audience can see it, and invite them to come and have a look. Put up signage and use it as a way of demonstrating what waste is being produced and how it is being dealt with. It's all too easy for everyone, every day of their lives, to throw things into a bin and forget about what happens next.

Unless it has been burnt, every piece of plastic you have ever thrown out in your life still exists. By showing the audience what has to happen to the stuff they throw away, you are making a potent statement.

Reclamation Stations and Recycle Islands

Rather than thinking of your bins as just sets of vessels with some nice signs on them for people to pop their rubbish into, make a bit of a song and dance about the whole deal, and create 'reclamation stations' or 'recycle islands'.

These beautifully presented (and possibly staffed) waste hubs can then be focal points for your waste efforts. They can be grand affairs with just a few set up, or each and every set of bins can have some theatre

Figure 9.31 Hurricane Festival in Germany's 'recycle islands'.
Source: FKP Scorpio.

added to it. Put an umbrella on a post, place a steward by the bins, wrap the front up in some great 'skirting' or build a bespoke surround into which your bins will fit. Put up a 3m × 3m marquee and ask attendees to hand their waste over the counter or place it into specially cut-out holes in the counters under which the bins sit.

At *Hurricane Festival* in Germany, they create 'recycle islands'. These are made out of fencing (which is used on site anyway). They are placed at crossroads in the camp-site, and split into four different waste streams. Through their various initiatives, *Hurricane Festival* collected 191, 078 cans from campsites! In all they sorted 35 tonnes of waste into separate material streams. Fantastic work. They have also created green campsites – read more about these on the book's website.

Cigarette Butts

It is commonly cited that globally, trillions (yes, you read correctly, *trillions*) of cigarette butts are littered every year. (A thousand million is a billion; a thousand billion is a trillion.) If people drop butts at the same rate at events as they do year-round, a massive number of butts could hit the ground over a multi-day event. It takes years for a cigarette butt to break down and there are many studies on the detrimental environmental impacts as a conse-quence of cigarette butt litter, from toxic chemicals to ingestion by wildlife.

Let us do some calculations. It is estimated that in the UK 23 billion butts are dropped a year.[27] With a popu-lation of around 61 million, that's 377 butts per person per year. Let us say one cigarette butt a day per person give or take. It's quite simple to work out your butt drop numbers.

Event day × attendees = butt drop potential!

At a three-day event with 50,000 attendees you're looking at 150,000 cigarette butts. A one-day event with 10,000 people = 10,000 butts.

Production areas, back of house, outside catering tents, outside dressing-rooms (or inside), outside offices and loading docks behind stages are all likely areas where smokers will congregate.

Many events hand out portable ashtrays. There are a number of options on the market, from the cute little 'Butts Out' containers that look like Tic Tac packages, through to awesome flat ones made of recycled material. Some people see these as possibly causing yet another waste problem.

It really does depend on the predisposition for butt littering by your attendees. Handing a portable ashtray to a smoker who has an auto response to flick it on the ground, and getting them to change their habit, would be a wonderful result.

With restrictions increasing on smoking in public places and on worksites, it is becoming a different landscape for many event organisers. Certainly where these restrictions are in place it means concentrated areas

Figure 9.32 Ashtrays from 44-gallon drums with chicken-wire and sand in the bottom. Genius at Glastonbury Festival.

Photo: Meegan Jones.

of smokers and their waste. It's definitely easier to plan where to put the bins. I have seen a 'corral' set up at an event inside which workers had to stand and smoke. It looked hilarious, but it is a whole lot better than a face full of second-hand smoke if you're working flat out on the event site.

Boom Festival in Portugal hand out thousands of personal 'ashcans' to festival-goers who smoke. These help to reduce the cigarette butt litter. However, the organisers warn that although this kind of issues management is very important, the organisers should not be hypocritical by handing these receptacles out to patrons while not addressing the huge volume of production waste they create themselves.

The following are some things to consider when planning to manage cigarette butt waste:

✓ Know your waste: calculate the likely number of cigarette butts littered.
✓ Communicate with staff, crew and attendees where the acceptable locations are for smoking, and what the penalty is for disregarding this and for littering.
✓ Identify where the smoking will occur and put the right receptacles in place.
✓ Place ashtrays on tables at bars and hospitability areas where smoking is allowed.
✓ Put butt bins or outdoor ashtrays in locations outside buildings where smokers will gather or in designated smoking areas.
✓ Hand out personal ashtrays to staff, crew, and possibly to attendees. If it works for your image, you could even put branding on personal ashtrays to hand out or sell as merchandise.
✓ Use tins (new paint tins, or even a 44-gallon drum) for cigarette bins. Place sand in the bottom and secure chicken-wire across the top to stop other waste entering. Clip smaller tins onto the side of larger bins using a clamp.

Sponsor and Partner Opportunities

• Engage your beverage suppliers to be active participants in your recycling operations.
• Invite local recycling groups to be part of your operations and to set up information stalls.

• Engage local government, state or national recycling and composting programmes to be part of your campaign to promote recycling.
• Take on any existing recycling or composting branding, logos or messaging from your region, to strengthen your messaging.
• Invite a brand, beverage or otherwise, to sponsor recycling and composting.
• Include branding on bins or signs, logos on waste staff, etc.
• Create a partnership with community gardens or other group which promotes composting, and possibly have them as the recipient of the finished compost.
• Bring on board a reuse centre, scrap store or other group that promotes reuse and repurposing to create your décor.
• Partner with scouts, welfare agencies, charity shops, etc., to be recipients of any abandoned, donated or salvaged items from your event's audience and production operations, including food from catering.

PERFORMANCE REPORTING

Measuring waste created is something just about every event does, and if you're not already measuring and reporting your waste results, it should be one of your immediate must dos.

To understand your waste management performance, you will need to measure the volumes of waste produced. Key metrics to measure and report are as follows:

• total waste produced
• total waste sent to landfill
• total waste sent to incineration
• total waste recycled (by material stream if possible)
• total biodegradable waste composted/AD
• total of other waste (e.g. e-waste, hazardous); total waste salvaged and sent for reuse/repurposing
• total percentage of waste diverted from landfill
• waste per person per day or per event
• reduction in waste created or waste diverted from landfill from waste initiatives.

The GHG impact of waste management can also be measured. Applicable reportable aspects may include the following:

- biodegradable waste created and lost to landfill
- GHG emissions from landfilled biodegradable waste
- GHG emissions from waste haulage (transport).

In addition, consider reporting waste by disposal method and across various stages of the event's life cycle. You may also report resources lost to landfill that could have been reclaimed, salvaged or recycled. You may also report by distinct precinct or event activation location.

Tonnage versus Volume

Waste can be reported by volume (e.g. cubic metres or yards, or even litres) or by weight (e.g. kgs, pounds, tonnes). It gets tricky when you have more than one location and some are removing single bins and reporting by volume (such as a 240L bin) with others decanting waste into skips and reporting by weight. To work to a common metric, I would suggest going with weight. However, as each material has a different weight, sometimes tonnage can be deceiving, so make a decision on how to express your waste metrics based on what will most accurately represent your situation. If you are reporting waste by weight and have a waste authority locally, check what their materials conversion factors are. If a waste contractor reports waste results for you, check

Table 9.3 Waste Conversion Factors

WASTE CONVERSION FACTORS: kg per m3

1 cubic metre general waste	150	Cans	26
Mixed recycling, including card and glass	63	Plastic bottles	10
Mixed recycling, including card, no glass	50	Plastic bottles and cans	18
Mixed paper and card	100	Food	150
Glass	150	1 cubic metre = 1000L	

WASTE CONVERSION FACTORS: into kg

240L General	36	660L glass	99
240L Mixed recycling, with card and glass	15.12	660L cans only	17.16
240L Mixed recycling, with card, no glass	12	660L plastic bottles only	6.6
240L Mixed paper and card	24	660L plastic bottles and cans only	11.88
240L Glass	36	1100L general	165
240L Cans only	6.24	1100L mixed recycling, with card and glass	69.3
240L Plastic bottles only	2.4	1100L mixed recycling with card, no glass	1.1
240L Plastic bottles and cans only	4.32	1100L mixed paper and card	110
660L General	99	1100L glass	165
660L Mixed recycling, with card and glass	41.58	1100L cans only	28.6
660L Mixed recycling, with card, no glass	33	1100L plastic bottles only	11
660L Mixed paper and card	66	1100L plastic bottles and cans only	19.8

what volume-to-weight conversion factors they are using. Ensure you report the key assumptions and methodologies used. Everyone seems to be a little different. Table 9.3 gives the factors I use which have been gleaned from several sources I have harmonised. Apologies to those of you working in yards and pounds.

Waste Metric Gathering

The key indicator included in the *Global Reporting Initiative Event Organizers' Sector Supplement*[28] that relates to measuring waste performance is as follows:

EN22 TOTAL WEIGHT OF WASTE BY TYPE AND DISPOSAL METHOD, AND INITIATIVES TO MANAGE WASTE AND THEIR RESULTS.

With this indicator you are not only reporting on the volumes (or weight) of waste by various disposable methods, but also on the following:

- waste avoidance, reduction and diversion initiatives undertaken
- waste avoided due to initiatives and efficiency improvements.

Where does one source the data you need to report your waste volumes? The waste contractor and disposal services are the obvious place. Relevant information may include evidence such as the following:

- transfer station, MRF or landfill weigh-bill receipts
- collection dockets which form part of invoicing.

Certainly scrutinise and sense-check any data provided by your waste contractor and cleaning service provider. The reason is that often these companies will send waste to a waste facility and they will then use that facility's year-round performance result. For example, they will claim an '80 per cent' recycling rate, which is the facility's results, not that of your waste.

If your waste or cleaning contractor parrots a figure back to you, you will need to ask whether it means either of the following:

1 The facility successfully extracts 80 per cent out of a possible 100 per cent of recyclable material going through the facility (i.e. an 80 per cent success rate).

2 The facility extracts 100 per cent of all possible recyclable material coming through, and, of all the waste, there is 80 per cent which is in fact recyclable.

You can see from the above scenario that figures can mean all sorts of things. The biggest question when such facility-based recycling results are presented as an indicator of how successful recycling will be at an event, if we use this waste/cleaning contractor, is, "*What exactly do you mean by this figure and how is it relevant to my event?*" A simple question, but it often stumps them.

It really is important to undergo careful scrutiny of potential performance claims being made by waste contractors and cleaning companies eager to secure your gig.

Now let us look ahead to the other end of the event and doing the actual wrangling of your waste data. Documenting how you have arrived at your figures and final outcomes, and the methodology and assumptions used, is an important feature of any reporting. This should be disclosed *by you* in your performance report, and reciprocally, *to you*, by any contractors working out the figures on your behalf. So what could these methodologies be? Let us walk through some scenarios.

'Bin-lift' Option

This is where bins are placed throughout the location of your event and, when full, are replaced by an empty one. The full bins are lined up back of house and emptied one at a time into a truck. In this scenario the event/venue is charged per 'bin lift'. Tracking waste volumes is done by the invoice or activity report.

You will need the following information to get accurate waste metrics:

- number of bins emptied
- size of bins (often expressed in litres)
- whether bins were full, or what proportion were full
- what waste is actually in bins.

Using the above information, you can then calculate weight or volume of waste. For example, if 10 240L bins are emptied, all at 75 per cent capacity, consisting of mixed recycling without glass, our calculation looks like this: 10 × 0.75 × 12kg = 90kg.

'Bin-emptying' Option

This is where bins stay *in situ* and cleaners remove bin bags from them. Alternatively in this option, bins may be physically removed and emptied into bulk storage skips or containers. Either way, the waste will be eventually removed in bulk and your figures will come back by weight.

In this situation, there's not much you need to do except ensure that the waste removal company knows to weigh your waste. If for some reason weighing it is not possible, then the calculation will proceed as follows.

You will need to know the following:

- size of bulk storage container (volume in cubic metres)
- number of times the storage skip/container is emptied, or number of actual bulk containers
- what the actual waste in the bins/skip is (cast your eye over whether it is reasonably 'packed full' rather than a couple of big, light, chunky items artificially filling it up).

Thus, for a skip which is 5 cubic metres, with mixed recycling, no glass, at 80 per cent capacity, our calculation looks like this: 5 × 0.8 × 50 × 5 = 100kg.

Waste Auditing

In some event scenarios, knowing the true waste results will require a waste audit.

For example, if you are sending commingled recycling to a MRF for further separation and you know there may be some contamination, you won't know your true recycling figures unless you do a waste audit onsite before sending your rubbish away (unless you have a massive event that will take over the MRF for a number of days).

Once your commingled recycling hits the MRF, it will be added to all the other waste coming in and it will be

impossible to work out what the contamination rate was, let alone the percentages of different recyclable materials such as plastics, aluminium, glass, etc.

Here is another scenario. Imagine you have your recycling bins set out, these are tipped into a skip and that skip is sent to the MRF and weighed as it arrives. If you take this figure, you will be reporting under the assumption that every single thing that went into the recycling bin was indeed recyclable. We all know that contamination occurs, and this simple fact may render your recycling proclamations less than accurate.

In addition, you may wish to report by material stream. Why would you want to do that? Some of your materials may be shipped offshore for onward processing into new materials, and some may be processed right there in the same city as the event. If you have effectively analysed the waste backstory in the event destination, you may have made procurement or operational decisions that look to optimise the use of materials that will be processed locally rather than shipped offshore. Thus it would be good to know recyclable resource recovery by material stream.

Figure 9.33 The Unitarian Universalist Association General Assembly event green team audits waste back-of-house at the Phoenix Convention Center before compacters are emptied by haulers. This ensures that any material not properly sorted front of house by volunteers and attendees can be caught and diverted from landfill, or prevented from contaminating recycling and composting streams.
Source: Shawna McKinley.

So what to do? Conduct a waste audit. If you want to gauge your true recycling rates, you will need to have someone monitoring the contents of bins and bags of waste before they land in the skip or waste truck. You don't need to do this for every bag of rubbish, but select sample bags across the course of the event to scrutinise. Have them opened up and the various waste streams in each bag counted; for example:

- each type of plastic
- aluminium
- metal
- glass
- cardboard/paper
- Tetrapak
- general waste contamination
- biodegradable waste contamination.

On completion of a good sample size you will have percentages of recycling categories which you can then apply to the total recycling tonnage provided by your MRF.

Other onsite waste audit techniques will include monitoring your systems as to how they are working and to either fix in real time or have information to plan for improvements next time. Things to look out for include the following:

- Is your bin signage working? Are people able to follow it easily?
- Are traders putting the right items in the right bins or skips back of house, or are they bucking the system?
- Are waste staff behaving as planned? Do they need further inductions, incentives or other management techniques to get them to handle waste as planned?
- Are bins in the right locations? Are there enough?

Conduct visual inspections of the interiors of bins and participant behaviour. Photograph contents, contamination and actions.

If you can resource it, have someone at the event who is focused on observing non-conformities and correcting things in real time.

Additional Reporting

The actual weight or volume of waste created is a main metric that needs to be measured. However, there are other aspects to be considered as part of your waste story that should also be reported. Behaviour change and lasting legacy are such aspects.

Within sustainability reporting on waste performance you will need to tell your story and show pictures, as well as present numerical data.

Detail in your performance report the approach you adopted for particular issues management. Include what was effective, what wasn't and analysis on why, along with lessons learned. In addition, include how you will embed continual improvement.

For additional aspects to consider reporting on, we can turn to the *Global Reporting Initiative Event Organizers' Sector Supplement* for guidance. Here are some of the indicators I have selected that may have some relevance for your more-than-obvious performance reporting.

EN27 PERCENTAGE OF PRODUCTS SOLD AND THEIR PACKAGING MATERIALS THAT ARE RECLAIMED BY CATEGORY.

This indicator relates particularly to food and beverage packaging. If you have intentionally put in a reusable or returnable cup or crockery system, consider reporting on the success of the programme.

SO1 PERCENTAGE OF OPERATIONS WITH IMPLEMENTED LOCAL COMMUNITY ENGAGEMENT, IMPACT ASSESS-MENTS AND DEVELOPMENT PROGRAMMES.

If your waste-based initiatives reach out into the community and perhaps leave a legacy, such as kick starting awareness programmes, or give leverage to fledgling programmes looking for some profile, this is something to consider reporting on.

EO9 TYPE AND SUSTAINABILITY PERFORMANCE OF SOURCING INITIATIVES.

If your sourcing initiatives include an impact on waste creation and diversion, then this would be a cross-cutting reportable item. You would report on the sourcing initiative, but the impact of the sourcing initiative's success would be closely tied to waste creation or diversion, and thus these results would be reported within the waste performance section of your report.

EO11 NUMBER, TYPE AND IMPACT OF SUSTAINABILITY INITIATIVES DESIGNED TO RAISE AWARENESS, SHARE KNOWLEDGE AND IMPACT ON BEHAVIOUR CHANGE AND RESULTS ACHIEVED.

EO12 NATURE AND EXTENT OF KNOWLEDGE TRANSFER OF BEST PRACTICE AND LESSONS LEARNED.

Learning and information sharing can be a tool for long-term and lasting behavioural, social, cultural, institutional and technological change. If your event waste initiatives have at their heart behaviour change as a legacy – within the supply chain, the local industry or indeed with attendees – then these indicators may help you to frame reporting around this aspect.

EO13 NUMBER, TYPE AND IMPACT OF PHYSICAL AND TECHNOLOGICAL LEGACIES.

If your waste initiatives have left physical resources to achieve improved waste results in legacy (e.g. within the venue, the destination, or the local event industry), then this indicator may help you to frame your reporting.

Goals and Targets

Setting objectives for your waste performance is one of the first things you should do. However, I have left the discussion of this until the end of the chapter as, without a full understanding of what is possible, it would be premature to talk about goals, objectives and targets.

The first thing to do is to set an overarching goal or ambition for your waste-related event outcomes. For example:

- to achieve a Zero Waste event
- to manage waste within a Towards Zero Waste philosophy

- to facilitate a changing waste agenda in the host destination.

Next, establish a strategy. This may include such strategy moments as:

- to view waste as a resource and at-event waste management as a resource recovery exercise
- to plan in end-of-life for all potential waste streams to ensure recovery is used as input to new materials
- to reduce waste creation and maximise diversion from landfill.

The next step is to write down objectives and targets. This is where the numbers come in. First, let us talk about waste created and reduction targets. Examples could be as follows:

- reduce total waste created by 20 per cent
- increase recycled waste from 40 per cent to 80 per cent of total waste created
- increase biodegradable waste sent to landfill by 50 per cent
- reduce per attendee waste from 1.5kg to 1.2kg.

Be aware that if you have parallel goals to move from, say, disposable serviceware to reusables, or substitute bottled water with refills, your total possible recyclable waste will reduce. Total waste will reduce too. So be careful with this target, as you will need to accurately reflect targets with planned actions.

Other targets which would tie to behaviour change or other legacy aspects may include the following:

- reduce contamination of recycling bins (from non-recyclables) to 5 per cent from 30 per cent
- increase number of food outlets that have in-kitchen biodegradable waste separation to 100 per cent from 50 per cent
- increase number of food outlets that sign up to the take-back system for reusable serviceware to 70 per cent from 50 per cent.

QUESTIONS

Definitions

Define the following terms:

1 Waste-to-energy.
2 Repurpose.
3 MRF.
4 Binfrastructure.
5 Bin lift (as opposed to) bin emptying.

Simple Answer

1 What is the difference between recycled and recyclable? How does achieving each state expend resources? Your answer will differ depending on the material you are focusing on.
2 Suggest three specific ways of better engaging cleaning and waste removal staff. Remember your joint goal.
3 Draw up a table in which you list the different possibilities for waste disposal (e.g. Reuse, recycling, composting, landfill). In separate columns list an advantage, a disadvantage and a logistical requirement of this approach.
4 Name five ways in which a multi-stream bin system may be let down by bad communication.
   Isolate three principles of effective binfrastructure communication.
5 What are the advantages and disadvantages of reporting an event's waste in terms of weight versus in terms of volume?

Case Studies

1 Evaluate and identify the relevant waste streams at the last event in which you were involved or attended.
2 Ensure you are familiar with the waste hierarchy on page 239. In light of the last event in which you were involved or attended, provide three examples of a resource or item that fits, or could have fitted, into each level of the hierarchy.
3 Complete the checklist on page 234 as it applies to your event scenario. Suggest other items that could or should be added to the list.
4 Research a festival or event considered at the forefront of event sustainability. What are some of the significant waste systems they have in place? Could you implement any of these systems in your event? What would be required to make them work? What are some of the challenges to progress in this aspect of your event?
5 Think about paper usage in the administration component of your event. How could this be minimised?
6 What is your event's personality? Answer with reference to the questions on page 292. How might this personality influence your choice of initiatives and/or how you might adapt them to your patrons?
7 Using an event in which you are involved (or, if this is not possible, one with which you are familiar), design a set of waste performance goals or ambitions. Note the hierarchy presented on page 313. Starting from an ambition you should then outline a strategy (including strategy moments) and subsequently the objectives and targets of each of these moments.

Further Research

1 Research the waste facilities available (Collectors, MRFs, reuse centres, composting facilities, etc.) in the region of your event.
2 Conduct a brief feasibility study on the cost of disposal of compostable and recyclable waste versus sending to landfill.
3 Analyse your event, breaking it down into its relevant departments and contractors. Identify the types and estimated amounts of waste generated in the running of the event. Use pages 276–78 as a suggestion.
4 Research a waste initiative (e.g. *Love Food Hate Waste* or *RREUSE* or *Love Your Tent*) that is active in your region or country. How could it benefit your event in the future? Identify the impediments to this initiative being applied to your event.
5 What are the options available in your area for

compostable reusable or recyclable cutlery? Which is most suitable to your event? Why?

6 Research a recent waste audit of your event, or, if possible, an event with which you are familiar. Analyse the language used by the waste contractors and the event organisers in reporting their recycling rates. Do these statements mean what you think they mean? Ensure you are familiar with the ways in which the language of recycling can be construed to obscure meaning. Provide two hypothetical examples of reported recycling rates that, despite using the same figures, mean very different things.

NOTES

1 Ciplat, Lombardi, Platt, June 2008. 'Stop Trashing the Climate, p. 4: www.stoptrashingtheclimate.org, accessed October 2008. Originally sourced from Brenda Platt and Neil Seldman, Institute for Local Self-Reliance, *Wasting and Recycling in the U.S. 2000*, GrassRoots Recycling Network, 2000, p. 13. Based on data reported in Office of Technology Assessment, Managing Industrial Solid Wastes from manufacturing, mining, oil, and gas production, and utility coal combustion (OTA-BP-O-82), February 1992, pp. 7, 10, accessed December 2008.

2 European Union, Landfill Directive: ec.europa.eu/ environment/waste/compost/, accessed December 2012.

3 Norwegian Biodegradable waste to landfill ban: www. environment.no/Topics/Waste/, accessed December 2012.

4 Zero Waste Plan: www.scotland.gov.uk/Publications/2010/ 06/08092645/0.

5 California – PUBLIC RESOURCES CODE, SECTION 42648-42648.7: www.leginfo.ca.gov/cgi-bin/displaycode? section=prc&group=42001-43000&file=42648-42648.7, accessed January 2013.

6 City of Boulder: www.bouldercolorado.gov/files/Special% 20Events%20ZW%20Rebate%20App.pdf, accessed January 2013.

7 International Aluminum Institute: recycling.world-aluminium.org, accessed September 2008.

8 Captain Charles J. Moore: www.algalita.org/about-us/bios/ charles.html.

9 FEVE Life Cycle Assessment for container glass: www. feve.org.

10 Biopak: www.biopak.com.au.

11 DEFRA, 2007. Waste Strategy for England 2007: www. defra.gov.uk/environment/waste/strategy/strategy07/pdf/ waste07-strategy.pdf, accessed September 2008.

12 WRAP, May 2008, *The Food We Waste*: www.wrap.org. uk/downloads/The_Food_We_Waste_v2__2_.0e2b7c17. 5635.pdf, accessed September 2008.

13 Love Food Hate Waste: england.lovefoodhatewaste.com/ content/about-food-waste-1.

14 Zero Waste International Alliance: zwia.org.

15 London 2012 Zero Waste Events Protocol: www.london 2012.com/documents/sustainability/london-2012-zero-waste-events-protocol.pdf.

16 Zero Waste Events: zerowasteevents.org.

17 The Bottle Bill: www.bottlebill.org.

18 Global Food Losses and Food Waste: www.fao.org/ docrep/014/mb060e/mb060e00.pdf, accessed May 2013.

19 Fork It Over: Food Donation food rescue finder: www. oregonmetro.gov/index.cfm/go/by.web/id=742.

20 OzHarvest Food Rescue: www.ozharvest.org.

21 Second Bite: www.secondbite.org.

22 Fare Share: www.fareshare.org.uk.

23 FoodCycle: www.foodcycle.org.uk.

24 Food Banks Canada: www.foodbankscanada.ca.

25 Green Restaurant Association: www.dinegreen.com.

26 MassDEP: www.rsgmag.com/public/425.cfm.

27 CSR Solutions: www.csrsolutions.co.uk/litter_cigarette. htm, accessed September 2008.

28 *Global Reporting Initiative's Event Organizers' Sector Supplement*: www.globalreporting.org/reporting/sector guidance/sector-guidance/event-organizers.

There's a smell down here that will outlast religion.

Kenny

Figure 10.1 Boom Festival is held beside a lake in Portugal and ensures that waterways are protected.

Source: Boom, Jakob Kalor.

10

WATER

Water scarcity is an important issue for many regions of the world, and certainly protection of watershed and waterways from contamination by event activities should be a priority for all producers. Responsible water use and wastewater management is an integral part of any event's sustainability agenda.

Whether your event is in an indoor venue, a park, a school, club grounds or in a greenfield site, your event will use clean water and produce wastewater.

Sustainable best practice requires you to reduce demand on water sources, strain on sewer systems and to protect natural water bodies from the effects of your event activities.

If you live in a dry region the reality of water scarcity will be part of your everyday life. Water restrictions are commonplace. Even in seemingly wet countries such as the UK where you imagine water supply not to be a problem, they are experiencing the direct impact of water shortages and it's being felt in the hip pocket. In any region where there are water shortages, the cost of water increases helps to incentivise water conservative behaviour by users.

The major issues when looking at sustainable water management are as follows.

1 Water Conservation

Ensuring responsible and conservative use of water is a fundamental aspect of any sustainably produced event. Respecting and adhering to local water conservation protocols (or indeed regulations) is especially important if your event is in a rural area where livelihoods depend on adequate water supply.

2 Wastewater Management

Just as there are inputs, there will be considerable outputs. Events produce large peaks in wastewater. Including grey water capture and reuse and restricting toxic substances in wastewater, and being sympathetic to local wastewater treatment facilities, are pathways towards sustainable event wastewater treatment.

3 Protect Bodies of Water

Protecting bodies of water from event activities, including solid and liquid waste, foot and vehicle impacts, erosion and habitat destruction or disturbance are key.

There is a direct climate change impact on water production, as pumping, delivery and wastewater treatment consume a significant amount of energy and therefore production of greenhouse gas emissions (GHG). In arid countries that use desalination for water provision, there is a direct, and considerable, GHG impact for water production.

When beginning your journey of sustainable water use and management for your event, consider the following aspects:

- How will water be supplied to the event/venue?
- What is water required for during the entire event life cycle?
- What volume of water could be used at the event?
- What does this calculate to per person per day?
- How 'water intense' is your proposed event, activity, site or venue?
- What types of wastewater will be produced, and from what sources?
- What volume of wastewater (sewage and grey water) is likely to be produced?
- How can wastewater be disposed of? What is the 'usual' approach to wastewater disposal and can you innovate more sustainable techniques?
- Are there natural waterways in the immediate vicinity to the event site that need consideration and protection?
- Is the event held in a watershed (water-capture zone)?
- Are any chemical/toxic substances used and could they make their way into wastewater or natural water systems?
- If you are a property owner, what permanent water-saving and water-capture techniques can be put in place?

The following pages will reveal some innovative solutions to water conservation, use and management of wastewater. To put things in perspective, let us first look at the issues surrounding water scarcity to understand why we need to conserve water.

Water Scarcity

Water is necessary for securing livelihoods, for social and economic welfare and for protecting ecosystems. It allows food to grow to support the human population, and is essential for ongoing development and improvement in standards of living.

As the planet's population continues to grow, demands on ground and surface water supply grow with increased domestic, agricultural and industrial use. Arid regions are affected by water scarcity; however, with unpredictable climate patterns, more regions are finding themselves in drought.

Water scarcity occurs when demand outstrips availability of accessible ground and surface water. This is exacerbated when ground water has been polluted or has salination issues, or where surface water quality is affected through agriculture, industry and urban impacts. Scarcity also occurs when more than one community, especially neighbouring nations, are sharing the same main water supply and upstream communities are restricting availability to those downstream.

The *Food and Agriculture Organisation* (FAO) of the United Nations reports that water usage has been growing at more than twice the rate of population increase in the past century and that by 2025, 1.8 billion people will be living in countries or regions with absolute water scarcity and two-thirds of the world population could be under stress conditions.[1] The way forward to ensure water for all is through the following measures:

- Increasing productivity of the water we use (using it more efficiently, recycling grey water, etc.).
- Protection of ecosystems that naturally capture, filter, store and release water (rivers, lakes, forest watersheds, wetlands, ground water).
- International and governmental cooperation (all water sectors working together to agree on equitable allocation and management of water globally).

The FAO also reports that one in five people in the developing world lacks access to sufficient clean water, with a suggested minimum of 20 litres per day. The average water use in the West across all activities to support their lifestyles ranges between 200 and 600 litres per day.[1]

The rural poor in 'developing' countries are impacted most by water scarcity. As dams and canals are built, those living downstream are affected. As ground water is taken for industrial and commercial use, those who have previously accessed this reserve through pumps and wells find lowering water tables taking water out of their reach. Sanitation issues and water quality are of the biggest concern to those living in poverty and are the focus of many NGOs, as the lack of such a basic human requirement causes such compounding problems.

As you can see, water conservation and protection is vitally important to sustainable development and should be considered as an important part of your event – especially if water supply and equitable distribution is an issue in your event destination.

Where water is a concern or if you would like to enlighten event attendees about local or international water issues, invite one of the many water NGOs to participate in your water conservation operations and to be present at your event to promote their messages of water conservation, water equity and sanitation issues.

Let us now have a quick run-down of the different types of water that need to be managed at events.

Types of Water

The management of various types and stages of water may need to be considered, all the way from fresh drinking water supply to handling sewage. The different categories of water are as follows:

- **Clear water:** for drinking only, supplied from stand-pipes if water is 'potable' (drinkable) or from bulk dispensing tanks.
- **Blue water:** for washing, showering and other human contact activities. This can be bore water, from a dam, river, tanks or other supply. It is not suitable for drinking.
- **Grey water:** used water from showers or other washing operations. The water doesn't have any organic contamination. This grey water may be recycled to toilet flushing once filtered, used for non-contact activities, or stored onsite and used for irrigation.

- **Brown/black water:** effluent from toilets and sullage from food stalls or caterer wash-up. This usually goes straight into the sewer drain, septic tank, or, for temporary events, is kept in tanks until taken by 'suck trucks' that dispose of it into the municipal sewer system.

Health and Safety Regulations

Safety and hygiene are paramount to any decision an event makes about water supply, management and treatment. Each country and indeed each local municipal authority will have regulations on what can and cannot be done with water. The Environment Agency or Health Services Department will direct what you must adhere to.

For example, in some countries, surprisingly, 're-circ' toilets are allowed. (This is where the urine, mixed with chemical, is used to re-flush the toilet. Yuk!) But at another event I wanted to redirect the wastewater from showers to flush the toilets but this wasn't allowed by the Council. Do check with your local council and environmental agency on what is appropriate in your local area.

WATER USE AND CONSERVATION

Clean water may be supplied to your event by tanker trucks, mains water supply, captured rain-water, or drawn from ground or surface water sources. Whichever method you choose, water conservation and protection of waterways from contamination should be your goal.

Water is used and wastewater is produced at events through various production purposes. For many events, the organiser will have little control over the source of water, either due to narrow options, or because they are not in control of utilities at the venue.

None the less, regardless of where water is sourced from or who controls or manages supply, the following is a list of potential water uses at events:

- catering and food stalls
- cleaning
- toilets and showers
- hand-washing facilities

Box 10.1

WATER MANAGEMENT CHECKLIST

Water Conservation

❏ Reduce water pressure.
❏ Reduce water demand through water-saving devices.
❏ Reduce water demand through 'water-wise' grounds preparation and gardening.
❏ Have central stand-pipes and require water to be carried to food stalls.
❏ Use waterless urinals and toilets.
❏ Use hand-held misting sprays, rather than continually running misting stations.
❏ Supply hand sanitiser to reduce hand-wash water use.
❏ Use dust suppressant additives to reduce water volume used to dampen dust.
❏ Carry out water conservation messaging to your attendees and crew.

For property owners:

❏ Design water-capture and -saving techniques into landscape design.
❏ Use sustainable irrigation and water-wise grounds preparation techniques.
❏ Capture rain-water and store in tanks to reduce demand on mains or ground water supply.
❏ Use innovative ways to capture or conserve the use of potable water, such as condensate capture.

Wastewater Management

❏ Capture and treat grey water for reuse onsite.
❏ Use soak-aways, a reed bed or mechanical filtering of wastewater to enable onsite reuse.

❏ Reuse grey water onsite for non-contact uses.

Emissions to Water

❏ Use chemical-free cleaning products.
❏ Use biological rather than chemical toilet treatment products.
❏ Use non-toxic paints so that wash-up water is not full of toxic pigments.
❏ Protect waterways from accidental chemical or toxic spills by restricting the use of these materials.

Land Protection

❏ If disposing of grey water through run-off or soak-aways, ensure water is free of chemical contaminants. Position the soak -away at the required distance from waterways.
❏ Protect the riparian zone, the region between land and a waterway, from any activity or impact.
❏ Prevent excessive urination direct to the land or waterways.

Attendee Messaging

❏ Conduct a water conservation campaign at your event to encourage water savings by attendees at the event and in legacy.
❏ Conduct a waterways protection campaign at outdoor events to protect the riparian zone, prevent urination contamination and other harmful emissions to waterways or within watersheds.

Waste Reporting

❏ Total water consumed is measured and reported.
❏ Total wastewater created is measured and reported.
❏ Total water per person per day is reported.

Figure 10.2 The Oasis Bar by Global Inheritance focuses on bringing awareness to the complexities and challenges we face regarding the future of drinking water.

Source: Global Inheritance.

- stand-pipes and free drinking taps
- misting stations at hot and dry events
- dust settling
- grounds preparation and gardens
- vehicle or equipment wash-down
- inputs for construction or event activities.

If your event plan predicts that it is going to use more than its fair share of water, or is going to draw an unusually large amount of water from local water sources, investigating whether there is water scarcity in the proposed event destination should be one of your first tasks.

Water conservation can be achieved through the equipment used or the operating procedures implemented. Techniques for water conservation include the following:

- demand reduction through using water-efficient fixtures and fittings, such as low-flow nozzles and sensors or spring-load return taps;
- demand reduction through efficiencies in operating procedures and techniques;
- use water management systems that detect leaks or automate supply to such devices as garden sprinklers;
- demand substitution through sourcing water from non-potable supply;
- use waterless options such as composting toilets, waterless urinals and hand sanitiser;
- reduce water pressure;
- realise water conservation plans through engaging and educating water users.

Aside from using low-flow technology you can manipulate the amount of water used by not having it on tap. Not literally of course, but by not having free-flowing and limitless water available at everyone's beck and call. Such measures may include opening showers for public use only at certain times (and not having hot water!), and requiring food vendors to decant and transport water back to their sites.

Hired Venues

You will have little control over implementing anything at an existing building that you hire out for your event; however, choosing the right venue in the first place is something you can control. If you have chosen a sustainably built venue for your indoor event, water conservation techniques should already be in place.

You can also implement your own water-saving campaign at your event by layering a messaging programme over existing infrastructure to encourage water saving by participants. This comes into its own at conferences which have a high proportion of delegates staying in hotels, and specifically in the hotel where the conference is held. In this case the bulk of water use related to the event activities will be delegates' bathroom use. If the hotel doesn't already have in-room messaging about water conservation such as taking short showers or not requesting towels and sheets changed daily, then your event can produce this in-room messaging, or request it to be produced by the hotel.

Cleaning

High-pressure hoses encourage excessive water use by cleaners. Require cleaners to use mops and buckets rather than hoses. This will discourage overly zealous hosing as a cleaning technique, rather than using elbow grease!

Catering and Food Stalls

Supply water at central stand-pipes so that the physical transport of water in containers is necessary to get water to stalls. Vendors that operate at events regularly are usually set up and are used to having to transport water.

One popular system is a barrel on wheels that pulls along, so you won't be inconveniencing them too much. Don't allow hoses to run from stand-pipes to vendor sites, as this will complicate wastewater disposal logistics.

Dust Settling

A major water consumer at some outdoor events is for dust settling. Thousands of litres of water are sprayed on roads and tracks to prevent dust from rising during the running of a hot and dry event. You will see water tankers drive up and down dusty tracks to dampen down the ground. Within a short space of time the water evaporates, and the whole process needs to be repeated. During the preparations of a site for an event, dust suppression may also be necessary.

Dust-settling products have been developed for the mining, construction and equestrian industries, and are a perfect solution for events with a dust problem. Using a non-hazardous organic dust-settling agent mixed in with the water drastically increases the effectiveness of spraying, and therefore the volume of water and the number of repeated applications needed is reduced. These products cause the dust particles to cling to each other, and prevent them from floating up into the air. Ensure a non-toxic product is used rather than a chemical-heavy product. Track down a dust-settling product that is approved to be non-toxic to the environment.

Recycled water (grey water) or non-potable water may also be used in the water trucks rather than potable water, if your health regulations allow. You may need to put your grey water through a filtration process before being allowed to spray it.

Grounds Keeping

Events held in beautiful parks, gardens and landscaped rural locations, or indoor venues with gardens and grounds, should also consider the volume of water needed to keep these spaces in pristine green and shiny condition. Enquire about water conservation and any water recycling techniques used. Make sure they don't use sprayers and sprinklers in the heat of the day. Drip irrigation, mulching and a range of other water-saving techniques are commonplace in 'water-wise' grounds.

If you have gardens on an outdoor event site, or the opportunity to create them, consider bringing in a permaculture group to set up gardens. They can create grey water recycling systems, and use the compost created from your event's waste, even from the toilet waste (see composting toilets below). *Boom Festival* in Portugal and *Electric Picnic* in Ireland have done just that. If you are unaware of permaculture principles, I encourage you to do some research into this marvellous gardening technique. It's a whole new way of looking at self-sufficiency and the cycles of nature.

Misting Stations

At hot and dry events nothing can be better than walking through a misting station. This is where overhead sprinklers spray mist down on hot and bothered patrons. It is truly a wonderful experience; however, it is also quite a water-wasteful one. The alternative may be for volunteers with hand-held water sprays (scented with lovely oils) roving the crowd or set up in a central spot. They could also supply and apply sunblock. If you must have misting stations look for the most water-efficient ones.

Hand-sanitising Stations

Set up hand-sanitising stations near your toilets to provide the necessary sanitation service while reducing water use. There are some wonderful solvent-free options available on the market made from all-natural ingredients and alcohol free. Not that your attendees are likely to drink the sanitiser; however, I have seen it being used as a propellant to start fires. There's no need to use an alcohol-based product when great products are available such as *Quash*, *Citrofresh* and *SafeHands*. Set up these hand-sanitising stations back of house near the toilets for food service staff.

Stand-pipes and Hand-washing

Providing stand-pipes, free drinking taps and hand-washing facilities is essential for event attendees for their convenience, comfort and hygiene. It is also a good way of reducing the volume of plastic bottle waste created. Unless you have good drainage, grey water capture and taps that automatically shut off, you are likely going to see a quagmire develop around stand-pipes and sinks.

Ensure that taps have water-saving fittings such as a 'spring-load release' technique so that they have to be held open when being used and are automatically shut off when released. This will save water and prevent a muddy pit from forming.

Rain-water and Water Tanks

If you have a permanent site, it's a great idea to set up water tanks to capture and store rain-water (assuming you're in a location that has rain). This may need investment-heavy, industrial-sized tanks placed underground and out of view, with serious plumbing, piping and pumping. At a minimum you could have a domestic-scale water tank set up to demonstrate to attendees what may be possible in their own homes. By capturing your own rain-water, you are reducing reliance on mains or other water sources, or, more importantly, reducing the amount of water that needs to be delivered by tanker truck.

WATER-WISE STAKEHOLDERS

In persuading relevant stakeholders to change their behaviours to help support your water conservation and protection ambitions, you will need to be informative, inspiring, simple and demonstrative. That's not too much to ask, is it?

So who has a part to play in influencing the water conservation and protection outcomes of your event?

Event Director/Owner

At the very top of the organisational pyramid are those who make the foundation decision on the existence of the event, where it will be held and what its principal purpose and likely activities will be. Hopefully top management will be leading by example; however, if they have made an event decision which will cause heightened water-use issues, engage them to provide resources to reduce impacts.

Planners/Organisers

Planners and event organisers' sourcing and operational decisions will affect water impacts. These decisions include event design and siting, venue and destination.

Destination

Local government, water and environment authorities have a part to play in facilitating what is possible to achieve at your event, as well as setting the scene locally around water conservation and protection. These are the organisations that are likely to be active in water conservation campaigns; they will have the statistics you need, and possibly artwork and existing and relevant messaging for you to use. These organisations will also regulate what your event site or venue must adhere to with regard to water use, wastewater disposal and waterways protection.

Venues

The facility that hosts your events will have a huge part to play in water impacts management. As mentioned earlier, hopefully you will have included the water efficiency of a venue as part of your venue selection criteria. If the venue is not working on water-efficiency initiatives already, there may be a huge amount of work that can be done with them. Use your event to leave a lasting positive legacy of change in the venue. Work with them to inspire kitchen-based solutions. Likewise in hotels hosting events that also lodge attendees, work with them to offer the sheet and towel hold-back programme. There is a lot of existing information available for venues and hotels on how to put water-efficiency initiatives in place. Find a great source of information locally, or even a branded programme or certification they can aim to achieve.

Certainly one thing to do is to ask them to estimate the amount of water that will be used during your event. That will get them thinking!

Contractors/Vendors

Those supplying services, infrastructure or workforce and those providing products or services to event attendees have a part to play in successful and sustainable water conservation and protection. It will often be their staff who are using water, and who will be responsible for ensuring efficient operations. Vendors, particularly food traders, could be major users of water, as well as cleaning contractors. Make sure they know well in advance about the event's water conservation and protection agenda and how they are expected to operate. Provide water conservation and protection information in site or venue inductions.

Staff and Crew

Whether they are the event organiser's direct employees or freelance crew, the individual people involved in building and operating your event and venue are critical to its success. Ensure inductions are carried out with the workforce whenever they enter the site or venue for the first time, to include what the water conservation and protection objectives are for the event and the expected actions they are expected to take.

Attendees and Participants

Those who attend your event or those participating in it (such as talent or speakers) will be using water. Much of the work to streamline water conservation and protection will have been done in the planning and execution of the event or venue logistics by your production team. There will be actions which attendees and participants can undertake to help reduce water volumes and certainly to protect nearby waterways from event activities (trampling, urination, littering, etc.).

Suppliers

Include the embedded water footprint in products and materials used in your discussions with the supply chain to propose low water footprint options.

MESSAGING AND CAMPAIGNS

Apart from putting mechanical or logistical barriers in place to inhibit water consumption, convincing users that conserving water is important is your next challenge.

As with convincing them to use public transport or to recycle their bottles and cans, getting the message across and having event attendees, and importantly your production staff and event participants, actually conserving water will require the use of psychology and a dash of marketing.

If your event is in a country or region where water scarcity is an everyday concern, your job will be easier. Tools will be at hand from water conservation groups, the language you use will be established and the techniques to cut water use familiar.

If you're attracting people from outside the area who may not be used to water conservation techniques, engaging event attendees and having them actually change their water use habits will be especially important.

Contact the local water authority and see what water conservation materials they have that you can co-opt and with which to harmonise your water conservation messaging. Some destinations start telling visitors as soon as they enter the airport about their localised environmental issues and certainly water conservation is a common theme in water-scarce destinations.

The *Water – Use It Wisely* campaign was born out of Arizona where research showed that residents were looking for what to do. They were preaching to the converted so to speak. Residents of Arizona were well aware of water scarcity, and rather than being told about the need for water conservation were after simple actions they could do to reduce water consumption. Since its launch in 1999, more than 400 towns, cities, states, utilities, and private and public organisations have adopted the *Water – Use It Wisely* campaign, making it one of the largest conservation educational outreach programmes in the world. If you are holding an event in a region that has co-opted the *Water – Use It Wisely* programme, you would do well to bring it into your water conservation initiatives and messaging (wateruseitwisely.com).

Look for a branded water conservation programme in the event destination that you can involve in your event.

There are many tactics you can use to inform, engage, inspire and induce action by your stakeholders to play their part in conserving water and protecting waterways. The usual pre-event communications methods such as newsletters, inclusion on the website, emails and phone

Figure 10.3 Water messaging at Boom Festival in Portugal lets attendees know how their wastewater is treated.
Source: Jakob Kalor.

calls, will work for various stakeholder groups. You may wish to step it up a notch and include provisions or requirements in contracts, or launch branded awareness campaigns. No matter the method you use, remember to inform, inspire, call to action and demonstrate potential results.

The first thing to do is to inform your stakeholders of what the issue is, such as water scarcity in the local area, sensitive natural waterways and ecosystems adjacent to the event site, or the fact that all ground water will flow into drains and directly into the ocean.

Present the water-based issue clearly and simply. It is possible that your stakeholders will be aware of the issues, so you're just reinforcing it, but for those who are visitors to an event destination or site, it is likely that they won't be aware of local water-based environmental issues. Examples of issues include the following:

- The event is held in an arid land and water security is a major national issue.
- The event destination is experiencing seasonal water shortages and all activities are under water restrictions.
- The conference and exhibition centre is located adjacent to a sensitive wetland that must be protected from event activities.
- The region's farmers rely on a limited water supply locally and the event must not overdraw on it.
- All water supplied in the destination comes from desalination plants and contributes to GHGs emitted through producing the water we need for the event

The next step is to inspire stakeholders to take action. Show them what the impacts are of not acting. Make it personal, showing how their involvement makes a difference to water security or the protection of natural water assets. Recruit their commitment. Examples include the following:

- *With your help we can bring benefit to the destination hosting our event leaving a positive legacy, rather than our legacy being to place unnecessary demand on their precious water resources.*
- *With your help we can prevent any chance of litter,*

accidental spills or disruption to the sensitive natural ecosystem next to our event site.
- *With your help we can further reduce our event's greenhouse gas emissions by conserving water. By reducing your shower to x minutes, you'll not only save x litres of water but also save x kgs of greenhouse gases from being emitted.*

Next you will have to ask them to act. Make it simple. Make it to the point. One step at a time.

- Don't choose an event destination with water scarcity issues.
- Look for a venue with water conservation initiatives in place.
- Hire low-water volume or waterless urinals and toilets.
- Create hand-sanitiser stations.
- Include a consideration about water footprint of proposed materials and products used for the event in all procurement assessment decisions.
- Bring your roll-along bulk water mover.
- Instigate water conservation techniques in kitchens.
- Put the sign on your bed to ask room attendants not to change your bed sheets for the three days of the conference.
- Hang your towels up so you can reuse them rather than having them washed daily.
- Use the timer placed in your bathroom to reduce your showering time and water used.

Finally, demonstrate what you're talking about. Put it into context. Add some targets and goals. Ideas are as follows:

- If every one of our delegates requests their bed sheets not be changed over each night of our three-day conference, we will save XYZ water.
- By using 500ml flush portaloos we estimate to save XYZ litres of water over the event.
- Remember to only pull the flush handle once; for every pump you'll use 1 litre of water, and if everyone pulled the handle twice we would waste XYZ water and XYZ more trucks will need to remove the wastewater across the duration of the event. Remember: one pump please!

- If all traders capture their wastewater from kitchens and place it in the 1000-litre tanks using the sieve, we estimate to collect XYZ litres of water across the event. That water is being filtered and used for irrigation purposes after the event, saving XYZ of potable water. Remember: don't throw your water on the ground now, it'll cause a mess and we need it later.

Water conservation websites will give you lots of statistics about what action saves what amount of water. Choose the examples that work for your situation or do the maths yourself and create your own examples and statistics.

WASTEWATER

Wastewater can be classified as grey or black. It may disappear down the sink and into a city's sewer system or it may be in your face with 'suck trucks' carting grey water and sewage away. Some grey water will make its way straight into the ground water using soak-aways or be treated onsite through a variety of mechanisms.

Whichever method of wastewater disposal is applicable to your event, cleaning products and other chemicals that end up in the wastewater have the potential to cause a hazardous environmental impact.

Chemical-free wastewater should be your event's goal. In the following pages we will look at different types of wastewater created at your event. We will then discuss wastewater treatment options. We will also hear from organisers of leading events on the mechanisms they have put in place to manage and recycle grey water.

Figure 10.4 Hand-wash stations at Golden Plains Festival.

Source: Mik la Vage.

Emissions to Water

It may sound obvious to not use chemicals that will end up in your wastewater, especially if you're treating wastewater onsite or sending it to treatment facilities that use biological treatment methods.

But let's take a step back. Why do we want to prevent chemical contamination to wastewater? What will it actually do?

When water is disposed of directly onto land, if any chemicals are present in the wastewater, toxic residue will remain on the land and in the soil. Soil is a fantastic natural filter. It is not a problem to dispose of grey water that has no chemicals present into a soak-away or run-off as long as it is not within proximity to a waterway or on land with a high water table. However, grey water polluted with chemicals will leave these chemicals in or on the land that will eventually make their way into waterways through surface water run-off.

Any grey water disposed down roadside drains can make its way directly to waterways and oceans, depending on the drainage system of the area.

Chemicals commonly used in toilets will disturb the natural processes in sewerage-treatment plants, where biological not chemical treatment is used. The better option is to use biological treatment products or odour eaters, or to use waterless loos. Toilets are discussed below.

Sources of potential hazardous emissions to water at events include the following:

- personal products in showers and from hand-wash
- urination
- cleaning products
- catering wastewater
- paint wash-up water
- toilet treatment products.

Personal Products in Showers

If your event includes staying overnight, either in hotel accommodation or camping onsite, you should encourage the use of environmentally sound personal products: shampoo, body wash and hand wash.

You can progress this further by providing the products for use, perhaps leveraging a partnership with a commercial retail product. Include messaging about what the effluent's impacts could be if personal products are used that do not meet your recommended specifications.

Cleaning Products

Products used to clean bathrooms, floors, kitchens and any other surface or material need to be environmentally sound. The issues to consider are the raw materials used to make the product and the biodegradability of the resulting effluent. Another happy by-product of using environmentally sound products is not exposing your staff or your event attendees to unhealthy and toxic chemicals.

More details on choosing the right cleaning products are given in Chapter 8.

Paint Sullage

If there is a lot of painting done at your event during preparations, in your venue on an ongoing basis, or on your behalf in offsite workshops, you may wish to consider the impact of large amounts of paint being washed down the drain or poured onto the land.

To minimise potential problems it is advised that you use environmentally friendly paints so that no toxic pigments are present to potentially make their way into waterways or left as residue on land. There are many brands available and a quick Google will find them. For specifications on what to look for in environmentally friendly paint, see Chapter 8.

Catering Sullage

In temporary kitchens at events, wash-up and cooking water is created and will need a disposal plan. Grey water will also make its way into the biological treatment works in the local region, down the drain or via sullage trucks. Whether this sullage makes its way to a sewer-treatment plant or is filtered of solid matter and recycled onsite, it is recommended that caterers use environmentally sound, chemical-free cleaning products.

Permanent kitchens should also be mindful of the cleaning products they are using both for the health of their customers and for the impacts they have on water treatment.

Figure 10.5 Paint wash-up. If you are doing a lot of painting at your event site, first use water-based paint, but most importantly, set up a system for cleaning brushes so that the paint wastewater doesn't contaminate the land as in this photo.

Photo: Meegan Jones.

Most commercial-grade cleaning products will contain chemicals and solvents, both of which you will want to avoid if possible. Don't be misled by a lovely photo of a whale or unsubstantiated 'eco-friendly' claims on packaging. Look into the details when choosing or approving cleaning products for your event or venue. More information on cleaning products is given in Chapter 8.

Urination

Excessive amounts of urine can quickly make their way into waterways. Men at events with crowded toilets are often tempted to take a leak in any dark corner they can find. These dark corners quickly become stinky, fly-ridden places. If it rains, the urine can make its way to the water table, especially at those muddy events you often get in the UK. One thing's for sure: you don't want to get any splash-back from mud near main stages at these shows, as they become a toilet too!

Increased urine levels in waterways can be harmful to the delicately balanced ecosystem. Think about how easy it is to get the balance of a tropical fish tank out of whack. Thousands of people peeing in a stream will do the same thing.

In order to deter urination on the ground, you will need to carry out the following:

- provide enough loos
- provide urinals for men
- site them close to places where large numbers of people will be gathered for a long time
- light any dark corners to prevent men from urinating there.

Glastonbury Festival has a campaign '*Don't Take The Piss*' to try to discourage people urinating on the ground, in bushes and in the streams. The festival also tests the streams three times a day to ensure that no damage is being done or unacceptable amounts of urine are hitting them.

Over the years they have identified likely spots for renegade urinating, and have either lit these spots, placed installations in them, put signs all over them or put in urinals. The *Green Police* also stage theatrical arrests, approaching the offender mid-stream, giving them a cup to finish into, and then escorting them to the nearest toilet, which is usually very close.

Sponsor and Partner Opportunities

- Align with a water conservation organisation to co-promote your water conservation messaging.
- Approach a brand of hand sanitiser and offer a product placement opportunity. Free product could be made available at the toilets and the brand can also retail or give away personal sized products.
- Get a sunblock range to do promo around patron welfare. They can apply and simultaneously promote their products, along with offering the

'misting' service. There are some lovely all-natural, chemical-free sunblocks out there. Alternatively, get an essential oil or skin care brand to do the same. What you're offering here is an opportunity to align a potential sponsor product with a great experience – getting cooled down. You could alternatively invite a health organisation that promotes sun protection such as the Cancer Council to run this activity.

- Invite a cleaning product range to supply product to your event for cleaning and for showers and hand-wash in bathrooms. Again this offers a consumer-level product exposure opportunity.
- Align with a range of bathroom accessories that promote low-flow taps and showerheads to sponsor your water-saving initiatives even if they aren't related to taps and showers.
- Partner with a water tank company to supply permanent or loaned water tanks to dispense water.

WASTEWATER MANAGEMENT

Wastewater can be disposed of through a sewage-treatment plant, through onsite mechanical or natural treatment, or directly onto the land or into waterways. When talking about wastewater we are categorising it into two types: 'black or brown' which is sewerage and kitchen wastewater or 'grey' which is from cleaning such as showers and sinks.

Events that are not connected to municipal sewer lines will arrange for their wastewater to be pumped into tankers and taken by road to sewage-treatment plants, or to work out a way to dispose of it onsite. A decision needs to be made by these greenfield events whether they further separate black, brown and grey wastewater for different end uses.

As a permanent venue, this will have been thought through at the design and construction phases. Buildings that were designed with sustainable operations and

Figure 10.6 Wastewater treatment at Boom Festival, Portugal.

Source: Boom, João Curiti.

water-saving features will likely have grey water diversion and onsite reuse systems in place. You may also find venues that have retrofitted this technology. If you are hiring a venue and are interested in reporting on the wastewater story, you will need to ask the building operator.

If you are a venue owner looking for best practice solutions to managing grey, brown and black water on your premises, there is a world of information available. Look into local 'green' plumbers' network or one that can direct you to a company which can work with you on retrofitting grey and brown water capture and reuse for your building.

If you are an outdoor event producer and would like to look at treating grey water separately rather than send it to the treatment plant along with sewage, you have several options depending on your location and event or site type.

Grey water (as opposed to black/sewage) can be disposed of straight onto the land but it is important that wastewater is free of harmful substances and that there is adequate distance between point of disposal and the water table and waterways. This is to allow adequate filtering time through the earth.

Local government and environmental agency regulations will place a restriction on how grey water collection, sources of grey water creation and grey water disposal points can be directed to a waterway. This is to ensure that there is a chance for contaminants to be filtered before hitting the waterways. They will also dictate whether you can actually treat and reuse grey water on your site at all.

It is advised that you get expert assistance in setting up your grey water treatment systems for your event or venue.

Soak-aways

This is a big hole dug in the ground that fills up with wastewater, and naturally drains away back into the water table. Soak-aways need to be positioned away from waterways. The soil acts as a natural filter, and as the water drains away, any residue that was in the water will be left in the soil. In using this system for water disposal, it is very important that no chemicals or other contaminants are in the water.

Grey Water Treatment and Reuse

If you have decided that rather than send your water directly back to nature via soak-aways or through the sewage-treatment works, but want to give it another chance to do its job by recycling it for another immediate use then and there on your land, you will need to store, treat and re-store it and then it can be used to flush toilets, for dust suppression or for irrigation.

Grey water treatment processes can use a completely natural system such as a reed bed, a system of chambers and filters and mechanical filtering technology, and finally ultraviolet treatment. The choice of technique or combination of techniques used will depend on the site topography (gravity is helpful), the volume of water needing treatment, at what rate, what the intended end use is for the water, and if it will be used immediately, stored for later use, or simply be cleaned to be put back into the natural water system.

At *Glenworth Valley* in Australia, fresh water is delivered to the festival site shower blocks via an underground irrigation pipe system. The fresh water is sourced from a natural ground water spring beneath the property where the event is held. It is pumped up into a massive tank on the hill and then fed down into the pipe system. Grey water is removed directly from shower blocks and initially stored in 1000-litre capacity pallet tanks. It is then pumped into an underground grey water line to 25,000-litre-capacity storage tanks to be stored for future grounds preparation purposes.

Reed Beds

If you have the opportunity to build a reed bed filtration system, you will get top marks in your grey water management and recycling project. In this system reeds (water plants) are planted in a pond with a bed of crushed volcanic stone.

Grey water is sent into the pond once solid matter like ends of carrots and bits and pieces have been filtered out or allowed to fall as sediment in a septic tank or preliminary holding tank or pond. The reed's roots send oxygen back into the pond bed, and the contaminants in the water settle down there and are eaten by the microorganisms that thrive on a diet of both. A lovely film grows on the bottom of the reed bed pond.

Box 10.2

BOOM FESTIVAL WATER TREATMENT

Boom Festival Water Story

Over the years *Boom Festival*, an outdoor event with 30,000+ people running since 1997 in Portugal, has distinguished itself through activities developed in the area of environmental sustainability. Through a 'do-it-yourself' approach, based on the principles of Permaculture, and partnerships with the *Ecocentro IPEC* (www.ecocentro.org) of Brazil and some Portuguese universities, Boom Festival has led worldwide pioneering projects to deal with sensitive areas inherent to large-scale events.

Water is a top environmental issue at Boom, as the event is situated in a Portuguese inland area and, like all Southern European countries, conserving water resources is a big issue. The event is adjacent to a natural water body, *Lake Idanha-a-Nova*. Thus there are twin impacts of water consumption and water protection that need to be managed. Used water from showers, sinks and all washing can create serious problems of pollution if discharged untreated into the lake. To manage this critical issue, Boom has installed biological control and treatment facilities for all residual water. This includes all water from the restaurants, showers and kitchens at the festival.

Boom Festival has installed water-saving taps and showers to reduce the amount of water used and still provide appropriate sanitation. The taps are the first step to being responsible for water usage. The complete shower system generates a flux of 50 litres/minute. This means 72,000 litres of grey water per day. All this water is passed through the *'evapo-transpiration'* system and returned to its point of origin one year later – totally purified. After use in the showers and sinks, the water passes through a series of wet garden beds where it is allowed to evaporate while the roots of aquatic plants undertake the first cleaning of the water-removing minerals and storing them on their leaves. Later, these plants may be used as organic fertilisers on agricultural fields. Floating aquatic plants also work in digesting some of the excess minerals that come from soaps and other products used by people in the showers.

Boom provides environmentally sound products for use in the showers to minimise this. By controlling what ends up in grey water through the use of non-hazardous products, Boom can be certain that the management and disposal of their grey water is not harmful to the delicate arid landscape where the event is held. The remaining minerals are absorbed with the help of enzymes that are added to the water in the holding ponds, specially constructed to allow these biological cycles to develop. After enough time has passed, a complete ecosystem develops in the water and around it. This is the natural state of water, providing habitat for many animals and plants and thus sustaining life. The results are crystal-clear water ready for reuse as irrigation. No further treatment is required and all environmental regulations are met.

In 2012 Boom treated and recycled 100 per cent of the 5.3 million litres of grey water created by showers and sinks through their bio-remediation and evapo-transpiration systems – which can be reused on the site for irrigation.

www.boomfestival.org

Information in this case study has been supplied by Dr André Soares, EcoCentro & Boom (www.ecocentro.org).

If the combination of the reeds, the micro-organisms, and the specially prepared pond bottom of rocks do their job, the result will be clear, clean water which can flow out the other end of the pond and into a reserve tank ready to be used for irrigation, flushing loos or recycled water purposes, or simply returned to the natural water system if it's not needed onsite.

Figure 10.7 Muddy long-drop toilets.

Source: Meegan Jones.

AMENITIES

We all have our own toilet horror stories, whether on backpacking or camping adventures, at a music festival or country fair. Toilets at any event with large numbers of attendees have the potential to end up in a terrible state and cause trauma to those who have experienced the horror face on.

But it doesn't need to be that way. Pleasant, aromatic, clean and non-harmful temporary toilets exist. It's proven that it can be done.

Apart from the personal experiences of all of you who have crossed the threshold of a stinking, sweaty plastic bubble of hell and survived, the sustainability considerations for toilet wrangling at events include the following:

1. water use by amenities
2. chemical use in toilets
3. transport impacts of toilets and sewage
4. energy and processes for treatment of sewage
5. greenhouse gas emissions.

Water Use

I am sure you are aware that flushing toilets with unnecessarily large volumes of water, and water that is of drinking quality (potable), is a waste of a precious resource. Solutions to reducing the impact of the flush at home can include putting a brick or a full bottle of water in the cistern so that it lowers the flush volume. People pee in their gardens, or make home-made nitrogen-rich fertiliser. The old 'if it's yellow, let it mellow' is a technique used to reduce flushing volumes in many a hippy household.

However, none of these solutions is really that practical for a large-scale event that needs additional toilets hired in. The only solution to reducing the volume of water used at your event due to overzealous flushing of water down the loo is to ensure that you use the following:

✓ waterless urinals
✓ low-volume flushing toilets
✓ waterless toilets (composters).

Best in class when it comes to toilet flush volume for hired-in toilets is the 500ml flush. To put that in perspective for a permanently installed toilet, the low-flush variety are looking at a 6-litre flush, compared with the full-flush big brothers of about 12 litres.

So the first questions to ask of your venue or toilet supplier if you're concerned about water conservation and protection at your event are the following:

• What's the toilet flush volume?
• Where does the water we're flushing come from?
• Where does the flushed water go?

Chemical Use

Sewage-treatment plants use biological methods to treat sewage. Sewage is first placed in settling ponds so that heavy matter can sink and oils float to the top. These are removed and then the effluent goes to the secondary stage where suspended or dissolved biological matter is digested by micro-organisms. Once they have done their job, further treatment can occur such as the use of ultraviolet light or chlorination for disinfection which will kill off these micro-organisms before being discharged, or diverted for irrigation or other municipal purposes.

The problem the event industry may pose to sewage-treatment facilities is that events cause a spike in deposits, as it were. If your toilets are laced with chemical disinfectants you are going to kill off prematurely the very micro-organisms used to treat sewage. So if your event produces large amounts of sewage that will be taken to a local and relatively small treatment facility, care should be taken to treat your toilets with appropriate products. Check with the local sewage-treatment plant if there is any effect your 'deposit' will have on their operations.

The function of the chemicals used in portable toilets is in any case primarily odour masking. It is not always necessary for your toilet supplier to use harsh toxic chemical treatments in their loos. They may have a preference for using a particular product because it's tried and tested, but there are many non-harmful and yet very effective biological alternatives. These include products such as www.southlandorganics.com/article/portable-toilet-odors. Research to see what options are available for the temporary treatment of toilets where your events are held. It should be noted that if biological treatments are used, excessive use of disinfectants to clean the toilets will negate the effectiveness of these natural products.

Another problem in the use of chemical treatment products is health and safety for the toilet workers and cleaners. In the rush of a high-pressure event, safe handling of chemicals may not always happen. You will need to minimise the risk of accidents, spills and splashes of any toilet chemicals used.

GHG Emissions

The treatment of sewage creates methane as a part of the natural process. When the micro-organisms break down the biological matter floating or dissolved in effluent, they give off methane (that's why it smells so bad). Methane is a greenhouse gas, and a strong one at that. Read more about methane in Chapter 7. The creation of this methane is unavoidable; however, capturing it to be used for renewable energy is an option.

The treatment of sewage waste has been given a GHG 'emissions factor' – which is the GHGs created per litre of wastewater treated. This takes into account both the methane, which is naturally emitted, along with energy needed to run the processing plants. So if you feel that your event will be creating an inordinate amount of sewage over and above what a normal day for these participants would, ahem, produce, then you may wish to include the GHG emissions due to treatment of your event's sewage waste. This follows the angle *Kenny* takes in the opening minutes of the movie where he's enquiring about the amount of drinking and 'curries' at the event!

Transport of sewage and the actual toilets themselves will also contribute to overall GHG emissions for your event. If you are causing significant additional transport for your toilets and sewage, then this GHG impact should be included in your event's GHG inventory.

Permanent Toilets

At indoor events, you won't need to worry too much about toilets, since as an event organiser you will have little control over adjusting what the venue has already permanently in place. Questions to ask however are as follows:

- What is the flush volume for the toilets?
- Do they have dual flush options?
- Are any chemical products used in the toilets?
- What cleaning products are used?
- Are water-efficient or waterless urinals used?
- Is toilet paper made from 100 per cent post-consumer recycled paper content, and chlorine-free bleached?
- Are disposable paper towels provided or energy-efficient hand dryers?
- Are hand-washing facilities water efficient and in place, and is hand sanitiser available to reduce the need for water?

A positive outcome of all this questioning would be for the venue to review and alter their toilet products and also to look at installing water-saving flush controls.

Venue owners and managers have lots of work to do to make their toilets as low impact as possible. The questions an organiser would ask you are a hint towards the issues for consideration. The simplest actions a permanent venue can do to improve their toilet-related sustainability credentials are to look at adjusting flush volumes to as low as possible, and to review any cleaning or toilet chemicals used. Taking things a step further is to look at non-potable water sources for flushing toilets.

Of course if you're designing a building from a standing start and are situated in a location that warrants this, look to compost toilets.

Do a feasibility analysis in order to make the best toilet technology decision for your venue. For example, if the municipal mains sewer lines lead to world-class treatment facilities in terms of sustainability outcomes such as methane capture for renewable energy and treated effluent being used for irrigation or even potable water, you may be better off opting into the mains solution, rather than trying to create a bespoke solution onsite.

Temporary Toilets

If you are an event organiser who has the job of ordering the temporary toilets, it is recommended that you stop reading now and go out and hire the Australian movie *Kenny*. It will offer you some comic relief, and also a sense of perspective before you delve into the unknown depths of toilet technology. I had the great pleasure of escorting the man himself around Reading Festival and it was a career highlight to introduce Kenny in character to a real-life version of himself: Dean!

For outdoor events, we are in a whole different universe. There are myriad portable toilet options, including the following:

- portaloos (single units)
- cabin toilets (blocks of toilets)
- long-drops or pit toilets
- urinals (waterless or flushing)
- compost toilets.

Single Units

The portaloo will probably always be a familiar sight at outdoor events, as they are cheap to hire, offer an easy solution for the event organiser, and if managed and emptied on time, are generally hassle free.

Portaloos or porta potties come in flushing, chemical, vacuum, and (top of my personal 'disgusting' list) the 'recirc' variety, where a urine and chemical cocktail is used as the flushing liquid.

The flushing variety will have a foot or hand pump to reduce water flush. The chemical loos are like a pit toilet,

Figure 10.8 The author takes Kenny for a turn around the toilets at Reading Festival.

Source: Meegan Jones.

where a shallow level of chemical and water is in the holding tank, and there is no flushing involved.

These are the ones that have the rich blue liquid at the bottom and have that distinct smell that wafts over all who pass by. These are also the toilets where you get – excuse me but it's funny – the famed mountains of 'bangers and mash' as it were. No further illustration required.

Vacuum technology such as the toilets used on aircraft is now available in portable toilets. They are odour free, use minimal water and don't use chemicals. Winner all round. Check out *Andy Loos* for their suite of vacuum units in the UK (www.andyloos.co.uk).

Single units do take up a lot of space on the back of a truck, and therefore the transport impact of moving them around can be significant.

There are some innovations happening with portaloos such as solar power to provide lighting and power for pumps, so look out for these also. If you want to get thematic, I quite like the range at *Callahead*. Look at the *Toiletree* (www.callahead.com).

You may also be interested in the *Firefly* motion-activated, solar-powered light for portable toilets (www.fireflysolarlights.com).

Cabin Toilets

Cabin toilets are the swankiest of the temporary toilet options and come in a variety of styles and luxury levels. They are hitched onto the back of a truck and towed to your event. They can be full flushing toilets that you would have at home, a recirc system as per the single units described above, a low-flush chemical single flush or vacuum. They have a holding tank at the bottom of the cabin and, depending on the length of the event and the usage rate, these will need to be emptied during the day, or could alternatively have enough holding capacity to get through your event.

The USA, due to demand for luxury rest rooms by the film industry, has probably got the best selection around.

If you go with single units or cabin toilets for your temporary toilets, again it comes down to finding out the following. If suppliers offer 'green' claims, judge them against this list:

- flush volume
- cleaning products used
- odour control products used
- toilet paper used
- non-alcohol hand sanitiser available
- spring-load return taps
- LED lighting and energy efficient operation
- solar powered
- how many fit on a truck
- how far they're travelling.

Long-drops

Long-drops were developed at UK festivals. They are essentially a large-volume pit toilet with a massive holding tank, which services a dozen or more individual toilet cubicles. The tank has a shallow level of chemical and water to attempt to mask the smell.

They are generally roofless, which helps with the level of smell. They need emptying at least once a day depending on how much they are used.

They are quite large stand-alone units and if they need to be transported from show to show, the impact can be significant. However, they are a convenient solution for large-volume capacity requirements. The size of the holding tank means that emptying the tank is not needed as frequently as for portaloos. They use minimal water to operate, as there is no flushing involved. As they are used, the level of the tank contents rises until it gets to the high tide mark, when they are emptied. The most important thing to remember when using these toilets is: 'don't look down'.

They do have the unfortunate feature of someone having to get inside them with a pressure hose in order to clean them at the end of the show.

Waterless Urinals

Waterless urinals are a great way of keeping the guys out of the cubicle toilets, separating the urine from the solid waste (when using compostable loos – see below) and of reducing water consumption if you have flush loos. You should always plan to back up your cubicles with waterless urinals.

The *Standing Room Only* (SRO) waterless urinal is suited for events to minimise queues, as these units can turn over a high volume of attendees. Each SRO has a total waste capacity of 480 litres (equates to approximately 1600 uses). The waterless urinal shown in Figure 10.9 has four urinal positions in a trough-style format.

The *Uritonnoir* is also a fantastic outdoor event waterless urinal solution (see Figure 10.10).

Compost Toilets

Compost toilets are environmentally friendly alternatives to water or chemical intensive toilets. Essentially a dry toilet, they are chemical free, odour free and, when operated at their best, reduce transportable waste by 80 to 90 per cent. This reduction in transport of sewage is achieved if the waste is composted onsite at your event. That is not as scary as it seems. The sewage is collected in individual tanks beneath each toilet. The liquid waste (urine) is drained away.

Depending on volume, lay of the land, soil type, proximity to waterways, etc., this urine can actually be piped into the ground and left to soak away with no damage to the natural environment. The alternative is for it to be collected in holding tanks and taken away by a

Figure 10.9 Standing Room Only waterless urinal (www.instanttoilets.com.au).

Source: Instant Toilets.

sewage tanker. The remaining solid waste (poo, sawdust shavings and toilet paper) stays in the container (generally a wheelie bin or other solid container that is sealable). It is seeded with microbes and worms/worm eggs and sealed shut. The system is aerobic, and there is other hardware and expertise needed to activate the composting process, so don't just try to replicate what I have explained above. This is a basic explanation and each type of compost toilet operator uses a slightly different set-up.

Depending on your weather conditions, clean compost is available in three to twelve months. For an event that is repeated annually this is perfect, as the bins can be emptied of the matured compost and used in gardens on the event grounds. The empty bins are then ready for use

Box 10.3

WATERLESS STRAW BALE URINALS BY L'URITONNOIR

French company *Faltazi* has invented *L'Uritonnoir*, an ingenious idea which uses specially shaped funnels inserted into the side of straw bales as waterless urinals for outdoor events. The remaining product – urine (nitrogen) and straw (carbon) – can be composted in six to twelve months.

A single *Uritonnoir* looks like a wide funnel with a tapered spike on the end and is either pre-made from stainless steel or folded together from a flat polypropylene sheet. A bale of straw is used as the stand. The spike on the end is inserted into the straw and then secured with a strap that wraps around the entire bale. Depending on the size of the bale, you can add as many *Uritonnoirs* as you need.

The size and number of bales of straw is dependent on the number of patrons and the length of the event. The bales should be sited upon gravel pits which have been dug to 20cm, to ensure no seepage occurs. The width of the straw bales also acts as an odour inhibitor. While the idea appears to be easily replicable, you are highly recommended to use this company's expertise and experience, as they've done the research to ensure that this human waste stream is handled hygienically and safely.

www.uritonnoir.com

at the next event. The compost that is produced is 'faecal content' free and the process includes testing the final product to prove it is safe for use.

Comfy Crappers in the UK have developed a pay-to-poo powder room-style toilet set-up. This is a great solution for events wanting to showcase composting toilets and to offer a boutique toilet experience for their patrons.

The whole area is kept spotlessly clean and is a toilet oasis in what is usually a sea of toilet misery at many shows. They also set up a precinct that has information about how compost loos work (www.comfycrappers.com).

My favourite for making a real impact on the sustainability of your event are the toilets created by *Natural Event* (www.naturalevent.com). This excellent option for outdoor events was developed, tested and perfected in Australia, at mainstream music festivals, psychedelic trance festivals and ute musters. They flat pack, so that there are further savings in transport of the infrastructure to your event. Eighty toilets can fit on the same-sized truck as 16 portaloos. They operate in Australia, the UK and Europe.

These loos have been permanently installed at the *Falls Festival* in Australia. They are flush free and water less, which saves well over 50k litres of fresh drinking water at each event (enough to fill 150,000 stubbies!). By treating and composting the waste on site, there is no need for transporting and dealing with it in a treatment plant and it doesn't get pumped out into the ocean.

Toilets and Sewage Transport

The transport of sewerage to treatment plants is also a significant environmental impact. Trucking thousands, sometimes millions, of litres of liquid waste from your event to the nearest treatment plant or sewer line access point will add significantly to your overall transport GHG emissions. Apart from the waste, the actual portable toilets must be moved to the event, further adding to the emissions impact. Remember that reducing water for flushing drastically reduces transportable sewage waste volumes. Likewise, choosing portable toilets that fit the largest number of cubicles per lorry will reduce transport impacts. There are several options in the marketplace, and it is likely that more toilet operators or enterprising businesses will develop their own solutions. Events which own their own land should seriously consider permanent installation of these units.

Figure 10.10 L'Uritonnoir, straw bales as waterless urinals for outdoor events.
Source: L'Uritonnoir.

Showers

Events which provide showers for their patrons are going to have the dual challenges of water supply and waste-water management. Influencing users to reduce water consumption (take short showers) and to use only natural and non-harmful personal products are key. The main areas which will impact on the sustainable management of showers are as follows:

- devising ways to reduce water consumption
- managing grey water
- water heating methods
- user messaging.

Water Heating

It is reported by the UK's *Waterwise*[5] that heating water is responsible for 25 per cent of domestic CO_2 emissions. It makes sense to think that in a commercial environment, although perhaps not 25 per cent, water heating (through electricity or gas) is going to be a significant contributor to your CO_2 emissions. Therefore, if you reduce the volume of water consumed for showers, you will reduce the energy needed to heat the water, and consequently the CO_2 emissions that result from this. Options to reduce the impact of water heating for both permanent or temporary showers are as follows:

- coin-operated systems so that hot water is only available on demand
- solar heating

Box 10.4

COMPOST TOILETS AT BOOM FESTIVAL, PORTUGAL

To reduce water use and to produce life-giving compost to use in the festival's gardens, *Boom Festival* has developed composting toilets.

In comparison to a conventional toilet which uses litres of water to flush, compost toilets are water free. The waste falls into composting chambers located in the bottom part of the construction, where the biological process solves what would have otherwise been a problem for the festival to dispose of.

After using the toilet, dry organic matter such as sawdust is added by the user. The mixture of human waste and sawdust initiates the process of composting, responsible for eliminating all of the pathogenic micro-organisms (that can cause diseases). The process of composting occurs in containers that are sealed with metal, as it retains solar heat. The inner temperature reaches 60 degrees Celsius, enough to guarantee the complete elimination of pathogenic micro-organisms. The gases released in this process exit via a central exhaust piping that leaves the air inside the toilet free of odours.

The next step in the system of human waste recycling is to put the waste into customised composting beds using composting accelerators. The beds have been developed by the team at Boom Festival using references and inspiration from many places, including EcoCentro IPEC,[2] Joe Jenkins,[3] Compostera[4] and Humus Sapiens. The matured compost is used on gardens at the event site, completing a beautiful closed loop. Each year Boom Festival creates about 5 tonnes of compost from the toilets, and saves an estimated 190,000 litres of water which would have been used for flushing.

www.boomfestival.com

Information in this case study has been supplied by Dr André Soares, EcoCentro & Boom Festival (www. ecocentro.org).

- wood pellet heating
- instantaneous gas heating.

Permanent Showers

At permanent venues, showers, water supply and waste-water systems are likely already in place and event organisers who don't own the venue may not have much opportunity to influence these installations.

Those events held at venues with permanent showering facilities, such as sports stadiums, exhibition centres, hotels, conference centres, etc., will need to concentrate on user messaging to encourage reduced water use.

If you are an owner/operator, perhaps owning the sports field or exhibition centre and also run events there, or an outdoor festival that owns the land, you should be looking to retrofit your water systems. There are many resources available, including websites, books, manuals,

and of course consultants, to advise you on the best system for your venue. The main points you need to consider are as follows.

Water Supply and Storage

If in a location that has rain, install rain-water tanks to capture rain from roofs. This water may be used for irrigation, in showers and toilets, and, depending on quality, for drinking. Reducing reliance on water supplied through the municipal water supply will reduce costs, as well as reduce GHG emissions. Energy is required to capture, store, treat and transport water through the municipal supply. Reduce your consumption of mains water, and you reduce your environmental impact. That is even more important if your water supply is from desalination.

Water Reduction Mechanisms

Ways to do this are to reduce water pressure, install low-flow showerheads, and put timers on showers. You can use taps that are press and release. These run the shower for about 30 seconds and the user needs to keep pressing the button to reactivate the shower. This is a fantastic way to dampen enthusiasm for a long, hot, steamy shower!

Grey Water Reuse

Install a grey water drainage system that doesn't end up with your toilet waste. Capture, store and treat this water before using it for irrigation, dust suppression or to flush toilets.

Falls Festival treats 100 per cent of the 250,000 litres of wastewater created onsite through the 40 onsite showers and wastewater points with soak-away trenches. Soak-away drainage trenches are located at each of the shower blocks with 50 per cent of water treated by soakage. Any excess that cannot be handled by the localised soak-aways is placed in a large centralised soak-away trench. If it's particularly dry and there isn't much moisture content in the earth, the soak-away system works significantly quicker. At the end of the event there are usually about 100,000 litres left to treat which is managed throughout the year through the soak-away trenches (www.fallsfestival.com.au).

Temporary Showers

Things become trickier, and yet much more exciting opportunities present themselves, when you bring in temporary showers. If you own the land your event is on and wish to install permanent showers, water capture and wastewater recycling, the options become really interesting and there are even greater opportunities to showcase a model system at work. Like permanent showers, water supply, water conservation, water heating and wastewater management are going to be your main areas of concern. The options you have are as follows:

- single-unit port-a-showers (look like the loos)
- cabin showers
- shower tents
- solar showers
- passive solar showers.

Single units, cabin showers and shower tents are all straightforward, mainstream, hire-in products. The water is heated by gas or diesel generators supplying electricity to heaters To reduce water use ensure the following:

Box 10.5

WATER SUPPLY AND TREATMENT AT WOODFORDIA

Woodford Folk Festival occurs annually at 'Woodfordia' land leased by the *Queensland Folk Federation*. An iconic event on the Australian festival calendar, Woodford is known for its excellence in environmental sustainability.

All water is sourced, treated and stored on the *Woodfordia* site. Over the past 15 years they have invested heavily in underground reticulation of the water supply.

Water for drinking purposes is provided from dams onsite. The water treatment system includes flocculation, sand and filters, and finally a chlorine contact tank. Frequent testing of the supply dam and treated water samples prior to the festival are undertaken by the local authorities. All water reticulated through the site is potable.

All wastewater on the site is treated as 'black water' in the one system, with an underground sewerage system installed throughout the site along with a purpose-built wastewater treatment plant. This has reduced the need to transport waste to offsite treatment plants and almost eliminated the use of pump trucks.

Wastewater at *Woodford* is being recycled through the onsite treatment facility and used for irrigation purposes in a major revegetation project for the property, which was previously an over-farmed and deforested dairy farm.

www.woodfordfolkfestival.com

- no hot water
- low-flow showerheads
- short shower policy
- press and release taps.

We move from run-of-the-mill shower solutions to more environmentally conscientious showers when looking to the sun. Solar water heating is available for domestic use and operators (boutique or solar installers) are setting up alternatives for event organisers to use the power of the sun to heat their water. Truly passive water heating can also be set up for smaller needs. Any black receptacle such as piping or bladders, left lying in the sun, will heat water. Get creative and come up with ways to heat water in a DIY fashion.

Read about the wonderful shower and toilet solution that Greg Peele, self-confessed frustrated want-to-be architect, has created for *Meredith Music Festival* and *Golden Plains*, held in a drought-affected area in rural Victoria, Australia on the book's website.

PERFORMANCE REPORTING

To measure your performance and set key sustainability indicators for water, you will need to measure the following in litres or cubic metres:

- volume of potable water used
- volume of non-potable water used
- volume of bottled water used
- volume of grey water produced and recycled
- volume of sewage/black water produced.

For events needing temporary sanitation and water supply report on the following:

- number of toilets (by type and number of seats)
- total flush volume per toilet (by type)
- number of water refill stations (and number of taps)
- number of water-filled bollards (road blocks) and volume of each.

You may additionally choose to report on the water saved due to conservation measures. For example:

- estimated water saved due to waterless urinals
- estimated water saved due to compost toilets
- estimated water saved due to water saving devices
- potable water saved due to the use of recycled water.

You may also choose to measure the GHG impacts of water supply and disposal, including the following:

- GHG emissions from water production (particularly important if provided through desalination)
- GHG emissions for sewage treatment
- transport impact of water cartage
- transport impact of sewage/wastewater cartage.

When reporting these statistics it is informative to present them in terms of per person per day. Use this figure to reflect against typical per capita water consumption in the destination (use the householder figure for the destination as an appropriate comparison rather than the national figure, which will include industry and agriculture).

In addition, look to your industry association to see if there are benchmarks on water use for your type of venue or event.

Water Volume

Water use can be reported in cubic metres or in litres. Choose which unit of measure you will report in and ensure consistency. There are 1000 litres in a cubic metre of water.

Obtaining this figure should be straightforward. Ask for a meter reading by the venue owner before or after your event.

If you have a greenfield site or similar with plumbing contractors on the job, make sure you pre-warn them that you will be needing this information. If water is supplied by tanker, again this information will be easy to gather from your supplier. If rain-water is collected and stored in tanks, have meters installed so that you can report on the amount of water used from this source. If grey water is treated and reused, again, installing meters is necessary for accurate usage reporting.

Sewage/Black Water

Measuring sewage volume at indoor events with flushing toilets will be a difficult exercise unless you take over the entire venue and effluent is metered.

You can estimate figures however by working out how many times a day participant may go to the loo and multiplying that number by the volume of each flush of the toilet.

For events that need to cart sewage away in tanker trucks, this will be an easy figure to obtain from your contractor.

If you are using composting toilets, you should do a comparison on how much would have been sent to the sewage-treatment plant if you had conventional loos. Report this as 'water saved' and 'sewage diverted'.

Grey Water

If your wastewater ends up with your sewage, down the drain or in a sewer truck for haulage, the above explanation fits.

However, if you are capturing grey water, treating and recycling it, you should take accurate measures of volume so that you can report on the potable water not used, along with the energy and transport saved in treatment if sent with sewage.

GHG Emissions

It is theoretically a simple process to calculate GHG emissions as a result of water production and sewage treatment.; that is, if you have the 'emissions factor' for water production and sewage treatment in your region.

If you wish to report on this, you will need to establish what those emissions factors are. Do this by first researching emissions factors for your country to see if they are published for water production and sewage treatment.

If your source of water is very specific, approach the supplier to see if they have investigated the GHG impact of their water production.

Likewise, if your sewage goes to a specific treatment facility, you may wish to find out if they have also published emissions factors.

This is quite important to get right, as national figures are average and take into account all varieties of treatment technologies. Some facilities harvest the methane created from treatment to power the plant. Others have installed renewable energy supply. In these cases they will have reduced GHG emissions factors than other facilities and certainly lower than the national average.

Include the transport impact of carting potable water in tanker trucks to your event. In addition, include haulage of sewage/wastewater by truck away from your event. This will be a simple case of accessing the emissions factor of the truck used to cart (use the *SEMS Transport Tool*[6] with embedded GHG factors for all vehicle types). Multiply the emissions factor by the number of trips and distance for each trip.

GRI Performance Indicators

The *Global Reporting Initiative* establishes indicators for sustainability reporting, and includes several water-specific indicators. GRI indicators that you may wish to report on are as follows:

EN8 TOTAL WATER WITHDRAWAL BY SOURCE, CONSERVATION AND IMPROVEMENT INITIATIVES AND RESULTS.

This indicator was originally only *'Total water withdrawn by source'*. The *Event Organizers' Sector Supplement* (EOSS) has also included the additional wording of *'conservation and improvement initiatives and results'*. This encourages those in the event industry to not only report on the total water withdrawn, but also on the conservation or other improvement initiatives they have undertaken and the results achieved. Where the indicator says 'by source' for the event industry this may mean by tanker truck, by municipal mains, from captured rain-water, from ground water (wells or bores) or surface water (e.g. rivers/lakes) or from recycled grey water. The EOSS has also included *bottled water* as a reportable metric. This cross-cuts with both purchasing and waste reporting. An objective of many events is to reduce the volume of bottled water used and increase the volume of refillable water vessels (cups, bottles). Therefore, by reducing bottled water you will probably increase the volume of potable water used. This should be explained in your water reporting.

EN10 PERCENTAGE AND TOTAL VOLUME OF WATER RECYCLED AND REUSED.

This indicator is used to report both the water recycled and reused by your organisation or recycled water used by your organisation that has been recycled by others. For example, your event or venue may capture grey water from showers and kitchens, treat it onsite and use it for irrigating grounds. Alternatively, the venue or event may use water supplied by the local water authority, but they have recycled wastewater at centralised treatment facilities and provide potable or non-potable water back to users through municipal mains.

Report on all recycled and reused water, whether under your control (i.e. captured and recycled and reused by your event or venue), supplied by a third party (i.e. recycled water from centralised municipal supply), or even grey water that is captured by your event or venue, recycled by your organisation but reused by others (e.g. you may recycle grey water and it is used to irrigate neighbouring agricultural lands or gardens).

EN21 TOTAL WATER DISCHARGE BY QUALITY AND DESTINATION, AND IMPROVEMENT INITIATIVES AND RESULTS.

The essence of this indicator is the quality of wastewater discharged and where you are discharging it. For example, is the wastewater contaminated with cleaning chemicals or paint? Is it discharged into the land vial soak-away, or into a tanker truck, directly to sewer mains or to storm water drains, making its way to natural waterways?

As with EN8, this indicator has also had the wording 'and improvement initiatives and results' added to it by the EOSS. Events are encouraged to report on the initiatives they have taken to improve the quality and to reduce the total quantity of wastewater produced.

Additional Reporting

The actual volume of water consumed, water saved and wastewater created are main metrics that need to be measured and reported. However, there are other aspects to be considered as part of your water story that should also be reported. Behaviour change and lasting legacy are such aspects.

Within sustainability reporting on water performance you will need to tell your story and show pictures, as well as present numerical data.

Detail in your performance report the approach you adopted for particular issues management. Include what was effective, what wasn't and analysis on why, along with lessons learned. In addition, include how you will embed continual improvement.

For additional aspects to consider reporting on, we will turn to the *Global Reporting Initiative Event Organizers' Sector Supplement* for guidance. Here are some indicators that may have relevance:

EN9 WATER SOURCES SIGNIFICANTLY AFFECTED BY WITHDRAWAL OF WATER.

If your event or venue is likely to withdraw 5 per cent or more water volume annually from a specific water source, this should be reported. For example, an event held in a rural area which has water scarcity issues may withdraw significant volumes from local water sources. This is most likely relevant for mega-events.

EN23 TOTAL NUMBER AND VOLUME OF SIGNIFICANT SPILLS.

It is incumbent upon any organisation that has a significant spill to report it. This includes substances such as oil, fuel, waste or chemicals, which may negatively impact on bodies of water, or is within the watershed.

EO13 NUMBER, TYPE AND IMPACT OF PHYSICAL AND TECHNOLOGICAL LEGACIES.

If your water initiatives have left physical resources to achieve improved water conservation or wastewater quality and reduction results in legacy (e.g. within the venue, the destination, or the local event industry), this indicator may help you frame your reporting.

EN25 IDENTITY, SIZE, PROTECTED STATUS, AND BIODIVERSITY VALUE OF WATER BODIES AND RELATED HABITATS SIGNIFICANTLY AFFECTED BY THE REPORTING ORGANISATION'S DISCHARGES OF WATER AND RUN-OFF.

The event or venue should identify where bodies of water may be affected by their water discharges or run-off. For example, a river may be at risk from litter entering it if the event is windy and solid waste becomes airborne. Streams may be at risk of pollution from urination. Beaches my be at risk of contamination if solid or liquid waste makes its way into them through storm water drains.

The process of identifying the likely bodies of water to be at risk will also be an exercise in stakeholder engagement, as, for example, the community may be concerned with a particular body of water and its protection in relation to your event activities. If this is the case, the (successful or unsuccessful) protection of this body of water from your event activities should be reported.

EO11 NUMBER, TYPE AND IMPACT OF SUSTAINABILITY INITIATIVES DESIGNED TO RAISE AWARENESS, SHARE KNOWLEDGE AND IMPACT ON BEHAVIOUR CHANGE AND RESULTS ACHIEVED.

EO12 NATURE AND EXTENT OF KNOWLEDGE TRANSFER OF BEST PRACTICE AND LESSONS LEARNED.

Learning and information sharing can be a tool for long-term and lasting behavioural, social, cultural, institutional and technological change. If your event water initiatives have at their heart behaviour change as a legacy – within the supply chain, the local industry or indeed with attendees – then these indicators may help you frame reporting around this aspect.

Goals and Targets

The first thing to do is to determine the significance and relevance of the water-related issues and impacts for your event or venue, particularly in relation to destination-based water issues and concerns.

Next is to set overarching goals for water-related performance outcomes. For example:

- to reduce the event or venue's water footprint
- to leave no lasting water withdrawal impacts
- to support water conservation and the protection agenda in the host destination.

Next is to establish a strategy. This may include the following:

- engage water users in reduction techniques
- use the event or venue as a vehicle to promote water reduction in the local citizenship
- use the event or venue as a catalyst for innovative water conservation or treatment techniques.

Next is to write down objectives and targets. This is where the numbers come in. Examples may be as follows:

- reduce total potable water used by 20 per cent
- increase grey water captured, treated and reused onsite from 5 per cent to 20 per cent
- eliminate chemical contamination from all waste-water
- reduce per attendee water consumption to 20 litres per day
- reduce total bottles of water sold.

QUESTIONS

Definitions

Define the following terms:

1 Potable water.
2 Grey water.
3 Blue water.
4 Brown/black water.

Simple Answer

1 What is the process of evapotranspiration?
2 Name six things recycled grey water can be used for at an event such as yours.
3 (a) Create a table comparing the toilets profiled on pages 334–9 by identifying two advantages and two disadvantages of each type of toilet.
  (b) Which type(s) of toilet(s) is/are most suitable for your event? Is this the most environmentally sustainable type of toilet?
  (c) What are the barriers to your event using these best practice toilets?
4 What is a soak-away?
5 (a) Name three ways in which a progressive water management system may be let down by bad communication.
  (b) Isolate three principles of effective water management communication.
  (c) Design a sign for hotel patrons at your event. What water-saving actions should they be taking within the hotel? What is the most effective language in which to express this?

Case Studies

1 What are the emissions factors for water production and sewage treatment in your area?
2 Using the water usage questions on page 319, provide a profile of your event's water usage.
3 Using the water management checklist on page 321, indicate which management devices your event has implemented and for those that it hasn't, annotate the checklist with what would be required – infrastructurally, socially and financially – to make it happen.
4 Who are the stakeholders involved in the management of the water resources exploited at your event? What are their main priorities in terms of business/attendance? How do these potentially conflict with the implementation of best practice water management systems? How can this be remedied?
5 What are the main issues in terms of sustainable water management for your event (water conservation, wastewater management, protection of nearby bodies of water)?

Further Research

1 (a) Research another environmentally progressive event like Meredith Music Festival. Outline the event's most important innovations.
  (b) What social, geographical or governmental obstacles has the event had to negotiate and how has it done so?
  (c) Could you implement any of these at your festival?
  (d) What would be required to make them work?
  (e) What are some of the challenges to progress in this aspect of your event?
2 Leaving aside basic amenities, analyse your event, breaking it down into its relevant departments and contractors. Identify the types and estimated amounts of water used and wastewater generated in the running of the event.
3 Research environmentally sound, chemical-free cleaning products available for use in catering kitchens. What claims are being made by manufacturers?

NOTES

1 The Food and Agriculture Organisation (FAO) of the United Nations: www.fao.org/nr/water/issues/scarcity.html, accessed January 2009.

2 EcoCentro IPEC | Instituto de Permacultura e Ecovilas do Cerrado: www.ecocentro.org.

3 Joseph Jenkins – Humanure: josephjenkins.com.

4 Compostera long-term composting toilets: www.compostera.eu.

5 Waterwise UK: www.waterwise.org.uk, accessed January 2009.

6 SEMS Transport Calculator is available with purchase of the SEMS Tool: www.semstoolkit.com.

11

STANDARDS AND CERTIFICATIONS

Aligning with the progression of sustainability management within the event industry is the creation and maturity of event-specific sustainability certifications and standards. These can be great tools to take an ad hoc approach to issues management to a systematic approach, offering credible external recognition for performance outcomes.

Event organisers, be they community, corporate or government, are all embracing the opportunity to show sustainability-in-action at their events, to reduce the impacts of their event's production, and to enhance the enduring legacies.

For reputable and independent assessment and recognition of commitment to sustainability and verifiable performance outcomes, the industry is turning to certifications, standards and awards programmes.

The first recognition programmes were award-based. Industry association *Yourope* (music events in Europe) launched its (still running) *Clean n Green Award*. This was quickly followed by the *A Greener Festival Award*, from the UK-based organisation of the same name.

Over in Australia, the development of the *SEMS Tool* was simultaneously being completed and this was the first tool developed which integrated a management system framework with an action list component, measurement calculators and broad sustainability (rather than just environmental or GHG-only) focus.

In 2007, the first of the management system standards was released – *BS 8901:2007 Specification for a sustainable event management system with guidance for use*. This was updated in 2009.

In 2008, also in the UK, the music industry climate change group *Julie's Bicycle* launched their *Industry Green* framework and accompanying recognition programme and online tool.

Across in North America around the same time, *EcoLogo Events* was launched. In Canada, things ignited in the 'standards' world with two new standards: *Canadian Standards* and the standards body from Quebec, *Bureau de normalisation du Québec*, both launching standards in 2010, *CSA Z2010-10* and *BNQ 9700-253* respectively.

Around this time, a tool and accompanying certification programme *Eventi Sosentibili* in Italy was launched and in the USA the sports sector saw the creation of the *Council for Responsible Sport's ReSport Certification*.

In June 2012, born out of the 2009 version of *British Standard BS 8901* came the international standard *ISO 20121: Event Sustainability Management Systems*. There are also many awards through general event industry associations for 'greening' given out at annual conferences. We are also seeing country-specific certifications starting to emerge. Coming up is further detail on many of the standards, certifications and awards mentioned above. The remainder of the chapter will include, in great detail, how to implement and successfully achieve conformity with *ISO 20121*, what I consider to be the overarching standard that all events should aspire to in order to achieve conformity.

CERTIFICATIONS

BNQ 9700-253

Quebec developed the standard in responsible event management: *BNQ 9700-253 Sustainable Development – Responsible Event Management* in June 2010, in answer to an industry need recognised by BNQ to establish "acknowledged rules of technology regarding compliance with the principles of sustainable development in responsible event management". The BNQ standard serves as a reference framework for a voluntary certification programme. It allows third parties to independently assess the conformity of an event organiser's event management practices. Event organisers holding a valid certificate of conformity earn the right to use the BNQ's event classification labels. A total of 56 performance criteria are included, combined into the following five event categories:

- Choice of suppliers
- Material, energy and water source management
- Residual material management
- Choice of food products
- Means of transportation.

www.bnq.qc.ca/en/certif/detail_
programme/detail_9700-253.html

CSA Z2010-10

The *CSA Z2010 – Requirements and Guidance for Organizers of Sustainable Events* standard integrates management and sustainability practices into a practical application for a wide variety of cultural, business, and sporting events and festivals.

Based on the sustainability efforts of the *Vancouver 2010 Olympic Games*, *CSA Z2010 – Requirements and Guidance for Organizers of Sustainable Events* was published as a practical standard for a wide variety of cultural, business, and sporting events and festivals.

This standard specifies requirements for organising and executing sustainable events, and provides guidance on how to continually improve the performance of events contributing to sustainable development (www.csa.ca).

ASTM/APEX Standards

The *ASTM/APEX Standards* are a set of nine formal, voluntary standards developed for the meetings, conventions, exhibitions and events industry. The standards were created in partnership with *ASTM International*, an ANSI-accredited standards development organisation. The standards provide event planners and suppliers with prescriptive, measurable specifications for producing events in a more sustainable manner. The nine standards cover the following areas:

- Accommodations
- Audio-visual
- Communication and marketing material
- Destinations
- Exhibits
- Food and beverage
- Meeting venue
- Onsite office
- Transportation.

Inside of each of the nine standards (sometimes called 'sector standards') eight impact areas are targeted:

- Staff management and environmental policy
- Communications
- Waste
- Energy

- Air quality
- Water
- Procurement
- Community partners.

www.conventionindustry.org

SEMS Tool + Audit

The *SEMS Tool + Audit* offers both a tool to plan, monitor, measure, check, act and report upon the sustainability performance of your organisation and events. You may also be audited and gain conformity to *ISO 20121: Event Sustainability Management Systems* Standard using the SEMS Tool.

The *SEMS Tool + Audit* focuses first on organisational principles, then on office and event performance. It is an integrated system offering a management system framework and a performance outcome assessment.

Questions are asked within the tool, with each question and category of questions weighted according to the event profile, with qualifying questions answered upon set-up, enabling prioritisation of issues for your unique situation.

Questions are in commonsense clusters, and where a specific question relates to a requirement of the management system standard *ISO 20121*, this is highlighted. Each question comes with guidance, including in many cases downloadable template examples of procedure and process documentation required for *ISO 20121* compliance.

Evidence is uploaded to the tool, offering a one-stop location to build your management system documentation and also a time-saving portal for future auditing and certification. Question categories include the following:

- Commitment and resourcing
- Reporting and continual improvement
- Commitment and resourcing
- Office: building, power, waste, water, business travel, procurement
- Planning
- Messaging and education
- Communications
- Destination

- Venue and accommodation
- Local environment and local community
- Economic and legacy
- Fair, safe and accessible
- Event activities
- Procurement: policy, suppliers and reporting; infrastructure, construction and décor; food and beverage; printing and paper; merchandise, gifts and rewards
- Waste: prevention; segregation; salvage and reuse; measurement and reporting
- Power: conservation; supply; measurement and emissions
- Water: scarcity and protection of water bodies; conservation; measurement and reporting
- Transport: attendees; event production; measurement and emissions.

www.semstoolkit.com

Industry Green

The *Industry Green* framework is the creative industry's greenhouse gas (GHG) emissions reduction programme; it is a voluntary certification scheme that enables companies to demonstrate climate responsibility. *Industry Green* targets the areas where the biggest impacts can be made, such as venues, CD packaging, festivals, offices, travel.

Industry Green is represented by the '*ig mark*', which identifies a service and/or product as committed to reducing GHG emissions while undertaking other climate-responsible actions. The *Industry Green* framework was developed and is managed by *Julie's Bicycle*, a not-for-profit company established in 2007 to support the UK music industry in tackling climate change (www.juliesbicycle.com/industry-green).

Eventi Sostenibili®

Eventi Sostenibili® is a Corporate Social Responsibility project; it is a tool supporting organisers in the actual and onsite reduction of an event's related environmental impact. With *Sustainable Event Screening®* software, *Eventi Sostenibili®* allows one to systematically manage the event environmental features:

- Organisation secretariat
- Site and sustainable mobility
- Location
- Food and beverage
- Stage design and service
- Accommodation.

www.eventisostenibili.it

ReSport Certification

ReSport Certification from the Council for Responsible Sport formally recognises a significant achievement: the successful completion of a socially and environmentally responsible sporting event. Standards may be achieved in areas ranging from waste management and climate impact to community involvement, health promotion and more (www.councilforresponsiblesport.org).

Austrian Eco-label for Green Meetings

An eco-label has been created which demonstrates externally the environmentally conscious management and the social way of acting of a meeting organiser. The guideline sets environmental and social standards for the event-organising enterprise as well as for all individual aspects of a meeting.

- Mobility and CO_2 offsetting
- Accommodation
- Event locations (including venue, power, water, natural setting protection)
- Procurement, material and waste management for the event
- Exhibitors/exhibition stand builders
- Catering/restaurants
- Communication
- Social aspects
- Event technology.

www.greenmeetings.umweltzeichen.at

A Greener Festival

The *Greener Festival Award* is based around the twin aims of promoting greener practices and promoting sustainability. It is available to any festival which can meet the requirements of a 56-question checklist and commit to an 'A–Z' of green priorities. *A Greener Festival* has a team of independent environmental auditors to visit festivals in the UK and around the world to check on participating festivals' progress.

The website *A Greener Festival* has established a system in the UK to assess the sustainability performance of festivals. They have a checklist against which to measure events. If they meet their standards, the festival is awarded the *A Greener Festival Award*.

The website is also an excellent forum for those in the industry wishing to share ideas around making their events more sustainable (www.agreenerfestival.com).

Green'n'Clean Award

In 2006/7, *Yourope*, the European Festival Association, launched environmental guidelines for music festivals. The original printed booklet *Green'n'Clean* has been supplemented by a new online tool, providing festival organisers with customised environmental advice plus a *Green'n'Clean Award* for festivals which achieve a defined number of criteria in terms of environmental measures (www.yourope.org).

Green Operations Award

In 2012, the *Green Operations Award* was created as part of the European Festival Award, rewarding the event that has made the most significant contribution or achievement towards developing more sustainable events. The panel is made up of experts who are not directly linked to any specific festival (out of the previous year's winner) and who look at practices and systems introduced at their event, development of good practices, a specific innovation, or continuous improvements over a number of years (go-group.org).

Figure 11.1 Green Operations Award winner at the European Festival Awards We Love Green Festival 2012 (www.welovegreen.fr).

Source: Go Group and mikebreeuwer.com.

ISO 20121 EVENT SUSTAINABILITY MANAGMENT SYSTEMS

To support the requirement for events to be produced with regard for people, planet and profit, the new international standard *ISO 20121* provides a framework to effectively manage event sustainability issues, enhance positive legacies and embed continual improvement. Rather than being a checklist, *ISO 20121* requires a systematic approach to addressing sustainable development issues in relation to event planning. It may be applied to an organisation, an event organiser, a single event or a venue.

Successful implementation of an event sustainability management system will ensure continual performance improvement and strategic management of issues rather than an ad hoc approach. It facilitates improved sustainability performance. Documentation of processes and disclosure of performance is key.

ISO 20121: Events Sustainability Management Systems is a standard developed by participating 'standards bodies' from various countries around the world. It is a management system standard and is similar in structure to other international standards, such as *ISO 14001* (Environmental Management Systems) and *ISO 9001* (Quality Management Systems).

While these other management system standards are not specific to any particular industry sector, *ISO 20121* has been written for the event industry, specifically about the topic of sustainability and the role the event industry plays in enhancing sustainable development.

The purpose of the standard is to provide a framework to implement a system to manage an event's sustainability issues. It's not a checklist and it's not just about counting greenhouse gas emissions.

The complexity of your event sustainability management system need only mirror the complexity of your event-related activities.

What Are the Steps?

In the following pages I will drill down into each of the steps, cross-matching it with the relevant clause in the standard, as well as alerting you to documentation requirements and what an auditor may be looking for if you choose to go for external assessment of conformity. The steps include the following:

1　Getting top management commitment and leader-ship.
2　Defining the organisation's governing principles of sustainable development.
3　Informing and engaging stakeholders, and under-standing their needs and expectations.
4　Providing resources, including competencies, time and budget.
5　Establishing awareness and designating roles and responsibilities.
6　Establishing policy.
7　Identifying and evaluating issues.
8　Establishing objectives and plans to achieve them.
9　Creating procedures and processes, and document-ing evidence of requirements.
10　Implementing plans, and taking action to correct and improve performance.
11　Performance measurement.
12　Management review and continual improvement.

The first step is getting commitment. You will need to be committed to the process of improved sustainability performance. That means the boss needs to commit: the 'top management' as they are called in the standard.

The next step is to identify and engage stakeholders. They can be internal stakeholders, such as your fellow colleagues in your event team, or external stakeholders, from suppliers to local government or event attendees.

Resources and competencies will need to be provided. You will need to know what is necessary to do the job and you will need to know what you need to know in order to be able to do it.

Identifying issues is a must and your team will need the skills necessary to identify issues competently, going through a diagnostic process and understanding the issues is really important.

After you have gone through this process you will need to establish policy and set objectives and targets.

When you're engaging with stakeholders and iden-tifying issues, you may need to go back to the boss and seek more commitment.

Establishing policy may change once you have unpacked or identified more issues or engaged with stake-holders, and so you can see how it may become cyclical.

Managing your issues for improved performance comes next. This involves the implementation of your sustainability initiatives and plans.

Maintaining communications and documenting everything that you have in place is also a requirement of the standard.

Ensure that monitoring and evaluating progress and a management review of performance is undertaken. As part of this process you should also complete an internal audit to ensure you are meeting the requirements of the standard and of your stated commitments.

And the clincher really is embedding continual improvement into your plans, so that you can manage future events and issues with further improved perfor-mance and achieve greater results.

Development History

So where did this standard come from? For a standard to become an international standard, it usually begins life as a standard of a particular country.

In 2007 *British Standards* released the first global standard for sustainability in events with the launch of *BS 8901:2007*. *British Standards* proposed their standard for internationalisation to the *International Standards Organisation* (ISO), which was accepted.

Standards bodies around the world were invited to 'participate' in or 'observe' the development of *ISO 20121* from the *British Standard BS 8901*. Those who chose to participate created 'mirror committees', consisting of event industry associations and stakeholder groups.

As the standard was developed through its various stages, these mirror committees acted as conduits to their country's event industry, gathering industry feedback and public comment.

The impetus for the standard to be finalised was the

London 2012 Olympics. This was achieved, with the standard launched in June 2012, just in time for the Games.

Why do we need it?

Resource depletion and its twin solid waste creation, fossil fuel use, greenhouse gases, climate change, plastic in the oceans, species extinction, toxic compounds running down our rivers into our oceans, desertification, polluted ground water, unknown effects of nanoparticles and genetic modification, felling of forests, damming of rivers, factory farming, feedlots and sow crates, uncontrolled industrialisation and urbanisation, displacement of peoples, war, famine, water scarcity, child workers, and modern-day slavery.

These issues and more are pressuring industry and government to address sustainability.

As the level of understanding of sustainable development increases in society and in the events industry specifically, we will see a growing need to formalise the processes necessary to address the sustainability impacts of our event activities.

Taking a systematic approach to problem solving is a natural next step as our industry gains understanding and becomes more sophisticated in the management of sustainable development impacts and issues.

The establishment of a management system framework provides a proven pathway to identifying and successfully managing an organisation's sustainable development issues and, importantly, to embed this learning into the organisation for continued improved success.

Implementing a management system means you will not miss any important steps in identifying event sustainability issues, impacts, risks and opportunities. It will facilitate or set up a higher likelihood of success in meeting sustainable development goals. It means you are not treating issues in an ad hoc way; rather you will track through the process systematically, leaving no stone unturned.

The *ISO 20121* standard is not mandatory; however, it is envisaged that it will become minimum accepted practice in the event industry. By implementing the standard you will improve sustainability performance, have a robust and verifiable framework to manage issues and be able to demonstrate responsible business practice to your stakeholders.

Meet Expectations

Those who attend events, along with talent and performers, sponsors, government and the wider community, are all increasingly expecting events and the venues that host them to be operated sustainably. Implementing *ISO 20121* assures stakeholders that you have your systems in place to allow great performance.

Save Money

Shrinking budgets and a need for leaner events using fewer resources and reducing expenditure while still maintaining quality production outcomes has turned producers towards sustainable event production practices. Taking a pragmatic approach to issues management will uncover where savings can be made.

Corporate Imperative

Matching corporate policy with event production, ensuring production practices meet the organisation's CSR goals, shareholder expectations and board directives, also drives event producers to embrace sustainable event management principles.

Reputation

Gaining competitive advantage and meeting client and sponsor requirements in a competitive industry are driving producers, venues and the supply chain to implement an event sustainability management system and conform to *ISO 20121*.

When I asked in an exam how a management system could benefit an event organisation, Steve McCoy provided this eloquent answer:

> *A management system benefits the sustainability performance of an event by providing event owners and organisers with a way to:*
>
> - *identify regulatory requirements and best practice trends*
> - *set goals rationally*
> - *craft well-considered implementation plans*

- *determine knowledge gaps and design effective training programmes*
- *integrate change management processes*
- *determine and provide adequate resources*
- *craft sound methods for tracking progress against deadlines*
- *implement thorough self-assessment processes leading to accountability, incentive and visible support structures, and continually improving performance/returns.*

Who is it for?

The standard has been designed to be flexible, so that it can apply to all types of events and the supply chains that service them. If you have any kind of event-related activity, then the standard is right for you.

Event Owner/Sponsor

Those organisations that own events, but which contract external organisations to manage and deliver their events, can implement an event sustainability management system for all their organisation's event-related activities.

A good example is a corporation requiring business events to be produced throughout the year but which contracts various companies to do the event production.

Another example is a company that sponsors events and has brand activation at events, or which may in fact create events around its own product/company or brands.

In these cases the organisation would have an event sustainability management system in place to cover all event-related activities for the company.

These organisations may additionally require that the event organiser they contract, events they agree to fund through sponsorship, venues they choose to host their events, or other areas of the supply chain are all also compliant with *ISO 20121*.

Events

One-off or recurring events, whether owned and self-managed, or managed by an external organisation, can have an event sustainability management system in place and become compliant with the requirements of the standard. The scope or boundary would be the event's activities, rather than other year-round event activities by the organising company or event owner.

In some circumstances an organisation is created just for the production and delivery of a single event, and in this case the management system would apply to both the event and the organising entity, which are in reality one and the same, as the organising body has no other activities apart from the event in question.

Event Organiser

Companies that are contracted to produce events on behalf of clients can become compliant with the standard. The event organising company will have a management system in place that guides the production of events they manage. It is expected that this group will make up the bulk of the entities implementing the standard.

Venues

Venues that host a client's events, or that run venue-owned events, can implement an event sustainability management system and conform to the requirements of the standard.

Examples of venues may be hotels with conferencing and gala ballroom facilities, parks and gardens, purpose-built conference centres, stadia and arenas, leisure complexes, sports grounds, exhibition centres, and the huge variety of boutique, unique, small to medium venues.

Suppliers

Those that supply products and services to the event industry can also achieve compliance to the standard for their event-related activities.

These may include labour supply companies such as waste and security staffing, waste companies, power companies, staging and infrastructure, amenities providers, décor and dressing, and of course likely candidates – caterers, food and beverage stallholders, and bar operators.

ISO 20121 CLAUSE BY CLAUSE

Organisational Context

One of the first clauses in the standard is *4.1 Understanding of the organisation and its context* which requires both internal and external issues that may be relevant to the organisation's purpose or affect its ability to meet the intended outcomes of the event sustainability management system to be determined.

This is any internal and external issue that may *influence* the ability of the organisation to meet its sustainability goals and the auditor, when undertaking the conformity assessment, should consider these issues.

Consider external or internal issues that may limit the ability to do all that is necessary to manage issues at a best practice level. This could include things such as the following:

- the non-existence of solutions in your region
- a head office corporate policy under which you have to operate
- a climate of unrest in an area which makes some aspects impossible to achieve
- a requirement to have sponsors which may conflict with some of the operational sustainability ambitions
- a cultural aspect which may impinge on best practice
- safety concerns.

An auditor will carry out a document review to see where your organisational context has been documented such as in a policy or strategy. In addition, interviews with staff members will also provide an opportunity to explain the context with the auditor and information on where else this context is documented or declared.

Interested Parties

The next is *Clause 4.2 Understanding the needs and expectations of interested parties* and requires you to identify and address stakeholders and their needs and expectations.

The production of most events relies on the coming together of many stakeholders external to the core event-producing organisation. There will be many people, entities and organisations which will be either interested in or have an impact on the sustainability performance of the organisation and its event activities. This may include supply chain, attendees, participants, regulatory authorities, clients, sponsors, media, talent, local community, staff, contractors, caterers, neighbouring businesses, and NGOs.

Having these many stakeholder groups engaged in and committed to the event sustainably processes will be pivotal to the success of your plans. They are integral to the identification of event sustainability issues – the issues identified through the engagement process will inform aspects of your objective setting, policy, actions and operational control.

By purposefully planning the recruitment of stakeholders into your event's sustainability plans, you will have a greater chance of success.

The communication and engagement process will also have the twin benefit of educating your event's stakeholders as to the deeper issues around sustainability, and (hopefully) ignite their active participation in developing solutions alongside you.

To meet the requirements of this clause the organisation must have a *procedure* in place for identifying and engaging those who have an interest in your event sustainability management system, and to include their needs and expectations in the planning and delivery of your event. This last part is especially important. The function of engagement and awareness is one thing; truly listening to your stakeholders and understanding their needs and identifying their expectations is where it's at. The *SEMS Tool* contains a sample Interested Party Identification, Engagement and Communications procedure.

Commitment to sustainable development principles, and implementing sustainable practices, along with how the stakeholders may be involved, should be communicated.

These stakeholders or 'interested parties' should have access to the following:

- the sustainability policy
- information on their contribution to the effectiveness of the event sustainability management system, sustainability performance and its benefits

- the implications of not engaging with sustainability practices.

In order to achieve all of this, a *procedure* should be prepared, which identifies the steps taken in first identifying and second engaging with interested parties. The reason for this, remember, is to help to uncover issues for management.

You should also realise that the 'needs and requirements' of interested parties may be based on opinion rather than fact. This leads to relevance of issues, and away from significance or size. If an interested party believes something is a big issue, then it is! This will in turn lead into the evaluation or prioritising of issues, which is addressed in *Clause 6.1.2* (see below).

A requirement of this clause is also that you document the outcomes of the consultation with stakeholders. Examples could be minutes from meetings, newsletters, survey results and action plans.

In assessing conformity with this clause, auditors will:

- Undertake a document review of procedure and other process documentation.
- Review the list of stakeholders you have identified and assess the communications routes used. They will be looking for verbal, written, contracts, newsletters, website information, pdf information sheets, meetings, onsite signage, inductions, surveys, feedback routes, etc.
- Look for examples of outcomes of interested party engagement, either documented, in practice, and through interviews.
- Undertake interviews as evidence that there is an awareness about the procedure and process among those implementing them.

Determine Scope

Before you launch into setting up your management system you will need to define what will be included and what will not.

Clause 4.3 Determining the scope of the event sustainability management system requires that the boundaries and applicability of the event sustainability management system are determined, so that an adequate scope of the system can be defined. Questions to consider include the following:

- Does the management system cover a single event, a company and their year's worth of events, or an event organiser who will apply a management system to all their client's events?
- Are you only concerned with what happens within the four walls of your venue, or are you scoping in all the activities in which attendees to your event will be involved (e.g. delegates at a conference)?

By articulating this scope, boundary or frame of reference you can then establish parameters within which all your event sustainability concerns will fall.

It is up to the organisation to decide what is included in the scope of its event sustainability management system.

This will include all event activities that are under your control or significant influence. Certainly the scope shouldn't be so narrow as to exclude elements that stakeholders would think are your responsibility. Nor should it be so broad that it would be impossible to control practical aspects, communicate with all interested parties, train the team, collect all the performance data, etc.

Just because you cannot control something completely, the issue or impact may still have considerable significance and be deemed relevant by your stakeholders. Do they see it as your responsibility? If so, you must factor these potential sustainability impacts, issues, risks and opportunities into your plans.

Remember: what is included in your management system needs managing! Don't be too wimpy though and scope everything out, and then call yourself a brilliant performer!

The organisation may choose to exclude aspects of the event planning cycle that are already considered in great detail by other areas of the organisation. This would be particularly relevant where there are legal or regulatory requirements, for example, around workplace health and safety, risk assessments, attendee safety, security, etc.

Example Scope for Event Owner

For an organisation that owns and manages a single event or umbrella event, the scope of the event sustainability management system could include the following:

- The year-round office/organisation-based activities.
- All events in XYZ Organisation controlled venues.

Excluded from the scope could be the following:

- Event activities that occur in venues which are not under the direct managerial or operational control of the organisation, but which are hired/host events under the organisation's event umbrella.
- Workplace health and safety, as this is dealt with in detail already by another department.
- Food health and safety, as this is handled by the catering manager who liaises with the local council health inspectors and is a regulatory requirement.
- Safety and crowd control for attendees, as this is already managed by the safety department and is a requirement of the event licence with insurers, council and police.

Example Scope for Event Organiser

For an event organising company that manages events for clients, the scope could include the following:

- Requirements as they relate to the company's principles of sustainable development, staff, policies, procedures and processes.
- All procedure and process documentation with sustainability relevance that forms the basis of all company operational practices for general event planning and delivery.
- All office-based procurement for the organisation.

Where a client indicates that they wish their event to be produced sustainability:

- Policy is related to the client event.
- Objectives are formed for the client event.
- Interested parties are identified and engaged for the client event.

- Issues are identified, and plans of action put in place for managing these issues, for the client event.
- Operational control, nonconformities and corrective action for the client event.

In assessing conformity to this clause the auditor will look for a written description of the scope. This could be a stand-alone statement or preamble to a document.

Principles, Purpose, Values

Clause 4.5 Sustainable development principles, statement of purpose and values requires that the organisation include considerations, at a minimum, in their governing principles of sustainable development for stewardship, inclusivity, integrity and transparency.

By declaring a statement of sustainable development principles to which the organisation subscribes, the organisation is confirming the values by which it runs. These values form a bridge between the principles and the operations of the organisation.

Whenever there are decisions to be made which may have a sustainability impact, the organisation should refer back to their values (guiding sustainable development principles) to assess whether the operational decision conflicts with the values of the organisation.

There must be a document that lays this out and includes the primary purpose and values of the organisation. This may be encompassed in a Sustainability Policy, or it may be a separate statement. Potentially it could be laid out in, for example, the leading page to an annual report or the 'about us' section of an organisation's website.

Establishing the higher principles to which the organisation subscribes will make decision making easier down the track. So what are these principles?

Sustainable development is defined as being able to meet the needs of the present without depleting resources or harming natural cycles for future generations.

Planning for sustainability provides a framework which links economic, social, environmental and governance matters.

Sustainable development principles may include aspects such as Inclusivity, Integrity, Stewardship, Transparency, Labour Standards, Human Rights and Legacy.

Embracing these principles at an organisational level is the first step; next comes embedding these principles into the operational, procurement (and possibly content) aspects of event production. The principles should guide strategy and decision-making processes right down to operational aspects of an event.

Refer to Chapter 1 for more details on how the principles of sustainable development can be interpreted for the event industry.

In auditing this clause the auditor will be looking for a document that lays out the governing sustainable development principles, and which includes the primary purpose and values of the organisation.

This may be embedded in a policy, an annual report, or on the website as a statement. The organisation may also be signed up to accords or protocols, such as the *UN Global Compact* or other campaigns or pledge-style programmes.

The auditor may also question relevant staff member/s about this to ensure the principles are known by staff.

Leadership and Commitment

Clause 5.1 Leadership and commitment requires, as it plainly says, leadership and commitment, and for this to be clearly demonstrated.

The boss (or whoever gives the final nod – the board, sponsors, clients, local councillors, department head, etc.) must give the go-ahead and offer the team the encouragement and support they need to ensure successful sustainability outcomes.

The standard offers a specific set of ways in which top management must demonstrate leadership and commitment. The use of the word 'shall' in this clause means that the following criteria must be in place:

- that the event sustainability policies and objectives are compatible with the strategic direction of the organisation;
- that the event sustainability management system is integrated into organisational processes;
- provision of resources needed for the management system's implementation;
- communicating the importance of sustainability management and conforming to standard;

- ensuring that the intended outcomes of the management system are met (that's a pretty big one!);
- directing and supporting individuals' contribution to the management system;
- promoting continual improvement;
- supporting management to demonstrate leadership.

By committing to sustainability, top management is showing leadership. Top management should ensure that processes and programmes are in place to engage everyone who has a role in sustainability performance to become involved and to 'buy into' successfully reaching objectives. Examples of demonstrating commitment could be as follows:

- having staff undertake sustainable event training;
- engaging someone to support the sustainability vision of the organisation;
- for the role of sustainability manager to be created;
- the formation of a greening team;
- ensuring sustainability is placed on an equal level with creative and financial decisions;
- resources are provided through time and knowledge, to ensure that sustainability is addressed;
- sustainability impacts are included in all major operational and procurement decisions as a matter of policy and staff are trained to understand the issues;
- that the importance of including sustainability considerations in decisions and the implementation of the management system is communicated to all relevant internal and external parties;
- that the top management direct staff to address sustainability issues and adhere to the Sustainability Policy for the organisation;
- that the idea of continual improvement is promoted by top management through establishing incremental goals and improvements each year;
- ensuring that all relevant departments address sustainability and are empowered to do so;
- undertaking a management review.

In assessing conformity to this clause an auditor will look for evidence that the top management are involved in or support the uptake of the management system framework, such as:

- the directive coming from the top to 'go green';
- challenges or requests from top management to the team to improve sustainability performance;
- training provided;
- management review undertaken;
- staff empowered and competent to embrace sustainability and make decisions.

The auditor may also question relevant staff member/s to get their opinion on the commitment of and leadership by top management.

Policy

Clause 5.2 Policy requires that top management establish and document a sustainable development policy. This is an unusual title for a policy for an event organisation, and during the development of the standard it was hotly contested. The policy in actuality is a policy to detail how you will manage sustainability; however, the title 'sustainable development policy' infers that you are managing sustainable development. As your event or organisation can only contribute to or support the enhancement of sustainable development, then really what is called for in this clause is a bog-standard Sustainability Policy.

The clause goes on to detail what is required in this policy and it makes it clear that it is really talking about a normal old Sustainability Policy. The additional requirements within this clause require that the policy be appropriate to the purpose of the organisation, provide a framework for setting objectives, and include continual improvement.

It must include a commitment to leadership within the field of event sustainability management, reference the organisation's statement of purpose and values, and its governing principles of sustainable development.

The policy should also be the foundation of sustainability management of event-related activities and consider operational aspects such as supply chain management, all stages of the event planning life cycle, engagement of interested parties and legacy components.

If it is the first year that you are addressing sustainability (in events or organisation-wide) then it is OK to have a vision rather than a policy. Alternatively, your policy in these early stages of sustainability maturity

within the organisation may include your vision rather than hard-and-fast 'rules' or must-takes.

See Chapter 1 for more details on how to create a policy for your organisation.

This clause specifies that the policy must be formally documented and be communicated within the organisation and be available to interested parties as appropriate.

The auditors will simply be looking for the existence of a policy and will review that policy to make sure it contains all the relevant information the standard says it should. They will also be looking for proof that it is communicated in multiple ways, not just hosted on your shared server in the organisation's computer system.

Roles and Responsibilities

Clause 5.3 Organizational roles, responsibilities and authorities requires that responsibilities and authorities for roles that are managing various aspects of sustainability issues, processes and outcomes are assigned and communicated, and that evidence that these roles are assigned exists.

Each person responsible for elements of the event planning cycle and event operation must be clearly assigned the appropriate role for implementing the sustainable event management system.

One person may guide the rest of the team, or each team member may be delegated a specific duty. A guiding hand or overall coordinator may be required when first adopting a sustainable event management system to work towards embedding the processes and procedures into the team and the event planning cycle.

Evidence of this clause being in place, and things an auditor will look for, could include the following:

- an organisational hierarchy chart;
- an action list with people's names or roles against them;
- a written description of overarching delegation of roles;
- inclusion by all departments in sustainability oversight;
- creation of agenda items at meetings where department representatives are responsible for addressing their department's sustainability responsibility;

- description of who reports on which areas of sustainability performance.

Identify Issues

Clause 6.1 Actions to address risks and opportunities requires that you have a *procedure* explaining how you will tackle issues identification and requires of course that you therefore have processes in place to do so. It also requires that you document the outcomes of the issues identification process.

Within this clause there are two subclauses. The gist of *6.1.1 General* is that you ensure you map back your issues identification to include the organisational context identified and explained in *Clause 4.1*, and the needs and expectations of interested parties identified and determined in *Clause 4.2*. In addition, it highlights that the issues identification process should include consideration for the organisation's governing principles of sustainable development that have, of course, been declared earlier through compliance with *Clause 4.5*.

Clause 6.1.2 Issue identification and evaluation is where the nuts and bolts of the issues identification process occur. Note that the standard talks about 'risks and opportunities' as well as 'issues'. It is also talking about 'sustainable development' issues or risks/opportunities – for you and I within the context of managing an event or event organisation, this means the four pillars of sustainability (environmental, economic, social, cultural), and the associated risks, opportunities, issues and impacts.

So what is the issue and who is responsible? Who cares about it and how big an issue is it really? Working out what should be focused on, what is relevant, where the biggest gains will be and where the 'must-takes' are (regardless of the size of the impact) is next.

Conduct a thorough analysis of your event and organisation's 'business as usual' performance. You're looking for risks and opportunities, and don't forget that issues can be positive or negative. There may be barriers to improvement and that is of course an issue. Legalities and regulations may impact on plans. This process will also allow you to uncover what you are already doing well. Understand which issues have greatest significance – just how big are the potential impacts, especially if you fail to act? Identifying and acknowledging issues is key. You

may decide on a staged approach to managing issues over the course of several editions of your event. Just make sure you declare that you're aware.

Refer to Chapter 3 for more ways you can tackle this huge subject. The important feature of this clause is that a formal procedure must be written up along with relevant process documentation.

An auditor will be looking for a formal procedure to "*identify its sustainable development issues and to evaluate their significance. . .*" and for evidence (or documented proof) of processes being in place and that they are being followed.

Using the *SEMS Tool* is one way of showing evidence of an issues identification process, as many aspects of the *SEMS Tool* are checklist in nature, tracking through many potential issues for consideration. The *SEMS Tool* also has a sample procedure you can use as the basis of your organisation's procedure for issues identification and evaluation.

Objectives

Clause 6.2 Event sustainability objectives and how to achieve them requires the organisation to establish objectives and supporting targets.

Setting objectives and supporting targets provides not only an end goal, but can help gauge how you have improved and whether your undertakings are having a positive effect.

If you're in the first year of implementing sustainability at your event, you will be in baselining mode. Your overarching objective will include gathering performance data in order to establish a baseline from which to assess future improvement.

Establishing *Key Sustainability Performance Indicators* is another aspect to setting objectives.

As with all objectives, event sustainability objectives should be specific, measurable, achievable, reasonable and time-bound (SMART!). They need to align with your sustainability policy, stated purpose of the organisation and its sustainable development principles. Importantly, objectives and targets must be communicated.

The specific mention of 'legacy' in this clause may require you to build in considerations for and objectives and targets based around legacy. See the 'Legacy' performance indicators in the *Global Reporting Initiative Event Organizers' Sector Supplement* and Chapter 12 (this volume) for more explanation.

It is also a requirement of this clause that maps back to your objectives and targets, namely that you have determined what will be done to meet the objectives and targets, what resources will be required, who is responsible, when it will be completed and how the results will be evaluated. This is all stated in *Clause 6.2* and has obvious synergies with the following:

- What will be done? (*6.1 Actions to address risks and opportunities*)
- What resources will be required? (*7.1 Resources*)
- Who will be responsible? (*5.3 Organizational roles, responsibilities and authorities*)
- When will it be completed? (*6.1 Actions to address risks and opportunities*)
- How will the results be evaluated? (*9 Performance evaluation*)

The auditor will look for evidence that the organisation has stated objectives, communicated them and worked towards actually achieving them. The event sustainability objectives could be outlined in the Sustainability Policy and this is one place where the auditor will look. Specific objectives could also be included in the departmental action plans.

The sustainability manager or similar should cross-check against performance of objectives at meetings with relevant departments and in the Greening Committee meetings, and an auditor will look for evidence that this has been done.

Objectives and their fulfilment should also be assessed in the management review, and in the analysis, interpretation and reporting of performance. An auditor will look for proof that this has also been undertaken.

The auditor will be looking to ensure that objectives, targets and performance indicators are relevant, that data collection is robust, and that analysis and interpretation of results is accurate and representative of the situation and performance outcomes.

The sustainability performance report for your event or organisation will state the performance outcomes against objectives and the auditor will be looking for

this to be in place. Look at the measurement and reporting section of relevant chapters for what objectives could be.

Resources

Clause 7.1 Resources requires that resources be allocated. For sustainability goals to be fully implemented into the organisation and the event planning cycle, top management must ensure that the time, budget, resources and skills are provided to enable this to be achieved.

Success may be inhibited if enough time is not allocated to do the required planning, research and sourcing, and if the team doesn't have the knowledge: they 'won't know what they don't know'.

If additional budget is required to procure or contact the most sustainable option this may need to be allocated. If logistical, material or other operational requirements are needed to see the initiatives to fruition, these must be supported and supplied.

- Staffing: Are there enough people to do it?
- Competency: Do they know what they are doing?
- Training: Staff training and onsite inductions?
- Infrastructure: Is the necessary equipment available?
- Technology: Apps, video conferencing, intranet?
- Finance: Budget allocated?

An auditor will be asking:

- Does everything look rushed?
- Do the team know what they are doing?
- Are there solutions available?

Competence

Clause 7.2 Competence requires the organisation to determine the competencies necessary for those people under their control doing work related to the event's sustainability performance.

The team members making purchasing, logistical and planning decisions must have the skills and knowledge to reach the most sustainable decision for the organisation and event, based on the policies and directives set down by the organisation.

With the right knowledge they will be able to successfully scrutinise the supply chain and proposals, ask the right questions and guide the event to the most sustainable outcome. If the team does not have these skills, staff training, ongoing professional development or contracting an external consultant are options.

If the competence isn't in place, then the clause asks for the organisation to take action to get that competence into the team. This may be training relevant event staff or the engagement of a consultant to lead the team forward. If you have a sustainability manager or coordinator on staff, conduct quarterly information sessions and in-house workshops with the rest of the team to complement any formal training.

The clause asks that a log of competency-building actions, such as training, be kept.

It is advised to encourage relevant persons to join the *Sustainable Event Alliance* and to network with peers through *Linked In Events Sustainability Practitioners*, so that those leading the charge in your team around event sustainability can keep up to date with the latest solutions and initiatives.

Awareness

Clause 7.3 Awareness requires anyone doing work under the organisation's control should actually be aware of the organisation's event sustainability policy. That makes sense.

It is also required that those doing work under the organisation's control actually know what their role is with regard to sustainability performance, how they can contribute and what effect that contribution will have on the final sustainability performance outcomes.

A good way of ensuring awareness is through inclusion in employment or engagement contracts, through inductions (into the office or the site), through all communications methods and through performance reviews.

If teams don't do what they were meant to do, the implications of this must be fully communicated – for example, if the waste team don't put the right bag of rubbish in the right skip, their action could cause the entire load of recycling to be rejected, and this needs to be communicated to them to drill home the importance of their part in an effective waste management process.

Auditors will be looking for proof that team members, contractors and service providers all know the part they have to play in the sustainability performance outcomes of the event or organisation. This may include clauses in employment/engagement contracts, action lists or other documentation that states their expected duties.

Auditor will also be looking for your communication of the consequences of not acting with staff. Auditors may also conduct interviews with staff to prove that there is in fact awareness of the various duties and expectations.

Communication

Clause 7.4 Communication requires that a *procedure* be in place for communications with external suppliers and interested parties. This procedure needs to include what it will communicate, when to undertake communication, with whom to communicate, and how to communicate.

Apart from this, the clause says you must liaise with various stakeholders to work out the best way to actually communicate with them over various subjects, considering the level of interest they have in these subjects. Sometimes meetings will work, or emails, maybe formal presentations, workshops, or through an information sheet or contract.

When communicating with stakeholders, this clause requires, where relevant, that your communication with them includes the following:

- your governing principles of sustainable development
- the purpose of the event
- how you will be managing sustainability to ensure improved performance
- what the issues are, along with your objectives and targets
- how they might be involved in meeting your objectives and targets
- relevance to them
- how you are doing performance-wise
- feedback from other stakeholders that is relevant.

The *SEMS Tool* contains a sample procedure you can follow.

The auditors will be looking for the existence of this procedure and evidence that it contains all the above points. They will also review whether it is adequate for the size and complexity of the organisation's event activities.

Documentation

Clause 7.5 Documentation requires that documentation be in place for relevant procedures, processes and outcomes as per the requirements of the standard.

Throughout the standard there are many mentions of the word 'shall'. Where this refers to a 'procedure' or to 'documentation', this *must* be addressed.

If you are using the *SEMS Tool* in the relevant question, there is mention in guidance or in the question itself, where a procedure or other documentation is required. Very helpful.

There must be clear delegation of roles, including communications channels, and responsibility for decision-making, operational control and task responsibility. This must be documented.

All processes relating to the management of issues in relation to the sustainability performance of the event/ organisation's event activities must be documented.

Documentation may include procedures for issues or interested parties' identification, or the identification of relevant legal or other requirements. Documentation of processes includes delegation of roles and respon-sibilities, action lists, processes and procedures for implementation of event activities and operations.

It is always assumed that procedures which are docu-mented are actually implemented, and that they are maintained and revised periodically.

Ensure you have processes in place which are docu-mented, especially for dealing with nonconformities at the event site during the event. It is essential that you have processes in place, and documented, to deal with potential high-risk (to sustainability outcomes) situations.

Ensure that all documentation is available to those who need it, through various and appropriate methods.

In addition, ensure that documents are:

*   protected from being lost or destroyed
*   appropriately titled

*   include dates or version number
*   mention who wrote them
*   include who is responsible for their implementation and signed if necessary
*   up to date
*   in relevant and accessible formats
*   are relevant to the situation.

Any documentation that has been created external to the organisation but deemed necessary for operational control (e.g. legal requirements, regulations for use of venues/sites, etc.) should likewise be disseminated and stored appropriately.

As mentioned in the list above – but which needs to be reiterated – is the importance of controls being in place to ensure that obsolete or old versions of docu-mentation are not accidentally used. Therefore electronic copies should be so named/filed and a log of who has the documentation kept so that updates can be distributed to all relevant parties.

Auditors will review all the 'shall' clauses within the standard and if any require documentation and you don't have it in place, you will receive a nonconformity note from the auditor. Other, more process-oriented docu-mentation that is particular to your situation will be more of a grey-area for the auditor. However, documentation is like honey to a bee for an auditor, so make sure you cross all your t's and dot all your i's.

See the summary of documentation required by *ISO 20121*, prepared by *GreenShoot Pacific*: www.greenshoot pacific.com/downloads.

Operational Control

Clause 8.1 Operational planning and control requires that processes are in place to manage issues and implement actions identified in *Clauses 4.1, 4.2* and *6.1*.

In order to effectively implement the organisation's policy, plans and procedures with regard to sustainable event management, the organisation must have 'processes' in place.

Clause 8.1 stipulates the processes to implement the actions you identified need to be taken in *Clause 6.1*.

This is standard operating procedure for any event; however, *ISO 20121* details this requirement in *Clause*

8.1, in case, as an event producer, you have forgotten that you will need to use some kind of planned process to do what is necessary.

Planning and documenting the processes is suggested, which would mean, for example, documenting the steps for the recycling programme. This makes perfect sense – see the requirement of documented processes as the 'action plan' for your sustainability initiatives.

Of course most events will have this material wrapped up in their very comprehensive (we hope) event management plan. Where the sustainability aspect is already included in the existing event management plan/s then refer to these. Don't try and rewrite processes if they already exist.

You may have some aspects where they are add-on or overlay to general event production practice and so would not form part of your normal event management plan; for example, the green stewards who interface with patrons for your front-of-house compostable waste collection initiative. In this case, follow the lead of all other process documentation that is in place for your event, and create a similar document that outlines the processes needed – in other words, the action plan for the green steward programme. Imagine if you left the organisation, and someone else needed to run the programme next year. This is the documentation that is required for 'Operational Control'.

It also applies if third parties deliver any processes. Following the same example, if you contracted a steward workforce supplier to arrange the stewarding programme they should provide you with process documentation on how they are going to manage the programme.

Moving a level up from processes and back up to procedures – the overarching 'instruction manual' on the steps to planning a process – you may also need to have procedures in place where you feel their absence will mean that the issue will not be managed appropriately without such a procedure being written down.

Processes that are likely to be included in general event planning which are innately part of sustainability, have some cross-over with, or need to be updated to include sustainability issues and considerations, include the following:

- traffic management
- energy management
- water management
- catering
- procurement
- biodiversity protection
- destination and venue choice
- accessibility
- security
- emergency procedures
- workplace health and safety
- inductions
- risk management
- waste management
- cleaning and sanitation
- communications.

It is suggested that you read *Clause 8.1* in full, as there are several other requirements detailed. (Make sure you read every clause in full.)

The auditor (generally this time it will be an event sustainability sector specialist who would be part of the audit team) will have to contextualise the event and the organisation's situation and determine whether you have adequately identified and managed issues that relate to your particular circumstances.

Modified Services

Clause 8.2 Dealing with modified services requires that issues, objectives, targets and plans are reviewed and amended where necessary, where new or modified activities, products or services, or changing operational circumstances are in place.

When a management system is set up, issues are identified, objectives set, plans put in place, and procedures and processes documented and implemented. However, if an organisation makes changes, some of these elements will need to be reviewed and modified as deemed necessary.

Changes could include the following:

- Ownership of the company and purpose or sustainable development principles are altered.
- The venue, destination or site for the event changes.
- The sponsor or funding source changes.
- The theme or content of the event changes.

- The choice of partner product providers, such as beverage sponsors, changes.
- There is a reduction or increase of budget, staffing or other resources.
- The availability of new solutions (e.g. a composting facility coming on line, a new organic range of produce available locally, or new service providers or caterers).
- Changes to external services, such as local transport solutions.

When a change occurs, you would simply detail these changes and show how plans, objectives, processes, procedures, etc., have been changed.

Supply Chain Management

Clause 8.3 Supply chain management requires that the sustainability intent of the organisation and supply chain requirements are included in tender or other documentation. It is also required that suppliers are informed of how they will be assessed with regard to sustainability requirements.

Ensure that the event tender documentation clearly outlines the organisation's commitment to sustainability and requests all respondents to outline their policies. Include these guidelines in tender documentation or additional information documentation.

Those that source products and services on behalf of the organisation must justify their sourcing choices based on considering the sustainability requirements in place by the organisation.

Those individuals or organisations involved in the production of the event, such as subcontractors, suppliers, stall holders, exhibitors and talent, should have sustainability involvement, compliance and performance expectations included in their contracts. Penalties or incentives may be included.

An auditor will be looking for a description of your sourcing process, a copy of your Sustainable Sourcing Policy and evidence of communication with the supply chain around sustainability requirements. This would include materials and supplies, infrastructure and equipment hire, along with service providers (e.g. catering, waste, energy). In addition, justification for sourcing which conflicts with principles must be offered.

Preparing a procurement checklist and process which enables those making sourcing decisions to measure up the sustainability credentials against the requirements of the organisation in their sustainability policy is a great start. More information on the supplier management process is given in Chapter 8.

SD Principles and Performance

Clause 9.1 Performance against governing principles of sustainable development requires you to have an approach mapped out on how you will actually track and review progress against your governing principles of sustainable development, and statement of purpose and values, with a desire to continuously improve.

This is high-level stuff and is looking at when you distil everything down, how your performance adds up to supporting your governing sustainable development principles.

In this approach, you would set out what the most important aspects are for consideration and describe key indicators of performance or milestones to be met, which will in turn be indicators of progress.

This is different from the performance outcomes such as measuring the amount of waste, etc. It is more holistic, with the report to match this clause's requirements being more storytelling than data crunching.

For example, in Table A3 of the standard, the *Maturity Matrix* approach is presented. This is where the stages of continual improvement towards meeting the principle against each of the sustainable development principles are mapped out in full. Against 'stakeholder identification and engagement' it lists three measures: minimal, improving and engaged.

Create a sliding scale of improvement, for each of the key aspects of your work, relating to the overarching pillars or foundation sustainable development principles.

Then write down a description or show graphically, or offer check boxes for ticking off on a scale. Table 11.1 shows an example.

In this approach you could set up a review of your performance against your governing principles of sustainable development.

Include the headings of the overarching principles and then underneath each, describe the issue, aspect or objective, and how you are working towards achieving it. Remember: you may be reviewing the success of your procedure's implementation, rather than the actual outcomes of the issue's management.

An auditor will look for your approach to assessing performance against your governing sustainable development principles and will want to see some structure and paperwork around this.

Performance Results

Clause 9.2 Monitoring, measurement, analysis and evaluation requires the following:

- the identification of what needs to be monitored and measured;
- the methods for monitoring, measurement, analysis and evaluation;
- when the monitoring and measuring shall be performed;
- when the results from monitoring and measurement shall be analysed and evaluated;
- that documentation of the results is kept;
- evaluation of the actual performance of the management system's effectiveness based on the performance results.

To understand the sustainability performance of an organisation's event activities or of a specific event, analysis must be undertaken and metric performance calculated.

In order to track improvement you must know from where you have begun – a 'baseline'. So establishing where you are now, identifying what actions you need to take, explaining how you put those actions in place, and what the results of those actions were, all make up part of your performance monitoring and sustainability performance report.

The *Global Reporting Initiatives Event Organizers' Sector Supplement* also includes metrics to measure against but goes far beyond the obvious environmentally based physical impacts such as waste, energy and GHGs.

Think about what you would want to report on, then back-track to work out how you are going to address the issues so that you can report on them at the end of the event.

The calculators in the *SEMS Tool* are mechanisms used to collect some of the physical impact data such as waste, water, energy, transport and related GHGs. You will also need a document that describes how you will go about the data collection and interpretation. In addition, the tools and methodologies you use must be sound, rigorous and accurate.

An auditor will be looking for evidence of a measurement system and data-collection process being in place.

Audit

Clause 9.3 Internal audit requires the organisation to conduct an internal audit to assess its conformity to the requirements of the standard. An internal audit allows you to ensure that your management system is complete, relevant, up to date, is effective, and is being implemented. Take the following steps:

- Review the documentation that is required to be in place, and ensure it is current and accessible. Use this opportunity to consider if any changes to your situation have occurred since the document was originally produced, and make modifications to encompass any new issues, objectives or plans.
- Check that awareness is in place by all those individuals and entities involved in implementing the system, procedures and processes.
- Check that the plans, procedures and processes are actually being implemented.
- Review the performance measurement process, its relevance, accuracy and level of robustness.

Where documentation, procedures or processes are a requirement of the standard and are not available, these will also be recorded as 'nonconformities' and corrective action will need to be taken to fix this.

Where there are deviations from procedures or policies observed, these will be also reported as 'nonconformities'. Corrective action will need to be taken to move back to the procedures and policies held by the organisation.

Table 11.1 Example of sustainable development principles assessment framework

Environmental stewardship

1 = 'minimum involvement'; 3 = 'improved commitment'; 5 = 'full engagement'.		1	2	3	4	5
Reduce energy demand	Energy demand reduction behaviour change campaign for energy users is in place. Although reductions have been achieved, it seems to be only moderate in the uptake by stakeholders.		X			
Increase renewable energy use	We have been unsuccessful in increasing renewable energy use as our generator suppliers are unwilling to switch fuels. More engagement is needed or more research into alternative suppliers needs to be undertaken.	X				
Reduce waste volume	Waste volume has reduced marginally.					

Inclusivity

1 = 'minimum involvement'; 3 = 'improved commitment'; 5 = 'full engagement'.		1	2	3	4	5
Stakeholder consultation	Our procedure for identifying stakeholders is set up to ensure their involvement in identifying issues and addressing their needs and expectations. This procedure has been embraced wholeheartedly by our event management team and the level of 'buy-in' by community groups and local governmental departments has dramatically increased from previous years. Evidence of this is the amount of 'in-kind' support the council now provides the event, and the drastic increase in volunteers sourced from local community groups.					X
Access for disadvantaged groups	We have identified that low-income and single-parent families have difficulty enjoying our event as there is a substantial ticket price and our family ticket is based on two adults. We have worked hard to create a programme whereby a new level of tickets is available for those on government benefits, or who are single parents. As these ticket packages are traceable, we have seen through this and through at-event observation that these groups are now enjoying the event more than ever before.	X				

Then continue on in this fashion.

Internal audits of a management system based on *ISO 20121* may be performed by those from within the organisation, or by external parties. In either case, those conducting the audit should be competent and in a position to do so impartially and objectively.

If you are a small organisation and still want to do a robust audit, choose someone that doesn't have any responsibility for the activity being audited – you can share the auditing role throughout your team, with each member taking on the auditing role for the various parts.

Funnily enough, when you go for an external audit, the auditor will look to ensure you have actually conducted an internal audit. Greenshoot Pacific have created an easy-to-use Internal Audit tool: internalaudit. greenshootpacific.com.

Management Review

Clause 9.4 Management review requires the planned dates or intervals of a management review to be recorded and that the outcomes of these reviews and evidence of these occurring are documented. For example, this may include placement of sustainability performance on the agenda at top management meetings and/or board meetings.

Top management must do more than give the go-ahead; they must also demonstrate engagement and commitment to sustainability, and conducting an effective management review is demonstration of this.

The management review of sustainability performance should include an assessment of the organisation's adherence to its governing principles of sustainable development and this can only be done at the highest level. Note cross-overs with *Clause 9.1*.

This should be reviewed by the heads of each department and by the uppermost management of the organisation. Where there is a board, an executive summary (or the full Sustainability Report) should be tabled at an appropriately timed board meeting. The board should minute its response and any directive to change either sustainable development principles or decisions made in adhering to them.

When undergoing a planning and management review (at whatever level of management), any occurrences of nonconformity to principles, objectives, policies and strategies must be addressed and corrective action taken to resolve it.

The inclusion of consideration for continual improvement and new goals, objectives and targets for performance at these reviews and the formal setting of new aims and documented evidence of the outcomes of the review are also steps to undertake.

An auditor will look for evidence that the management review has been scheduled and undertaken.

Nonconformities

Clause 10.1 Nonconformity and corrective action requires you to have a procedure in place that outlines the authority, schedule and process for identifying and correcting nonconformity to the standard. This includes the documentation required, the implementation of procedures and processes, and awareness of requirements.

The review of effectiveness and efficiency of the event sustainability management system includes the identification, review and planning for corrective action of nonconformities. When looking at operational control, this may occur in real time during the execution of the event. When looking at other event life cycle issues and aspects, identification of nonconformities and corrective action may occur during the planning of the event, or during the post-event performance evaluation, internal audit or management review.

Identification of nonconformities, of the existence of appropriate documentation and the implementation of procedures should be done through the internal audit process.

Identification of nonconformities of the requirements, including awareness by those doing work under the control of the organisation along with the effective implementation of the processes outlined in the management system, should be undertaken through ongoing monitoring of the management system.

Nonconformities should be documented, including who is responsible for correcting the nonconformity, who will review action taken, and timetables for both.

Corrective action should be taken by a designated person/department.

The key point to take away from this process is that, of course, learning has been achieved and new processes established for future activity control.

Improvement

Clause 10.2 Improvement requires that continual improvement is embedded in the management system implementation, review and ongoing action.

This is straightforward in that the document review/management review/internal audit would evaluate the effectiveness, currency and awareness of the existing management system.

Nonconformity correction plans, or plans for dealing with modified services, would be evidence of continual improvement.

Likewise, improvement in performance results, increasing objectives and targets, and expanding the scope may all be viewed as continual improvement.

In addition, more effective communications and

engagement, improved competency in the team in sustainability, and more sustainable sourcing may also be viewed as continual improvement.

It should be noted that this is where an auditor's (most likely a sector specialist) opinion may come into play. It is acceptable for all issues not to be identified, all operational control not to be put in place, all measurement not to be done, for communications not to be complete or effective if there are plans to improve this in the future.

ISO 20121 CONFORMITY CLAIMS

So how to achieve conformity with the standard – can you become 'certified'?

Conformity with *ISO 20121* means your organisation or event has met the requirements of the standard in implementing an event sustainability management system. You can achieve conformity in one of three ways: first- , second- or third-party assessments.

First Party

This is where an organisation assesses its own system and makes a self-declaration of conformity with the requirements of the standard. In first-party conformity assessment someone from within your organisation will review the event sustainability management system in place, effectively conducting an internal audit.

For self-assessment claims to be credible, the organisation should ensure that these claims are supported by the existence of a robust, internally transparent and well-documented system.

Consider how you will 'prove' your conformity if your claims are questioned by internal or external stakeholders.

The *SEMS Tool* is the perfect way to identify, manage, document and report performance – it is a one-stop shop for management system implementation. By using the *SEMS Tool* you can be confident that your conformity claims are valid and viewed as authentic.

Who is First Party For?

First-party conformity assessment is suitable for small or simple events and event organisers, who wish only to self-declare their sustainability performance and outcomes. In addition, those events just beginning their sustainability journey and creating a management system for the first time will begin with an internal audit and self-declaration before putting themselves forward for external audit.

Steps to First-Party Certification

The following are steps in undergoing a first-party conformity assessment to *ISO 20121* using the *SEMS Tool*:

1 Buy a copy of the standard.
2 Read the standard and the annex guidance.
3 Define the scope of your management system.
4 Frame your system against a sample event activity.
5 Purchase the SEMS Tool.
6 Implement the management system.
7 Map conformity against the standard's requirements.
8 Make conformity claims.

Who Conducts the Audit?

The person who takes on the first-party/internal audit role must understand the requirements of *ISO 20121*. They should also have adequate experience and competency to be able to identify and understand event sustainability issues so that they can interpret the implementation of the management system considering the context of the organisation, external and internal issues, all framed against the organisation's sustainable development principles.

Conformity Claims

When assessing conformity to the requirements of *ISO 20121*, your organisation will most likely wish to make public claims of conformity.

It is not permitted for you to use the ISO logo, so don't go online and copy the ISO logo and place it on any communications material.

Events should use the following claim for events conforming to the standards:

> XYZ Event has been self-assessed to be planned and managed to conform to the requirements

of the international standard ISO 20121: Event Sustainability Management Systems.

For the supply chain, namely those who conduct physical operations at events, such as caterers or waste or cleaning companies, conformity can also be achieved; your scope would be simply narrowed down to the activities over which you have control.

For an event organising company that produces many events throughout the year, it is appropriate to have conformity by the organisation, rather than each event. The audit must be framed against a typical sample event. If you produce more than one type of event, you will need to assess your management system across each event type. Use the following claim for organisations and supply chain:

XYZ Organisation is self-assessed to plan and manage its event activities to conform to the requirements of the international standard ISO 20121: Event Sustainability Management Systems.

Second Party

In a second-party conformity assessment an individual or organisation external to but in some way related to your organisation or event reviews your conformity with the requirements of the standard.

It is expected that this will be the most popular form of conformity assessment. Data integrity, transparency and consistency are central to implementing an effective management system.

A *SEMS Audit* and second-party conformity assessment to the requirements of *ISO 20121* gives validation to your sustainability claims. Once you have completed the tool, uploaded the appropriate evidence and filled in the calculators, you should apply to *SEMS* for auditing, and receive a customised quote. A *SEMS Audit* 'credit' is then applied to your dashboard and you simply click the 'submit for audit' button to begin.

Who is Second Party For?

Second-party conformity assessment is suitable for events and event organisers of all sizes and types who wish to have an independent assessment of their sustainability claims and performance. Reputable second-party conformity schemes allow you to be audited by industry experts in event sustainability trained in implementing and auditing *ISO 20121*.

Steps to Second-Party Certification

The following are steps to undergoing a second-party conformity assessment using the *SEMS Tool*:

1 Buy a copy of the standard.
2 Read the standard and the annex guidance.
3 Define the scope of your management system.
4 Frame your system against a sample event activity.
5 Purchase the *SEMS Tool*.
6 Use the *SEMS Tool* to assist in implementing your management system.
7 Upload all evidence.
8 Conduct an internal audit/self-assessment.
9 Request a quote for second-party assessment.
10 Submit for audit.
11 A desktop audit is conducted, and a live audit is conducted if necessary.
12 Conformity assessment confirmed and communications material provided.
13 Promote your achievement.

A qualified SEMS auditor will be assigned to your assessment. The auditor will systematically review your submissions and supporting evidence and documentation for conformity with the requirements of *ISO 20121*.

Once the auditor is satisfied that the SEMS score correctly reflects the status of the event, and that all the requirements for conformity to *ISO 20121* are in place, they will confirm the SEMS result and recommend conformity assessment be awarded.

Who Conducts the Audit?

Second-party auditors should have successfully completed competency assessments in event sustainability subject knowledge, management system implementation and audit process.

It is recommended that they are *Sustainable Event Alliance Accredited Professionals* with experience in implementing *ISO 20121*, and have been trained in audit processes and the requirements of the standard.

Conformity Claims

Post-event or post-assessment the following wording may be used for events:

> XYZ Event is planned and managed using a Sustainable Event Management System and is independently assessed to conform to the requirements of ISO 20121: Event Sustainability Management Systems.

For event organisers and supply chain organisations:

> XYZ Organisation plans and manages our event activities using a Sustainable Event Management System and is independently assessed to conform to the requirements of ISO 20121: Event Sustainability Management Systems.

Third Party

In a third-party conformity assessment a Certifying Body (CB) undertakes the audit. CBs are usually accredited by their nation's accreditation authority. This means that 'accredited' third-party audits can be undertaken. At the time of writing, there was no 'accredited' scheme for certifying bodies for *ISO 20121* and thus only 'unaccredited' certification is currently available.

You will see that I have introduced the word 'certification' rather than conformity assessment. 'Certification' only applies to third-party audits, and in a true sense should only be applied to *accredited* third-party audits.

So beware of any schemes offering *ISO 20121* 'certification' if they are not (1) official third-party CBs; and (2) there is actually an accredited third-party assessment scheme in place approved by the nation's accreditation authority or the *International Accreditation Forum* (www.iaf.nu).

The *SEMS Tool* may be used to put your management system in place and be ready for third-party auditing,

Using the SEMS Tool streamlines the conformity assessment process. All evidence is held within the tool, ensuring that steps to third-party conformity assessment are as simple as possible.

The auditor will use the built-in audit function of the tool to review the evidence and map it back to the requirements of the standard. Third-party conformity assessment requires this documentation review, interviews with key staff and stakeholders, and an observation audit at a live event.

Who is Third Party For?

Third-party conformity assessment is suitable for large events, event organisers, venues, and those with major public stakeholders or major public funding.

Third-party audits are the most expensive, as there are a minimum number of 'audit days' prescribed by the accredited scheme, and CBs charge higher fees than second-party assessors. It is anticipated that third-party audits will be taken up by very large or very high-profile events.

Steps to Third-Party Certification

The following are the steps required in undergoing a third-party conformity assessment to *ISO 20121* using the SEMS Tool:

1   Buy a copy of the standard.
2   Read the standard and the annex guidance.
3   Define the scope of your management system.
4   Establish your management system.
5   Purchase and use the *SEMS Tool* to assist in implementing your management system.
6   Upload all evidence.
7   Conduct an internal audit/self-assessment.
8   Request a quote for a third-party audit.
9   Submit for external audit.
10 A desktop documentation audit is conducted.
11 A live audit is conducted, including interviews and event activity observation.
12 Conformity assessment is confirmed, certification awarded and communications material provided.
13 Promote your achievement.

Who Conducts the Audit?

The audit will be conducted by an audit team, which in most cases would include an accredited ISO auditor from a certifying body supplemented by an event sustainability specialist. This way, you can be assured that your audit team has the breadth of sector experience and auditing rigour required for a robust and comprehensive audit.

Auditor Competency

As sustainability is pushed to the top of the agenda for the event industry, coupled with the launch of standards and certifications, more events will be applying for the auditing of their management systems and/or performance.

The trick to a great audit, that offers value to your organisation, and certainly that is worth the money you will spend on it, is the quality of the audit team.

It is up to us as an industry to demand that certifying bodies provide an audit team with the appropriate competencies and sector-relevant experience.

The successful uptake and effective implementation of this standard and others may be influenced by the quality of audits or auditors. While the standard was not produced just for auditing, but primarily for implementation and improved performance, its recognised organisations will want to have their implementation of the standard independently assessed for conformity with the requirements of the standard.

If the certifying body does not have auditors employed or contracted who have experience in full-breadth sustainability, especially as is relates to the event sector, then they should engage sector specialists. These sector specialists should have independent recognition of their competency, for example, through the *Sustainable Event Alliance Accredited Professionals* programme or other industry led programmes as they develop. The auditor team should comprise an individual, or group of individuals who collectively have experience in implementing *ISO 20121*, and who have been trained in audit process and the requirements of the standard.

All members of the audit team should have successfully completed competency assessments in event sustainability subject knowledge, management system implementation and the audit process.

Suggested competencies in the audit team to be able to adequately assess your treatment of sustainability issues and implementation of your management system include the following:

- Event experience.
- Event sustainability experience.
- Best practice implementation.
- Sustainable development knowledge.
- Legal and regulations knowledge.
- Practical and academic experience.
- Management system implementation.
- Audit process understanding.
- Industry recognition of expertise.

See Chapter 1 for details on specific sector competencies that both those auditing, as well as those planning, managing and implementing the sustainability aspects of your organisation, should hold.

QUESTIONS

1   Choose three of the existing awards or certification programmes described in this chapter and search for an event or organisation that has successfully achieved certification. Review the details of this event's conformity or sustainability attributes which lead to it being awarded or certified.

ISO 20121: Event Sustainability Management Systems

• Obtain a copy of the standard and answer the questions below.

Clause 4.1 Understanding of the Organisation and its Context

• Explain internal and external factors which may affect the organisation achieving its event sustainability objectives. List one positive and one negative aspect.

Clause 4.2 Interested Parties

• Provide an example of text that could be included in a procedure for Clause 4.2.
• Give an example of a technique to communicate event sustainability policy, processes or responsibilities, with:

   • staff
   • traders
   • venue/site
   • attendees

How could an organisation plan and document the identification and engagement of interested parties?

Clause 4.3 Scope

What could be included in the scope of a management system for:

• an event organising company (e.g. PCO);

• a multi-day arts festival run by a not-for-profit committee, held across multiple venues in a city;
• a conference run by a multinational company for its employees?

Clause 5.1 Leadership and Commitment

• How can top management demonstrate commitment to the event sustainability management system?

Clause 5.3 Organizational roles, responsibilities and authorities

• Describe the relevant types of roles and associated sustainability tasks in the event types with which you are involved. Ensure you match this to the requirements of this clause.

Clause 6.1 Actions to Address Risks and Opportunities

• What tools may be used for identification planning actions to manage risks and opportunities (issues)?
• What documentation is required under this clause?

Clause 6.1.3 Legal and other Requirements

• Name the applicable acts, laws, regulations, or voluntary codes which may be applicable for events held in the region in which you are located.

Clause 6.2 Event Sustainability Objectives and How to Achieve Them

• What ten *GRI EOSS* performance indicators would you see as most relevant for the region or sector of the event industry that you primarily work in and plan to audit?

Clause 7.1 Resources

• Give examples of the types of resources which could be provided to fulfil this clause, in your chosen event sector.

Clause 7.2 Competency

- What competencies are required by those undertaking work related to the event sustainability management system? Are there existing industry associations which state competencies?
- What documentation could be in place to log the competencies required and/or the competencies in place by those doing work under the organisation's control?

Clause 7.3 Awareness

- Who needs to be aware of the organisation's sustainability policy and their principles of sustainable development?
- How could this be communicated?

Clause 7.4 Communication

- Explain what may be included in the procedure required by this clause.

Clause 7.5 Documentation

- List the documentation that is *required* by this standard.

Clause 8.1 Operational Planning and Control

- Given your chosen event sector, what type of processes would need to be in place?
- What type of documentation would be suitable for these processes? Give examples.

Clause 8.3 Supply Chain Management

- What steps does an organisation need to take to ensure appropriate supply chain management regarding sustainability?
- What documentation could flow between organisation and supplier?

Clause 9.1 Performance against Governing Principles of Sustainable Development

- How could an organisation evaluate its performance against governing principles of sustainable development?
- How could the organisation's approach to this review be formally documented?

Clause 9.2 Monitoring, Measurement, Analysis and Evaluation

- Given the event sector you usually work in or plan to work in, what should be monitored and measured?
- Choose one aspect and describe the methods used for monitoring, measuring, analysis and evaluation of the aspect.

Clause 9.3 Internal Audit

- What should be included in an internal audit plan? How could this be documented?
- Who should conduct the internal audit?

Clause 9.4 Management Review

- What should be included in a management review?

Clause 10.1 Nonconformity and Corrective Action

- Give examples of potential nonconformities.
- Describe the difference between the nonconformity of a standard's requirements and the nonconformity of the implementation of a requirement.

Clause 10.2 Continual Improvement

- Give examples of continual improvement across several clauses of this standard.

12

LEGACY

An important aspect of event sustainability performance is its enduring legacies, such as demonstrating sustainability-in-action, encouraging changing behaviours, and leaving new skills and resources with the host community.

Legacy and leadership may be seen as another aspect of an event's sustainability performance – taking a leading role in change-making to enhance sustainable development and leave lasting legacies through the decisions made and actions taken by the event.

As the event industry reaches so many people globally, our activities are an important touch-point between the principles of sustainable development, the way we demonstrate it in action at our events, and the lasting impressions we have on our attendees and other stakeholders. We have both a responsibility and an opportunity to influence changes in opinions and behaviours through interaction with the event.

Therefore, the enduring positive legacy an event has at a local, national or even global level is an important aspect of sustainability performance for organisers to consider. These legacies can be intangible or 'soft', such as knowledge transfer or changing behaviours, or tangible or 'hard', such as infrastructure, resources and technolo-

gies. Legacies can be immediate, and able to be seen, experienced and measured during the project's life cycle, or anticipated future legacies or of a more indirect nature.

A soft or hard event legacy is anything that has a lasting physical, social, environmental or economic impact which endures. Positive legacies may be the result of initiatives purposefully planned and carried out by the event organiser to achieve a certain legacy outcome, or be the consequences of the day-to-day actions of the organiser. Legacy outcomes may also be the result of initiatives created by external parties, such as local government or industry associations.

Events of all sizes can leave a lasting legacy, which may include the following:

- Individual, organisational and cultural change in attitudes and behaviours
- Improved or additional physical infrastructure
- New approaches to planning and convening events

- Creating demand for new jobs, skills and business opportunities
- Positive direct and indirect economic benefits to the region
- Immediate environmental benefits, such as rehabilitation
- Indirect environmental benefits, such as sustainable sourcing's long-term impacts.

Mega-events are those that own the space in terms of great legacy opportunities. They are at high risk of leaving huge negative legacies in terms of investment in infrastructure that is mothballed soon after the end of the event.

Cities that have geared up for mega-sports events invest huge sums of money in new infrastructure, some which lie dormant or fall into disrepair.

The 1994 *Lillehammer Winter Olympic Games* in Norway were the first Games to explicitly include environmental impacts in their planning, and to embrace the newly crafted principles of sustainable development and contribution the Games could make, thus touching on lasting potential positive legacies.

It was the *Sydney Olympics* in 2000 that fully embraced environmental considerations across all planning aspects and which had an eye on future lasting legacies – both in knowledge transfer on how to achieve such environmental performance and in physical enduring assets. It took an area of land in central Sydney that was not being used to its full potential and rehabilitate it while simultaneously creating a much-needed mega-event space in the city. While the facility may not be used to its fullest potential at all times, it is still, nearly 15 years later, a well-utilised and useful precinct for events, from concerts to major sporting fixtures.

It was the Olympic movement that first started to formalise the concept of 'legacy', and at a symposium in 2002 on the legacy of the Olympic Games, they created a loose definition:

> [T]he effects of the legacy have many aspects and dimensions, ranging from the more commonly recognized aspects – architecture, urban planning, city marketing, sports infrastructures, economic and tourist development – to others that are just as, if not more important, but that are less recognised. In particular, it is necessary to point out the importance of so called intangible legacies, such as production of ideas and cultural values, intercultural and non-exclusionary experiences (based on gender, ethnicity or physical abilities), popular memory, education, archives, collective effort and voluntarism, new sport practitioners, notoriety on a global scale, experience and know-how, etc. These intangible legacies also act as a motor for the tangible ones to develop a long-term legacy.[1]

London 2012 Olympics took things to a whole new level with their legacy intent. They struck out on the front foot with legacy being an end-game as much as the Games themselves. The revitalisation of an area of East London as Olympic Park lay at the heart of the physical legacy planning (www.londonlegacy.co.uk).

What was particularly useful to the industry, and something previously only passed from one Olympic host city to the next, was the *London Learning Legacy* project. This gathered up all the information on ambitions, experiences and lessons learned, and is neatly and candidly packed on the *London Learning Legacy* website. There is a wealth of information in terms of sustainability learning from strategic focus, right down to aspects such as material choice to replace PVC in signage and overlay (learninglegacy.independent.gov.uk).

Of course the majority of events are not of the size or scale of the Olympic Games, but positive legacy outcomes can result from any type of event. Positive legacy outcomes can be a happy by-product of all your good work, or they can be designed in and intentful.

LEGACY PLANNING

Actively planning-in the desired positive physical, environmental, social and economic legacy outcomes begins at the design stage of the event life cycle; and so we circle back to the start of this book, and the concept of beginning with the end in sight. You have formalised your organisation's principles, purposes and values, and identified how your event/s can make a positive contribution to sustainable development. You have undergone an issues identification process, and understood the needs and expectations of your stakeholders from community and government, through to supply chain and attendees. The context in which your organisation and event operates has been clearly defined, and you understand the nuances of the host destination, and identified relevant best or expected practice in the production of your event and the management of its impacts and outcomes.

All of this work will set you up for being able to clearly identify where the lasting legacy opportunities lie and how you can design-in policies, objectives and initiatives to enable these to come to fruition.

The list of potential positive hard and soft legacies is endless, and is as long and as deep as are the sustainable development topics, needs of the community, state of the supply chain, or resources and capabilities of your organisation, staff and crew.

KNOWLEDGE TRANSFER

Events are an amazing platform to express ideas, have new experiences and leave lasting impressions. In fact, in many cases this is exactly what the event is designed to do. No matter the event's purpose, subject matter or planned activities, all have the opportunity to transfer knowledge about sustainability and to expand ideas and experiences, which will lead to a positive contribution to sustainable development.

Through the implementation of policies, objectives, initiatives and campaigns an event can leave a lasting impact of inspiration, new knowledge and changed behaviours on those involved with the production of the event (e.g. staff, crew, contractors, traders, supply chain, venues, local government, sponsors and performers). The lasting legacy is for this new learning to be taken forward to the next events with which these participants are involved.

Initiatives to raise awareness of sustainability among event participants may include the following:

- site inductions and briefings
- pre-event information sessions with major suppliers, contractors and venues
- inclusion of sustainability information in staff/crew handbooks

- development of an online resource and informational intranet portal
- creation of guidelines, action plans and checklists
- branded awareness-raising campaigns around specific sustainability issues
- hosting of webinars, workshops and conferences around sustainable production practices
- production of performance reports, including lessons learned.

Included in the knowledge transfer concept is not just initiatives to raise awareness about sustainability and sustainable development or behaviour-changing initiatives getting those involved in producing the event to change their ways or inspiring attendees to do things differently in their homes, workplaces and communities. Legacy outcomes may also be the sharing of new ways of producing events, best practices and lessons learned across the full length and breadth of event production, from safety and security, to sourcing, waste management and even performance reporting. Consider how you will leave a legacy of new knowledge to your industry sector or those who will produce the event the next time (new staff or a new organising committee).

BEHAVIOUR CHANGE

The following pages give some examples of plug-and-play legacies which many events could include in planning to lead to positive enduring legacies with attendees, event staff, supply chain and venues.

Sustainable Food

Use your event to showcase and promote the consumption of local, seasonal, chemical-free, sustainably harvested, organic and/or Fairtrade food. Serve it, sell it, promote it. Partner with local farmers' markets, farm-to-plate programmes, food cooperatives, or other local and sustainable food sourcing programmes.

The legacy:

✓ Attendees are inspired to source local, seasonal, sustainable food in their everyday lives.

✓ Farmers' markets or farm gate vegetable 'box' programmes are supported.

✓ Local sustainable produce is promoted and supported.

✓ Venues, hotels and temporary caterers commit to sustainable food sourcing.

✓ Sustainable food sourcing is included in future event policies.

✓ Sustainable products, cafés and caterers receive more business due to increased awareness.

Waste

Use your event to demonstrate how it is possible to reduce waste creation to minimal levels by planning-in waste avoidance. Promote per person waste figures for the event to showcase to attendees how they are getting on. Demonstrate diversion from landfill and incineration by having at-event waste segregation that includes attendee participation. Partner with *Zero Waste* (www.zwia.org) or other waste campaigns locally, such as recycling, composting, salvage and reuse programmes or organisations. Provide them with a space at your event, or include them in your event waste activities. Use the event to demonstrate excellence in recycling, composting and salvage, and inspire event attendees to do the same in their everyday lives.

The legacy:

✓ Inspire your event attendees to consider the choices they make which create avoidable waste.

✓ Inspire attendees to look at ways they can prevent waste from being created at work and at home.

✓ Increased participation in waste campaigns at home and at work by event participants.

✓ Support local waste initiatives, and give strength to their messaging and campaigns.

✓ Influence venues, contractors and vendors to adopt more effective waste reduction and diversion practices.

✓ Improve knowledge of event production staff on effective waste reduction techniques.

✓ Establish best practice processes for future event organisers to adopt.

✓ Educate event staff on best practice for at-event waste reduction and segregation.

✓ Establish best practice guidance on event waste reduction and segregation for the venue/site/destination.

Energy

Use your event to demonstrate how being energy efficient in planning, use and equipment choice is possible. Show power-free options. Use LED lighting. Use natural light. Implement power-down policies. Partner with energy conservation education programmes or with energy-efficient product companies. Offer an outlet at your event to promote energy-saving programmes and products. Use your event to promote alternatives to reliance on fossil-fuelled energy supply. Use solar power, biofuelled generators, wind, pedal, kinetic, hydrogen fuel-cell, micro-hydro or mains/grid renewable energy. Partner with renewable energy mains/grid suppliers to promote their renewable energy products. Offer a forum for renewable energy innovations and technologies to be showcased at your event.

The legacy:

✓ Inspire attendees to look at their energy consumption habits. Get attendees thinking about turning the lights off and opening their curtains and blinds in offices and homes during the day, and instigating their own power-down policies.

✓ Inspire event attendees to switch to renewable energy tariff/supply at home and at work, and to offer their support to programmes and innovations through their voting and political choices.

✓ Inspire venues and vendors to adopt energy conservation practices.

✓ Encourage venues to permanently switch to renewable energy tariffs and/or offer renewable energy tariffs to event organisers.

✓ Improve event production staff and power users' understanding of how to conserve energy and achieve efficiencies.

✓ Enhance viability of the market for renewable energy suppliers to the event industry.

✓ Increase knowledge within the venue and event industry of energy impacts and renewable energy options.

✓ Establish renewable energy targets or policies for the venue or future events.

Mass Transit/Walk/Cycle

Use your event to encourage the uptake of sustainable transport options. Incentivise event attendees to get out of cars and taxis, and onto public transport, bikes or walking. Partner with local transport initiatives and offer a platform at your event for these programmes to promote themselves. Inspire attendees to choose sustainable transport options in their everyday lives.

The legacy:

✓ Increased use of public transport in a city.
✓ Support for the implementation of cycle ways or more bike parking.
✓ Support for the local car-share programme.
✓ Increased use of cycle rickshaws or bike hire in tourist areas.
✓ Inspire local government and venues to work together to ensure enhanced urban connectivity using sustainable transport options.
✓ Enhance understanding of the importance of sustainable transport options by event staff and future event organisers.
✓ Establish sustainable transport policies and objectives for future events, or for the venue or destination.

Offset Air Travel GHGs

If your event requires participants to travel by air to attend, create an option for them to offset GHG emissions. Consider bundling it with ticket purchase. Offset event production air travel (talent, speakers, crew), or 'go halves' with talent at a minimum. Choose offsetting projects to channel your funds to and promote the benefits of the project outcomes to event participants.

The legacy:

✓ Have event participants take responsibility for their air travel choices and GHG impacts by continuing to offset all their air travel.
✓ Positive social and environmental benefits achieved through funding for offset projects.

✓ Enhanced understanding of GHGs and air travel impacts, by event producers and the event industry.
✓ Enhanced understanding of the offsetting market so that informed choices are made in the future around offsetting projects and initiatives.

Water

Practise responsible water habits and ensure conservative water use and protection of waterways. Partner with water-wise programmes and campaigns to promote water conservation and waterways protection. Offer the event as a platform for promotion of their messages. Inspire attendees to consider their own water-use habits and for them to be water-wise in their everyday lives.

The legacy:

✓ Inspire attendees to use water-saving devices at home and at work.
✓ Encourage attendees to sign up to local water conservation programmes at home and at work.
✓ Improve understanding by attendees of how grey water systems or water-wise gardening can help with water conservation.
✓ Increase knowledge by event staff and future event organisers on water consumption impacts and water conservation techniques.
✓ Set policies and objectives for water conservation for future events.

Go Bottled Water-free

Reduce resource consumption, energy, waste and water impacts through providing water refill stations or glasses and jugs of water, rather than selling or providing packaged bottled water. Partner with 'take back the tap'-style campaigns or create your own. Inspire event attendees to always use refillable water bottles rather than buying packaged water.

The legacy:

✓ Your example could be what is needed to turn an entire venue, or even town, to significant reductions in bottled water use and resulting waste.
✓ Encouraging ongoing use of refillable water bottles.

✓ Reduced disposable water bottle waste.

✓ Inspire event staff and future event producers to include this important aspect in future event production.

Buy Sustainable Stuff

Scrutinise all your procurement and choose the most sustainable options. Choose eco-labelled, non-toxic, fair labour, fair trade, local, sustainably manufactured, cruelty-free, sustainable materials, low carbon footprint, and low water footprint products. Partner with sustainable products both to use for the event as well as offering exposure at your event to attendees. Partner only with sponsors and funding partners which enhance and support the event's sustainability performance. Support the local economy by preferentially purchasing locally. Create a procurement framework that ensures those making purchasing decisions for your event are actively seeking local solutions, and potentially work with the supply chain to enable them to service your event. Depending on the size and duration of your event, you may work with local business incubation organisations to help create supply chain solutions within the local economy. These suppliers should have the ability to endure as going concerns once your event is over.

The legacy:

✓ Through your great procurement choices, expose attendees to these products and relevant options for their everyday lives.

✓ Support viability of markets for these items, including local markets.

✓ Educate venues and the event industry on suitable sustainably sourced options for future use, including 'must-takes' such as products and items produced or manufactured locally.

✓ Encourage the establishment of policies and objectives for future sustainable sourcing at events and venues.

✓ Improve knowledge on sustainable sourcing issues by event production staff for consideration at future events.

Support Campaigns

Offer your event as a vehicle to promote relevant and aligned sustainable development campaigns, initiatives, organisations or programmes. Seek those local to the event destination or aligned with your event's content or attendees. Partner with charities, local campaigns or other organisations, and offer exposure for their messages as well as enhancing your reputation.

The legacy:

✓ Inspire participation in campaigns and organisations by event attendees.

✓ Improve the success of these programmes through offering a platform at your event.

REPORTING LEGACY

An event's positive legacy is an important aspect to include in sustainability performance reporting.

The *Global Reporting Initiative* (GRI) has developed guidance on reporting event sustainability performance, including 'Legacy', in the *Event Organizers' Sector Supplement*. This new aspect of legacy was added with three new indicators, categorised into 'soft' and 'hard' legacies.

Aspect: Legacy

EO11: NUMBER, TYPE AND IMPACT OF SUSTAINABILITY INITIATIVES DESIGNED TO RAISE AWARENESS, SHARE KNOWLEDGE AND IMPACT ON BEHAVIOUR CHANGE AND RESULTS ACHIEVED.

Reporting to this indicator requires placing metrics around the 'number, type and impact' of awareness-raising, behaviour-changing and knowledge-sharing initiatives. List the actual sustainability initiatives by both your organisation and related third parties to raise awareness, share knowledge and encourage changed behaviours. Report on the changed behaviour evidenced during the life cycle of the event. This may include things such as number of stakeholders that have actively involved themselves successfully in voluntary initiatives (e.g. energy consumption reductions, sustainable sourcing, changed operational practices, etc.), or number of staff members trained or inducted into sustainability policies and processes. In addition, report on any initiatives instigated by stakeholders as a result of their experience with your sustainability initiatives and any resulting changed behaviours that will endure; for example, the creation of new policies within venues, use of new equipment or operational processes by contractors, or instigation of new event sustainability requirements or resources by local government.

You could view the legacy outcomes described above as 'back of house'. This indicator also looks at awareness-raising, behaviour-changing and knowledge-sharing initiatives directed at 'front of house' – those not involved in the production of the event, but rather with the event attendee base, the wider community or the host destination.

EO12: NATURE AND EXTENT OF KNOWLEDGE TRANSFER OF BEST PRACTICE AND LESSONS LEARNED.

This indicator is specifically looking at how an event transfers knowledge of best practice and lessons learned to future events teams and the event industry generally. While the previous indicator is about initiatives created to raise awareness about sustainability and effect change, this indicator is about transferring knowledge on event production, not exclusively sustainability knowledge, to the industry and to future producers of the event. This is particularly relevant for events that are rotated through different countries or regions, such as world congresses and sporting events with large geographical coverage. This indicator is looking for evidence that the lessons learned and best practice examples are collated and available publicly for all stakeholders who would wish to access them. While this should be a given for events held by or in the public interest, it does not omit commercially operated events from also benevolently sharing their best practices and lessons learned on production aspects, including security and safety practices, inclusivity and accessibility, sourcing and staff competency development.

When reporting to this indicator, identify the knowledge items that are collated and available for stakeholders' access. Identify the format in which the information is available and the ways in which its existence has been promoted. If known, report also on the impacts of this information being shared; for example, other organisations, host cities, or event producers taking on the information provided to inform their event production practices.

EO13: NUMBER, TYPE AND IMPACT OF PHYSICAL AND TECHNOLOGICAL LEGACIES.

This indicator is more straightforward than the previous two, as physical and technological legacies are easily identifiable, and most likely have been designed-in at the outset with legacy outcomes in mind. When reporting to this indicator list the physical legacies such as buildings, infrastructure or transport systems that have been constructed for the event and that will be continued to be used in legacy after the event. Tied in with physical legacies are technological legacies, and this can be the information systems and security systems, or technological assets such as sound and lighting equipment. Some technological advancements or systems may have been innovated at an event; for example, a new way to manage crowds or security monitoring. The innovation of these practices may have been in coordination with a supplier and the plan is to bring these new systems to scale for implementation at future events. These technological and systems legacies should also be reported under this indicator.

Physical assets of a slightly less 'physical' nature could be new organisations or operating entities such as those organisations that take over custody of the physical assets left in legacy. These should also be reported on. An example of this is the *London Legacy Development Corporation* established to transition the Olympic site into future use by the city.

Anticipated indirect benefits as a result of the physical and technological legacies should also be reported. This may include increased tourism and accompanying economic benefits, attraction of more events to a destination as a result of the new assets, establishment of new businesses or innovation hubs as a result of the new technologies, increased job opportunities as a consequence of revitalisation efforts, or availability of new resources at reduced costs.

In addition to the three new indicators under the aspect of 'legacy', the following GRI indicators are part of other aspects of the GRI reporting framework, but cross over with legacy. See the *GRI Event Organizers' Sector Supplement* for more details on these indicators, or further explanation in the relevant chapters of this book.

Aspect: Economic

EO1: DIRECT ECONOMIC IMPACTS AND VALUE CREATION AS A RESULT OF SUSTAINABILITY INITIATIVES.

EC1: DIRECT ECONOMIC VALUE GENERATED AND DISTRIBUTED, INCLUDING REVENUES, OPERATING COSTS, EMPLOYEE COMPENSATION, DONATIONS AND OTHER COMMUNITY INVESTMENTS, RETAINED EARNINGS, AND PAYMENTS TO CAPITAL PROVIDERS AND GOVERNMENTS.

EC8: DEVELOPMENT AND IMPACT OF INFRASTRUCTURE INVESTMENTS AND SERVICES PROVIDED PRIMARILY FOR PUBLIC BENEFIT THROUGH COMMERCIAL, IN-KIND OR PRO BONO ENGAGEMENT.

EC9: UNDERSTANDING AND DESCRIBING SIGNIFICANT INDIRECT ECONOMIC IMPACTS, INCLUDING THE EXTENT OF IMPACTS.

Aspect: Environment

EN26: INITIATIVES TO MITIGATE ENVIRONMENTAL IMPACTS OF EVENTS, PRODUCTS AND SERVICES, AND EXTENT OF IMPACT MITIGATION.

EN30: TOTAL ENVIRONMENTAL PROTECTION EXPENDITURES AND INVESTMENTS BY TYPE.

EO3: SIGNIFICANT ENVIRONMENTAL AND SOCIO-ECONOMIC IMPACTS OF TRANSPORTING ATTENDEES AND PARTICIPANTS TO AND FROM THE EVENT, AND INITIATIVES TAKEN TO ADDRESS THE IMPACTS.

Aspect: Society

SO1: PERCENTAGE OF OPERATIONS WITH IMPLEMENTED LOCAL COMMUNITY ENGAGEMENT, IMPACT ASSESSMENTS AND DEVELOPMENT PROGRAMMES.

SO10: PREVENTION AND MITIGATION MEASURES IMPLEMENTED IN OPERATIONS WITH SIGNIFICANT POTENTIAL AND ACTUAL NEGATIVE IMPACTS ON LOCAL COMMUNITIES.

NOTE

1 *Provisional Remarks, Conclusions And Recommendations*, International Symposium on Legacy of the Olympic Games, 1984 to 2000, 14–16 November 2002.

INDEX